CW01657758

THE ART WORLD DIRECTORY

1999/2000 26TH EDITION

PUBLISHED BY art REVIEW

Published by: Art Review Ltd., Hereford House, 23/24 Smithfield Street, London EC1A 9LF.
Tel: 0171-236 4880. Fax: 0171-236 4881. e-mail info@art-review.co.uk Ws http://www.art-review.co.uk
ISBN 0904831272

Every effort has been made to ensure the accuracy of the information contained in the Directory. However, it is advisable to check with galleries prior to visiting.

Editorial	**Abigail Grater**
Classified Executive	**Patrick Adams**
Advertisement Manager	**Louisa Utting**
Production	**Alex John**
	Neil Pereira
Compilation	**Megan Hughes**
Financial Controller	**Dilip Chauhan**
Publisher	**David Fox**
Database Consultants	**DB Consulting**
Reprographics	**Saffron Reprographics Ltd 0171-251 8338**
Printed and bound by	**B R Hubbard Printers Ltd 01246 410701**

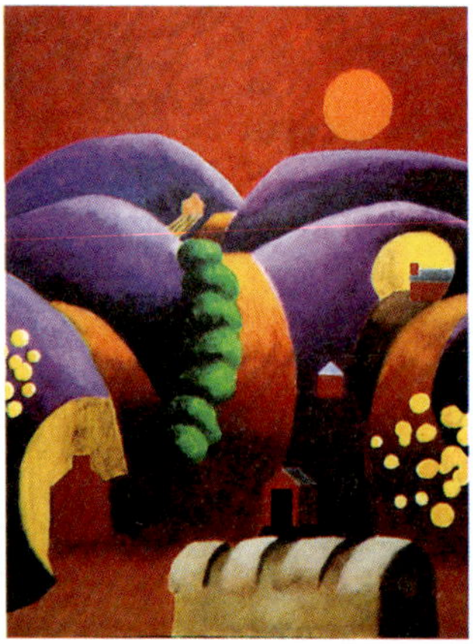

Porthclais

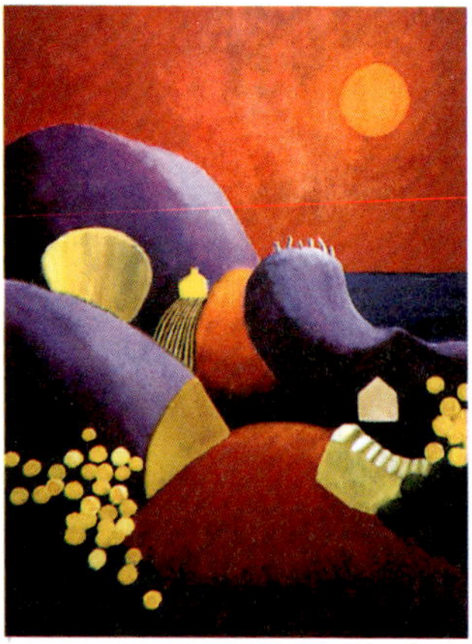

Melin Trefin

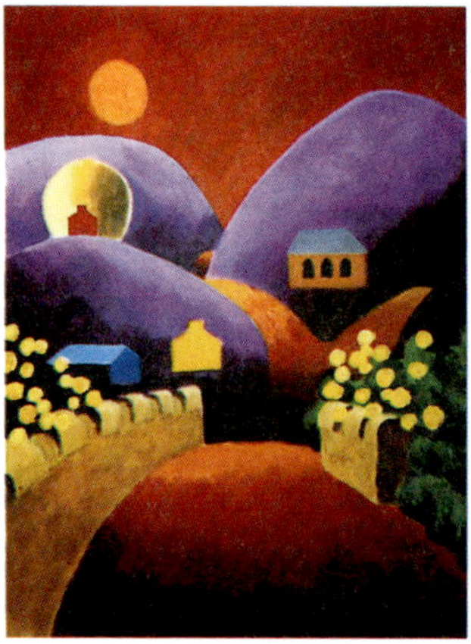

Felin Ganol

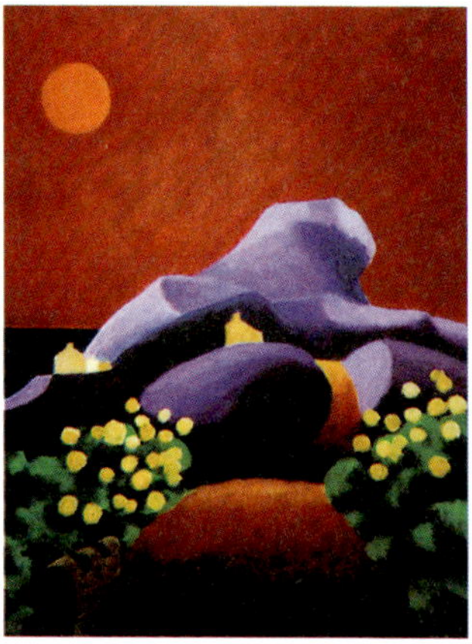

Garn Fawr

HOW TO USE THE NEW EDITION 1999/2000

New readers of The Art World Directory will find the following a useful guide when using the Directory.

GALLERIES AND EXHIBITION SPACES. Where this has been supplied, establishments are designated 'C' for a purely commercial enterprise, 'P' for a public gallery or museum or 'PS' for a public gallery or museum holding selling shows.

SERVICES AND FACILITIES OFFERED. Many establishments will offer additional services such as art consultancy, framing, art for offices and commissioning services. These are listed as part of each establishment's entry.

WORK STOCKED AND SOLD. Where provided, the media in which commercial establishments specialise is listed as part of their entry.

PRICE RANGE. A guide to commercial establishments' price range may also be found as part of their entry.

ART SERVICES. The back sections of the Directory are devoted to a full range of art service providers. Use this section to find the service you require.

INDICES. At the back of the Directory will you find a number of useful indices to help you find the gallery, media, artist or price range of your choice. These include:

Art Under £1,000. This section lists commercial establishments who also sell work priced at £1,000 or less.

Commercial Galleries by Media. Use this section to find galleries stocking work in your chosen media.

Commercial Gallery Artists. This section lists by gallery, a sample of the artists whose work is sold by that establishment.

Artists' Index. This section lists by artist, the establishments which sell the artist's work.

Gallery Services. This section lists additional services offered by many galleries and commercial establishments.

General Index. The alphabetical index to all entries listed in the Directory.

CONTENTS

THE ART WORLD DIRECTORY
1999/2000 26TH EDITION

Dear Reader,

Welcome to the 26th edition of the Art Review Art World Directory. The Directory aims to make art buying and exhibition visiting an easier and more rewarding process for the experienced art collector and those new to the visual arts who may need help in getting started.

We have amended and added to the Directory for this new edition and trust that you will find it an even more useful guide to the UK visual arts scene.

We are again very much indebted to the galleries and art service providers throughout the UK who have kindly given their advice and support during the preparation of this new edition.

Yours faithfully,

David Fox Publisher

paint and *prejudice*

Twentieth century British art at the Imperial War Museum

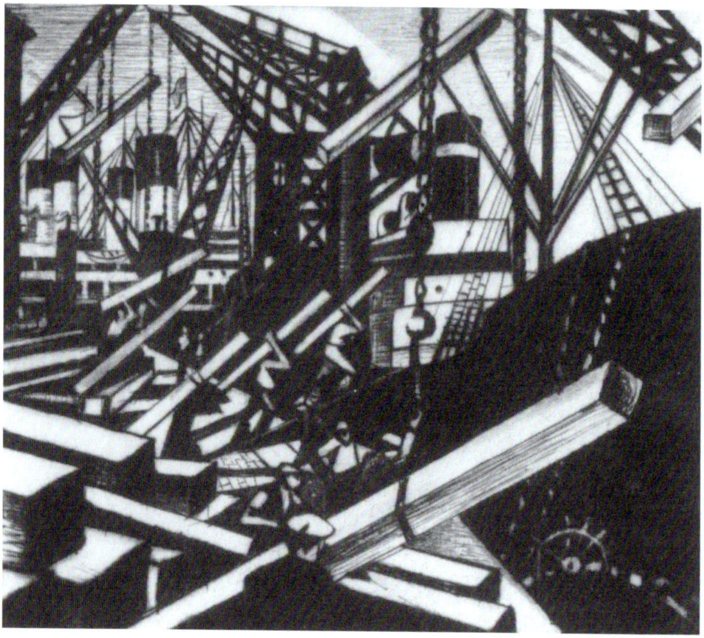

CRW Nevinson *Southampton 1916*

Imperial War Museum
Lambeth Road
London SE1 6HZ

Department of Art
Research and Archives
10.00 - 17.00
Monday - Friday

Museum open
seven days a week
10.00 - 18.00
admission £5.20
free after 16.30
tel 0171 416 5320

Art exhibitions during 1999 include **Ian Hamilton Finlay : A Wartime Garden** (19 March - 31 May) and **CRW Nevinson : The Twentieth Century** (from 28 October). Other exhibitions: **From the Bomb to the Beatles : Postwar Britain 1945-1965** opens 25 March.

IMPERIAL WAR MUSEUM

Graham Clarke

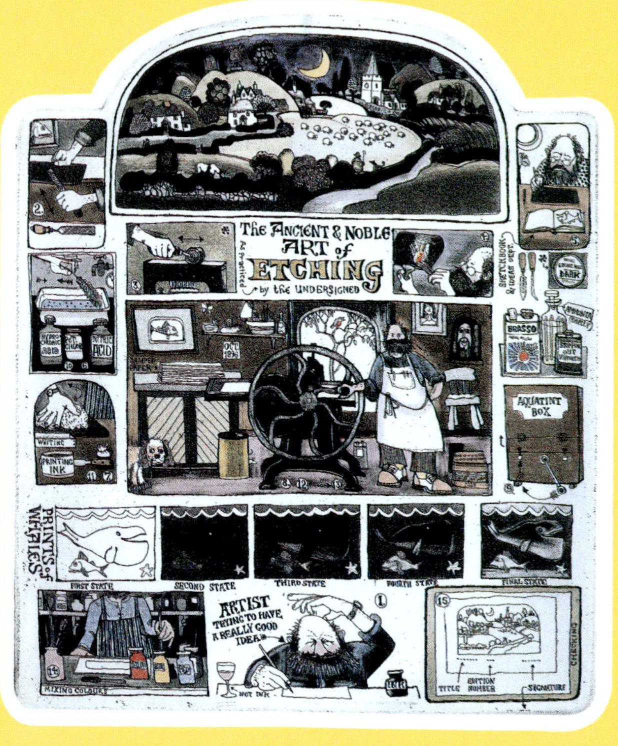

Etching and the Prints of Whales

Edition of 300 copies plus 30 artists' proofs.
Image size 248mm x 212mm.

Contact: Up the Garden Studio, Green Lane,
Boughton Monchelsea, Maidstone, Kent ME17 4LF

Phone: 01622 743938 Fax: 01622 747229
E-mail: info@grahamclarke.co.uk Website: www.grahamclarke.co.uk

Studio open by appointment.

CALENDAR OF EXHIBITIONS

THE ART WORLD
DIRECTORY

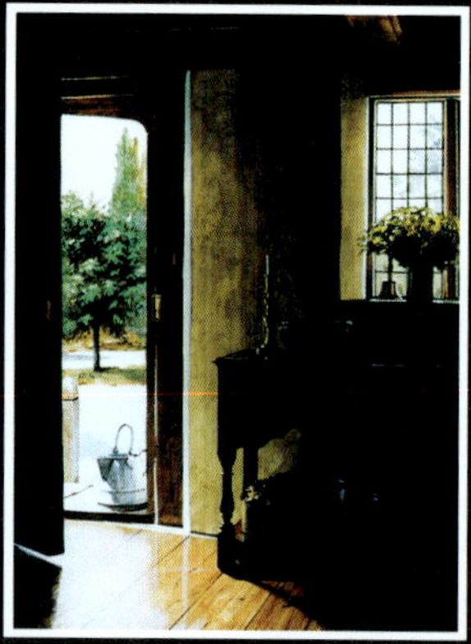

NATIONAL TOURING EXHIBITIONS

These exhibitions, organised by the Hayward Gallery on behalf of the Arts Council, will be touring Britain during 1999/2000 – call 0171-921 0887 for details of venues and dates.

Disasters of War: Callot, Goya, Dix – three series of etchings

Head First: Portraits from the Arts Council Collection

Here to Stay: Arts Council Collection Purchases from the 1990s

Printmaking in Paris: Picasso and his Contemporaries

Secret Victorians: work by contemporary British and US artists on 'Victorian' themes

Spotlight on Antony Gormley

Spotlight on Terry Frost

Spotlight on Gillian Wearing

Thinking Aloud, curated by Richard Wentworth

Patrick Caulfield: *The Poems of Jules Laforgue* – prints

Goya: *The Disparates* – prints

David Hockney: *Grimm's Fairy Tales* – prints

Käthe Kollwitz: Artist of the People

Matisse: *Jazz*

Networking: Art by Post & Fax

On the Road: the art of engineering in the age of the car

Picasso: *Histoire Naturelle* – etchings

Pop Prints from the Arts Council Collection

Printers Inc.: Recent British Prints

Screen: work by Young British Artists

Edward Weston: photographs

OTHER EXHIBITIONS

This is a selection of exhibitions due to take place from April 1999 to March 2000 at public and commercial galleries throughout Britain.

Exhibitions are listed under the month in which they start, so if you want to know what's on in a particular month, don't forget also to check previous months for continuing exhibitions.

It is advisable to contact the venue before visiting in order to ensure that details have not changed since publication.

Key: **selling exhibitions**
non-selling exhibitions

CONTINUING FROM PREVIOUS MONTHS

Doreen Fletcher
Ogilvy & Estill, Conwy (01492 592292)
to 11 April

Aubrey Beardsley: Centenary Exhibition
Walker Art Gallery, Liverpool (0151-478 4199)
to 11 April

Frank Lloyd Wright
Art Gallery & Museum, Kelvingrove, Glasgow (0141-287 2699)
to 11 April

Patrick Caulfield
Hayward Gallery, London (0171-960 4242)
to 11 April

Picasso and Matisse
Fitzwilliam Museum, Cambridge (01223 332900)
to 11 April

Gerald Laing: sculpture
Fine Art Society, London (0171-629 5116)
to 15 April

New Work 1999: group show
Loggia Gallery, London (0171-828 8963)
to 16 April

Landscapes: Mixed Show
Rebecca Hossack Gallery, London (0171-436 4899)
to 17 April

Janet Hodgson: History Lesson – video installation
Bluecoat Gallery, Liverpool (0151-709 5297)
to 17 April

Paintings by Francis Boag, Fiona Dick and Bel McCoig; ceramic animals by Paul Smith
Gallery Heinzel, Aberdeen (01224 625629)
to 17 April

Arts of Japan
British Museum, London (0171-636 1555)
to 18 April

Roman Baroque Drawings; Building the British Museum
British Museum, London (0171-636 1555)
to 18 April

Monet in the 20th Century
Royal Academy of Arts, London (0171-300 8000)
to 18 April

Pleasures of Peace: Craft, Art & Design in Britain c.1940-70
Sainsbury Centre for Visual Arts, Norwich (01603-456060/593199) and touring
to 18 April

Peter Illsted: paintings & mezzotints
Lumley Cazalet, London (0171-491 4767)
to 23 April

Henri Michaux (1899-1984): works on paper
Whitechapel Art Gallery, London (0171-522 7888)
to 25 April

Portraits by Ingres
Sainsbury Wing, National Gallery, London (0171-839 3321/747 2885)
to 25 April

Scottish Rugs Old & New; pottery by Thomas Lochhead
Crawford Arts Centre, St. Andrews (01334 474610) and touring
to 25 April

Terry Winters: abstract paintings
Whitechapel Art Gallery, London (0171-522 7888)
to 25 April

First Impressions 99: work by Art & Design students
New Walk Museum, Leicester (0116-247 3042)
to 28 April

Peter Potworowski (1898-1962): paintings
Connaught Brown, London (0171-408 0362)
to 30 April

Recent Acquisitions from the NatWest Group Art Collection
Lothbury Gallery, London (0171-726 1795)
to 30 April

Poetic License: European Quilt Art
Ruskin Gallery, Sheffield (0114-203 9416)
to 1 May

A Scottish Grand Tour: topographical exhibition of famous landmarks
Malcolm Innes Gallery, Edinburgh (0131-558 9544/5)
to 1 May

Arturo di Stefano: Strands
Djanogly Art Gallery, Nottingham (0115-951 3189)
to 2 May

Buddhist Art from Tibet: the E.M. Scratton Collection
Ashmolean Museum, Oxford (01865 278000)
to 2 May

Edward Falkener: A Victorian Orientalist
British Museum, London (0171-636 1555)
to 2 May

Francis Bacon: Works on Paper and Paintings
Tate Gallery, London (0171-887 8000)
to 2 May

At Home with Contemporary Art: the Nancy Balfour Collection
Norwich Castle Museum, Norwich (01603 493655)
to 3 May

The King's Head: portraits of Charles I
The Queen's Gallery, Buckingham Palace, London (0171-839 1377)
to 3 May

Recent Acquisitions of American Prints
Fitzwilliam Museum, Cambridge (01223 332900)
to 3 May

Manchester Academy of Fine Artists
Bury Art Gallery & Museum (0161-253 5878)
to 8 May

Memhet Gueler: semi-abstract paintings
Huddersfield Art Gallery, Huddersfield (01484 226300)
to 8 May

Avigdor Arikha: retrospective
Scottish National Gallery of Modern Art, Edinburgh (0131-556 8921)
to 9 May

Cefyn Burgess: textiles
Harley Gallery, Worksop (01909 501700)
to 9 May

Head Masters: paintings and sculpture on the theme of the head
The Red Gallery, Southsea (01705 793924)
to 9 May

Henri Cartier-Bresson: Portraits – Tête-à-Tête
Scottish National Gallery of Modern Art, Edinburgh (0131-556 8921) and touring
to 9 May

The Homes of Football: photographs by Stuart Clarke
Kirkcaldy Museum & Art Gallery (01592 412860) and touring
to 9 May

Philip Mead & Alan Rogers: work produced in Rajestan
Glynn Vivian Art Gallery, Swansea (01792 655006)
to 9 May

Sea Dreams: Art Salutes the Boat
Usher Gallery, Lincoln (01522 527980)
to 9 May

Andreas Gursky: photographs 1994-8
Dean Gallery, Scottish National Gallery of Modern Art, Edinburgh (0131-624 6332)
to 16 May

Vertigo: The Strange New World of the Contemporary City
The Old Fruitmarket, Glasgow (0141-287 7346 for details)
to 16 May

Simon Lewty: Towards Drawing
City Art Gallery, Worcester (01905 25371)
to 18 May

Ray Atkins & The Figure (1958-1998)
Royal Cornwall Museum, Truro (01872 272205)
to 22 May

Orazio Gentileschi at the Court of Charles I
Sunley Room, National Gallery, London (0171-839 3321/747 2885)
to 23 May

Performances: photographs by David Buckland
National Portrait Gallery, London (0171-306 0055)
to 23 May

Kenny Hunter: sculptures
Scottish National Portrait Gallery, Edinburgh (0131-556 8921)
to 30 May

Curve: photomontages by Mark Johnston
Scottish National Portrait Gallery, Edinburgh (0131-556 8921)
to 30 May

Cornish Art & Craft of the '90s
Beatrice Royal Art Gallery, Eastleigh (01703 610592)
to 31 May

Jackson Pollock: retrospective
Tate Gallery, London (0171-887 8000)
to 6 June

From Cozens to Palmer: Exhibition Watercolours
Ashmolean Museum, Oxford (01865 278000)
to 13 June

Girtin in the North
Harewood House, Leeds (0113-288 6331)
to 13 June

Twin Perspectives: contemporary Indian miniatures
Birmingham Museum & Art Gallery (0121-303 2834)
to 13 June

Rembrandt and the Passion
Fitzwilliam Museum, Cambridge (01223 332900)
to 20 June

Chris Burden: The Two Minute Airplane Factory
Tate Gallery, London (0171-887 8000)
to 27 June

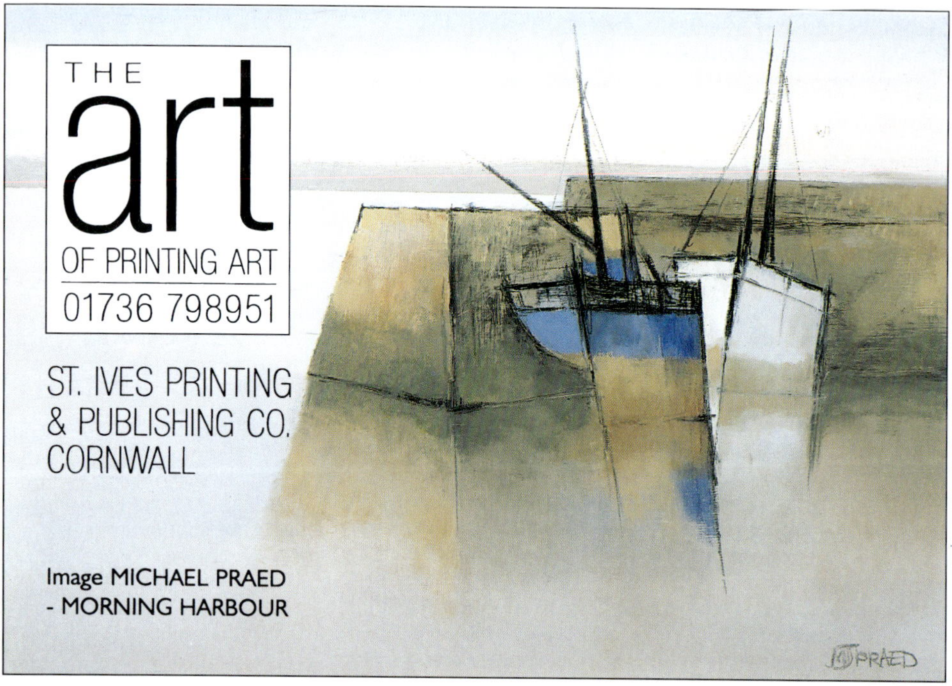

THE
art
OF PRINTING ART
01736 798951
ST. IVES PRINTING
& PUBLISHING CO.
CORNWALL
Image MICHAEL PRAED
- MORNING HARBOUR
PRAED

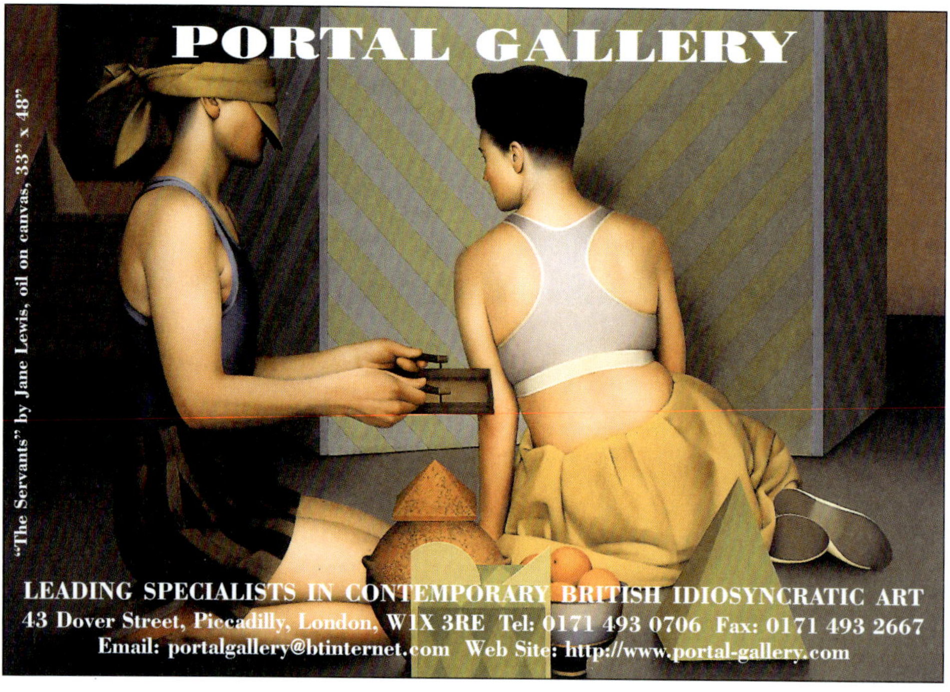

PORTAL GALLERY
"The Servants" by Jane Lewis, oil on canvas, 33" x 48"
LEADING SPECIALISTS IN CONTEMPORARY BRITISH IDIOSYNCRATIC ART
43 Dover Street, Piccadilly, London, W1X 3RE Tel: 0171 493 0706 Fax: 0171 493 2667
Email: portalgallery@btinternet.com Web Site: http://www.portal-gallery.com

Sex, Drugs and Rock & Roll: The Last 50 Years of British Art
Cecil Higgins Art Gallery, Bedford (01234 211222)
to 11 July

St. Ives Artists and their Friends in the North
Harewood House, Leeds (0113-288 6331)
to 18 July

Arts of the Sikh Kingdoms
Victoria & Albert Museum, London (0171-938 8500)
to 25 July

The Animal Construction Company: architecture & design made by animals
Hunterian Museum, University of Glasgow (0141-330 4221)
to 20 August

Shadow of the Beekeeper: new work by Bill Woodrow
Lothbury Gallery, London (0171-726 1795)
to 27 August

Silver and Syrup: selections from the history of photography
Canon Photography Gallery, Victoria & Albert Museum, London (0171-938 8500)
to 30 August

The Harris Museum Project: a series of specially commissioned new artworks
Harris Museum & Art Gallery, Preston (01772 258248)
to autumn 1999

Modern British Art from the Tate Collection
Tate Gallery, Liverpool (0151-709 3223)
to 2000

Arts of Korea
British Museum, London (0171-636 1555)
to 2000

Violent Incident: violent works from the Tate
Tate Gallery, Liverpool (0151-709 3223)
to March 2000

From the Bomb to the Beatles: post-war Britain 1945-1965
Imperial War Museum, London (0171-416 5000)
to 29 May 2000

APRIL 1999

Gordon K. Mitchell RSW RGI
Roger Billcliffe Gallery, Glasgow (0141-332 4027)
during April

Chelsea Harbour Sculpture '99: Jean Robert Ipoustéguy
Chelsea Harbour, London (0171-439 2822 for details)
April to September

In the Line of Fire: installation by Mildred Howard
The City Gallery, Leicester (0116-254 0595)
1 April to 8 May

Into the Light: Photographic Printing after the Darkroom
Royal Photographic Society, Bath (01225 462841)
1 April to 6 June

Simon Norfolk: For Most Of It I Have No Words
Royal Photographic Society, Bath (01225 462841)
1 April to 6 June

Evolution Isn't Over Yet: Scottish contemporary artists
The Fruitmarket Gallery, Edinburgh (0131-225 2383)
2 April to 29 May

Netsuke & miniature carvings from Japan
City Art Gallery, York (01904 551861)
3 April to 16 May

Mountain
Wolverhampton Art Gallery, Wolverhampton (01902 552055)
3 April to 19 June

Daphne Reynolds: mezzotints and works on paper
Christchurch Mansion, Ipswich (01473 253246)
4 April to 16 May

Josef Albers: Prints from the Estate
Alan Cristea Gallery, London (0171-439 1866)
6 April to 8 May

Jeffrey Blondes: paintings of Scottish landscapes
Ingleby Gallery, Edinburgh (0131-556 4441)
7 April to 15 May

Iain Faulkner
Albemarle Gallery, London (0171-499 1616)
8 April to 24 April

Clive Blackmore
New Academy Gallery, London (0171-323 4700)
8 April to 30 April

Kamal Shah: oil paintings from Kenya
Meghraj Gallery, London (0171-269 5500)
8 April to 7 May

100 Giants of Chair Design: miniatures by the Vitra Design Museum
Collins Gallery, Glasgow (0141-548 4145)
8 April to 8 May

Royal Photographic Society
Vennel Gallery, Irvine (01294 275059)
8 April to 8 May

A Million Brushstrokes: miniatures by 120 artists
Llewellyn Alexander, London (0171-620 1322)
9 April to 8 May

Master Drawings from the National Gallery of Scotland
National Gallery of Scotland, Edinburgh (0131-556 8921)
9 April to 13 June

William Gillies (1898-1973)
Lillie Art Gallery, Milngavie (0141-578 8847)
10 April to 8 May

Philip Wilson Steer: A Very English Impressionist; New English Art Club
Atkinson Art Gallery, Southport (01704-533133, ext. 2111)
12 April to 6 June

19th C Scottish Landscapes
Bourne Fine Art, Edinburgh (0131-557 4050)
12 April to end May

Mat Barber-Kennedy RI & Colin Kent RI: paintings
Linda Blackstone Gallery, London (0181-868 5765)
14 April to 1 May

Kandinsky
Royal Academy of Arts, London (0171-300 8000)
14 April to 4 July

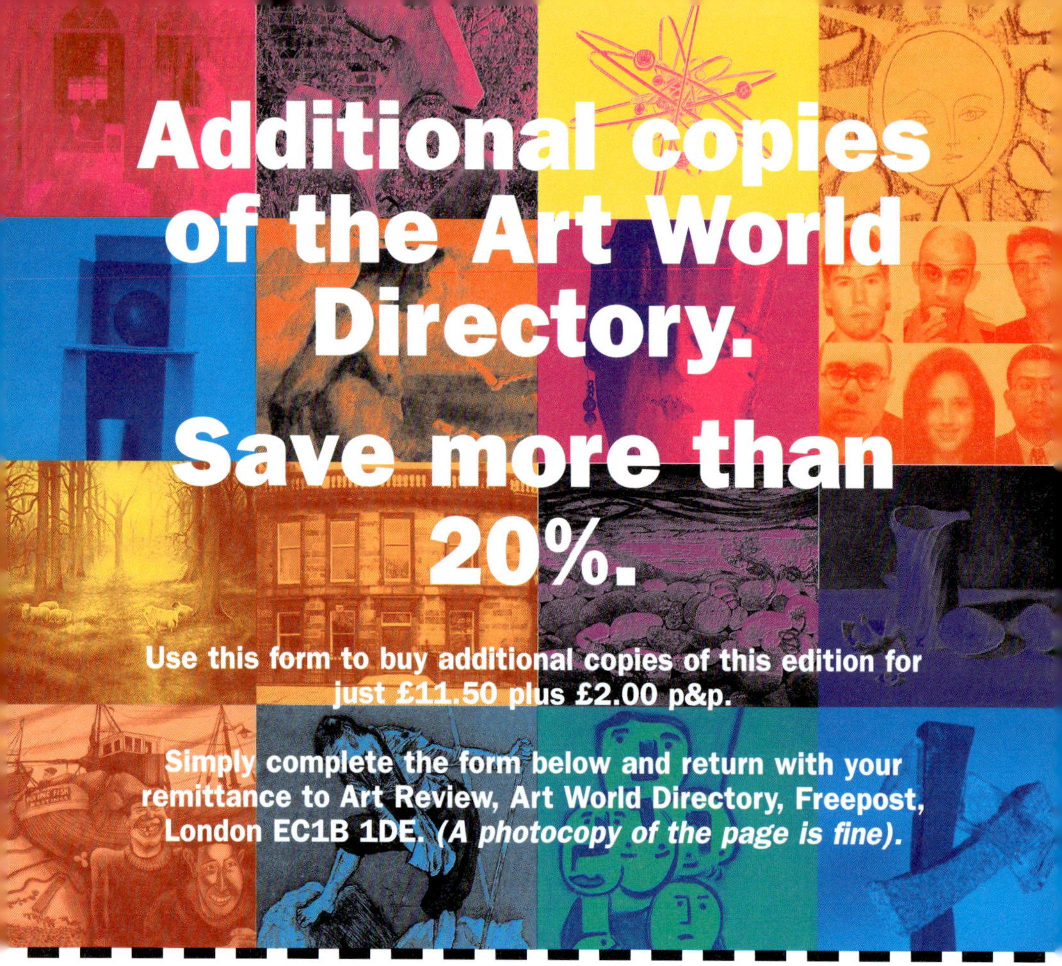

Art World Directory Additional Copies Order Form.

Please send me ________ additional copy(ies) of the 1999/2000 Art World Directory @ £11.50 plus £2.00 p&p each.*

I enclose my remittance for **£** ____________________ made payable to Art Review Ltd.

Please debit my ☐ Access ☐ Visa ☐ Amex ☐ Mastercard

Card No: ______________________________ Expiry Date ________________

Signature ______________________________ Date ________________

Name ____________________ Address ______________________________

____

______________________________ Postcode ________________

Tel ______________________________ (in case of queries only)

*The postage and packing cost relates to UK orders only, European p&p £3.00, Overseas £6.00.

Ref: AWDF1

David Bailey: Birth of the Cool
Barbican Art Gallery, London
(0171-638 4141)
15 April to 27 June

Willi Kissmer
Parkview Fine Paintings
(0117-970 6265)
16 April to 8 May

David Merrills
Ogilvy & Estill, Conwy (01492 592292)
16 April to 9 May

Mariannita Luzzati
Purdy Hicks, London (0171-401 9229)
16 April to 15 May

Wearable Art: jewellery and textiles
Contemporary Applied Arts, London
(0171-436 2344)
16 April to 29 May

Stephen Conroy: recent paintings and prints
Marlborough Fine Art, London
(0171-629 5161)
16 April to 4 June

Paul Reid: paintings and drawings
The Rendezvous Gallery, Aberdeen
(01224 323247)
17 April to 1 May

Hsiao-Mei Lin
Adam Gallery, Bath (01225 480406)
17 April to 10 May

The Elders: Brother Everald Brown & Stanley Greaves – contemporary Caribbean art
Christchurch Mansion, Ipswich
(01473 253246)
17 April to 31 May

Personal Effects: Sculpture and Belongings – contemporary
Angel Row Gallery, Nottingham
(0115-947 6334)
17 April to 5 June

Towers and Colonnades: the architecture of Cuthbert Brodrick
City Art Gallery, Leeds (0113-247 8248)
17 April to 20 June

Anna Gaskell: photographs, drawings & film
Museum of Modern Art, Oxford
(01865 722733)
18 April to 27 June

James McIntosh Patrick (1907-1998): Memorial Exhibition; also etchings by Samuel Palmer
Fine Art Society, London (0171-629 5116)
19 April to 21 May

Heather Rollinson: mystical paintings
Tolbooth Art Centre, Kirkcudbright
(01557 331643)
20 April to 2 May

Eva Rippon: paintings
Castle Douglas Art Gallery, Kirkcudbright
(01557 331643)
21 April to 5 May

Martin Oxley: paintings & drawings 1989-99
Artsway, Sway (01590 682260)
21 April to 23 May

Ralph Brown, Ken Smith, Joseph O'Reilly & Martin Cooper: paintings & sculptures
Bruton Gallery, Leeds (0113-242 2323)
21 April to 2 June

Secret Passion to Noble Fashion: Portrait Miniatures
Holburne Museum, Bath (01225 466669)
21 April to 18 July

Anne Desmet: Towers and Transformations – prints
Peter Scott Gallery, Lancaster University
(01524 593057) and touring
22 April to 28 May

Emma Woffenden: glass
Barrett Marsden Gallery, London
(0171-336 6396)
23 April to 5 June

Melanie Keevil: new ceramics
The Ice House, Holland Park, London
(0171-361 3010)
24 April to 9 May

Six Artists: members of Free Painters & Sculptors
Loggia Gallery, London (0171-828 8963)
24 April to 14 May

Contemporary Cornish Abstraction
Falmouth Art Gallery, Falmouth
(01326 313863)
24 April to 22 May

John Byrne: new watercolours
art.tm, Inverness (01463 712240)
24 April to 22 May

RSA 173rd Annual Exhibition
Royal Scottish Academy, Edinburgh
(0131-225 6671)
24 April to 11 July

Mary Jackson
Alresford Gallery, Alresford
(01962 735286)
25 April to 18 May

Holly Warburton: recent work
Leighton House, London (0171-602 3316)
26 April to 8 May

4 young artists new to the Gallery
The Edinburgh Gallery, Edinburgh
(0131-557 5227)
26 April to 19 May

Flexible Furniture
Podium Gallery, Glasgow School of Art
(0141-353 4500)
26 April to 20 May

Jack Milroy
Art First, London (0171-734 0386)
27 April to 13 May

'Mac' of the *Mail*: cartoons
Rae-Smith Gallery, London
(0171-836 7424)
27 April to 15 May

The Art of Fashion: clothing in contemporary & historical paintings
Hove Museum & Art Gallery
(01273 290200)
28 April to 27 June

New Art for a New Era: Malevich's Vision of the Russian Avant-Garde
Barbican Art Gallery, London
(0171-638 4141)
29 April to 27 June

Clementina, Lady Hawarden: photographs 1857-64
Canon Photography Gallery, Victoria & Albert Museum, London (0171-938 8500)
29 April to 30 August

Andrew Smith
Kingfisher Gallery, Edinburgh
(0131-557 5454)
30 April to 21 May

Hamish Fulton: texts and photographs
Crawford Arts Centre, St. Andrews
(01334 474610)
30 April to 13 June

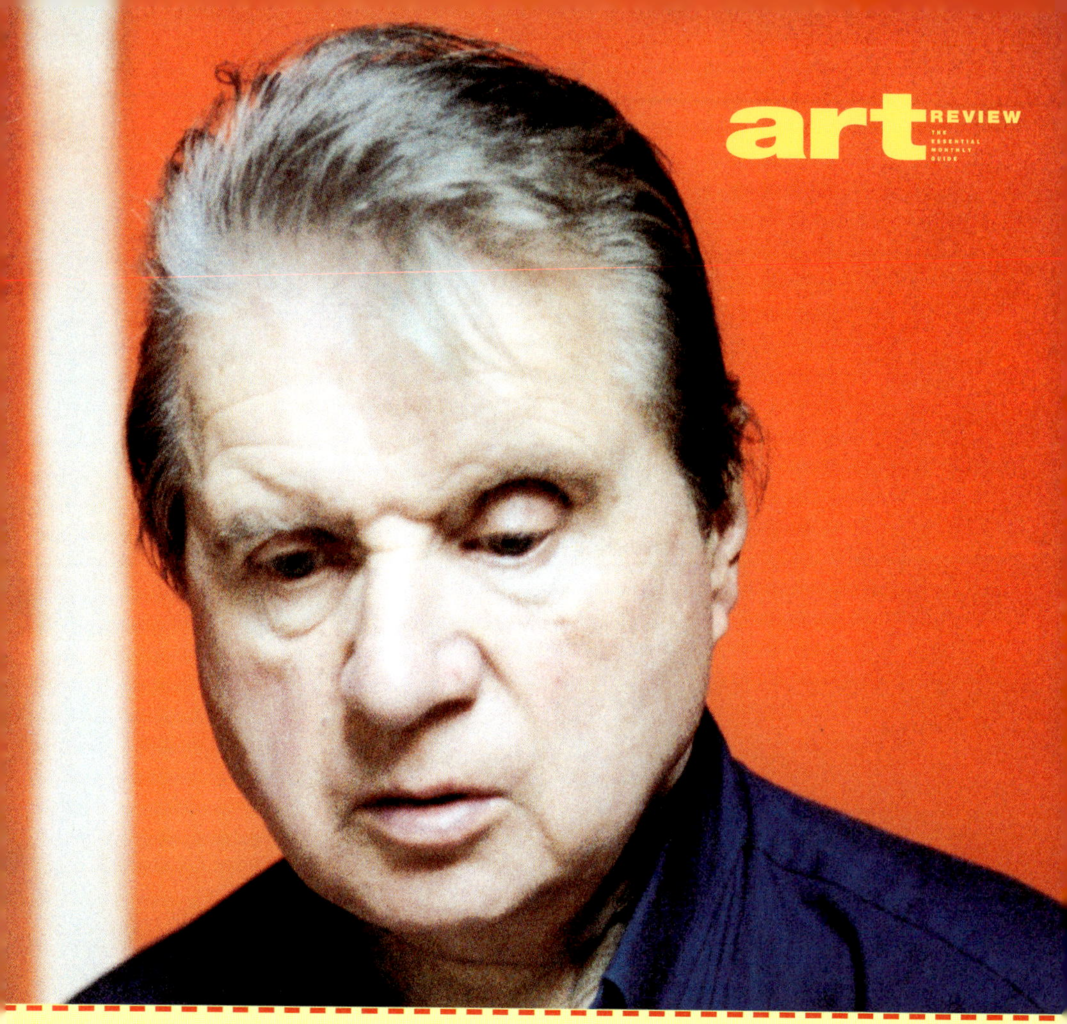
art
REVIEW

Julia Carter Preston: pottery
Walker Art Gallery, Liverpool
(0151-478 4199)
30 April to 13 June

Marc Newson: design
McLellan Galleries, Glasgow
(0141-331 1854)
30 April to 19 June

Van Dyck: *The Five Eldest Children of Charles I*, 1599
Walker Art Gallery, Liverpool
(0151-478 4199)
30 April to 18 July

Architecture of Democracy: parliamentary architecture
McLellan Galleries, Glasgow
(0141-331 1854)
30 April to 25 July

MAY 1999

Ceri Richards: drawings
Martin Tinney Gallery, Cardiff
(01222 641411)
during May

Sir William McTaggart (1903-81): paintings
Ewan Mundy Fine Art, Glasgow
(0141-248 9755)
during May

Paul Helleu: drypoints
Lumley Cazalet, London (0171-491 4767)
during May & June

Roger Ackling
Sainsbury Centre for Visual Arts, Norwich (01603-456060/593199)
May to July

Paradise Street Commissions: contemporary work
Bury Art Gallery & Museum
(0161-253 5878)
May to November

Richard Walker: new paintings
Talbot Rice Art Gallery, Edinburgh
(0131-650 2210)
1 May to 1 June

Pookie & the Animal Shelf: puppets & illustrations
Durham Art Gallery, Durham
(0191-384 2214)
1 May to 13 June

Victor Pasmore
Tate Gallery, Liverpool (0151-709 3223)
1 May 1999 to March 2000

Neil Palisser: figurative paintings & pastels
Cupola Gallery, Sheffield (0114-285 2665)
3 May to 29 May

Tajammul Hussain: contemporary Islamic paintings
Ashmolean Museum, Oxford
(01865 278000)
4 May to 30 May

Tim Pomeroy: new sculpture & drawings
McHardy Sculpture Company, London
(0171-403 7555)
5 May to 23 May

Caroline Bailey: new works
The Gallery, Manchester's Art House, Manchester (0161-237 3551)
5 May to 29 May

Firm Impressions: Royal Society of Painter-Printmakers annual show, featuring Jennifer Dickson
Bankside Gallery, London (0171-928 7521)
5 May to 31 May

Jonathan Hood: paintings
Gallery Heinzel, Aberdeen (01224 625629)
7 May to 5 June

Mactotem: the Duke of Sutherland Monument
Inverness Museum & Art Gallery (01463 237114) and touring
7 May to 5 June

Examining Pictures: an analysis of international contemporary painting
Whitechapel Art Gallery, London
(0171-522 7888)
7 May to 27 June

The Popular Print in England, 16th to 19th century; Castiglione in Context
British Museum, London (0171-636 1555)
7 May to 30 August

O Caledonia! Sir Walter Scott and the Creation of Scotland
Scottish National Portrait Gallery, Edinburgh (0131-556 8921)
7 May to 17 October

Innerspace: mixed craftwork from the Cockpit Workshops
The Orangery, Holland Park, London
(0171-361 3010)
8 May to 16 May

Johan Muyle: Transformations
University of Brighton Gallery, Brighton
(01273 643012)
8 May to 29 May

John Virtue: gestural paintings
Newlyn Art Gallery, Newlyn
(01736 363715)
8 May to 5 June

Surveillance: installation by Mark Doman
Huddersfield Art Gallery, Huddersfield
(01484 226300)
8 May to 19 June

Changing Places: photographs by Stephen Gill
Orleans House Gallery, Twickenham
(0181-892 0221)
8 May to 4 July

Food: Design and Culture
Art Gallery & Museum, Kelvingrove, Glasgow (0141-287 2699)
8 May to 22 August

City Life: contemporary prints, paintings, watercolours
Bartley Drey Gallery, London
(Lena Boyle, 0171-373 8247 for details)
9 May to 22 May

Richard Oliver: Tableaux Vivants
Museum of Modern Art, Wales, Machynlleth (01654 703355)
10 May to 5 June

Ethel Walker: paintings
Thackeray Gallery, London
(0171-937 5883)
11 May to 28 May

Gillian Ayres: prints
Alan Cristea Gallery, London
(0171-439 1866)
11 May to 5 June

Lines of Desire: contemporary international drawing
The City Gallery, Leicester
(0116-254 0595) and touring
13 May to 26 June

Cities on the Move
Hayward Gallery, London
(0171-960 4242)
13 May to 27 June

Ray Richardson: English Bull Terriers
Cambridge Contemporary Art, Cambridge
(01223 324222)
14 May to 29 May

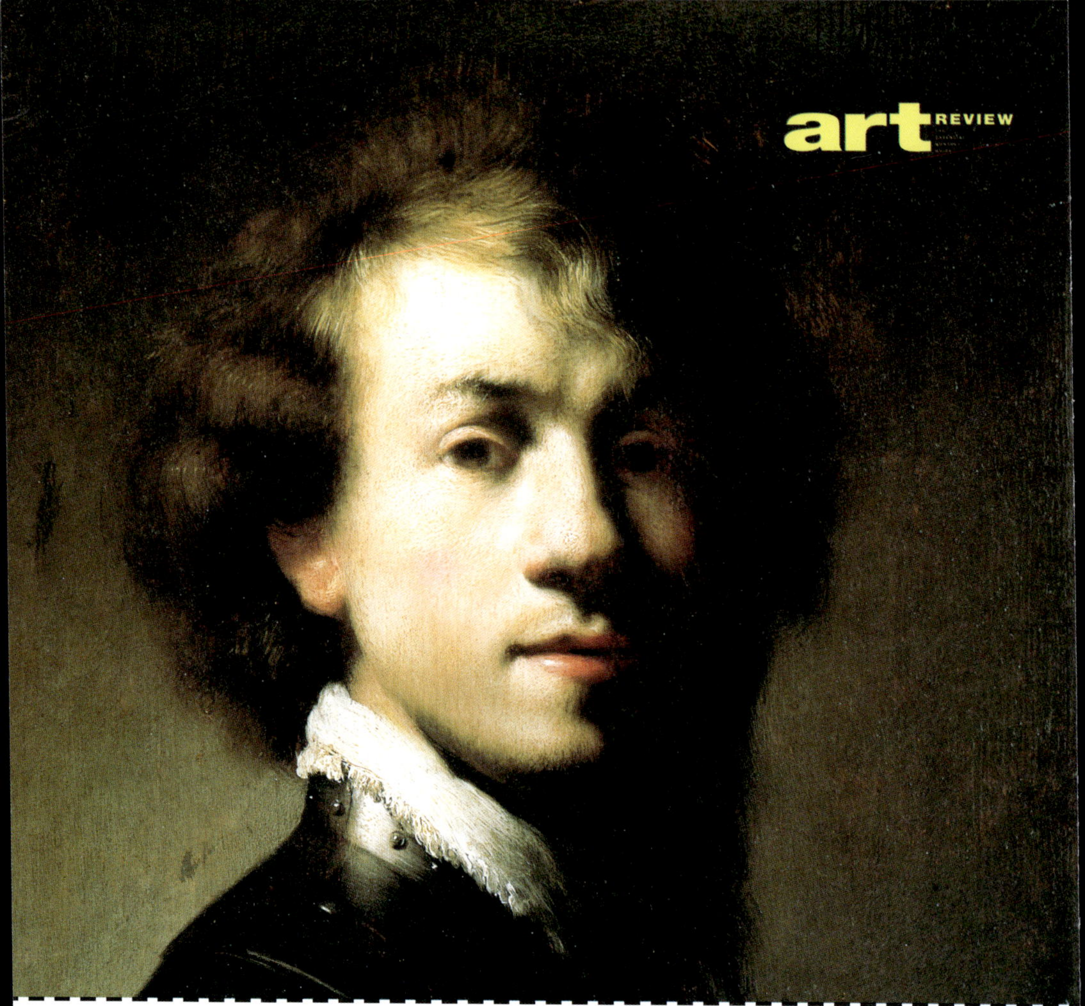
art REVIEW

Paper sculptures by Susan Cutts; wood jewellery by Rachel Groombridge
Hitchcocks, Alresford
(01962 734762)
14 May to 31 May

Mies van der Rohe: Architecture and Design in Stuttgart, Barcelona, Brno
The Burrell Collection, Glasgow
(0141-649 7151)
14 May to 29 August

Andrew Dodds: drawings, watercolours & prints
Chappel Galleries, Chappel
(01206 240326)
15 May to 4 June

William Selby
Adam Gallery, Bath (01225 480406)
15 May to 7 June

Representing the People: contemporary Chinese figurative painting
Aberystwyth Arts Centre, Aberystwyth
(01970 622895) and touring
15 May to 19 June

Richard Hamilton: Printmaking and New Technology
Glasgow Print Studio, Glasgow
(0141-552 0704)
15 May to 26 June

Tony Philips: Guide to the 20th Century – paintings, etchings & drawings
City Art Gallery, Worcester
(01905 25371)
15 May to 26 June

The Incisive Eye: Colin See-Paynton – wood engravings
Hereford Museum and Art Gallery
(01432 260000)
15 May to 27 June

Kate Malone: The Allotment – ceramics
Gainsborough's House, Sudbury
(01787-372958) and touring
15 May to 27 June

A Swiss Painter in Italy: Abraham Louis Rodolphe Ducros (1748-1810)
Norwich Castle Museum, Norwich
(01603 493655)
15 May to 11 July

Take 4: New Perspectives on British Quilt Art
Glynn Vivian Art Gallery, Swansea
(01792 655006)
15 May to 11 July

Roger Barnes: recent jewellery; plus mixed exhibition of rings
Craft Centre & Design Gallery, City Art Gallery, Leeds (0113-247 8241)
15 May to 17 July

Coo Gellar: prints influenced by patterns in rock strata
The Yard Gallery, Wollaton Park, Nottingham (0115-915 3653)
15 May to 8 August

Treasures from Collections in the East of England
Fitzwilliam Museum, Cambridge
(01223 332900)
18 May to 1 August

Victorians with Mark Jerram
Wykeham Galleries, Stockbridge
(01264 810364)
18 May to 5 June

Paintings by Ken Paine from the Michael Simonow Collection
Holburne Museum, Bath (01225 466669)
19 May to 18 July

Terence Wilson Fletcher
Parkview Fine Paintings (0117-970 6265)
20 May to 12 June

Annu Naik: oil paintings from India
Meghraj Gallery, London
(0171-269 5500)
21 May to 18 June

Raphael and his Circle
The Queen's Gallery, Buckingham Palace, London (0171-839 1377)
21 May to 10 October

As Dark as Light: work by Yuko Shiraishi, Gia Edzveradze & Garry Fabian Miller on the theme of the solar eclipse (11/8/99)
Tate Gallery St. Ives (01736 796543)
21 May to 31 October

Helena Morgan: New Directions
Loggia Gallery, London (0171-828 8963)
22 May to 11 June

Edward Chamberlaine: ceramics
The Red Gallery, Southsea
(01705 793924)
22 May to 20 June

Baltic Passage: recent paintings by Lys Hansen
Kirkcaldy Museum & Art Gallery
(01592 412860)
22 May to 18 July

Urban: 20th-century works from the Tate Liverpool
Nottingham Castle Museum & Art Gallery, Nottingham (0115-915 3700)
22 May to 18 July

Michael Whittlesea
Alresford Gallery, Alresford
(01962 735286)
23 May to 15 June

Musicians Art: Mile Davis, John Illesley, Tico Torres, Ronny Wood
The Gallery, Manchester's Art House, Manchester (0161-237 3551)
24 May to 7 June

Brian Grimwood
The Coningsby Gallery, London
(0171-636 7478)
25 May to 5 June

Angus McEwan & Robert Saunders
The Leith Gallery, Edinburgh
(0131-553 5255)
25 May to 12 June

Annual Modern Masters Exhibition, including works on paper by William Scott
Ingleby Gallery, Edinburgh
(0131-556 4441)
26 May to 19 June

Mike Francis: Recent Works
Whitford Fine Art, London
(0171-930 9332)
26 May to 30 June

Pindaro Cabrera: work by this Canadian artist
Landings Gallery, Edinburgh
(0131-225 1501)
26 May to 2 July

Ruth Stage
New Grafton Gallery, London
(0181-748 8850)
27 May to 19 June

CALENDAR OF EXHIBITIONS

Diverse Landscapes: Angela Hughes and Paul Gallagher
University Gallery, University of Northumbria, Newcastle (0191-227 4424)
28 May to 2 July

Paintings by Christine Woodside RSW; ceramics by Emma Hollands; jewellery by Lesley Strickland; Print Room exhibition: 'The Need to Draw'
The Open Eye Gallery, Edinburgh (0131-557 1020)
29 May to 17 June

Freestate: 15 artists explore statehood and independence
art.tm, Inverness (01463 712240)
29 May to 3 July

The Artist and the Model from Etty to Spencer
City Art Gallery, York (01904 551861) *and touring*
29 May to 11 July

Morning Light: landscape painting by John Park and others
Harris Museum & Art Gallery, Preston (01772 258248)
29 May to 23 July

John Coplans: A Self-Portrait 1984-97
Dean Gallery, Scottish National Gallery of Modern Art, Edinburgh (0131-624 6332)
29 May to 25 July

Whistler: Friends and Foes – prints 1850-1930
Birmingham Museum & Art Gallery (0121-303 2834)
29 May to 1 September

John Lancaster
Peterborough Museum & Art Gallery (01733 343329)
30 May to 15 July

JUNE 1999

Burt Brill & Cardens Graduate Shows
University of Brighton Gallery, Brighton (01273 643012)
during June

Peter Howson
Roger Billcliffe Gallery, Glasgow (0141-332 4027)
during June

Post-Impressionist and Modern Master paintings, drawings and sculptures
Connaught Brown, London (0171-408 0362)
during June and July

Degree Show
Gray's School of Art, Aberdeen (01224 263600)
1 June to 6 June

Chen Chi-Kwan: paintings
Ashmolean Museum, Oxford (01865 278000)
1 June to 27 June

Jessie M. King (1875-1949)
Tolbooth Art Centre, Kirkcudbright (01557 331643)
4 June to 17 July

Neil Brownsword, Stephen Dixon, Mo Jupp, Christy Keeney: new ceramics
Contemporary Applied Arts, London (0171-436 2344)
4 June to 17 July

Worlds Within: fantasy in art from Dürer to Klinger
Barber Institute of Fine Arts, Birmingham (0121-414 7333)
4 June to 27 August

Going Out in Style: coffins from Africa
Art Gallery & Museum, Kelvingrove, Glasgow (0141-287 2699)
4 June to 29 August

Innocence and Decadence: flowers as symbols in turn-of-the-century Northern Europe
Pallant House Gallery, Chichester (01243 774557)
4 June to 5 September

David Woodford: paintings
Royal Cambrian Academy, Conwy (01492 593413)
5 June to 4 July

Contemporary German and American Art from the Froehlich Collection
Tate Gallery, Liverpool (0151-709 3223)
5 June to 30 August

Israeli Contemporary Art
The Fruitmarket Gallery, Edinburgh (0131-225 2383)
5 June to 11 September

English Watercolours
Malcolm Innes Gallery, London (0171-839 8083/4)
7 June to 12 June

Sergei Paradjanov (1924-90): paintings, drawings & collages
Leighton House, London (0171-602 3316)
7 June to 3 July

Renaissance Master Bronzes from the Ashmolean: the Fortnum Bequest
Ashmolean Museum, Oxford (01865 278000)
7 June to 16 July

RA Summer Exhibition
Royal Academy of Arts, London (0171-300 8000)
7 June to 15 August

Beatrice d'Este
Christ Church Picture Gallery, Oxford (01865 276172)
7 June to 25 August

Filippo Lauri's Roman Fan
Christ Church Picture Gallery, Oxford (01865 276172)
7 June to 25 August

Leonardo da Vinci: drawings
Christ Church Picture Gallery, Oxford (01865 276172)
7 June to 25 August

Not the Royal Academy: annual 'salon des refusés'
Llewellyn Alexander, London (0171-620 1322)
7 June to 4 September

David Hockney: new prints
Alan Cristea Gallery, London (0171-439 1866)
8 June to 24 July

The Prophetic Vision: prints & drawings on Christian themes
Ashmolean Museum, Oxford (01865 278000)
8 June to 15 August

Alan Simpson: paintings from Israel and Provence
Linda Blackstone Gallery, London (0181-868 5765)
9 June to 26 June

Victor Pasmore: Memorial Retrospective Exhibition
Marlborough Fine Art, London (0171-629 5161)
9 June to 30 July

Rembrandt by himself
Sainsbury Wing, National Gallery, London (0171-839 3321/747 2885)
9 June to 5 September

Degree Show
Peter Scott Gallery, Lancaster University (01524 593057)
10 June to 23 June

Royal Scottish Academy Show
Albemarle Gallery, London (0171-499 1616)
10 June to 26 June

Jean MacAlpine & Sutton Taylor
Hart Gallery, London (0171-704 1131)
10 June to17 July

Gordon & Nancy Baldwin: ceramics & paintings
Barrett Marsden Gallery, London (0171-336 6396)
11 June to 24 June

Alexander Thomson: Unknown Genius – architecture
The Lighthouse, Glasgow (0141-287 7346 for details)
11 June to 22 August

Murray Johnston: Landscapes
Scottish National Portrait Gallery, Edinburgh (0131-556 8921)
11 June to 5 September

Degree Show
Edinburgh College of Art, Edinburgh (0131-221 6032)
12 June to 22 June

Green Waters: Ian Hamilton Finlay, Ian Stephen and Graham Rich
An Lanntair, Stornoway, Isle of Lewis (01851 703307)
12 June to 3 July

Philippe Lavandy: photographs of the Highlands
Inverness Museum & Art Gallery (01463 237114) and touring
12 June to 3 July

David Wheeler: new paintings
Wakefield Art Gallery, Wakefield (01924-305900)
12 June to 18 July

Simryn Gill: sculpture & mixed media
Bluecoat Gallery, Liverpool (0151-709 5297)
12 June to 24 July

Revealing Views: Images from Ireland
Royal Photographic Society, Bath (01225 462841) and touring
12 June to 29 August

Nicola Hicks: new and retrospective sculpture
Ferens Art Gallery, Hull (01482 613902)
12 June to 30 August

William Selby
Bruton Gallery, Leeds (0113-242 2323)
16 June to 18 August

From Stubbs to Freud: Ten Years of Collecting, 1989-99
Hunterian Art Gallery, University of Glasgow (0141-330 5431)
16 June to 16 October

Methodist Art Collection: 20th-century masters
Atkinson Art Gallery, Southport (01704-533133, ext. 2111)
17 June to 17 July

Home to the Clyde: marine paintings
McLean Museum & Art Gallery, Greenock (01475 715624)
19 June to 9 October

Degree Show
Duncan of Jordanstone College of Art, Dundee (01382 345330)
20 June to 26 June

John Horwill: retrospective of paintings
Wrexham Arts Centre, Wrexham (01978 292093)
20 June to 31 July

Starting a Collection
Art First, London (0171-734 0386)
22 June to 8 July

Caroline McAdam Clark
Thackeray Gallery, London (0171-937 5883)
22 June to 9 July

Leonid Pasternak (1862-1945): paintings
Ashmolean Museum, Oxford (01865 278000)
22 June to 22 August

The Quality of Mercy: video stills by Rodriguez King Dorset
Stables Gallery at Orleans House, Twickenham (0181-892 0221)
23 June to 11 July

A Brush with Nature: The Gere Collection of Landscape Oil Sketches
Sunley Room, National Gallery, London (0171-839 3321/747 2885)
23 June to 30 August

Artists of Today & Tomorrow
New Grafton Gallery, London (0181-748 8850)
24 June to 4 September

Artists' Gardens: Charles Jencks & Ian Hamilton Finlay
Crawford Arts Centre, St. Andrews (01334 474610)
25 June to 22 August

Degree Show
Glasgow School of Art, Glasgow (0141-353 4500)
26 June to 2 July

Fragments of Nature: paintings & collages by Sarah Lugg
The Ice House, Holland Park, London (0171-361 3010)
26 June to 11 July

Nottingham University Summer Exhibition
Djanogly Art Gallery, Nottingham (0115-951 3189)
26 June to 18 July

Images 23: British illustration
Aberystwyth Arts Centre, Aberystwyth (01970 622895)
26 June to 24 July

Stephen Partridge: video & digital art
Dick Institute, Kilmarnock (01563 526401)
26 June to 7 August

Great Dutch Paintings from the National Gallery
City Art Gallery, Leeds (0113-247 8248)
26 June to 29 August

The World of the Incas
Birmingham Museum & Art Gallery (0121-303 2834)
26 June to 31 August

Four Centuries of Sculpture
Ferens Art Gallery, Hull (01482 613902)
26 June to 26 September

Devon Guild of Craftsmen Summer Exhibition
Devon Guild of Craftsmen, Bovey Tracey (01626 832223)
27 June to 5 September

CALENDAR OF EXHIBITIONS

Yirrkala: bark paintings & prints
Rebecca Hossack Gallery, London (0171-436 4899)
28 June to 31 July

Gwen Raverat
Fitzwilliam Museum, Cambridge (01223 332900)
29 June to 12 September

Japanese Warrior Prints by Kuniyoshi
Ashmolean Museum, Oxford (01865 278000)
29 June to 19 September

Design in the Digital Age
Victoria & Albert Museum, London (0171-938 8500)
30 June 1999 to 3 January 2000

Sculpture: Owen Young, Ian Hamilton Finlay, Andy Goldsworthy & others
Ingleby Gallery, Edinburgh (0131-556 4441)
30 June to 25 July

JULY 1999

Elemental Vessels: ceramics by Loretta Braganza
Ruskin Gallery, Sheffield (0114-203 9416)
July to September

Lydia Bauman: retrospective of paintings
Falmouth Art Gallery, Falmouth (01326 313863)
3 July to 31 July

Andrew Vass, Hugh Webster & Christopher Northall: paintings
Gainsborough's House, Sudbury (01787-372958)
3 July to 29 August

The Tinkler-Gypsies: 18th & 19th C gypsy life in Galloway
Stranraer Museum, Stranraer (01776 705088)
3 July to 4 September

Joseph Beuys: multiples
Scottish National Gallery of Modern Art, Edinburgh (0131-556 8921)
3 July to 19 September

Chocolate in Contemporary Art
Gracefield Arts Centre, Dumfries (01387 262084) and touring
4 July to 1 August

Touch: tactile sculptures by Jan Niedojadlo
Wolverhampton Art Gallery, Wolverhampton (01902 552055)
5 July to 4 September

George Ehret: Flower Painter Extraordinary
Fitzwilliam Museum, Cambridge (01223 332900)
6 July to 26 September

Tactile Territory: interactive sculpture by Jan Niedojadlo
Hove Museum & Art Gallery (01273 290200)
7 July to 22 August

Gakonga J Gakonga (Kenya) and Joe Amenichi (Nigeria)
Landings Gallery, Edinburgh (0131-225 1501)
7 July to 10 September

A Month in the Summer: Anglo-Asian culture
Whitechapel Art Gallery, London (0171-522 7888)
8 July to 8 August

Colin See-Paynton: The Incisive Eye – wood engravings 1980-1996
Peter Scott Gallery, Lancaster University (01524 593057)
8 July to 13 August

Brenda Lenaghan
Kingfisher Gallery, Edinburgh (0131-557 5454)
9 July to 30 July

French Drawings from the Collection of Jeffrey E. Horvitz
National Gallery of Scotland, Edinburgh (0131-556 8921)
9 July to 5 September

Flesh and Blood: oil paintings by Terry Curling
Chappel Galleries, Chappel (01206 240326)
10 July to 31 July

Les Matthews: paintings
Guild Gallery, Bristol (0117-926 5548)
10 July to 31 July

Mac Gregory, Antony Micallef, Patience Foster & Katy Bailey: new works
Woodbine Cottage Gallery, Whaplode Drove, Spalding, Lincs (01406 330693)
10 July to 1 August

Antony Kerr: 75th Birthday Retrospective – paintings
Hereford Museum and Art Gallery (01432 260000)
10 July to 30 August

Cynthia Pell (1933-1977): A Retrospective
Orleans House Gallery, Twickenham (0181-892 0221)
10 July to 5 September

117th Annual Summer Exhibition
Royal Cambrian Academy, Conwy (01492 593413)
10 July to 12 September

Alfred Hitchcock (1899-1980: Centenary Exhibition
Museum of Modern Art, Oxford (01865 722733)
11 July to 3 October

Dialogue of the Present: mixed media & installation by Arab women
Pitshanger Manor & Gallery, London (0181-567 1227) and touring
14 July to 14 August

Watercolour 21: open competition
Bankside Gallery, London (0171-928 7521)
15 July to 15 August

Abracadabra: International Contemporary Art
Tate Gallery, London (0171-887 8000)
15 July to 26 September

Open Exhibition: small works
University Gallery, University of Northumbria, Newcastle (0191-227 4424)
16 July to 13 August

Ooh La La! Photographs by Martin Parr
Harley Gallery, Worksop (01909 501700)
17 July to 12 September

The Sixties: design, fashion, science and the Beatles in Elgin
Elgin Museum, Elgin (01343 543675)
17 July to 31 October

Contemporary Glass and work from the Guild of Glass Engravers
Durham Art Gallery, Durham (0191-384 2214)
19 June to 1 August

36 Modèles pour Maison: small house designs by European architects
Glasgow School of Art, Glasgow (0141-353 4500)
19 July to 30 August

Jessie M. King (1875-1949)
Glasgow School of Art, Glasgow (0141-353 4500)
19 July to 30 August

Ettore Sottsass and friends: post-war Italian design
Glasgow School of Art, Glasgow (0141-353 4500)
19 July to 24 September

A Pot of Gold: an extraordinary man, his home and collection
Cecil Higgins Art Gallery, Bedford (01234 211222)
20 July to 21 November

Joseph Beuys: Drawings
Royal Academy of Arts, London (0171-300 8000)
22 July to 16 September

Chuck Close: Full Moon
Hayward Gallery, London (0171-960 4242)
22 July to 19 September

Lucy Casson: metalwork; Rushton Aust: textiles
Contemporary Applied Arts, London (0171-436 2344)
23 July to 11 September

Philippe Starck: Retrospective
The Lighthouse, Glasgow (0141-287 7346 for details)
23 July to 31 October

African Caribbean Arts
The Potteries Museum & Art Gallery, Stoke-on-Trent (01782 232323)
24 July to 26 September

Surrealism: works from the Tate Gallery
Norwich Castle Museum, Norwich (01603 493655)
24 July to 3 October

Flowers in Art in the 20th Century
Harewood House, Leeds (0113-288 6331)
24 July to 31 October

Printmaking Open
Cupola Gallery, Sheffield (0114-285 2665)
26 July to 28 August

Dutch Landscape Paintings from Dulwich Picture Gallery
Holburne Museum, Bath (01225 466669)
26 July to 19 September

New Artists
Gallery Heinzel, Aberdeen (01224 625629)
30 July to 28 August

Alvar Aalto in Seven Buildings
Gallery of Modern Art, Glasgow (0141-229 1996)
30 July to 10 October

Metamorphisis: new paintings by Michael Cooper
Crypt Gallery, Seaford (01323 891461)
31 July to 14 August

Chart: Roger Ackling, Eileen Lawrence, Nick Rands, Stephen Turner
Angel Row Gallery, Nottingham (0115-947 6334)
31 July to 11 September

Kiki Smith
The Fruitmarket Gallery, Edinburgh (0131-225 2383)
31 July to 11 September

James MacKeown & Leonard Beard
West Wales Arts Centre, Fishguard (01348 873867)
end July to mid September

AUGUST 1999

Sir David Wilkie and his Circle; Will Maclean: A Retrospective
Bourne Fine Art, Edinburgh (0131-557 4050)
during August (Festival Exhibition)

Caroline Hunter
Dundas Street Gallery, Edinburgh (01835 830518 for details)
1 August to 8 August

Frances Richardson; Johnny Warrangkula; mixed Aboriginal stock
Rebecca Hossack Gallery, London (0171-436 4899)
2 August to 11 September

Jemima Blackburn (1823-1909): watercolours and drawings
Malcolm Innes Gallery, Edinburgh (0131-558 9544/5)
4 August to 14 August

Northern Graduates
Curwen Gallery, London (0171-636 1459)
5 August to 28 August

James Morrison: new paintings
The Scottish Gallery, Edinburgh (0131-558 1200)
6 August to 1 September

Margaret Ballantyne
Kingfisher Gallery, Edinburgh (0131-557 5454)
6 August to 3 September

Small Works by RSA Members
Royal Scottish Academy, Edinburgh (0131-225 6671)
6 August to 19 September

Paintings by Jack Knox RSA RGI and contemporary Scottish masters; crafts by Malcolm Martin; jewellery by Catherine Currell
The Open Eye Gallery, Edinburgh (0131-557 1020)
7 August to 2 September

Changing Pages: pop-up books
Durham Art Gallery, Durham (0191-384 2214) and touring
7 August to 19 September

Peter Prendergast: new paintings
Midlands Arts Centre, Birmingham (0121-440 3838) and touring
7 August to 19 September

The John Kobal Photographic Portrait Awards
Royal Photographic Society, Bath (01225 462841) and touring
7 August to 26 September

John Anthony Park and the Painters of Light: early 20th-century St. Ives artists
Falmouth Art Gallery, Falmouth (01326 313863)
7 August to 2 October

Transatlantic Connections: 12 American artists
Gracefield Arts Centre, Dumfries (01387 262084)
8 August to 5 September

Gary Hume: new paintings
Dean Gallery, Scottish National Gallery of Modern Art, Edinburgh (0131-624 6332)
11 August to 17 October

CALENDAR OF EXHIBITIONS

Grineal: giant sand sculpture
Dick Institute, Kilmarnock (01563 526401)
14 August to 9 October

Frank Bramley RA: paintings by the Victorian artist
Usher Gallery, Lincoln (01522 527980)
15 August to 24 October

A Scottish Panorama
Malcolm Innes Gallery, Edinburgh (0131-558 9544/5)
18 August to 4 September

Keith Wallace: new paintings
Crypt Gallery, Seaford (01323 891461)
21 August to 29 August

New Fibre Art: Body Parts
City Art Gallery, Worcester (01905 25371)
21 August to 2 October

Architectural and Ornament Prints & Drawings 1500-1850
Scottish National Gallery of Modern Art, Edinburgh (0131-556 8921)
25 August to 7 November

Thomasin Smith: paintings and ceramic sculptures
The City Gallery, Leicester (0116-254 0595)
27 August to 2 October

Mhairi Sutherland: Blackout – photographic/video work
Crawford Arts Centre, St. Andrews (01334 474610)
27 August to 17 October

Hi Fibre: International Basketmaking
Brighton Museum & Art Gallery (01273 290900) and Hove Museum & Art Gallery (01273 290200)
28 August to 17 October

The Royal Society of Painter-Printmakers 1880-1999
Ashmolean Museum, Oxford (01865 278000)
31 August to 31 October

Drawn from Literature
Christ Church Picture Gallery, Oxford (01865 276172)
31 August to 10 November

SEPTEMBER 1999

Sculpture by Dennis Shields; paintings by Peter Nardini
Vennel Gallery, Irvine (01294 275059)
during September

Kirsty Wither: new paintings
Gatehouse Gallery, Glasgow (0141-620 0235)
during September

Alighiero e Boetti: *arte povera*
Whitechapel Art Gallery, London (0171-522 7888)
during September and October

Mimmo Paladino: New Prints
Alan Cristea Gallery, London (0171-439 1866)
during September and October

Animate and Fascinate: contemporary animation
Collins Gallery, Glasgow (0141-548 4145)
4 September to 9 October

Denis Thorpe: Fifty Years of Photojournalism 1948-1998
Royal Photographic Society, Bath (01225 462841)
4 September to 10 October

Relief Printing Today
Gainsborough's House, Sudbury (01787-372958)
4 September to 31 October

Edward Seago: War Paintings & Watercolours
Fine Art Society, London (0171-629 5116)
6 September to 1 October

Paul Ryan
Curwen Gallery, London (0171-636 1459)
8 September to 2 October

Jill Crowley: ceramics
Morley College, London (0171-450 9226)
9 September to 30 September

Andrzej Jackowski
Purdy Hicks, London (0171-401 9229)
10 September to 9 October

Landmarks in Print Collecting: Connoissears and Donors at the British Museum; The Light of Nature: landscape drawings and watercolours by Van Dyck and his contemporaries
British Museum, London (0171-636 1555)
10 September to 28 November

Head Strong & Telling Tales: mixed media by Guy Burch
The Orangery, Holland Park, London (0171-361 3010)
11 September to 19 September

Herefordshire Photographic Festival
Hereford Museum & Art Gallery (01432 260000) and throughout the region
11 September to 9 October

Annual Open Exhibition
City Art Gallery, Leeds (0113-247 8248)
11 September to 10 October

Art & Craft to celebrate the opening of the new extension
Beatrice Royal Art Gallery, Eastleigh (01703 610592)
11 September to 24 October

James Holland (1799-1970): the John Constable of Stoke-on-Trent
The Potteries Museum & Art Gallery, Stoke-on-Trent (01782 232323)
11 September to 7 November

Computers and Printmaking
Birmingham Museum & Art Gallery (0121-303 2834)
11 September to 28 November

Craig Cooper: 50 canvases
Bury Art Gallery & Museum (0161-253 5878)
11 September to 23 October

Sir John Soane (1753-1837): architecture
Royal Academy of Arts, London (0171-300 8000)
11 September to 3 December

Jazz Prints and Pop Prints
Peterborough Museum & Art Gallery (01733 343329)
11 September to 10 October

Van Dyck (1599-1641)
Royal Academy of Arts, London (0171-300 8000)
11 September to 10 December

GaelForce: season of Celtic-rooted arts and culture
Gracefield Arts Centre, Dumfries (01387 262084) and throughout the region
12 September to 10 October

Grinneas Nan Eilean: Islands open
An Lanntair, Stornoway, Isle of Lewis (01851 703307)
13 September to 2 October

Stephanie Dingle: new works
The Gallery, Manchester's Art House, Manchester (0161-237 3551)
15 September to 9 October

Robert Wlérick: Model of Therese
Bruton Gallery, Leeds (0113-242 2323)
15 September to 16 November

It Won't be Long: The Rediscovery of Ron Traeger, Michael Cooper and John Cowan
Canon Photography Gallery, Victoria & Albert Museum, London (0171-938 8500)
16 September 1999 to 30 January 2000

Maria van Kesteren: wood
Barrett Marsden Gallery, London (0171-336 6396)
17 September to 30 October

Walter Keeler: recent ceramics
Contemporary Applied Arts, London (0171-436 2344)
17 September to 30 October

The Shape of Colour: Red
The Lighthouse, Glasgow (0141-287 7346 for details)
17 September to 21 November

Road Works: ceramics by Loraine Rutt
The Ice House, Holland Park, London (0171-361 3010)
18 September to 9 October

David Cox: watercolours
Royal Cambrian Academy, Conwy (01492 593413)
18 September to 17 October

Textures of Memory: contemporary cloth work
Angel Row Gallery, Nottingham (0115-947 6334)
18 September to 30 October

Everyone's a Winner: South West Arts Annual Award winners
Devon Guild of Craftsmen, Bovey Tracey (01626 832223)
18 September to 31 October

Malcolm Bowman: paintings
Wakefield Art Gallery, Wakefield (01924-305900)
18 September to 31 October

Innocence and Cruelty: engraved glass by Ronald Pennell
Wolverhampton Art Gallery, Wolverhampton (01902 552055)
18 September to 13 November

Mosaic: A Living Art – An Anglo-Indian Celebration
Ruskin Gallery, Sheffield (0114-203 9416)
18 September to November/December

Thomas Gainsborough: Diligence under the Appearance of Chance
Christ Church Picture Gallery, Oxford (01865 276172)
20 September to 15 December

Chandler/Whiteside and Hill
Medici Galleries, London (0171-837 7099)
21 September to 7 October

Sickert Prints and Drawings
Fitzwilliam Museum, Cambridge (01223 332900)
21 September to 20 December

Jim Harold: exhibition based on casts of classical sculpture
Talbot Rice Art Gallery, Edinburgh (0131-650 2210)
24 September to 30 October

On Show 12: open exhibition
Usher Gallery, Lincoln (01522 527980)
24 September to 28 November

The John Moores Liverpool Exhibition 21
Walker Art Gallery, Liverpool (0151-478 4199)
24 September 1999 to 9 January 2000

East Coast: Erosion & Corrosion – recent paintings in egg tempera by Rob Milliken
Woodbine Cottage Gallery, Whaplode Drove, Spalding, Lincs (01406 330693)
25 September to 18 October

Ken Elias: paintings of Glynneath in the '50s
Wrexham Arts Centre, Wrexham (01978 292093)
25 September to 6 November

Trace: The 1999 Liverpool Biennial of Contemporary Art
Tate Gallery, Liverpool (0151-709 3223)
25 September to 7 November

David Measures: recordings & paintings of farmland habitats
The Yard Gallery, Wollaton Park, Nottingham (0115-915 3653)
25 September to 14 November

The Earl Haig OBE ARSA
Mainhill Gallery, Jedburgh (01835 830518)
26 September to 10 October

Ana Maria Pacheco: paintings & sculpture
National Gallery, London (0171-839 3321) between dates below, then on UK tour: contact Pratt Contemporary Art (01732 882326) for details
29 September 1999 to 9 January 2000

John Hoyland RA
Royal Academy of Arts, London (0171-300 8000)
30 September to 31 October

OCTOBER 1999

Charles Camoin (1878-1965): works on paper
Connaught Brown, London (0171-408 0362)
during October

Harry Holland: new paintings
Martin Tinney Gallery, Cardiff (01222 641411)
during October

Jim Hardie and Pam So: installation
Vennel Gallery, Irvine (01294 275059)
during October

John Creed: steelwork & metalwork
Roger Billcliffe Gallery, Glasgow (0141-332 4027)
during October

Perspectives of Glasgow
Gatehouse Gallery, Glasgow (0141-620 0235)
during October

Root Festival: performance and time-based art
Ferens Art Gallery, Hull (01482 613902)
during October

Victoria Crowe: paintings
Thackeray Gallery, London (0171-937 5883)
during October

Joseph Beuys: Multiples
Barbican Art Gallery, London (0171-638 4141)
October to December

When Time Began to Rant and Rage: 20th-century Irish figurative painting
Barbican Art Gallery, London (0171-638 4141)
October to December

CALENDAR OF EXHIBITIONS

Blue
Walsall Museum & Art Gallery (01922 653116)
October 1999 to January 2000

Sculptures by Stanley Dove; Modern Master Graphics
Cambridge Contemporary Art, Cambridge (01223 324222)
1 October to 16 October

Terry Duffy
Ogilvy & Estill, Conwy (01492 592292)
1 October to 24 October

Melita Denaro
Adam Gallery, Bath (01225 480406)
2 October to 25 October

Baa: wool-based craft
art.tm, Inverness (01463 712240)
2 October to 6 November

Counting Sheep: the role of sheep in cultural contexts
Inverness Museum & Art Gallery (01463 237114) and touring
2 October to 6 November

50 Years a Potter: David Eeles and the Eeles Pottery in Dorset
Royal Cornwall Museum, Truro (01872 272205)
2 October to 13 November

Disaster! – images of epic destruction
Harris Museum & Art Gallery, Preston (01772 258248)
2 October 1999 to 15 January 2000

Alberto Morrocco OBE RSA RGI RSW (1917-1998): paintings
The Scottish Gallery, Edinburgh (0131-558 1200)
4 October to 27 October

Eleri Mills: Figures in an Ancestral Landscape
Museum of Modern Art, Wales, Machynlleth (01654 703355)
4 October to 4 November

The Fine Art of Medicine: links between art & medicine
Hunterian Museum, University of Glasgow (0141-330 4221)
4 October to 24 December

The Apocalypse: prints by Dürer and Duvet
Fitzwilliam Museum, Cambridge (01223 332900)
5 October 1999 to March 2000

Ann Oram: new paintings
Portland Gallery, London (0171-321 0422)
6 October to 22 October

A Decade: furniture & interiors by Nina Moeller & Pat Booth
The Orangery, Holland Park, London (0171-361 3010)
7 October to 20 October

A Cabinet of Curiosities from the Collections of Peter Blake
Morley College, London (0171-450 9226)
7 October to 11 November

Art & Science 2000 Exhibitions
Peter Scott Gallery, Lancaster University (01524 593057)
7 October 1999 into 2000

John Mackechnie: Urban Myth – lens-based screenprints
Glasgow Print Studio, Glasgow (0141-552 0704)
9 October to 13 November

Bob Brown
Alresford Gallery, Alresford (01962 735286)
10 October to 2 November

Ian Weatherhead
Wykeham Galleries, Stockbridge (01264 810364)
12 October to 23 October

Godfrey Tonks
Medici Galleries, London (0171-837 7099)
12 October to 27 October

Pastel Society 100th Birthday Exhibition: invited members
Linda Blackstone Gallery, London (0181-868 5765)
13 October to 30 October

Lucio Fontana
Hayward Gallery, London (0171-960 4242)
14 October 1999 to 9 January 2000

A Grand Design: The Art of the Victoria & Albert Museum
Victoria & Albert Museum, London (0171-938 8500)
14 October 1999 to 16 January 2000

Estelle Thompson
Purdy Hicks, London (0171-401 9229)
15 October to 20 November

Mingalay: paintings, drawings, photo's & film by Julie Brooks
Collins Gallery, Glasgow (0141-548 4145)
16 October to 13 November

Pam Johnson: aboriginal art
Gracefield Arts Centre, Dumfries (01387 262084)
16 October to 13 November

Millennium Calendar Exhibition: paintings by East Ayrshire artists
Dick Institute, Kilmarnock (01563 526401)
16 October to 27 November

Symbiosis: Bashir Makhoul and Alnoor Mitha
Huddersfield Art Gallery, Huddersfield (01484 226300)
16 October to 27 November

The influence of music and dance on the work of J.D. Fergusson
The Fergusson Gallery, Perth (01738 441944)
16 October 1999 to 19 April 2000

Michelangelo Pistoletto: The Shifting Perspective
Museum of Modern Art, Oxford (01865 722733)
17 October 1999 to 2 January 2000

Renaissance Florence: The Art of the 1470s
Sainsbury Wing, National Gallery, London (0171-839 3321/747 2885)
20 October 1999 to 16 January 2000

Enid Mitchell FRBS: sculpture
Guild Gallery, Bristol (0117-926 5548)
23 October to 13 November

Helen Parrott: textiles and paperworks
Cupola Gallery, Sheffield (0114-285 2665)
25 October to 27 November

John Yardley RI: new oils and watercolours
Llewellyn Alexander, London (0171-620 1322)
28 October to 13 November

Model Life: sculptures by Matthew Miller, Guy Holder & Bruce Williams
Brighton Museum & Art Gallery (01273 290900)
28 October to 7 December

C.R.W. Nevinson: The Twentieth Century
Imperial War Museum, London (0171-416 5000)
28 October 1999 to end January 2000

Matthias Stom: 17th-century Dutch painter
Barber Institute of Fine Arts, Birmingham (0121-414 7333)
29 October 1999 to 16 January 2000

NOVEMBER 1999

Two Painters: Sandy Murphy RSW and Helen Wilson RGI
Gatehouse Gallery, Glasgow (0141-620 0235)
during November

Post-Impressionist and Modern Master paintings, drawings and sculptures
Connaught Brown, London (0171-408 0362)
November 1999 to January 2000

Paul Slater & Tony McSweeney
The Coningsby Gallery, London (0171-636 7478)
2 November to 13 November

Anne Magill
Medici Galleries, London (0171-837 7099)
2 November to 18 November

Dennis Page
Wykeham Galleries, Stockbridge (01264 810364)
2 November to 20 November

Barbara Rae
Art First, London (0171-734 0386)
2 November to 25 November

Sixties Sculpture: Clive Barker
Whitford Fine Art, London (0171-930 9332)
3 November to 12 December

Barry Atherton
New Academy Gallery, London (0171-323 4700)
4 November to 26 November

Ken Howard RA
New Grafton Gallery, London (0181-748 8850)
4 November to 27 November

The Art of Bloomsbury: Roger Fry, Vanessa Bell and Duncan Grant
Tate Gallery, London (0171-887 8000)
4 November 1999 to 30 January 2000

Mackintosh Sketches
Hunterian Art Gallery, University of Glasgow (0141-330 5431)
5 November 1999 to 29 January 2000

Magna Brava! The Magnum Women Photographers
Scottish National Portrait Gallery, Edinburgh (0131-556 8921)
5 November 1999 to 30 January 2000

Paintings by Marj Bond RSW; prints by Kenna Crawford; jewellery by Amanda Doughty
The Open Eye Gallery, Edinburgh (0131-557 1020)
6 November to 25 November

Yorkshire Photographic Unit
Wakefield Art Gallery, Wakefield (01924-305900)
6 November to 5 December

African Decorative Art
Devon Guild of Craftsmen, Bovey Tracey (01626 832223)
6 November to 18 December

A Retrospective Future: innovative craftwork
Craft Centre & Design Gallery, City Art Gallery, Leeds (0113-247 8241)
6 November 1999 to 16 January 2000

Chris Orr: prints
Craft Centre & Design Gallery, City Art Gallery, Leeds (0113-247 8241)
6 November to 29 February

Thirza Kotzen
Curwen Gallery, London (0171-636 1459)
10 November to 4 December

Contemporary Sporting Art
Malcolm Innes Gallery, London (0171-839 8083/4)
11 November to 20 November

20th Century Art from the Museum's Collection
Birmingham Museum & Art Gallery (0121-303 2834)
12 November 1999 to 26 March 2000

Coastal Collection: sculpture by Robert Callender
An Lanntair, Stornoway, Isle of Lewis (01851 703307)
13 November to 11 December

Rob McLauren: new paintings
Talbot Rice Art Gallery, Edinburgh (0131-650 2210)
13 November to 18 December

The Allotment: new ceramics by Kate Malone
City Art Gallery, Worcester (01905 25371)
13 November 1999 to 8 January 2000

Wales Drawing Biennale
Wrexham Arts Centre, Wrexham (01978 292093)
13 November 1999 to 8 January 2000

Drawings and Prints from Northern Europe
Christ Church Picture Gallery, Oxford (01865 276172)
15 November 1999 to 30 January 2000

Graham McKean
The Leith Gallery, Edinburgh (0131-553 5255)
16 November to 27 November

Botticelli: *The Mystic Nativity*
Room 1, National Gallery, London (0171-839 3321/747 2885)
18 November 1999 to end January 2000

Alastair Salvesen Art Scholarship Exhibition
Royal Scottish Academy, Edinburgh (0131-225 6671)
19 November to 15 December

Identity Crisis: The 90s Defined
The Lighthouse, Glasgow (0141-287 7346 for details)
19 November 1999 to 13 February 2000

The Plate Show
Collins Gallery, Glasgow (0141-548 4145)
20 November to 23 December

Christmas Exhibition: Glasgow Print Studio artists
Glasgow Print Studio, Glasgow (0141-552 0704)
20 November to 24 December

Keith Andrew: landscape paintings
Rhyl Library Museum & Art Gallery, Rhyl (01745 353814) and touring
20 November 1999 to 8 January 2000

Into the New: Art for the Next Millennium
The Potteries Museum & Art Gallery, Stoke-on-Trent (01782 232323)
20 November 1999 to 9 January 2000

Pacesetters
Peterborough Museum & Art Gallery (01733 343329)
20 November 1999 to 5 February 2000

Derek McGuire
Landings Gallery, Edinburgh (0131-225 1501)
24 November 1999 to 14 January 2000

Frans Wesselman
Ogilvy & Estill, Conwy (01492 592292)
26 November to 24 December

Artists at Home: The Holland Park Circle (1850-1900)
Leighton House, London (0171-602 3316)
29 November 1999 to 26 February 2000

All Our Yesterdays
Cecil Higgins Art Gallery, Bedford (01234 211222)
30 November 1999 to 27 February 2000

DECEMBER 1999

Eileen Agar (1899-1991): Surrealist paintings
Dean Gallery, Scottish National Gallery of Modern Art, Edinburgh (0131-624 6332)
1 December 1999 to 27 February 2000

The Scottish Colourists
Portland Gallery, London (0171-321 0422)
2 December to 23 December

Millennium Show
Albemarle Gallery, London (0171-499 1616)
2 December 1999 to 31 January 2000

Susan Cohn: jewellery & metalwork
Glasgow School of Art, Glasgow (0141-353 4500)
3 December to 31 December

Charles Mahoney: paintings & works on paper
Harris Museum & Art Gallery, Preston (01772 258248)
4 December 1999 to 29 January 2000

Light Fantastic: Royal Society of Painter-Printmakers & Royal Watercolour Society
Bankside Gallery, London (0171-928 7521)
4 December 1999 to 30 January 2000

Jack Morrocco: paintings; 'Little Silver Darlings': paintings in silver frames, silver sculpture & other silver items
The Leith Gallery, Edinburgh (0131-553 5255)
7 December 1999 to 15 January 2000

Size Immaterial: Handheld Sculpture of the 1990s
British Museum, London (0171-636 1555)
7 December 1999 to April 2000

J.D. Fergusson Arts Award Trust Winner
The Fergusson Gallery, Perth (01738 441944)
10 December 1999 to 1 April 2000

Landscape Watercolours 1760-1830
Birmingham Museum & Art Gallery (0121-303 2834)
11 December to 28 February

Obscene Powers: exhibition and conference
John Hansard Gallery, Southampton (01703 592158)
14 December 1999 to 5 February 2000

Crossover: the painting & illustration of David Armitage
Brighton Museum & Art Gallery (01273 290900)
18 December 1999 to 6 February 2000

The Apocalypse and the Shape of Things to Come
British Museum, London (0171-636 1555)
18 December 1999 to 29 April 2000

JANUARY 2000

Richard Walker
New Academy Gallery, London (0171-323 4700)
during January 2000

Club Culture I
Ruskin Gallery, Sheffield (0114-203 9416)
January to February 2000

Classical Indian Sculpture
Walsall Museum & Art Gallery (01922 653116)
January to March 2000

Peoples Portraits: 50 portraits by members of the Royal Society of Portrait Painters
Mall Galleries, London (0171-930 6844) and touring
11 January to 22 January 2000

New Frontiers: the history of British landscape painting
City Art Gallery, Worcester (01905 25371)
15 January to 11 March 2000

The Year 1900: Art at the Crossroads
Royal Academy of Arts, London (0171-300 8000)
15 January to 3 April 2000

Pick of the Best IV: painting & craft by top graduates
Beatrice Royal Art Gallery, Eastleigh (01703 610592)
23 January to March 2000

FEBRUARY 2000

Aracely Alarcon
Albemarle Gallery, London (0171-499 1616)
during February 2000

Sally Moore: new paintings
Martin Tinney Gallery, Cardiff (01222 641411)
during February 2000

Madola: Esculturas
Museum of Modern Art, Wales, Machynlleth (01654 703355)
February to March 2000

Recycled Art from South Africa
Harley Gallery, Worksop (01909 501700)
2 February to 5 March 2000

Panamarenko
Hayward Gallery, London (0171-960 4242)
10 February to 9 April 2000

Jock MacInnes: first London solo exhibition
Portland Gallery, London (0171-321 0422)
11 February to 2 March 2000

MARCH 2000

David McClure RSA RSW RGI (1926-1998): Memorial Exhibition – paintings
The Scottish Gallery, Edinburgh (0131-558 1200)
during March 2000

Roderic Barrett: paintings – 80th Birthday Exhibition
Chappel Galleries, Chappel (01206 240326)
during March 2000

Makers' Dozen: craft work
Brighton Museum & Art Gallery (01273 290900)
during March and April 2000

Anita Klein: paintings
Cambridge Contemporary Art, Cambridge (01223 324222)
10 March to 25 March 2000

FAIRS & FESTIVALS

THE ART WORLD
DIRECTORY

The following is a selection of fine art and craft fairs and arts festivals taking place in the coming year. Whilst many are open to visitors on the day, it is necessary to reserve places for some specialist festivals: please contact the organisers for information.

For a free leaflet covering over 50 leading arts festivals, send an A5 SAE to:
British Arts Festivals Association,
The Library (3rd Floor),
77 Whitechapel High Street,
London E1 7QX.

APRIL 1999

Chelsea Art Fair

Chelsea Old Town Hall, Kings Road, London.
Details available on the Web at http://www.penmanfairs.demon.co.uk, or contact Penman Art Fairs, tel 01444 482514, fax 01444 483412, email cp@penmanfairs.demon.co.uk
Art fair now in its 4th year. 47 galleries showing Old Master to contemporary work in two and three dimensions (admission £6 including catalogue). Exhibits are vetted for quality and accuracy of description. Open weekdays 11-8, Sat 11-7, Sun 11-5.
Complimentary tickets for Private Views available on request.
22 to 25 April

London Original Print Fair

Royal Academy of Arts, London.
Details: 0171-300 8000
Now in its 14th year, this is Europe's only specialist print fair to span the five centuries of printmaking from the earliest medieval woodcuts to the most recent work by contemporary artists.
24 dealers of the highest calibre.
22 to 25 April

The Craft Movement Contemporary Craft Fair

Battersea Arts Centre, London.
Details: 01373 813333.
High quality contemporary crafts chosen by a rigorous selection procedure. Ceramics, textiles, glass, jewellery, metal, wood & furniture.
24 to 25 April

Glasgow Art Fair

George Square, Glasgow.
Details: 0141-553 1937
Scotland's only art fair and the largest fair dedicated to art outside London(admission £3 adults, £2 concessions). Now in its fourth year, with over 40 of Britain's finest art dealers selling original works of art by both celebrated and lesser-known artists at prices from £50 upwards. This year, as part of Glasgow 1999: UK City of Architecture and Design, the Fair also includes an exhibition, 'The Art of Design'. Open Thur 10.30-7, Fri & Sat 10.30-8, Sun 12-7.
29 April to 2 May

MAY 1999

The Art of Living Spring Fair

The Kilvert Gallery, Ashbrook House, Clyro, Radnorshire, via Hereford HR3 5RZ.
Details: tel/fax 01497 820831
A celebration of the best in decorative arts for home and garden, supported by Sir John Harvey Jones and Sir Roy Strong. Also includes demonstrations, painting classes and a sculpture exhibition. Open 10-7, last admission 6pm.
1 to 3 May

Brighton Festival

Various venues in Brighton.
Details: Brighton Festival, 21-22 Old Steine, Brighton, East Sussex BN1 1EL (01273 676926)
England's biggest arts festival.
1 to 23 May

Living Crafts

Hatfield House, Hatfield, Hertfordshire AL9 5NQ.
Details: 01705 426523
Around 500 of Britain's top craftsmen and women demonstrating and selling a wide range of crafts from rural to highly sophisticated and traditional to state-of-the-art, in 12 giant marquees (admission £6.50 adults, £3 children). Living Crafts celebrates its 25th anniversary this year, with presentations and demonstrations by members of the British Artist Blacksmiths Association, who will set up forges for the event, and the Embroiderers Guild, which also celebrates its 25th anniversary. Open daily 10-6.
6 to 9 May

The International Fine Art Fair

The Seventh Regiment Armory, Park Avenue at 67th Street, New York City, USA.
Details available on the Web at http://www.haughton.com, or contact Haughton Fairs, 31 Old Burlington Street, London W1X 1LB, tel 0171-734 5491, fax 0171-494 4604, email info@haughton.com
Western art: paintings, drawings and sculpture, c.1300 to the 1960s, from European countries including France, Italy, Germany, Belgium, Spain, Britain, The Netherlands and the United States. Open Fri, Sat, Mon & Tue 11-8, Sun & Wed 11-7.
7 to 12 May

Newbury International Spring Festival

Newbury, Berkshire.
Details: Newbury Spring Festival, 1 Bridge Street, Newbury, Berkshire RG14 5BE (01635 32421/528766)
Music, opera, film, visual arts and family events.
8 to 22 May

Bury St. Edmunds Festival

Bury St. Edmunds, Suffolk.
Details: Festival Office,
Borough Offices, Angel Hill,
Bury St Edmunds,
Suffolk IP33 1XB (01284 757099)
Mixed arts festival.
14 to 30 May

The West of England Art Fair

The Pavilion, Bath.
Details: contact Caroline Penman,
tel 01444 482514,
fax 01444 483412,
email cp@penmanfairs.demon.co.uk,
or Duncan Phillips,
tel 01297 443355,
fax 01297 442541,
email duncanphillips@btinternet.com
New annual art fair with a good mix of work by major artists of the present and the past in two and three dimensions (admission: £4). 38 dealers from throughout the UK will be selling work at prices from £50 to £50,000. Open Thur-Sat 10.30-6, Sun 10.30-5. Complimentary tickets and 2-for-1 offers available on request.
13 to 16 May

Salisbury Festival

Salisbury, Wiltshire.
Details: Salisbury Festival,
75 New Street,
Salisbury SP1 2PH
(01722 323888)
Music, theatre, circus, sculpture and more.
22 May to 5 June

The Craft Movement Contemporary Craft Fair

The Queen Charlotte Hall,
Richmond-upon-Thames.
Details: 01373 813333
High quality contemporary crafts chosen by a rigorous selection procedure. Ceramics, textiles, jewellery, glassware, metal, wood & furniture.
29 to 31 May

JUNE 1999

The Summer Fine Art and Antiques Fair

Olympia, London.
Details: 0171-370 8234
This prestigious fair, now in its 26th year, features high quality paintings, prints, watercolours, pottery, porcelain, silver, glass, books, manuscripts, textiles, carpets, furniture and statuary. Careful vetting of exhibits by a panel of experts ensures accuracy of identification, so the public can buy with confidence. Prices range from the affordable to the exclusive.
3 to 13 June
(closed 7 June)

The Grosvenor House Art & Antiques Fair

Great Room, Grosvenor House,
Park Lane, London W1A 3AA.
Details available on the Web at http://www.grosvenor-antiquesfair.co.uk,
or from the organisers at the above address, tel 0171-399 8100,
fax 0171-495 8747, email
grosvenor-antiquesfair@msn.com
Britain's pre-eminent fair in the international world of art and antiques, now in its 65th year and attracting an audience of some 20,000 visitors (admission plus handbook £16 single, £27 double; £8 for admission only during final two hours each day; concessions available). The world's leading dealers will be exhibiting works of art from antiquity to the 20th century, and this year each exhibitor has been asked to exhibit a *fin-de-siècle* item from their area of expertise. Prices range from £100 to over £1 million, and quality is assured by the vetting of every exhibit. In addition, there will be loan exhibitions from the Royal Collection and from the private collection of Surrealist art patron Edward James.
Open 9 June 11am-5pm; 10, 11 & 14 June 11am-8pm; 12, 13 & 15 June 11am-6pm.
A charity gala evening, in aid of the British Red Cross, will be held on 9 June – call 0171-201 5144 for details.
9 to 15 June

The International Ceramics Fair and Seminar

The Park Lane Hotel, Piccadilly,
London W1.
Details available on the Web at
http://www.haughton.com,
or contact Haughton Fairs,
31 Old Burlington Street,
London W1X 1LB,
tel 0171-734 5491,
fax 0171-494 4604,
email info@haughton.com
A synthesis of academia and commerce, now in its 18th year. Organised in three sections, the event comprises: a loan exhibition of 18th-century British porcelain from private collections; a series of 15 lectures covering a vast range of aspects of the history of world ceramics by academics and curators from all over the world; and a fair of contemporary work with over 40 exhibitors from 9 countries. Open Fri-Sun 11-8, Mon 11-7.
11 to 14 June

artLONDON

Duke of York's Barracks,
King's Road, London SW3.
Details: Ebury Events,
Unit F2,
The 1927 Bulding,
2 Michael Road,
London SW6 2AD
(0171-736 5546)
New art fair for 20th-century and contemporary British and international art, with about 65 exhibitors selling a comprehensive range of figurative and abstract paintings, sculpture, works on paper and other media.
16 to 20 June

City of London Festival

Details: City of London Festival, Bishopsgate Hall, 230 Bishopsgate, London EC2M 4HW (0171-377 0540)

A large variety of events in stunning heritage venues, many of which are not normally open to the public. Programme includes concerts, opera, dance, theatre, comedy, exhibitions, cinema, architectural and garden walks, readings and workshops.

22 June to 15 July

JULY 1999

The Art of Living Summer Fair

Cabbages & Kings, Centre for Garden Design, Wilderness Farm, Wilderness Lane, Hadlow Down, East Sussex TN22 4HU.
Details from The Kilvert Gallery, Ashbrook House, Clyro, Radnorshire, via Hereford HR3 5RZ (tel/fax 01497 820831).

A celebration of the best in decorative arts for home and garden, housed in the converted 18th-century stables, cartshed and piggery as well as in small marquees (admission £5). Supported by Sir John Harvey Jones and Sir Roy Strong. Demonstrations, painting classes and work for sale by specially selected artists, makers and plantsmen, as well as a first class restaurant. Open 11-6, last admission 5pm.

2 to 4 July

International Potters Festival

Aberystwyth Arts Centre, University of Wales, Ceredigion SY23 3DE (01970 622882)
Details from Aberystwyth Arts Centre at the above address or on the Web at http://www.ftech.net/-carrog/ipc.htm

Biennial event at Aberystwyth Arts Centre on the campus of the University of Wales, surrounded by beautiful countryside and overlooking Cardigan Bay. Founded in 1987, the festival attracts ceramicists, potters, students and collectors from all over the world, and comprises demonstrations, hands-on events, kiln-building, firings, lectures, debates, exhibitions, videos, tradestands, entertainment and good food. Book early to avoid disappointment.

2 to 4 July

Lichfield International Arts Festival

Various venues in & around Lichfield.
Details: Lichfield Festival, 7 The Close, Lichfield, Staffs WS13 7LD (01543 257298)

Mixed arts festival.

8 to 18 July

Greenwich & Docklands International Festival

East London.
Details: 6 College Approach, Greenwich, London SE10 9HY (0181-305 1818)

Free outdoor spectaculars as well as ticketed events including theatre, music, dance and visual arts. The 1999 programme celebrates a cultural partnership with Sydney, Australia.

9 to 18 July

Art in Action

Waterperry House, nr. Wheatley, Oxford OX33 9JZ.
Details: SAE to Art in Action, 96 Sedelscombe Road, London SW6 1RB (0171-381 3192)

Open-air event attracting some 25,000 visitors over four days. More than 250 artists and craftsmen of the highest quality will be selling and demonstrating their work, with examples from both western and non-western cultures. Practical classes are available: book on the day. Excellent food, plus live music and dance performances.

15 to 18 July

Gallery Week '98

Nationwide.
Details and regional leaflets: contact Engage, National Association for Gallery Education, 1 Herbal Hill, Clerkenwell, London EC1R 5EJ (0171-278 8382)

Over 400 galleries and museums, from local establishments to national institutions, will be hosting a variety of events to attract a wider audience to art. The themes of this year's Gallery Week are: Science and Creativity (the overlap between science and art); Art in Space (relationships between art and the built environment); and Seeing Out Loud (reading, talking and writing about art).

17 to 25 July

National Eisteddfod of Wales

Llanbedrgoch, Anglesey.
Details: contact Robyn Tomos, National Eisteddfod of Wales Arts & Crafts Officer, tel 01222 763777

Exhibition of contemporary art, crafts, sculpture, installation, video, photography, fashion etc. by contributors who are of Welsh descent, are based in Wales or speak or write Welsh.

31 July to 7 August

AUGUST 1999

Edinburgh International Festival

Venues throughout Edinburgh.
Details from Edinburgh International Festival, 21 Market Street, Edinburgh EH1 1BW (0131-473 2001)

Cultural feast featuring some of the world's greatest artists and companies.

15 August to 4 September

The Craft Movement Contemporary Craft Fair

The Guildhall, Winchester.
Details: 01373 813333
High quality contemporary crafts chosen by a rigorous selection procedure. Ceramics, textiles, glass, jewellery, metal, wood and furniture.
28 to 30 August

SEPTEMBER 1999

The Contemporary Print Fair

Concourse Gallery, Barbican Centre, London EC2.
Details available on the Web at http://www.artnet.co.uk, or contact Clive Jennings, 6a Goodge Place, London W1P 1FL, tel 0171-436 4007, fax 0171-436 2755, email clivej@artnet.co.uk for information and a free catalogue
The best of printmaking today: over 1,000 original prints by around 250 artists, spanning the entire 20th century, on sale from dealers and publishers. All the major print media, with prices from under £50 to over £5,000.
Autumn: contact Clive Jennings (address above) for exact dates

The Craft Movement Contemporary Craft Fair

Kensington Town Hall, London.
Details: 01373 813333
High quality contemporary crafts chosen by a rigorous selection procedure. Ceramics, textiles, glass, jewellery, metal, wood and furniture.
11 to 12 September

The 20th Century British Art Fair

Royal College of Art, London.
Details: contact Gay Hutson, tel 0181-742 1611, fax 0181-995 5094
Founded in 1988, this is the only fair for British art covering the period 1900 to the present day, and is held at the Royal College of Art, a venue associated internationally with the best in British art. Some 60 leading galleries and dealers will be participating.
22 to 26 September

The Craft Movement Contemporary Craft Fair

Camden Centre, London.
Details: 01373 813333
High quality contemporary crafts chosen by a rigorous selection procedure. Ceramics, textiles, jewellery, glassware, metal, wood and furniture.
25 to 26 September

Southwark Festival

Southwark, London.
Details: 16 Winchester Walk, London SE1 9AQ (0171-403 7474)
Exhibitions, classes, lectures, workshops, concerts and other events on a theme of Russia and the Mysterious East.
27 September to 16 October

OCTOBER 1999

City of London Art Fair

Honourable Artillery Company, Armoury House, 39 City Road, London EC1.
Details available on the Web at http://www.penmanfairs.demon.co.uk, or contact Penman Art Fairs, tel 01444 482514, fax 01444 483412, email cp@penmanfairs.demon.co.uk
Art fair with a good mix of old and new, in a unique setting: a 1738 palladian house in 7 acres of grass in the heart of the City of London, not normally open to the public (admission £6 including catalogue). 35 galleries and artists selling mainly 20th-century and contemporary work in two and three dimensions. Exhibits are vetted for quality and accuracy of description. Open weekdays 11-8, Sat 11-6, Sun 11-5.
Complimentary tickets for Private Views available on request.
7 to 10 October

Chelsea Crafts Fair

The Old Town Hall, Kings Road, London.
Details from the Crafts Council, 0171-278 7700
The 20th annual fair, organised by the Crafts Council (admission charge to be decided). Around 230 makers selling high quality work including jewellery, ceramics, furniture, textiles, glass, wood, toys, fashion and accessories. The Fair is organised in two sections: Week 2 has different exhibitors to Week 1.
12 to 17 October and 19 to 24 October

The International Fine Art & Antique Dealers Show

The Seventh Regiment Armory, Park Avenue at 67th Street, New York City, USA.
Details available on the Web at http://www.haughton.com, or contact Haughton Fairs, 31 Old Burlington Street, London W1X 1LB, tel 0171-734 5491, fax 0171-494 4604, email info@haughton.com
Art and antiques from all periods and countries, including pictures, sculpture, manuscripts, furniture, pottery and porcelain, glass, jewellery, silver, textiles, ethnographica and antiquities. Open Fri, Sat & Mon-Wed 11-8, Sun & Thur 11-7.
15 to 21 October

NOVEMBER 1999

The Craft Movement Contemporary Craft Fair

The Concert Halls, Blackheath.
Details: 01373 813333
High quality contemporary crafts chosen by a rigorous selection

procedure. Ceramics, textiles, jewellery, glassware, metal, wood and furniture.
6 to 7 November

The Winter Fine Art and Antiques Fair
Olympia, London.
Details: 0171-370 8234
Around 230 leading dealers exhibiting and selling high quality antiques and outstanding works of art. Careful vetting of exhibits by a panel of experts ensures accuracy of identification, so the public can buy with confidence.
15 to 21 November

The Craft Movement Contemporary Craft Fair
Battersea Arts Centre, London.
Details: 01373 813333
High quality contemporary crafts chosen by a rigorous selection procedure. Ceramics, textiles, jewellery, glassware, metal, wood and furniture.
20 to 21 November

DECEMBER 1999

The Craft Movement Contemporary Craft Fair
The Queen Charlotte Hall, Richmond-upon-Thames.
Details: 01373 813333
High quality contemporary crafts chosen by a rigorous selection procedure. Ceramics, textiles, jewellery, glassware, metal, wood and furniture.
3 to 5 December

JANUARY 2000

ART2000, The London Contemporary Art Fair
Business Design Centre, 52 Upper Street, Islington, London N1 0QH.
Details: contact Lucy Field, tel 0171-359 3535, fax 0171-288 6446, email lucyf@business-design-centre.com
The biggest contemporary art fair in the UK presents over 100 galleries, featuring work on sale by the best-known contemporary artists as well as promising recent graduates.
8 to 17 January (dates to be confirmed)

FEBRUARY 2000

The Spring Fine Art and Antiques Fair
Olympia, London.
Details: 0171-370 8234
Around 160 of the world's leading dealers exhibiting and selling high quality antiques and 20th-century works of art.
Careful vetting of exhibits by a panel of experts ensures accuracy of identification, so the public can buy with confidence.
22 to 27 February

MARCH 2000

The Contemporary Print Show
Concourse Gallery, Barbican Centre, London EC2.
Details available on the Web at http://www.artnet.co.uk, or contact Clive Jennings, 6a Goodge Place, London W1P 1FL, tel 0171-436 4007, fax 0171-436 2755, email clivej@artnet.co.uk for information and a free catalogue
The best of printmaking today: over 1,000 original prints by around 250 artists, presented in exhibition format and on sale from galleries and publishers (admission: free). All the major print media, with prices from under £50 to over £5,000.
Spring 2000 – contact Clive Jennings (address above) for exact dates

The International Asian Art Fair
The Seventh Regiment Armory, Park Avenue at 67th Street, New York City, USA.
Details available on the Web at http://www.haughton.com, or contact Haughton Fairs, 31 Old Burlington Street, London W1X 1LB, tel 0171-734 5491, fax 0171-494 4604, email info@haughton.com
Asian and Islamic works of art, sculpture, ceramics and textiles from the Far East including China, Japan and Korea as well as Southeast Asia, India and the Middle East. Open Thur-Sat & Mon 11-8, Sun & Tue 11-7.
24 to 29 March

Battersea Contemporary Art Fair
Battersea Old Town Hall, London SW11.
Details: 0171-228 0741 or 0171-642 5318
The largest artists' art fair in the UK, with artists selling their own work direct to the public at truly affordable prices (no commission goes to the organisers). Paintings, sculptures, limited edition prints and photographs from highly traditional to cutting edge.
26 to 27 March (dates to be confirmed)

COMPETITIONS

THE ART WORLD
DIRECTORY

This is only a selection of the competitions, awards and bursaries available, ranging from cash prizes and travel scholarships to opportunities for exhibitions and publishing. Further information can be obtained through art colleges, regional arts boards, local artists' groups and libraries. It is advisable to check before submitting work or sending money.

ALASTAIR SALVESEN ART SCHOLARSHIP

This is an enablement scholarship, offered by the Royal Scottish Academy, which comprises up to £8,000 in travel funds and a three-week exhibition, for an artist aged 25-35 who trained at a Scottish college of art.
Details: SAE in November to Alastair Salvesen Scholarship, Royal Scottish Academy, The Mound, Edinburgh EH2 2EL.

BG WILDLIFE PHOTOGRAPHER OF THE YEAR

SUBMISSIONS BY 14 MAY
Competition organised by *BBC Wildlife Magazine* and the Natural History Museum, aiming to find the best wildlife pictures taken by photographers worldwide. Winning and commended photographs appear in a Natural History Museum exhibition from late October to February before touring worldwide, and are published in a commemorative book. Adult and junior categories are available; prizes total £14,000.
Details: call 0171-938 8714.

BRITISH SCHOOL AT ROME

APPLICATIONS BY DECEMBER
This residential centre for research in the humanities and the practice of visual arts and architecture offers scholarships ranging from 3 to 9 months, including the 9-month Abbey Scholarship in Painting, the Rome Scholarships in the Fine Arts, the Arts Council of England Helen Chadwick Fellowship, the Henry Moore Sculpture Fellowship at the BSR, the RIBA Rome Scholarship in Architecture and Urbanism and the Sargant Fellowship for Fine Arts.
Details: SA label to Registrar, The British School at Rome, Piazzale Winston Churchill 5 (gia via Gramsci 61), 00197 Rome, Italy.

COUTTS CONTEMPORARY ART FOUNDATION AWARDS

Established in 1992 as part of the bank's 300th anniversary celebrations, the awards are made biennially (the next year being 2000) at the discretion of the Foundation's Art Advisory Committee. Submissions are not required, and winners tend to be artists of international standing.
Details: Dr. Sabina R. Korfmann-Bodenmann, Manager, Coutts Contemporary Art Foundation, Talstrasse 59, CH-8022 Zürich, Switzerland.

DALER-ROWNEY AWARDS

Daler-Rowney make various awards at national and regional exhibitions. See *The Art Paper*, available free of charge from art stores in March, June and October, for competitions.

DELFINA STUDIO TRUST

APPLICATIONS BY JANUARY
The Trust provides 18 free studio spaces: British artists are awarded two years' space and others one year with accommodation.
Details: The Administrator, The Delfina Studio Trust, 50 Bermondsey Street, Southwark, London SE1 3UD.

THE DISCERNING EYE

Works not larger than 20" in any direction are invited from artists 'not yet household names'. Prizes and an exhibition are available.
Details: A4 SAE to Exhibition/ Competition Organisers and PR, Parker Harris Partnership, PO Box 279, Esher, Surrey KT10 8YZ (tel: 01372 462190, fax: 01372 460032, email: info@parkerharris.co.uk).

EUROPEAN PUBLISHERS AWARD FOR PHOTOGRAPHY

An open competition for an unpublished book project by a photographer, now in its 6th year. Open to photographers worldwide. The winning book is published in five European countries.
Details: SAE to European Publishers Award, Dewi Lewis Publishing, 8 Broomfield Road, Heaton Moor, Stockport SK4 4ND.

FINE ART TRADE GUILD BUSINESS AWARDS SCHEME

Winners in several nominated art and trade categories are presented with an artist-designed trophy in the spring.
Details: SAE to Robin Rudolph, Fine Art Trade Guild, 16 Empress Place, London SW6 1TT (tel 0171-381 6616, fax 0171-381 2596).

FULBRIGHT POSTGRADUATE AWARDS

APPLICATIONS BY NOVEMBER
Graduate students may apply for a year's postgraduate funding in the

USA. A maintenance grant, full tuition fees and transatlantic travel will be awarded to outstanding candidates.
Details: A4 SAE (39p) to the British Programme Administrator, Fulbright Commission, 62 Doughty Street, London WC1N 2LS (tel: 0171-404 6880, website http://www.fulbright.co.uk).

THE HUNTING ART PRIZES

Over 1,000 artists annually enter this prestigious competition which offers generous cash prizes and an exhibition at the RCA, followed by a tour.
Details: A4 SAE to Exhibition/ Competition Organisers and PR, Parker Harris Partnership, PO Box 279, Esher, Surrey KT10 8YZ (tel: 01372 462190, fax: 01372 460032, email: info@parkerharris.co.uk).

JERWOOD PAINTING PRIZE

This major award is given for excellence in painting, with an exhibition of the shortlisted prizewinners' work in London.
Details: A4 SAE to Exhibition/ Competition Organisers and PR, Parker Harris Partnership, PO Box 279, Esher, Surrey KT10 8YZ (tel: 01372 462190, fax: 01372 460032, email: info@parkerharris.co.uk).

THE JOHN KINROSS MEMORIAL FUND

APPLICATIONS BY APRIL
Students at Scottish colleges studying painting, sculpture and architecture are eligible to apply for a three-month scholarship to Florence in memory of the late John Kinross.
Details: SAE to The Secretary, Royal Scottish Academy, The Mound, Edinburgh EH2 2EL.

JOHN KOBAL PHOTOGRAPHIC PORTRAIT AWARD

APPLICATIONS BY 5 JUNE
This annual award is open to anyone over the age of 18 submitting any photographic portrait (to be interpreted in its loosest sense). Prize money totals £5,500, which includes the top prize of £2,500, the Fuji Film Technical Award of £500 and a variety of other awards. The winning work is published, and exhibitions are held at the National Portrait Gallery (October-January) and various regional galleries.
Details: SAE to The Award Administrator, John Kobal Foundation, PO Box 3838, London WC1X 0NP.

JOHN MOORES LIVERPOOL EXHIBITION

This is a leading biennale of contemporary painting. There

Attendant Facts **by Gus Cummins RA, winner of last year's Hunting Art Prize**

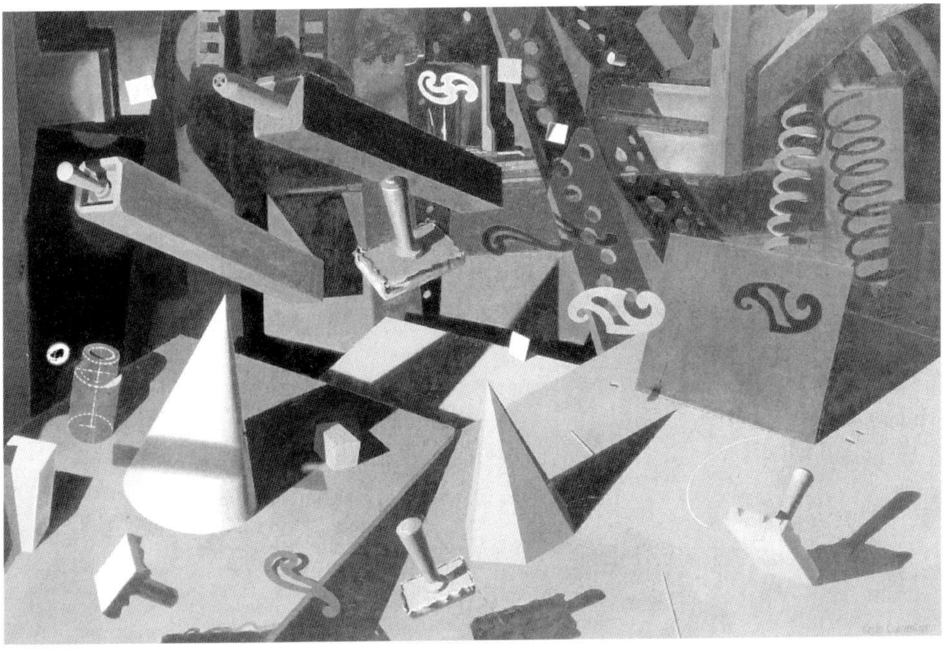

are a £25,000 purchase prize, 10 prizes of £1,000 and an exhibition at the Walker Art Gallery, for works in any medium except traditional watercolour and no larger than 10ft by 12ft in any direction. Next exhibition: 24 September 1999 to 9 January 2000. Details: available from spring 1999 – SAE to The Exhibition Secretary, Walker Art Gallery, William Brown Street, Liverpool L3 8EL.

JULIET GOMPERTS MEMORIAL SCHOLARSHIPS

APPLICATIONS BY END JANUARY

Young figurative and landscape artists, aged over 23 and under 45, are invited to apply for scholarships to attend courses for up to six weeks at the Verrocchio Arts Centre in Tuscany. The value is approximately £2,000. Also, the £500 Janet Konstam Travelling Fellowship is awarded to the best applicant for travel and research in Italy after the tenure of the Juliet Gomperts Scholarship.
Details: SAE to Artists' Residencies in Tuscany, 31 Addison Avenue, London W11 4QS.

KRASZNA-KRAUSZ BOOK AWARDS

These international awards are made annually to encourage and recognise outstanding achievements in the publishing and writing of books on photography and the moving image (film, television and video). Prize money totalling more than £10,000 is awarded in January.
Details: Andrea Livingstone, 122 Fawnbrake Avenue, London SE24 0BZ (tel/fax: 0171-738 6701, email: k-k@dial.pipex.com).

LAING ART COMPETITION

In this major annual competition, thousands of pounds worth of prizes are given for landscapes or seascapes, with an exhibition in London and at various regional centres, starting in January.
Details: Laing Art Competition, John Laing plc, Maxted House, 13 Maxted Road, Hemel Hempstead, Herts. HP2 7DX.

THE LINBURY PRIZE FOR STAGE DESIGN

Commissions and cash awards, sponsored by one of the Sainsbury family charitable trusts, are made biennially to final-year graduate and post-graduate theatre design students from selected colleges. Finalists will exhibit in the autumn. Current entry period: 1999.
Details: Liz Martell, Kallaway, 0171-221 7883.

THE MACMILLAN PRIZE FOR A CHILDREN'S PICTURE BOOK

Art students in higher education are eligible to enter works that are original and will provide children with much enjoyment in this annual competition.
Details: SAE to Marketing Dept, Macmillan Children's Books, 25 Eccleston Place, London SW1W 9NF.

THE MORRISON SCOTTISH PORTRAIT AWARD

APPLICATIONS BY MID-JULY

This is a biennial award, now in its 6th year, offering a prize fund of £6,250 which includes a top award of £5,000. It is open to painters and sculptors living or working in Scotland. The 1999 finalists will have their work exhibited in the Royal Scottish Academy in the autumn.
Details: Royal Scottish Academy, The Mound, Edinburgh EH2 2EL (0131-225 6671).

THE NATIONAL ART LIBRARY ILLUSTRATION AWARDS

SUBMISSIONS BY JULY

Organised by the National Art Library and sponsored by the Enid Linder Foundation, these annual awards are for book and magazine illustrations published in the calendar year preceding the date of the award (ie. 1999 awards for 1998 books and magazines). Overall winner (£2,500), two second prizewinners (one for book and one for magazine illustration), four distinguished mention awards. December-February exhibition.
Details: Dr. Leo Defreitas, National Art Library, The Victoria & Albert Museum, South Kensington, London SW7 2RL.

NATIONAL EISTEDDFOD OF WALES

SUBMISSIONS BY 14 FEBRUARY

The Eisteddfod hosts a large contemporary art and crafts exhibition. Awards include: Gold Medal and £5,000 in Fine Art; Gold Medal and £5,000 in Craft and Design; Young Artist/Craftsman Scholarship of £1,500. Any person born in Wales, of Welsh parentage, able to speak or write the Welsh lan guage or who has lived or worked in Wales for the three years prior to the date of the Eisteddfod is eligible.
Details: Eisteddfod Office, 40 Parc Ty Glas, Llanishen, Cardiff CF4 5WU (01222 763777).

NATIONAL PRINT EXHIBITION 2000

RECEIVING DAYS EARLY JANUARY 2000

February open exhibition at the Mall Galleries, London, offering 11 prizes for outstanding printmakers.
Details: SAE to Mall Galleries, 17 Carlton House Terrace, London SW1Y 5BD.

NATWEST ART PRIZE

SUBMISSIONS BY 31 JANUARY

The NatWest Art Prize, sponsored and organised by the NatWest Group, is one of Britain's major art prizes. Concentrating on painting and drawing, it is open to artists aged 35 years and under, who are living, working or studying in Britain. It aims to encourage creative innovation and technical skills in composition, drawing and use of colour. There is a First Prize of £26,000, plus ten further awards of £1,000. The eleven finalists' work is shown in a summer exhibition at the Lothbury Gallery, London.
Details: check the press for advertisements in Autumn.

NEW ART AWARD

Founded with the intention of recognising and helping young artists in their final year of post-graduate study, this award offers cash prizes and a London show. NB: not held annually.
Details: SAE to Lynne Stern and Linnet Feilding, c/o 107 Hartfield Road, London SW19 3TJ.

NEW DESIGNERS AWARDS

This is part of the New Designers Exhibition held annually in July at the Business Design Centre, Islington. In 1999, Part I (3D work) takes place from July 8-11, with Part II (2D work) from July 15-18. Business and sponsors from throughout the UK select winners from the exhibition representing the best graduates from British design courses.
Details: Lucy Field, 0171-359 3535.

NEW ENGLISH ART CLUB

RECEIVING DAYS 1 & 2 OCTOBER 1999

November open exhibition at the Mall Galleries in London offering a number of awards plus Marks & Spencer subsidies for entries by recent art students.
Details: SAE to Mall Galleries, 17 Carlton House Terrace, London SW1Y 5BD.

NORTHERN ARTS

APPLICATIONS THROUGH-OUT THE YEAR

Northern Arts is the regional arts board for the five counties of the Northern region, covering Cumbria, County Durham, Teeside, Northumberland and Tyne & Wear, and operates a number of projects and schemes.
Details: 0191-281 2866 – for general information, ask for ext. 134; for Visual Arts, ext. 111; for Film, Media and Literature, ext. 132; for Performing Arts, ext. 106; for Lottery and Communications, ext. 118; and for Northern Production Fund, ext. 114.

THE OPEN DRAWING COMPETITION, CHELTENHAM

Competition for professional artists which awards cash prizes every year during an exhibition held at Cheltenham & Gloucester College of Higher Education.
Details: large SAE to Sara Neish-Barker, Exhibition Administrator, School of Fine Art, Cheltenham & Gloucester College of Higher Education, Albert Road, Cheltenham, Glos GL52 3JG.

PASTEL SOCIETY

SUBMISSIONS IN LATE JANUARY

March open exhibition for members and non-members at the Mall Galleries in London, with 12 awards.
Details: SAE to Mall Galleries, 17 Carlton House Terrace, London SW1Y 5BD.

QUEEN ELIZABETH SCHOLARSHIP TRUST

APPLICATIONS BY 15 JANUARY

Aimed at furthering education in crafts and trades, scholarships are granted (ranging from £2,500 to £12,000) every June. Application forms available from September.
Details: A4 (31p) SAE to the Secretary, The Queen Elizabeth Scholarship Trust, 7 Buckingham Gate, London SW1E 6JY.

ROYAL ACADEMY SUMMER EXHIBITION

SUBMISSIONS BY THE SPRING

Annual open exhibition sponsored by Diageo, which usually attracts around 12,000 paintings, sculptures, prints and architectural designs, of which about 10% are hung. Over 60% of the works hung are sold during the course of the exhibition. Awards and prizes include: the Charles Wollaston Award (£25,000) for the most distinguished work in the exhibition; the Bovis/Architects Journal Awards (£7,500) for architecture; the Jack Goldhill Award (£8,000) for sculpture; t he Diageo Award (£5,000) for a commission from a first-time exhibitor; the Dupree Family Award (£2,500) for a painting or sculpture by a woman artist; the Worshipful Comany of Chartered Architects Award (£1,000) for a measured architectural drawing; and the Nordstern Award (£1,000), in association with the

London Original Print Fair, for a print in any medium.
Details: send SAE to
Summer Exhibition Office,
The Royal Academy of Arts,
Burlington House, Piccadilly,
London W1V 0DS.

ROYAL INSTITUTE OF OIL PAINTERS

RECEIVING DAYS 22 & 23 OCTOBER 1999

Open exhibition in late December at the Mall Galleries in London for members and non-members, with a number of prizes awarded.
Details: SAE to Mall Galleries,
17 Carlton House Terrace,
London SW1Y 5BD.

ROYAL INSTITUTE OF PAINTERS IN WATERCOLOURS

SUBMISSIONS IN LATE FEBRUARY

Open exhibition at the Mall Galleries in London in the Spring. Many prizes on offer.
Details: SAE to Mall Galleries,
17 Carlton House Terrace,
London SW1Y 5BD.

ROYAL OVER-SEAS LEAGUE OPEN EXHIBITION

There will be no open exhibition in 1999, but a new competition will be arranged for the year 2000.
Details: SAE to Department of Cultural Affairs, Royal Over-Seas League, Over-Seas House,
Park Place, St. James's Street,
London SW1A 1LR.

ROYAL SCOTTISH ACADEMY ANNUAL EXHIBITION

SUBMISSIONS BY MARCH

The annual exhibition, sponsored by Maclay Murray & Spens, Solicitors, takes place from 24 April to 11 July. It includes painting, printmaking, architecture and sculpture, with numerous awards in all categories including the M. S. Macfarlane Charitable Trust prizes for painting and sculpture and the McGrigor Donald Sculpture Award.
Details: SAE to The
Administrative Secretary,
The Royal Scottish Academy,
The Mound, Edinburgh EH2 2EL.

ROYAL SOCIETY OF BRITISH ARTISTS

RECEIVING DAYS 13 & 14 AUGUST 1999

Autumn open exhibition at the Mall Galleries in London, with nine awards on offer.
Details: SAE to Mall Galleries,
17 Carlton House Terrace,
London SW1Y 5BD.

ROYAL SOCIETY OF MARINE ARTISTS

RECEIVING DAYS 10 & 11 SEPTEMBER 1999

Open exhibition in October at the Mall Galleries in London of works featuring the sea, with three prizes on offer.
Details: SAE to Mall Galleries,
17 Carlton House Terrace,
London SW1Y 5BD.

ROYAL SOCIETY OF PORTRAIT PAINTERS

SUBMISSIONS IN MID MARCH

Annual open exhibition held in May, at the Mall Galleries in London, offering three prestigious awards for portraiture: the Ondaatje Prize (£5,000) for the most distinguished painting in the exhibition; the Carroll Foundation Young Portrait Painters Award (£3,000) for a painter under 35; and the new Prince of Wales's Award for Portrait Drawing (£2,000), sponsored by Prince Charles.
Details: SAE to Mall Galleries,
17 Carlton House Terrace,
London SW1Y 5BD.

RSA ART FOR ARCHITECTURE

APPLICATIONS FOUR TIMES A YEAR

Grants are available to those involved in building or landscape projects to appoint, at the outset of a project, artists as part of the design team.
Details: Project Manager,
RSA Art for Architecture,
8 John Adam Street,
London WC2N 6EZ.

RSA STUDENT DESIGN AWARDS

SUBMISSIONS BY END NOVEMBER

Awards in the form of Attachment or Travel awards are made to students submitting winning designs in response to the briefs offered in the Projects Book, which is published in September.
Details: contact RSA Design,
8 John Adam Street,
London WC2N 6EZ.

SCOTTISH ARTS COUNCIL

The Scottish Arts Council funds various projects covering the visual arts, combined arts, placements and travel, crafts and photography and commissions. There are also exhibition schemes.
Details: The Scottish Arts Council,
12 Manor Place,
Edinburgh EH3 7DD
(Help Desk 0131-240 2443/2444 – Mon-Fri 10-2 & 2-4, answering machine outwith hours).

SINGER & FRIEDLANDER/ *SUNDAY TIMES* WATERCOLOUR COMPETITION

SUBMISSIONS IN JUNE

A competition and selected exhibition for works "upholding the finest traditions of contempo-

rary British watercolour painting." Finalists' exhibitions are held at the Mall Galleries and in several regional centres, and prizes are worth a total of around £25,000.
Details: A4 SAE to Exhibition/ Competition Organisers and PR, Parker Harris Partnership, PO Box 279, Esher, Surrey KT10 8YZ (tel: 01372 462190, fax: 01372 460032, email: info@parkerharris.co.uk).

SOCIETY OF WILDLIFE ARTISTS

RECEIVING DAYS 18 & 19 JUNE 1999

Summer open exhibition at the Mall Galleries in London of work depicting wildlife, with six prizes on offer.
Details: SAE to Mall Galleries, 17 Carlton House Terrace, London SW1Y 5BD.

SOUTH EAST ARTS

Information services and funding schemes covering the visual arts, crafts and photography.
Details: contact The Administrative Assistant, Visual & Media Arts, South East Arts, Union House, Bridge Road, Tunbridge Wells, Kent TN4 8HF.

MORE COMPETITIONS OVERLEAF...

Self Portrait **by Paul Brason RP, winner of the Ondaatje Prize at last year's Royal Society of Portrait Painters Annual Exhibition**

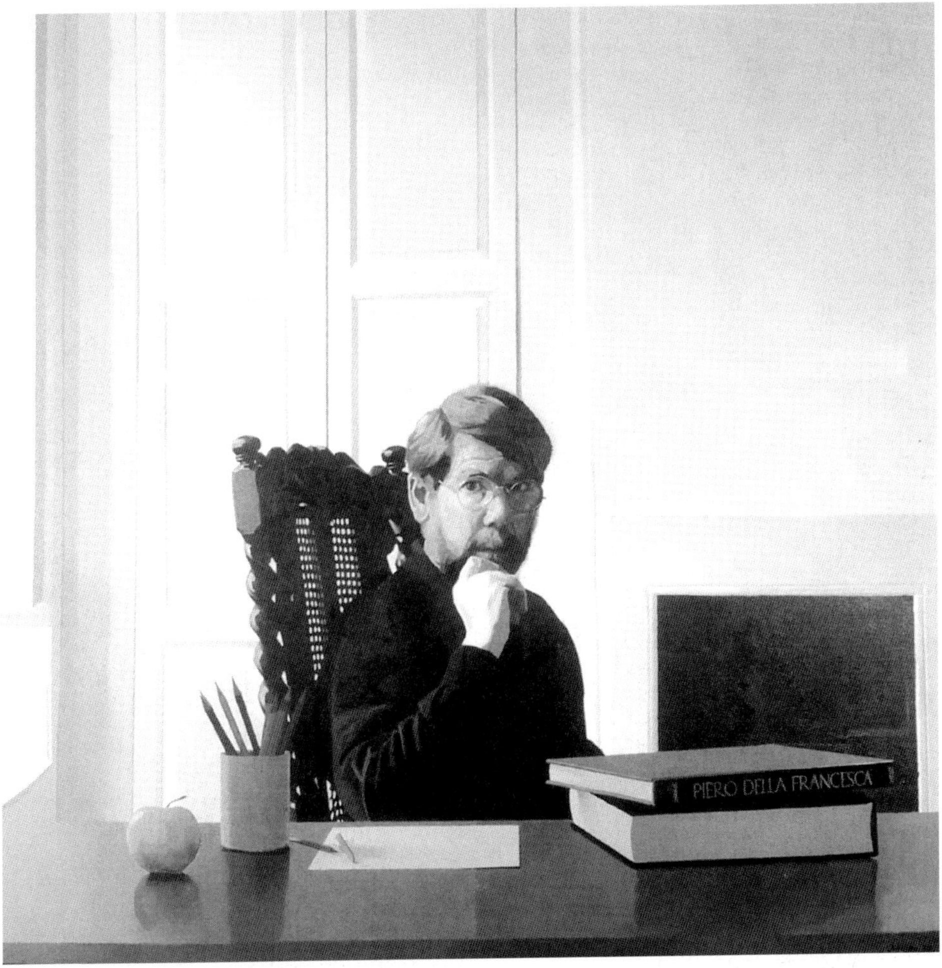

SOUTH WEST ARTS

SUBMISSIONS THROUGHOUT THE YEAR

Like most regional arts boards, this invites artists from the region to submit applications for various schemes.
Details: Bradninch Place, Gandy Street, Exeter EX4 3LS.

STOCKPORT OPEN EXHIBITION

SUBMISSIONS BY JULY

Works made by artists in the North West are exhibited annually and merit awards are made.
Details: SAE to Exhibitions Officer, Stockport Art Gallery, Wellington Road South, Stockport SK3 8AB.

THE TURNER PRIZE

This annual prize, supported by the Patrons of New Art, is usually sponsored by Channel 4. Nominations from the public are invited and four British contemporary artists under 50 are chosen by a selection panel for a popular finalists' exhibition at the end of each year on the strength of the previous year's exhibitions. A large cash prize (£20,000) is awarded at the Tate Gallery.
Details: The Turner Prize, Tate Gallery, Millbank, London SW1P 4RG.

WATERCOLOUR C21

SUBMISSIONS BY JUNE 11; HANDING-IN DAYS JUNE 28 & JUNE 29

New open painting competition organised by the Royal Watercolour Society, encouraging innovative approaches to the use of watercolour. Artists are invited to submit three framed, glazed water-based paintings on paper, and successful entries will be exhibited at Bankside Gallery, London from July 13 to August 15, alongside works by internationally acclaimed artists. Prizes are awarded, with a total value of over £10,000.
Details: contact Bankside Gallery, 48 Hopton Street, London SE1 9JH (0171-928 7521).

WINSOR & NEWTON AWARDS

Winsor & Newton sponsor several awards including the ROI Young Artists' Award and the Royal Institute of Painters in Watercolours Award. The prizes consist of art materials up to the value of £1,000. Both award winners are shown at an exhibition at the Mall Galleries in London.
Details: UK Marketing Department, Winsor & Newton, Whitefriars Avenue, Harrow, Middlesex HA3 5RH.

YORKSHIRE ARTS

SUBMISSIONS THROUGHOUT THE YEAR

Artists from the region are invited to submit applications for various schemes covering the visual arts, crafts, photography, film-making, multimedia and broadcasting.
Details: Visual & Media Arts Unit, Yorkshire Arts Board, 21 Bond Street, Dewsbury, West Yorkshire WF13 1AX.

LONDON COMMERCIAL GALLERIES

All entries in this section are sorted alphabetically by gallery.

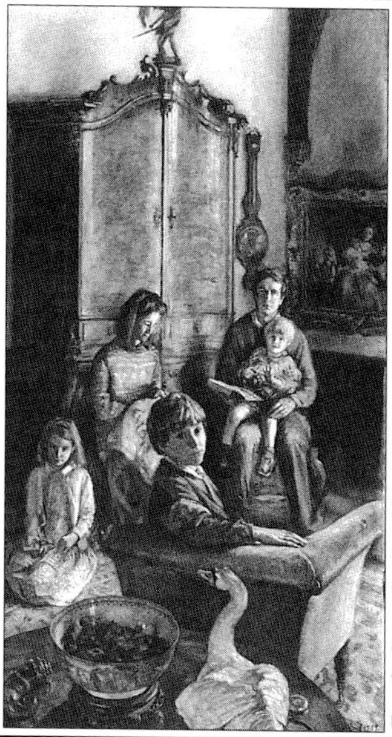

Family Group by Jane Bond RP, NEAC.

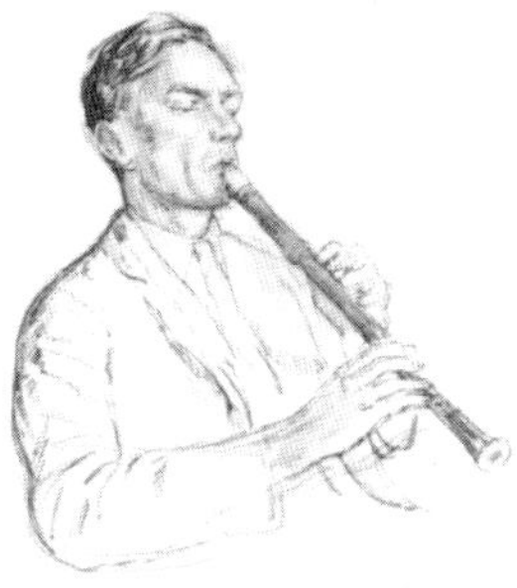

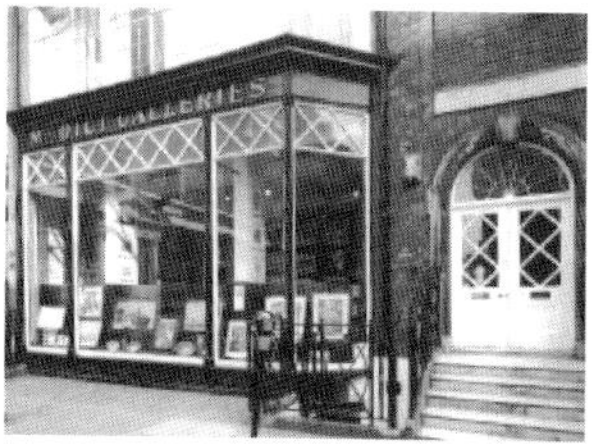

11 Duke Street Ltd
11 Duke Street, London SW1Y. **Fax:** *0171-976 2733.*

180 Gallery
182 Westbourne Grove, London W11 2RH.
Tel: *0171-229 9309.* **Fax:** *0171-243 7215.*

507 Gallery
507 Kings Road, Chelsea, London SW10 0TX.

Aaron Gallery
34 Bruton Street, London W1X.
Tel: *0171-499 9434.*

Abbott & Holder
30 Museum Street, London WC1A 1LH.
Tel: *0171-637 3981.* **Fax:** *0171-631 0575.*
Email *abbott.holder@virgin.net*
Ws *http://www.artefact.co.uk/AaH.html*
Opening times: *Mon-Sat 9.30-6, Thurs 9.30-7.*
Nearest Underground: *Tottenham Court Road.*
Personnel: *Partners:* Phillip Athill, John Abbott.
Over 1000 English watercolours,, drawings and prints (with some oils) 1780-1990 displayed on three gallery floors. Founded in 1936 our policy has always been to sell pictures that can be bought from income and our price range is from £50-£5,000.
We have an in-house conservator and are happy to give free advice of cleaning, restoring and framing. Every seven weeks we issue a LIST introducing 300 works to stock and announcing any particular exhibition we are featuring.
Our LISTS are free and will be sent in application.
Services and Facilities:
Art Consultancy. Framing. Gallery space for hire. Restoration. Valuation.
Work Stocked and Sold:
Pr.
Price range: £50 - £5,000.
For artists see *Commercial Gallery Artists.*

Ackermann & Johnson
Lowndes Lodge Gallery, 27 Lowndes Street, London SW1X 9H7.
Tel: *071-235 6464.* **Fax:** *0171-823 1057.*

Actaeon Gallery
15 Motcomb Street, London SW1X 8LB.
Tel: *0171-259 5095.* **Fax:** *071 259 5069.*

Adam Gallery
62 Walcot Square, London SE11.
Tel: *0171-582 1260.*

Addison Ross Gallery
40 Eaton Terrace, London SW1 W8TS.
Tel: *0171-730 1536, 0171-730 6353.*
Fax: *0171-823 5081.*

Adonis Art
1B Coleherne Road, London SW10.
Tel: *0171-460 3888.*

Adrian Sassoon
14 Rutland Gate, London SW7 1BB.
Tel: *0171-581 9888.*
Fax: *0171-823 8473.*

Agnew's
43 Old Bond Street, London W1X 4AB.
Tel: *0171-629 6176.* **Fax:** *0171-629 4359.*

Ainscough Contemporary Art
Drayton Gardens, London SW10 9QS.
Tel: *0171-341 9442.*

The Air Gallery
32 Dover Street, London W1X 3RA.
Tel: *0171-409 1255 / 1516 / 1395.*
Fax: *0171-409 1856.*

Alan Cristea Gallery
31 Cork Street, London W1X 2NU.
Tel: *0171-439 1866.* **Fax:** *0171-734 1549.*
Opening times: *Mon-Fri 10-5.30, Sat 10-1.*
Nearest Underground: *Green Park.*
Personnel: *Director:* Alan Cristea.

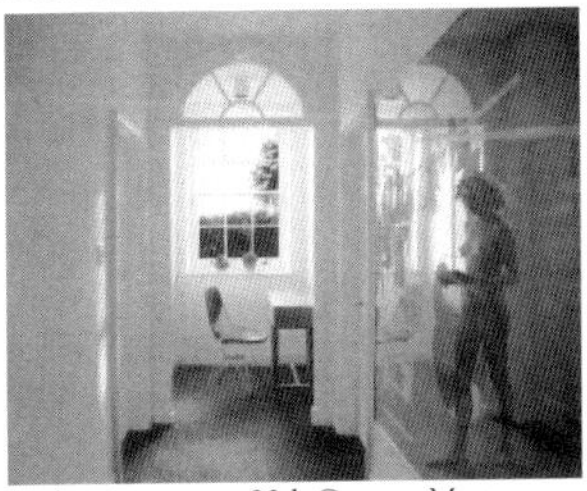

Dealers in top-rate 20th Century Master Graphics including Braque, Gabo, Léger, Matisse, Miró, Nicholson and Picasso.
Dealers in important contemporary artists including Ayres, Baldessari, Baselitz, Bochner, Buckley, Chillida, Close, Flanagan, Frankenthaler, Hockney, Johns, Judd, Kirkeby, Langlands & Bell, Lichtenstein, Mangold, Mansen, Manser, Nauman, Oldenburg, Opie, Pasmore, Penck, Rauschenberg, Rosenquist, Scully, Self, Stella, Tapies, Turnbull, Warhol and Winters. Publishers of major contemporary artists including Blake, Caulfield, Craig-Martin, Davey, Dibbets, Dine, Fulton, Hamilton, Hodgkin, Hoyland, Inshaw, Jones, McKeever, Milroy, Moon, Motherwell, Paladino, Salle, Sultan, Tilson, Walker and Woodrow. Exhibitions about once a month including, for 1999, one-man exhibitions of Patrick Caulfield, Gillian Ayres, Mimmo Paladino and Howard Hodgkin.
Services and Facilities:
Art Consultancy. Art for Offices. Disabled Access.
Work Stocked and Sold:
Ab. Pr.
Price range: £150 - £150,000.
For artists see *Commercial Gallery Artists.*

Albany Gallery
1 Bury Street, London SW1Y.
Tel: *0171-839 6119.*

Albemarle Gallery
49 Albemarle Street, London W1X 3FE.
Tel: *0171-499 1616.* **Fax:** *0171-499 1717.*
Ws *http://www.i-i.net/albemarlegallery*
Opening times: *Mon-Fri 10-6. Sat 10-4.*
Nearest Underground: *Green Park.*
Personnel: *Managing Director:* Tony Pontone. *Manager:* Kate Daniel. *Gallery Assistant:* Mayumi Bolton.
Specialising in contemporary figurative European, British and American artists, with particular emphasis on Spain.
The gallery has a reputation for lively and exciting one man and group shows, supported by full colour illustrated catalogue, and also for introducing artists hitherto never seen before in the UK. The gallery's activities has attracted the attention of international collectors and boasts a mailing list in excess of 6,000, growing daily. The '99 exhibition programme comprises 15 major exhibitions.
Enquiries should be directed to Tony Pontone, Managing Director or Kate Daniel, Gallery Manager.
Services and Facilities:
Art Consultancy. Art for Offices. Commissioning Service.
Work Stocked and Sold:
Pa.
Price range: £1,000 - £50,000.
For artists see *Commercial Gallery Artists.*

Alchemy Gallery
157 Farringdon Road, London EC1R 3AD.
Tel: *0171-278 5666.* **Fax:** *0171-278 9666.*

Alex Wengraf
The Old Knoll, Eliot Hill, London SE13 7EB.
Tel: *0181-852 4552.*
Fax: *0181-852 4554.*

Alexander Gotz
35 Connaught Square, London W2.
Tel: *0171-724 4435.* **Fax:** *0171-262 9891.*

Alexandra Gallery
Alexandra Palace Garden Centre, London N22 4BB.
Tel: *0181-444 2674.*

Alternative Art Market
47a Bushfield Street, Spitalfields, London E1 6AA.
Tel: *0171-375 0441.* **Fax:** *0171-375 0484.*
Opening times: *Sundays 10-5.*
Nearest Underground: *Liverpool Street.*
Personnel: *Director:* Maggie Pinhorn.
The Alternative Art Market is held every Sunday from April to December in the Old Spitalfields Market in the East End of London.
We exhibit work by contemporary artists who sell directly to the public. Each artist is allocated their own 3 sided unit. Work in all media is accepted. Submit to Alternative Arts who select. Send in slides/photos and CV.
Services and Facilities:
Art Consultancy. Art for Offices. Commissioning Service. Disabled Access.
Work Stocked and Sold:
Cer. Ph. Pr. Sc. Tx.
Price range: £10 - £1,000.
For artists see *Commercial Gallery Artists.*

The Alton Gallery
2a Suffolk Road, Barnes, London, SW13 9PH.
Tel: *0181-748 0606.*

Andrew Edmunds Prints & Drawings
44 Lexington Street, London W1R 3LH.
Tel: *0171-437 8594.*

Animation Art Gallery
13-14 Great Castle Street, London W1X.
Tel: *0171-255 1456.*

The Animation Gallery
Gray's Antique Market, London W1Y 1AR.
Tel: *0171-493 3779.*

Anna Bornholt Gallery
3-5 Weighhouse Street, London W1Y 1YL.
Tel: *0171-499 6114.*

Anna-Mei Chadwick
64 New King's Road Parson's Green, London SW6 4LT.
Tel: *0171-736 1928.*

Anne Faggionato
Fourth Floor, 20 Dering Street, London W1R.
Tel: *0171-493 6732.* **Fax:** *0171-493 9693.*
Opening times: *Mon-Fri 10-6.*
Nearest Underground: *Bond Street, Oxford Circus.*
Personnel: *Director:* Anne Faggionato. Emma Percy-Davis.
Dealers in impressionist, modern and contemporary paintings, sculpture and works on paper.
Services and Facilities:
Art Consultancy.
Work Stocked and Sold:
Dr. Pa. Ph. Sc.
For artists see *Commercial Gallery Artists.*

Annely Juda Fine Art
23 Dering Street, (off New Bond Street), London W1R 9AA.
Tel: *0171-629 7578.* **Fax:** *0171-491 2139.*
Opening times: *Mon-Fri 10-6, Sat 10-1.*
Nearest Underground: *Bond Street*
Contemporary British and international artists including: Roger Ackling, Anthony Caro, Chillida, Christo, Alan Charlton, Prunella Clough, Nathan Cohen, Gloria Friedmann, Hamish Fulton, Funakoshi, Alan Green, Nigel Hall, David Hockney, Christine Hatt, Werner Haypeter, Al Held, Honegger, Malcolm Hughes, Iida, Kadishman, Kawamata, Leon Kossoff, Darren Lago, Edwina Leapman, Catherine Lee, Estate of Kenneth and Mary Martin, John McLaughlin, Michaeledes, Morellet, David Nash, Saito, Toko Shinoda, Yuko Shiraishi.
Also specialising in Russian Constructivism, Bauhaus, de Stijl, etc., Arp, Gabo, Kliun, Lissitzky, Malevich, Moholy Nagy, Mondrian, Rodchenko, Schwitters, Vantongerloo, Vordemberge-Gildewart.
Services and Facilities:
Art Consultancy. Art for Offices. Commissioning Service. Valuation.
Work Stocked and Sold:
Dr. Pa. Sc.
For artists see *Commercial Gallery Artists.*

Anthony d'Offay Gallery
9, 21 & 23 & 24 Dering Street, off New Bond Street, London W1R 9AA.
Tel: *0171-499 4100.*
Fax: *0171-493 4443.*

Anthony Mould Ltd
173 New Bond Street, London W1.
Tel: *0171-491 4627.*

Anthony Reynolds
5 Dering Street, London W1R 9AB.
Tel: *0171-491 0621.*

The Art Supermarket
28 Islington Park Street, London N1 1PX.
Tel/Fax: *0171-359 2750*
Email *artsuper@aol.com*
Opening times: *By appointment.*
Nearest Underground: *Highbury & Islington (3 Mins). Buses 4, 19, 30, 43.*
Personnel: *Directors:* James West, Steve Hamblen.
We exhibit contemporary painting by an extensive selection of British and international artists within major department stores, currently showing in London at Harvey Nichols in Knightsbridge and Dickens and Jones on Regent Street.
An immense choice of work is also always on hand at our office premises. We eschew much of the conventional wisdom on how to sell fine art and aim instead to make work of quality available to a considerably wider audience at lower than usual prices.
Our group of 80 artists includes: David Atkins, Naomi Avsec, Celio Braga, Lydia Bauman, David Boyne, Rosana Casano, Kevin Chapman, Joseph Codina, Cecile Colombo, Lucian Cooper, Manuel de Val, John Duffin, David Eustace, Mark Halsey, Alex Knubley, Mhairi McGregor, Emerson Mayes, Christine Milne, Jordi Prat, Marion Notman, James Read, Sabala, Ian Thompson, Janet Waring, Sarah West.
Services and Facilities:
Art for Offices. Commissioning Service.
Work Stocked and Sold:
Pa.
Price range: £135 - £345.
For artists see *Commercial Gallery Artists.*

Artemis Fine Arts Limited
15 Duke Street, St James's, London SW1Y 6DB.
Tel: *0171-930 8733.* **Fax:** *0171-839 5009.*

Arthaus
Old School House, 12 Pop Street, London SE1 3PR.
Tel: *0171-232 1097.*

Arthouse
140 Lewisham Way, London SE14.
Tel: *0181-694 9011.*

Arthur Tooth & Sons
13 Dover Street, London W1X.
Tel: *0171-499 6753.*

Artlondon
Suite958, 28 Old Brompton Road, South Kensington, London SW7 3SS.
Tel: *0171-485 2273, Mobile 0385-707427.*
Fax: *0171-419 9033.*

Artmonsky Arts
108A Boundary Road, St. Johns Wood, London NW8 0RH.
Tel: *0171-604 3990.* **Fax:** *0171-604 3991.*

The Association Gallery
81 Leonard Street, London EC2A 4QS.
Tel: *0171-739 3631.* **Fax:** *0171-739 8707.*
Email *aop@dircon.co.uk*
Ws *http://www.aophoto.co.uk*
Opening times: *Mon-Fri 9.30-6, Sat 12-4.*
Nearest Underground: *Old Street, exit 4.*
Personnel: *Gallery Administrator:* Alex Steele-Mortimer.

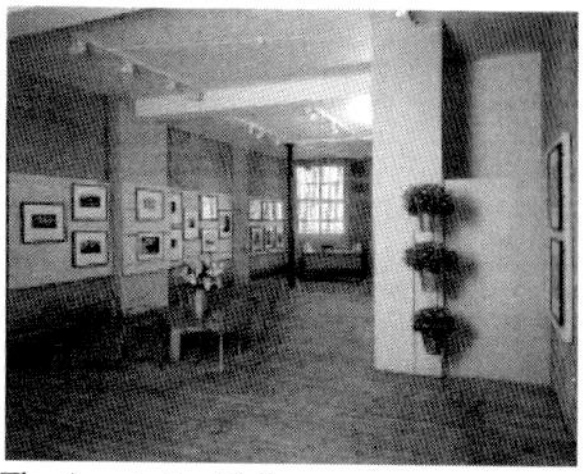

The Association Gallery stages contemporary photographic exhibitions on a variety of themes. The gallery is part of the Association of Photographers, and represents photographers working in advertising and editorial photography. The gallery displays and sells both commissioned and personal work.
Services and Facilities:
Disabled Access. Gallery space for hire.
Work Stocked and Sold:
Ab. Ph.
Price range: £75 - £700.

Atelier One
1-5 Maple Place, London W1P 5FX.
Tel: *0171-323 3350.* **Fax:** *0171-636 5282.*

Audley Art
20 The Mall, Upper Street, Islington, London N1.
Tel: *0171-704 9507.*

Austin Desmond Fine Art
Pied Bull Yard, 68-69 Great Russell Street, London WC1B 3BN.
Tel: *0171-242 4443.*

bada@
Tel: *0171-480 5952.*

Ballantyne & Date
38 Museum Street, London WC1A.
Tel: *0171-242 4249.*

Bar Room Bar
48 Rosslyn Hill, London NW3.
Tel: *0171-435 0808.*

The Barnes Gallery
51 Church Road, Barnes, London, SW13 9HH.
Tel: *0181-741 1277.*

Barry Davies Oriental Art
1 Davies Street, London W1Y 1LL.
Tel: *0171-408 0207.* **Fax:** *0171-493 3422.*
Email *bdoa@btinternet.com*
Ws *http://www.antiques-on-line.com/barry-davies*
Opening times: *Mon-Fri 10-6.*
Nearest Underground: *Bond Street or Green Park.*
Barry Davies Oriental Art has been one of the principal dealers in antique Japanese art for over 20 years. Our ability to source extraordinary and unique works of art of outstanding quality world-wide has given us the reputation

of being one of the most respected and competitive dealers in Oriental art.

Barry Davies Oriental Art Ltd

We invite you to visit our spacious Mayfair gallery where you will find a wide range of items including netsuke by all major artists, inro and other fine lacquer wares, 17th and 18th century porcelain, including Nabeshima and Kakiemon, Meiji masterpieces, screens, swords and sword fittings.
Services and Facilities:
Art Consultancy. Disabled Access. Valuation.

Bartley Drey Gallery
62 Old Church Street, Chelsea, London, SW3 6DP.
Tel: *0171-352 8686.*
Fax: *0171-351 2921.*

Battersea Art Centre
176 Lavender Hill, London SW11 5QF.

BCA Boukamel Contemporary Art
9 Cork Street, London W1X 1PD.
Tel: *0171-734 6444.* **Fax:** *0171-287 1740.*
Email BCA@netcomuk.co.uk
Ws *http://www.bca-gallery.com*
Opening times: *Mon-Fri 10-6, Sat 10-2.*
Nearest Underground: *Green Park.*
Personnel: *Director:* B. Boukamel.

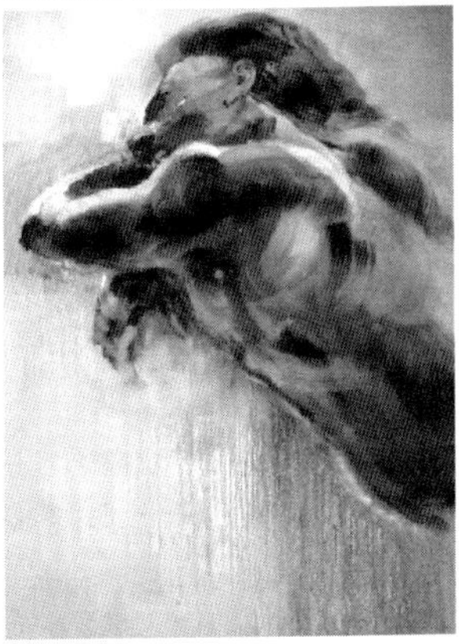

Contemporary British and European Art - representing: Philip Braham, Ernesto Tatafiore, Rainer Fetting, Ken Currie, Markus Lüpertz, Luciano Castelli, Gérard Garouste, Joumana Mourad, Daniel Spoerri, A.R. Penck, Elvira Bach, François Delebecque, Adrian Wiszniewski, Gérard Traquandi, E.R. Nele, Hélène Delprat.
Work Stocked and Sold:
Dr. Pa. Ph. Pr. Sc.
Price range: £500 - £50,000.
For artists see *Commercial Gallery Artists.*

Beardsmore Gallery
22-24 Prince Of Wales Road, Kentish Town, London NW5 3LG.
Tel: *0171-485 0923.*
Fax: *0171-267 0824.*

Beaux Arts London
22 Cork Street, London W1X 1HB.
Tel: *0171-437 5799.* **Fax:** *0171-437 5798.*
Opening times: *Mon-Fri 10-6, Sat 10-2.*
Nearest Underground: *Green Park, Piccadilly Circus, Oxford Circus.*
Personnel: *Directors:* Reg Singh, Patricia Singh, Robin Page.
Nine exhibitions a year. Modern: Frank Auerbach, Kenneth Armitage, Michael Ayrton, John Bellany, Lynn Chadwick, Elisabeth Frink, Terry Frost, Barbara Hepworth, Ivon Hitchens, Roger Hilton, Peter Lanyon, Jonathan Leaman, Henry Moore, John Piper, William Scott, Keith Vaughan. Contemporary: Gwen Hardie, Andy Harper, Philip Harris, Roger Kelly, Ray Richardson, David Spiller.
Services and Facilities:
Art for Offices. Commissioning Service.
Work Stocked and Sold:
Dr. Pa. Pr. Sc.
Price range: £4,000 - £100,000.
For artists see *Commercial Gallery Artists.*

Beldam Gallery
Brunel University, Wilfred Brown Building, Cleveland Road, Uxbridge, UB8 3PH.
Tel: *01895-273482.* **Fax:** *01895-203250.*

Belgrave Gallery
53 England's Lane, London NW3 4YD.
Tel: *0171-722 5150.* **Fax:** *0171-722 0858.*

Bengstrom
Studio 2N, Cooper House, 2 Michael Road, London SW6 2AD.
Tel: *0171-731 2815, Mobile 0370-966741.*
Fax: *0171-610 9212.*

Benjamin Hargreaves
90 Kenyon Street, London SW6 6LB.
Tel: *0171-385 7757.*

Berkeley Square Gallery
23a Bruton Street, London W1X 8JJ.
Tel: *0171-493 7939.* **Fax:** *0171-493 7798.*

Bernard Jacobson Gallery
14a Clifford Street, London W1X 1RF.
Tel: *0171-495 8575.*
Fax: *0171-495 6210.*

Big Art Issue
P.O. Box 2DR, London W1A 2DR.
Tel: *0171-503 7236.* **Fax:** *0171-503 6869.*

Blackheath Gallery
34a Tranquil Vale, Blackheath, London, SE3 0AX.
Tel: *0181-852 1802.*

Blackman's Place
14 All Saints Road, London W11.
Tel: *0171-243 4372.*

The Bloomsbury Workshop Ltd
12 Galen Place, off Bury Place, London, WC1A 2JR.
Tel: *0171-405 0632.*

The Blue Gallery
93 Walton Street, London SW3 2HP.
Tel: *0171-589 4690.* **Fax:** *0171-589 4729.*

Bob Lawrence Gallery
93 Sloane Street, London SW1W.
Tel: *0171-730 5900.*

Bolton Street Gallery
28 Bolton Street, London W1Y 7PD.
Tel: *0171-629 9933.* **Fax:** *0171-493 5561.*

Boundary Gallery, Agi Katz Fine Art
98 Boundary Road, London NW8 0RH.
Tel: *0171-624 1126.* **Fax:** *0171-681 7663 or 0171-624 1126.*
Opening times: *Wed- Sat 11-6 and by appointment.*
Personnel: *Director & Owner:* Agi Katz. *Gallery Assistant:* Louise Homes.

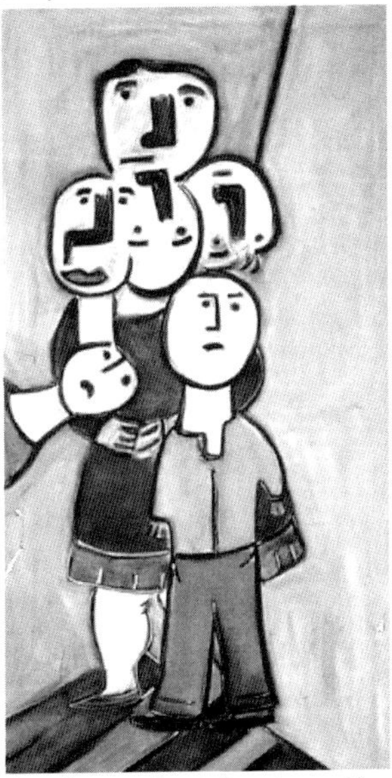

The gallery specialises in figurative art with emphasis on good draughtsmanship and strong use of colour. There are two periods of specialisation. 1. Modern British (1910 - 1950) including Bomberg, Brodzky, Dubsky, Epstein, Gotlib, Kramer Meninsky, Wolmark. Specialised knowledge of Anglo-Jewish artists - works in stock (available for sale) and will show by request. 2. Contemporary artists include Phillipa Clayden, Josef Herman, Morris Kestelman, Sonia Lawson, Albert Louden, Ana Maria Pacheco, Neil MacPherson, Peter Prendergast, David Tress. Eight thematic or solo exhibitions a year. Catalogues published 3-4 times a year.
Services and Facilities:
Art Consultancy. Art for Offices. Commissioning Service. Framing. Restoration. Valuation.
Work Stocked and Sold:
Pa. Pr.
Price range: £300 - £6,000.
For artists see *Commercial Gallery Artists.*

The Bow House Gallery
35 Wood Street, Barnet, EN5 4BE.
Tel: *0181-441 5841.* **Fax:** *0181-441 5841.*

Opening times: *Thurs-Sat 10-5, Sun 2-5 (during exhibitions).*
Nearest Underground: *High Barnet*
Personnel: John Brown. Pauline Brown.

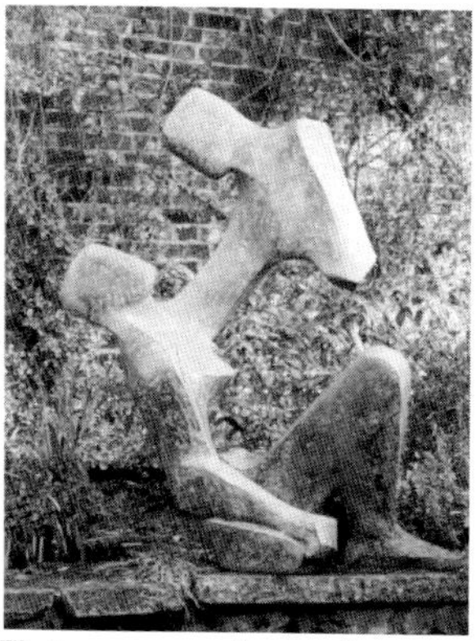

We aim to present a wide range of paintings and sculpture by professional artists and to provide affordable art for home or work place through a series of exhibitions, which includes Sculpture in the Garden shows in spring and summer.
Services and Facilities:
Art Consultancy. Commissioning Service.
Work Stocked and Sold:
Cer. Pa. Pr. Sc.
Price range: £150 - £5,000.
For artists see *Commercial Gallery Artists.*

BritArt.com
Tel: *0181-809 5127.* **Fax:** *0181-809 5354.*

Brixton Art Gallery
35 Brixton Station Road, London SW9 8PB.
Tel: *0171-733 6957.*

Browns Design Associates Ltd.,
29 Queen Elizabeth Street, London SE1 2LP.

Browse and Darby Gallery
19 Cork Street, London W1X 1HB.
Tel: *0171-734 7984.* **Fax:** *0171-437 0750.*

The Bruton Street Gallery
28 Bruton Street, London W1X 7DB.
Tel: *0171-499 9747.* **Fax:** *0171-409 7867.*
Ws *http://www.artnet.com/bruton.html*
Opening times: *Mon-Fri 10-6, Sat 12-4 out of hours by appointment.*
Nearest Underground: *Green Park.*
Contemporary exhibitions every month in Galleries 1 and 2, featuring paintings and sculpture by European Contemporary artists. One-man shows by young British artists in Gallery 3. Art consultants to architects, designers, and corporate buyers. Paintings for investment portfolios and first-time collectors. On-site presentation given. Commissions for painting and sculpture undertaken.
Services and Facilities:
Commissioning Service.
Work Stocked and Sold:
Pa. Sc.
Price range: £1,000 - £40,000.
For artists see *Commercial Gallery Artists.*

The Cable Street Gallery
Thames House, 566 Cable Street, Limehouse, London E1 9HB.
Tel: *0171-790 1309.* **Fax:** *0171-790 1309.*

Cadogan Contemporary Art
108 Draycott Avenue, South Avenue, London, SW3 3AE.
Tel: *0171-581 5451.* **Fax:** *0171-589 3222.*
Email *alight@artcad.co.uk*
Ws *http://www.artcad.co.uk*
Opening times: *Mon-Wed 10-7, Thurs-Sat 10-6.*
Nearest Underground: *South Kensington.*
Modern contemporary art.
Work Stocked and Sold:
Pa. Sc.
For artists see *Commercial Gallery Artists.*

Camberwell Gallery
169 Camberwell Road, London SE5.
Tel: *0171-740 6161.*

Camden Art Gallery
22 Church Street, London NW8.
Tel: *0171-262 3613.* **Fax:** *0171-723 2333.*

Camerawork: Gallery and Darkroom
121 Roman Road, London, E2 0QN.
Tel: *0181-980 6256.*

Cassien de Vere Cole Fine Arts
50 Elgin Crescent, London W11 2JJ.
Tel: *0171-221 9161.* **Fax:** *0171-221 1082.*

Cato Miles Wynn
60 Lower Sloane Street, London SW1W.
Tel: *0171-259 0306.*

Catto Gallery
100 Heath Street, Hampstead, London NW3 1DP.
Tel: *0171-435 6660.* **Fax:** *0171-431 5620.*

CCA Galleries Ltd
517-523 Fulham Road London SW6 1HD.
Tel: *0171-386 4900.* **Fax:** *0171-386 4919.*
Opening times: *Mon-Sat 9.30-5.30.*
Nearest Underground: *Fulham Broadway.*
Personnel: *Retail Director:* Marian Orchard-Webb. *Gallery Manager:* Marianna Lavery. *Publishing Dept.:* Teffany Tooke.
Leading publishers of limited edition silkscreens, etchings and lithographs. Catalogue of new publications produced twice a year. Exciting programme. Artists include Donald Hamilton-Fraser, Annora Spence, Sir Terry Frost, Richard Spare.
Services and Facilities:
Art Consultancy. Art for Offices. Framing.
Work Stocked and Sold:
Gla. Pr.
Price range: £45 - £3,500.
For artists see *Commercial Gallery Artists.*

Centaur Gallery
82 Highgate High Street, Highgate, London, N6.
Tel: *0181-340 0087.*

Centre 181 Gallery
181 King Street, London W6.
Tel: *0181-748 3020.*
Fax: *0181-741 3869.*

Chaucer Fine Arts
45 Pimlico Road, London SW1W.
Tel: *0171-730 2972.*

Chinese Contemporary
11 New Burlington Place, London W1X 1FA.
Tel: *0171-734 9808.* **Fax:** *0171-734 9818.*

Chris Beetles
8 & 10 Ryder Street, St. James's, London SW1Y 6QB.
Tel: *0171-839 7551.* **Fax:** *0171-839 1603.*

Christopher Drake
Flat 1, 19 Mason's Yard, Duke Street, St. James's, London SW1Y 6BU.
Tel: *0171-839 1198.*

Christopher Hull Gallery
17 Motcomb Street, London SW1X 8LB.
Tel: *0171-235 0500.* **Fax:** *0171-235 7912.*

Cinegrafix Gallery
4 Copper Row, Tower Bridge Piazza, London SE1.
Tel: *0171-234 0566.*

The City Gallery
26 Copthall Avenue, London EC2R 7DN.
Tel: *0171-256 5815.* **Fax:** *0171-256 6002.*

Clarges Gallery
1st Floor, 158 Walton Street, London SW3 2JZ.
Tel: *0171-584 3022.*

Clink Wharf Gallery
Clink Street, London SE1 9DG.
Tel: *0171-357 8355.*

Collins & Hastie Ltd
5 Park Walk, London SW10 0AJ.
Tel: *0171-351 4292.* **Fax:** *0171-351 7929.*

Colnaghi
15 Old Bond Street, London W1X 4LJ.
Tel: *0171-491 7408.* **Fax:** *0171-491 8851.*

Colville Place Gallery
1 Colville Place, London W1P 1HN.
Tel: *0171-436 1330.* **Fax:** *0171-436 1339.*

The Commercial Gallery
109 Commercial Street, London E1 6BG.
Tel: *0171-392 9031.* **Fax:** *0171-377 8915.*

The Coningsby Gallery
30 Tottenham Street, London W1 9PN.
Tel: *0171-636 7478.* **Fax:** *0171-580 7017.*
Opening times: *Mon-Fri 11-6.*
Nearest Underground: *Goodge Street*
Personnel: Andrew Coningsby.

the coningsby gallery

Specialists in the exhibition and marketing of contemporary art photographers, illustrators and fine artists who work, or are interested in working, in the applied arts markets of advertising, design and publishing. Wide variety of

hire and promotional options.
Services and Facilities:
Art Consultancy. Art for Offices. Commissioning Service. Gallery space for hire.
Work Stocked and Sold:
App. Cra. Dr. Pa. Ph. Pr. Sc.
Price range: £200 - £8,000.
For artists see *Commercial Gallery Artists.*

Connaught Brown
2 Albemarle Street, London W1X 3HF.
Tel: *0171-408 0362.* **Fax:** *0171-495 3137.*

Connoisseur Gallery
14 Holland Street, London W8.
Tel: *0171-937 0788.*

Contemporary Applied Arts
43 Earlham Street, Covent Garden, London WC2H 9LD.
Tel: *0171-836 6993.*

The Contemporary Art Gallery/Group
59 Ebury Street, London SW1W 0NZ.
Tel: *0171-730 6407.* **Fax:** *0171-823 6521.*

Contemporary Ceramics
William Blake House, 7 Marshall Street, London, W1V 1LP.
Tel: *0171-437 7605.* **Fax:** *0171-287 9954 / 437 7605.*

Coombs Contemporary
Tower Bridge Piazza, 1a Copper Row, Butlers Wharf, London SE1 2LH.
Tel: *0171-403 6866.*

Coskun & Co. Ltd.
56a Walton Street, London SW3 1RB.
Tel: *0171-581 9056.* **Fax:** *0171-581 1336.*

Crafts Council Shop
Victoria and Albert Museum, South Kensington, London SW7 2RL.
Tel: *0171-589 5070.*

Crane Kalman Gallery
178 Brompton Road, London SW3 1HQ.
Tel: *0171-584 7566/225 1931.* **Fax:** *0171-584 3843.*

Cubitt Gallery
2-4 Caledonia Street, London N1.
Tel: *0171-278 8226.*

Curwen Gallery
4 Windmill Street, (off Charlotte Street), London W1P 1HF.
Tel: *0171-636 1459.* **Fax:** *0171-436 3059.*
Email *gallery@curwen.demon.co.uk*
Ws *http://www.curwen.demon.co.uk*
Opening times: *Mon-Fri 10-6, Sat 11-5 (closed Bank Holiday Weekends).*
Nearest Underground: *Goodge Street/Tottenham Court Road.*
Personnel: *Directors:* Jill Hutchings, John Hutchings. *Contact:* Caroline Brown.
Exhibition programme features Contemporary British Art, Modern Masters & International Graphics. Artists include: Edward Bawden, Kenneth Blackburn, Glyn Boyd Harte, Phoebe Dingwall, Kieron Farrow, Jonathan Gibbs, Don Holden, Lallitha Jawahirilal, Stanley Jones, Thirza Kotzen, Ruth Martin, Jennifer McRae, Laimonis Mierins, Yuji Oki, Robin Richmond, Sophia Rizvi, Paul Ryan, Johannes von Stumm, Kenichi Tominaga, Marjan Woulda.

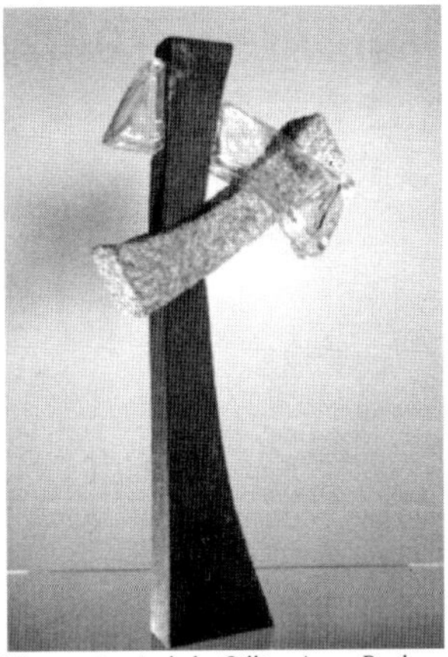

Master prints include: Gillian Ayres, Basil Beattie, Prunella Clough, Elizabeth Frink RA, Barbara Hepworth, Josef Herman RA, John Hoyland RA, Albert Irvin, Henry Moore, John Piper and Ceri Richards.
Services and Facilities:
Art Consultancy. Art for Offices. Commissioning Service. Framing.
Work Stocked and Sold:
Dr. Pa. Pr. Sc.
Price range: £40 - £20,000.
For artists see *Commercial Gallery Artists.*

The Cut Gallery
82 The Cut, London SE1 8LW.
Tel: *0171-207 8388.* **Fax:** *0171-207 8390.*

Daggett Gallery
153 Portobello Road, London, W11 2DV.
Tel: *0171-229 2248.*

Daniel Hunt
60 Lower Sloane Street, London SW1W.
Tel: *0171-259 0304.*

Daniel Katz Ltd
59 Jermyn Street, St. James's, London SW1Y 6LX.
Tel: *0171-493 0688.* **Fax:** *0171-499 7493.*
Email *danny@katz.co.uk*
Ws *http://www.katz.co.uk*
Opening times: *Mon-Fri 9-6.*
Nearest Underground: *Green Park.*
Personnel: *Director:* Daniel Katz. Stuart Lochhead. Rebecca Bailey.
European sculpture and works of art from the Renaissance 17th and 18th centuries including bronze statuettes, marble and terracotta figures and old master paintings. Sales to all major museums worldwide plus collectors and private clients.
Services and Facilities:
Art Consultancy.
Work Stocked and Sold:
Pa. Sc.
Price range: From £5,000.
For artists see *Commercial Gallery Artists.*

Danielle Arnaud Contemporary Arts
123 Kennington Road, London SE11 6SF.
Tel: *0171-735 8292.* **Fax:** *0171-735 8292.*

Danusha Fine Arts
30 Warrington Crescent, London W9 1EL.
Tel: *0171-286 4832.* **Fax:** *0171-266 1639.*
Opening times: *Viewing by appointment all year.*
Personnel: *Managing Director:* Tamara Bassi.

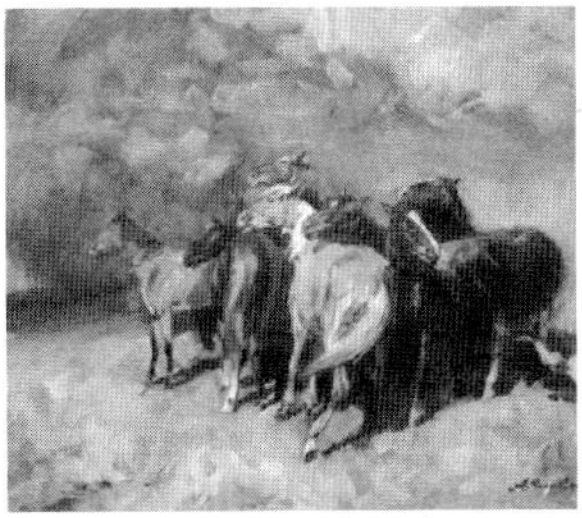

Realism & Impressionism from Ukraine. The names of such artists as Malevitch, Archipenko, Buriiuk, Ermolov, Exter - pioneers of Avant-gard Art - are well known to art specialists. However, not everyone knows that these artists were all born in Ukraine, where they lived and worked at different times. Their creativity had an important influence on the development of Ukrainian art. Even during the period of socialist realism their ideas produced a new generation of talented artists like Tetyana Yablonska, Grygoriy Shyshko, Evgeniy Volobuev, Tetyana Holimbievska, Andriy Yalanskyi, Petro Magro, Gayane Atayan, Volodymyr Zhugan, Valentin Znoba.
Services and Facilities:
Art Consultancy. Commissioning Service.
Work Stocked and Sold:
Pa.
Price range: £200 - £5,000.
For artists see *Commercial Gallery Artists.*

David Gill Gallery
60 Fulham Road, London, SW3.
Tel: *0171-371 8115 / 0171-589 5946.*

David Messum Fine Art
8 Cork Street, London W1X 1PB.
Tel: *0171-408 0243/0171-437 5545.*
Fax: *0171-491 3162/0171-734 7018.*

Davies & Tooth
The Air Gallery, 32 Dover Street, London W1X 3RA.
Tel: *0171-409 1516.* **Fax:** *0171-409 1856.*

Dissenters Chapel and Gallery
Kensal Green Cemetary, Harrow Road, London W10 4RA. **Tel:** *0171-402 2749.*

Douwes Fine Art
38 Duke Street, St. James's, London, SW1Y 6DF. **Tel:** *0171-839 5795.* **Fax:** *0171-839 5904.*

Dover Street Gallery
13 Dover Street, Green Park, London W1X 3PH. **Tel:** *0171-409 1540.*

Duncan Campbell Contemporary Art
15 Thackeray Street, Kensington, London W8 5ET. **Tel:** *0171-937 8665.*

Duncan R. Miller Fine Arts
17 Flask Walk, Hampstead, London NW3 1HJ. **Tel:** *0171-435 5462.* **Fax:** *0171-431 5352.*

E M Arts
36 Tregunter Road, London SW10.

East West
8 Blenheim Crescent, London W11 1NN. **Tel:** *0171-229 7981.* **Fax:** *0171-221 0741.*

Eastern Art Gallery
40 Bloomsbury Way, London, WC1A 2SE. **Tel:** *0171-430 1072.*

Editions Graphiques
3 Clifford Street, London, W1X 1RA. **Tel:** *0171-734 3944.* **Fax:** *0171-437 1859.*

Edward Cohen
40 Duke Street, London SW1Y. **Tel:** *0171-839 5180.*

Electrum Gallery
21 South Molton Street, London, W1Y 1DD. **Tel:** *0171-629 6325.* **Fax:** *0171-435 9806.*

England and Co.
14 Needham Road, Westbourne Grove, London, W11 2RP. **Tel:** *0171-221 0417.* **Fax:** *0171-221 4499.*

Enid Lawson Gallery
36a Kensington Church Street, London W8 4BX. **Tel:** *0171-937 8444.* **Fax:** *0171-376 0552.*

Entwistle
6 Cork Street, London W1X 2EE. **Tel:** *0171-734 6440.* **Fax:** *0171-734 7966.*

Ermitage
14 Hay Hill, London W1X. **Tel:** *0171-499 5459.*

Finchley Fine Art Galleries
983 High Road, North Finchley, London N12 8QR. **Tel:** *0181-446 4848.*
Opening times: *Mon, Tues, Thurs, Fri, Sat, Sun 12.30-7. Wed by appt.*
Nearest Underground: *Woodside Park.*
Personnel: *Proprietor:* S. Greenman.

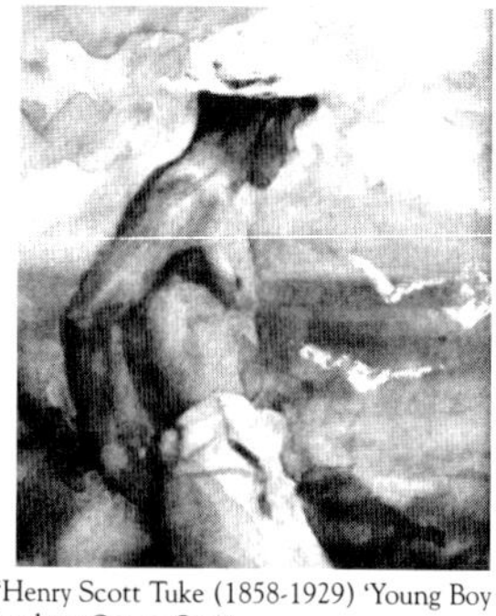

"Henry Scott Tuke (1858-1929) 'Young Boy Looking Out to Sea'"

"Established 1972." 200 plus 18th-20th century English watercolours and paintings displayed in four galleries together with good quality Georgian, Victorian and Edwardian furniture, pottery, porcelain, smalls etc. Services: Valuations, Insurance/Probate. Restoration watercolours, paintings, cleaning, relining, framing and mounting.
Services and Facilities:
Framing. Restoration. Shop. Valuation.
Work Stocked and Sold:
Cer. Dec. Dr. Fur. Gla. Pa. Pr. Sc. Tx. Wd.
Price range: £50 - £10,000.
For artists see *Commercial Gallery Artists.*

Fine Art Society
148 New Bond Street, London, W1Y OJT. **Tel:** *0171-629 5116.*

Fischer Fine Art
49 Carlton Hill, London NW8 0EL. **Tel:** *0171-328 6502.* **Fax:** *0171-625 8341.*

Fleur de Lys Gallery
227a Westbourne Grove, London W11 2SE. **Tel:** *0171-727 8595.* **Fax:** *0171-727 8595.*

Florence Trust Studios
St. Saviour's, Aberdeen Park, Highbury, London N5 2AR.
Tel: *0171-354 4771.* **Fax:** *0171-354 4771.*
Nearest Underground: *Highbury & Islington.*
Personnel: *Director:* Rod McIntosh.
The Florence Trust is based at St. Saviour's, Aberdeen Park, a Grade 1 listed 1866 Victorian Gothic church. The Studios offer visual artists studio awards, from 2-9 months, in an open plan environment where they can work intensively and engage in critical exchange. Regular exhibitions are held at the Trust and we have "Open Studio" events with invited guest artists exhibiting. Studio talks and slide presentations are also planned throughout the year. We have a comprehensive slide index of the artists we support, available for view by appointment. The studios and exhibition area are available for outside hire.
Services and Facilities:
Commissioning Service. Friends/Society. Gallery space for hire. Lectures. Workshop Facilities.
Work Stocked and Sold:
Dr. Pa. Sc.
Price range: £100 - £6,000.

Flowers East
199-205 Richmond Road, London E8 3NJ.
Tel: *0181-985 3333.* **Fax:** *0181-985 0067.*
Email *flowerseast@compuserve.com*
Opening times: *Tues-Sun 10-6.*
Nearest Underground: *Bethnal Green, + 253/106 buses.*
Personnel: *Chairman:* Angela Flowers. *Managing Director:* Matthew Flowers. *Directors:* Karen Demuth, Huei Flowers. *Director of Graphics:* Marian Stone.
Angela Flowers Gallery opened in Soho in 1970, with the aim of introducing young contemporary British artists and promoting established artists who deserved greater recognition. In 1988 the gallery moved to London's East End and became Flowers East. Since then it has acquired Plc status & expanded into one of the biggest and most important commercial galleries in the country.

Flowers East

Flowers East has two large gallery spaces and represents more than thirty-five artists, from young newcomers to major international figures. There is also a separate graphics department which publishes and sells limited edition prints by a wide range of contemporary artists.
Services and Facilities:
Art Consultancy. Art for Offices. Bookshop. Commissioning Service. Guided Tours. Parking.
Work Stocked and Sold:
Ab. Dr. Pa. Pr. Sc.
Price range: £100 - £100,000.
For artists see *Commercial Gallery Artists.*

Flying Colours Gallery
PO Box 9361, Chelsea, London SW3 3ZJ. **Tel:** *0171-351 5558.* **Fax:** *0171-351 5548.*

Footstool Restaurant Gallery
St. John's Smith Square, Westminster, London SW10 0AJ. **Tel:** *0171-222 2168.*

Foyles Art Gallery
2nd Floor, 113-119 Charing Cross Road, London, WC2H 0EB. **Tel:** *0181-518 7685.*

Francis Graham-Dixon Gallery
P.O. Box 21100, London N16 0WQ.
Tel: *0181-809 1999.* **Fax:** *0181-809 1999.*
Email *fg-d@dircon.co.uk*
Opening times: *By appointment.*
Personnel: *Director:* Francis Graham-Dixon.
Annual programme of exhibitions of primarily British and European contemporary artists. Artists represented/stocked - Emily Andersen, Sybille Berger, Willard Boepple, John Carter, Jane Dixon, Jennifer Durrant, Julia Farrer, Sheila Girling, Clyde Hopkins, Bryan Ingham, Jiri Kolár, Oleg Kudryashov, Merlin James, John McLean, Mali Morris, Derek Roberts, Kikuo Saito, Sophie Smallhorn, Amanda Thesiger, Virginia Verran, Johanes Zechner.
Services and Facilities:
Art Consultancy. Commissioning Service. Valuation.
Work Stocked and Sold:
Dr. Pa. Ph. Pr. Sc.
Price range: £250 - £25,000.
For artists see *Commercial Gallery Artists.*

Francis Kyle Gallery
9 Maddox Street, London, W1R 9LE. **Tel:** *0171-499 6870.*

Frederick Mulder
83 Belsize Park Gardens, London NW3 4NJ. **Tel:** *0171-722 2105.*

Frivoli
7a Devonshire Road, London W4 2EU.
Tel: *0171-742 3255.* **Fax:** *0171-994 7372.*
Opening times: *Mon-Sat 10-6, Thur 10-7.*
Work Stocked and Sold:
Cer. Cra. Fur. Gla. Jew. Tx. Wd.

Frost & Reed
2-4 King Street St. James's London Sw1Y 6QP.
Tel: *0171-839 4645.* **Fax:** *0171-839 1166.*

Futuraneon, Interior Designers & Artists
11 Chase Side, London N14 5BP.
Tel: *0181-882 6181.* **Fax:** *0181-886 1810.*

Gagliardi Gallery
509 Kings Road, Chelsea, London SW10 0TX.
Tel: *0171-352 3663.* **Fax:** *0171-351 6283.*

Galerie Besson
15 Royal Arcade, 28 Old Bond Street, Green Park, London, W1X 3HB.
Tel: *0171-491 1706.* **Fax:** *0171-495 3203.*

Galerie Moderne / le Style Lalique
9-10 Halkin Arcade, Motcomb Street, Belgravia, London SW1X 8JT.
Tel: *0171-245 6907.* **Fax:** *0171-245 6341.*
Opening times: *Mon-Fri 10-6 or by appointment.*
Nearest Underground: *Knightsbridge/Hyde Park Corner.*
Personnel: *Gallery Director:* Mark Waller. Alison Allen.

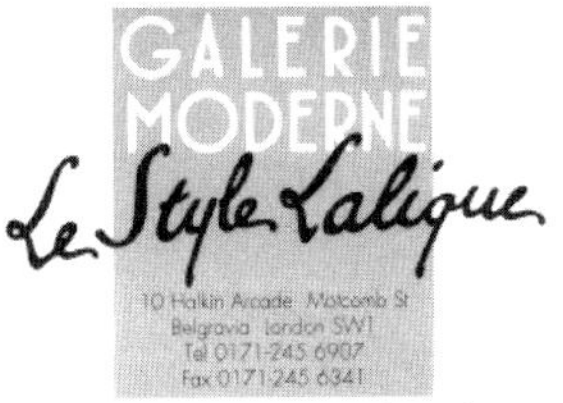

Specialists in Pre-War René Lalique glass, scent bottles, tableware lighting fixtures, designs, car mascots, jewellery and statuettes. Automobile Art, posters and lithographs from 1890-1940.
Price Range - Above £500.
Work Stocked and Sold:
Dr. Gla.
Price range: £500 - £50,000.
For artists see *Commercial Gallery Artists.*

Galerie Valerie Knightsbridge
215 Brompton Road, London SW3 2EJ.
Tel: *0171-823 9971 or 0956-310780.*

Galleria Enterprise
606 King's Road. London SW6 2DX.
Tel: *0171-371 9940.* **Fax:** *0171-371 9950.*

Gallery 75
75 Heath Street, Hampstead, London NW3 6UG.
Tel: *0171-431 8711.* **Fax:** *0171-625 6100.*

Gallery Differentiate
45 Shad Thames, Tower Bridge Piazza, London SE1 2NJ.
Tel: *0171-357 8909/403 9050.* **Fax:** *0171-357 8909.*

Gallery Duncan Terrace
24 Duncan Terrace, London N1 8BS.
Tel: *0171-837 5856.*
Fax: *0171-278 2140.*

Gallery K
101-103 Heath Street, London NW3 6SS.
Tel: *0171-794 4949.* **Fax:** *0171-431 4833.*

Gallery Lingard
Walpole House, 35 Walpole Street, London SW3 4QS.
Tel: *0171-730 9233.* **Fax:** *0171-730 9152.*

Gallery M
London Fields, 282 Richmond Road, London E8 3QS.
Tel: *0181-986 9922.* **Fax:** *0181-985 0067.*

The Gallery of Architecture
6 Turnpin Lane, Greenwich, London SE10 9JA.
Tel: *0181-293 3617.* **Fax:** *0181-305 2064.*

Gallery of Modern Art
9 Barmouth Road, London SW18 2DT.
Tel: *0181-875 1481.* **Fax:** *0181-875 1481.*
Opening times: *Mon-Thurs 10-4, and by appointment.*
Nearest Underground: *BR: Wandsworth Town.*
Personnel: *Art Director:* Bea Newbery.
Commercial Gallery almost exclusively abstract art. Full range of sizes, prices, new and established artists. App. 4-5 exhibitions per year. Widely known for very high standards and very reasonable prices. Also act as agents for modern art, prints, graphic work, large and small paintings, sculpture, also ceramic and glass sculpture. Suppliers to interior designers, architects, institutions and general public. Available of above number at all times for enquiries. The gallery has a national and international list of painters, sculptors and graphic artists of very high standards and also include new artists in their four yearly exhibitions.
Work Stocked and Sold:
Cer. Dr. Gla. Pa. Pr. Sc.
Price range: £50 - £5,000.
For artists see *Commercial Gallery Artists.*

The Gallery
168 Pentonville Road, London N1.
Tel: *0171-837 8490.*

Gavin Graham Gallery
47 Ledbury Road, London W11 2AA.
Tel: *0171-229 4848.* **Fax:** *0171-792 9697.*

Georgina Turner Fine Art
Haus, 23-25 Mortimer Street, London W1.
Tel: *00331-45670334.*

Gimpel Fils
30 Davies Street, London W1Y 1LG.
Tel: *0171-493 2488.* **Fax:** *0171-629 5732.*

Gladwell & Co.
69 Queen Victoria Street, London EC4N.
Tel: *0171-248 3824.*

The Greenhouse at the Drill Hall
16 Chenies Street, London WC1E 7EX.
Tel: *0171-631 1353.*

Grosvenor Gallery
18 Albemarle Street, London W1X 3HA.
Tel: *0171-629 0891.* **Fax:** *0171-491 4391.*
Opening times: *Mon-Fri 10-5.*
Nearest Underground: *Green Park.*
Personnel: *Director:* Mr Ray Perman.
20th century painting and sculpture.
Services and Facilities:
Art for Offices.
Work Stocked and Sold:
Pa. Sc.

Grosvenor Prints
28-32 Shelton Street, London, WC2H 9HP.
Tel: *0171-836 1979.*

Guy Morrison
91a Jermyn Street, London, SW1Y.
Tel: *0171-839 1454.*

Hales Gallery
70 Deptford High Street, London SE8 4RT.
Tel: *0181-694 1194.* **Fax:** *0181-692 0471.*
Opening times: *Mon-Sat 10-5.*
Nearest Underground: *Deptford, New Cross.*
Personnel: Paul Hedge. Paul Maslin.

halesgallery

Hales Gallery was co-founded by former Goldsmiths' graduate Paul Hedge. It has provided a platform for many young British artists, including the Chapman brothers, Sarah Jones and John Frankland. Hales Gallery artists include Tomoko Takahashi, Keith Wilson and Ian Dawson, both included in the latest Saatchi publication, The New Neurotic Realism, and Jonathan Callan, who, along with Dawson, was featured in the latest SAKS Fifth Avenue Project Art, London Now, in New York. In addition, Andrew Bick, Claude Heath and David Leapman were all shortlisted for this year's Jerwood Painting Prize and Martin McGinn won the EAST International '98 Prize.
Services and Facilities:
Café.
Work Stocked and Sold:
Dr. Pa. Ph. Pr. Sc.
Price range: £150 - £10,000.
For artists see *Commercial Gallery Artists.*

Hall & Knight
15 Duke Street, St. James's, London SW1Y 6DB.
Tel: *0171-839 4090.* **Fax:** *0171-839 4091.*

Hamilton Forbes Fine Art
The Garden Market, Chelsea, London, SW10 0XE.
Tel: *0171-937 2577.*

Hamilton's Gallery
13 Carlos Place, London W1Y 5AG.
Tel: *0171-499 9493.* **Fax:** *0171-629 9919.*

Hanga Ten
Hurlingham Studios, Ranelagh Gardens, London SW6 3PA
Tel: *0171-371 9677, Mobile: 0780-115 1981.*
Fax: *0171-371 9677.*
Email *japanart@hangaten.demon.co.uk*
Opening times: *By appointment.*
Nearest Underground: *Putney Bridge.*
Personnel: Hely Norton.
Hanga Ten is a new gallery specialising in

modern and contemporary Japanese prints, hand-picked in Japan.

版画店 *Hanga Ten*
Contemporary Japanese Prints

Artists represented include many internationally known printmakers such as SHINODA Toko, ENDO Susumu and TAKAHASHI Rikio, but also those at the beginning of their careers. Techniques cover all printing methods: woodblock, silkscreen, lithograph, intaglio and combination processes. Artistic expression is also diverse, ranging from minimalist and abstract compositions to traditional Japanese themes. All the artists have one thing in common: their immense creative talent and the quality of their work, a reflection of their technical excellence and the genius of Japan's papermakers.
Work Stocked and Sold:
Pr.
Price range: £35 - £3,000.
For artists see *Commercial Gallery Artists.*

Hanging Space
36a Newington Green, Islington, London, N16 9PR.
Tel: *0171-249 7727.* **Fax:** *0171-249 7727.*
Email *Tpoynings@aol.com*
Ws *Skypages*
Opening times: *Tue-Fri 12-8, Sat 11-4.*
Nearest Underground: *Canonbury.*
Personnel: *Owner & Director:* Rebecca Thompson.

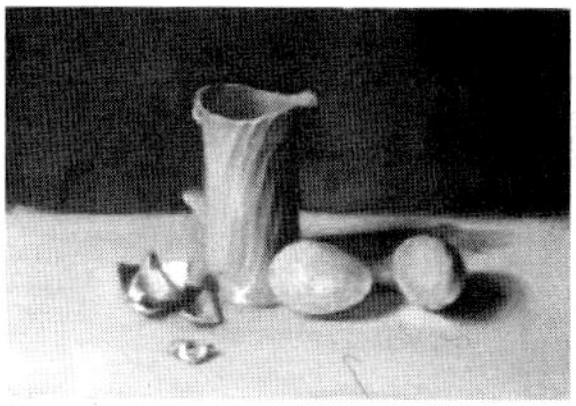

New gallery situated on Newington Green in large converted Georgian building. Monthly exhibitions of contemporary painting, textiles, sculpture and jewellery with private views for members. Huge variety of styles and themes.
Services and Facilities:
Art Consultancy. Art for Offices. Commissioning Service. Friends/Society. Gallery space for hire. Parking.
Work Stocked and Sold:
Dr. Jew. Pa. Ph. Pr. Sc.
Price range: £100 - £3,500.
For artists see *Commercial Gallery Artists.*

Hanina Gallery
180 Westbourne Grove, London W11 2RH.
Tel: *0171-243 8877.* **Fax:** *0171-243 0132.*

Hardware Gallery
162 Archway Road, Highgate, London N6 5BB.
Tel: *0181-341 6415.* **Fax:** *0181-348 0561.*

Hart Gallery
113 Upper Street, Islington, London N1 1QN.
Tel: *0171-704 1131.* **Fax:** *0171-704 1707.*
Opening times: *Tues, Wed, Thurs, Fri 11-7. Sat 11-6. Sun 2-6.*
Nearest Underground: *Angel.*
Personnel: *Directors:* John Hart, Katherine Hart.
Hart Gallery exhibits and promotes a range of contemporary painting, sculpture and ceramics. Established in Nottingham (0115-963 8707) in 1989 and opened in London in 1994. To promote the gallery artists the gallery has forged links with other private and public galleries both in the UK and abroad and regularly exhibits at Art Fairs. A range of artist's monographs have been published including Kenneth Draper, Tom Wood and David Blackburn. Exhibitions change monthly both in the downstairs painting/sculpture gallery and in the upstairs ceramics gallery.
Services and Facilities:
Art Consultancy. Art for Offices. Disabled Access. Lectures.
Work Stocked and Sold:
Cer. Dr. Pa. Ph. Pr. Sc.
Price range: £100 - £20,000.
For artists see *Commercial Gallery Artists.*

Hazlitt, Gooden & Fox
38 Bury Street, St. James's, London, SW1Y 6BB.
Tel: *0171-930 6422.* **Fax:** *0171-839 5984.*

The Heifer Gallery
3 Calabria Road, Highbury, London N5 1JB.
Tel: *0171-226 7380.*

Hicks Gallery
2 Leopold Road, Wimbledon, London SW19 7BD. **Tel:** *0181-944 7171.*

Highgate Fine Art
26 Highgate High Street, London N6 5JG.
Tel: *0181-340 7564.* **Fax:** *0181-347 7010.*
Email *hfal26@aol.com*
Opening times: *Tue-Sat 10-6, Sun, Mon - by appointment.*
Nearest Underground: *Archway.*
Personnel: Noël Oddy. Fiona Hutson.
20th Century paintings, drawings, prints and small sculpture. New exhibitions every three weeks. Two/three large mixed shows yearly. In addition to British painters, the HFA programme now includes solo exhibitions by French, German, Norwegian, Russian, Italian and Spanish painters - a combination which has established the gallery as a small centre of international repute. In 1998-9, HFA has also pioneered the preparation and publication of copious catalogues for artists, with bilingual commentaries illustrating their different groups of work acting as a sales aid and permanent record. Details of these and invitations to Private Views on application.
Services and Facilities:
Art Consultancy. Commissioning Service. Framing. Valuation.
Work Stocked and Sold:
Dr. Pa. Pr. Sc.
Price range: £50 - £20,000.
For artists see *Commercial Gallery Artists.*

Hilary Chapman, 20th Century Gallery
821 Fulham Road, London SW6 5HG.
Tel: *0171-731 5888.* **Fax:** *0171-731 5888.*
Opening times: *Mon-Fri 10-6, Sat 10-1.*
Nearest Underground: *Parsons Green.*
Personnel: Hilary Chapman.
Specialist print dealer in late nineteenth and early twentieth century British prints. Stock includes etchings, engravings, lithographs, wood-engravings and colour prints by major and minor artists of the period up to the 1950's.

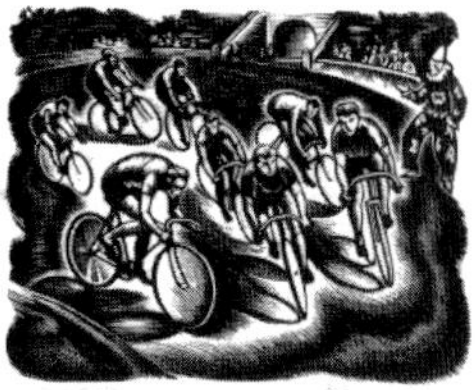

At least two exhibitions are held each year and illustrated lists issued periodically. Please send details to the gallery to be included on the mailing list. Exhibitions for 1999 include 'The Colour Woodcuts of John Edgar Platt, 1886-1967' (Oct/Nov).
Services and Facilities:
Art for Offices. Framing. Shop. Valuation.
Work Stocked and Sold:
Pr.
Price range: £50 - £1,000.
For artists see *Commercial Gallery Artists.*

Hildegard Fritz-Denneville Fine Arts
31 New Bond Street, London, W1Y 9HD.
Tel: *0171-629 2466.* **Fax:** *0171-408 0604.*
Nearest Underground: *Bond Street.*
Personnel: Mrs Fritz-Denneville.
Hildegard Fritz-Denneville Fine Arts has been established for 25 years and is a member of the Society of London Art Dealers. The gallery has developed expertise in German and Austrian art, and specialises in German Romantics, Nazarenes and Expressionists, as well as in French Impressionists.
Work Stocked and Sold:
Dr. Pa. Pr.
For artists see *Commercial Gallery Artists.*

Hirschl Contemporary Art
Suite 3, 7 Sheffield Terrace, London W8 7NG.
Tel: *0171-727 4401.* **Fax:** *0171-792 9173.*

Honor Oak Gallery
52 Honor Oak Park, London SE23 1DY.
Tel: *0181-291 6094.*
Opening times: *Tues-Fri 9.30-6, Sat 9.30-5.*
Nearest Underground: *Honor Oak Park.*
Personnel: *Director:* John Broad.

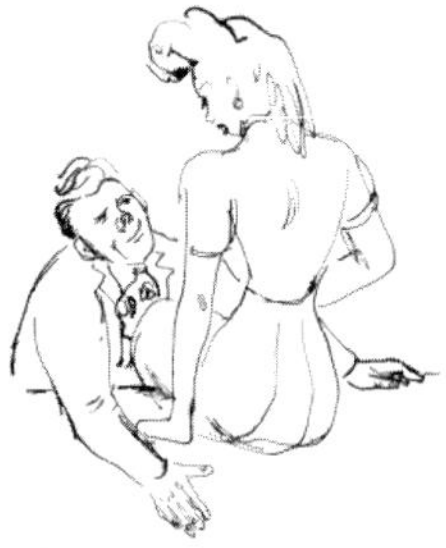

Prints, drawings, watercolours and paintings by 20th century artists: Norman Ackroyd,

Rosemary Benson, June Berry, Paul Bisson, Elizabeth Blackadder, Graham Crowley, Gill Day, Jenny Devereux, Paul Drury, Margareta Berger-Hamerschlag, A.S. Hartrick, Thomas Hennell, John Houston, Rudolph Kortokraks, Karolina Larusdottir, Clare Leighton, Vincent Lines, Charles Lloyd, Phyllis Mahon, George Mayer-Marton, Tiffany McNab, Terence Millington, Donald Myall, Charlotte Novitz, John O'Connor, Trevor Price, Edward Stamp, Robin Tanner, Erich Wagner, Richard Wardle, Gerd Winner, Adrian Wiszniewski, etc. Agent for Glasgow Print Studio.
Services and Facilities:
Commissioning Service. Framing. Restoration.
Work Stocked and Sold:
Dr. Pa. Pr.
Price range: £12 - £2,000.
For artists see *Commercial Gallery Artists.*

Houldsworth Fine Art
1-5 Needham Road, London W11 2RP.
Tel: *0171-243 1500.*
Fax: *Please phone for new fax number.*
Ws *http://www.art-connection.com*
Opening times: *Please telephone.*
Personnel: Pippy Houldsworth.

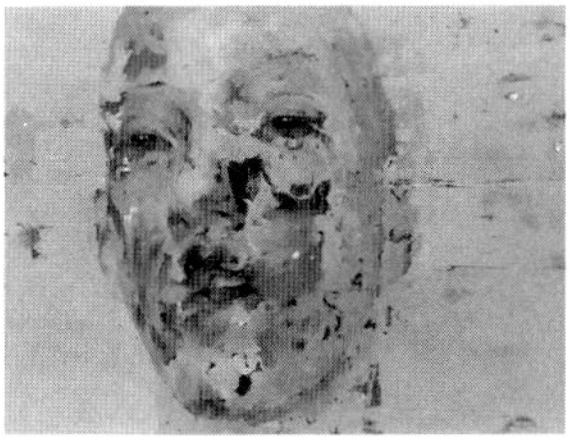

Contemporary art. Representing Robin Connelly, Jonathan Delafield Cook, Richard Henman, Gavin Lockheart, Paul McPhail, Matthew Radford, Peter Randall-Page, Jason Spivak, Karl Weschke, Uwe Wittwer.
Services and Facilities:
Art Consultancy. Art for Offices.
Work Stocked and Sold:
Dr. Pa. Ph. Pr. Sc.
Price range: £300 - £20,000.
For artists see *Commercial Gallery Artists.*

Hugo Ball
33c Corinne Road, Tufnell Park, London N19 5EZ.

Hybrid
98 Columbia Road, London E2.
Tel: *0171-613 2628.*

Hyde Park Gallery
16 Craven Terrace, London W2 3QD.
Tel: *0171-402 2904.*

IAP Fine Art
65 Roman Road, London E2 0QN.
Tel: *0181-980 0100.* **Fax:** *07070-645297.*

Ice House
Central Library, Phillimore Walk, London W8 7RX. **Tel:** *0171-361 2295.*

Independent Art Space
23a Smith Street, London SW3.
Tel: *0171-259 9232.*

Institute of Fine Art
5 Kirby Street, Hatton Garden, London EC1N.
Tel: *0171-831 4048.*

International Art Project
57 Moreton Street, London SW1V.
Tel: *0171-976 6200.*

Iona Antiques
PO Box 285, London E8 4RE.
Tel: *0171-602 1193.* **Fax:** *0171-371 2843.*

James Colman Fine Arts
The Tower, 28 Mossbury Road, London SW11 2PB.
Tel: *0171-924 3860.* **Fax:** *0171-924 3860.*

Michael David
Lynton House, 48 Lynton Road, Rayners Lane, Harrow, HA2 9NN

James Roundell
58 Jermyn Street, London SW1Y.
Tel: *0171-499 0722.*

James West Fine Art
28 Islington Park Street, London N1 1PX.

Japan Print Gallery
43 Pembridge Road, London W11.
Tel: *0171-221 0927.*

Jason & Rhodes
4 New Burlington Place, London W1F 1XB.
Tel: *0171-434 1768.* **Fax:** *0171-287 8841.*

Jay Jopling
White Cube, 44 Duke Street, St. James's, London SW1Y 6DD.
Tel: *0171-930 5373.* **Fax:** *0171-930 9973.*

Jeremy Hunt Fine Art
32 Dover Street, London W1X 3RA.
Tel: *0171-409 1165/0171-629 3748.*
Fax: *0171-409 1856.*

Jill George Gallery
38 Lexington Street, Soho, London W1R 3HR.
Tel: *0171-439 7319 / 439 7343.* **Fax:** *0171-287 0478.*
Email *jillgeorgegallery@compuserve.com*
Opening times: *Mon-Fri 10-6, Sat 11-5.*
Nearest Underground: *Piccadilly/ Oxford Circus*
Personnel: *Director:* Jill George.

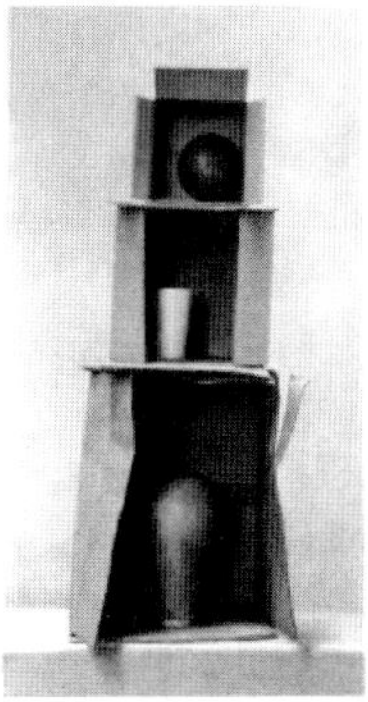

British contemporary art. Paintings, drawings, watercolours, limited edition prints and monoprints from the established artist to the recent graduate. The gallery handles both figurative and abstract originals and prints. Participates in national and international art fairs. Art Consultancy and commissions organised on behalf of the artists. Exhibition every five weeks throughout the year.
Services and Facilities:
Art Consultancy. Art for Offices. Commissioning Service.
Work Stocked and Sold:
Dr. Pa. Pr.
Price range: £100 - £20,000.
For artists see *Commercial Gallery Artists.*

Joanna Barnes Fine Arts
14 Mason s Yard, Duke Street, St James's, London SW1Y 6BU.
Tel: *0171-930 4215.* **Fax:** *0171-839 8307.*

John Bloxham Fine Art
117 St. Johns Hill, London SW11 1SZ.
Tel: *0171-924 7500.* **Fax:** *0171-733 4451.*

John Denham Gallery
50 Mill Lane, West Hampstead, London NW6 1NJ.
Tel: *0171-794 2635.* **Fax:** *0171-794 2635.*

John Hunt
15 King Street, St. James's, London SW1Y 6QU.
Tel: *0171-839 2643.* **Fax:** *0171-839 2643.*

John Martin of London
38 Albemarle Street, London W1X 3FB.
Tel: *0171-499 1314.* **Fax:** *0171-493 2842.*

John Mitchell & Son
160 Bond Street, London W1Y 9PA.
Tel: *0171-493 7567.*

Jonathan Cooper
Park Walk Gallery, 20 Park Walk, London, SW10 OAQ.
Tel: *0171-351 0410.* **Fax:** *0171-351 0410.*
Opening times: *Mon-Fri 10-6.30, Sat 11-4.*
Nearest Underground: *South Kensington.*
Personnel: Jonathan Cooper. Henrietta Dudley.
19th and 20th century English and European paintings and watercolours. Modern British and contemporary. Sole agents for Jay Kirkman, William Newton, Kate Nessier, Michael Austin.
Services and Facilities:
Art Consultancy. Framing. Restoration. Valuation.
Work Stocked and Sold:
Pa. Ph.
Price range: £120 - £25,000.
For artists see *Commercial Gallery Artists.*

Jonathan Potter
125 New Bond Street, London W1Y 9AF.
Tel: *0171-491 3520.* **Fax:** *0171-491 9754.*
Email *jpmaps@ibm.net*
Opening times: *Weekdays 10-6.*
Nearest Underground: *Bond Street.*
Our very large, fine quality, stock includes original antique maps, plans and charts of all areas of Britain and the World. Prices range

from around £50 to several thousand pounds per item for museum quality pieces. Maps, city plans or sea charts make elegant, unusual office or restaurant decoration of genuine worth.

Catalogues issued and a search service offered for items not in stock. Framing service. We are members of BADA, ABA, PBFA and LAPADA.
Services and Facilities:
Art for Offices. Framing.
Work Stocked and Sold:
Pr.
Price range: £50 - £10,000.
For artists see *Commercial Gallery Artists.*

The Jonathan Wylder Gallery and Studio
2 Motcomb Street, Belgravia, London SW1X.
Tel: *0171-245 9949.* **Fax:** *0171-245 9949.*

Julian Hartnoll
14 Masons Yard, off Duke Street, St. James's, London SW1Y 6BU.
Tel: *0171-839 3842.*
Fax: *0171-930 8234.*

Julian Lax
37-39 Arkwright Road, London NW3 6BJ.
Tel: *0171-794 9933.* **Fax:** *0171-431 5845.*
Opening times: *By appointment.*
Nearest Underground: *Hampstead, Finchley Road.*
Personnel: *Director:* Julian Lax.

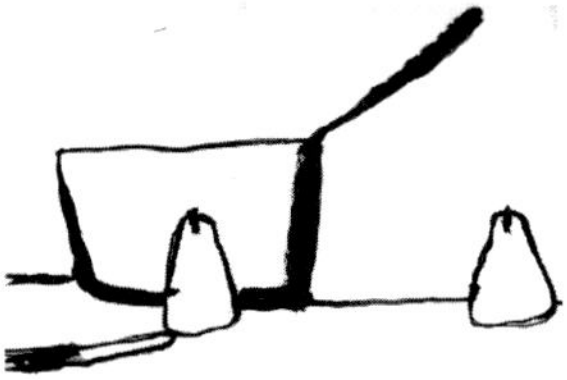

Julian Lax - Modern European Prints, Modern and Contemporary British Prints, Paintings, Drawings and Sculpture. European: Buffet, Chagall, Léger, Matisse, Miró, Picasso and Rouault. British: Auerbach, Blake, Colquhoun, Frink, Heron, Hockney, Hodgkin, Kossoff, Moore, Nevinson, Nicholson, Pasmore, Piper, Roberts, Scott, Sutherland and Vaughan.
Services and Facilities:
Art Consultancy. Art for Offices. Framing. Parking. Restoration. Valuation.
Work Stocked and Sold:
Dr. Pa. Pr. Sc.
Price range: £100 - £30,000.
For artists see *Commercial Gallery Artists.*

Julian Simon Fine Art
70 Pimlico Road, London SW1W 8LS.
Tel: *0171-730 8673.* **Fax:** *0171-823 6116.*

Kaleidoscope
64-66 Willesden Lane, London, NW6 7SX.
Tel: *0171-328 5833.* **Fax:** *0171-624 2913.*
Opening times: *Tues-Sat 10-6.*
Nearest Underground: *Kilburn.*
Personnel: *Director:* Karl Barrie.

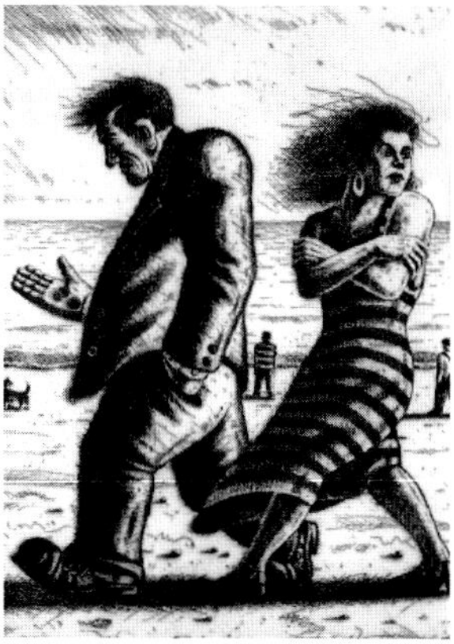

Established over 25 years the gallery shows a wide range of work from early 19th century to the present day. With a constantly changing stock aiming to show established artists along side raw beginners Kaleidoscope is a popular call for both dealers and collectors. The gallery is incorporated with Scope Antiques (situated next door) which stocks unusual items often complimentary to the art side of the business. Sometimes group exhibitions are organized with invited artists being given a specific theme. Past successful shows include 'The Political Circus', 'Erotica' etc. We welcome enquiries from new artists but insist on photographs or slides in the first instance.
Services and Facilities:
Framing. Restoration. Valuation.
Work Stocked and Sold:
Cer. Dr. Pa. Pr. Wd.
Price range: £50 - £4,000.
For artists see *Commercial Gallery Artists.*

Karen Griffiths
Chenil Galleries, 181-183 Kings Road, London SW3 5EB.
Tel: *0171-352 8002.*

Kathryn Bell/Fine Art Consultancy
Studio 123D, Canalot Production Studios, 222 Kensal Road, London W10 5BN.
Tel: *0181-960 0070.* **Fax:** *0181-960 0209.*

Keith Nickol
58 Sandringham Flats, Charing Cross Road, London WC2H 0BL.
Tel: *0171-836 0216, Mobile 041-141 4602.*

Knapp Gallery
Regents College, Inner Circle, Regents Park, London NW1.

L'Acquaforte
49a Ledbury Road, London, W11.
Tel: *0171-221 3388.*

L'Art Abstrait
18a The Circle, Queen Elizabeth Street, London SE1.
Tel: *0171-403 9360.*

La Galerie
225 Ebury Street, London, SW1W.
Tel: *0171-730 9210.*

Lamont Gallery
67 Roman Road, Bethnal Green, London E2 0QN.
Tel: *0181-981 6332.* **Fax:** *0181-983 0144.*

Le Chat Noir Gallery
35 Albemarle Street, Mayfair, London W1X 3FB.
Tel: *0171-495 6710.* **Fax:** *0171-495 6710.*

Lefevre Gallery
30 Bruton Street, London, W1X 8JD.
Tel: *0171-493 2107.* **Fax:** *0171-499 9088.*

The Leger Galleries Ltd
13 Old Bond Street, London, W1X 3DB.
Tel: *0171-629 3538.*

Lena Boyle Fine Art
40 Drayton Gardens, London SW10 9SA.
Tel: *0171-373 8247.* **Fax:** *0171-370 7460.*
Opening times: *By appointment only.*
Nearest Underground: *Gloucester Road, South Kensington.*
Personnel: *Director:* Lena Boyle. John Boyle.
Modern British and contemporary paintings, drawings, watercolours and original Limited Edition Prints. Sculpture, boxes, ceramics.
Services and Facilities:
Art Consultancy. Art for Offices. Commissioning Service.
Work Stocked and Sold:
Cer. Dec. Dr. Pa. Pr. Wd.
Price range: £75 - £6,000.
For artists see *Commercial Gallery Artists.*

Lennox Gallery (London)
77 Moore Park Road, London SW6 2HH.
Tel: *0171-736 3326, Exhibitions: 01349-884083.*

Lenz
401 Langham House, 302 Regent Street, London W1R 6HH.
Tel: *0171-580 4242 or 01954-231006.* **Fax:** *0171-580 4792.*

Lesley Craze Gallery
34 Clerkenwell Green, London EC1R 0DU.
Tel: *0171-608 0393.* **Fax:** *0171-251 9200.*

Linda Anne Landers & Spoon Print Press
337 Westbourne Park Road, London W11 1EG.
Tel: *0171-229 2763.*

Linda Blackstone Gallery
The Old Slaughterhouse, R/O 13 High Street, Pinner, HA5 5QQ.
Tel: *0181-868 5765.* **Fax:** *01923-897153 or 0181-868 4465.*
Email *artgallery@blackstone.co.uk*
Ws *http://www.blackstoneart.com*
Opening times: *Wed-Sat 10-6.*

Nearest Underground: *Pinner (Metropolitan Line - Watford Branch).*
Personnel: *Proprietor:* Linda Blackstone. *Artistic Co-ordinator:* Debra Manifold.

the Linda Blackstone GALLERY

Established 1985. High quality representational paintings, ceramics and sculpture by contemporary British artists. Continually changing exhibition punctuated by 6 major exhibitions a year.
Subjects include: landscape, marine, wildlife and the figure. Gallery artists include: Richard Bolton, Michael Cadman RI ARCA, Ashton Cannell RSMA, Patrick Cullen PS, NEAC, Pamela Davis RMS, Jackie Simmonds, Janet Ledger, Stephanie Harrison RMS, Ken Paine PS, J. Richard Plincke RI, Jacquie Turner, Debra Manifold PS, Leo McDowell RI, Colin Kent RI, Mat Barber Kennedy RI, Catherine Brennand RI, Robert King RI RSMA, Alan Simpson RSMA, John Lidzey, Sue Read RI.
Fine art framing and restoration.
In 1988 staged a special exhibition of paintings, prints and cards by British Artists (including Ken Howard RA and Norman Ackroyd RA) to commemorate the 50th Anniversary of the state of Israel. Their first visit and first impressions of the Holy Land.
Services and Facilities:
Art for Offices. Commissioning Service. Framing. Parking. Restoration.
Work Stocked and Sold:
Ab. Cer. Pa. Pr. Sc.
Price range: £100 - £5,000.
For artists see *Commercial Gallery Artists.*

Lisson Gallery
67 Lisson Street and 52-54 Bell Street, London NW1 5DA.
Tel: *0171-724 2739.* **Fax:** *0171-724 7124.*
Email *contact@lisson.co.uk*
Ws *http://www.lisson.co.uk*
Opening times: *Mon-Fri 10-6, Sat 10-5.*
Nearest Underground: *Edgware Road, Marylebone.*
Personnel: *Chairman:* Nicholas Logsdail. *Executive Directors:* Barry Barker, Jill Silverman van Coenegrachts.

LISSON GALLERY
LONDON

Artists include: Edward Allington, Art & Language, John Baldessari, Pierre Bismuth, Christine Borland, Victor Burgin, Scott Burton, James Casebere, James Coleman Mat Collishaw, Tony Cragg, Grenville Davey, Richard Deacon, Lili Dujourie, Ceal Floyer, Gaylen Gerber, Douglas Gordon, Dan Graham, Rodney Graham, John Hilliard, Mark Hosking, Shirazeh Houshiary, Peter Joseph, Donald Judd, Anish Kapoor, On Kawara, John Latham, Sol Lewitt, Simon Linke, Robert Mangold, Jason Martin, Allan McCollum, John McCracken, Jonathan Monk, Anna Mossman, Juan Muñoz, John Murphy, Avis Newman, Julian Opie, Tony Oursler, Giulio Paolini, Simon Patterson, Thomas Schütte, Lee Ufan, Jan Vercruysse, Richard Wentworth, Franz West, Jane & Louise Wilson.
For artists see *Commercial Gallery Artists.*

Llewellyn Alexander (Fine Paintings) Ltd
124-126 The Cut, Waterloo, London SE1 8LN.
Tel: *0171-620 1322/1324.* **Fax:** *0171-928 9469.*

Loggia
15 Buckingham Gate, London SW1E 6LB.
Tel: *0171-828 5963.*

Logos Art Gallery
20 Barter Street, London, WC1A 2AH.
Tel: *0171-404 7091.*

London Contemporary Art Ltd
132 Lots Road, Chelsea, London, SW10 0RJ.
Tel: *0171-351 7696.*

London Print Studio
(formerly London Print Workshop) 425 Harrow Road, London W10 4RD.
Tel: *0181-969 3247.* **Fax:** *0181-964 0008.*
Email *lpw@200.co.uk*
Ws *http://www.200.co.uk/~z8000007*
Opening times: *Mon-Fri 10-6, Sat 1-5.*
Nearest Underground: *Westbourne Park.*
Personnel: *Director:* John Phillips.

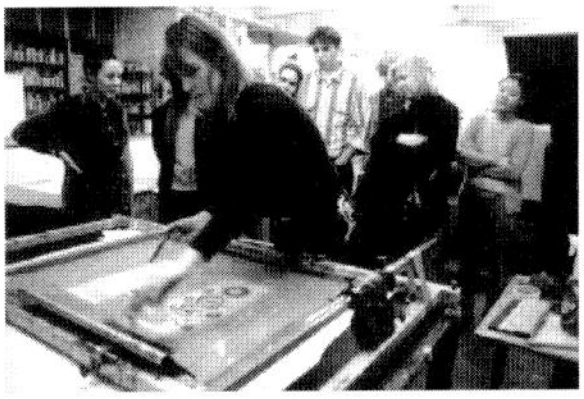

Specialist centre for printmaking and the graphic arts: comprises printmaking studio, computer graphics facility and gallery. LPW runs a programme of exhibitions, short courses and events.
It provides open access resource for artists using screenprint, intaglio, relief printing, and computer graphics facilities. Professional staff are on hand to provide support.
Charges from £4.74 (Cons.) for a 3-hour session. A wide selection of artists' prints are available for sale in the gallery.
Services and Facilities:
Disabled Access. Lectures. Workshop Facilities.
Work Stocked and Sold:
Pr.
Price range: £50 - £5,000.

Long & Ryle Art International
4 John Islip Street, London, SW1P 4PX.
Tel: *0171-834 1434.* **Fax:** *0171-821 9409.*

Lucy B. Campbell Gallery
123 Kensington Church Street, London, W8 7LP.
Tel: *0171-727 2205.*

Lumley Cazalet
33 Davies Street, London W1Y 1FN.
Tel: *0171-491 4767.* **Fax:** *0171-493 8644.*
Opening times: *Mon-Fri 10-6.*
Nearest Underground: *Bond Street.*
Personnel: *Directors:* Camilla Cazalet, Caroline Lumley , Catherine Hodgkinson.

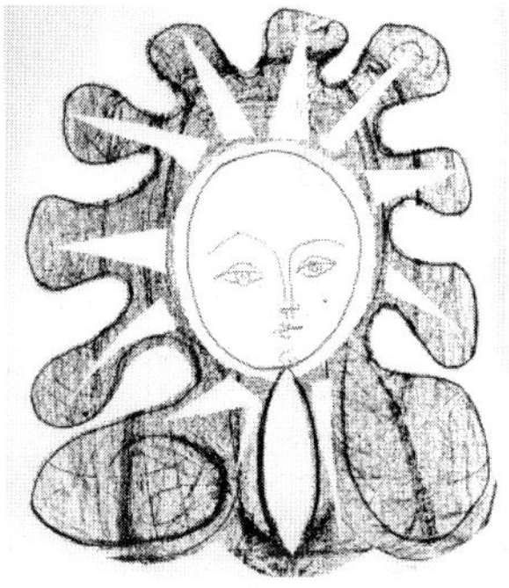

Original prints by 20th C. European masters including Braque, Chagall, Frink, Hockney, Matisse, Miró, Picasso. Late 19th Century.prints, including Belleroche, Helleu, Tissot. Drawings by Matisse. Sculpture and drawings by Frink.
Work Stocked and Sold:
Dr. Pr. Sc.
Price range: £50 - £300,000.
For artists see *Commercial Gallery Artists.*

Lutz Riester
P.O. Box 2769, London W2 6ZJ.
Tel: *0171-258 3467.*

M.J. Putman
151 Lavender Hill, London, SW11 5QJ.
Tel: *0171-228 9087.*

The Maas Gallery
15a Clifford Street, London W1X 1RF.
Tel: *0171-734 2302.* **Fax:** *0171-287 4836.*

Malcolm Innes Gallery
7 Bury Street, St. James's, London SW7Y 6AL.
Tel: *0171-839 8083/4.* **Fax:** *0171-839 8085.*

Mall Arcade
Camden Passage, Islington, London N1.
Tel: *0171-930 1904.* **Fax:** *0171-839 7509.*

Manya Igel Fine Arts
21-22 Peter's Court, Porchester Road, London W2 5DR.
Tel: *0171-229 1669/8429.* **Fax:** *0171-229 6770.*

Marble Arch Art Gallery
14 Old Quebec Street, London, W1H.
Tel: *0171-629 5159.*

Marina Henderson Gallery
11 Langton Street, London, SW10.
Tel: *0171-352 1667.*

The Mark Gallery
9 Porchester Place, Marble Arch, London W2 2BS.
Tel: *0171-262 4906.* **Fax:** *0171-224 9416.*

Markovitch Gallery
108A Boundary Road, St. Johns Wood, London NW8 0RH. **Tel:** *0171-372 1333.*

Marlborough Graphics
6 Albemarle Street, London W1X 4BY.
Tel: *0171-629 5161.* **Fax:** *0171-495 0641.*
Ws *http://www.icollector.com*
Opening times: *Mon-Fri 10-5.30, Sat 10-12.30.*
Nearest Underground: *Green Park.*
Personnel: *Director:* David Case. Nicola Togneri.

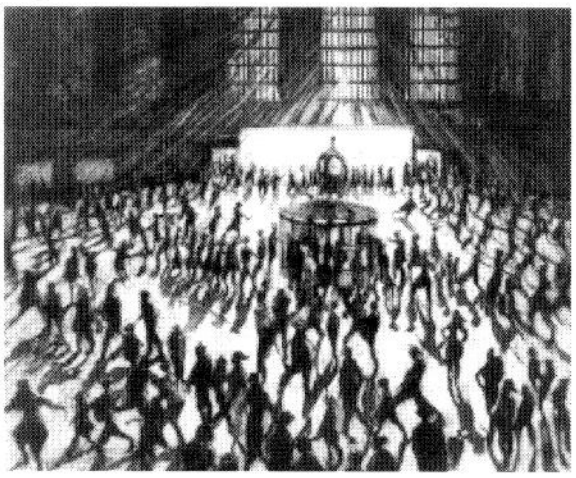

London's leading publishers of contemporary limited edition prints. Also stock European Modern Master Prints including Bacon, Hepworth, Matisse, Miro, Moore, Nicholson, Picasso and Sutherland.
Gallery artists represented include Arikha, Auerbach, Conroy, Davies, Freud, Hambling, Jacklin, Kiff, Kitaj, Le Brun, Olton, Pasmore, Paul, Piper and Rego. Forthcoming publications will include lithographs by Stephen Conroy and etchings and monoprints by Bill Jacklin both of whom will have exhibitions in 1999.
Services and Facilities:
Art Consultancy. Art for Offices. Framing. Valuation.
Work Stocked and Sold:
Ab. Dr. Ph. Pr.
Price range: £300 - £60,000.
For artists see *Commercial Gallery Artists.*

Marlene Eleini
#12-69 Westbourne Terrace, London, W2 3UY.
Tel: *0171-706 0373.* **Fax:** *0171-706 1241.*
Email *meleini@x-stream.co.uk*
Opening times: *Wed-Thur 11-6 and by appointment.*
Nearest Underground: *Lancaster Gate, Paddington.*
Personnel: *Director:* Marlene Eleini. *Administrator:* Adrian George.
Contemporary and modern art.
Services and Facilities:
Art Consultancy. Art for Offices. Commissioning Service.
Work Stocked and Sold:
Dr. Pa. Ph. Pr. Sc.
Price range: £300 - £40,000.
For artists see *Commercial Gallery Artists.*

Marsden Contemporary Art
21 Dulwich Village, London SE21 7BT.
Tel: *0181-488 4169.* **Fax:** *0181-693 2700.*

Martyn Gregory
34 Bury Street, St. James's, London SW1Y 6AU.
Tel: *0171-839 3731.* **Fax:** *0171-930 0812.*
Opening times: *10-6.*
Nearest Underground: *Green Park.*
British watercolours and paintings; China Trade pictures.

Matthiesen Fine Art Limited
7/8 Mason's Yard, Duke Street, London SW1Y 6BU.
Tel: *0171-930 2437.* **Fax:** *0171-930 1387.*
Email *OldMastersLondon@Compuserve.com*
Ws *http://www.Europeanpaintings.com*
Opening times: *Mon-Fri 10-6. By appointment only.*
Nearest Underground: *Green Park & Piccadilly.*
Personnel: *Director:* Patrick Matthiesen.
Museum quality Italian, French and Spanish Old Master paintings 1330-1848. Specialising in Italian painting in London and French painting in New York. Exhibition catalogues available. In association with Stair Sainty Matthiesen Inc., 22 E. 80th St., New York, NY 10021, USA. Tel (212) 288 1088, fax (212) 628 2449.
Services and Facilities:
Art Consultancy.
Work Stocked and Sold:
Pa.
Price range: £30,000 - £5,000,000.
For artists see *Commercial Gallery Artists.*

Matts Gallery
42-44 Copperfield Road, London E3 4RR.
Tel: *0181-983 1771.* **Fax:** *0181-983 1435.*

Mayor Gallery
22a Cork Street, London W1X 1HB.
Tel: *0171-734 3558.* **Fax:** *0171-494 1377.*

McDonald Wyckaert
The Georgian Group, 6 Fitzroy Square, London W1P 6DX. **Tel:** *0171-706 3387.*

The McHardy Sculpture Company
Cardamom Building, Shad Thames, London SE1 2YR.
Tel: *0171-403 7555.* **Fax:** *0171-378 7300.*
Email *nevagi@compuserve.com*
Ws *http://www.mchardy-sculpture.com*
Opening times: *Tue-Sat 11-5, Sun 12-5.*
Nearest Underground: *London Bridge, Tower Hill.*
Personnel: *Contacts:* Agi & Neville Cohen.

The McHardy Sculpture Company

The gallery at Butlers Wharf by Tower Bridge has a continual display of more than 100 pieces including figurative and abstract works from distinguished names and new discoveries. McHardy Sculpture Company can help all those with an interest in sourcing the work of contemporary sculptors at realistic prices.
Services and Facilities:
Art Consultancy. Art for Offices. Commissioning Service.
Work Stocked and Sold:
Sc.
Price range: £150 - £10,000.
For artists see *Commercial Gallery Artists.*

Medici Galleries
7 Grafton Street, London W1X 3LA.
Tel: *0171-629 5675.* **Fax:** *0171-495 2997.*
Opening times: *Mon-Fri 9-5.30.*
Nearest Underground: *Green Park.*
Personnel: *Manager:* Ian Lewis. Jenny Kerr.

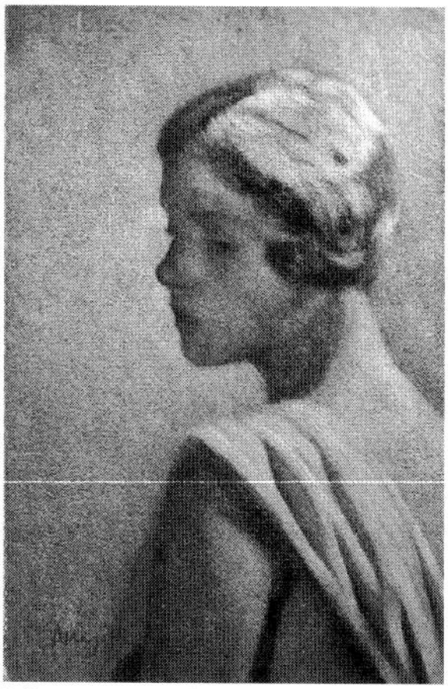

Offering a rare combination of services, The Medici Galleries have been a West End landmark since 1910. The upper gallery has a changing display of original contemporary art - oils, watercolours, miniatures and craft - with exhibitions several times a year. Signed limited edition, reproduction and children's prints are available in the lower gallery, as is a framing service offering a wide choice of mounts and frames. Rooms in the lower gallery are devoted to displaying Fine Art Greeting Cards, postcards, stationary, carved book ends and art and children's books. A Personalised Christmas Card service is available from August.
Services and Facilities:
Art Consultancy. Art for Offices. Commissioning Service. Framing. Gallery space for hire. Shop.
Work Stocked and Sold:
Cra. Pa. Pr.
Price range: £200 - £15,000.
For artists see *Commercial Gallery Artists.*

Meghraj Gallery
Meghraj Court, 18 Jockey's Fields, London WC1R 4BW.
Tel: *0171-831 6881.* **Fax:** *0171-404 8288.*

Mercury Gallery
26 Cork Street, London W1X 1HB.
Tel: *0171-734 7800.* **Fax:** *0171-287 9809.*
Email *mercury@netcomuk.co.uk*
Ws *http://www.mercury-gallery.co.uk*
Opening times: *Mon-Fri 10-5.30, Sat 10-12.30 (except during Summer Show).*
Nearest Underground: *Green Park, Piccadilly.*
Personnel: *Directors:* Gillian Raffles, Gordon Samuel.
Large stock of Modern British Art, including: Burra, Eardley, Gaudier-Brzeska, Redpath, Spencer, Vaughan, Wallis, Wyndham Lewis and Wood. Contemporary gallery artists exhibiting: Samira Abbassy, Elizabeth

Blackadder RA,RSA, Janet Boulton, Robert Callender, David Gentleman, John Houston, Barry Hirst, Michael Kenny, RA, Simon Laurie, David Remfry, Mick Rooney, RA, Eric Rimmington, Carol Ann Sutherland. Young painters' work during mixed shows.
Services and Facilities:
Art Consultancy. Art for Offices.
Work Stocked and Sold:
Ab. Cer. Dr. Pa. Pr. Sc.
Price range: £100 - £100,000.
For artists see *Commercial Gallery Artists.*

Merrifield Studios
112 Heath Street, Hampstead, London NW3 1AA.
Tel: *0171-794 0343/0171-431 0794.*
Fax: *0171-435 8039.*

Michael Elcke
2 Old Bond Street, London, W1X.
Tel: *0171-495 2687.*

Mil Arté
98 Mill Lane, West Hampstead, London NW6 1NF.
Tel: *0171-681 9136.* **Fax:** *0171-435 1005.*

Milne & Moller
35 Colville Terrace, London W11 2BU.
Tel: *0171-727 1679.*

Mina Renton Fine Art
50 Eresby House, Rutland Gate, London SW7 1BG.
Tel: *0171-584 1907.* **Fax:** *0171-584 1907.*

Modern African Gallery
102 Park Street, London, W1Y.
Tel: *0171-629 7528.*

Momtaz Islamic Art
79A Albany Street, Regent's Park, London NW1 4BT. **Tel:** *0171-486 5411.*

Montpelier Sandelson
4 Montpelier Street, London SW7 1EZ.
Tel: *0171-584 0667.* **Fax:** *0171-225 2280.*

Morley Gallery
61 Westminster Bridge Road, London SE1 7HT.
Tel: *0171-450 9226.* **Fax:** *0171-928 4074.*
Opening times: *Mon 1-6, Tues, Thurs, Fri 10-6, Wed 10-8, closed Bank Holidays; please contact gallery for details of Saturday openings.*
Nearest Underground: *Lambeth North, Waterloo BR.*
Personnel: *Exhibitions Organiser:* Jane Hartwell.
Exhibitions of contemporary art every 3-6 weeks. Annual programme includes: painting, drawing, prints, sculpture, photography, ceramics and textiles. Work selected annually by committee. Details of exhibitions listed in Art Review.
Work Stocked and Sold:
Cer. Cra. Dr. Pa. Ph. Pr. Sc. Tx.
Price range: £50 - £10,000.

Nairi Sahakian Contemporary Art
34 Burton Court, Franklin's Row, London SW3 4SZ.
Tel: *0171-730 0432.* **Fax:** *0171-831 9489.*

Narwhal Inuit Art Gallery
55 Linden Gardens, Chiswick, London W4 2EH.
Tel: *0181-747 1575.* **Fax:** *0181-742 1268.*
Email *narwhalman@aol.com*
Opening times: *By appointment seven days a week.*
Nearest Underground: *Turnham Green.*
Personnel: *Directors:* Ken Mantel, Tija Mantel.

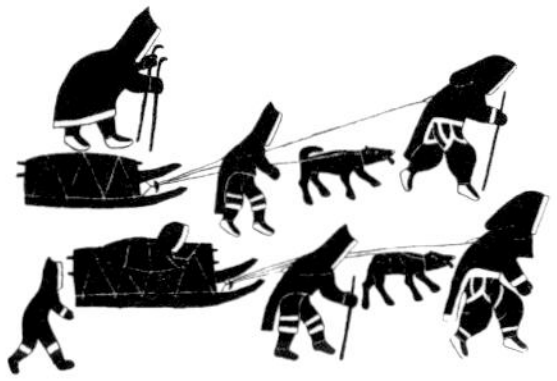

Permanent exhibition specialising in Inuit (Eskimo) art from Canada (Nunavut) and Greenland. Carvings in soapstone, jadeite, relic bone, caribou horn and musk ox horn. Plus original drawings and editioned graphics from 1955 to present day. Reference books, videos, audio tapes, touring educational exhibitions and slide-based lectures. Museum and corporate clients welcome. Teacher education packs 6-18 year olds, plus in service assistance. Also registered as NIAEF (Narwhal Inuit Art Education Foundation) a charity to promote the understanding of Inuit life and tradition through contemporary art and issues.
Services and Facilities:
Art for Offices. Friends/Society. Lectures. Valuation.
Work Stocked and Sold:
Ab. Dr. Pr. Sc.
Price range: £50 - £2,500.
For artists see *Commercial Gallery Artists.*

Neffe-Degandt
32a, St. George Street, London W1R 9FA.
Tel: *0171-493 2630, 0171-629 9788.*
Fax: *0171-493 1379.*

New Academy Gallery and Business Art Galleries
34 Windmill Street, Fitzrovia, London W1P 1HH.
Tel: *0171-323 4700.* **Fax:** *0171-436 3059.*
Email *gallery@curwen.demon.co.uk*
Ws *http://www.curwen.demon.co.uk*
Opening times: *Mon-Fri 10-6, Thurs until 8, Sat 11-5. Closed Sun and Bank Holiday weekends.*
Nearest Underground: *Goodge St/Tottenham Court Road.*
Personnel: *Directors:* John Hutchings, Jill Hutchings. *Contact:* Pryle Behrman.
Exhibits and promotes a wide range of contemporary British painting, sculpture, original prints. Regular exhibiting artists include: Barry Atherton, Jo Barry, Clare Bigger, Clive Blackmore, Naomi Blake, John Brokenshire, Roger Cecil, Clare Chinnery, Jane Corsellis, Alexander Creswell, Peter Dover, Bernard Dunstan RA, Frederick Gore RA, Alistair Grant, Donald Hamilton Fraser RA, Brenda Hartill, Susan-Jayne Hocking, Sarah Holliday, Andrew Macara, Padraig Macmiadhachain, Anita Mandl, Michèle Noach, Linda Norris, John Piper, Jacqueline Rizvi, Hans Schwarz, Keith Roberts, Zoe Rubens, Richard Walker, Jago Max Williams and Peter Wray.

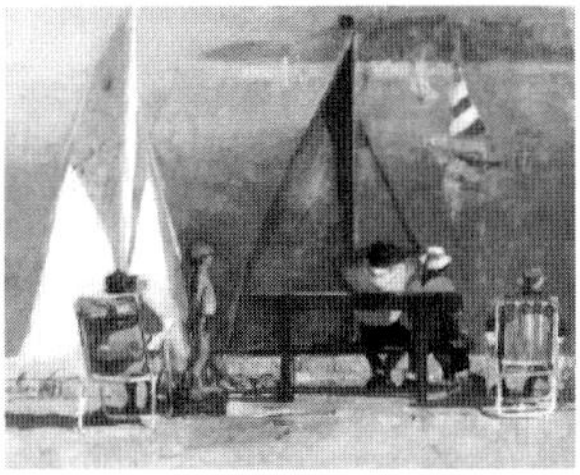

We offer a comprehensive service to businesses including free advice on purchases, a flexible hire scheme and on-site presentations; and undertake commissions (painting of portraits, houses, Christmas cards etc.) for both business and private individuals.
Services and Facilities:
Art Consultancy. Art for Offices. Commissioning Service. Framing.
Work Stocked and Sold:
Dr. Pa. Pr. Sc.
Price range: £20 - £20,000.
For artists see *Commercial Gallery Artists.*

New Art Centre
168 Sloane Street, London, SW1X.
Tel: *0171-235 5844.*

New Grafton Gallery
49 Church Road, Barnes, London SW13 9HH.
Tel: *0181-748 8850.* **Fax:** *0181-748 9818.*
Opening times: *Tues-Sat 10-5.30.*
Founded 1968. Mainly figurative English painting and drawing by living artists; also English painting 1900-40 and permanent Portrait Centre. Mark Adlington, Julian Bailey, Jason Bowyer, Oliver Campion, Sue Campion, Tom Coates, Anthea Craigmyl & Fred Cuming, Jane Dowling, Fred Dubery, Mary Fedden, Christa Gaa, Reg Gammon, Peter Greenham, Christopher Hall, Colin Hayes, Josef Herman, Susan-Jayne Hocking, Ken Howard, John Nash, Paul Newland, Richard Pikesley, Mick Rooney, Liam Spencer, Sarah Spencer, Ruth Stage, Pip Todd Warmoth, Josephine Trotter, Carel Weight, Jacqueline Williams.
Services and Facilities:
Art Consultancy. Commissioning Service. Disabled Access. Parking. Valuation.
Work Stocked and Sold:
Dr. Pa.
Price range: £100 - £10,000.
For artists see *Commercial Gallery Artists.*

Nicholas Treadwell Gallery
17 Punderson's Gardens, Bethnal Green, London, E2 9RU.
Tel: *0171-613 3600.* **Fax:** *0171-613 3700.*
Email *nick.treadwell@superhumanism.com*
Opening times: *4/6 exhibitions a year and by appointment.*
Nearest Underground: *Bethnal Green.*
Personnel: *Director:* Nicholas Treadwell.
Established in 1963, the Treadwell Gallery moved back into London in 1996, after twelve years outside, spent in a Kent Mansion and then a Bradford Mill. The Gallery follows a

strictly figurative policy, Art about life and People, with an emphasis on work of an entertaining nature.

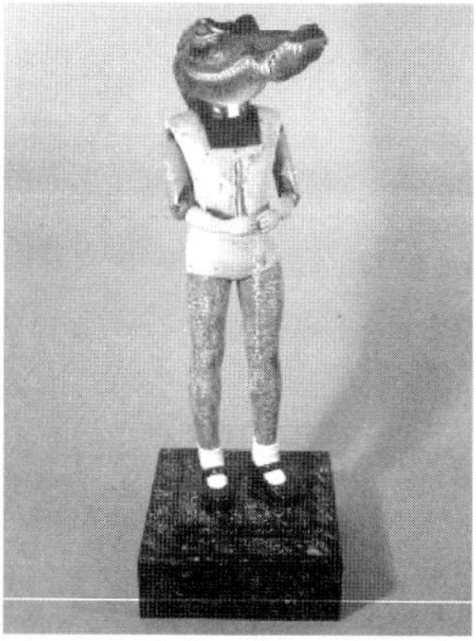

It has a strong Sculptural bias, with more than half of the twenty or so Artists, currently represented, being Sculptors. Live Art and Music Events are organised on a Bi-Monthly Basis.
Services and Facilities:
Commissioning Service. Lectures.
Work Stocked and Sold:
Cer. Dr. Pa. Sc.
Price range: £250 - £12,000.
For artists see *Commercial Gallery Artists.*

The Northcote Gallery
110 Northcote Road, Battersea, London, SW11 6QP.
Tel: *0171-924 6741.*

O'Shea Gallery
120a Mount Street, London W1Y 5HB.
Tel: *0171-629 1122.*

The October Gallery
24 Old Gloucester Street, London WC1N 3AL.
Tel: *0171-242 7367.* **Fax:** *0171-405 1851.*
Email *octobergallery@compuserve.com*
Ws *http://www.ecotechnics.edu/indexog.html*
Opening times: *Tues-Sat 12.30-5.30.*
Nearest Underground: *Holborn/Russell Square.*
Personnel: *Artistic Director:* Elisabeth Lalouschek. *Director:* Chili Hawes.
The October Gallery represents a range of artists from the international avant-garde. The gallery offers an extensive selection of contemporary paintings, drawings, prints, photographs and sculpture by artists from Africa, the Americas, Asia and Europe.
Artists include Pablo Amaringo, El Anatsui, Carol Beckwith, William S. Burroughs, Leroy Clarke, Ira Cohen, Sokari Douglas Camp, Ablade Glover, Emmanuel Taiwo Jegede, Elisabeth Lalouschek, Manuel Mendive, Z. O. Oloruntoba, Julieta Rubio, Mickael Bethe-Selassie, Laila Shawa, Wijdan, Gerald Wilde, Aubrey Williams and Xu Zhong Min. The October Gallery café serves food from around the world and is open at lunch time, Tues-Sat 12.30-2.30. Education Programme.
Services and Facilities:
Art Consultancy. Art for Offices. Bookshop. Café. Craftshop. Friends/Society. Gallery space for hire. Workshop Facilities.
Work Stocked and Sold:
Dr. Pa. Ph. Pr. Sc.
Price range: £100 - £10,000.
For artists see *Commercial Gallery Artists.*

Offer Waterman & Co. Fine Art Ltd
20 Park Walk, London SW10 0AQ.
Tel: *0171-351 0068.* **Fax:** *0171-351 2269.*

Olimpia Theodoli Fine Prints
14 Dover Street, London W1X 3PH.
Tel: *0171-491 9196.* **Fax:** *0171-491 9197.*
Email *othedolifineprints@compuserve.com*
Opening times: *Open every day by appointment.*
Nearest Underground: *Green Park, Piccadilly.*
Fine prints for all pockets.
Services and Facilities:
Restoration. Valuation.
Work Stocked and Sold:
Ab. Dr. Ph. Pr.
Price range: From £100.
For artists see *Commercial Gallery Artists.*

Oliver Hoare
Flat 3 7 Onslow Gardens, London SW7 3LY.
Tel: *0171-835 1600.* **Fax:** *0171-373 5787.*

Orangery
Central Library, Phillimore Walk, London W8 7RX. **Tel:** *0171-361 2295.*

Oriel Contemporary Art
25 Princess Road, Regents Park, London NW1 8JR.
Tel: *0171-483 1375.* **Fax:** *0171-483 1363.*

Osbourne Studio Gallery
13 Motcomb Street, London SW7X 8LB.
Tel: *0171-235 9667/8.*

Paisnel Gallery
22 Mason's Yard, Duke Street, St. James's, London SW1Y 6BU.
Tel: *0171-930 9293.* **Fax:** *0171-930 7282.*

Park Gallery
26 Connaught Street, London W2 2AF.
Tel: *0171-262 2588.* **Fax:** *0171-262 2587.*

Park Walk Gallery
20 Park Walk, London SW10 0AQ.
Tel: *0171-351 0410.*

Parker Gallery
28 Pimlico Road, Chelsea, London, SW1W 8LJ.
Tel: *0171-730 6768.* **Fax:** *0171-259 9180.*

Partridge Fine Arts
144 New Bond Street, London, W1Y.
Tel: *0171-629 0834.*

Paton Gallery
London Fields, 282 Richmond Road, London E8 3QS.
Tel: *0181-986 3409.* **Fax:** *0181-986 0811.*

Paul Hawkins Gallery
4 Davies Street, London W1Y 1LY.
Tel: *0171-499 7009.* **Fax:** *0171-499 2265.*

Paul Mason Gallery
149 Sloane Street, London, SW1X 9BZ.
Tel: *0171-730 3683/7359.*

Paul Smith/R. Newbold Gallery
Paul Smith Press Office, 33 Longacre, London WC2E 9LA. **Tel:** *0171-240 0009/32.*

Peter Gwyther Gallery
29 Bruton Street, Mayfair, London W1X 7DB.
Tel: *0171-495 4747.* **Fax:** *0171-495 6232.*

Philip Graham Contemporary Art
9a-11 Bonhill Street, London, EC2A.
Tel: *0171-920 0350.*

Piano Nobile
129 Portland Road, Holland Park, London W11 4LW. **Tel:** *0171-229 1099.*

Piccadilly Gallery Ltd.
43 Dover Street, London W1X 3RE.
Tel: *0171-629 2875.* **Fax:** *0171-499 0431.*
Email *art@piccadillygall.demon.co.uk*
Ws *http://www.piccadillygall.demon.co.uk*
Opening times: *Mon-Fri 10-5.30, Sats by appointment.*
Nearest Underground: *Green Park.*
Personnel: *Directors:* R.G. Pilkington, Eve Pilkington, Christabel Pool.
Founded 1953. Exhibitions changing monthly. Symbolist works, 20th C. British and European drawings and watercolours. Contemporary British figurative painters; Adrian Berg RA, Anthony Green RA, Martin Greenland, Julie Held, John Kelly John Morley, Michael Murfin, Graham Ovenden, Alan Parker, Peter Turnbull, Matilda Tumim, William Wilkins, etc.
Services and Facilities:
Disabled Access.
Work Stocked and Sold:
Dr. Pa.
Price range: £200 - £20,000.
For artists see *Commercial Gallery Artists.*

Piers Feetham Gallery
475 Fulham Road, London SW6 1HL.
Tel: *0171-381 5958.* **Fax:** *0171-381 3031.*
Opening times: *Tues-Fri 10-1, 2-6, Sat 10-1.*
Nearest Underground: *Fulham Broadway.*
Personnel: Piers Feetham. Caroline McAdam Clark.

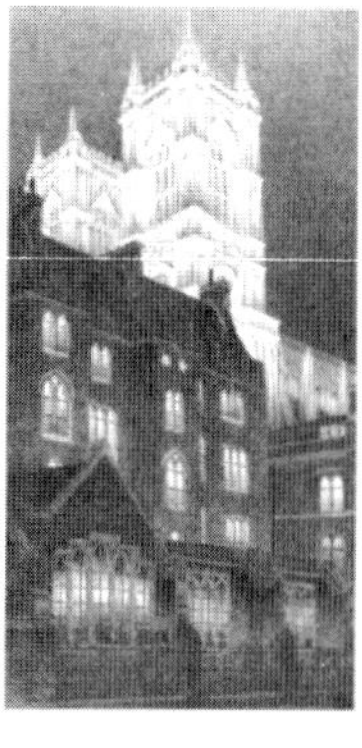

The gallery holds eight to nine mixed and solo exhibitions a year, by contemporary British artists - with a special emphasis on drawings. Regular Xmas mixed show! "The Artist as Decorator", small and large decorated and decorative items. The gallery also comprises a long-established and comprehensive framing business, specialising in conservation framing; also paper conservation, oil restoration and antique frame restoration services.
Services and Facilities:
Framing. Restoration.
Work Stocked and Sold:
Dr. Pa.
Price range: £100 - £1,500.

The Pike Gallery
145 St John's Hill, London, SW11 1TQ.
Tel: *0171-223 6741.*

Pitshanger Manor Gallery
Mattock Lane, Ealing, London, W5 5EQ.

Plantation House
31-35 Fenchurch Street, London, EC3M 3DX.
Tel: *0171-623 2935.*

Plazzotta Ltd
10 Shalcomb Street, London SW10 0HY.
Tel: *0171-352 7493.* **Fax:** *0171-352 7493.*
Email *oconor@plazzotta.co.uk*
Ws *http://www.plazzotta.co.uk*
Opening times: *The office and storeroom are open by appointment.*
Nearest Underground: *Sloane Square, Earls Court.*
Personnel: *Director:* Richard S. O'Conor.

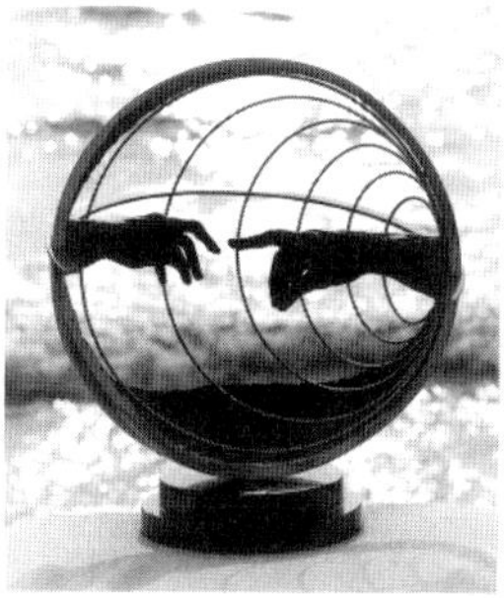

We are a small family run company specialising in the work of the late Italian sculptor Enzo Plazzotta (1921-1981). There remains a considerable and varied stock of sculpture within the artist's declared editions. The fully illustrated hardback catalogue raisonné is for sale at £15 plus postage and our current price list of available sculpture can be sent on request. Subjects range from mythology, ballet, horses, human form and Christian themes. With sizes from 8 inches to monumental. The office and storeroom are open by appointment.
Services and Facilities:
Valuation.
Work Stocked and Sold:
Ab. Sc.
Price range: £400 - £50,000.
For artists see *Commercial Gallery Artists.*

Polak Gallery
21 King Street, St James's, London, SW1Y 6QY.
Tel: *0171-839 2871.*

Portal Gallery
43 Dover Street, Piccadilly, London W1X 3RE.
Tel: *0171-493 0706.* **Fax:** *0171-493 2667.*
Email *portalgallery@btinternet.com*
Ws *http://www.portal-gallery.com*
Opening times: *Mon-Fri 10-5.30, Sat 10-4.*
Nearest Underground: *Green Park.*
Personnel: *Directors:* Lionel Levy, Jess Wilder.

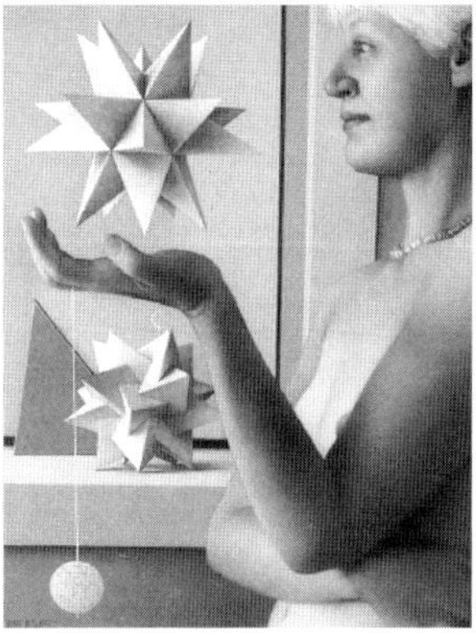

The gallery specialises in idiosyncratic, figurative painting by contemporary British artists. Started in 1959, Portal has long been a venue for the work of quirky and imaginative artists such as John Byrne, Beryl Cook, Haydn Cornner, Nick Cudworth, Steve Easby, Jane Lewis, Lizzie Riches, Mick Rooney and many others. The gallery has eight solo exhibitions each year, theme shows and a permanent exhibition of Portal painters.
Services and Facilities:
Commissioning Service. Shop.
Work Stocked and Sold:
Pa. Pr.
Price range: £500 - £20,000.
For artists see *Commercial Gallery Artists.*

Portland Gallery
9 Bury Street, St. James's, London, SW1Y 6AB.
Tel: *0171-321 0422.* **Fax:** *0171-321 0230.*

Posk Gallery
238 King Street, London, W6 0RF.
Tel: *0181-741 1940.* **Fax:** *0181-746 3798.*
Nearest Underground: *Ravenscourt Park*
Personnel: *Director:* J. Baranowska.
The POSK Gallery provides exhibitions of works (all kinds of media) from artists of all nationalities. The price of hiring the gallery is £36 plus VAT (£42.30) per week for the members of POSK - and £48 plus VAT (£56.40) for non-members plus 15% commission from the price of sold exhibits.
The POSK Gallery will advertise all exhibitions free of charge in art magazines "Galleries" and "Art Review", also in papers of the Polish Social and Cultural Association Ltd., and in the Polish Cultural Institute. Artists who wish to exhibit should send a short curriculum vitae and five colour photographs of their work. Exhibitors are solely responsible for printed material, advertising and invitations. Exhibitions are changed fortnightly.
Services and Facilities:
Bar. Café. Disabled Access. Gallery space for hire. Restaurant.
Work Stocked and Sold:
Cer. Cra. Dr. Jew. Pa. Ph. Pr. Sc.
Price range: £100 - £1,800.
For artists see *Commercial Gallery Artists.*

Primrose Hill Gallery
81 Regents Park Road, London NW1 8UY.
Tel: *0171-586 3533.*

Proud Galleries
5 Buckingham Street, London WC2N 6BS.
Tel: *0171-839 4942.*
Fax: *0171-839 4947.*

Pryory Art
240 Belsize Road, London NW6 4BT.
Tel: *0171-604 4455.*
Opening times: *Mon-Fri 10.30-5.30, Sat by appointment.*
Nearest Underground: *Kilburn Park/West Hampstead.*
Personnel: *Managing Director:* Andy Worth.

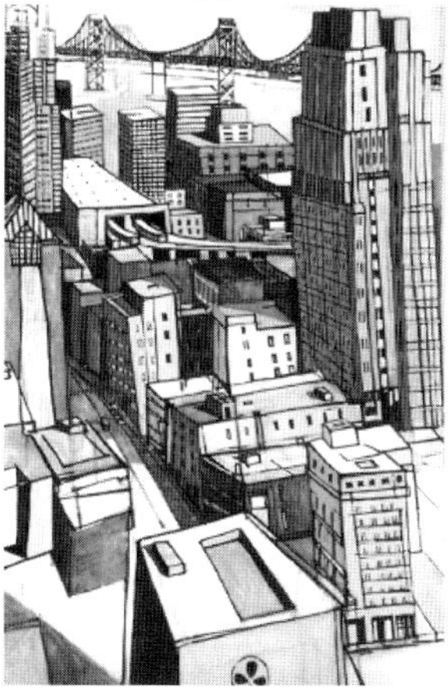

Pryory Art provides a constantly changing showcase of contemporary art drawn from Hampstead's wealth of local talent alongside established artists from home and abroad. The emphasis is on affordable art of highest standard sculpture, ceramics and jewellery are

also featured. Many exciting events and demonstrations scheduled for 1999/2000. Call for details.
Services and Facilities:
Art Consultancy. Art for Offices. Framing. Gallery space for hire.
Work Stocked and Sold:
Cer. Cra. Dr. Jew. Pa. Ph. Pr. Sc. Tx.
Price range: £200 - £2,000.
For artists see *Commercial Gallery Artists.*

Pyms Gallery
9 Mount Street, Mayfair, London W1Y 5AD.
Tel: *0171-629 2020.* **Fax:** *0171-629 2060.*
Opening times: *Mon-Fri 10-6 and by appointment.*
Nearest Underground: *Green Park, Bond Street.*
Personnel: Alan Hobart. Mary Hobart.

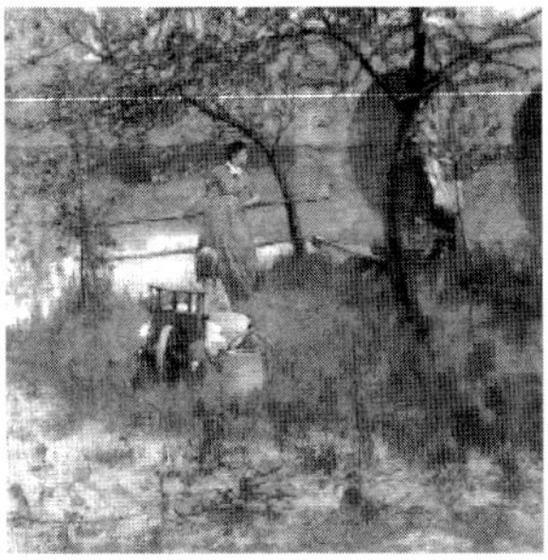

Specialising in British and Irish 18th, 19th and 20th century paintings and 19th century French paintings. Regular exhibitions, catalogues available. Requests for information and for notification of exhibitions and events welcome. Insurance valuations of single works and collections. Advice on commission purchases and cleaning and restoration of paintings. Members of British Antique Dealers Association. Exhibitors at Grosvenor House Art and Antiques Fair. Members Society of London Art Dealers.
Work Stocked and Sold:
Dr. Pa.
Price range: £200 - £1,000,000.
For artists see *Commercial Gallery Artists.*

Quantum Contemporary Art
The Old Imperial Laundry, 71 Warriner Gardens, London SW11 4XW.
Tel: *0171-498 6868.* **Fax:** *0171-498 7878.*

R. K. Gallery
65 Sheen Lane, Sheen, London SW14 8AD.
Tel: *0181-876 8137.*

Rafael Valls Gallery
6 Ryder Street, London, SW1Y.
Tel: *0171-930 0029.*

Railings Gallery
5 New Cavendish Street, London W1M 7RP.
Tel: *0171-935 1114.* **Fax:** *0171-486 9250.*

Rebecca Hossack Gallery
Fitzrovia, 35 Windmill Street, London W1P 1HH.
Tel: *0171-436 4899.* **Fax:** *0171-323 3182.*
Email *rebecca@hossackgallery.demon.co.uk*
Opening times: *Mon-Sat 10-6.*
Nearest Underground: *Goodge Street.*
Personnel: *Director:* Rebecca Hossack. *Contact:* Tom Greatrex.

The Rebecca Hossack Gallery is one of the most innovative galleries in central London with a reputation for showing top quality non-European art as well as the best of British Contemporary artists. The leading European gallery for Australian Aboriginal art and for the art of the Kalahari Bushmen, the Rebecca Hossack Gallery has a full range of such work - both paintings and prints - always in stock including pieces by Clifford Possum, Jimmy Pike, Gertie Huddlestone, Emily Kngwarreye and Mathias Kauage. Contemporary Scottish artists are also a strong focus of the gallery (Abigail McLellan, Joseph Davie and Alasdair Wallace). British Contemporary art shown includes painting (figurative and abstract), sculpture, ceramics (Deborah Prosser, Ann Stokes) and furniture (Camilla Meddings). The gallery is opening a new space dedicated to showing work from the Australian Print Network and Dreamweaver Australian Aboriginal Art Rugs.
Services and Facilities:
Art Consultancy. Art for Offices. Commissioning Service. Framing. Gallery space for hire. Valuation.
Work Stocked and Sold:
Ab. Cer. Cra. Dec. Dr. Fur. Jew. Pa. Ph. Pr. Sc. Tx. Wd.
Price range: £200 - £6,000.
For artists see *Commercial Gallery Artists.*

The Red Dot
22b Bellevue Road, Wandsworth Common, London SW17 7EB.
Tel: *0181-672 6086/0181-675 8110.*

Redchurch Galleries (John Hunt Galleries)
47-49 Redchurch Street, London E2 7DJ.
Tel: *0171-739 7333.* **Fax:** *0171-739 7333.*

Redfern Gallery
20 Cork Street, Burlington Gardens, London, W1X 2HB. **Tel:** *0171-734 1732/0578.*

Reel Poster Gallery
First Floor, 22 Great Marlborough Street, London W1V 1AF.
Tel: *0171-734 4303.* **Fax:** *0171-734 4260.*

Richard Day
173 New Bond Street, London, W1Y.
Tel: *0171-629 2991.*

Richard Philip
59 Ledbury Road, London, W11 2AA.
Tel: *0171-727 7915.*

Richard Salmon Ltd
Studio 4, 54 South Edwardes Square, London, W8 6HW.
Tel: *0171-602 9494.* **Fax:** *0171-371 6617.*

Riverside Room
Old Town Hall, Whittaker Avenue, Richmond, TW9 1TP.
Tel: *0181-332 0534.* **Fax:** *0181-940 7568.*

Rona Gallery
1/2 Weighhouse Street, London W1Y 1YL.
Tel: *0171-491 3718.* **Fax:** *0171-491 4171.*

Ropner Gallery
136 Wandsworth Bridge Road, London SW16 2UL.
Tel: *0171-736 2524.*

Rowley Gallery Contemporary Arts
115 Kensington Church Street, London W8 7LN.
Tel: *0171-229 5561, 01420-542 885.*
Fax: *0171-229 5561.*

The Royal Collection Trust
Stable Yard House, St. James's Palace, London SW1A 1JR.
Tel: *0171-930 4832.* **Fax:** *0171-839 8168.*

Royal College of Art
Kensington Gore, London SW7 2EU.
Tel: *0171-584 5020 / 0171-590 4444.*
Fax: *0171-584 8217.*

Royal Exchange Art Gallery
14 Royal Exchange, London EC3V 3LL.
Tel: *0171-283 4400.*

Royal Over-Seas League
Over-Seas House, Park Place, St. James's Street, London SW1A 1LR.
Tel: *0171-408 0214 x219.* **Fax:** *0171-499 6738.*

Russian Arts Gallery - GZHEL (UK)
257 High Street, Acton, London W3 9BY.
Tel: *0181-993 9096.* **Fax:** *0181-993 5989.*

Ruth Piper
Studio 11, Waterside, 99 Rotherhithe Street, London SE16 4NF. **Tel:** *0171-252 1130.*

Sabin Galleries
Campden Lodge, 82 Campden Hill Road, London W8 7AA. **Tel:** *0171-937 0471.*

Sackville Gallery
26 Sackville Street, London W1X 1DA.
Tel: *0171-734 8104.* **Fax:** *0171-734 8104.*

Sandra Lummis Fine Art
Flat 7, 17 Haslemere Road, London N8 9QP.
Tel: *0181-340 2293.*

Sara Davenport Gallery
206 Walton Street, London, SW3 3JG.
Tel: *0171-225 2223.*

The Schuster Gallery
P.O. Box 14849, London, NW2 5WU.
Tel: *0181-830 1311.*

Scolar Fine Art
Mecklenburgh House, 11 Mecklenburgh Square, London WC1N 2AD.
Tel: *0171-837 6300.* **Fax:** *0171-837 6322.*

Shenda Amery Studio
25A Edith Grove, London SW10 0LB.
Tel: *0171-351 1775.* **Fax:** *0171-351 1775.*

Sho Gallery
73 Curtain Road, Shoreditch, London EC2
Tel: *0171-7291590.*

Simmons Gallery
53 Lambs Conduit Street, London WC1N 3NB.
Tel: *0171-831 2080.* **Fax:** *0171-831 2090.*
Opening times: *Mon-Fri 10.30-5.30 or by appointment.*
Nearest Underground: *Russell Square or Holborn.*
Personnel: *Directors:* Howard Simmons, Frances Simmons.

SIMMONS GALLERY

Sculpture, medals and coins - the only specialist gallery for contemporary medals in the UK. Apart from solo and group exhibitions, we always have exciting international work for sale in a relaxed setting. Visitors are warmly encouraged to touch and handle the small sculpture. We also offer a commissioning service.
Services and Facilities:
Art Consultancy. Art for Offices. Commissioning Service. Valuation.
Work Stocked and Sold:
Dec. Jew. Sc.
Price range: £5 - £5,000.
For artists see *Commercial Gallery Artists.*

Simon Capstick-Dale Fine Art
23a St. James Street, London SW1A 1HA.
Tel: *0171-839 4070.* **Fax:** *0171-839 4077.*
Email *simoncdale.aol.com*
Opening times: *Mon-Fri 10-6, Saturday by appointment.*
Nearest Underground: *Green Park.*

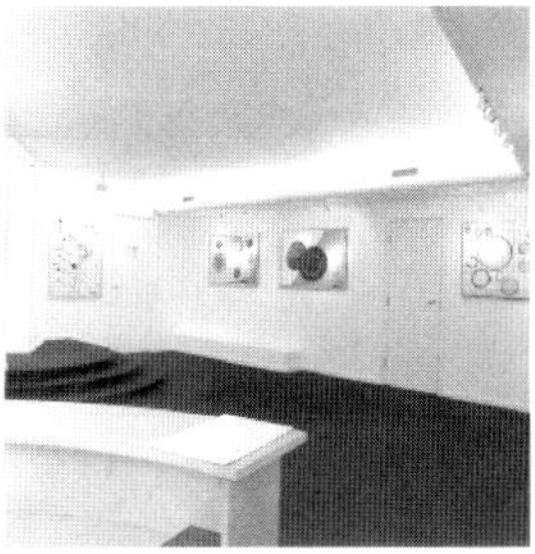

Simon Capstick-Dale Fine Art Ltd, London and 128 East 72nd Street, New York, NY 10021, Tel: 001-212 628 2067. Art dealers and gallery buying , selling and exhibiting 20th century works of art including impressionist, modern and contemporary paintings, watercolours, drawings and sculpture.
Work Stocked and Sold:
Dr. Pa. Pr. Sc.
For artists see *Commercial Gallery Artists.*

Simon Dickinson
58 Jermyn Street, London SW1Y 6LX.
Tel: *0171-493 0340.* **Fax:** *0171-493 0796.*

Sims Reed
43a Duke Street, St. James's, London SW1Y 6DD.
Tel: *0171-493 5660.*

Sloane Graphics Ltd.
6 Harben Parade, Finchley Road, London NW3.
Tel: *0171-586 0189.*

The Special Photographer's Company
21 Kensington Park Road, London W11 2EU.
Tel: *0171-221 3489.*
Fax: *0171-792 9112.*

Spink-Leger
5 King Street, St .James's, London SW1Y 6QS.
Tel: *0171-930 7888.* **Fax:** *0171-839 4853, 4850.*

Spink-Leger Pictures
13 Old Bond Street, London W1X 3DB.
Tel: *0171-629 3538/9.*

St. James's Fine Arts
72 New Bond Street, London W1Y 9DD.
Tel: *0171-355 1096.* **Fax:** *0171-495 3017.*

St. James's Prints
15 Piccadilly Arcade, London SW1Y 6NH.
Tel: *0171-495 6487.*

St. Martins Gallery
St. Martins-in-the-Fields, Trafalgar Square. London WC2N 4JJ.
Tel: *0171-839 4342.* **Fax:** *0171-839 5163.*

Stables Gallery
Gladstone Park, Dollis Hill Lane, Cricklewood, London NW2 6HT. **Tel:** *0181-452 8655.*

StART Gallery
493 Fulham Palace Road, London SW6.
Tel: *0171-371 0909.*

Stephanie Hoppen
17 Walton Street, London SW3.
Tel: *0171-589 3678.* **Fax:** *0171-581 5744.*

Stephen Friedman Gallery
25-28 Old Burlington Street, London W1X 1LN. **Tel:** *0171-494 1434.*

Stephen Somerville Ltd
14 Old Bond Street, London W1X 3DB.

Stern Art Dealers
46 Ledbury Road, London W11 2AB.
Tel: *0171-229 6187.* **Fax:** *0171-229 7016.*
Email *pisaro@global-net.co.uk*
Ws *http://www.stern-art.com*
Opening times: *Mon-Sat 10-6.*
Nearest Underground: *Notting Hill Gate.*
Personnel: *Director:* David Stern.
The gallery displays on its two floors over 400 19th and 20th century paintings. The ground floor is dedicated entirely to 19th century Victorian & European oil paintings covering a wide range of subjects.The lower gallery exhibits works by Camille Pissarro and his descendants covering eight artists from four generations.

Stern Art Dealers
19th & 20th Century Paintings

Works on display include oil paintings and works on paper.
Services and Facilities:
Art Consultancy. Framing. Restoration. Valuation.
Work Stocked and Sold:
Dr. Pa. Sc.
Price range: £500 - £15,000.
For artists see *Commercial Gallery Artists.*

Strategic Art
21 Douglas Street, London SW1P.

The Strong Print Room
University College London, Gower Street, London WC1E 6BT. **Tel:** *0171-387 7050.*

Studio 3 Gallery
75 Leonard Street, London EC2A 4QJ.
Tel: *0171-739 2024.*

Studio Nine
9 Marylands Road, London W9 2DU.
Tel: *0171-266 3729.* **Fax:** *0171-286-2305.*

Studio Sienko
57a Lant Street, London SE1 1QN.
Tel: *0171-403 1353.* **Fax:** *0171-357 6976.*

Swan Fine Art
120 Islington High Street, London N1.
Tel: *0171-226 5335, 0171-359 2225.*

T.A.G. Sale Co. Ltd
Ladbroke Hall, 79 Barlby Road, London W10.
Tel: *0181-932 7210.*

Tadema Gallery
10 Charlton Place, Camden Passage, London N1 8AJ.
Tel: *0171-359 1055.* **Fax:** *0171-359 1055.*
Opening times: *Wed & Sat 10-5 or by appointment.*
Nearest Underground: *Angel.*
Personnel: *Directors:* Sonya Newell-Smith, David Newell-Smith.

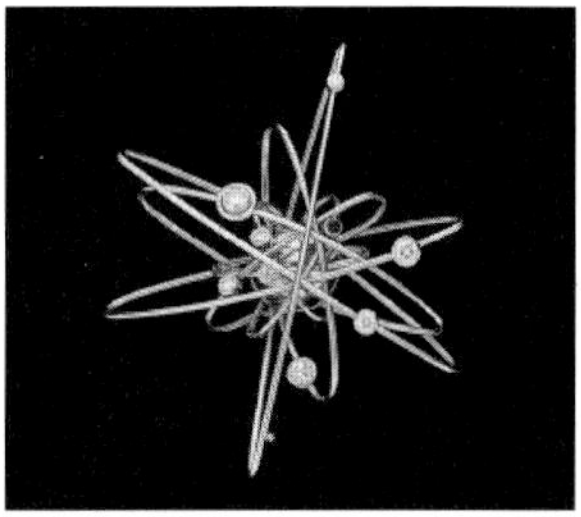

Late 19th- and 20th-century jewellery from Art Nouveau, Art Deco and Arts & Crafts to artist-designed jewels c.1960; also post-war abstract art.
Work Stocked and Sold:
Jew. Pa.

Talisman Fine Arts
82 Mill Lane, West Hampstead, London NW6 1NL.
Tel: *0171-794 4266.* **Fax:** *0171-435 65.*

Taylor Galleries
1 Bolney Gate, London SW7.
Tel: *0171-581 0253.*

Tekay Fine Art
36A Hillfield Park, Muswell Hill, London N10.

Thackeray Gallery
18 Thackerey Street, Kensington Square, London W8 5ET.
Tel: *0171-937 5883.* **Fax:** *0171-937 6965.*

Thameside Studio
109 Oxo Tower Wharf, Barge House, London SE1.
Tel: *0171-928 7411.*

Theo Waddington Fine Art
5a Cork Street, London W1X 1PB.
Tel: *0171-494 1584.* **Fax:** *0171-287 0926.*

Third Floor Art Gallery, Whiteleys
Queensway, London W2 4YN.

Thomas Heneage
42 Duke Street, St James's, London, SW1Y 6DJ.
Tel: *0171-930 9223.*

Thompson's Gallery
18 Dover Street, London W1X 3PB.
Tel: *0171-629 6878.* **Fax:** *0171-629 6181.*

Thornton Bevan Arts
130 Percy Road, London W12 9QL.
Tel: *0181-740 8084.*
Fax: *0181-740 8084.*

Throssells
13 Broad Street, Teddington, TW11 8QZ.
Tel: *0181-943 4248.*

Tian Art
36 Beauchamp Place, London SW3.
Tel: *0171-823 8088.*

The Timothy Taylor Gallery
1 Bruton Place, London W1.
Tel: *0171-409 3344.*

Todd Gallery
1-5 Needham Road, London W11 2RP.
Tel: *0171-792 1404.* **Fax:** *0171-792 1505.*

The Tom Blau Gallery
21 Queen Elizabeth Street, London, SE1 2PD.
Tel: *0171-378 1300.*

Tom Tempest Radford
16 Devonshire Row, London EC2M.
Tel: *0171-377 8004.*

The Tower/James Colman Fine Art
The Tower, 28 Mossbury Road, London, SW11 2PB.
Tel: *0171-924 3860.*
Fax: *0171-924 3860.*

Tricycle Gallery
Tricycle Theatre, 269 Kilburn High Road, London NW6 7JR.
Tel: *0171-372 6611.* **Fax:** *0171-328 0795.*

Trowbridge Gallery
555 Kings Road, London SW6.
Tel: *0171-371 8733.*

Tryon & Swann Gallery
23-24 Cork Street, London W1X 1HB.
Tel: *0171-634 6961, 0171-734 2256.* **Fax:** *0171-287 2480.*

Unicorn Pictures Ltd.
"Space 8" Hollywood Road, London SW10 9HY
Tel: *0171-376 3195.* **Fax:** *0171-351 5100.*
Opening times: *Tue-Sat 11-8, Sun 12-5.*
Nearest Underground: *Fulham Broadway, South Kensington.*
Personnel: *Director:* John Simmons FRSA. *Consultants:* Maurizio Castronovo, Michelle Dennison. *Artist Liaison:* Madeleine Honor.

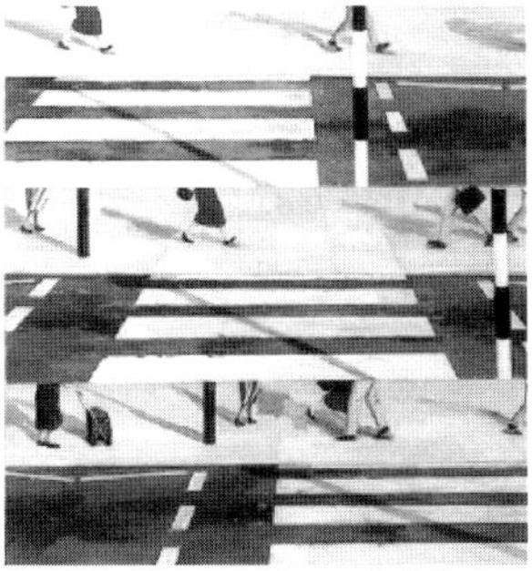

Art enthusiasts eager to know which fast-rising painters and sculptors are being collected and commissioned by canny collectors should get on Unicorn's 'inside track' mailing list, to see the series of "The Future Famous" exhibitions.
Unicorn Pictures, the award-winning art projects consultancy, has combined its resource of 'young masters' and corporate client supporters with Space 8 Gallery's network of young artists and local art connoisseurs.
Services and Facilities:
Art Consultancy. Art for Offices. Commissioning Service.
Work Stocked and Sold:
Cer. Gla. Pa. Pr. Sc. Tx.
Price range: £300 - £8,000.
For artists see *Commercial Gallery Artists.*

Victoria Gallery
158 Hermon Hill, London, E18 1QH.
Tel: *0181-989 1195.*

Victoria Miro London
21 Cork Street, London W1X.
Tel: *0171-734 5082.*

Vyvyan Robinson & Co.
235 Regent Street, London W1R.
Tel: *0171-495 6642.*

W.H. Patterson Fine Arts
19 Albemarle Street, London, W1X.
Tel: *0171-629 4119.*

Waddington Galleries
11,12 & 34 Cork Street, London W1X 2LT.
Tel: *0171-437 8611, 0171-439 6262.* **Fax:** *0171-734 4146.*

The Walk
23 King Edward Walk, London SE1 7PR.
Tel: *0171-928 3786.* **Fax:** *0171-261 1541.*
Opening times: *Tues-Sun 1.30-6 during exhibitions. By appointment at other times.*
Nearest Underground: *Lambeth North.*
Personnel: *Directors:* Ranabir Chanda, Gillian Salmon.

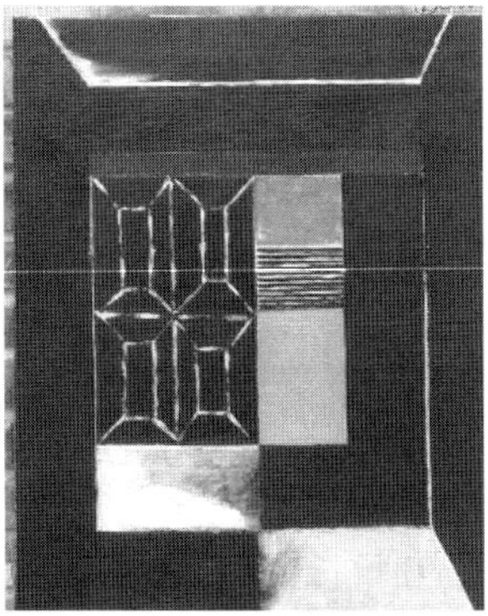

The Walk has a policy of encouraging relatively unknown, contemporary artists whose work uses a range of media. Their approaches can be traditional as well as experimental, exploratory and challenging. Group and solo shows are held in the attractive exhibition area. The Walk proposes to make original art affordable to a very wide range of people. Prices are within the range £275-£6,000. A full programme of exhibitions is planned for 1999/2000. Details of forthcoming events are available on request. Works in stock: Bartlett, Carr, Milne, Clarke and Snow.
Services and Facilities:
Art Consultancy. Art for Offices. Commissioning Service.
Work Stocked and Sold:
App. Dr. Pa. Ph. Pr. Sc.
Price range: £275 - £6,000.
For artists see *Commercial Gallery Artists.*

Walpole Gallery
38 Dover Street, London, W1X 3RB.
Tel: *0171-499 6626.*

Walton Contemporary Art
188 Walton Street, London SW3 2JL.
Tel: *0171-581 9011.* **Fax:** *0171-581 0585.*

Waterhouse & Dodd
110 New Bond Street, London, W1Y 9AA.
Tel: *0171-491 9293.*

Waterman Fine Art
74a Jerymn Street, St. James's, London SW1Y 6NP.
Tel: *0171-839 5203.* **Fax:** *0171-321 0212.*

Waterside Workshops
99 Rotherhithe Street, London, SE16 4NF.
Tel: *0171-237 0017.*

Weiss Gallery
1b Albemarle Street, London W1X.
Tel: *0171-409 0035.*

Well Hung Gallery
39 Ledbury Road, Notting Hill, London W11 2AA.

Wellington Gallery
1 St. Johns Wood High Street, London, NW8.
Tel: *0171-586 2620.*

White Cube
44 Duke Street, St. James's, London SW1Y 6DD.
Tel: *0171-930 5373.* **Fax:** *0171-930 9973.*

White Horse Gallery
Upstairs at The White Horse, 1-3 Parson's Green, London SW6 4UL.
Tel: *0171-736 2115, 07970-810168.* **Fax:** *0171-610 6091.*

Whitfield Fine Art
180 New Bond Street, London W1Y.
Tel: *0171-499 3592.*

Whitford Fine Art
6 Duke Street, St James's, London SW1Y 6BN.
Tel: *0171-930 9332.* **Fax:** *0171-930 5577.*
Email *whitfordfineart@btinternet.com*
Ws *http://www.artnet.com/whitford.html*
Opening times: *10-6.*
Nearest Underground: *Green Park, Piccadilly Circus.*
Personnel: Yvonne Elphick.

WHITFORD
FINE ART

Whitford Fine Art specialises in 20th century paintings, sculpture and designer furniture from the sixties.
Services and Facilities:
Art Consultancy.
Work Stocked and Sold:
Fur. Pa. Pr. Sc.
Price range: £400 - £500,000.
For artists see *Commercial Gallery Artists.*

Wigmore Fine Art
104 Wigmore Street, London W1H 9DR.
Tel: *0171-224 1962.* **Fax:** *0171-224 1965*

Wilkins & Wilkins
1 Barrett Street, London W1M.
Tel: *0171-935 9613.*

William Beadleston Incorporated
13 Masons Yard, St James's, London, SW1Y.
Tel: *0171-321 0495.*

William Hardie Gallery
15a Blythswood Square, Glasgow G2 2BG.
Tel: *0141-221 6780.* **Fax:** *0141-248 6237.*

William Thuillier
14 Old Bond Street, London W1X 3DB.
Tel: *0171-499 0106.* **Fax:** *0171-233 8965.*
Email *thuillart@aol.com*
Ws *http://www.thuillart.com*
Opening times: *10-6 by appointment.*
Nearest Underground: *Green Park.*
Personnel: *Proprietor:* William Thuillier.
Old Master paintings and drawings 1600-1850.
Services and Facilities:
Art Consultancy. Restoration. Valuation.
Work Stocked and Sold:
Pa.
Price range: £500 - £150,000.

William Weston Gallery
7 Royal Arcade, Albemarle Street, London, W1X 4JN.
Tel: *0171-493 0722.*

Williams & Son
2 Grafton Street, London W1X.
Tel: *0171-493 5751, 0171-493 4985.*

Wilson Stephens Fine Art
11 Cavendish Road, London NW6 7XT.
Tel: *0181-459 0760.*
Fax: *0181-459 0760.*

Wiseman Originals
34 West Square, Lambeth, London SE11 4SP.
Tel: *0171-587 0747.* **Fax:** *0171-793 8817 / 9917.*
Email *wisemanoriginals@compuserve.com*
Ws *http://www.wisemanoriginals.com*
Opening times: *Any time by appointment.*
Nearest Underground: *Lambeth North.*
Personnel: *Director:* Caroline Wiseman. Garth Wiseman. Lucia Lindsay.
Specialises in affordable art by modern masters.
Deals from home which is used as gallery space. Good selection of original prints by modern European masters including Buffet, Braque, Calder, Chagall, Matisse, Miró, Picasso and modern and contemporary British including Auerbach, Frink, Hodgkin, Hockney, Frost, Hepworth, Nicholson, McLean, Pasmore, Piper, Moore, Sutherland, Bellany and Scott.
Also recently opened in America: Wiseman Originals LLC, The Wiseman Art House, The Square, Old Chatham, (PO Box 31), New York 12136, Tel: (Int+1) 518 794 6131, Fax: (Int+1) 518 794 6140.
Services and Facilities:
Art Consultancy. Art for Offices. Commissioning Service. Framing. Valuation.
Work Stocked and Sold:
Dr. Pa. Pr.
Price range: £300 - £30,000.
For artists see *Commercial Gallery Artists.*

Wolseley Fine Arts
12 Needham Road, Notting Hill, London W11 2RP.
Tel: *0171-792 2788.* **Fax:** *0171-792 2988.*
Email *WolseleyFineArts@btinternet.com*
Opening times: *Open during exhibitions at least Tues-Sat 2-5. Otherwise by appointment.*
Nearest Underground: *Notting Hill.*
Personnel: *Director:* Rupert Otten. *Director:* Hannene van der Werf.
Dealers in 20th century works on paper by British and European masters from France, Belgium, and Holland. Specialist in all works by Eric Gill, David Jones, Edgar Holloway, John Buckland Wright and Eugeen van Mieghem. Wolseley Contemporary represents Gretta, Brian Yale, Paul Klemann and exhibits carved lettering and calligraphy.

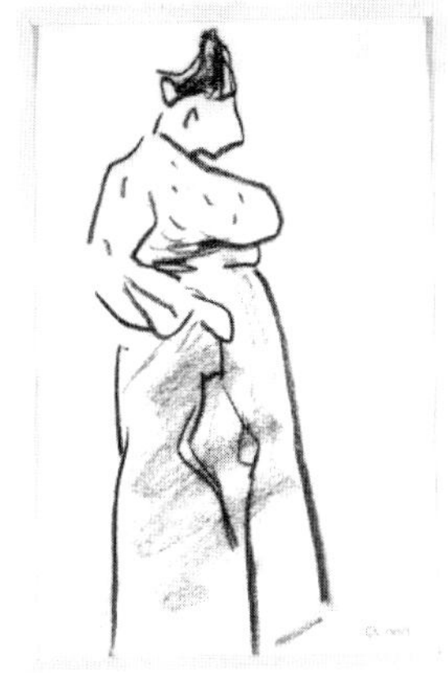

Fairs include: Art on paper Fair, British 20th Century Fair. Works on Paper, New York, and TEFAF, Basel.
Services and Facilities:
Art Consultancy. Commissioning Service. Valuation.
Work Stocked and Sold:
Dr. Pa. Pr. Sc.
Price range: £50 - £30,000.
For artists see *Commercial Gallery Artists.*

Woodlands Art Gallery
90 Mycenae Road, Blackheath, London SE3 7SE.
Tel: *0181-858 5847.* **Fax:** *0181-858 5847.*

The Wykeham Galleries
51 Church Road, Barnes, London, SW13 9HH.
Tel: *0171-351 4449.*

Zelda Cheatle Gallery
99 Mount Street, London W1Y 5HF.
Tel: *0171-408 4448.*
Fax: *0171-497 8911.*

Zella Gallery
2 Park Walk, Fulham Road, London SW10 0AD.
Tel: *0171-351 0588.* **Fax:** *0171-352 4752.*
Opening times: *Mon-Sat 9.30-6, Sun 11.30-5.30.*
Personnel: Mrs M. Gore.
Well known gallery, established 1971, that specialises in finding and promoting young artists. Contemporary printmaking by gallery artists on show in lower gallery. Upper gallery showcases solo exhibitions throughout the year, painting, photography and works on paper. Works priced from £80-£2,000. For further information contact: Eva Tait.
Services and Facilities:
Art Consultancy. Art for Offices. Framing.
Work Stocked and Sold:
Pa. Ph. Pr.
Price range: £50 - £2,000.
For artists see *Commercial Gallery Artists.*

Zenith Gallery
41 Balham High Road, London, SW12 9AN.
Tel: *0181-675 7570.*

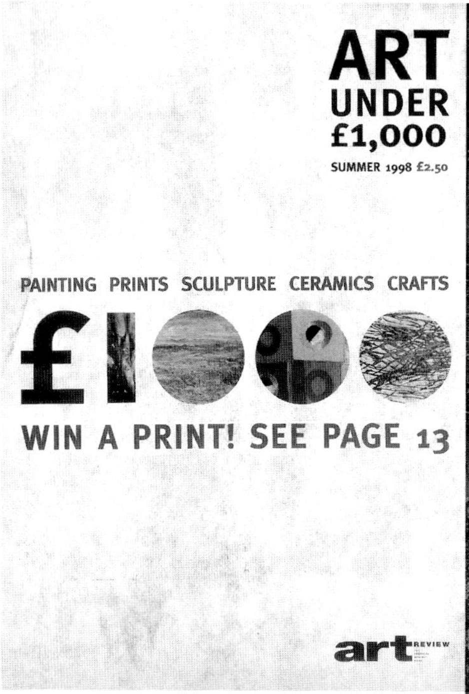
ART
UNDER
£1,000
SUMMER 1998 £2.50
PAINTING PRINTS SCULPTURE CERAMICS CRAFTS
WIN A PRINT! SEE PAGE 13
art REVIEW

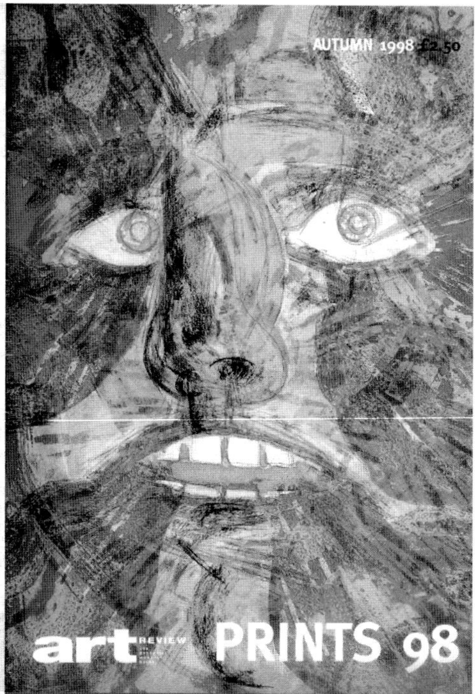
AUTUMN 1998 £2.50
art REVIEW
PRINTS 98

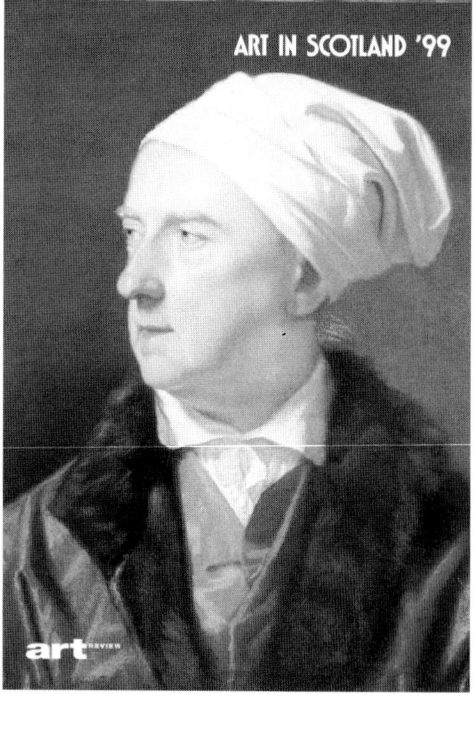
ART IN SCOTLAND '99
art REVIEW

LONDON PUBLIC GALLERIES

All entries in this section are sorted alphabetically by gallery.
Where this information has been provided, entries are designated 'P' for public gallery or museum or 'PS' for a public gallery or museum holding selling shows.

198 Gallery *PS*
194-198 Railton Road, Herne Hill, London SE24 0LU.
Tel: *0171-978 8309.* **Fax:** *0171-652 1418.*
Email *198gallery@globalnet.co.uk*
Ws *http://www.globalnet.co.uk/~198glry*
Opening times: *Mon-Sat 11-6.*
Nearest Underground: *BR: Herne Hill. Buses 3, 37, 68, 68A, 196, 332.*
Personnel: *Administration:* Zoe Linsley-Thomas. *Education:* Paul Howard.

198 Gallery, education and training resource. Contemporary art by artists from diverse cultural backgrounds, wide range of media including new technologies. Education centre offers programmes for schools/colleges/training for adults in arts/new technologies, agency for artists in schools/hospitals/public commissions. Eight exhibitions per annum, shop offers original paintings, prints, ceramics, sculpture, stools, Benin bronzes, from around the world.
Services and Facilities:
Commissioning Service. Disabled Access. Friends/Society. Gallery space for hire. Lectures. Shop. Workshop Facilities.
Work Stocked and Sold:
Cer. Dr. Pa. Ph. Pr. Sc. Tx. Wd.
Price range: £50 - £5,000.
For artists see *Commercial Gallery Artists.*

Architecture Foundation *P*
30 Bury Street, London SW1Y.
Tel: *0171-839 9389.*

The Ark (Museum of Garden History) *P*
220 Lambeth Road, London SE7 7JY.
Tel: *0171-582 890...?.*

Bank of England Museum *P*
Bank of England, Threadneedle Street, (public entrance Bartholomew Lane), London EC2R 8AH.
Tel: *0171-601 5545 (information desk; Minicom 0171-601 5140).* **Fax:** *0171-601 5808.*
Email *museum@bankofengland.co.uk*
Ws *http://www.bankofengland.co.uk*
Opening times: *10-5 all year. Closed weekends and Public and Bank Holidays. Open on the day of the Lord Mayor's Show.*
Nearest Underground: *Bank (Northern, Central, Docklands Light Railway, Waterloo and City). BR: Liverpool Street, Fenchurch Street, Cannon Street.*
Personnel: *Assistant Curator:* June Greenhalf.
The Museum is housed within the Bank of England right at the heart of the City of London. It traces the history of the Bank from its foundation by Royal Charter in 1694 to its role today as the nation's central bank. Displays include: gold; banknotes; 18th century banking hall and state of the art interactive video systems on the Bank and its roles, as well as foreign exchange dealing games.
Services and Facilities:
Disabled Access. Guided Tours. Lectures. Museum Shop.

Bankside Gallery *PS*
48 Hopton Street, Blackfriars, London SE1 9JH.
Tel: *0171-928 7521.* **Fax:** *0171-928 2820.*
Email *RE&RWS@bankside-gallery.demon.co.uk*
Opening times: *During exhibitions Tues 10-8, Wed-Fri 10-5, Sun 1-5.*
Nearest Underground: *Blackfriars, Southwark (new station opens May 1999).*

Bankside Gallery is the home of the Royal Watercolour Society and the Royal Society of Painter-Printmakers. This friendly gallery runs a changing programme of exhibitions of contemporary watercolours and original prints. Members of the two societies are elected by their peers and represent a tradition of excellence reaching back two hundred years. Their work embraces both established and experimental practices and the exhibitions balance these different approaches. Informal 'Artists Perspectives' take place every Tuesday evening during the course of an exhibition. Practical courses and tutorials are held every year by artist members of the two societies. Full details are available from the Gallery. Admission: £3.50, concessions £2. Free admission to Friends.
Services and Facilities:
Art for Offices. Bookshop. Commissioning Service. Friends/Society. Gallery space for hire. Lectures. Shop.
Work Stocked and Sold:
Pa. Pr.
Price range: £40 - £2,000.

Barbican Art Gallery
Gallery Floor, Level 3, Barbican Centre, London EC2Y 8DS.
Tel: *0171-588 9023.* **Fax:** *0171-628 0364.*
Ws *http://www.uk-calling.co.uk*
Opening times: *Mon, Thur-Sat 10-6.45, Tues 10-5.45, Wed 10-7.45, Sun + Public Hols 12-6.45.*
Nearest Underground: *Moorgate, Barbican, St.Pauls, Liverpool Street.*
Personnel: *Curator:* John Hoole.
Barbican Art Gallery, a leading international art exhibition venue located in the heart of the City, presents an annual programme of up to six shows covering a diverse range of subjects including Impressionist painting, interactive new media, photography, sculpture and fashion.

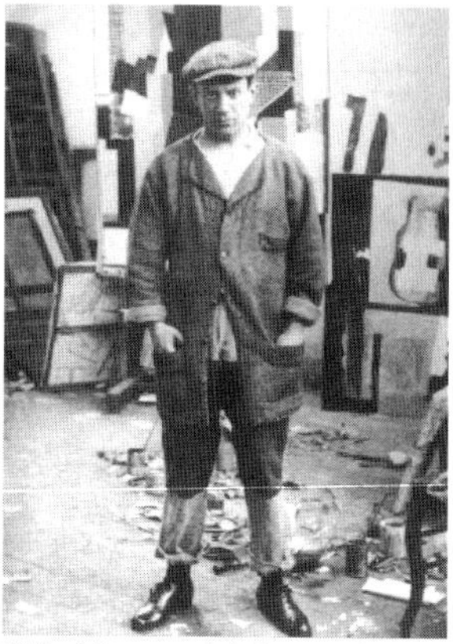

1999 exhibitions include Picasso and Photography (29 Jan-28 Mar) focusing on the extent to which Picasso drew upon this medium in his work, David Bailey: Birth of the Cool (15 Apr-27 Jun), Malevich's Vision of the Russian Avant Guarde (29 Apr-27 Jun) and exhibition displaying work of leading Russian artists of Malevich's era, and for the first time in Britain Joseph Beys' complete Multiples will be seen in their entirety (Oct-Dec). Admissions £5.00/£3.00 reductions.
Services and Facilities:
Bar. Bookshop. Disabled Access. Guided Tours. Lectures. Parking. Restaurant. Workshop Facilities.

Barbican Centre *PS*
Silk Street, London EC2Y 8DS.
Tel: *0171-382 7105 (weekdays before 5pm). 0171-638 4141.* **Fax:** *0171-628 0364.*
Opening times: *Please call for details.*
Nearest Underground: *Moorgate, Barbican, St.Pauls, Liverpool Street.*
BARBICAN ART GALLERY - LEVEL 3.
CONCOURSE GALLERY - LEVEL 0.
FOYER GALLERY - LEVEL 0.
GROUND FLOOR FOYER - LEVEL 0.
Services and Facilities:
Bar. Bookshop. Café. Disabled Access. Gallery space for hire. Parking. Restaurant.

Ben Uri Art Society *PS*
126 Albert Street, London NW1 7NE.
Tel: *0171-482 1234.* **Fax:** *0171-482 1414.*
Email *benuri@ort.org*
Ws *http://www.ort.org/benuri/*
Opening times: *Closed Jewish Holy days and Bank Holidays, otherwise by arrangement.*
Nearest Underground: *Camden Town.*
Personnel: *Director:* Jo Velleman.
The aim of the society, which is a registered charity founded in 1915, is to promote Jewish art as part of the Jewish cultural heritage. The Gallery provides a showcase for contemporary exhibitions, as well as works from the Society's own permanent collection of over 800 works by Jewish artists including Auerbach, Bomberg, Epstein, Gertler, Kossoff,

Kramer and Pissarro. A new catalogue of the Collection was published in 1994 and all works are accessible on CD ROM. The Society is presently in temporary office accommodation, pending the building of a new Jewish Arts and Cultural Centre in Camden Town.
Services and Facilities:
Art for Offices. Café. Disabled Access. Friends/Society. Gallery space for hire. Lectures.
For artists see *Commercial Gallery Artists.*

Bethnal Green Museum of Childhood
Cambridge Heath Road, London E2 9PA.
Tel: *0181-983 5200, recorded info. 0181-980 2415.* **Fax:** *0181-983 5225.*
Email *m.baker@vam.ac.uk*
Ws *http://www.vam.ac.uk/bgm/welcome.html*
Opening times: *Mon-Thurs, Sat & Sun 10-5.50. Closed every Friday, May Day Bank Holiday, 24-26 December, 1 January.*
Nearest Underground: *Bethnal Green.*
The National Museum of Childhood at Bethnal Green is a fascinating blend of toys and other nursery objects that belong to the experience of childhood.
The ground floor is packed full of playthings, ranging from dolls' houses, dolls and games to teddy bears, toy soldiers and trains, dating from the 17th century to the present day.
The upper gallery explores the process of growing up from birth through to the teenage years, including prams, party dresses and T-shirts. Admission free.
Services and Facilities:
Café. Guided Tours. Museum Shop.

Bhownagree and Today Galleries *PS*
The Commonwealth Experience, Commonwealth Institute, Kensington High Street, London W8 6NQ.
Tel: *0171-603 4535.* **Fax:** *0171-602 7374.*

British Museum *P*
Great Russell Street, London WC1B 3DG.
Tel: *0171-636 1555.*

Camden Arts Centre *P*
Arkwright Road, London, NW3 6DG.
Tel: *0171-435 2643 / 5224.* **Fax:** *0171-794 3371.*

Carlyle's House *P*
24 Cheyne Row, London SW3 5HL.
Tel: *0171-352 7087.*

Chalk Farm Gallery *P*
20 Chalk Farm Road, London NW1 8AG.
Tel: *0171-267 3300.* **Fax:** *0171-267 3300.*

Chisenhale Gallery *P*
64 Chisenhale Road, London E3 5QZ.
Tel: *0181-981 4518.* **Fax:** *0181-980 7169.*

Chiswick House *P*
Burlington Lane, London W4 2RP.
Tel: *0181-995 0508.* **Fax:** *0181-742 3104.*

Courtauld Institute Galleries *P*
Somerset House, Strand, London WC2R 0RN.
Tel: *0171-837 2526 .*
Fax: *0171-873 2589.*

Crystal Palace Museum *P*
Anerley Hill, London SE19 2BA.
Tel: *0181-676 0700.*

Delfina *P*
50 Bermondsey Street, London SE1 3UD.
Tel: *0171-357 6600.* **Fax:** *0171-357 0250.*
Personnel: David Gilmour.
Temporary exhibitions of modern and contemporary art.

Design Museum *P*
28 Shad Thames, London SE1 2YD.
Tel: *0171-403 6933, 0171-378 6055 (recorded info.).* **Fax:** *0171-378 6540.*
Opening times: *Daily 11.30-6. Admission £5.25 and £4.00 concessions.*
Personnel: *Communications Manager:* Naomi Simpson.
Visitors of all ages can rediscover one hundred years of design, view state-of-the art innovations from around the globe and enjoy an extensive programme of critically acclaimed exhibitions on design and architecture. We have a riverside café and a shop.
Services and Facilities:
Café. Disabled Access. Friends/Society. Gallery space for hire. Lectures. Museum Shop. Shop. Workshop Facilities.

Estorick Collection of Modern Italian Art
Northampton Lodge, 39A Canonbury Square, London N1 2AN.
Tel: *0171-704 9522.* **Fax:** *0171-704 9531.*
Email *curator@estorickcollection.com*
Ws *http://www.estorickcollection.com*
Opening times: *Wed-Sat 11-6, Sun 12-5.*
Nearest Underground: *Highbury & Islington.*
Personnel: *Curator:* Alexandra Noble.
A new museum which opened in January 1998 in a handsome, Grade II, Georgian villa showing a permanent collection of early 20th century Italian art including world famous works by the Futurists, Boccioni, Balla, Carra, Severini and Russolo. Other artists represented include de Chirico, Modigliani, and Morandi and sculptors Medardo Rosso, Giacomo Manzu and Marino Marini. There is a changing exhibition and education programme. Group and school visits are always welcome, but must book in advance. Art reference library by appointment. Access for wheelchair users on two floors only. Zwemmers gallery shop and Cafe Panini open museum hours.
Services and Facilities:
Café. Disabled Access. Friends/Society. Gallery space for hire. Guided Tours. Shop.

Geffrye Museum *P*
Kingsland Road, London, E2 8EA.
Tel: *0171-739 9893.* **Fax:** *0171-729 5647.*

Goethe-Institut London *P*
50 Princes Gate, Exhibition Road, London SW7 2PH.
Tel: *0171-411 3445.* **Fax:** *0171-581 0974.*

Goldsmiths' Hall *P*
Foster Lane, London EC2V 6BN.
Tel: *0171-606 7010.*
Fax: *0171-606 1511.*

Guildhall Art Gallery *P*
Aldermanbury, London EC2P 2EJ.
Tel: *0171-606 3030 /332 1632 / 332 1856 (direct line).* **Fax:** *0171-600 3384.*

Hayward Gallery
Belvedere Road, London SE1 8XZ.
Tel: *0171-928 3144.* **Fax:** *0171-401 2664.*
Ws *http://www.hayward-gallery.org.uk*
Opening times: *10-6 daily, Tues-Wed 10-8.*
Nearest Underground: *Waterloo/Embankment.*
Personnel: *Director:* Susan Ferleger Brades.
Exhibitions of international stature are the hallmark of the Hayward Gallery, with a programme featuring the works of modern masters, thought-provoking historical shows and the most exciting names in contemporary art. Exhibitions for 1999: Patrick Caulfield (4th February-11th April), Cities on the Move (13th May-27th June), Chuck Close (22nd July-19th September), Full Moon (22nd July-19th September), Lucio Fontana (14th October-9th January 2000).
Admission: £6, £4 concessions. Further information on 0171-928 3144.
Services and Facilities:
Bookshop. Café. Disabled Access. Friends/Society. Lectures. Parking.

Hogarth's House Foundation *P*
Hogarth's House, Hogarth Lane, Great West Road, London W4 2QN.
Tel: *0181-994 6757/570 0622.* **Fax:** *0181-862 7602.*

The Horniman Museum and Gardens
100 London Road, Forest Hill, London SE23 3PQ.
Tel: *0181-699 1872.* **Fax:** *0181-291 5506.*
Email *enquiry@horniman.demon.co.uk*
Ws *http://www.horniman.demon.co.uk*
Opening times: *Mon-Sat 10.30-5.30, Sun 2-5.30 (except over Christmas).*
Nearest Underground: *Forest Hill (from London Bridge).*
Personnel: *Director:* Janet Vitmayer.
Director of Finance and Operational Services: Jennifer Beaver.

THE HORNIMAN MUSEUM & GARDENS

An enjoyable experience for all set in the striking art nouveau building by Harrison Townsend. The museum consists of three permanent exhibitions - The Music Room, The Living Waters Aquarium and The Natural History Gallery which includes Ethnographic displays. A new permanent exhibition is set to open soon called African Worlds, along with a temporary exhibition called The Collectors Gallery. The museum also houses a Conservation Centre - C.U.E., landscaped gardens, a beautiful conservatory, nature trails and an animal enclosure. The museum hosts

a variety of concerts, theatrical pieces, workshops and activities for children and adults alike. Admission is free.
Services and Facilities:
Café. Disabled Access. Friends/Society. Museum Shop. Workshop Facilities.

Imperial War Museum
Lambeth Road, London SE1 6HZ.
Tel: *0171-416 5211 (voicemail).* **Fax:** *0171-416 5215.*
Email *art@iwm.org.uk*
Ws *http://www.iwm.org.uk*
Opening times: *Daily 10-6, free after 4.30.*
Nearest Underground: *Lambeth North, Elephant and Castle.*
Personnel: *Director General:* Robert Crawford.
The temporary art exhibition gallery which has been closed during redevelopment reopens at the end of October 1999 with a full-scale retrospective of C R W Nevinson. While 'Gassed' is on loan to the Tate Gallery's Sargent exhibition and its USA tour in 1999, a series of small shows in the Sargent Gallery will include Ian Hamilton Finlay's sculpture 'A Wartime Garden'. In October 2000, a major exhibition will focus on John Piper as artist and intellectual in the Forties. The permanent collection will be on display but please ring to check if visiting to see a specific work.
Services and Facilities:
Café. Disabled Access. Friends/Society. Museum Shop.

Institute of Contemporary Arts *P*
The Mall, London SW1Y 5AH.
Tel: *0171-839 6751, 873 0061, box office 0171-930 3647.* **Fax:** *0171-873 0051.*

Kensington Palace *P*
Kensington Gardens, London W8 4PX.
Tel: *0171-937 7079.* **Fax:** *0171-376 0198.*

Kenwood House *P*
The Iveagh Bequest, Hampstead Lane, London NW3 7JR.
Tel: *0171-973 3891.*

Kingsgate Gallery *PS*
114 Kingsgate Road, London NW6 2JG.
Tel: *0171-328 7878.* **Fax:** *0171-328 7878.*
Opening times: *Sat & Sun 12-6 and by appointment.*
Nearest Underground: *West Hampstead.*
Personnel: *Gallery Director:* Stephen Williams.

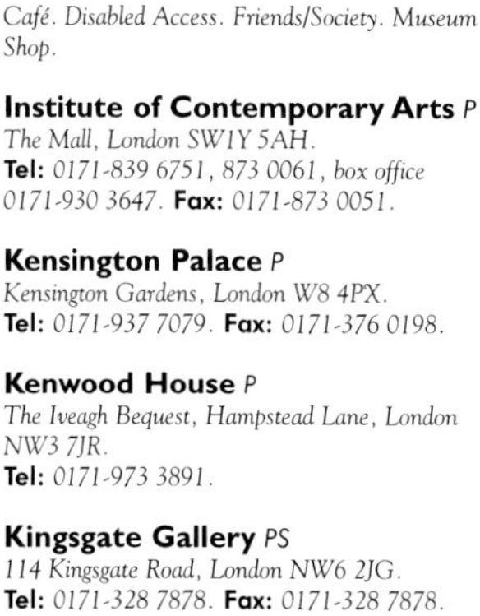

Contemporary work shown in a split level space. 2-4 week exhibitions. The exhibition programme is decided at quarterly meetings and is particularly interested in group proposals. It is part of the charitable organisation Kingsgate Workshops Trust.
During 1998 Kingsgate took part in the Woman In Focus Festival, organised "20/20" - a large group show sponsored by Boots Opticians which asked artists to explore the theme of vision. Artists who have shown at the gallery during 1998 include: Renata Aller, Tabatha Andrews, Martin Appleton, Karen Bedford, Ken Butler, Paul Eachus, Tina Gallifent, Peter Jeffrey, Holly Lynton, Kasia Morawska, Anthea Nicholson, Celia & Sophia Hayes, Leonora Robinson, Josie Taylor, Eugenia Vronskaya.
Services and Facilities:
Art Consultancy. Commissioning Service. Framing.

Kufa Gallery *PS*
26 Westbourne Grove, London W2 5RH.
Tel: *0171-229 1928.* **Fax:** *0171-243 8513.*
Email *kufa@dircon.co.uk*
Opening times: *Tues-Sat 10-6.*
Nearest Underground: *Bayswater, Queensway.*
Personnel: *Manager:* Walid Atiyeh.

A non-profit making organisation, specialising in Islamic/Middle Eastern Art and Architecture, including art exhibitions, poetry & musical evenings and cultural lectures and talks. The gallery hall is available for hire for similar events.
Services and Facilities:
Gallery space for hire. Lectures.
Work Stocked and Sold:
Ab. App. Cer. Cra. Dec. Dr. Pa. Ph. Pr. Tx.

Lauderdale House Community Arts Centre *PS*
Waterlow Park, Highgate Hill, London N6 5HG.
Tel: *0181-348 8716/341 2032.* **Fax:** *0181-341 4892.*
Opening times: *Tues-Fri 11-4, Sun 12-5. (check events). Sats (dependent on private bookings).*
Nearest Underground: *Archway (Northern Line).*
Personnel: *Director:* Carolyn Naish. *General Manager:* Katherine Ives. *Arts Education Assistant:* Lucy Ribeiro.

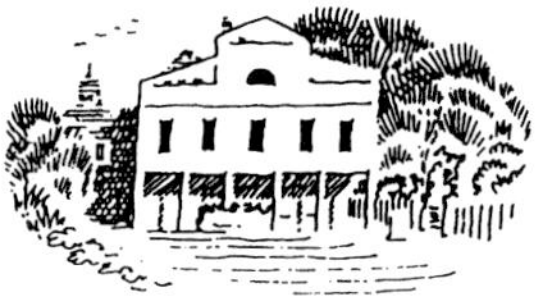

Old Tudor building from 1580, set in Waterlow Park. Reopened in 1978 by Lauderdale House Society Charity. Community Arts and Education Centre. Approx. 38 exhibitions a year, admission free, varying from fine art, photography, local history, to special exhibitions by local groups, societies and schools. Four gallery spaces for hire as follows - Lower Gallery £300, Upper Gallery £170, Entrance Hall £110, and Long Gallery £300. These prices are for a fortnight (Mon to Mon) and include a Private View evening. Space can be shared among artists, no commission on sales and no selection, but artists must manage show professionally. Limited Disabled Access.
Services and Facilities:
Friends/Society. Gallery space for hire. Restaurant. Workshop Facilities.

Leighton House Museum *PS*
12 Holland Park Road, London W14 8LZ.
Tel: *0171-602 3316.* **Fax:** *0171-371 2467.*
Opening times: *Mon-Sat 11-5.30.*
Nearest Underground: *High St. Kensington.*

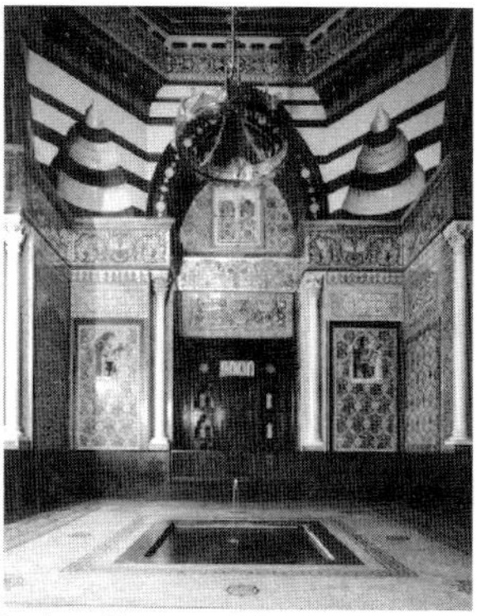

Leighton House was the home of, Frederic, Lord Leighton (1830-1896) The great classical painter and president of the Royal Academy. The house was built between 1867-1879 to designs by George Aitchison and is the expression of Leighton's vision of a private palace devoted to art. The Arab Hall is the centrepiece of Leighton House with dazzling gilt mosaics and authentic Isnik tiles. The opulent fantasy extends throughout the other rooms of the house, culminating in Leighton's studio, the heart and purpose of the house. Leighton House contains a fine collection of Victorian art and may be booked for concerts, lectures, receptions and private functions. The galleries adjoining Leighton House may be hired for exhibitions. They are recently refurbished and work should be submitted to the curator. Wide and extensive exhibition programme.
Services and Facilities:
Friends/Society. Gallery space for hire. Guided Tours. Lectures. Museum Shop.

London Institute Gallery *PS*
65 Davies Street, London W1Y 2DA.
Tel: *0171-514 8083.* **Fax:** *0171-514 6131.*
Email *marcom@linst.ac.uk*
Opening times: *Mon-Fri 10-8.*
Nearest Underground: *Bond Street.*
Personnel: *Gallery Manager:* Anna Malyckyj.
The London Institute Gallery presents an

ambitious programme of exhibitions across a range of art and design disciplines that reflect the diversity of activities taking place within the Institute's five colleges - Camberwell, Central Saint Martins, Chelsea, London College of Fashion and London College of Printing.

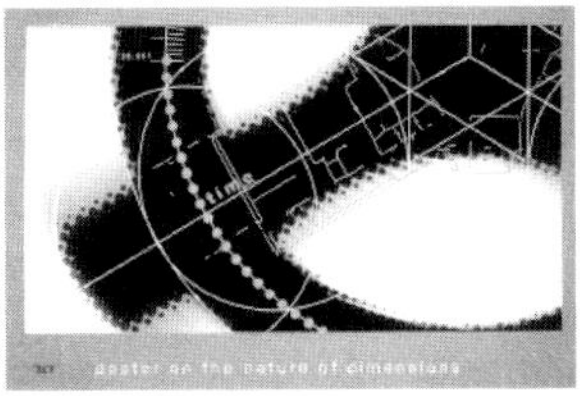

The Gallery acts as a focal point for the work of the Institute's staff, students and alumni as well as a venue for national and international touring exhibitions.

Lothbury Gallery *PS*
41 Lothbury, London EC2P 2BP.
Tel: *0171-726 1642/1643.*
Opening times: *Mon-Fri 10-4.*
Nearest Underground: *Bank underground, Moorgate, Liverpool Street (BR), Cannon Street.*
Personnel: *Curator:* Rosemary Harris. *Assistant:* Lynne Richards. *Office Administrator:* Daksha Patel.
The Lothbury Gallery displays works from the Nat West Group Art Collection and a series of changing exhibitions. This important corporate art collection has been established over many years for display in our offices. It includes work from the seventeenth century to the present day with a focus on twentieth century post-war British art. The Collection includes work by such artists as Frank Auerbach, Adrian Berg, David Hockney, Albert Irvin, Patrick Caulfield, Gillian Ayres, Jason Martin and Mark Francis. Nat West also holds an annual major painting competition which is open to all artists under 35 who are living, working or studying in Britain.

Mall Galleries *PS*
Federation of British Artists, 17 Carlton House Terrace, London SW1Y 5BD.
Tel: *0171-930 6844.* **Fax:** *0171-839 7830.*
Opening times: *Daily 10-5.*
Nearest Underground: *Charing Cross/Piccadilly Circus.*

MALL
GALLERIES

The Mall Galleries is home to the Federation of British Artists, the umbrella organisation for nine of Britain's leading Art Societies. Besides the annual exhibitions held by each society, the FBA hosts a varied and exciting programme of exhibitions and events throughout the year. These include The National Print Exhibition which is an open exhibition featuring the work of invited artists, and members of the Royal Society of Painter-Printmakers, together with selected work from the open submission. Lectures, demonstrations and workshops are held throughout the year to complement the exhibitions. In addition, two major art competitions are held at the Mall Galleries: The Singer & Friedlander/Sunday Times Watercolour Competition and the Laing Painting Competition. Artists' prizes and awards are offered by many of the societies. The FBA also operates a Fine Art and Portrait Commissions and Advisory Service. For details on any of the above, please contact the administrative address. Please see also entry under Gallery Space for Hire and entries under Art Consultants and Art Societies.
Services and Facilities:
Art Consultancy. Commissioning Service. Friends/Society. Gallery space for hire. Guided Tours. Lectures. Workshop Facilities.
Work Stocked and Sold:
Dr. Pa. Pr. Sc.
Price range: £200 - £20,000.

Mall Galleries
The Mall, Nr. Admiralty Arch, London SW1Y.
Tel: *0171-930 6844.* **Fax:** *0171-839 7830.*
Opening times: *10-5 Daily (incl. Sundays).*
Nearest Underground: *Charing Cross*
Personnel: *Chairman:* Tom Muir. *Chief Executive:* John Molony. *Company Secretary:* John Sayers. *General Manager:* John Deston.
Royal Institute of Painters in Water Colours (RI), Royal Society of British Artists (RBA), Royal Society of Marine Artists (RSMA), Royal Society of Portrait Painters (RP), Royal Institute of Oil Painters (ROI), New English Art Club (NEAC), Pastel Society (PS), Society of Wildlife Artists (SWLA), Hesketh Hubbard Art Society (HH). The Mall Galleries are the venue for the annual exhibitions of eight art societies (as listed above). It also hosts workshops, art competitions, and independent one man and small group shows.
Services and Facilities:
Art Consultancy. Commissioning Service. Friends/Society. Gallery space for hire. Guided Tours. Lectures. Workshop Facilities.

Marble Hill House *P*
(English Heritage) Richmond Road, Twickenham, TW1 2NL.
Tel: *0181-892 5115.*

Museum of Installation
175 Deptford High Street, London SE8 3NU.
Tel: *0181-692 8778.* **Fax:** *0181-692 8122.*
Email *moi@dircon.co.uk*
Ws *http://www.moi.dircon.co.uk*
Opening times: *Tue-Fri 12-5, Sat 2-5.*
Nearest Underground: *Deptford.*
Personnel: *Directors:* Nicola Oxley, Nicolas de Oliveira, Michael Petry. *Assistant Director:* Jeremy Wood. *Administrator:* Calan Stanley. *Project Assistants:* David Howells, Sarah Loriot.
The Museum of Installation is an artist led organisation and registered charity set up in 1990 as a unique institution dedicated to the research, production and dissemination of installation. MOI has initiated 60 exhibitions and projects at sites in the UK, Europe and the United States. At its base in London MOI has begun to compile the first major archive of installation and the book "Installation Art" has been published by Thames and Hudson.

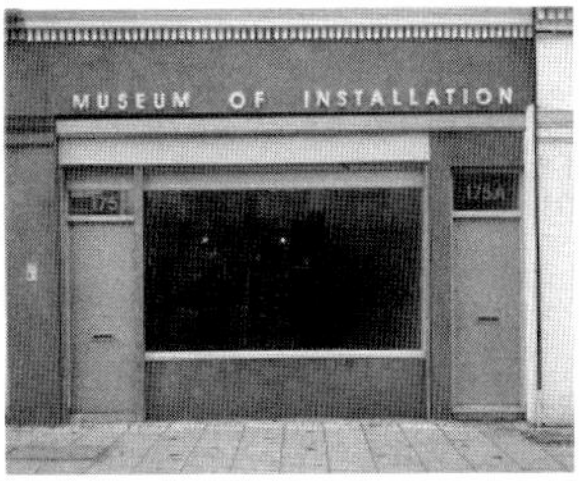

MOI is committed to the cross fertilisation of theory and practice, and to encourage new artists and new audiences to engage with contemporary art practice.
Services and Facilities:
Art Consultancy. Commissioning Service. Guided Tours. Lectures. Workshop Facilities.

The Museum of London *PS*
150 London Wall, London, EC2Y 5HN.
Tel: *0171-600 3699.* **Fax:** *0171-600 1058.*
Email *info@museumoflondon.org.uk*
Ws *http://www.museumoflondon.org.uk*
Opening times: *Mon-Sat 10-5.50, Sun 12-5.50.*
Nearest Underground: *St. Paul's, Barbican, Moorgate.*

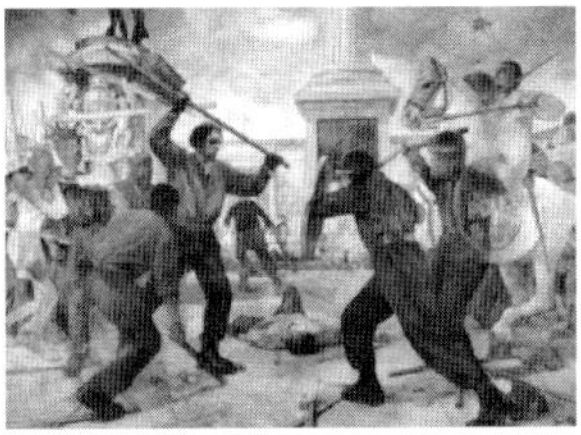

The Museum of London has a large collection of paintings, prints, drawings and photographs spanning from the 16th century to the 1990s. For the last ten years, the Museum has been actively pursuing contemporary collecting, at times commissioning artists. The themes of housing, the changing landscape of London, and social conflicts have emerged high on this new agenda. A programme of loan exhibitions complement the work that is being done through the Museum's collections: Tim Rice, Magda Segal, David Hepher and Mark Cazalet are some of the artists (including photographers) whose work has been shown at the Museum of London.
Services and Facilities:
Café. Commissioning Service. Disabled Access. Friends/Society. Lectures. Museum Shop. Restaurant.

Museum of Mankind *P*
The Ethnography Dept. of the British Museum, Burlington Gardens, London W1.
Tel: *0171-437 2224.*

Museum of the Moving Image *P*
BFI on the South Bank, Waterloo, London SE1 8XT. **Tel:** *0171-928 3232 box office, 0171-620 2025 minicom, 0171-401 2636 museum information, 0171-815 1331/2 press office.*

Museum of Women's Art *P*
Correspondence: 2nd Floor North, 55-63 Goswell Road, London EC1V 7EN.
Tel: *0171-251 4881.*
Fax: *0171-251 4882.*

National Army Museum *P*
Royal Hospital Road, Chelsea, London SW3 4HT.
Tel: *0171-730 0717.* **Fax:** *0171-823 6573.*

National Gallery *P*
Trafalgar Square, London WC2N 5DN.
Tel: *0171-747 2885.*
Email *information@ng-london.org.uk*
Ws *http://www.nationalgallery.org.uk*
Opening times: *Daily 10-6, Weds until 9pm. Closed New Year's Day, Good Friday, 24-26 Dec.*
Nearest Underground: *Charing Cross, Leicester Square, Embankment. All buses to Trafalgar Square.*
Personnel: *Director:* Neil MacGregor.
The Collection numbers over 2,200 works and covers Western European painting from 1260 to 1900, including works by Leonardo, Titian, Rubens, Rembrandt, Turner, Constable, and the Impressionists.
Exhibitions and displays; many educational events: quizzes for children, lectures, audio-visuals and guided tours. Admission free, except for some major exhibitions. Micro Gallery computer information room. Gallery Guide Soundtrack (CD Audio commentary on the collection).
Services and Facilities:
Bookshop. Café. Disabled Access. Guided Tours. Lectures. Museum Shop. Restaurant. Shop.

National Maritime Museum, Queen's House and Old Royal Observatory *P*
Romney Road, Greenwich, London SE10 9NF.
Tel: *0181-858 4422.* **Fax:** *0181-312 6632.*

National Portrait Gallery *PS*
St. Martin's Place, London WC2H 0HE.
Tel: *0171-306 0055.* **Fax:** *0171-306 0058.*
Ws *http://www.npg.org.uk*
Opening times: *Mon-Sat 10-6, Sun 12-6.*
Nearest Underground: *Charing Cross, Leicester Square.*
Personnel: *Director:* Dr Charles Saumarez Smith.
The National Portrait Gallery was founded in 1856 to collect the likenesses of famous British men and women. Today the collection is the most comprehensive of its kind and constitutes a unique record of men and women who created (and are still creating) the history and culture of the nation. The gallery houses over 9,000 works, as well as an immense archive.
There are oil paintings, watercolours, drawings, sculptures, caricatures and photographs. The gallery continues to develop its role through changing displays, a programme of temporary exhibitions and an annual portrait competition for young artists.
Services and Facilities:
Bookshop. Café. Disabled Access. Friends/Society. Gallery space for hire. Guided Tours. Lectures. Museum Shop. Shop. Workshop Facilities.

Orleans House Gallery *PS*
Riverside, Twickenham, TW1 3DJ.
Tel: *0181-892 0221.* **Fax:** *0181-744 0501.*
Email *jane.dalton@virgin.net*
Ws *http://www.guidetorichmond.co.uk/orleans.html*
Opening times: *Apr-Sept Tues-Sat 1-5.30, Sun 2-5.30, (Oct-Mar closes at 4.30). Sun & Bank Holidays 2-5.30.*
Nearest Station: *St. Margaret's from Waterloo.*
Personnel: *Curator:* Jane Dalton. *Assistant Curator:* Rachel Tranter.

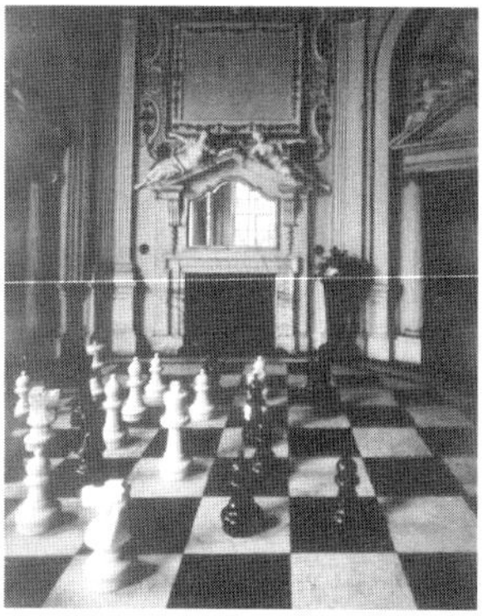

Our exhibitions programme showcases contemporary artists and makers, and draws in loans from Art Museums across the UK or from Richmond Borough's own collections. We hold 5/6 exhibitions per year, which are created in-house or in partnership with other Galleries. The 1999 programme includes large-scale photographic work by Stephen Gill, and a collaboration with the Museum of Women's Art to publicise the work of artist Cynthia Pell. In the smaller Stables Gallery, which is open during from April to September, we work exclusively with local interest groups and local artists, to provide an outlet for expression and discussion.
Services and Facilities:
Craftshop. Disabled Access. Lectures. Parking. Workshop Facilities.
Work Stocked and Sold:
App. Cer. Cra. Dec. Gla. Jew. Pa. Ph. Pr. Tx.
Price range: £30 - £2,000.

Percival David Foundation *P*
53 Gordon Square, London WC1H 0PD.
Tel: *0171-387 3909.* **Fax:** *0171-383 5163.*

Photographers' Gallery *P*
5-8 Great Newport Street, London WC2H 7HY.
Tel: *0171-831 1772 minicom.* **Fax:** *0171-836 9704.*

Polish Cultural Institution *P*
34 Portland Place, London W1N 4HQ.
Tel: *0171-636 6032.* **Fax:** *0171-637 2190.*
Opening times: *Mon-Fri 10-4, Thurs 10-8.*
Personnel: *Director:* Mrs Aleksandra Czapiewska. *Deputy Director:* Ms Elzbieta Lyszkowska.
Exhibitions including Polish paintings, graphics, photography, posters, tapestry and folk art. Space available for hire for events connected with Poland and Polish art.
Services and Facilities:
Gallery space for hire. Lectures.

Pump House Gallery *PS*
Battersea Park, London SW11 4NJ.
Tel: *0181-871 7572.* **Fax:** *0181-228 9062.*
Opening times: *Oct-Mar: Wed-Fri 11-3, Sat & Sun 11-4; April-Sept: Wed-Sat 11-4, Sun 11-6.*
Nearest Underground: *Sloane Square. BR: Battersea Park Station (one stop from Victoria or Waterloo). Buses: 19, 39, 44, 45, 137, 170.*
Personnel: *Acting Manager:* Susie Gray.

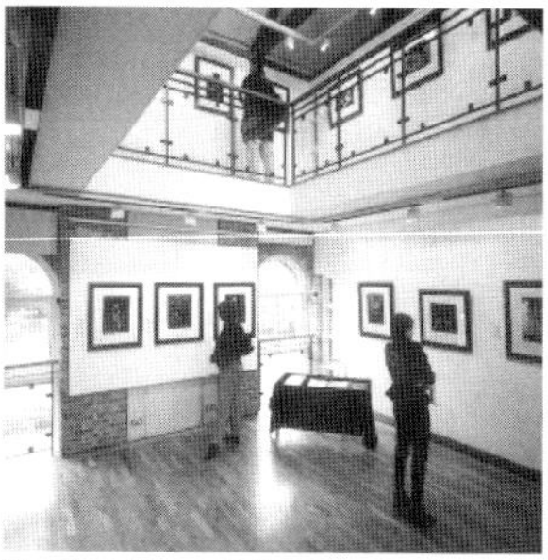

The Pump House Gallery is situated beside the lakes in Battersea Park, just south of the Thames over Chelsea Bridge. The gallery runs an annual programme of about 20 exhibitions by contemporary artists, which emphasises variety in media and style. Hire rates are currently £150 per week April - September, £125 per week October - March. 25% commission on sales.
Services and Facilities:
Gallery space for hire. Shop.
Work Stocked and Sold:
Cra. Dr. Pa. Ph. Pr.
Price range: £50 - £5,000.

Queen's Gallery *P*
Buckingham Palace. London SW1A 1AA.
Tel: *0171-799 2331 / 0171-839 1377.*

Royal Academy of Arts *PS*
Burlington House, Piccadilly, London W1V 0DS.
Tel: *0171-300 8000.* **Fax:** *0171-300 8001.*
Ws *http://www.RoyalAcademy.org.uk*
Opening times: *Mon-Sun 10-6.*
Nearest Underground: *Piccadilly Circus/Green Park.*
Personnel: *Press & Promotions Officer:* Katharine Jones.

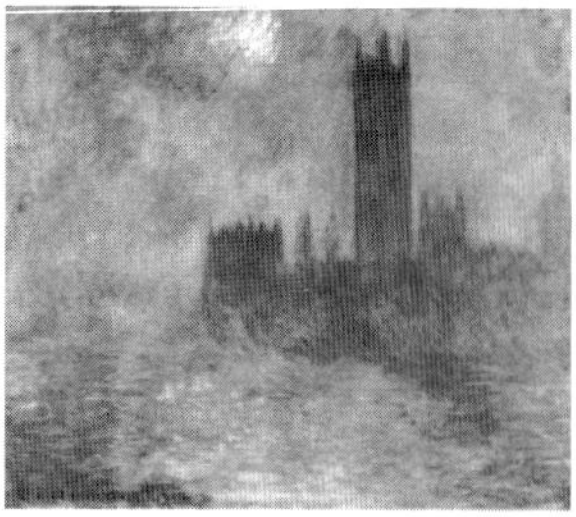

Founded in 1768, The Royal Academy is the

oldest arts institution in the UK, governed by its artist members. Its exhibition programme includes the annual Summer Exhibition of work by living artists and internationally acclaimed travelling exhibitions.
Services and Facilities:
Bookshop. Café. Disabled Access. Framing. Friends/Society. Guided Tours. Lectures. Museum Shop. Restaurant. Shop.

Saatchi Collection *P*
98a Boundary Road, London NW8 0RH.
Tel: *0171-624 8299.* **Fax:** *0171-624 3798.*

Serpentine Gallery *P*
Kensington Gardens, London W2 3XA.
Tel: *0171-402 6075/0343 / 0171-823 9727.*
Fax: *0171-402 4103.*

Sir John Soane's Museum *P*
13 Lincoln's Inn Fields, London WC2A 3BP.
Tel: *0171-430 0175.* **Fax:** *0171-831 3957.*

The Sladmore Gallery - 19th and 20th Century Bronze Sculpture. *P*
32 Bruton Place, Berkeley Square, London W1X 7AA.
Tel: *0171-499 0365.* **Fax:** *0171-409 1381.*

Small Mansion Arts Centre *PS*
Gunnersbury Park, Popes Lane, Acton, London, W3 8JQ.
Tel: *0181-993 8312.*

South London Gallery
65 Peckham Road, London, SE5 8UH.
Tel: *0171-703 6120.* **Fax:** *0171-252 4730.*
Email *mail@southlondonart.com*
Ws *http://www.southlondonart.co.uk*
Opening times: *Tues, Wed & Fri 11-6, Thus 11-7, Sat & Sun 2-6.*
Nearest Underground: *Elephant & Castle, Oval.*

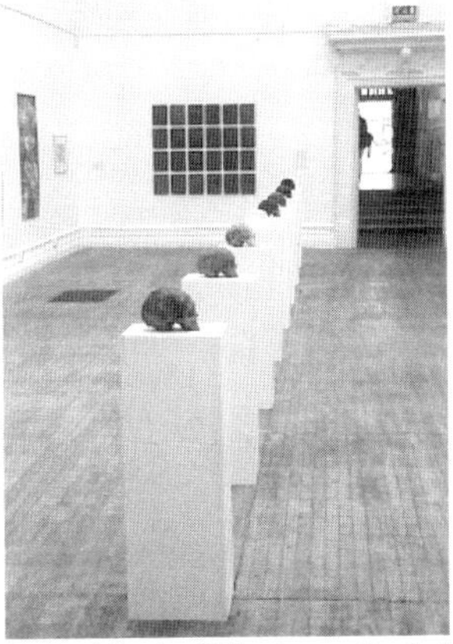

The South London Gallery is one of London's foremost contemporary art exhibition spaces, committed to a challenging curatorial programme showing the work of local, national and international living artists. It also holds in storage an extensive collection that extends from work by John Everett Millais and Frederic Leighton to contemporary artists including Anish Kapoor, Tracey Emin and Tom Phillips. In the past four years, exhibitions of work by artists including Gilbert and George, Anselm Kiefer, Bill Viola and Tracey Emin have established the South London Gallery as an important national and international forum for the extension of the debate around contemporary art.
The gallery also provides a range of debates, seminars, talks and performances by key figures in the fields of art journalism, broadcasting and curatorship.
Recent speakers at the gallery have included Richard Cork, art critic for The Times, sculptor Anthony Gormley, Gill Hedley, Director of the Contemporary Arts Society and Tim Marlow, Editor of Tate Magazine and television arts presenter.
Services and Facilities:
Lectures.

St. Marylebone Crypt Gallery *P*
St. Marylebone Parish Church, 17 Marylebone Road, London NW1 5LT.
Tel: *0171-935 6374.* **Fax:** *0171-935 6374.*

Strang Print Room *P*
University College London, London WC1E 6BT.
Tel: *0171-387 7050 ext 2540.*
Fax: *0171-813 2803.*

Studio Glass Gallery *P*
63 Connaught Street, London W2 2AE.
Tel: *0171-706 3013, 3069.*

Tate Gallery *P*
Millbank, London SW1P 4RG.
Tel: *0171-887 8000/8008.*
Fax: *0171-887 8007.*

TWO10 Gallery
The Wellcome Trust, 210 Euston Road, London NW1 2BE.
Tel: *0171-611 8888.* **Fax:** *0171-611 8562.*
Email *k.arnold@wellcome.ac.uk*
Ws *http://www.wellcome.ac.uk*
Opening times: *Mon-Fri 9-6 (closed weekends and public holidays).*
Nearest Underground: *Euston.*
Personnel: *Exhibitions Manager:* Dr Ken Arnold. *Exhibitions Officer:* Denna Jones.

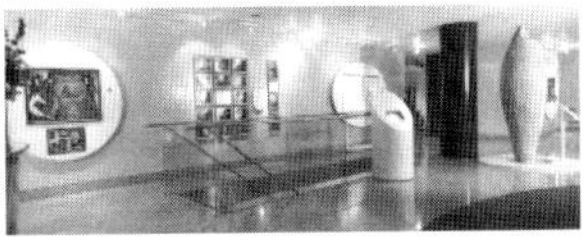

The TWO10 Gallery presents temporary exhibitions on the interaction between contemporary medical science and art. Recent exhibitions have included 'Before Birth: the art and science of life in the womb' and 'Multiplicity: 24 artists look at cloning'. TWO10 exhibitions are available for loan to other museums. Admission free. Limited disabled access.

Venezuelan Embassy *P*
Bolívar Hall, 54-58 Grafton Way, London W1P 5LB.
Tel: *0171-388 5788.*
Fax: *0171-383 3253.*

Victoria and Albert Museum The National Museum of Art and Design
Cromwell Road, South Kensington, London SW7 2RL.
Tel: *0171-938 8500.*
Fax: *0171-938 8341.*
Ws *http://www.vam.ac.uk*
Opening times: *Daily 10-5.45. Open every day except 24, 25 & 26 December. New Guided Tour Times: Daily 10.30, 11.30, 12.30, 13.30, 14.30,15.30.*
Nearest Underground: *South Kensington.*
The V&A holds one of the world's largest and most diverse collections of the decorative arts. A 146 galleries contain unrivalled collections dating from 3,000 BC to the present day. Furniture, fashion, textiles, paintings, silver, glass, ceramics, sculpture, jewellery, books, prints and photographs illustrate the artistic life of many different cultures from around the world. The exciting programme of exhibitions for 1999 include; The Arts of the Sikh Kingdoms, 25 March 1999 - 25 July 1999; and A Grand Design: The Art of the Victoria and Albert Museum, 14 October 1999 - 16 January 2000. Free family activities on selected days. Guided tours, disabled access, shop, restaurant, Friends society, galleries and rooms available for hire.
Admission: Full £5.00, senior citizens £3.00. Admission is free for those under 18, full-time students, pre-booked educational groups, disabled people with carer and the unwaged. Entry is free daily between 16.30 and 17.45.
Services and Facilities:
Café. Craftshop. Disabled Access. Friends/Society. Gallery space for hire. Guided Tours. Lectures. Museum Shop. Restaurant. Shop.

Wallace Collection *P*
Hertford House, Manchester Square, London W1M 6BN.
Tel: *0171-935 0687.*
Fax: *0171-224 2155.*

Westminster Gallery *P*
Central Hall, Storey's Gate, London SW1 9NH.
Tel: *0171-222 2723, 0171-222 8010.*
Fax: *0171-222 6883.*

Whitechapel Art Gallery *P*
Whitechapel High Street, London E1 7QX.
Tel: *Recorded information: 0171-522 7878, other enquiries, 0171-522 7888.*
Fax: *0171-377 1685.*

William Morris Gallery and Brangwyn Gift *P*
Lloyd Park, Forrest Road, Walthamstow, London, E17 4PP.
Tel: *0181-527 3782.*
Fax: *0181-527 7070.*

NOTES

ENGLISH REGIONAL GALLERIES

The regional galleries section is sorted by region, starting with the South West and finishing with the North. On the following pages you will find indices by Region/County/Town and Town/County/Region.

Where this information has been provided, galleries are designated 'C' for commercial, 'P' for public gallery or museum or 'PS' for a public gallery or museum holding selling shows.

THE ART WORLD
DIRECTORY

REGION/ COUNTY/ TOWN INDEX

Sandy

Cambridgeshire
Bourn
Cambridge
Ely
Huntingdon
Peterborough
Wisbech

Essex
Brentwood
Buckhurst Hill
Chelmsford
Colchester
Harlow
Ilford
Saffron Walden
Southend-on-Sea
Westcliff-on-Sea

Hertfordshire
Barnet
Berkhamsted
Hatfield
Hemel Hempstead
Hitchin
Letchworth
Much Hadham
Royston
Sawbridgeworth
St. Albans
Stevenage
Ware
Watford

Lincolnshire
Boston
Gainsborough
Lincoln
Spalding
Stamford

North Lincolnshire
Scunthorpe

Norfolk
Aylsham
Burnham Deepdale
Castle Acre
Diss
Gorleston on Sea
Great Yarmouth
Holt
Hunstanton
King's Lynn
Kings Lynn
Mundesley
Norwich
Wells-next-the-Sea

Suffolk
Aldeburgh
Bury St. Edmunds
Cransford
East Bergholt
Felixstowe
Halesworth
Ipswich
Lowestoft
Newmarket
Saxmundham
Southwold
Sudbury
Woodbridge

East Midlands

Derby
Derby

Derbyshire
Buxton
Chesterfield
Ilkeston
Wirksworth

Leicester
Leicester

Leicestershire
Ashby de-la-Zouch
Lutterworth
Market Harborough

Northamptonshire
Kettering
Northampton
Towcester
Wellingborough

Nottinghamshire
Newark
Nottingham
Ravenshead
Worksop

Rutland
Uppingham

West Midlands

Birmingham
Birmingham

Coventry
Coventry

Dudley
Dudley
Kingswinford

Hereford & Worcester
Bewdley
Broadway
Bromsgrove
Cradley
Great Malvern
Hereford
Kidderminster
Leominster
Ombersley
Worcester

Sandwell
Wednesbury

Shropshire
Bishops Castle
Bridgnorth
Ellesmere
Ludlow
Shrewsbury
Telford

Staffordshire
Burton upon Trent
Leek
Newcastle-under-Lyme
Stafford

Stoke-on-Trent
Stoke-on-Trent

Warwickshire
Alcester
Henley-in-Arden
Leamington Spa
Rugby
Stratford-upon-Avon
Warwick

Wolverhampton
Wolverhampton

North West

Bolton
Bolton

Bury
Bury

Cheshire
Northwich
Prestbury
Sandbach
Warrington
Winsford

Lancashire
Accrington
Blackburn
Blackpool
Burnley
Chorley
Lancaster
Preston

Liverpool
Liverpool

Manchester
Manchester

Oldham
Oldham

Rochdale
Rochdale

Salford
Salford

Sefton
Southport

St. Helens
St. Helens

Stockport
Stockport

Tameside
Stalybridge

Wigan
Leigh

Wirral
Bebington
Birkenhead
Heswall

Yorkshire & Humberside

Bradford
Bradford
Keighley

Calderdale
Halifax
Todmorden

Doncaster
Doncaster

Hull
Hull

Humberside
Kingston Upon Hull

Kirklees
Batley
Dewsbury
Huddersfield
Mirfield

Leeds
Leeds
Wetherby

Rotherham
Rotherham

Sheffield
Sheffield

Wakefield
Wakefield

York
York

East Riding of Yorkshire
Beverley
Bridlington
Goole

North Yorkshire
Harrogate
Helmsley
Knaresborough
Richmond
Scarborough
Settle
Thirsk
Whitby

West Yorkshire
Halifax
Huddersfield
Ilkley

Northern

Cumbria
Alston
Ambleside
Carlisle
Cockermouth
Coniston
Egremont
Kendal
Keswick
Penrith
Whitehaven
Workington

Durham
Barnard Castle
Castle Eden
Darlington
Durham

Hartlepool
Hartlepool

Middlesbrough
Middlesbrough

Newcastle-upon-Tyne
Gateshead
Newcastle-upon-Tyne

North Tyneside
Wallsend

Northumberland
Alnwick
Belford
Berwick Upon Tweed
Cramlington
Hexham
Rothbury
Stamfordham
Warkworth

Redcar and Cleveland
Guisborough
Redcar
Saltburn By The Sea

Stockton on Tees
Billingham
Stockton on Tees

Sunderland
Sunderland
Washington

North Tyneside
North Shields

South Tyneside
Jarrow
South Shields

TOWN/ COUNTY/ REGION INDEX

A

B

Berwick Upon Tweed *(Northumberland)*
Northern
Beverley *(East Riding of Yorkshire)*
Yorkshire & Humberside
Bewdley *(Hereford & Worcester)*
West Midlands
Bideford *(Devon)*
South West
Biggleswade *(Bedfordshire)*
Eastern
Billingham *(Stockton on Tees)*
Northern
Billingshurst *(West Sussex)*
South East
Birkenhead *(Wirral)*
North West
Birmingham *(Birmingham)*
West Midlands
Bishops Castle *(Shropshire)*
West Midlands
Blackburn *(Lancashire)*
North West
Blackpool *(Lancashire)*
North West
Bolton *(Bolton)*
North West
Boston *(Lincolnshire)*
Eastern
Bourn *(Cambridgeshire)*
Eastern
Bournemouth *(Bournemouth)*
Southern
Bourton on the Water *(Gloucestershire)*
South West
Bovey Tracey *(Devon)*
South West
Bracknell *(Berkshire)*
Southern
Bradford *(Bradford)*
Yorkshire & Humberside
Brentwood *(Essex)*
Eastern
Bridgnorth *(Shropshire)*
West Midlands
Bridlington *(East Riding of Yorkshire)*
Yorkshire & Humberside
Bridport *(Dorset)*
South West
Brighton *(Brighton & Hove)*
South East
Bristol *(Bristol)*
South West
Broadway *(Hereford & Worcester)*
West Midlands
Bromham *(Bedfordshire)*
Eastern
Bromsgrove *(Hereford & Worcester)*
West Midlands
Buckfastleigh *(Devon)*
South West
Buckhurst Hill *(Essex)*
Eastern
Budleigh Salterton *(Devon)*
South West
Burnham Deepdale *(Norfolk)*
Eastern
Burnley *(Lancashire)*
North West
Burton upon Trent *(Staffordshire)*
West Midlands
Bury *(Bury)*
North West
Bury St. Edmunds *(Suffolk)*
Eastern
Buxton *(Derbyshire)*
East Midlands

C

Calne *(Wiltshire)*
Southern
Cambridge *(Cambridgeshire)*
Eastern
Camelford *(Cornwall)*
South West
Canterbury *(Kent)*
South East
Carlisle *(Cumbria)*
Northern
Castle Acre *(Norfolk)*
Eastern
Castle Eden *(Durham)*
Northern
Chalford *(Gloucestershire)*
South West
Chelmsford *(Essex)*
Eastern
Cheltenham *(Gloucestershire)*
South West
Chesterfield *(Derbyshire)*
East Midlands
Chichester *(West Sussex)*
South East
Chipping Norton *(Oxfordshire)*
Southern
Chipping Sodbury *(South Gloucestershire)*
South West
Chobham *(Surrey)*
South East
Chorley *(Lancashire)*
North West
Christchurch *(Hampshire)*
Southern
Cirencester *(Gloucestershire)*
South West
Cockermouth *(Cumbria)*
Northern
Colchester *(Essex)*
Eastern
Coniston *(Cumbria)*
Northern
Cookham *(Berkshire)*
Southern
Coventry *(Coventry)*
West Midlands
Cradley *(Hereford & Worcester)*
West Midlands
Cramlington *(Northumberland)*
Northern
Cransford *(Suffolk)*
Eastern

D/E

Darlington *(Durham)*
Northern
Dartmouth *(Devon)*
South West
Derby *(Derby)*
East Midlands
Devizes *(Wiltshire)*
Southern
Dewsbury *(Kirklees)*
Yorkshire & Humberside
Diss *(Norfolk)*
Eastern
Ditchling *(East Sussex)*
South East
Doncaster *(Doncaster)*
Yorkshire & Humberside
Dorchester *(Dorset)*
South West
Dudley *(Dudley)*
West Midlands
Durham *(Durham)*
Northern
East Bergholt *(Suffolk)*
Eastern
East Grinstead *(West Sussex)*
South East
East Molesey *(Surrey)*
South East
Eastbourne *(East Sussex)*
South East
Eastleigh *(Hampshire)*
Southern
Egremont *(Cumbria)*
Northern
Ellesmere *(Shropshire)*
West Midlands
Ely *(Cambridgeshire)*
Eastern
Eton *(Berkshire)*
Southern
Exeter *(Devon)*
South West

F/G

Falmouth *(Cornwall)*
South West
Farnham *(Surrey)*
South East
Felixstowe *(Suffolk)*
Eastern
Folkestone *(Kent)*
South East
Frome *(Somerset)*
South West
Gainsborough *(Lincolnshire)*
Eastern
Gateshead *(Newcastle-upon-Tyne)*
Northern
Gillingham *(Kent)*
South East
Gloucester *(Gloucestershire)*
South West
Godalming *(Surrey)*
South East
Gomshall *(Surrey)*
South East
Goole *(East Riding of Yorkshire)*
Yorkshire & Humberside
Goring-on-Thames *(Oxfordshire)*
Southern
Gorleston on Sea *(Norfolk)*
Eastern
Gosport *(Hampshire)*
Southern
Great Malvern *(Hereford & Worcester)*
West Midlands
Great Yarmouth *(Norfolk)*
Eastern
Guildford *(Surrey)*
South East

Guisborough *(Redcar and Cleveland)*
Northern

H/I

Halesworth *(Suffolk)*
Eastern
Halifax *(Calderdale)*
Yorkshire & Humberside
Harlow *(Essex)*
Eastern
Harrogate *(North Yorkshire)*
Yorkshire & Humberside
Hartlepool *(Hartlepool)*
Northern
Hassocks *(East Sussex)*
South East
Hastings *(East Sussex)*
South East
Hatfield *(Hertfordshire)*
Eastern
Havant *(Hampshire)*
Southern
Haywards Heath *(West Sussex)*
South East
Helmsley *(North Yorkshire)*
Yorkshire & Humberside
Helston *(Cornwall)*
South West
Hemel Hempstead *(Hertfordshire)*
Eastern
Henley-in-Arden *(Warwickshire)*
West Midlands
Henley-on-Thames *(Oxfordshire)*
Southern
Hereford *(Hereford & Worcester)*
West Midlands
Heswall *(Wirral)*
North West
Hexham *(Northumberland)*
Northern
Hitchin *(Hertfordshire)*
Eastern
Holt *(Norfolk)*
Eastern
Horsham *(West Sussex)*
South East
Hove *(Brighton & Hove)*
South East
Huddersfield *(Kirklees)*
Yorkshire & Humberside
Hull *(Hull)*
Yorkshire & Humberside
Hunstanton *(Norfolk)*
Eastern
Huntingdon *(Cambridgeshire)*
Eastern
Ilford *(Essex)*
Eastern
Ilkeston *(Derbyshire)*
East Midlands
Ilkley *(West Yorkshire)*
Yorkshire & Humberside
Ipswich *(Suffolk)*
Eastern

J/K

Jarrow *(South Tyneside)*
Northern
Keighley *(Bradford)*
Yorkshire & Humberside
Kendal *(Cumbria)*
Northern
Keswick *(Cumbria)*
Northern
Kettering *(Northamptonshire)*
East Midlands
Kidderminster *(Hereford & Worcester)*
West Midlands
King's Lynn *(Norfolk)*
Eastern
Kings Lynn *(Norfolk)*
Eastern
Kingston Upon Hull *(Humberside)*
Yorkshire & Humberside
Kingston upon Thames *(Surrey)*
South East
Kingswinford *(Dudley)*
West Midlands
Knaresborough *(North Yorkshire)*
Yorkshire & Humberside

L/M

Lacock *(Wiltshire)*
Southern
Lancaster *(Lancashire)*
North West
Langford *(Bedfordshire)*
Eastern
Leamington Spa *(Warwickshire)*
West Midlands
Leatherhead *(Surrey)*
South East
Lechlade *(Gloucestershire)*
South West
Leeds *(Leeds)*
Yorkshire & Humberside
Leek *(Staffordshire)*
West Midlands
Leicester *(Leicester)*
East Midlands
Leigh *(Wigan)*
North West
Leighton Buzzard *(Bedfordshire)*
Eastern
Leominster *(Hereford & Worcester)*
West Midlands
Letchworth *(Hertfordshire)*
Eastern
Lewes *(East Sussex)*
South East
Lincoln *(Lincolnshire)*
Eastern
Liverpool *(Liverpool)*
North West
Lowestoft *(Suffolk)*
Eastern
Ludlow *(Shropshire)*
West Midlands
Luton *(Bedfordshire)*
Eastern
Lutterworth *(Leicestershire)*
East Midlands
Lyme Regis *(Dorset)*
South West
Maidenhead *(Berkshire)*
Southern
Maidstone *(Kent)*
South East
Manchester *(Manchester)*
North West
Marazion *(Cornwall)*
South West
Market Harborough *(Leicestershire)*
East Midlands
Marlborough *(Wiltshire)*
Southern
Marlow *(Buckinghamshire)*
Southern
Middlesbrough *(Middlesbrough)*
Northern
Midhurst *(West Sussex)*
South East
Milton Keynes *(Buckinghamshire)*
Southern
Mirfield *(Kirklees)*
Yorkshire & Humberside
Montacute *(Somerset)*
South West
Much Hadham *(Hertfordshire)*
Eastern
Mundesley *(Norfolk)*
Eastern

N/O

Nailsworth *(Gloucestershire)*
South West
New Alresford *(Hampshire)*
Southern
New Malden *(Surrey)*
South East
Newark *(Nottinghamshire)*
East Midlands
Newbury *(Berkshire)*
Southern
Newcastle-under-Lyme *(Staffordshire)*
West Midlands
Newcastle-upon-Tyne *(Newcastle-upon-Tyne)*
Northern
Newmarket *(Suffolk)*
Eastern
Newport *(Isle of Wight)*
Southern
North Shields *(North Tyneside)*
Northern
Northampton *(Northamptonshire)*
East Midlands
Northwich *(Cheshire)*
North West
Norwich *(Norfolk)*
Eastern
Nottingham *(Nottinghamshire)*
East Midlands
Oldham *(Oldham)*
North West
Ombersley *(Hereford & Worcester)*
West Midlands
Oxford *(Oxfordshire)*
Southern

P/Q

Painswick *(Gloucestershire)*
South West
Par *(Cornwall)*
South West
Penrith *(Cumbria)*
Northern
Penzance *(Cornwall)*
South West
Peterborough *(Cambridgeshire)*

Eastern
Petersfield *(Hampshire)*
Southern
Plymouth *(Devon)*
South West
Polperro *(Cornwall)*
South West
Poole *(Poole)*
Southern
Portland *(Dorset)*
South West
Portsmouth *(Hampshire)*
Southern
Prestbury *(Cheshire)*
North West
Preston *(Lancashire)*
North West

R

Rainham *(Kent)*
South East
Ramsgate *(Kent)*
South East
Ravenshead *(Nottinghamshire)*
East Midlands
Reading *(Berkshire)*
Southern
Redcar *(Redcar and Cleveland)*
Northern
Redhill *(Surrey)*
South East
Reigate *(Surrey)*
South East
Richmond *(Surrey)*
South East
Ringwood *(Hampshire)*
Southern
Rochdale *(Rochdale)*
North West
Rochester *(Kent)*
South East
Rothbury *(Northumberland)*
Northern
Rotherham *(Rotherham)*
Yorkshire & Humberside
Royston *(Hertfordshire)*
Eastern
Rugby *(Warwickshire)*
West Midlands
Ryde *(Isle of Wight)*
Southern
Rye *(East Sussex)*
South East

S

Saffron Walden *(Essex)*
Eastern
Salford *(Salford)*
North West
Salisbury *(Wiltshire)*
Southern
Saltburn By The Sea *(Redcar and Cleveland)*
Northern
Sandbach *(Cheshire)*
North West
Sandwich *(Kent)*
South East
Sandy *(Bedfordshire)*
Eastern
Sawbridgeworth *(Hertfordshire)*
Eastern
Saxmundham *(Suffolk)*
Eastern
Scarborough *(North Yorkshire)*
Yorkshire & Humberside
Scunthorpe *(North Lincolnshire)*
Eastern
Seaton *(Devon)*
South West
Selbourne *(Hampshire)*
Southern
Settle *(North Yorkshire)*
Yorkshire & Humberside
Sevenoaks *(Kent)*
South East
Sheffield *(Sheffield)*
Yorkshire & Humberside
Sherborne *(Dorset)*
South West
Shrewsbury *(Shropshire)*
West Midlands
Sidcup *(Kent)*
South East
South Shields *(South Tyneside)*
Northern
Southampton *(Southampton)*
Southern
Southend-on-Sea *(Essex)*
Eastern
Southport *(Sefton)*
North West
Southsea *(Hampshire)*
Southern
Southwold *(Suffolk)*
Eastern
Spalding *(Lincolnshire)*
Eastern
St. Albans *(Hertfordshire)*
Eastern
St. Helens *(St. Helens)*
North West
St. Ives *(Cornwall)*
South West
Stafford *(Staffordshire)*
West Midlands
Stalybridge *(Tameside)*
North West
Stamford *(Lincolnshire)*
Eastern
Stamfordham *(Northumberland)*
Northern
Stevenage *(Hertfordshire)*
Eastern
Stockbridge *(Hampshire)*
Southern
Stockport *(Stockport)*
North West
Stockton on Tees *(Stockton on Tees)*
Northern
Stoke-on-Trent *(Stoke-on-Trent)*
West Midlands
Stow-on-the-Wold *(Gloucestershire)*
South West
Stratford-upon-Avon *(Warwickshire)*
West Midlands
Stroud *(Gloucestershire)*
South West
Sudbury *(Suffolk)*
Eastern
Sunderland *(Sunderland)*
Northern
Swanage *(Dorset)*
South West
Swindon *(Swindon)*
Southern

T/U

Taunton *(Somerset)*
South West
Telford *(Shropshire)*
West Midlands
Thirsk *(North Yorkshire)*
Yorkshire & Humberside
Tiverton *(Devon)*
South West
Todmorden *(Calderdale)*
Yorkshire & Humberside
Topsham *(Devon)*
South West
Torrington *(Devon)*
South West
Totnes *(Devon)*
South West
Towcester *(Northamptonshire)*
East Midlands
Truro *(Cornwall)*
South West
Tunbridge Wells *(Kent)*
South East
Uppingham *(Rutland)*
East Midlands

V/W/Y

Virginia Water *(Surrey)*
South East
Wakefield *(Wakefield)*
Yorkshire & Humberside
Wallingford *(Oxfordshire)*
Southern
Wallsend *(North Tyneside)*
Northern
Ware *(Hertfordshire)*
Eastern
Warkworth *(Northumberland)*
Northern
Warrington *(Cheshire)*
North West
Warwick *(Warwickshire)*
West Midlands
Washington *(Sunderland)*
Northern
Watford *(Hertfordshire)*
Eastern
Wedmore *(Somerset)*
South West
Wednesbury *(Sandwell)*
West Midlands
Wellingborough *(Northamptonshire)*
East Midlands
Wells *(Somerset)*
South West
Wells-next-the-Sea *(Norfolk)*
Eastern
West Byfleet *(Surrey)*
South East
Westcliff-on-Sea *(Essex)*
Eastern
Weston Super Mare *(North Somerset)*
South West
Wetherby *(Leeds)*
Yorkshire & Humberside

South West

Bath & North East Somerset

BATH

Adam Gallery C
13 John Street, Bath, BA1 2JL.
Tel: *01225-480406.* **Fax:** *01225-480406.*
Email *adamgallery@clara.net*
Opening times: *Mon-Sat 9.30-5.30.*
Personnel: *Directors:* Paul Dye, Philip Dye. Vanessa Wells, James McDonagh.

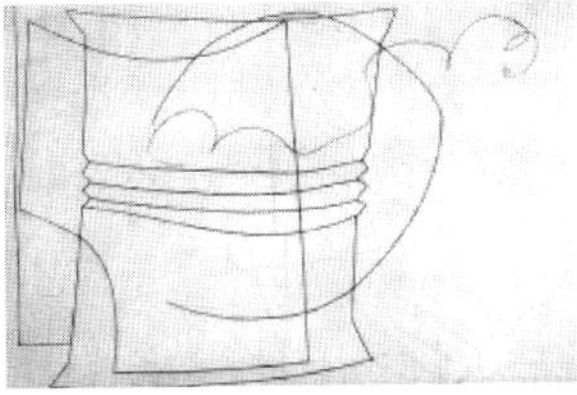

20th Century British Art including Ben Nicholson, Patrick Heron, William Scott, Roger Hilton, John Piper, Henry Moore, Sir Robin Philipson, Algernon Newton, David Hockney, Terry Frost, John Hoyland, Ivon Hitchens and Alan Davie. Also large stock of work by leading contemporary artists including Susan Foord, William Selby, Marj Bond, Melita Denaro, Gail Harvey, Richard Cartwright, Colin Kent, Hsiao-Mei Lin, Judith Cain, James Judge, Leo McDowell and Padraig Macmiadhachain.
Services and Facilities:
Art Consultancy. Art for Offices. Framing. Restoration. Valuation.
Work Stocked and Sold:
Dr. Pa. Pr. Sc.
Price range: £500 - £50,000.
For artists see *Commercial Gallery Artists.*

American Museum in Britain P
Claverton Manor, Bath, BA2 7BD.
Tel: *01225-460503.* **Fax:** *01225-480726.*

Anthony Hepworth Fine Art Gallery
Ivy House, Cavendish Road, Sion Hill, Bath, BA1 2UE. **Tel:** *01225-442917.*

Beaux Arts C
12/13 York Street, Bath, BA1 1NG.
Tel: *01225-464850.* **Fax:** *01225-422256.*
Opening times: *Mon-Sat 10-5.*
Personnel: *Directors:* Anna-Liza Singh, Colin Carlin.

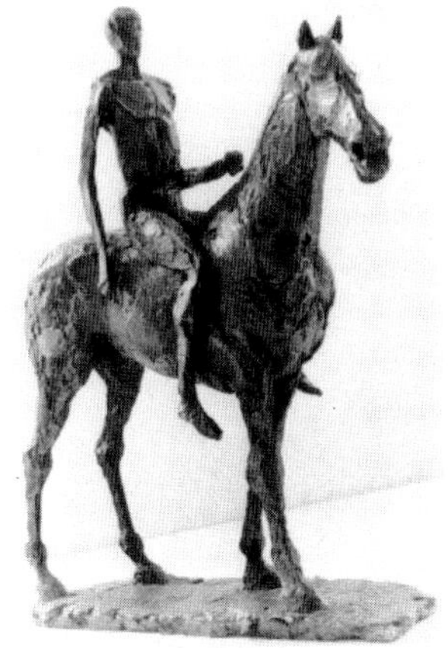

Beaux Arts is the longest established commercial gallery in Bath and is the sister gallery of Beaux Arts, London. The gallery specialises in work of major 20th Century British painters and sculptors as well as leading modern ceramicists. Established artists and sculptors include Norman Adams, Frank Auerbach, Michael Ayrton, John Bellany, Lynn Chadwick, Mary Fedden, Elisabeth Frink, John Piper, the St. Ives School, and young Scottish artists. The Gallery regularly shows leading artists of the younger generation, including, Patrick Barker, Nicola Bealing, Lucy Boydell, Lin Jammet, Anita Klein, Jennifer McRae, Julian Paltenghi, Ray Richardson, Patricia Volk and many others.
Services and Facilities:
Art Consultancy. Art for Offices. Commissioning Service.
Work Stocked and Sold:
Cer. Dr. Pa. Pr. Sc.
Price range: £50 - £10,000.
For artists see *Commercial Gallery Artists.*

Beckford's Tower and Museum P
Lansdown, Bath, BA1 9BH.
Tel: *01225-422212.*

Bough & Lime
Crossleaze Farm, Nr Woolley, Bath, BA1 8AU.
Tel: *01225-859772.* **Fax:** *01225-859088.*

Facade C
5-8 Saville Row, Bath, BA1.
Tel: *01225-723636.*

Hitchcock's C
10 Chapel Row, Bath, BA1 1HN.
Tel: *01225-330646.*

The Holburne Museum of Art PS
Great Pulteney Street, Bath, BA2 4DB.
Tel: *01225-466669.* **Fax:** *01225-333121.*
Opening times: *6 Mar-11 Dec 11-5 weekdays, Sun 2-5.30 (including bank holidays). Closed Mondays, Nov to Easter. Group bookings by appointment.*
Nearest Station: *Bath Spa.*
Personnel: *Directors:* Barley Roscoe, Barbara Milner .

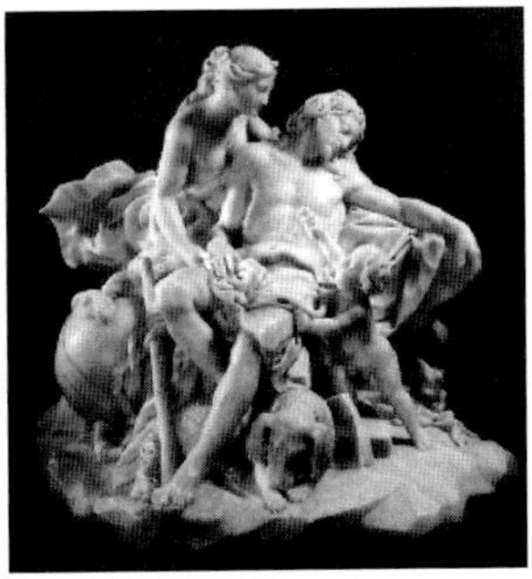

The superb art collections in this famous 18th century building were formed by Sir William Holburne. Widely known for his silver, he also collected paintings, Italian bronzes such as the famous Susini owned by Louis XIV, maiolica, porcelain, glass, furniture and portrait miniatures. His legacy has been enriched by gifts and bequests, including Guardi and Turner landscapes and portraits by Stubbs, Ramsay, Zoffany and Gainsborough.
Bath connections are represented by Angelica Kauffman's portrait of Henrietta Laura Pulteney, Hone's miniature of Beau Nash and Joseph Plura's 1752 marble masterpiece, made in Bath depicting Diana and Endymion. Major temporary art exhibitions complement the displays.
Services and Facilities:
Art Consultancy. Bookshop. Café. Disabled Access. Friends/Society. Gallery space for hire. Guided Tours. Lectures. Museum Shop. Parking. Restaurant. Workshop Facilities.

Kelston Fine Arts C
Kelston House, College Road, Lansdown, Bath, BA1 5RY.
Tel: *01225-424224.*

Larkhall Fine Art C
9 Cambridge Mews, Bath, BA1 6QE.
Tel: *01225-329030.*

Museum of East Asian Art P
12 Bennett Street, Bath, BA1 2QL.
Tel: *01225-464640.* **Fax:** *01225-461718.*

Peter Hayes Contemporary Art
2 Cleveland Bridge, Bath, BA1 5DH.
Tel: *01225-466215.*

Rooksmoor Gallery
31 Brock Street, Bath, BA1 2LN.
Tel: *01225-420495.*

Rostra Gallery C
5 George Street, Bath, BA1 2EH.
Tel: *01225-448121.*
Fax: *01225-447421.*

The Royal Photographic Society
The Octagon Galleries, Milsom Street, Bath, BA1 1DN.
Tel: *01225-462841.* **Fax:** *01225-448688.*

Six Chapel Row Contemporary Art
Six Chapel Row, Bath, BA1 1HN.
Tel: *01225-337900.*
Fax: *01225-336577.*

St. James's Gallery, C
9b Margaret's Buildings, Bath, BA1 2LP.
Tel: *01225-319197.*

Trimbridge Galleries
2 Trimbridge, Bath, BA1 1HD.
Tel: *01225-466390.*

Victoria Art Gallery P
Bridge Street, Pulteney Bridge, Bath, BA2 4AT.
Tel: *01225-477772.*
Fax: *01225-477231.*

Bristol

BRISTOL

3D Gallery
13 Perry Road, Bristol BS1 5BG.
Tel: *0117-929 1363.*

Alexander Gallery C
122 Whiteladies Road, Clifton, Bristol BS8 2RP.
Tel: *0117-973 4692.* **Fax:** *0117-940 6991.*

Arnolfini Gallery C
16 Narrow Quay, Bristol BS1 4QA.
Tel: *0117-929 9191.*
Fax: *0117-925 3876.*

Bristol Museum and Art Gallery P
Queen's Road, Bristol BS8 1RL.
Tel: *0117-922 3571.*
Fax: *0117-922 2047.*

Empire and Commonwealth Museum P
Clock Tower Yard, Temple Meads, Bristol BS1 6QH.
Tel: *0117-925 4980/292688.*
Fax: *0117-925 4983.*

Guild Gallery C
68 Park Street, Bristol BS1 5JY.
Tel: *0117-926 5548.*
Opening times: *Mon-Sat 9.30-5 except Sun and Bank Hols.*
Nearest Station: *Temple Meads, Bristol.*
Personnel: *Gallery Organiser:* John Stops.

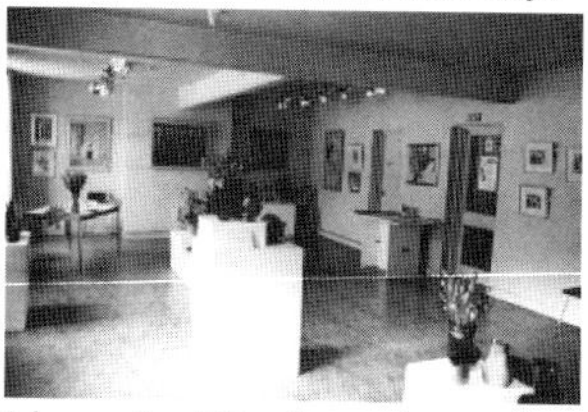

A large and well-lit gallery on the second floor of the Bristol Guild of Applied Art. It is rented by exhibitors and no commission is charged on sales. There are monthly exhibitions by mainly, but not exclusively, West Country artists and craftspeople, individually or in small groups. A large multi-media exhibition is held every Christmas. There is now a small gallery next to our craft dept. which holds occasional exhibitions by craftsmen.
Services and Facilities:
Café. Craftshop. Gallery space for hire. Restaurant. Shop.
Work Stocked and Sold:
App. Cer. Cra. Dr. Pa. Sc.
Price range: £100 - £500.

Michael Stewart Galleries
24 The Mall, Clifton, Bristol BS8 4DS.
Tel: *0272-706265.* **Fax:** *0272-706268.*

Michael Wright Fine Art
Holloway House, 14 New Road, Pill Bristol BS20 0AD

Niche Frames
26 Stokes Croft, Bristol BS1 3QD.
Tel: *0117-942 2213.* **Fax:** *0117-942 3016.*

Parkview Fine Paintings C
24 The Mall, Clifton, Bristol BS8 4DS.
Tel: *0117-970 6265.* **Fax:** *0117-970 6268.*

Royal West of England Academy C
Queen's Road, Clifton, Bristol BS8 1PX.
Tel: *0117-973 5129.* **Fax:** *0117-923 7874.*
Opening times: *Mon-Sat: 9-5.30, Sun 2-5.*
Nearest Station: *Bristol Temple Meads.*
Personnel: *Academy Secretary:* Rachel Fear.
Exhibitions mainly by practising artists, representing a "broad church" are shown throughout the year in the RWA's beautiful Victorian toplit galleries, arranged by RWA Council. Annual open Autumn Exhibition attracts thousands of submissions, with approximately 700 selected and hung, the majority for sale. Open Print and Sculpture Exhibitions are held triennially. Several student bursaries are awarded annually. Galleries are available for hire for evening functions. Friends' associa-

RWA
Royal West of England Academy

tion organises lectures, visits and holidays. Coffee available during exhibitions.
Services and Facilities:
Disabled Access. Friends/Society. Gallery space for hire. Lectures. Shop.
Work Stocked and Sold:
Pa. Pr. Sc.

Sir William Russell Flint Gallery
Broad Street, Wrington, Bristol BS18 7LA.
Tel: *0117-940 5440.*

Watershed Exhibitions
Watershed Media Centre, 1 Canons Road, Bristol BS1 5TX.
Tel: *0117-927 6444, 925 3845.*
Fax: *0117-921 3958.*
Email *info@watershed.demon.co.uk*
Ws *http://www.watershed.co.uk*
Opening times: *Gallery 1 daily 12 noon-8pm, 7 days a week.*
Nearest Station: *Bristol Temple Meads.*
Personnel: *Exhibitions Officer:* Jackie Puzey. *Marketing:* Louise Gardner, Gina Bowen.
Open 7 days a week Watershed is situated in the heart of the city centre of Bristol and offer a lively exhibition programme of photography, film and digit work plus events, courses and a relaxing and friendly cafe/bar which all contributes to making it one of Bristol's most frequently visited and popular venues.
Services and Facilities:
Bar. Café. Disabled Access. Gallery space for hire. Guided Tours. Lectures. Workshop Facilities.

Cornwall

CAMELFORD

North Cornwall Museum & Gallery P
The Clease, Camelford,
Tel: *01840-212954.*

FALMOUTH

Falmouth Art Gallery PS
Municipal Buildings, The Moor, Falmouth, TR11 2RT.
Tel: *01326-313863.* **Fax:** *01326-312662.*
Opening times: *Open all year (except Bank Holidays) Mon-Fri 10-5, Sat 10-1.*
Personnel: *Curator:* Catherine Wallace. *Assistant:* Alix Hooper. *Assistant:* Shelley Brett.
Permanent collection includes 200 works of art from Maritime prints and paintings (1600 - 1950) to Victorian and Edwardian paintings

by artists like Burne-Jones, Munnings, Waterhouse, Laura Knight and H.S. Tuke. The display of the collection is rotated every six months. The gallery holds 10 temporary exhibitions per year including contemporary solo and group shows and historic, general, local artistic subjects plus two touring. Now open after major renovation and expansion of exhibiting space providing disabled access via new lift. Also new shop selling local artists' work on permanent basis and books, postcards and posters. Admission Free.
Services and Facilities:
Disabled Access. Guided Tours. Lectures. Shop.
Work Stocked and Sold:
Ab.

Falmouth Arts Centre
24 Church Street, Falmouth, TR11 3EG.
Tel: *01326-314566.* **Fax:** *01326-211078.*

HELSTON

Creftow Gallery C
6 Church Street, Helston, TR13 8TE.
Tel: *01326-572848.*

Mullion Gallery
Nansmellyon Road, Mullion, Helston, TR12 7DQ.
Tel: *01326-241170.*

MARAZION

Avalon Art C
West End, Marazion, TR17 0EL.
Tel: *01736-710161/711968.*
Opening times: *Tues-Sat 10.30-1.30 and 2-5 Oct to April and open 7 days a week in Summer.*
Personnel: Sally Scott. Lucie Bray.

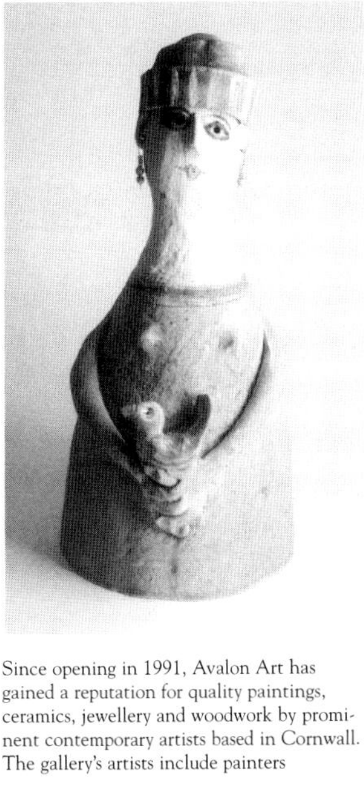

Since opening in 1991, Avalon Art has gained a reputation for quality paintings, ceramics, jewellery and woodwork by prominent contemporary artists based in Cornwall. The gallery's artists include painters Anthony Frost, Fred Yates, Jeremy Le Grice, Michael Praed, Emma Jeffrey, Robert Jones, Lucie Bray, Sue McDonald, Maggie Henshall, Mary Stork and Dot Searle; ceramics Shirley Foote, Debbie Prosser, Jill Bevan, Seth Marshall and Lucy Haynes; jewellery Jenny Yates, Amanda Ray and Lu Wray; woodworkers Lynn Muir and Kim Scott. Prints, cards, reproduction prints and artist's books are also in stock. We are opposite the National Trust property St. Michael's Mount.
Services and Facilities:
Disabled Access.
Work Stocked and Sold:
Ab. Cer. Cra. Jew. Pa. Pr. Sc. Wd.
Price range: £5 - £1,500.
For artists see *Commercial Gallery Artists.*

PAR

Mid-Cornwall Galleries
Discovery, Par, PL24 2EG.
Tel: *01726-812131.*

PENZANCE

The Bakehouse Gallery C
Old Bakehouse Lane, Chapel Street, Penzance,
Tel: *01736-332223, 369979.*

Newlyn Art Gallery PS
New Road, Newlyn, Penzance, TR18 5PZ.
Tel: *01736-363715.* **Fax:** *01736-331578.*
Opening times: *Mon-Sat 10-5.*
Nearest Station: *Penzance.*
Personnel: *Director:* Emily Ash.
Shop Manager: Blair Todd.
Newlyn Art Gallery has been established as a venue for exhibiting contemporary art for over 100 years, showing the best work by local, national and international artists. To compliment the exhibitions programme, the education programme includes talks, lectures, workshops and educational activities for schools and colleges. The gallery also presents a programme of events including music concerts, live arts, festival activities, art classes and a Summer Art Week of children's workshops. The gallery shop stocks a wide range of art books and magazines, greetings cards, ceramics, jewellery, prints and small paintings.
Services and Facilities:
Bookshop. Craftshop. Disabled Access. Friends/Society. Lectures. Shop. Workshop Facilities.
Work Stocked and Sold:
Ab. App. Cer. Cra. Dec. Dr. Jew. Pa. Ph. Pr. Sc. Tx. Wd.
Price range: £3 - £3,000.
For artists see *Commercial Gallery Artists.*

Round House Gallery
Sennen Cove, Lands End, Penzance, TR19 7DF.
Tel: *01736-871859.*

Shears Fine Art
58 Chapel Street, Penzance, TR18 4AW.
Tel: *01736-50501.*

Tony Sanders Penzance Gallery
14 Chapel Street, Penzance, TR18 4AW.
Tel: *01736-66620.*

Victoria Studios
Morrab Road, Penzance,
Tel: *01736-62228.*

POLPERRO

Peak Rock Artist's Studio & Gallery
Peak Rock Art Studio, The Harbour, Polperro, PL13 2QY.
Tel: *01503-72490.*

ST. IVES

Barbara Hepworth Museum P
Barnoon Hill, St. Ives,
Tel: *01736-796226.*

The Book Gallery
2a & 2b Bedford Road, St. Ives, TR26 1SP.
Tel: *01736-793545.*

Judi Emmanuel
30 Fore Street, St. Ives, TR26 1HE.
Tel: *01736-797303/798448.*

Mosaic Gallery
8 St. Andrews Street, St. Ives, TR26 1AH.
Tel: *01736-793459.*

New Craftsman C
24 Fore Street, St. Ives, TR26 1HE.
Tel: *01736-795652.*

The New Millenium Gallery
Street-An-Pol, St. Ives, TR26 2DS.
Tel: *01736-793121.*

Penhaven Gallery
4 St. Peters Street, St. Ives,
Tel: *01736-798147.*

Penwith Galleries PS
Back Road West, St. Ives, TR26 1NL.
Tel: *01736-795579.*
Opening times:
Tues-Sat 10-1, 2.30-5.
Admission: 50p.
Nearest Station: *St. Ives.*
Personnel: *Director:* Kathleen Watkins.
The Penwith Society was founded in 1949 by a group of notable contemporary artists in St. Ives and its seasonal exhibitions became a national showing place for contemporary work. The Society has an elected membership, limited to fifty and an unlimited associated membership. Its aims are to encourage practising artists and craftsmen in Cornwall and foster public interestin the arts. The gallery has charity status.
It is a unique complex of buildings including public galleries, print workshop, book shop, artists' studios and workshops. Continuous exhibitions of paintings sculpture and ceramics throughout the year.
Services and Facilities:
Art for Offices. Bookshop. Commissioning Service. Friends/Society. Shop. Workshop Facilities.
Work Stocked and Sold:
Ab. App. Cer. Cra. Dec. Dr. Jew. Pa. Pr. Sc. Wd.
For artists see *Commercial Gallery Artists.*

Picture House Galleries C
Island Square, St. Ives, TR26 1NT.
Tel: *01736-794423.*

Plumbline Gallery C
2 Barnoon Hill, St. Ives, TR26 1AD.
Tel: *01736-797771.*

Porthmeor Gallery
Porthmeor Road, St. Ives, TR26 1NP.
Tel: *01736-798412.*

Salthouse Gallery
Norway Square, St. Ives, TR26 1NA.
Tel: *01736-795003.*

Sims Gallery
22 Fore Street, St. Ives, TR26 1HE.
Tel: *01736-797148.* **Fax:** *01736-797148.*

St. Ives Society of Artists
Norway Gallery, Norway Square, St. Ives, TR26 1NA.
Tel: *01736-795582.*

Tate Gallery St. Ives
Porthmeor Beach, St. Ives, TR26 1TG.
Tel: *01736-796226.* **Fax:** *01736-794480.*
Ws *http://www.tate.org.uk*
Opening times: *Tues-Sun 10.30-5.30 & Mondays in July & August. Bank Holidays 10.30-5.30.*
Nearest Station: *St. Erth for St. Ives.*
Personnel: *Curator:* Michael Tooby. *Press & Information:* Ina Cole. *Education:* Susan Lamb.

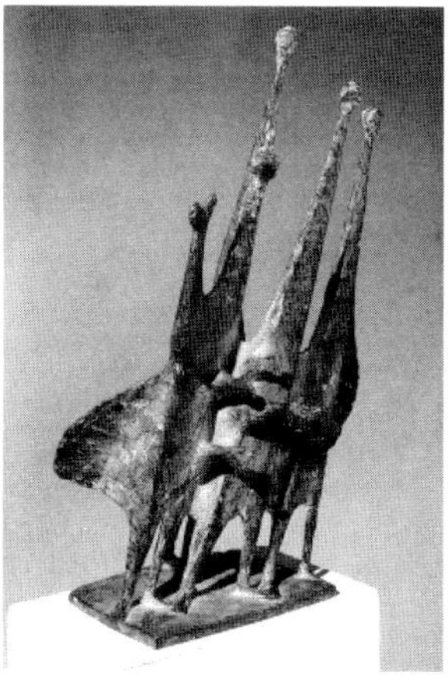

The Tate Gallery St. Ives opened in 1993 and presents changing displays of 20th century art from the Tate Gallery's collections, focusing on the post-war modern movement St. Ives is so famous for. Key artists represented in the collection include Alfred Wallis, Ben Nicholson, Barbara Hepworth, Naum Gabo, John Wells, Patrick Heron, Terry Frost and Wilhelmina Barns-Graham. In 1999 work by Bernard Leach, Shoji Hamada, Cecil Collins & Mark Tobey will also be shown. The displays are complemented by a series of exhibitions and artists' projects and residencies, which explore the diversity of working methods in art today. A major Contemporary Project has been planned to take place from May-Nov '99; Yuko Shiraishi and Gia Edsveradze will be creating new work in response to the solar eclipse, seen in its totality in W. Cornwall. The Barbara Hepworth Museum and Sculpture Garden in St. Ives is run by Tate Gallery St. Ives.
Services and Facilities:
Bookshop. Café. Disabled Access. Friends/Society. Guided Tours. Lectures. Museum Shop. Restaurant. Shop. Workshop Facilities.

Wills Lane Gallery
Wills Lane, St. Ives, TR26 1AF.
Tel: *01736-795723.*

TRURO

The Gallery Portscatho
Portscatho, Nr St Mawes, Truro, TR2 5HQ.
Tel: *01872-580719.* **Fax:** *01872-580719.*

Royal Cornwall Museum P
River Street, Truro, TR1 2SJ.
Tel: *01872-72205.*

The Royal Cornwall Museum P
River Street, Truro, TR1 2SJ.
Tel: *01872-72205.*

Devon

APPLEDORE

Gallerie Marin
31 Market Street, Appledore, EX39 1PP.
Tel: *01237-473679.*

BIDEFORD

The Appledore Crafts Company
5 Bude Street, Appledore, Bideford, EX32 1PS.
Tel: *01237-423547.*

Burton Art Gallery & Museum P
Kingsley Road, Bideford, EX39 2QQ.
Tel: *01237-471455.* **Fax:** *01237-471455.*

Cooper Gallery C
Cooper Street, Bideford, EX39 2DA.
Tel: *01237-477370.* **Fax:** *01237-423415.*

BOVEY TRACEY

Devon Guild of Craftsmen C
Riverside Mill, Bovey Tracey, TQ13 9AF.
Tel: *01626-832223.* **Fax:** *01626-834220.*
Email *devonguild@crafts.org.uk*
Ws *http:/www.crafts.org.uk*
Opening times: *Daily 10-5.30 (except Winter Bank Holidays), Café 10-5.*
Nearest Station: *Newton Abbot.*
Personnel: *Director:* Francis Byng. *Contact:* Tess Coulson.
The picturesque Riverside Mill, a grade II listed building, has a shop, Exhibition Gallery and café. The shop, selected for quality by the Crafts Council, displays a wide variety of contemporary crafts including ceramics, jewellery, furniture, textiles, prints and woodwork by members of the Devon Guild. The Exhibition gallery holds a regularly changing programme of themed exhibitions featuring

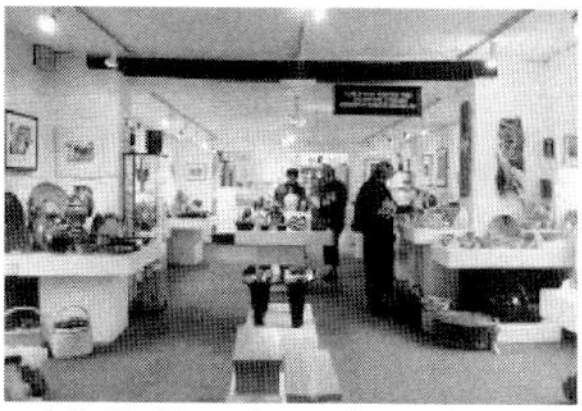

work by Guild members and invited contributors. The café serves delicious homemade food. Educational work with schools. Free adjacent parking.
Services and Facilities:
Café. Commissioning Service. Craftshop. Friends/Society. Lectures. Shop.
Work Stocked and Sold:
Cer. Cra. Dr. Fur. Gla. Jew. Pr. Sc. Tx. Wd.
Price range: £5 - £5,000.
For artists see *Commercial Gallery Artists.*

BUCKFASTLEIGH

Buckfast Abbey P
Buckfastleigh, TQ11 0EE.
Tel: *01364-642519.* **Fax:** *01364-643891.*

BUDLEIGH SALTERTON

Brook Gallery C
Fore Street, Budleigh Salterton, EX9 6NH.
Tel: *01395-443003.* **Fax:** *01395-446490.*

Otterton Mill Gallery C
Budleigh Salterton, EX9 7HG.
Tel: *01395-568521.*
Fax: *01395-568521.*
Opening times: *Daily 10.30-5.30 daily mid March-end October, 11.00-4.00 daily Nov-Mid March.*
Nearest Station: *Exmouth.*
Personnel: *Director:* Desna Greenhow.
Otterton Mill Gallery has an annual programme of fine arts and crafts exhibitions. The annual exhibition of furniture design is normally held in October. Frequent exhibitions include sculpture, both inside the gallery and in the courtyard, and the work of West Country craftspeople. Five studio-workshops include a pottery, weaving workshop, painting studio and wood turning and framing workshop. A co-operative craft shop is run by local craftspeople.
Services and Facilities:
Bookshop. Café. Craftshop. Framing. Gallery space for hire. Parking. Workshop Facilities.
Work Stocked and Sold:
Cer. Cra. Fur. Jew. Pa. Ph. Pr. Sc. Tx. Wd.
Price range: £10 - £1,500.
For artists see *Commercial Gallery Artists.*

DARTMOUTH

Facets C
14 Broadstone, Dartmouth, TQ9 9NR.
Tel: *01803-833534.*

Higher Street Gallery C
1 Higher Street, Dartmouth, TQ6 9RB.
Tel: *01803-833157.*

Simon Drew Gallery C
13 Foss Street, Dartmouth, TQ6 9DR.
Tel: *01803-832832.*
Fax: *01803-833040.*

EXETER

Boatyard Studios
76 Haven Road, St. Thomas, Exeter, EX2 8DP.
Tel: *01392-218704.*

Gordon Hepworth Gallery
Hayne Farm, Sandowne Lane, Newton St. Cyres, Exeter, EX5 5DE.
Tel: *01392-851351.*

Laurel Keeley Gallery
4 St. David's Hill, Exeter,
Tel: *01392-428128.*

The Look C
53 Queen Street, Exeter,
Tel: *01392-219855.*

Royal Albert Memorial Museum & Art Gallery PS
Queen Street, Exeter, EX4 3RX.
Tel: *01392-265858.*
Fax: *01392-421252.*
Email *R.E.Randall@exeter.ac.uk*
Ws *http://www.exeter.gov.uk*
Opening times: *Mon-Sat 10-5.*
Nearest Station: *Exeter Central.*
Personnel: *Head of Museums:* Katherine Chant. *Exhibitions Administrator:* Fay Squire. *Curator of Decorative Art:* John Madin. *Assistant Curator of Art:* Caroline Worthington. *Press & Events Officer:* Ruth Randall.
Large regional museum with collections of regional, national and international importance. Fine Art collection, Decorative Art collection, art from peoples around the world in the Ethnography collection, a programme of temporary exhibitions, workshops, lectures and children's activities. Important exhibitions 1999: 10th May-12th June 1999, Jan Niedojadlo, Huge and spectacular interactive sculptures made from recycled materials; 19th June 1999, Opening of three new World Cultures Galleries, A dazzling array of outstanding artefacts from every part of the world - from Tierra del Fuego to Alaska, Cape Town to Cairo, Tasmania to Hawaii, Borneo to Palestine and including objects from the voyages of Cook, Bligh and Vancouver; 26th June-4th September 1999, Mosaics - A Living Art, An Anglo-Italian Celebration, featuring work by 15 leading contemporary British and Italian artists; 18th September-27th November 1999, From Script to Print to Hypertext, Two millennia of Devon's written heritage; 11th December 1999-29th January 2000, Henri Cartier Bresson Portraits, 120 photographs representing a career spanning over 60 years.
Services and Facilities:
Café. Friends/Society. Lectures. Museum Shop. Shop.

Spacex Gallery
45 Preston Street, Exeter, EX1 1DF.
Tel: *01392-431786.*

Vincent Gallery C
15 Magdalen Road, Exeter, EX2 4TA.
Tel: *01392-430082.*

PLYMOUTH

Atlantic Gallery C
Armada Centre, Plymouth,
Tel: *01752-221600.*

The Chapel Gallery C
Saltram House, Plympton, Plymouth, PL7 1UH.
Tel: *01752-336546.* **Fax:** *01752-336474.*
Email *dsaltr@smtp.ntrust.org.uk*
Opening times: *28th March-1st October: 10-5 daily except Friday & Saturday, 2nd October-18th December: 11-4 every day.*
Nearest Station: *Plymouth.*
Personnel: *Gallery Manager:* Rebecca Green.
The Chapel Gallery stands at the North-West corner of Saltram House, and is set amongst the beautiful gardens of the National Trust Estate in Plympton, Devon. Since 1977 when the National Trust and the Plymouth Centre renovated the picturesque ruin, The Chapel has run as a Gallery, and has become a firm focus for work by professional West Country Artists and Craftspeople. The Chapel Gallery aims to provide Contemporary Arts and Crafts, and to promote the work of the regions new artists and craftspeople. The work displayed includes paintings, prints, ceramics, sculpture, textiles, furniture, glass, wood, jewellery, hand-knits, cards and books.
Services and Facilities:
Bookshop. Commissioning Service. Craftshop. Disabled Access. Gallery space for hire. Parking.
Work Stocked and Sold:
Ab. Cer. Cra. Dec. Dr. Fur. Gla. Jew. Pa. Pr. Sc. Tx. Wd.
Price range: £1 - £30,000.
For artists see *Commercial Gallery Artists.*

Plymouth Arts Centre PS
38 Looe Street, Plymouth, PL4 0EB.
Tel: *01752-206114.* **Fax:** *01752-206118.*

Plymouth City Museum & Art Gallery P
Drake Circus, Plymouth, PL4 8AJ.
Tel: *01752-264878.* **Fax:** *01752-264959.*

White Lane Gallery C
1 White Lane, The Barbican, Plymouth, PL1 2LP.
Tel: *01752-221450.*

SEATON

Marine House at Beer
Fore Street, Beer, Seaton, BS12 3EF.
Tel: *01297-625257.* **Fax:** *01297-625493.*

TIVERTON

Angel Gallery
1 Angel Terrace, Tiverton, EX16 6PD.
Tel: *01994-254778.*

TOPSHAM

The Ship Aground Gallery
36 Fore Street, Topsham, EX3 0HQ.
Tel: *01392-874505.*

TORRINGTON

Plough Gallery
Plough Arts Centre, The High Street, Torrington, EX38 8HQ.
Tel: *01805-622552.* **Fax:** *01805-624624.*

TOTNES

Dartington Arts Gallery PS
Dartington Hall, Totnes, TQ9 6DE.
Tel: *01803-867068.* **Fax:** *01803-868108.*
Opening times: *Mon-Fri 10.30-1, 2-5, Sat 2-5.*
Personnel: *Gallery Co-ordinator:* Kamya O'Keeffe.
Dartington Arts Gallery is situated on the 900-acre medieval Dartington Hall Estate and has a wall space of 77.8 m2. It is constantly invigilated during opening hours and has a Nacoss approved intruder alarm system. The gallery has a programme of innovative exhibitions supporting both local and national/international artists. The Gallery is part of the overall activities at Dartington Arts.
Services and Facilities:
Bar. Craftshop. Disabled Access. Gallery space for hire. Lectures. Parking. Restaurant. Workshop Facilities.

High Cross House
Dartington Hall, Totnes, TQ9 6ED.
Tel: *01803-864114.* **Fax:** *01803-867057.*

Marshall Arts Gallery
3 Warland, The Plains, Totnes, TQ9 5EL.
Tel: *01803-863533.*

Seymour Gallery
10 High Street, Totnes, TQ9 5RY.
Tel: *01803-864200.*

WINKLEIGH

Square Gallery C
Fore Street, Winkleigh, EX19 8HQ.
Tel: *01837-83145.*

Dorset

ABBOTSBURY

Abbotsbury Studios C
11a Rodden Row, Abbotsbury, DT3 4JL.
Tel: *01305-871876.*
Opening times: *Thus-Sat 1.30-5 or by appointment.*
Nearest Station: *Dorchester South.*
Personnel: *Artist:* John Skinner.
Work space of artist John Skinner. Courses in Contemporary Art, Creative Thinking for Business. Exhibition of John Skinner's work and exhibitions by artists of established or emerging national and international reputation, e.g. 1997 Jerwood shortlisted artist Rose Wylie 1998.

Services and Facilities:
Art for Offices. Commissioning Service. Gallery space for hire. Workshop Facilities.
Work Stocked and Sold:
Dr. Pa.
Price range: £100 - £8,000.
For artists see *Commercial Gallery Artists.*

Dansel Gallery C
Rodden Row, Abbotsbury, Weymouth, DT3 4JL.
Tel: *01305-871515.* **Fax:** *01305-871518.*

BEAMINSTER

Parnham House PS
Beaminster, DT8 3NA.
Tel: *01308-862204.* **Fax:** *01308-863494.*

BRIDPORT

Bridport Arts Centre
South Street, Bridport, DT6 3NR.
Tel: *01308-424204.*

Bridport Museum P
South Street, Bridport, DT6 3NR.
Tel: *01308-422116.* **Fax:** *01308-420659.*

DORCHESTER

The Gallery Dorchester C
20 Durngate Street, Dorchester DT1 1JP.
Tel: *01305-267408.* **Fax:** *01305-251429.*
Email *john.pearson1@virgin.net.uk*
Opening times: *Tues-Sat, 10-5.*
Nearest Station: *Dorchester South.*
Personnel: *Director:* Susie Pearson.

THE GALLERY DORCHESTER

Found in Dorchester's ancient Durngate Street, this gallery is on the ground floor of a 16th century building. Previously well known for representing established watercolourists, the owners now exhibit and promote original printmakers. Artists represented include: Jo Barry, Stephen Brown, Michael Cadman, Katie Clemson, Ros and David Cuthbert, Anne Desmet, Edwina Ellis, Jason Hicklin, Ron Jesty, Richard Pikesley, Peter Toms, Alan Simpson and others. Four to five exhibitions a year. Bespoke Framing and Conservation.
Services and Facilities:
Disabled Access. Framing. Restoration.
Work Stocked and Sold:
Dr. Pa. Pr. Sc.
Price range: £100 - £1,000.
For artists see *Commercial Gallery Artists.*

Gallery Gilbert C
48 High West Street, Dorchester, DT1 1UT.
Tel: *01305-263740.*

Thomas Henry Fine Art C
The Old Warehouse, Durngate Street, Dorchester, DT1 1JP.
Tel: *01305-250388.*

LYME REGIS

David Hibberd Fine Art
The Town Mill, Mill Lane, Lyme Regis, DT7 3PU.
Tel: *01297-443446.*

PORTLAND

Artworks Gallery C
133 Chiswell, Portland, DT5 1AP.
Tel: *01305-826191.*
Opening times:
Tue/Wed 8.30-6, Thur/Fri 8.30-8, Sat 8.30-3.30 and by appointment.
Nearest Station: *Weymouth.*
Personnel: *Manager:* Suzanne Yates.
Artworks Gallery is adjacent to the famous Chesil Beach and situated in the heart of Chiswell which is fast becoming a colony for artists. Internally the building consists of

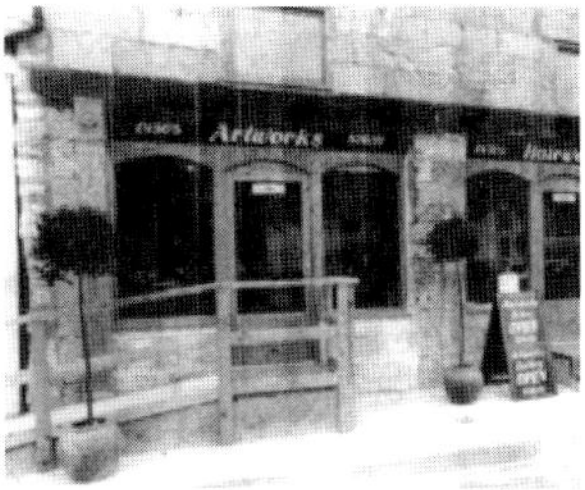

natural Portland stone walls and high beamed ceilings that provide a superb backdrop for the work of artists. There is ample free parking directly outside the gallery.
The Gallery represents a wide range of established and newly emerging artists from regional painters and print makers, abstract artists, ceramicists, outsider artists and performance artists. A wide selection of paintings, monoprints, drawings, ceramics, sculpture and multi media art shown throughout the year.
Services and Facilities:
Art for Offices. Commissioning Service. Disabled Access. Framing. Parking.
Work Stocked and Sold:
Cer. Dr. Pa. Ph. Pr. Sc.
Price range: £60 - £2,000.
For artists see *Commercial Gallery Artists.*

SHERBORNE

Alpha House Gallery C
South Street, Sherborne, DT9 3LU.
Tel: *01935-814944/850511.*
Fax: *01935-816717.*

SWANAGE

Alpha Gallery
21A Commercial Road, Swanage,
Tel: *01929-423692.*

White Yard Studio
3 Arcade Terrace, Swanage, BH19 1DE.
Tel: *01929-426621/426578.*

Gloucestershire

BOURTON ON THE WATER

Chestnut Gallery
High Street, Bourton on the Water,
Tel: *01451-820017.*

CHALFORD

Gallery Pangolin C
Unit 9, Chalford Industrial Estate, Chalford, GL6 8NT.
Tel: *01453-886527.* **Fax:** *01453-731499.*

CHELTENHAM

Axiom Centre for the Arts PS
57-59 Winchcombe Street, Cheltenham, GL52 2NE.
Tel: *01242-253183.* **Fax:** *01242-253183.*

Cheltenham Art Gallery & Museum P
Clarence Street, Cheltenham, GL50 3JT.
Tel: *01242-237431.*
Fax: *01242-262334.*

Holst Birthplace Museum P
4 Clarence Road, Cheltenham, GL52 2AY.
Tel: *01242-524846.*

Jonathan Poole C
Compton Cassey Gallery, Nr. Withington, Cheltenham, GL54 4DE.
Tel: *01242-890224.*
Fax: *01242-890479.*
Email
jonathanpoole@comptoncassey.demon.co.uk
Ws *http://www.jonathanpoole.co.uk*
Personnel: Jonathan Poole.
Maggie Mallen.
European representatives for John Lennon and Miles Davis Estates. Exhibition organisers with venues in Europe and the Middle East. Contemporary Sculpture, Paintings and Sculpture by Jonathan Poole and Bobby Plisnier.
Services and Facilities:
Art Consultancy. Art for Offices. Gallery space for hire. Valuation.
Work Stocked and Sold:
Dr. Pa. Pr. Sc.
Price range: £50 - £15,000.
For artists see *Commercial Gallery Artists.*

Manor House Gallery
16 Royal Parade, Bayshill Road, Cheltenham, GL50 3AY.
Tel: *01242-228330.*
Fax: *01242-228328.*

Montpellier Gallery C
27 The Courtyard, Montpellier Street, Cheltenham, GL50 1SR.
Tel: *01242-515165.*
Fax: *01242-515165.*

The Northleach Gallery
The Green, Northleach, Cheltenham, GL54 3EX.
Tel: *01451-860519.*

CIRENCESTER

Brewery Arts Centre C
Brewery Court, Cirencester, GL7 1JH.
Tel: *01285-657181.* **Fax:** *01285 644060.*

GLOUCESTER

Gloucester City Museum & Art Gallery P
Brunswick Road, Gloucester, GL1 1HP.
Tel: *01452-524131.* **Fax:** *01452-410898.*

Robert Opie Collection Museum of Advertising and Packaging P
Albert Warehouse, Gloucester Docks, Gloucester, GL1 2EH.
Tel: *01452-302309.* **Fax:** *01452-308507.*

LECHLADE

Filkins Gallery & Studio
Cross Tree, Filkins, Lechlade, GL7 3JL.
Tel: *01367-850385 (evenings).*

Kelmscott Manor P
Kelmscott, Lechlade, GL7 3HJ.
Tel: *01367-252486.* **Fax:** *01367-253754.*

NAILSWORTH

Hand Prints & Watercolour Gallery
3 Bridge Street, Nailsworth, GL6 0AA.
Tel: *01453-834967.*

PAINSWICK

Nina Zborowska C
Damsels Mill, Paradise, Painswick, GL6 6UD.
Tel: *01452-812460.* **Fax:** *01452-812912.*

STOW-ON-THE-WOLD

Fosse Gallery
The Square, Stow-on-the-Wold, GL54 1AF.
Tel: *01451-831319.*

John Blockley Gallery C
Church Street, Stow-on-the-Wold,
Tel: *01451-832564.* **Fax:** *01451-832564.*

The John Davies Gallery C
Church Street, Stow-on-the-Wold, GL54 1BB.
Tel: *01451-831698.*
Fax: *01451-832477.*
Opening times: *Mon-Sat 9.30-1.30, 2.30-5.30.*
Nearest Station: *Moreton in Marsh.*
Personnel: John Davies. Tony Retallack. Jeffrey Garrington.
Established 1977. A fresh, spacious and welcoming gallery offering contemporary and earlier 20th Century works from the traditional to the more progressive. Artists include David Prentice, Lionel Aggett, Peter Evans, Keith Dunkley, Sandy Murphy, Kurt Jackson and William Selwyn. Bronzes by Kate Denton, Kathleen Friedenberg, Deborah Scaldwell and Adrian Sorrell. Restoration in all media to museum level. Regular Exhibitions.
Services and Facilities:
Restoration.
Work Stocked and Sold:
Cer. Dr. Pa. Pr. Sc.
For artists see *Commercial Gallery Artists.*

Traffords C
Digbeth Street, Stow-on-the-Wold, GL54 1BN.
Tel: *01451-830424.*

STROUD

Stroud House Gallery
Station Road, Stroud, GL5 3AP.

Yew Tree Gallery C
Steanbridge Lane, Nr. Stroud, Slad, GL6 7QE.
Tel: *01452-813601.*

South Gloucestershire

CHIPPING SODBURY

Carousel Gallery
21a High Street, Chipping Sodbury, BS17 6AE.
Tel: *01454-312622.*

Somerset

FROME

The Black Swan Guild
2 Bridge Street, Frome, BA11 1BB.
Tel: *01373-473980.*

MONTACUTE

National Trust Montacute House P
Montacute, TA15 6XP.
Tel: *01935-823289.* **Fax:** *01935-823289.*

TAUNTON

Albemarle Centre Gallery
Albemarle Centre, Taunton, TA1 1BA.
Tel: *01823-252945.*

Brewhouse Theatre & Arts Centre C
Coal Orchard, Taunton, TA1 1JL.
Tel: *01823-274608.*
Fax: *01823-323116.*

Byram Gallery
Somerset College of Art & Technology, Wellington Road, Taunton, TA1 5AX.
Tel: *01823-283403.*

WEDMORE

The Studio Gallery
Poolbridge, Blackford, Wedmore, BS28 4PD.
Tel: *01934-713380.* **Fax:** *01934-712511.*

WELLS

Sadler Street Gallery C
7a Sadler Street, Wells, BA5 2RR.
Tel: *01749-670220.*

Wells Museum P
8 Cathedral Green, Wells, BA5 2UE.
Tel: *01749-673477.* **Fax:** *01749-676013.*

YEOVIL

80 South Street Gallery
Yeovil Community Arts Centre, 80 South Street, Yeovil, BA20 1QH.
Tel: *01935-32123.*

North Somerset

WESTON SUPER MARE

Hans Price Gallery
Weston Super Mare College, Creative Arts and Design, Knightstone Road, Weston-super-Mare, BS23 2AL.

The Time Machine
North Somerset Museum Service, Burlington Street, Weston-super-Mare, BS23 1PR.
Tel: *01934-621028.* **Fax:** *01934-612526.*

Southern

Berkshire

BRACKNELL

South Hill Park Arts Centre PS
Bracknell, RG12 7PA.
Tel: *01344-427272.* **Fax:** *01344-411427.*
Email *visual.art@southhillpark.org.uk*
Opening times: *Bracknell Gallery:- Wed-Fri 1-5 & 7-9.30pm, Sat 1-10pm, Sun 1-5. Mansion House:- Mon-Sat 9-11pm, Sun & Bank Holidays 12 noon-10.30pm.*
Nearest Station: *Bracknell.*
Personnel: *Visual Arts Co-ordinator:* Lucie May.

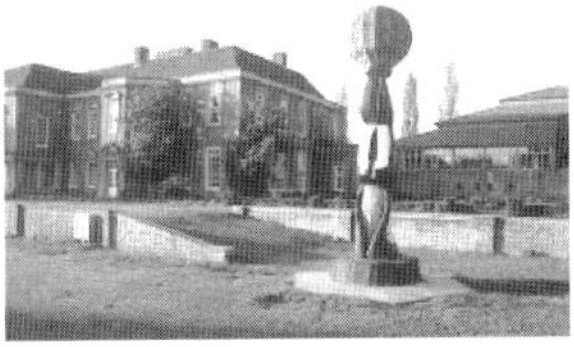

Mansion building and the purpose built Bracknell Gallery hosting a lively range of temporary fine art and craft exhibitions. The Bracknell Gallery programme ranges across major solo exhibitions to group and historical shows. Further spaces in the Mansion building present exhibitions by local artists, young artists and groups both formal and informal. Craft cabinets feature a range of work both by national and local makers. Also printmaking studio, jewellery studio and ceramics studio.
Services and Facilities:
Bar. Café. Disabled Access. Gallery space for hire. Parking. Restaurant. Workshop Facilities.
Work Stocked and Sold:
Cer. Cra. Jew. Pa. Ph. Sc.

COOKHAM

Stanley Spencer Gallery
Kings Hall, High Street, Cookham, SL6 9SJ.
Tel: *01628-520890 / 523484.*
Opening times: *Easter-Oct daily 10.30-5.30. Nov-Easter weekends and Bank Holidays 11-5.*
Nearest Station: *Cookham.*
Personnel: *Chairman:* Mr R. Hurley.

STANLEY SPENCER GALLERY

THE COLLECTION. The gallery's important collection includes a fine group of early religious paintings: 'The Betrayal' 1914, 'The Last Supper' 1920, 'St. Veronica Unmasking Christ' 1921 and 'Christ Overturning the Money Changers' Table' 1921. The gallery also owns figure painting from the 1930s, such as 'The Beatitudes of Love: Contemplation' 1937; portraits and later works. A recent major bequest of paintings and drawings from Barbara Karmel includes, 'Sarah Tubb and the Heavenly Visitors' 1933, a self-portrait 1923, 'Neighbours' 1936 and a landscape 'Beacon Hill' 1927. Admission: Adults 50p; Concessions 10p/25p. Gallery shop stocks facsimile drawings, colour reproductions, postcards and books.
Services and Facilities:
Bookshop. Disabled Access. Friends/Society. Guided Tours. Lectures. Museum Shop. Shop.

ETON

Contemporary Fine Art Gallery & Sculpture Park *C*
31 High Street, Eton, SL4 6AX.
Tel: *01753-854315, after 7pm 01753-830731.*
Fax: *01753-620390.*

MAIDENHEAD

Royal Borough Collection *P*
c/o Royal Borough of Windsor and Maidenhead, Town Hall, St. Ives Road, Maidenhead, SL6 1QS.
Tel: *01628-798888.*

NEWBURY

Arts Workshop
Northcroft Lane, Newbury, RG13 1BU.
Tel: *01635-47851.*

Newbury Museum *P*
The Wharf, Newbury, RG1 5AS.
Tel: *01635-3051.*

READING

Blakes Lock Museum *P*
Gasworks Road, Reading,
Tel: *01734-390918.*

Blond Fine Art *C*
Barnat Works, 1A Upper Redlands Road, Reading RG1 5JJ.
Tel: *0118-926 0880.* **Fax:** *0118-926 9101.*
Opening times: *By appointment.*
Nearest Station: *Reading.*
Personnel: Jonathon Blond.
British original prints 1920-80.
Services and Facilities:
Art Consultancy. Art for Offices.
Work Stocked and Sold:
Pr.
Price range: £50 - £2,500.
For artists see *Commercial Gallery Artists.*

Reading Museum and Art Gallery *P*
Blagrave Street, Reading, RG1 1QH.
Tel: *0118-939 9800/9898.*

Rising Sun Institute
30 Silver Street, Reading, RG1 2ST.
Tel: *01734-866788.*

WINDSOR

Century Gallery Datchet
The Shop on the Green, Datchet, Windsor, SL3 9JH.
Tel: *01753-581284.*

Eton Applied Arts *C*
81 High Street, Windsor, SL4 6AF.
Tel: *01753-860771.*

The Pembroke Gallery *C*
15A The Arches, Goswell Hill, Windsor, SL4 1RH.
Tel: *01753-868844.* **Fax:** *01344-876546.*

Windsor Arts Centre
The Old Court, St. Leonard's Road, Windsor, SL4 3DB.
Tel: *01753-859421.*

Bournemouth

BOURNEMOUTH

Riddetts of Bournemouth
26 Richmond Hill, Bournemouth BH2 6EJ.
Tel: *01202-555686.*

Russell-Cotes Art Gallery and Museum *PS*
East Cliff, Bournemouth BH1 3AA.
Tel: *01202-451800.* **Fax:** *01202-451851.*
Email *enquiries@russell-cotes.demon.co.uk*
Ws *To be announced soon.*
Opening times: *Tues-Sun 10-5.*
Personnel: *Senior Arts Officer:* Victoria Pirie. *Visual Arts Officer:* Mark Bills.
The Russell-Cotes Art Gallery and Museum houses an important collection of Victorian, Edwardian, Modern and Contemporary British and European fine art, and excellent decorative art, sculpture and ethnographic collections relevant to the original Victorian and Edwardian buildings. A distinguished group of contemporary craft and sculpture commissions is housed in the award-winning new museum extension and beautifully restored gardens. A highly regarded exhibition programme of contemporary and 19th Century fine art, and crafts is also held throughout the year. The Museum is closed for building work until Autumn 1998 when the new extension re-opens with the launch of the Craft Café and 1999 for East Cliff Hall and the Art Galleries.
Services and Facilities:
Art Consultancy. Art for Offices. Café. Commissioning Service. Disabled Access. Friends/Society. Guided Tours. Lectures. Museum Shop. Workshop Facilities.

TZB Southbourne Gallery *C*
2 Carbery Row, (Southbourne Road), Bournemouth BH6 3QR.
Tel: *01202-426967.*

Buckinghamshire

AYLESBURY

Buckinghamshire Art Gallery County Museum *PS*
Church Street, Aylesbury, HP20 2QP.
Tel: *01296-331441.* **Fax:** *01296-334884.*
Email *prussell@buckscc.gov.uk*
Opening times: *Mon-Sat 10-5, Sun 2-5.*
Nearest Station: *BR: Aylesbury.*
Personnel: *Head of Museum Service:* Alan Knox. *Exhibitions Officer:* Susanne Anderegg.
Voted Joint Museum of the Year, 1996. Awarded Special Commendation for 1997 European Museum of the Year. The Buckinghamshire County Museum opened in October 1995. As part of a multi-million pound redevelopment, a suite of exhibition galleries were added to show the best in regional, national and international art, craft, design and photography. A range of major exhibitions is held supplemented by a series of small, theme-based shows occasionally focusing on works from the collections. Educational events include workshops, lectures and talks - school packs and teacher oriented events are organised regularly. There is a small entrance charge to the museum. The gallery holds selling exhibitions of Buckinghamshire artists.
Services and Facilities:
Bookshop. Café. Disabled Access. Friends/Society. Guided Tours. Lectures. Museum Shop. Workshop Facilities.
Work Stocked and Sold:
App. Cer. Cra. Jew. Pa. Pr.
Price range: £50 - £3,500.

Discerning Collections, The Gallery *C*
Baldways Close, Wingrave, Aylesbury, HP22 4PB.
Tel: *01296-681471.* **Fax:** *01296-682869.*

Queen Park Arts Centre Gallery
Queens Park Road, Aylesbury, HP21 7RT.
Tel: *01296-243325.*

Waddesdon Manor - The Rothschild Collection
Waddesdon, Aylesbury, HP18 0JH.
Tel: *Recorded message:* *01296-651211,*

Booking Office: 01296-651226.
Fax: *01296-651142.*
Opening times: *Gardens, Aviary, Restaurant and Shops: Wed 3 March-Fri 24 Dec, Wed-Sun & Bank Holiday Mondays 10-5. House (including Wine Cellars): Thur 1 April-Sun 31 Oct, Thur-Sun, Bank Holiday Mondays & Weds in July & Aug 11-4. (Recommended last admission 2.30). Bachelors' Wing open Thur & Fri, & Weds in July & Aug 11-4 (access cannot be guaranteed.*
Waddesdon Manor won the Museum of the Year and Best National Trust Property awards in 1997 & England for Excellence Silver Award 1998. This French Renaissance-style château was built (1874-89) for Baron Ferdinand de Rothschild to display his vast collection of works of art. The Collection includes French Royal furniture, Savonnerie carpets and Sèvres porcelain as well as important portraits by Gainsborough and Reynolds and works by Dutch and Flemish masters of the 17th century. The formal gardens, parkland, Rococo-style aviary, wine cellars, shops and fully licensed restaurant are also open to the public. Lectures, garden workshops and special events take place throughout the year.
Services and Facilities:
Disabled Access. Guided Tours. Lectures. Museum Shop. Parking. Restaurant. Shop.

MARLOW

David Messum Fine Art
Lordswood, Marlow, SL7 2QS.

MILTON KEYNES

Arts Workshop Trust Ltd
The Barn Office, The Courtyard, Milton Keynes, MK14 5DZ.
Tel: *01908-663966.*

Fenny Lodge Gallery C
Simpson Road, Fenny Stratford, Bletchley, Milton Keynes, MK1 1BD.
Tel: *01908-835600 / 642207.*
Fax: *01908-647840.*

Milton Keynes Craft Guild C
The National Hockey Stadium, Silbury Boulevard, Central Milton Keynes, MK9 1HA.
Tel: *01908-694764.*

Stantonbury Gallery
Stantonbury Campus, Milton Keynes,
Tel: *01908-605536.*

WINGRAVE

The Gallery
2 Baldways Close, Wingrave, HP22 4PB.
Tel: *01296-681471.* **Fax:** *01296-682869.*

Hampshire

ALRESFORD

Alresford Gallery C
36 West Street, Alresford, SO24 9AU
Tel: *01962-735286.* **Fax:** *01962-735295.*

Candover Gallery C
22 West Street, Alresford, SO24 9AE.
Tel: *01962-733200.*

ALTON

Allen Gallery C
(Hampshire County Museums Service), 10-12 Church Street, Alton, GU34 2BW.
Tel: *01420-82802.*

ANDOVER

Andover Museum P
(Hampshire County Museums Service), 6 Church Close, Andover, SP10 1DP.
Tel: *01264-366283.*

BASINGSTOKE

Willis Museum and Art Gallery P
Market Place, Basingstoke, RG21 1QD.
Tel: *01256-465902.*

CHRISTCHURCH

Red House Museum and Art Gallery P
(Hampshire County Museums Service), Quay Road, Christchurch, BH23 1BU.
Tel: *01202-482860.*

EASTLEIGH

Eastleigh Museum P
25 High Street, Eastleigh, SO5 5LF.
Tel: *01703-643026.*

GOSPORT

Gosport Museum P
Walpole Road, Gosport, PO12 1LQ.
Tel: *01705-588035.*

HAVANT

Havant Museum P
East Street, Havant, PO9 1BS.
Tel: *01705-451155.*

Old Town Hall Arts Centre
East Street, Havant,

NEW ALRESFORD

Hitchcocks
11 East Street, New Alresford,
Tel: *01962-734762.*

PETERSFIELD

Academy Arts Centre C
Winton Road, Petersfield, GU32 3HA.
Tel: *01730-261624.* **Fax:** *01730-231499.*
Email *NIXY@COMPUSERVE.COM*
Opening times: *Mon-Sat 9-5.30.*
Nearest Station: *Petersfield.*
Personnel: *Gallery Director:* Nick Yellop. *Art Centre Manager:* Geoff Harris. *Exhibition Administrator:* Wendy Drake.
A recently expanded centre for the arts close to Petersfield town centre. Academy Art Centre comprises one of the largest artists materials suppliers in the south of England. Services include a bespoke picture framing department where decades of experience come together with extensive ranges of mouldings and mounts.
Our Contemporary Art Gallery specialises in original works of art, and provides Art Consultancy to Commerce and Industry for selection of suitable works of art for offices and reception areas. Further expansion of the Academy Art Centre in 1999 will herald an inspiring start to the millennium for the artists in Hampshire, Surrey and West Sussex.
Services and Facilities:
Art for Offices. Commissioning Service. Framing. Gallery space for hire. Parking. Shop.

PORTSMOUTH

Aspex Gallery
27 Brougham Road, Southsea, Portsmouth, PO5 4PA.
Tel: *01705-812121.*

Mountbatten Gallery
Guildhall Square, Portsmouth, PO1 2AD.
Tel: *01705-827261.*

Portsmouth City Museum & Records Office P
Museum Road, Portsmouth, PO1 2LJ.
Tel: *01705-827261.*
Email *xpcclsde@hants.gov.uk*
Ws *http://www.xpcclsde@hants.gov.uk*
Opening times: *Daily 10-5.30. last ticket 5.00. (closed 24-26 Dec) Free Admission.*
Displays of furniture and decorative art shown in a series of local history period room settings from 17th century to the 1950's. Local topographical paintings. Collection of 20th c. paintings, prints and sculpture shown in a new Fine and Decorative Art Gallery. Programme of regular changing exhibitions. Record Office: Contains official records of City of Portsmouth from 14th century. Collection of photographs, maps and postcards. Museum shop selling wide range of publications and gifts including contemporary craft work. Gardens/grounds, Corporate Art Lease Scheme.
Services and Facilities:
Bookshop. Disabled Access. Friends/Society. Lectures. Museum Shop. Parking. Shop.

RINGWOOD

Bettles Gallery C
80 Christchurch Road, Ringwood, BH24 1DR.
Tel: *01425-470410.* **Fax:** *01425-479002.*
Opening times: *Tues-Fri 10-5, Sat 10-1.*
Personnel: *Directors:* Gill Bettle, Roger Bettle.

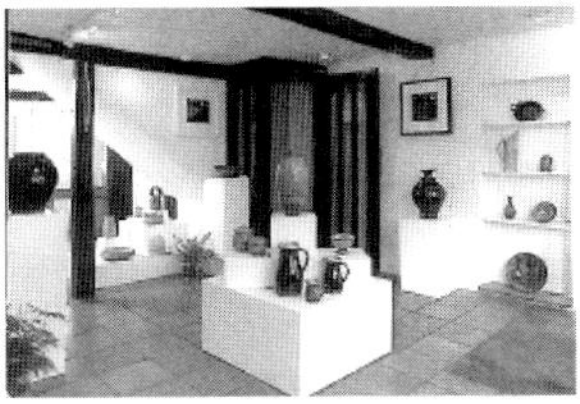

A small privately owned gallery specialising in the exhibition and sale of contemporary

ceramics and paintings in a 300-year-old building on the outskirts of Ringwood, which borders the New Forest. The work of leading potters and artists from around the British Isles is shown in nine annual exhibitions in addition to the comprehensive stock which is constantly changing. The gallery actively promotes the work of new makers alongside that of established craftsmen and artists and is pleased to arrange temporary displays for business venues etc.
Services and Facilities:
Commissioning Service. Parking.
Work Stocked and Sold:
Cer. Jew. Pa.
Price range: £10 - £1,000.
For artists see *Commercial Gallery Artists.*

SELBOURNE

Courtyard Gallery C
The Plestor, High Street, Selbourne, GU34 3JQ.
Tel: *01420-511334.* **Fax:** *01420-346822.*

SOUTHSEA

The Red Gallery C
98 Marmion Road, Southsea, PO5 2BB.
Tel: *01705-793924.*

STOCKBRIDGE

Courcoux & Courcoux Contemporary Art Ltd C
Nomads House, High Street, Stockbridge, SO20 6HE.
Tel: *01264-810717.* **Fax:** *01264-810481.*

Wykeham Galleries
High Street, Stockbridge, SO20 6HE.
Tel: *01264-810364.*
Fax: *01264-810182.*

WINCHESTER

Angelus Gallery
Winchester College, Winchester,
Tel: *01962-864242.*

Guildhall Gallery
The Broadway, Winchester,
Tel: *01962-840222.*

The Jaze Gallery
Great Minster Street, Winchester, SO23 9HA.
Tel: *01962-877601.*

Winchester Contemporary Art
3a Minster Street, Winchester, SO23 9HA.
Tel: *01962-877601.*

The Winchester Gallery
Park Avenue, Winchester, SO23 8DL.
Tel: *01962-852500.*

Isle of Wight

NEWPORT

The Quay Arts Centre
Sea Street, Newport, PO30 5BD.
Tel: *01983-528825.*

Seely Gallery
Lord Louis Library, Newport, PO30 1LL.
Tel: *01983-527655.*

RYDE

Ryde Library Gallery
George Street, Ryde, PO33 2JE.
Tel: *01983-62170.*

Oxfordshire

BAMPTON

Bampton Arts Centre
(West Oxfordshire Arts Association), Town Hall, Bampton,
Tel: *01993-850137.*

BANBURY

Banbury Museum P
8 Horsefair, Banbury, OX16 0AA.
Tel: *01295-259855.*

CHIPPING NORTON

Brian Sinfield Gallery C
150 High Street, Burford, OX18 4QU.
Tel: *01993-824464 / 830886.*
Fax: *01993-830707 / 824525.*
Email *brian@sinfieldg.freeserve.co.uk*
Opening times: *Tue-Sat 9.30-1, 2-5.30. (Mondays by appointment).*
Nearest Station: *Charlbury.*
Personnel: Brian Sinfield.
Ingrid Levrincova.
Established 1972. Mainly traditional contemporary and earlier 20th century paintings, some bronzes. Up to 8 exhibitions a year, usually accompanied by catalogues. Artists include Fred Cuming, Andrew Hemingway, Richard Smith, Diana Armfield, Sally Arnup, Olive Wootton, Sue Ryder, Jacqueline Williams, Don Cordery, P.J. Crook, Len Tabner, Joseph Herman, John Ward. Artists invited to send photographs.
Work Stocked and Sold:
Pa. Sc.
Price range: £400 - £15,000.
For artists see *Commercial Gallery Artists.*

Manor House Gallery C
West Street, Chipping Norton, OX7 5LH.
Tel: *01608-642620.* **Fax:** *01608-642240.*

The Theatre Gallery
2 Spring Street, Chipping Norton, OX7 4NL.
Tel: *01608-2349.*

GORING-ON-THAMES

Goring Mill Gallery C
Lock Approach, Goring-on-Thames, RG8 9AD.
Tel: *01491-875030.* **Fax:** *01491-872519.*
Opening times: *April-Dec Wed-Fri 10-4, Sat, Sun & Bank Hols 10-5. Jan-Mar Wed-Sun 10-4.*
Nearest Station: *Goring & Streatley.*
Personnel: Ron Bridle.
Original art and craftwork in a beautiful riverside setting. Part of a picturesque and historic Water Mill, recorded in the Domesday Book and painted by Turner, Goring Mill Gallery specialises in original work of only the most talented regional artists and craftspeople. Over 500 paintings, ceramics, sculptures and other craftworks by over forty selected professional and recreational artists. Most two

GORING MILL GALLERY

dimensional work is 'representational' art with an emphasis on atmospheric landscapes and riverscapes of the Thames Valley and surrounding countryside. Sensible prices between £50 and £1000.
Services offered include a commissioning service (portraits of people, animals and houses), craftwork commissions and bespoke framing.
Services and Facilities:
Art for Offices. Commissioning Service. Craftshop. Framing. Gallery space for hire.
Work Stocked and Sold:
Cer. Cra. Dec. Dr. Gla. Pa. Sc. Wd.
Price range: £50 - £1,000.
For artists see *Commercial Gallery Artists.*

HENLEY-ON-THAMES

Barn Galleries
Aston, Henley-on-Thames, RG9 3DX.
Tel: *01491-577786.* **Fax:** *01491-577786.*

Bohun Gallery C
15 Reading Road, Henley-on-Thames, RG9 1AB.
Tel: *01491-576228.* **Fax:** *01491-576228.*

Luxters Fine Art
Old Luxters, Hamleden, Henley-on-Thames, RG9 6JW.
Tel: *01491-638816.*

River and Rowing Museum
Mill Meadows, Henley-on-Thames, RG9 1BF.
Tel: *01491-415600.*

OXFORD

Ashmolean Museum of Art and Archaeology P
Beaumont Street, Oxford, OX1 2PH.
Tel: *01865-278000.* **Fax:** *01865-278018.*
Email *jonathan.moffett@ashmus.ox.ac.uk*
Ws *http://www.ashmol.ox.ac.uk/*
Opening times: *Tue-Sat 10-4, Sun 2-4. Admission Free.*
Nearest Station: *Oxford.*
Personnel: *Acting Director:* Dr P.R.S. Moorey.

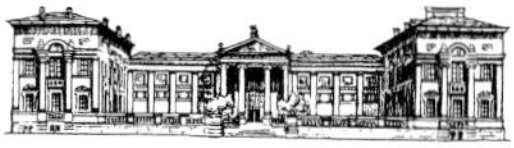

Founded 1683. The oldest Museum in the UK and the largest Gallery in Oxfordshire. Houses the University of Oxford's collections of European and Oriental fine and applied art; artifacts from Ancient Egypt, Greece and Rome, and northern Europe from the Dark

Ab Artists' Books **App** Applied Art **Cer** Ceramics **Cra** Crafts **Dec** Decorative **Dr** Drawing **Fur** Furniture

Ages up to the end of the Middle Ages; and Numismatics. Paintings range from the early Italian Masters through to the Pre-Raphaelites and French Impressionists. Major collections of Majolica, English Ceramics, European Silver. Temporary exhibitions and loan exhibitions. Education Service.
Services and Facilities:
Bookshop. Café. Disabled Access. Friends/Society. Guided Tours. Lectures. Museum Shop. Shop.
Work Stocked and Sold:
Pr.

Brampton Arts Centre
West Oxfordshire Arts Association, Town Hall, Brampton, Oxford,
Tel: *01973-85013??.*

Christ Church Picture Gallery *PS*
Christ Church, Oxford, OX1 1DP.
Tel: *01865-276172.* **Fax:** *01865-202429.*
Email *dennis.harrington@christ-church.ox.ac.uk*
Ws *http://www.chch.ox.ac.uk*
Opening times: *Mon-Fri 10.30-1 and 2-4.30, Sun 1-4.30, open until 5.30 Easter to Sept. Closed until 7th June 1999.*
Personnel: Christopher Baker. Brigid Cleaver.
Collection of Old Master paintings and drawings displayed in a modern gallery. Quattrocento Masters; works by Tintoretto, Veronese, the Carracci, Frans Hals and Van Dyck. Changing displays in the print room of works selected from over 2000 Old Master drawings and prints. Special temporary exhibitions. Guided tours each Thursday 2.15-3 and by advance request.
Services and Facilities:
Guided Tours. Museum Shop.

Elizabeth Harvey-Lee - Original Prints c.1490 - c.1940. *C*
1 West Cottages, Middle Aston Road, North Aston, Oxford, OX6 3QB.
Tel: *01869-347164.* **Fax:** *01869-347956.*

Museum of Modern Art *P*
30 Pembroke Street, Oxford, OX1 1BP.
Tel: *Recorded information : 01865-728608, Office 01865-722733.*
Fax: *Office: 01865-722573.*

Museum of Oxford *P*
St. Aldates, Oxford,
Tel: *01865-815539.*

Oxford Gallery *C*
23 High Street, Oxford, OX1 4AH.
Tel: *01865-242731.*

Stables Gallery
Green College, Woodstock Road, Oxford, OX2 6HG. **Tel:** *01865-274770.*

Wiseman Gallery
40/41 South Parade, Summertown, Oxford, OX2 7JZ.

WALLINGFORD

Wallingford Arts Centre
Kinecroft, Goldsmith Lane, Wallingford,
Tel: *01753-859336.*

WOODSTOCK

Objet D'Art
1 Market Place, Woodstock, OX20 1SY.
Tel: *01993-811819.*

Poole

POOLE

Poole Arts Centre *PS*
Seldown Gallery, Kingland Road, Poole BH15 1UG.
Tel: *01202-665334.*
Opening times: *10-5.*
Nearest Station: *Poole.*
Personnel: *Programme Director:* Alistair Wilkinson.

Poole**arts**centre

Gallery space (30 Linear metres) available on a low commission basis to artists wishing to exhibit photography or new media work. Please send exhibition proposals including images.
Services and Facilities:
Bar. Café. Gallery space for hire. Restaurant.

Waterfront Museum *P*
High Street, Old Town, Poole BH15 1BW.
Tel: *01202-683138.*

Southampton

SOUTHAMPTON

Beatrice Royal Art Gallery,
Nightingale Avenue, Eastleigh, Southampton SO5 3JJ.
Tel: *01703-610592.* **Fax:** *01703-411427.*

The First Gallery
1 Burnham Chase, Bitterne, Southampton S018 5DG.
Tel: *01703-462723.*

On Line Gallery *C*
76 Bedford Place, Southampton SO15 2DF.
Tel: *01703-330660.* **Fax:** *01703-330660.*

Swindon

SWINDON

Swindon Museum & Art Gallery *P*
Bath Road, Swindon SN1 4BA.
Tel: *01793-493181.* **Fax:** *01793-541685.*

Wiltshire

CALNE

Bowood House
Calne, SN11 0LZ.
Tel: *01249-812102.*

DEVIZES

The Gallery
Handel House, Sidmouth Street, Devizes, SN8 1JQ. **Tel:** *01672-52860.*

Garton & Co. *C*
Roundway House, Devizes, SN10 2EG.
Tel: *01380-729624.*

LACOCK

Fox Talbot Museum of Photography *PS*
Lacock, SN15 2LG.
Tel: *01249-730459.* **Fax:** *01249-830472.*

MARLBOROUGH

The Antique & Book Collector *C*
Katharine House, The Parade, Marlborough, SN8 1NE. **Tel:** *01672-514040.*
Opening times: *Mon-Sat 9.45-5.30.*
Nearest Station: *Swindon.*
Personnel: *Director:* Christopher Gange.

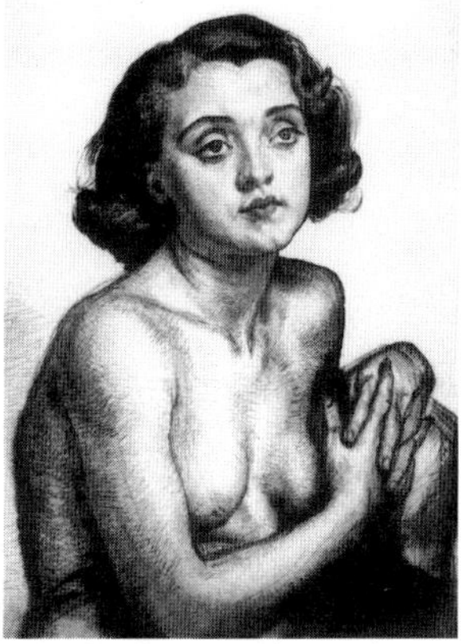

Modern British prints and drawings always in stock: Eric Gill, David Jones, Laura Knight, F.L. Griggs, H. Gaudier-Brzeska, Orovida Pissarro, Stanley Spencer, Duncan Grant, Roger Hilton, Barbara Jones, Robin Tanner, Keith Vaughan, Eric Fraser, Gertrude Hermes and others.
Exhibitions twice a year in this field. We also deal in good quality unusual antiques and antiquities, as well as fine second hand and rare books.
Services and Facilities:
Bookshop.
Work Stocked and Sold:
Ab. Dr. Pa. Pr.
Price range: £75 - £2,000.
For artists see *Commercial Gallery Artists.*

Bajazzo Gallery
8 St. Martins, Marlborough, SN8 1AR.
Tel: *01672-512860.*

Marlborough Studio Art Gallery
4 Hughenden Yard, High Street, Marlborough, SN8 1LT.
Tel: *01672-514848.*

SALISBURY

The Jerram Gallery C
7 St. John Street, Salisbury, SP1 2SB.
Tel: *01722-412310.* **Fax:** *01722-323577.*
Email *jerramgal@aol.com*
Opening times: *Tues-Sat.*
Nearest Station: *Salisbury (main line)*

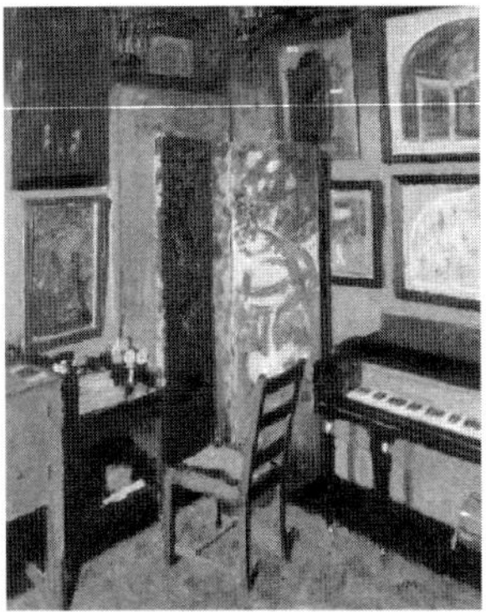

Primarily British paintings and watercolours 1850-1950. Contemporary artists - pictures and sculpture. Small selection of wood engraving. Six exhibitions held per year, contemporary and earlier. Also exhibit at London fairs. Situated just outside the Cathedral Close.
Services and Facilities:
Art Consultancy. Art for Offices. Commissioning Service. Restoration.
Work Stocked and Sold:
Dr. Pa. Sc.
Price range: £75 - £10,000.
For artists see *Commercial Gallery Artists.*

Margaret Turner Gallery
15 St. Ann's Street, Salisbury, SP1 2DP.
Tel: *01722-333501.*

Salisbury Arts Centre
Bedwin Street, Salisbury, SP1 3UT.
Tel: *01722-321744.*

South East

Brighton & Hove

BRIGHTON

Barlow Collection of Chinese Art P
University Library, University of Sussex, Falmer, Brighton, BN1 9QE. **Tel:** *01273-606755.*

Brighton Museum and Art Gallery PS
Church Street, Brighton, BN1 1UE.
Tel: *01273-603005/202900/290900.*
Fax: *01273-779108.*

First Light
3 Nile Street, Brighton, BN1 1HW.
Tel: *01273-327344.*

Gardner Centre Gallery C
University of Sussex, Falmer, Brighton, BN1 9RA.
Tel: *01273-685447.*
Fax: *01273-678551.*

Hugo Barclay C
7 East Street, Brighton, BN1 1HP
Tel: *01273-321694.*
Fax: *01273-725959.*

Phoenix Gallery
10-14 Waterloo Place, Brighton, BN2 2NB.
Tel: *01273-603700.*

Preston Manor P
Preston Park, Brighton, BN1 6SD.
Tel: *01273-292770.*

Royal Pavilion P
Pavilion Buildings, Brighton, BN1 1EE.
Tel: *01273-290900.*
Fax: *01273-292871.*

University of Brighton Gallery
Grand Parade, Brighton, BN2 2JU.
Tel: *01273-643012.*
Fax: *01273-643128.*

HOVE

Hove Museum & Art Gallery P
19 New Church Road, Hove, BN3 4AB.
Tel: *01273-290200.*
Fax: *01273-292827.*

Kent

CANTERBURY

Drew Gallery
16 Best Lane, Canterbury, CT1 2JB.
Tel: *01227-458759.*

The Herbert Read Gallery
KIAD at Canterbury, New Dover Road, Canterbury, CT1 3AN.
Tel: *01227-769371 ext 240.*
Fax: *01227-451320.*

Nevill Gallery C
43 St. Peter's Street, Canterbury, CT1 2BG.
Tel: *01227-765291.*
Ws *http://www.nevillgallery.com*
Opening times: *Mon-Sat 10-5.*
Nearest Station: *Canterbury.*
Contemporary British and European paintings:- oils, watercolours, etchings and limited edition prints. Established in 1969 we have several shows a year where we devote the whole of the ground floor to the work of one artist. Readers who wish to be informed of future shows should forward their name and address to the Nevill Gallery.

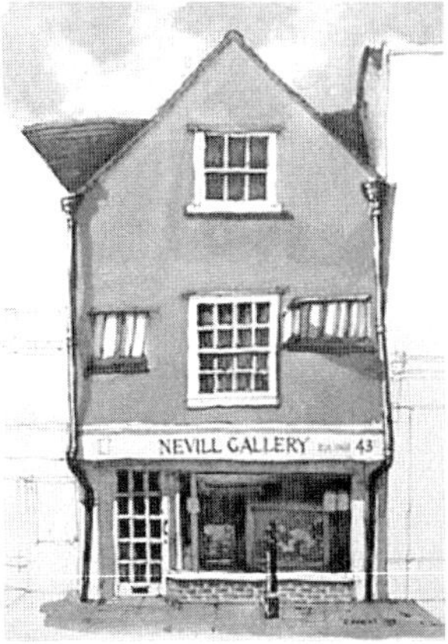

Services and Facilities:
Framing. Restoration.
Work Stocked and Sold:
Pa. Pr.
For artists see *Commercial Gallery Artists.*

Royal Museum & Art Gallery P
High Street, Canterbury, CT1 2JE.
Tel: *01227-452747.*

FOLKESTONE

Folkestone Museum P
2 Grace Hill, Folkestone, CT20 1HD.
Tel: *01303-850123.*
Fax: *01303-242907.*

Metropole Arts Centre PS
The Leas, Folkestone, CT20 2LS.
Tel: *01303-255070.*
Fax: *01303-244706.*
Opening times:
Apr-Oct: Mon-Sat 10-5, Sun 2.30-5; Nov-Mar: Tue-Sat 10-4, Sun 2.30-5.
Personnel: *Director:* Ann Fearey.
10 major exhibitions per year with an emphasis on contemporary painting, photography and sculpture (admission free). The Arts Centre programmes include a Children's Festival (April), Kent Literature Festival (September), Classical Concert Series, Annual Short Story Writing Competition (send SAE for entry form from Feb '99), Art History Lectures and one-off events throughout the year. Sales area and coffee shop. Free parking on The Leas.
Services and Facilities:
Café. Craftshop. Friends/Society. Lectures. Parking.
Work Stocked and Sold:
Cer. Pa.
Price range: £5 - £3,000.

GILLINGHAM

Gillingham Library Gallery
High Street, Gillingham, ME7 1BG.
Tel: *01634-281066.*
Fax: *01634-855814.*

Ab Artists' Books **App** Applied Art **Cer** Ceramics **Cra** Crafts **Dec** Decorative **Dr** Drawing **Fur** Furniture

Space Frame Gallery C
Gillingham Adult Education Centre Green Street, Gillingham, ME7 1XA.
Tel: *01634-856439.*

MAIDSTONE

Bearsted Gallery
The Green, Bearsted, Maidstone, ME14 4DN.
Tel: *01622-744130.*

The Gallery
KIAD at Maidstone, Oakwood Park, Maidstone, ME16 8AG.
Tel: *01622-757286.* **Fax:** *01622-692003.*

Graham Clarke C
White Cottage, Green Lane, Boughton Monchelsea, Maidstone, ME17 4LF.
Tel: *01622-743938.* **Fax:** *01622-747229.*
Opening times: *Open by appointment.*
Personnel: Dawn Masters.
Graham Clarke's 'Up The Garden Studio' is open by appointment. Graham Clarke the artist, writer and humorist, one of Britain's most popular and best-selling printmakers, has created some five hundred images of English rural life and history, and of the Englishman's view of Europe. He has been widely exhibited in Britain and abroad, examples of his work being held by royal, public and private collections in addition to those hanging on the walls of homes all over the world. His original etchings which are produced entirely by hand using traditional processes in strictly limited editions are available together with his watercolours, books, and greetings cards. Price lists and illustrations of recent images will be sent on request.
Work Stocked and Sold:
Ab. Dr. Pa. Pr.
Price range: £50 - £2,000.
For artists see *Commercial Gallery Artists.*

Maidstone Library Gallery
St. Faith's Street, Maidstone, ME14 1LH.
Tel: *01622-752344.* **Fax:** *01622-754980.*

RAINHAM

Christopher Turner C
4 Caledonian Court, Rainham, ME8 0DG.
Tel: *01634-231465.*
Fax: *01634-231465.*

RAMSGATE

Addington Street Studio & Gallery
49 Addington Street, Ramsgate, CT11 9JJ.
Tel: *084-359 7405.*

Ramsgate Library Gallery
Guildford Lawn, Ramsgate, CT11 9AY.
Tel: *01843-593532.*
Fax: *01843-293015.*

ROCHESTER

The Gallery
KIAD at Rochester, Fort Pitt, Rochester, ME1 1DZ.
Tel: *01634-830022.*
Fax: *01634-829461.*

Medway Towns Galleries PS
c/o Head of Arts, Civic Centre, Strood, Rochester, ME20 4AW. **Tel:** *01634-727777.*

Strood Library Gallery
32 Bryant Road, Strood, Rochester, ME2 3EP.
Tel: *01634-718161.* **Fax:** *01634-718161.*

SANDWICH

The Hunt Gallery C
33 Strand Street, Sandwich, CT13 9DS.
Tel: *01304-612792 or 01227-722287.*
Fax: *01227-721969.*
Email *www.huntgallery@hotmail.com*
Ws *http://www.thehuntgallery.com*
Opening times: *By appointment.*
Personnel: *Director:* Rosemary Hunt.

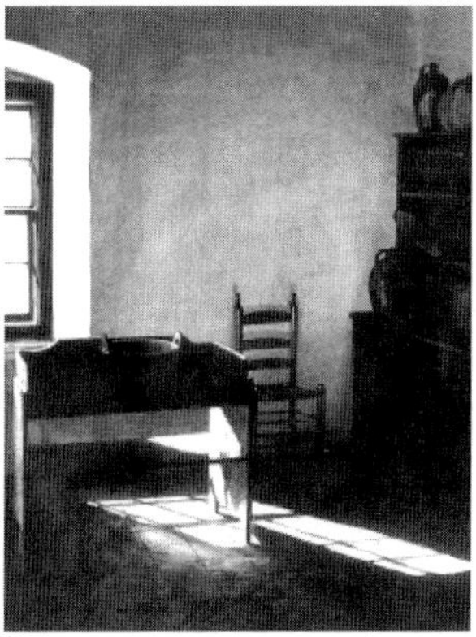

We have a permanent but constantly changing exhibition of work by the contemporary English painter Michael John Hunt. Topographical, architectural and interior paintings with an emphasis on accurate draughtsmanship.
Work Stocked and Sold:
Pa.
Price range: £100 - £10,000.
For artists see *Commercial Gallery Artists.*

SEVENOAKS

Bank Street Gallery
3-5 Bank Street, Sevenoaks, TN13 1UW.
Tel: *01732-458063.*

Pratt Contemporary Art/Pratt Editions C
The Gallery, Ightham, Sevenoaks, TN15 9HH.
Tel: *01732-882326/884417.*
Fax: *01732-885502.*
Opening times: *Gallery open seven days a week by appointment.*
Nearest Station: *Charing Cross to Sevenoaks or Victoria to Borough Green.*
Personnel: *Directors:* Bernard Pratt, Susan Pratt.
Established 1976. Printers and publishers of original limited edition prints (see Print Publishers and Dealers) working directly with artists: screenprints, etchings, drypoints, woodcuts, monotypes, artists' books. Proofing and editioning service. Sculpture, Paintings and Drawings by artists represented. Artists include: Ana Maria Pacheco, Seyed Edalatpour, Julian Grater, Akram Rahmanzadeh, Kristian Krokfors, Mick Rooney RA, Michael Kenny RA, Marcus Rees Roberts, Denise Walker, Leonam Nogueira Fleury, Richard Davies. Print Studios.

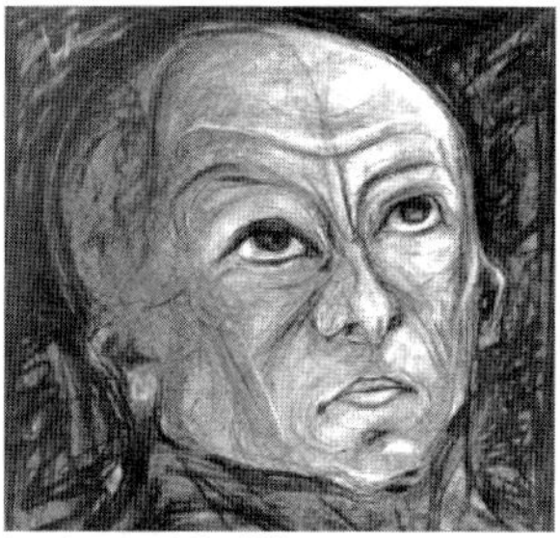

Services and Facilities:
Art Consultancy. Commissioning Service. Framing.
Work Stocked and Sold:
Ab. Dr. Pa. Pr. Sc.
Price range: £50 - £150,000.
For artists see *Commercial Gallery Artists.*

SIDCUP

H.Arts C
39 Sidcup Hill, Sidcup, DA14 6HJ.
Tel: *0181-308 9290.* **Fax:** *0181-308 9290.*
Opening times: *Mon-Sat 9.30-5.*
Nearest Station: *Sidcup.*
Personnel: *Owner:* Tony Hart.

H.ARTS

The gallery displays paintings and sculpture by the owner and a growing number of young and interesting artists. The woodcarvers art is headed up by a permanent display of works by the award winning artists Bill Prickett and others. H. Arts produce and display limited edition. Pieces taken from the original woodcarvings. Commissions for pictures, sculpture and woodcarving are welcome.
Services and Facilities:
Art Consultancy. Commissioning Service. Framing.
Work Stocked and Sold:
Dec. Dr. Pa. Sc. Wd.
Price range: £30 - £1,000.
For artists see *Commercial Gallery Artists.*

TUNBRIDGE WELLS

Fairfax Gallery C
23 The Pantiles, Tunbridge Wells, TN2 5TD.
Tel: *01892-525525.* **Fax:** *01892-525525.*

Nicholas Bowlby
9 Castle Street, Tunbridge Wells, TN1 1XJ.
Tel: *01892-510880.* **Fax:** *01892-510880.*

Squeaky Door
1 The Pantiles, Tunbridge Wells, TN2 5TD.
Tel: *01892-518024.*

Trinity Gallery
Church Road, Tunbridge Wells, TN1 1JP.
Tel: *01892-525111.* **Fax:** *01892-525112.*

Tunbridge Wells Museum & Art Gallery *P*
Civic Centre, Mount Pleasant, Tunbridge Wells, TN1 1JN.
Tel: *01892-526121 / 547221.*
Fax: *01892-534227.*

WHITSTABLE

Whitstable Museum & Art Gallery *P*
Oxford Street, Whitstable, CT5 1DB.
Tel: *01227-276998.* **Fax:** *01227-772379.*

Surrey

CHOBHAM

The Bank Gallery *C*
73-75 High Street, Chobham, GU24 8AF.
Tel: *01276-857369.*

EAST MOLESEY

The Molesey Gallery *C*
46 Walton Road, East Molesey, KT8 ODQ.
Tel: *0181-979 6464 or 0181-941 2706.*

FARNHAM

CCA Galleries *C*
13 Lion and Lamb Yard, West Street, Farnham, GU9 7LL.
Tel: *01252-722231.* **Fax:** *01252-733336.*
Opening times: *Mon-Sat 9-5.30.*
Leading publishers of limited edition silkscreens, etchings and lithographs. Catalogue of new publications produced twice a year. Exciting programme. Artists include Donald Hamilton-Fraser, Annora Spence, Sir Terry Frost, Richard Spare.
Services and Facilities:
Framing.
Work Stocked and Sold:
Cra. Pa. Pr.
Price range: £45 - £3,500.

Farnham Maltings Gallery
Bridge Square, Farnham, GU9 7QR.
Tel: *01252-713637.* **Fax:** *01252-718177.*

Foyer Gallery / James Hockey Gallery *PS*
Surrey Institute of Art and Design, Falkner Road, Farnham, GU9 7DS.
Tel: *01252-892668 / 01252-892646.*
Fax: *01252-892667.*
Email *ckapteijn@surrart.ac.uk*
Ws *http://www.surrart.ac.uk*
Opening times: *Foyer Gallery daily 9.30-5. James Hockey Gallery daily 10-4.30, Sat 10-4, Sun closed.*
Nearest Station: *Farnham.*
Personnel: *Galleries Co-ordinator:* Christine Kapteijn.
The Foyer Gallery and James Hockey Gallery are operated as public galleries. They are committed to the accessibility of the visual arts to all, including those with special needs. The Galleries show a wide range of exhibitions, including art, craft, design and related media, both from Britain and from abroad. They aim to promote work of lasting importance, which will contribute to the public and professional debate. Many of the educational events organised in conjunction with the exhibitions programme, are open to a broad audience from the community, fostering the audience and arts professionals of the future.
Services and Facilities:
Art for Offices. Disabled Access. Guided Tours. Lectures. Parking. Restaurant.

New Ashgate Gallery *C*
Wagon Yard, Lower Church Lane, Downing Street, Farnham, GU9 7PS.
Tel: *01252-713208.*
Fax: *01252-737398.*
Email *gallery@newashgate.datanet.co.uk*
Opening times: *Mon-Sat 10-5.*
Nearest Station: *Farnham.*
Personnel: *Director:* Susan Szabanowicz. *Manager:* Joanne Barber.

New Ashgate Gallery

The gallery exhibits work by well-established professional contemporary artists and crafts people, whilst also promoting emerging younger talents. Monthly changing exhibitions, and a large stock of paintings, prints, sculpture, ceramics, jewellery, glass, wood textiles.
Services and Facilities:
Art Consultancy. Art for Offices. Commissioning Service. Craftshop. Disabled Access. Framing. Friends/Society. Lectures. Parking. Restoration. Shop.
Work Stocked and Sold:
App. Cer. Cra. Dr. Fur. Gla. Jew. Pa. Pr. Sc. Tx. Wd.
Price range: £30 - £5,000.
For artists see *Commercial Gallery Artists.*

GODALMING

Godalming Museum *P*
109a High Street, Godalming, GU7 1AQ.
Tel: *01483-426510.*

GOMSHALL

Gomshall Gallery *PS*
Station Road, Gomshall, GU5 9LB.
Tel: *01483-203795.*
Fax: *01483-203282.*

GUILDFORD

Guildford House Gallery
155 High Street, Guildford, GU1 3AJ.
Tel: *01483-444740.*
Fax: *01483-444742.*

Jonleigh Gallery
The Street, Wonersh, Guildford, GU5 0PF.
Tel: *01483-893177.*

KINGSTON UPON THAMES

The Stanley Picker Gallery for the Arts *P*
Kingston University, Middle Mill Island, Knights Park, Kingston upon Thames, KT1 2QJ.
Tel: *0181-547 8074.*
Fax: *0181-547 8068.*

LEATHERHEAD

Studio Art House *C*
16 Church Road, Leatherhead, KT22 8AY.
Tel: *01372-377173.*

NEW MALDEN

Gallery Focus *C*
Unit 2 Apex Tower, 9 High Street, New Malden, KT3 3DQ.
Tel: *0181-336 0761 / 942 9914.*
Fax: *0181-336 2674.*

REDHILL

The Cider House Gallery *C*
Norfolk House, 80 High Street, Bletchingly, Redhill, RH1 4PA.
Tel: *01883-742198.*
Fax: *01883-744014.*

REIGATE

Bourne Gallery *C*
31-33 Lesbourne Road, Reigate, RH2 7JS.
Tel: *01737-241614.*
Fax: *01737-223291.*
Ws *http://www.bournegallery.com*
Opening times: *Tue-Sat 10-5. Closed Mondays & Lunch 1-2pm.*
Nearest Station: *Redhill*
Personnel: *Directors:* John Robertson, Ian Read, Linda Read.
26,000 paintings... that's how many Victorian and traditional pictures we have sold in the past twenty-seven years. A remarkable achievement for a gallery tucked away in a quiet side street of a market town. Today, we continue to stock original works priced from under £200 to over £20,000. If you are looking for a particular artist or would like to join us for a glass of champagne at our next exhibition please write for our brochure now or call in (phone for directions).
Services and Facilities:
Art Consultancy. Art for Offices. Commissioning Service. Restoration. Shop. Valuation.
Work Stocked and Sold:
Dr. Pa.
Price range: £150 - £50,000.
For artists see *Commercial Gallery Artists.*

RICHMOND

Henry Boxer
98 Stuart Court, Richmond Hill, Richmond, TW10 6RJ.
Tel: *0181-948 1633.*
Fax: *0181-948 1633.*

Piano Nobile *C*
26 Richmond Hill, Richmond, TW10 6QX.
Tel: *0181-940 2435.*

VIRGINIA WATER

The Gallery C
13 Station Approach, Virginia Water, GU25 4DP.
Tel: *01344-844460.* **Fax:** *01344-844785.*
Email *Carpathian@btinternet.com*
Ws *http://www1.btwebworld.com/carpathian/*
Opening times: *Wed-Fri 10.30-3.30, Sat 10-6 or later, Sun 12-6.*
Nearest Station: *Virginia Water.*
Personnel: *Directors:* Bryan Forbes, Richard Dolinski, Andrew Dolinski, Peter Nagy, Nanette Forbes.

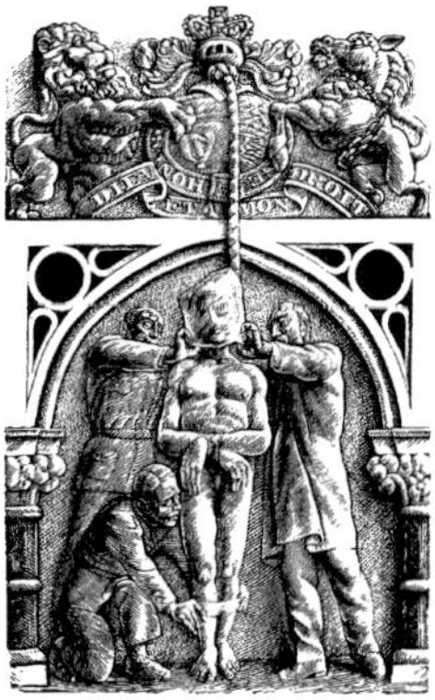

Regular exhibitions by both local and international artists hosted in a unique atmosphere. We cater for traditional and contemporary art in mixed media. Artists can be seen at work in the gallery and commissions are accepted. The Rostrum Library contains rare and limited edition books, art books and fine prints. A bespoke framing service is available. The gallery boasts a working private press producing our own fine limited edition books. Enquiries for commissions are welcomed.
Services and Facilities:
Art for Offices. Bookshop. Commissioning Service. Disabled Access. Framing. Gallery space for hire. Parking. Restoration. Shop. Workshop Facilities.
Work Stocked and Sold:
Ab. Cer. Dec. Dr. Gla. Pa. Ph. Pr. Sc.
Price range: £50 - £6,000.
For artists see *Commercial Gallery Artists.*

WEST BYFLEET

T. P. I. Gallery
32 Station Approach, West Byfleet, KT14 6NF.
Tel: *01932-351733.* **Fax:** *01932-341472.*

WEYBRIDGE

Edward Cross Gallery
128 Oatlands Drive, Weybridge, KT13 9HL.

WOKING

Gallery Knaphill
40 High Street, Knaphill, Woking, GU21 2PY.
Tel: *01483-476230.*

East Sussex

DITCHLING

Ditchling Gallery
30 High Street, Ditchling, BN6 8TA.

EASTBOURNE

Towner Art Gallery and Local Museum PS
Manor Gardens, High Street, Old Town, Eastbourne, BN20 8BB.
Tel: *01323-417961 (Admin.) & 411688 (Info. Service).*
Fax: *01323-648182.*
Email *townergallery@eastbourne.gov.uk*
Opening times: *Tues-Sat 12-5, Sun & Bank Hol. Mon. 2-5. Closed Mon, Good Friday, 24-27th Dec & New Year's Day.*
Personnel: *Head of Cultural Services:* Fiona Robertson. *Arts Administrator:* Sarah Blessington.
Housed in an elegant 18th Century building, the Towner is set in delightful gardens. There is a lively and innovative programme of exhibitions from historical to contemporary art in all media, accompanied by education projects. The art collection includes works by: Joseph Wright of Derby, Picasso, Christopher Wood, Frances Hodgkins, Ivon Hitchens, John Virtue, Estelle Thompson, Tacita Dean and Karen Knorr, a selection of which is always on show and there is a gallery devoted to Eric Ravilious. The South East Arts Collection of Contemporary Art is housed at the Towner.
Services and Facilities:
Disabled Access. Friends/Society. Gallery space for hire. Guided Tours. Lectures. Shop.

HASSOCKS

Ditchling Museum P
Church Lane, Ditchling, Hassocks, BN6 8TB.
Tel: *01273-844744.*

HASTINGS

Hastings Museum and Art Gallery P
Johns Place, Cambridge Road, Hastings, TN38 1ET.
Tel: *01424-721202 / 781155.*
Fax: *01424-781165.*

Riviera Gallery
6 Pelham Arcade, Hastings, TN34 3AE. **Tel:** *01424-427088.*

LEWES

Charleston Gallery C
Charleston Farmhouse, Nr. Firle, Lewes, BN8 6LL.
Tel: *01323-811265/811626.*
Fax: *01323-811628.*

Firle Place
Lewes, BN8 6LP.
Tel: *01273-858188.*

Star Gallery C
Castle Ditch Lane, Lewes, BN7 1YJ.
Tel: *01273-480218.* **Fax:** *01273-488241.*
Opening times: *Mon-Sat 10.30-5.30, closed Suns and Bank Holidays.*
Nearest Station: *Close to the castle and railway station, just off the High Street.*
Personnel: *Director:* Patricia Cooper.

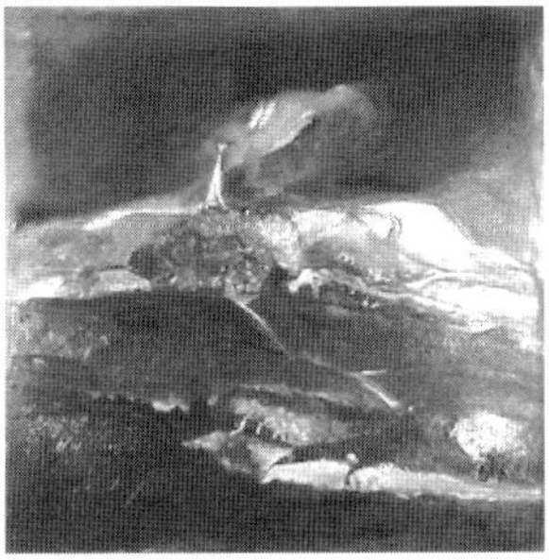

Popular gallery with a reputation for showing British and International contemporary art. The gallery enthusiastically encourages the work of new artists with talent. Six major exhibitions a year plus group shows and summer craft exhibition. Artists showing in 1998 include Henrietta Dubrey, Tom Hammick, Mary Fedden, Mick Rooney RA, William Bowyer RA, Michael Cooper, Anthony Whishaw RA, Harold Mockford, Peter Messer, John Blight, Anne de Geus. Star Gallery is set on the ground floor of the Victorian Star Brewery building amidst artists' and designers' workshops and studios, many of which are open to the public.
Services and Facilities:
Disabled Access. Framing. Gallery space for hire. Restoration. Workshop Facilities.
Work Stocked and Sold:
Cer. Cra. Dr. Gla. Pa. Pr. Sc.
Price range: £50 - £5,000.
For artists see *Commercial Gallery Artists.*

The Workshop C
164 The High Street, Lewes, BN7 1XU.
Tel: *01273-474207.*

RYE

Rye Art Gallery C
Stormont Studio, Ockman Lane, Rye, TN31 7JY.
Tel: *01797-223218.* **Fax:** *01797-225376.*

West Sussex

ARUNDEL

Trinity Art Gallery
18B Tarrant Street, Arundel, BN18 9DJ.
Tel: *01903-883689.*
Fax: *01903-884309.*

BILLINGSHURST

Lanards Gallery C
Okehurst Lane, Billingshurst, RH14 9HR.
Tel: *01403-782692.*

CHICHESTER

Mitre Gallery
Chichester College of Higher Education, College Lane, Chichester, PO19 1PE.
Tel: *01243-816000.*
Fax: *01243-536011.*

Pallant House Gallery Trust
9 North Pallant, Chichester, PO19 1TJ.
Tel: *01243-774557.*
Fax: *01243-536038.*

Re: Pallant House
6 Northlands House, Salthill Road, Chichester, PO19 3PY.

EAST GRINSTEAD

The Antique Print Shop *C*
11 Middle Row, High Street, East Grinstead, RH19 3AX.
Tel: *01342-410501.*

HAYWARDS HEATH

Ashdown Gallery *C*
49-53 Sussex Road, Haywards Heath,
Tel: *01444-412827.*

HORSHAM

Caufold Gallery *C*
Caufold, Horsham, RH
Tel: *01403-864237.*

Christ's Hospital Theatre Foyer *PS*
Christ's Hospital, Horsham, RH13 7LE.
Tel: *01403-252547.*
Fax: *01403-211580.*

Horsham Arts Centre *PS*
North Street, Horsham, RH12 1RL.
Tel: *01403-259708 / 268689.*
Fax: *01403-211502.*
Opening times: *Mon-Sat 10-7, Sun 5-7.*
Nearest Station: *Horsham.*
Personnel: *Visual Art Co-ordinator:* Belinda Holden.

HORSHAM Arts CENTRE

Contemporary art work shown in two exhibition spaces. The programme is made up of invited artists, touring shows, opens and group proposals. Exhibitions usually run in four week periods. An Education Outreach Programme linked to the exhibitions runs for children and adults. In 1998 shows included the following artists: Dan baldwin, Pernille Holm-Mercer, Helen Moon, Chris Smith, David Halliwell, Chris Harrison, Steve Pyke, Francesca Clarke, Catherine Golding.
Services and Facilities:
Bar. Café. Commissioning Service. Parking. Workshop Facilities.
Work Stocked and Sold:
Dr. Pa. Ph. Pr.
Price range: £20 - £5,000.

MIDHURST

Peters Barn Gallery *C*
South Ambersham, Midhurst, GU29 0BX.
Tel: *01798-861388.* **Fax:** *01798-861581.*
Opening times: *By appointment Nov-May 1st, May-Oct Tue-Fri 2-6, Sat, Sun & Bank Hols 11-6.*
Nearest Station: *Chichester, Petersfield, Pulborough, Haslemere - then taxi or bus.*
Personnel: *Directors:* Gabrielle & Annabel.

PETER'S BARN GALLERY

Small very attractive gallery within a large wild garden. Wooded walks by stream and pond. Very peaceful setting. Showing work by known, established and up & coming artists, both inside the barn and out. From the A272 - 3m. East of Midhurst & 3m. West of Petworth, take road opposite the Half Way Bridge Pub. Sign posted to South Ambersham, Graffham & Selham. After 1 mile take first right to South Ambersham & Selham Church. Continue 1 mile, turn right at T-junction in South Ambersham. Peters Barn is 200 yards on the left. From Chichester take A286. Turn right 1/2m out of Cocking to Heyshoff & Graffham. 2m on turn left to Ambersham at the cross roads. Peters Barn on left after 1 mile.
Services and Facilities:
Disabled Access. Parking.
Work Stocked and Sold:
Ab. App. Cer. Dr. Gla. Jew. Pa. Pr. Sc.
Price range: £10 - £7,000.
For artists see *Commercial Gallery Artists.*

WORTHING

Worthing Museum & Art Gallery *P*
Chapel Road, Worthing, BN11 1HP.
Tel: *10903-236552 ext 2526.*
Fax: *01903-236552.*

Eastern

Bedfordshire

BEDFORD

Bedford Central Library Gallery
Harpur Street, Bedford, MK40 1PG.
Tel: *01234-350931.*

Bedford Museum *P*
Castle Lane, Bedford, MK40 3XD.
Tel: *01234-353323.* **Fax:** *01234-214599.*

Cecil Higgins Art Gallery and Museum *P*
Castle Close, Castle Lane, Bedford, MK40 3RP.
Tel: *01234-211222.* **Fax:** *01234-327149.*

The Gatehouse
Foster Hill Road, Bedford, MK41 7TD.
Tel: *01234-355870.*

BIGGLESWADE

Fairfield Gallery
Fairfield House, Biggleswade, SG18 0AA.
Tel: *01767-312176.*

BROMHAM

Bromham Mill Art Gallery *PS*
Bromham Mill, Bridge End, Bromham, MK43 8LP.
Tel: *01234-824330.* **Fax:** *01234-228315.*

LANGFORD

Loggia Gallery
Lansbury, 51a High Street, Langford, SG18 9RU.

LEIGHTON BUZZARD

Leighton Buzzard Theatre
Lake Street, Leighton Buzzard, LU7 8RX.
Tel: *01525-371788.*

LUTON

33 Arts Centre
33-35 Guildford Street, Luton, LU1 2NQ.
Tel: *01582-419 584.* **Fax:** *01582-459 401.*

The Gallery, Luton Central Library
St. George's Square, Luton, LU1 2NG.
Tel: *01582-30161.* **Fax:** *01582-24638.*

Luton Museum and Art Gallery *P*
Wardown Park, Luton,
Tel: *01582-746722.*

SANDY

Sculptor's Studio:Thane Studios
10 Vicarage Road, Waresley, Sandy, SG19 3DA.
Tel: *01767-650444.* **Fax:** *01767-650444.*

Cambridgeshire

BOURN

Wysing Arts *P*
Fox Road, Bourn, CB3 7TX.
Tel: *01954-718881.* **Fax:** *01954-718500.*
Email *info@wysing.demon.co.uk*
Ws *http://www.wysing.demon.co.uk*
Opening times: *7 days a week. Phone for details.*
Nearest Station: *Cambridge/Royston.*
Personnel: *Director:* Trystan Hawkins.
Wysing Arts is based nine miles south-west of Cambridge. Resources - 26 studios, large performance studio, fully equipped darkroom, ceramics studio, café and meeting rooms. On-site residential accommodation. Situated in eleven acres of open farm land, comprising three fields, Wysing commissions/exhibits sculpture and 'site specific' sculpture,

alongside a programme of exhibitions in our spacious Gallery. Open throughout the year please phone for details of our programme of exhibitions, workshops and space hire information. Four deadlines a year for exhibition

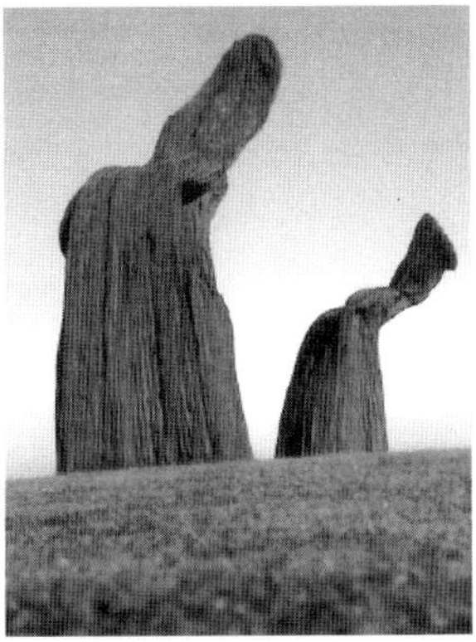

proposals. Commissions for sculpture advertised in arts press or send details to join our mailing list. Charity Number 1039555.
Services and Facilities:
Commissioning Service. Disabled Access. Gallery space for hire. Guided Tours. Parking. Workshop Facilities.

CAMBRIDGE

Broughton House Gallery C
98 King Street, Cambridge, CB1 1LN.
Tel: *01223-314960.* **Fax:** *01223-314960.*
Email *bhg@dircon.co.uk*
Ws *http://www.broughtonhouse gallery.uksw.com*
Opening times: *Mar-Dec Tues-Sat 10.30-5.30.*
Nearest Station: *BR: Cambridge; Bus Station: Drummer Street, Cambridge, 5 mins walk.*
Personnel: *Director:* Rosemary Davidson.

This modern gallery has been built into the ground floor of an 18th century house, opening onto a walled garden, in the centre of Cambridge. There are monthly exhibitions from March to December, each lasting three weeks (both one-man/woman and theme shows). Contemporary paintings and prints, also sculpture, from British and European, artists. A wide variety of paintings and prints always in stock (including Gwen Raverat wood engravings). Friends of the Broughton House Gallery scheme. Consultancy for private and business clients.
Services and Facilities:
Art Consultancy. Disabled Access. Friends/Society.
Work Stocked and Sold:
Pa. Pr. Sc.
Price range: £25 - £1,500.
For artists see *Commercial Gallery Artists.*

Cambridge Arts C
Willowhurst, Station Road, Fordham, Nr. Ely, Cambridge, CM7 5LW.
Tel: *01638-721884.* **Fax:** *01638-721885.*

Cambridge Contemporary Art C
6 Trinity Street, Cambridge, CB2 1SU.
Tel: *01223-324222.* **Fax:** *01223-315606.*
Email *cam.cont.art@dial.pipex.com*
Ws *http://www.artcambridge.co.uk*
Opening times: *Mon-Sat 9-5.30.*
Nearest Station: *Cambridge.*
Personnel: *Director:* Denise Collins. *Gallery Manager:* Rosy Gounaris.

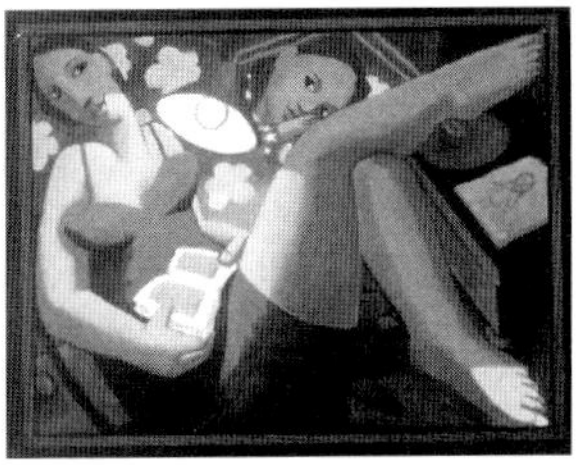

Cambridge Contemporary Art, the largest commercial art gallery in the city, offers the best of painting, sculpture, original prints and crafts by acknowledged masters, established artists and young talent. The work is highlighted through constantly changing displays and a varied exhibition programme. Our private and corporate customers benefit from a wide range of services making the gallery the first port of call for any art enquiry. Artists include: Karolina Larusdottir, Charlotte Cornish, Anita Klein, Jonathan Clarke, Stanley Dove, Eoghan Bridge, Aliisa Hyslop, Donald Hamilton Fraser, Dorothy Stirling, Marj Bond, Sheila McInnes, Elisabeth Frink, Ray Richardson, Craigie Aitchison, Henri Matisse, Marc Chagall, Bert Irvin and John Piper.
Services and Facilities:
Art Consultancy. Art for Offices. Commissioning Service. Craftshop. Disabled Access. Framing. Friends/Society. Restoration. Shop.
Work Stocked and Sold:
Ab. App. Cer. Cra. Dec. Fur. Gla. Pa. Pr. Sc. Tx. Wd.
Price range: £50 - £5,000.
For artists see *Commercial Gallery Artists.*

Cambridge Darkroom
Dales Brewery, Gwydir Street, Cambridge, CB1 2LJ.
Tel: *01223-312188 (01223-566725, 01223-350725).* **Fax:** *01223-312188.*

Conservatory Gallery C
6 Hills Avenue, Cambridge, CB1 7XA.
Tel: *01223-211311.* **Fax:** *01233-214588.*

Curwen Chilford Prints C
Chilford Hall, Linton, Cambridge, CB1 6LE.
Tel: *01223-893544.* **Fax:** *01223-893544.*

Fitzwilliam Museum
Trumpington Street, Cambridge, CB2 1RB.
Tel: *01223-332900.* **Fax:** *01223-332923.*
Opening times: *Tues-Sat 10-5; Sun 2.15-5. Closed Mon (except Easter Mon, Spring and Summer Bank Hols). Closed Good Friday, May Day Holiday and 24 Dec-1Jan inclusive.*
Personnel: *Director:* Duncan Robinson. *Education Officer:* Frances Sword.

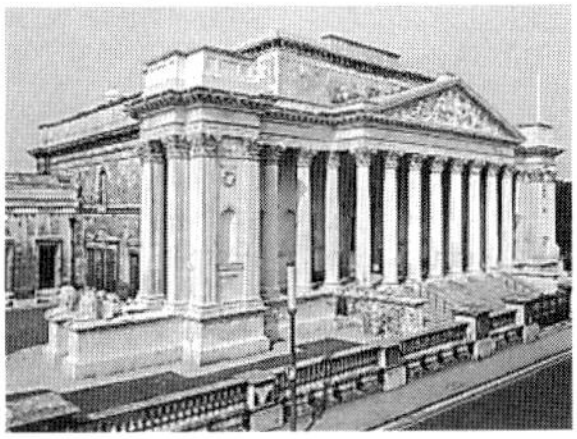

Antiquities from Egypt, Greece, Rome, and displays of Roman, Romano-Egyptian, Cypriot and Western Asiatic art; Applied arts including: ceramics, furniture, textiles; coins and medals; manuscripts and rare printed books; paintings, including masterpieces by Titian, Veronese, Brueghel, Rubens, Canaletto, Monet, Renoir, Cézanne; drawing, prints. Varied temporary exhibition programme, concerts, gallery talks. Disabled Access, preferably by arrangement. Guided tours Sun 2.30 and by arrangement. Admission Free.
Services and Facilities:
Café. Disabled Access. Friends/Society. Guided Tours. Lectures. Museum Shop. Shop.

The Gallery
23 High Street, Fen Ditton, Cambridge, CB5 8ST.
Tel: *012205-5264.*

The Heffer Gallery C
19 Sidney Street, Cambridge, CB2 3HL.
Tel: *01223-568403.* **Fax:** *01223-568410.*

Kettle's Yard
Castle Street, Cambridge, CB3 0AQ.
Tel: *01223-352124.* **Fax:** *01223-324377.*

Lynne Strover Gallery C
23 High Street, Fen Ditton, Cambridge, CB5 8ST.
Tel: *01223-295264.* **Fax:** *01223-295264.*

The Peter McMillen Gallery
168 Mill Road, Cambridge,
Tel: *01223-242037.* **Fax:** *01223-211275.*

Primavera C
10 King's Parade, Cambridge, CB2 1SJ.
Tel: *01223-357708.* **Fax:** *01223-576920.*
Opening times: *Mon-Sat 9.30-5.30.*
Personnel: *Director:* Ronald Pile.
Situated opposite Kings College in

Cambridge, Primavera has long been associated with the best in British craft and design. Ceramics (both functional and "one-off), furniture and paintings always on show in the basement galleries, alongside changing exhibitions throughout the year. Studio glass, metalwork and textiles on the ground floor, which also features an extensive range of contemporary British jewellery.
Services and Facilities:
Commissioning Service. Craftshop. Shop.
Work Stocked and Sold:
App. Cer. Cra. Fur. Gla. Jew. Pa. Sc. Tx. Wd.
Price range: £10 - £5,000.
For artists see *Commercial Gallery Artists.*

ELY

Keramikos
37 Mildenhall, Fordham, Ely, CB7 5NW.
Tel: *01638-721371.*
Fax: *01638-720375.*

The Stained Glass Museum P
North Triforium, Ely Cathedral, Ely, CB7 4DN.
Tel: *01353-667735.*
Fax: *01223-327367.*

HUNTINGDON

The Cottage Gallery C
11/12 High Street, Huntingdon, PF18 6TE.
Tel: *01480-411521.*
Fax: *01480-386521.*
Opening times: *Mon-Sat 9-5.30, Sun 10-4.*
Nearest Station: *Huntingdon.*
Personnel: *Manageress:* Amanda Burrell. *Proprietor:* John Nind. *Art Co-ordinator:* Sarah Rennison.

The Cottage Gallery, Huntington is situated in a historic listed building with two floors of gallery exhibition space, a sculpture garden and picture framing showrooms. We have an exciting range of exhibitions, approximately eight a year featuring the work of local and national artists. We are committed to creating a showcase for the work of contemporary applied arts and fine arts. The gallery garden is a beautiful peaceful space. You are invited to have coffee, look at the work of contemporary and traditional sculptors or just count the gallery goldfish. Admission to all our exhibitions is free and you are very welcome to come and browse.
Services and Facilities:
Art Consultancy. Art for Offices. Commissioning Service. Framing. Gallery space for hire. Lectures. Restoration. Shop. Valuation. Workshop Facilities.
Work Stocked and Sold:
App. Cer. Dec. Dr. Gla. Jew. Pa. Ph. Pr. Sc. Tx. Wd.
Price range: £20 - £10,000.
For artists see *Commercial Gallery Artists.*

L'bidi Studio
40 The Broadway, St. Ives, Huntingdon, PE17 4BN.
Tel: *01480-466886.*
Opening times: *Closed Thus & Suns.*

PETERBOROUGH

Annakin Fine Arts
Owlburn, Church Lane, Helpston, Peterborough,
Tel: *01733-252555.*

Peterborough Museum & Art Gallery P
Priestgate, Peterborough, PE1 1LF.
Tel: *01733-343329.*
Fax: *01733-341928.*

Yarrow Gallery
Art Department, Oundle School, Glapthorn Road, Oundle, Peterborough, PE8 4EN.
Tel: *01832-274034.*
Fax: *01832-274034.*

WISBECH

Skylark Studios C
Hannath Road, Tydd Gote, Wisbech, PE13 5ND.
Tel: *01945-420403.*

Essex

BRENTWOOD

Brandler Galleries C
1 Coptfold Road, Brentwood, CM14 4BM.
Tel: *01277-222269.*
Fax: *01277-222786.*
Email *art.british@dial.pipex.com*
Ws *http://www.thesaurus.co.uk/brandler*
Opening times: *Tues-Sat 10-5.30.*
Nearest Station: *Brentwood 400 yds, Shenfield 1 mile.*
Personnel: *Director:* John Brandler. Linda Rodrigues.

A friendly gallery just 2 miles from exit 28 on the M25 with free parking. A wide selection of prints and paintings by British old and modern masters. As we purchase virtually all our stock we have to choose the best examples. Without the London overheads our clients know they get a much better deal on the same artists, without having to fight to get into London with all its problems. We are happy to send photographs or E-Mail images before your trip. Clients include banks, insurance companies and collectors all wanting the best art at realistic prices.
Services and Facilities:
Art Consultancy. Art for Offices. Commissioning Service. Framing. Parking. Restoration. Valuation.
Work Stocked and Sold:
Cer. Dr. Pa. Pr. Sc.
Price range: £50 - £65,000.
For artists see *Commercial Gallery Artists.*

BUCKHURST HILL

Reynolds Fine Art C
59 Queens Road, Buckhurst Hill, IG9 5BU.
Tel: *0181-504 2244.*

CHELMSFORD

Chelmsford and Essex Regimental Museums P
Oaklands Park, Moulsham Street, Chelmsford, CM2 9AQ.
Tel: *01245-353066.*

Chelmsford Museum P
Old Cemetery Lodge, 1 Writtle Road, Chelmsford,
Tel: *01245-281660.*

COLCHESTER

Chappel Galleries
15 Colchester Road, Chappel, Colchester, CO6 2DE. **Tel:** *01206-240326.*

Dragonfly
The Old Bakery, Fordstreet, Aldham, Colchester, CO6 3PH. **Tel:** *01206-241043.*

Firstsite PS
The Minories art gallery, 74 High Street, Colchester, CO1 1UE.
Tel: *01206-577067.* **Fax:** *01206-577161.*
Opening times: *Mon-Sat 10-5. (Summer), 10-4 (Winter).*
Nearest Station: *Colchester North & Colchester Town.*

Firstsite is one of the leading organisations presenting contemporary visual art in the East of England. Based at the Minories art gallery, Firstsite runs a year-round programme of exhibitions ranging from local to international artists. The exhibitions and events cover a wide variety of art forms, from painting, sculpture and crafts to live art and architecture. All exhibitions are accompanied by an exciting and stimulating series of events, talks and workshops for all ages. Visitors also enjoy relaxing in our Garden Café and browsing through the books, cards and magazines in our bookshop. Families are always welcome. Admission is free.
Services and Facilities:
Bookshop. Café. Commissioning Service. Disabled Access. Friends/Society. Guided Tours. Lectures.
Work Stocked and Sold:
Ab. Pa.

Sir Alfred Munnings Art Museum *P*
Castle House, Dedham, Colchester, C07 6AZ.
Tel: *01206-322127.*
Fax: *01206-322127.*

University of Essex Gallery *P*
Wivenhoe Park, Colchester, CO4 3SQ.
Tel: *01206-284100 / 873333 / 872074 / 873260.* **Fax:** *01206-873598 / 873702.*

HARLOW

Addison Wesley Longman
Edinburgh Gate, Harlow, CM20 2JE.
Tel: *01279-623260.*

John Graham Fine Arts
19 The Rows, Stonecross, Harlow, CM20 1DD.
Tel: *01279-26672.*

ILFORD

Pailer Gallery *C*
83 Windsor Road, Ilford, IG1 1HG.

SAFFRON WALDEN

The Church Street Gallery
17 Church Street, Saffron Walden,
Tel: *01799-24422.*

Fry Public Art Gallery
Bridge End Gardens, Castle Street, Saffron Walden, CB10 1BD.
Tel: *01799-513779.*
Opening times: *2.45-5.30, Sat, Sun and Bank Holidays from Easter Sunday - end of October each year.*
Nearest Station: *Audley End.*
Personnel: Mr Nigel Weaver.

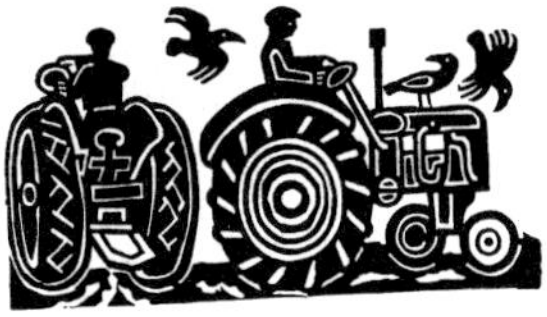

A unique collection of work by artists who have lived in and around Great Bardfield and Saffron Walden since 1930 - Edward Bawden, Eric Ravilious, Michael Rothenstein, John Aldridge, Michael Ayrton and others. Significant contemporary works are also included to show the area's continuing artistic tradition in oil, watercolour, prints, book illustration and design.
Two short special exhibitions associated with the North-West Essex artists each year alongside the permanent collection exhibition, and an invited artists exhibition and sale each November.
Also, oils and watercolours by L.G. Fry (1860-1933), Roger Fry and Anthony Fry. MGC and Charity Commission registered. Society membership (£5) to join mailing list. School Parties and Adult Groups out of normal opening times are welcome by pre-arrangement.
Services and Facilities:
Disabled Access. Friends/Society. Lectures. Museum Shop. Shop.

Newport Gallery
High Street, Newport, Saffron Walden, CB11 3QZ.
Tel: *01799-40623.*

Saffron Walden Museum *P*
Museum Street, Saffron Walden, CB10 1LL.
Tel: *01799-22494.*

SOUTHEND-ON-SEA

Focal Point Gallery *P*
Southend Central Library, Victoria Avenue, Southend-on-Sea, SS2 6EX.
Tel: *01702-612621 ext 207.*
Fax: *01702-469241.*

WESTCLIFF-ON-SEA

Beecroft Art Gallery *PS*
Station Road, Westcliff-on-Sea, SS0 7RA.
Tel: *01702-215130.*

Hertfordshire

BARNET

Contemporary Ceramics *C*
Whalebones, Wood Street, Barnet, EN5 48Z.
Tel: *0181-449 5288.*

Old Bull Arts Centre
68 High Street, Barnet, EN5 5SJ.
Tel: *0181-449 5189.*

BERKHAMSTED

Dower House Gallery
108 High Street, Berkhamsted, HP4 2BL.
Tel: *014427-2562.*

HATFIELD

Margaret Harvey Gallery and University Gallery *PS*
University of Hertfordshire, Faculty of Art & Design, College Lane, Hatfield, AL10 9AB.
Tel: *01707-285376.* **Fax:** *01707-285310.*
Email *m.shaul@herts.ac.uk*
Ws *http://www.herts.ac.uk/artdes/*
Opening times: *Mon-Fri 9.30-5.30, Sat 9.30-1.30.*
Nearest Station: *St. Albans.*
Personnel: *Exhibitions Officer:* M. Shaul.

UNIVERSITY GALLERY

MARGARET HARVEY GALLERY

Purpose built galleries showcasing work by artists, craftspeople and designers of a national and international standard. Operated by University of Herts Faculty of Art & Design. Brand new 250m2 gallery as part of Faculty of Art & Design's new facility on University's main campus at Hatfield.
Services and Facilities:
Café. Commissioning Service. Gallery space for hire. Lectures.
Work Stocked and Sold:
Ab. App. Cer. Cra. Dec. Dr. Pa. Ph.

HEMEL HEMPSTEAD

Old Town Hall *PS*
High Street, Hemel Hempstead, HP1 3AE.
Tel: *01442-228095.* **Fax:** *01442-234072.*
Opening times: *Mon-Thur 10-3, Fri-Sat 10am-11pm.*
Nearest Station: *Hemel Hempstead.*
Personnel: *Borough Arts Manager:* Sara Railson. *Exhibitions:* Claire Dolling.
Gallery restaurant featuring work by local and national artists. Mixed media exhibitions (24 a year), various sizes and prices, from £25-£500. Also small craft shop selling jewellery, pottery (bi-monthly turnaround).
Services and Facilities:
Art for Offices. Bar. Commissioning Service. Craftshop. Gallery space for hire. Parking. Restaurant.
Work Stocked and Sold:
App. Cer. Cra. Dec. Dr. Jew. Pa. Ph. Pr. Sc.
Price range: £25 - £500.
For artists see *Commercial Gallery Artists.*

HITCHIN

The Grosvenor Art Gallery
11 Bridge Street, Hitchin. **Tel:** *01462-33663.*

Hitchin Museum & Art Gallery *P*
Paynes Park, Hitchin, SG5 1EQ.
Tel: *01462-434476.*

LETCHWORTH

Letchworth Museum and Art Gallery *P*
Broadway, Letchworth, SG6 3PF.
Tel: *01462-685647.*

Vilas Fine Arts *C*
8-10 Leys Avenue, Letchworth, SG6 3EU.
Tel: *01462-677455.* **Fax:** *01462-677455.*

MUCH HADHAM

The Henry Moore Foundation
Dane Tree House, Perry Green, Much Hadham, SG10 6EE.
Tel: *01279-843333.* **Fax:** *01279-843647.*

ROYSTON

Manor Gallery
13 Angel Pavement, Royston, SG8 9AS.
Tel: *01763-45518.*

SAWBRIDGEWORTH

The Gowan Gallery *C*
3 Bell Street, Sawbridgeworth, CM21 9AR.
Tel: *01279-600004.*

ST. ALBANS

Arte - Gallery
26 George Street, St. Albans,
Tel: *01920-469620.*

Museum of St. Albans *P*
Hatfield Road, St. Albans, AL1 3RR.
Tel: *01727-56679.*

STEVENAGE

Boxfield Gallery *PS*
Stevenage Arts & Leisure Centre, Stevenage, SG1 1LZ.
Tel: *01438-766644.*
Fax: *01438-766675.*
Opening times: *Mon-Sun 9.30-10.*
Personnel: *Visual Arts Officer:* George Cass.
Boxfield Gallery, run by contract to Stevenage Borough Council, runs a varied programme of temporary exhibitions. Duration one month each, about four a year are contemporary shows, the remainder are mixed theme exhibitions. The gallery aims to increase public awareness and appreciation of art in general and to make the art gallery a welcoming and popular place. Gallery space 36 linear metres, height 3 metres. Gallery pays for preview, and hire cost.
At present work sold not a priority.
Craft Cabinets.
Services and Facilities:
Bar. Café. Craftshop. Disabled Access. Gallery space for hire. Restaurant.
Work Stocked and Sold:
Cer. Wd.

WARE

Loft Gallery
63 Cappell Lane, Stanstead Abbotts, Ware, SG12 8BX.
Tel: *01920-870013.*

Trading Places Gallery
11 New Road, Ware, SG12 7BS.
Tel: *01920-469620.*
Fax: *01920-463003.*

WATFORD

John Harsfield
25 Valley Rise, Watford, WD2 7EY.
Tel: *01923-675671/463123/226642.*

Watford Museum *P*
194 High Street, Watford, WD1 2HG.
Tel: *01923-32297.*

Lincolnshire

BOSTON

Blackfriars Art Centre
Spain Lane, Boston, PE21 6HP.
Tel: *01205-363108.*

The Guildhall Museum *P*
South Street, Boston, PE21 6HT.
Tel: *01205-365954.*

GAINSBOROUGH

Gainsborough Old Hall *P*
Parnell Street, Gainsborough, DN21 2NB.
Tel: *01427-612669.* **Fax:** *01427-612779.*

LINCOLN

Doddington Hall *P*
Doddington, Lincoln, LN6 4RU.
Tel: *01522-694308.* **Fax:** *01522-682584.*

Usher Gallery *PS*
Lindum Road, Lincoln, LN2 1NN.
Tel: *01522-527980.* **Fax:** *01522-560165.*
Opening times: *Mon-Sat 10-5.30, Sun 2.30-5. Admission charge.*
Nearest Station: *Lincoln.*
Personnel: *Principal Keeper:* Richard H. Wood. *Keepers:* Rosalyn Thomas, Judith Robinson, Janita Elton. *Education Officer:* Pauline Roberts.
This regional gallery houses collections of clocks and watches, miniatures, ceramics, silver and English glass. There are important collections of paintings by Peter de Wint (1784-1849), topographical paintings of Lincolnshire, the Alfred Lord Tennyson collection and English coins. As well as 20th c. works there is an inspiring programme of special exhibitions. The Gallery organises various educational activities and workshops based on the permanent collections and the temporary exhibitions programme. Further details are available from the Education Officer. Baby Changing facilities, Café (light refreshments). Founded 1927.
Services and Facilities:
Café. Disabled Access. Friends/Society. Guided Tours. Shop.

SPALDING

Woodbine Cottage Gallery *C*
Back Bank, Whaplode Drove, Spalding, PE12 0TT.
Tel: *01406-330693.*
Opening times: *Sat, Sun, Mon 10.30-5.30 or by appt.*
Nearest Station: *Spalding or Peterborough.*
Personnel: *Artist/Gallery Owner:* Liz Yorath. *Artist/Gallery Owner:* Rowan Yorath.

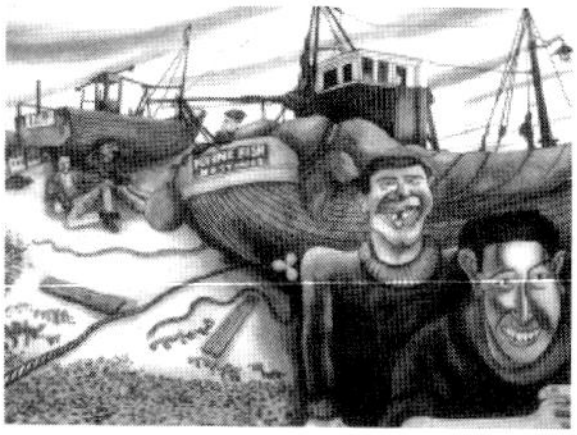

Woodbine Cottage Gallery is an old Fenland cottage, which until its renovation and conservation to a gallery had stood empty for sixteen years. It is situated in the village of Whaplode Drove, 10 miles from Spalding and 14 miles from Peterborough, in the South Holland area of Lincolnshire. Owned and run by Liz and Rowan Yorath, the gallery features changing exhibitions of high quality contemporary art at accessible prices. The wide range of media shown include wood engraving, etching, ceramics, bronze and glass sculptures, painting and drawing. For details of current and forthcoming exhibitions please telephone. Limited disabled access.
Services and Facilities:
Art for Offices. Commissioning Service. Parking.
Work Stocked and Sold:
Cer. Dr. Pa. Ph. Pr. Sc.
Price range: £50 - £1,500.
For artists see *Commercial Gallery Artists.*

STAMFORD

Burghley House
Stamford, PE9 3JY.
Tel: *01780-65262.*

Torkington Gallery
38 St. Peters Street, Stamford, PE9 2PF.
Tel: *01780-62281.*

North Lincolnshire

SCUNTHORPE

Normanby Hall Country Park
Normanby, Scunthorpe, DN15 9HU.
Tel: *01724-720226.*

Scunthorpe Museum & Art Gallery *P*
Oswald Road, Scunthorpe, DN15 7BD.
Tel: *01724-843533.*

Norfolk

AYLSHAM

Red Lion Gallery
Holman House, Market Place, Aylsham, NR11 6EJ.
Tel: *0263-732115.* **Fax:** *0263-732115.*

BURNHAM DEEPDALE

Brancaster Staithe and Burnham Deepdale/Micromouse Limited
Deepdale Farm, Burnham Deepdale, PE31 8DD.
Tel: *01485-210404.* **Fax:** *01485-210993.*

CASTLE ACRE

The Old Red Lion
Bailey Street, Castle Acre, PE32 2AG.
Tel: *017605-557.*

DISS

Palgrave Gallery
The Old Rectory, Rose Lane, Palgrave, Diss, IP22 1AP.
Tel: *01379-652056.*

GORLESTON ON SEA

Hardies Gallery and Art Shop
205/6 High Street, Gorleston on Sea, NR31 6RR. **Tel:** *01493-668003.*

GREAT YARMOUTH

Museums Galleries *P*
Central Library, Tolhouse Street, Great Yarmouth, NR30 2SH.
Tel: *01493-858900 / 745526.*
Fax: *01493-745459.*

HOLT

Judy Hines of Holt *C*
3 Fish Hill, Holt, NR25 6BD
Tel: *01263-713000.*

HUNSTANTON

Ringstead Gallery
Ringstead, Hunstanton, PE36 5JZ.
Tel: *01485-525316.*

KING'S LYNN

Deepdale Exhibitions
The Old Plough House, Burnham, Deepdale, Nr Brancaster, King's Lynn, PE31 8DD.
Tel: *01485-210801.*

Galeria Reflexions
56 Norfolk Street, King's Lynn, PE30 1AG.
Tel: *01553-760766.*

Houghton Hall
Estate Office, Houghton, King's Lynn, PE31 6UE.
Tel: *01485-528569.*

King's Lynn Arts Centre *PS*
27-29 King Street, King's Lynn, PE30 1HA.
Tel: *01553-774725.*
Fax: *01553-770591.*

KINGS LYNN

Unit 2 Gallery *C*
The Rural Workshops, Station Road, Docking, Kings Lynn, PE31 8LT.
Tel: *01485-518817.*
Opening times: *Tues-Sun 10-4.*
Nearest Station: *Kings Lynn.*
Personnel: *Director:* Tony Eeles.

UNIT 2 GALLERY

Exciting gallery in the heart of North West Norfolk presenting craftwork from East Anglia and around the UK especially ceramics and sculpture complemented by textiles, jewellery, automata etc. Crafts Council listed gallery.
Services and Facilities:
Craftshop. Disabled Access. Parking.
Work Stocked and Sold:
Cer. Cra. Gla. Jew. Pr. Sc. Tx. Wd.
Price range: £5 - £1,000.
For artists see *Commercial Gallery Artists.*

MUNDESLEY

St. Brannock's Gallery *C*
7 Cromer Road, Mundesley, NR11 8BE.
Tel: *01263-722622.* **Fax:** *01692-650330.*

NORWICH

Contact Gallery *C*
56 St. Benedicts Street, Norwich, NR2 4AR.
Tel: *01603-760219.*

Frederick Gallery *C*
The Raveningham Centre, Beccles Road, Raveningham, Norwich, NR14 6NU.
Tel: *01508-548688.* **Fax:** *01508-548958.*
Opening times: *Mon-Sun 11-5. Closed Tuesdays.*
Personnel: *Directors:* Adrian Woodard, Janet Woodard.
Rural location on the Norfolk/Suffolk border 3 miles north of Beccles off the B1140, close to A143/A146. The Gallery specialises in contemporary East Anglian artists and sculptors with over 200 exhibits permanently on display. Wide range of styles from traditional to modern impressionism and abstract. Regular special exhibitions. Gallery artists include John Burman, Paul Darley, Margaret Glass, Andrew King, Raymond Leech, Ross Loveday, John Patchett, David Quantrill, Tony Stocker, Kevin Thompson, Adrian Woodard and sculptors Andrew Campbell, Louise Richardson, Ann Richardson and Madeline Smith.
Studio Pottery.
Services and Facilities:
Commissioning Service. Disabled Access. Parking.
Work Stocked and Sold:
Cer. Dr. Pa. Sc. Wd.
Price range: £25 - £3,000.
For artists see *Commercial Gallery Artists.*

The King of Hearts
13-15 Fye Bridge Street, Norwich, NR3 1LJ.
Tel: *01603-766129.*

Mandell's Gallery
Elm Hill, Norwich, NR3 1HN.
Tel: *01603-629180.*

Norwich Castle Museum *P*
Norwich, NR1 3JU.
Tel: *01603-493624.* **Fax:** *01603-765651.*
Ws *http://www.norfolk.gov.uk/tourism/museums/museums/htm*
Opening times: *Mon-Sat 10-5, Sun 2-5.*
Nearest Station: *Thorpe, Norwich.*
Personnel: *Head of Museums:* Vanessa Trevelyan. *Curator:* Andrew W. Moore.
Headquarters of the Norfolk Museums Service. Sited prominently in the City centre, the museum houses an important collection of the Norwich School featuring works by John Crome and John Sell Cotman. Other major attractions include the annual Tate Gallery Collection Exhibition and its lively programme of events. Other attractions include displays of fine and decorative art from the 17th century to the present day, archaeology and natural history displays, battlements and dungeons tours daily and a lively exhibition and education programme. Also provide: Guided Tours on request.
Major exhibitions for 1999: 1) A Swiss Painter in Italy: Louis Ducros (1748-1810), a selection of watercolours from The Musée Cantonal des Beaux-Arts, Lausanne, Switzerland (15 May-11 July). 2) Surrealism, The Untamed Eye, a Tate Gallery Collection Exhibition (24 July-21 November).
Norwich Castle Museum is due to undergo major development under the Heritage Lottery Fund during late 1999/2000. If you are planning to visit towards the end of the year please telephone to confirm details.
Tel: 01603-498624.
Services and Facilities:
Art Consultancy. Art for Offices. Bookshop. Café. Craftshop. Disabled Access. Friends/Society. Guided Tours. Lectures. Museum Shop. Shop.

Norwich Gallery
Norwich School of Art and Design, St. George Street, Norwich, NR3 1BB.
Tel: *01603-610561.* **Fax:** *01603-615728.*

Sainsbury Centre for Visual Arts
University of East Anglia, Norwich, NR4 7TJ.
Tel: *01603-456060 (Galleries), 01603-593199 (Enquiries).* **Fax:** *01603-259401.*
Email *scva@uea.ac.uk*
Opening times: *Tue-Sun 11-5. Admission £2 (£1 concs.).*
Nearest Station: *Norwich.*
Personnel: *Director:* Nichola Johnson. *Head of Admin. & Services:* Kate Carreno. *Curator of Collections and Exhibitions:* Amanda Daly. *Head of Education:* Dr Veronica Sekules. *Head of Conservation & Collection Management:* Don Sale.
The museum and gallery of the University of East Anglia, designed by world famous architect Sir Norman Foster to house the Robert and Lisa Sainsbury Collection, which was given to the University in the 1970's. Modern European sculpture and painting, including works by Bacon, Degas, Epstein, Giacometti, Moore and Picasso are displayed alongside one of the finest collections of non-Western art outside London. The centre also has a lively programme of special exhibitions, events and education work.
An exciting and varied special exhibition programme is run throughout the year. The Centre has a coffee bar and gallery shop and offers facilities for special functions, meetings and conferences.
Services and Facilities:
Art for Offices. Bar. Bookshop. Café. Disabled Access. Friends/Society. Guided Tours. Lectures. Museum Shop. Parking. Restaurant. Shop.

WELLS-NEXT-THE-SEA

Holkham Picture Gallery
The Ancient House, Holkham, Wells-next-the-Sea.

School House Gallery *C*
Wighton, Nr. Wells-next-the-Sea, NR23 1AL.
Tel: *01328-820457.*
Opening times: *11.30-5.30 inclusive Sat, Sun and Bank Holidays. Closed Monday.*
Personnel: *Director:* Diana Cohen.
Contemporary paintings, watercolours,

drawings, limited edition prints and sculpture shown in an attractive space that was once the Wighton village school. 20th century British and European art of the highest quality, also work by foremost East Anglian artists. Four major exhibitions a year

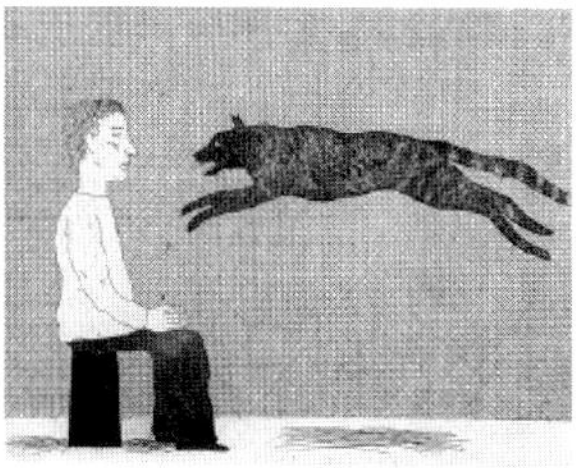

interspersed with constantly changing mixed shows. Situated two miles from Wells and the North Norfolk coast. Large car park.
Services and Facilities:
Parking.
Work Stocked and Sold:
Cer. Dr. Pa. Pr. Sc.
Price range: £100 - £3,000.
For artists see *Commercial Gallery Artists.*

Suffolk

ALDEBURGH

Thompson's Gallery
175 High Street, Aldeburgh, IP15 5AN.
Tel: *01728-453743.* **Fax:** *01728-452488.*

BURY ST. EDMUNDS

Chimney Mill Galleries
Chimney Mill, West Stow, Bury St. Edmunds,
Tel: *01284-778234.*

Manor House Museum *P*
Honey Hill, Angel Corner, Bury St. Edmunds, IP33 1UZ. **Tel:** *01284-757074.*

Moyses Hall Museum *P*
Cornhill, Bury St. Edmunds,
Tel: *01284-769834.*

Ottewell Art Gallery
50 St. Andrew's Street South, Bury St. Edmunds, IP33 3PH. **Tel:** *01284-61172.*

CRANSFORD

Boundary Gallery
Boundary House, Cransford.
Tel: *01728-723862.*

EAST BERGHOLT

Woodgates Gallery
Woodgates Road, East Bergholt, CO7 6RE.
Tel: *01206-298448.*

FELIXSTOWE

Artworks
Victoria Street, Felixstowe,
Tel: *01502-583521.*

HALESWORTH

Halesworth Gallery
Steeple End, Halesworth,
Tel: *01986-872409.*

IPSWICH

Christchurch Mansion *PS*
Christchurch Park, (Ipswich Museums and Galleries: Ipswich Borough Council). Ipswich, IP4 2BE.
Tel: *01473-253246.* **Fax:** *01473-210328.*

First Floor Gallery
at M. F. Frames Ltd, 10 St. Helens Street, Ipswich. **Tel:** *01473-225544.*

Ipswich Museums & Galleries Christ Church Mansion *PS*
(including Wolsey Art Gallery), Soane Street, Ipswich, IP4 5NB.
Tel: *01473-253246.*
Fax: *01473-210328.*

John Russell Gallery
4-6 Wherry Lane, Ipswich, IP4 1LG.
Tel: *01473-212051.* **Fax:** *01473-212051.*

Shelley Priory
Hadleigh, Ipswich,
Tel: *01206-337220.*

LOWESTOFT

The Art Centre Gallery
Regent Road, Lowestoft, NR32 1PA.
Tel: *01502-583521 ext 281.*

NEWMARKET

Equus Art Gallery
Sun Lane, Newmarket, CB8 8EW.
Tel: *01638-560445.*

The Newmarket Fine Art Gallery
Nell Gwynn Studio, Palace Street, Newmarket,
Tel: *94-660065.*

SAXMUNDHAM

Snape Maltings Gallery *C*
Snape Maltings Riverside Centre, Saxmundham, IP17 1SR.
Tel: *01728-688305.*
Fax: *01728-688930.*
Email *snapemalt@aol.com*
Opening times: *Mon-Sun all year round, 10-5 (6 during the summer).*
Nearest Station: *Saxmundham.*
Personnel: Julia Pipe.
Housed in a collection of 19th century maltings on the River Alde. Continuing mixed exhibition of paintings, artists' prints and British craft. Painting and craft courses in summer. Also six interesting shops, tea shop and pub. Additional space available to hire for exhibitions.
Services and Facilities:
Bar. Bookshop. Café. Craftshop. Disabled Access. Gallery space for hire. Parking. Shop.
Work Stocked and Sold:
Ab. Cer. Cra. Dr. Jew. Pa. Pr. Tx.
For artists see *Commercial Gallery Artists.*

SOUTHWOLD

New Gallery
10 Market Place, Southwold,
Tel: *01728-724269.*

Portland Studio
Portland House, High Street, Southwold, IP18 6AB.
Tel: *01502-723652.*

SUDBURY

Gainsborough's House *PS*
46 Gainsborough Street, Sudbury, CO10 2EU.
Tel: *01787-372958.*
Fax: *01787-376991.*
Opening times: *Tues-Sat 10-5, Sun 2-5. (closes at 4 Nov-March).*
Nearest Station: *Sudbury.*
Personnel: *Curator:* Hugh Belsey. *Assistant Curator:* Andrew Hunter.

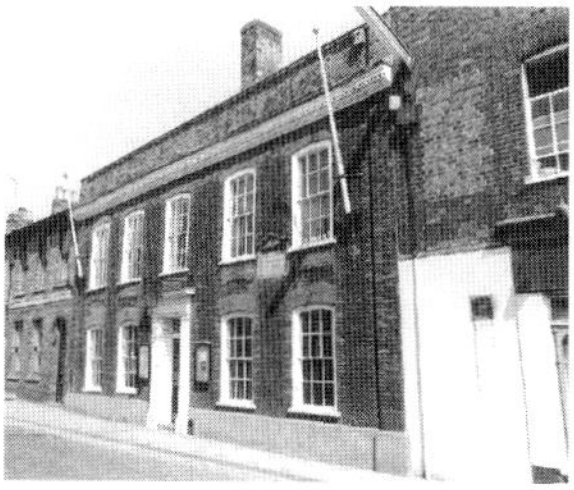

Georgian-fronted town house, the birthplace of Thomas Gainsborough, displays a substantial collection of paintings, drawings and prints from throughout the artist's career and houses a library and study collection of works on paper. Lively contemporary and historical exhibitions of regional and national interest are shown in galleries overlooking the charming garden. The open-access print workshop is available to individual artists and for summer courses. Disabled Access ground floor only.
Services and Facilities:
Friends/Society. Guided Tours. Lectures. Museum Shop. Workshop Facilities.
Work Stocked and Sold:
Pr.
Price range: £50 - £200.

The Phoenix Gallery
97 High Street, Lavenham, Sudbury, CO10 9PZ.
Tel: *01787-247356.*

WOODBRIDGE

The Barn Gallery
Mill Lane, Butley, Woodbridge, IP12 3PA.
Tel: *01394-450843.*
Fax: *01394-450843.*

The Deben Gallery
26 Market Hill, Woodbridge, IP12 4LU.
Tel: *013943-3216.*

The Fraser Gallery
62a New Street, Woodbridge, IP12 1DX.
Tel: *01394-387535.*

East Midlands

Derby

DERBY

The Arbor Darkrooms & Gallery C
Arboretum Lodge, Arboretum Square, Derby DE23 8FN.
Tel: *01332-299049.*

Art for All
Derby City General Hospital, Uttoxeter Road, Derby DE22 3NE.
Tel: *01332-340131 ext 5910.*

The Atrium Gallery
The Derwent Business Centre, Clarke Street, Derby DE1 2BU.

Derby Museum and Art Gallery P
The Strand, Derby DE1 1BS.
Tel: *01332-255586.* **Fax:** *01332-255804.*

Royal Crown Derby Museum P
Royal Crown Derby Porcelain Co. Ltd., 194 Osmaston Road, Derby DE3 8JZ.
Tel: *01332-712800.* **Fax:** *01332-712899.*

Derbyshire

BUXTON

Buxton Museum & Art Gallery P
Terrace Road, Buxton, SK17 6DJ.
Tel: *01298-24658.*

CHESTERFIELD

Chesterfield Museum & Art Gallery P
St Mary's Gate, Chesterfield, S41 7TY.
Tel: *01246-559727.* **Fax:** *01246-206667.*

Uno Gallery C
5 South Street, Chesterfield, S40 1QX.

ILKESTON

Bottle Kiln Gallery
High Lane East, West Hallam, Ilkeston, DE7 6HP. **Tel:** *0115-932 9442.*

Charles Stone Gallery of Contemporary Painting
Bottle Kiln Gallery, High Lane East, West Hallam, Ilkeston, DE7 6HP.
Tel: *0115-932 9442.*

Erewash Museum P
Ilkeston, DE7 5JA.
Tel: *01602 440440 ext 331.*

WIRKSWORTH

Modern Print Gallery
25 Market Place, Wirksworth, DE4 4ET.
Tel: *01629-824525.*

Leicester

LEICESTER

The City Gallery PS
90 Granby Street, Leicester LE1 1DJ.
Tel: *0116-254 0595.* **Fax:** *0116-254 0593.*

Gadsby Gallery
22 Market Place, Leicester LE1 5GF.
Tel: *0116-262 2410.*

Leicester Museum & Art Gallery P
53 New Walk, Leicester LE1 7EA.

Leicestershire

ASHBY DE-LA-ZOUCH

Ferrers Gallery C
Staunton Harold, Ashby de-la-Zouch, LE6 5RU.
Tel: *01332-863337.*

LUTTERWORTH

Cedar House Craft Shop & Gallery
Main Street, Peatling Pava, Lutterworth, LE17 5QA.
Tel: *0116-273 0482.*

MARKET HARBOROUGH

Coughton Galleries C
The Old Manor, Arthingworth, Market Harborough, LE6 8JD.
Tel: *01858-525436.* **Fax:** *01858-525535.*

The Frank Haynes Gallery
50 Station Road, Great Bowden, Market Harborough, LE16 7HN.
Tel: *01858-464862.*

Northamptonshire

KETTERING

Alfred East Art Gallery PS
c/o, The Coach House, Sheep Street, Kettering, NN16 8AN.
Tel: *01536-534274/534381/534394.*
Fax: *01536-410795/534370.*

NORTHAMPTON

Central Museum & Art Gallery PS
Guildhall Road, Northampton, NN1 1DP.
Tel: *01604-639415.* **Fax:** *01604-238720.*
Opening times: *Mon-Sat 10-5, Sun 2-5.*
Nearest Station: *Northampton.*
Personnel: *Curator:* S. Stone.
Central Museum, Northampton houses an unexpectedly fine collection of 15th-18th century art, including works by Guardi and Giordano. The rich British collection features early watercolours, and Norwich School and Pre-Raphaelite works. Modern and contemporary strands are represented by Sickert, John Nash, Sutherland, Moore and Hockney amongst others, and our print collection includes works by Pasmore and Nolan. Our outstanding ceramics collections comprise comprehensive ranges of both British and Oriental pottery and porcelain. The small collection of studio ceramics includes pieces by Ewen Henderson and Gordon Baldwin.
Services and Facilities:
Bookshop. Disabled Access. Friends/Society. Gallery space for hire. Guided Tours. Lectures. Museum Shop.

Four Seasons Gallery
39 St Giles Street, Northampton,
Tel: *01604-32287.*

Onsight Gallery
The Roadmender, 1 Lady's Lane, Northampton, NN1 3AH.

Weston Favell Library
Weston Favell Shopping Centre, Northampton,
Tel: *01604-413327.*

TOWCESTER

Blakesley Gallery C
Barton House, High Street, Blakesley, Towcester, NN12 8RE.
Tel: *01327-860282.* **Fax:** *01327-860282.*

Towcester Library
Richmond Road, Towcester, NN12 7EX.
Tel: *01327-50794.*

WELLINGBOROUGH

The Gallery
108 Midland Road, Wellingborough, NN8 1NB.
Tel: *01933-274215.*

Raunds Library
High Street, Raunds, Wellingborough, NN9 6HT.
Tel: *01933-623671.*

Wellingborough Library
Pebble Lane, Wellingborough, NN8 1AS.
Tel: *01933-225365.* **Fax:** *01933-44060.*

Nottinghamshire

NEWARK

Millgate Museum P
48 Millgate, Newark, NG24 4TS.
Tel: *01636-79403.*

Pierrepont Gallery
Thoresby Park, Nr Ollerton, Newark,
Tel: *01623-822365.* **Fax:** *01623-822301.*

NOTTINGHAM

Angel Row Gallery PS
Central Library Building, 3 Angel Row, Nottingham, NG1 6HP.
Tel: *0115-947 6334.* **Fax:** *0115-947 6335.*
Opening times: *Mon-Sat 11-6, Wed 11-7.*

Personnel: *Exhibitions Officer:* Deborah Dean.
Situated in central Nottingham, Angel Row Gallery shows an exciting and diverse programme of contemporary visual arts. A large gallery with three exhibitions spaces it promotes regional, national and international artists. An extensive programme of events and activities is organised in conjunction with the exhibitions. Bookshop stocks a wide range of art magazines, catalogues, postcards and greetings cards.
Services and Facilities:
Bookshop. Disabled Access. Friends/Society. Lectures.

Arnold Library
Front Street, Arnold, Nottingham, NG5 7EE.
Tel: *0115-920 2247.*

The Bonington Gallery PS
The Nottingham Trent University, Dryden Street, Nottingham, NG1 4FX.
Tel: *0115-948 6443 / 6131 (office), 0115-941 8418 ext. 2260 (gallery).* **Fax:** *0115-948 6403.*
Email *stella.couloutbanis@ntu.ac.uk*
Ws *http://www.ntu.ac.uk/gallery/*
Opening times: *Mon-Thur 10-5, Fri 10-4, Sat 10-5.*
Personnel: *Artistic Director:* Robert Ayers. *Exhibitions Organiser:* Stella Couloutbanis.

The **BONINGTON** *Gallery*

Situated within the Bonington Building of the University, the gallery is one of the foremost exhibition spaces for contemporary art in the Midlands.
The gallery presents a diverse programme of events encompassing both pure and applied contemporary Visual Arts, Crafts, Design, Performance and Dance.
Emphasis is placed upon programming work which is innovative and at the forefront of contemporary practice, encouraging the work of younger, emerging artists as well as established practitioners.
Services and Facilities:
Art for Offices. Disabled Access. Friends/Society. Lectures. Workshop Facilities.

Byard Gallery
9 Byard Lane, Nottingham,
Tel: *0115-950 0434.*

Nottingham Castle Museum & Art Gallery PS
The Castle, Nottingham, NG1 6EL.
Tel: *0115-915 3700 (General information).*
Fax: *0115-915 3653.*
Opening times: *Open daily, 10-5 (Nov-Feb, Fridays closed). Closed Christmas Day, Boxing Day & New Years Day.*
Nearest Station: *Nottingham.*
Personnel: *Director:* Michael Williams.
Founded 1878. A seventeenth century mansion on the site of the original Nottingham Castle, housing a strong collection of fine art from the seventeenth century to the present day. Featuring artists such as Bonington, Rossetti, Laura Knight and Lowry with a unique collection of Medieval alabasters. A lively programme of temporary exhibitions of historical and contemporary art, craft and textiles in newly refurbished galleries. Regularly

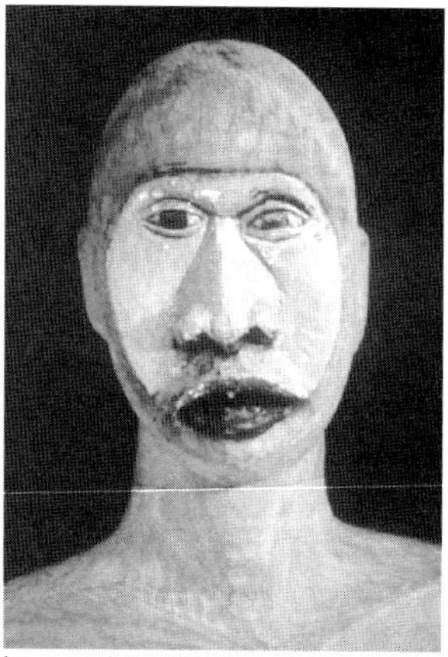

feature work for sale by up and coming painters, photographers and craftmakers and host an annual contemporary art auction. Crafts Council recommended shop selling a wide range of crafts. Also run a post-graduate level training programme for artists.
Services and Facilities:
Café. Commissioning Service. Craftshop. Disabled Access. Friends/Society. Gallery space for hire. Guided Tours. Lectures. Museum Shop.
Work Stocked and Sold:
Cra. Pa. Ph.

Djanogly Art Gallery PS
The University of Nottingham Arts Centre, University Park, Nottingham, NG7 2RD.
Tel: *0115-951 3192.* **Fax:** *0115-951 3194.*
Ws *http://www.nottingham.ac.uk/artscentre/*
Opening times: *Mon-Sat 11-5, Sun & Bank Hols 2-5.*
Nearest Station: *Nottingham.*
Personnel: *Director:* Joanne Wright. *Exhibitions Officer:* Neil Walker. *Marketing Officer:* Position vacant at present - due to appoint April '99. *Exhibitions Secretary:* Tracey Isgar.

DJANOGLY artgallery

The Djanogly Art Gallery originates historical and contemporary exhibitions and hosts a wide range of touring shows. Foyer exhibitions and craft cabinets extend the type of work shown. The gallery has an artist in residence - Heather Connelly until September 1999 - who leads workshops and education programmes in conjunction with the exhibitions.
Services and Facilities:
Bookshop. Café. Craftshop. Disabled Access. Lectures. Parking.

Focus Gallery
108 Derby Road, Nottingham, NG1 5FB.
Tel: *0115-953 7575.*

The Hart Gallery C
23 Main Street, Linby, Nottingham, NG15 8AE.
Tel: *0115-963 8707.*

Nottingham Playhouse Gallery
Wellington Circus, Nottingham, NG1 5AF.
Tel: *0115-941 9419.*

The West End Gallery C
St. Mary's Church, High Pavement, The Lace Market, Nottingham, NG1 1HF.
Tel: *0115-947 2476.*
Fax: *0115-947 2476.*
Email *stmary@john316.com.*
Opening times: *Tues-Sat 9-4.30.*
Nearest Station: *Nottingham.*
Personnel: *Community Arts Organiser:* Ruth Shelton.
'The West End Gallery' is situated within the nave of the ancient parish church of St. Mary in Nottinghams historic Lace Market. The gallery holds monthly group and solo shows of contemporary works by young local artists, community organisations, and more established national and international painters, photographers and sculptors. The gallery also supports students from the two local universities and holds degree shows. Workshops and talks take place throughout the year. 'The West End Gallery' is a non profit making organisation run by a volunteer Artist in Residence. The gallery shows all works that are in keeping with the setting of the space. We especially welcome visual arts dealing with issues of faith.
Services and Facilities:
Disabled Access. Gallery space for hire. Lectures.
Work Stocked and Sold:
Pa. Ph. Sc.
Price range: £20 - £1,000.
For artists see *Commercial Gallery Artists.*

Yard Gallery PS
Wollaton Park, Nottingham, NG8 2AE.
Tel: *0115-915 3920 (general enquiries).*
Fax: *0115-915 3932.*
Opening times: *Winter 11-4, Summer 11-5.*
Nearest Station: *Nottingham.*
Personnel: *Exhibition Co-ordinator:* Jim Waters.
The Yard Gallery is a space dedicated to exhibiting artists whose work is influenced by natural and environmental science. Artists are also encouraged to explore the extensive natural history collections at Wollaton Hall as a source of inspiration for new work. The cross-fertilisation of art and science in the gallery provides a fascinating marriage of the rigours of two traditionally diverse disciplines.
Services and Facilities:
Bookshop. Café. Craftshop. Disabled Access. Guided Tours. Lectures. Parking.

RAVENSHEAD

Longdale Gallery
Longdale Craft Centre, Museum and Restaurant, Longdale Lane, Ravenshead, NG15 9AH.
Tel: *01623-794858.*

WORKSOP

Harley Gallery *C*
Welbeck, Worksop, S80 3LW.
Tel: *01909-501700.*
Fax: *01909-488747.*

Rutland

UPPINGHAM

The Goldmark Gallery *C*
14 Orange Street, Uppingham, LE15 9SQ.
Tel: *01572-821424.*
Fax: *01572-821503.*
Opening times: *Daily 9.30-5.30 & Sun afternoons.*
Personnel: *Director:* M. M .Goldmark. Sally Jones.
2500 sq. ft. of the best in contemporary figurative British art. With neither Cork Street landlords nor an Armani habit to support, we offer competitive prices and no art bollocks.
Services and Facilities:
Art for Offices. Bookshop. Disabled Access. Framing.
Work Stocked and Sold:
Ab. Pa. Pr. Sc.
Price range: £250 - £3,000.
For artists see *Commercial Gallery Artists.*

West Midlands

Birmingham

BIRMINGHAM

The Angle Gallery
Dakota Buildings, James Street, off St. Paul's Square, Birmingham B3 1SD.
Tel: *0121-688 5515.*

Aston Hall *P*
Trinity Road, Aston, Birmingham B6 6JD.
Tel: *0121-327 0062.*
Fax: *0121-327 7162.*

The Barber Institute of Fine Arts *P*
The University of Birmingham, Edgbaston, Birmingham B15 2TS.
Tel: *0121-414 7333.*
Fax: *0121-414 3370.*
Email *info@barber.org.uk*
Ws *http://www.barber.org.uk*
Opening times: *Mon-Sat 10-5, Sun 2-5.*
Nearest Station: *New Street (Main line), University (Cross City Line).*
Personnel: *Director:* Professor Richard Verdi. *Senior Curator:* Paul Spencer-Longhurst. *Administrator:* Sophie Wilson.
One of the finest small picture galleries in the world housing an outstanding collection of old masters and modern paintings including masterpieces by Bellini, Rubens, Poussin, Murillo, Gainsborough, Rossetti, Whistler and Magritte. Among the Impressionist pictures are major works by Manet, Monet, Renoir, Degas, Gauguin and Van Gogh. The Institute regularly holds concerts, lectures and recitals - all of which are open to the public. It is also available for hire for seminars, receptions, concerts and private views.

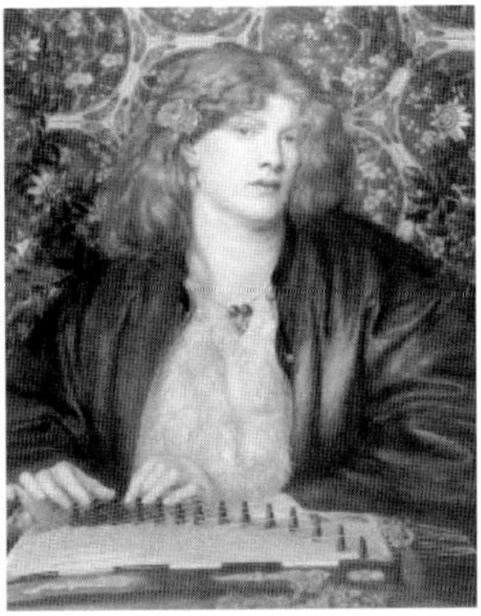

Services and Facilities:
Disabled Access. Friends/Society. Gallery space for hire. Guided Tours. Lectures. Museum Shop. Parking.
Work Stocked and Sold:
Pa.

Birmingham & Midland Institute
9 Margaret Street, Birmingham B3 3BS.
Tel: *0121-236 3591.*

Birmingham Museum and Art Gallery, including the Gas Hall Exhibition Gallery *PS*
Chamberlain Square, Birmingham B3 3DH.
Tel: *0121-303 2834/1966.*
Fax: *0121-303 1394.*
Opening times: *Mon-Thurs & Sat 10-5, Fri 10.30-5, Sun 12.30-5.*
Nearest Station: *Birmingham New Street.*
A spectacular Victorian building housing one of the world's finest collections of Pre-Raphaelite paintings. Older schools are represented by Dutch, Italian and French artists and other works from the 14th century to the present day. The museum has displays of ceramics and fine silver, and a new sculpture gallery. Other sections include Greek and Roman antiquities, objects from the Near East, Mexico and Peru and a life-size dinosaur in the natural history gallery. The Edwardian tea room offers a varied menu in elegant surroundings. 1999 offers a varied exhibition programme, including: 12 January-14 March: Heritage Regained - The Gilbert Collection of Silver; 8 February-18 April: Devious Devices; 4 February-16 May: George Chinnery in India and China; 13 March-13 June: Twin Perspectives; 14 May-12 September: The Science of Sport; June-September: The Incas; 11 September-24 October: Made in the Middle; October-December: 20th Century Art.
Services and Facilities:
Café. Disabled Access. Friends/Society. Gallery space for hire. Guided Tours. Museum Shop. Restaurant.

The Bond Gallery
Design & Studio Centre, The Bond Warehouse, 180-182 Fazeley Street, Birmingham B5 5SP.
Tel: *0121-753 2065.*

Carleton Gallery
91 Vivian Road, Harborne, Birmingham B17 0DR.
Tel: *0121-427 2487.*

Danford Collection of West African Art and Artefacts *P*
Centre for West African Studies, University of Birmingham, Birmingham B15 2TT.
Tel: *0121-414 5128.*
Fax: *0121-414 3228.*

Goate Gallery
57 Stephenson Street, New Street, Birmingham B2 4JH.
Tel: *0121-643 2624.*

Helios Gallery
25 Valentine Road, Kings Heath, Birmingham B14 7AN.
Tel: *0121-444 1585.*

Ikon Gallery *C*
1 Oozells Square, Brindeyplace, Birmingham B1 2HS.
Tel: *0121-248 0708.*
Fax: *0121-643 2254.*

MAC (Midlands Arts Centre) *PS*
Cannon Hill Park, Birmingham B12 9HQ.
Tel: *0121-440 4221.*
Fax: *0121-446 4372.*
Opening times: *Daily 9.30-11*
Personnel: *Exhibition Programmer:* Judy Dames.

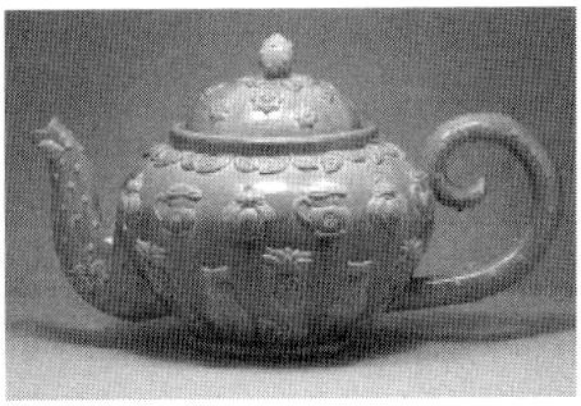

40 exhibitions a year, of which 20 originated and 20 touring. Two stewarded galleries plus three public spaces, with 194 lin. m. hanging space and 300 sq. m. floor space. Shows contemporary fine art, craft and photography from both artists of known stature and those in the early stages of a promising career. Visited by 12,000 people a week. Extensive programme of live performance, cinema, education and exhibitions. Has bar, restaurant and bookshop and set in a large park. Only one space does not have disabled access. Applications from individual artists and touring organisations welcomed. MAC is funded by Birmingham City Council and West Midlands Arts.
Services and Facilities:
Bar. Bookshop. Café. Disabled Access. Guided Tours. Lectures. Parking. Restaurant. Shop.

The Mine Fine Art Gallery
24 Temple Street, Birmingham B2 5DB.
Tel: *0121-643 8424.*

Warstone & Turner Fine Art C
67 Warstone Lane, Hockley, Birmingham B18 6NG.

Coventry

COVENTRY

Herbert Art Gallery & Museum P
Jordan Well, Coventry CV1 5QP.
Tel: *01203-832381 / 832386;*
Minicom: 01203-83240.
Fax: *01203-832410.*
Email *coventry.museums@dial.pipex.com*
Ws *http://www.coventry.org/coventrymuseums*
Opening times: *Mon-Sat 10-5.30, Sun 12-5.*
Nearest Station: *Coventry.*
Personnel: *Exhibitions & Events Officer:* Rosie Addenbrooke.
Coventry is associated with outstanding manufacturing skills, post war reconstruction and the legend of Lady Godiva. As a focus for the city's heritage, the Herbert Art Gallery & Museum offers a fascinating visit with international appeal. The 'Godiva City' exhibition is a lively interpretation of one thousand years of Coventry's history. Here, the tale is told through historical treasures, interactive games, archive films and objects to handle. An optional audiotape tour is available. You can see Graham Sutherland's working drawings for the famous Coventry Cathedral Tapestry, portraits of Lady Godiva through the centuries, sculpture by Henry Moore and Jacob Epstein and paintings by L.S. Lowry, John Collier and David Cox. Please telephone for details of our lively temporary exhibition programme, workshops, lectures and children's activities. The Herbert Art Gallery & Museum has a tea room, gift shop, toilets for people with disabilities, baby changing facilities and parking for orange badge holders. Admission is free.
Services and Facilities:
Café. Disabled Access. Friends/Society. Gallery space for hire. Lectures. Museum Shop.

Mead Gallery, Warwick Arts Centre
University of Warwick, Coventry CV4 7AL
Tel: *01203-22589.*
Fax: *01203-523883.*

Dudley

DUDLEY

Dudley Museum & Art Gallery P
St. James's Road, Dudley DY1 1HU.
Tel: *01384-815575.*
Fax: *01384-815576.*

KINGSWINFORD

Broadfield House Glass Museum P
Compton Drive, Kingswinford, DY6 9QA.
Tel: *01384-812745.*

Hereford & Worcester

BEWDLEY

Bewdley Museum P
The Shambles, Load Street, Bewdley, DY12 2AE. **Tel:** *01299-403573.*

BROADWAY

Anderson Gallery C
96 Upper High Street, Broadway, WR12 7AJ.
Tel: *01386-858086.* **Fax:** *01386-858086.*
Opening times: *Open Daily. Please telephone to confirm hours.*
Personnel: *Proprietor:* Ronald Anderson.
The Anderson Gallery in the very heart of the Cotswolds is a vibrant arena for contemporary paintings, sculpture, ceramics, jewellery and furniture. An exciting calender of exhibitions throughout the year ensures something fresh and interesting on each visit. Paintings, contemporary and modern British sit happily alongside a rich display of sycamore and walnut chairs, mirrors and bookshelves, twisted wire and glass candle-sticks, bronzes, ceramics, stone carvings and beautifully made jewellery. Ronald Anderson, a highly qualified art historian is able to advise on paintings for corporate acquisition, probate and insurance valuations.
Services and Facilities:
Art Consultancy. Art for Offices. Commissioning Service. Restoration. Valuation.
Work Stocked and Sold:
Cer. Cra. Dec. Dr. Fur. Gla. Jew. Pa. Sc. Wd.
Price range: £30 - £30,000.
For artists see *Commercial Gallery Artists.*

BROMSGROVE

The Jinney Ring Craft Centre C
Old House Farm, Hanbury, Bromsgrove, B60 4BU.
Tel: *01527-821272.* **Fax:** *01527-821869.*

CRADLEY

The Lower Nupend Gallery C
Nr. Malvern, Cradley, WR13 5NP.
Tel: *01886-880500/334.* **Fax:** *01886-880848.*

GREAT MALVERN

Malvern Art Gallery
Malvern Library, Graham Road, Great Malvern, WR14 2HW.
Tel: *016845-61223.*

HEREFORD

Brook Street Pottery C
Brook Street, Hay-on-Wye, Hereford, HR3 5BQ. **Tel:** *01497-821026.*

Hatton Art Gallery
Churchill House Museum, 3 Venns Lane, Hereford.
Tel: *01432-267409.* **Fax:** *01432-342492.*

Hereford City Museum and Art Gallery P
Broad Street, Hereford, HR4 9AU.
Tel: *01432-364691.*
Fax: *01432-342492.*

John McKeller C
23 Church Street, Hereford, HR1 2LR.
Tel: *01432-354460.*

Mappa Mundi and Chained Library P
5 College Cloisters, Cathedral Close, Hereford, HR1 2NG.
Tel: *01432-359880.* **Fax:** *01432-355929.*

Meridian Contemporary Arts C
13 High Town, Hay-on-Wye, Hereford, HR3 5AE.
Tel: *01497-821633.*

Old Chapel Gallery C
East Street, Pembridge, Nr Leominster, Hereford, HR6 9HB.
Tel: *01544-388842.*

KIDDERMINSTER

Hereford & Worcester County Museum P
Hartlebury Castle, Hartlebury, Kidderminster, DY11 7XZ.
Tel: *01299-250416.*

LEOMINSTER

Lion Gallery C
15b Broad Street, Leominster, HR6 8BT.
Tel: *01568-614644.*

OMBERSLEY

Ombersley Gallery C
Church Terrace, Nr Droitwich, Ombersley, WR9 0EP.
Tel: *01905-620655.*

WORCESTER

City Museum & Art Gallery P
Foregate Street, Worcester,
Tel: *01905-25371.*

Regent Galleries C
22 Reindeer Court, Worcester, WR1 2DS.
Tel: *01905-21300.*

Worcester City Art Gallery & Museum P
Foregate Street, Worcester, WR1 1DT.
Tel: *01905-25371.*

Sandwell

WEDNESBURY

Wednesbury Museum & Art Gallery P
Holyhead Road, Wednesbury, WS10 7DF.
Tel: *0121-556 0683.*
Fax: *0121-505 1625.*

Shropshire

BISHOPS CASTLE

Longhouse Gallery
25 The High Street, Bishops Castle,
Tel: *01588-638147.*

BRIDGNORTH

Clode Gallery
New Market Building, Listley Street, Bridgnorth, WV16 4AW.
Tel: *01746-768338.* **Fax:** *01746-768481.*

ELLESMERE

Ellesmere Arts Centre
Ellesmere College, Ellesmere, SY12 9AB.
Tel: *01691-622828.*

LUDLOW

Feathers Gallery
20 The Bull Ring, Ludlow, SY8 1AA.
Tel: *01584-875390.*

Silk Top Hat Gallery
4 Quality Square, Ludlow, SY8 1AR.
Tel: *01584-875363.*

SHREWSBURY

Artifex C
Porch House, Swan Hill, Shrewsbury, SY1 1NQ.
Tel: *01743-241031.*

Gateway Galleries Gateway Education & Arts Centre
Chester Street, Shrewsbury, SY1 1NB.
Tel: *01743-55159.*

Grove Contemporary Arts C
Ruyton XI Towns, Shrewsbury, SY4 1LA.
Tel: *01939-260377.*
Opening times: *11-5 During major exhibitions - other times by appointment.*
Nearest Station: *Shrewsbury.*
Personnel: *Proprietor:* Yvonne Cooper.

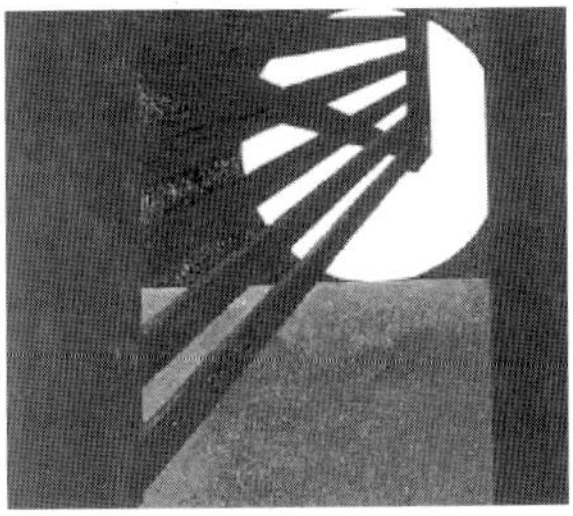

Grove Contemporary Arts has as its primary intent the exhibiting of quality work in a part of the world where there is little opportunity to view or to purchase contemporary art. The policy of staging a limited number of exhibitions prevents the pressure felt by many galleries to be always open and selling. Grove Contemporary Arts is in the enviable position of being able to concentrate on displaying work for its artistic merit rather than its immediate commercial viability, and seen in the conjunction of the proprietor's 'home-gallery' (Victorian elegance grafted on the traditional timbered cottage) - contemporary works work.
Services and Facilities:
Parking.
Work Stocked and Sold:
Dr. Pa. Sc.
Price range: £50 - £3,000.
For artists see *Commercial Gallery Artists.*

TELFORD

Elton Gallery
Ironbridge Gorge Museum, Coalbrookedale, Telford, TF8 7DG.
Tel: *01952-433522.*

The Gallery
Spout Farm House, Telford Town Park, Telford,
Tel: *01952-290240.*

Staffordshire

BURTON UPON TRENT

Brewhouse
Union Street, Burton upon Trent, DE14 1EB.
Tel: *01283-67720.*

Round House Gallery C
38 High Street, Tutbury, Burton upon Trent, DE13 9LS.
Tel: *01238-814964.*

LEEK

Leek Art Gallery
Nicholson Institute, Stockwell Street, Leek, ST13 6HQ.
Tel: *01538-399181.*

NEWCASTLE-UNDER-LYME

Hood & Broomfield Fine Art
29 Albert Street, Newcastle-under-Lyme, ST5 1JP.
Tel: *01782-626859.*

Newcastle-Under-Lyme Museum & Art Gallery P
Brampton Park, Newcastle-under-Lyme, ST5 0QP.
Tel: *01782-619705.*

Wavertree Gallery
Berkeley Court, Borough Road, Newcastle-under-Lyme, ST5 1TT.
Tel: *01782-712686.*

STAFFORD

The Shire Hall Gallery P
Market Square, Stafford, ST16 2LD.
Tel: *01785-278345.* **Fax:** *01785-278327.*

Shugborough
Ancestral home of the Earls of Milford, Stafford, ST17 0XB **Tel:** *01889-881388.*

Stoke-on-Trent

STOKE-ON-TRENT

City Museum and Art Gallery, Stoke on Trent P
Bethesda Street, Hanley, Stoke-on-Trent ST1 3DW.
Tel: *01782-232323.* **Fax:** *01782-205033.*

Wedgwood Museum P
Barlaston, Stoke-on-Trent ST12 9ES.
Tel: *01782-204141.* **Fax:** *01782-204666.*

Warwickshire

ALCESTER

Coughton Court P
Alcester, B49 5JA. **Tel:** *01789-400777*
Visitor info: 01789-762435.
Fax: *01789-765544.*

HENLEY-IN-ARDEN

The Gallery Upstairs C
Torquil, 81 High Street, Henley-in-Arden.
Tel: *01564-792174.*

LEAMINGTON SPA

Leamington Spa Art Gallery & Museum P
Avenue Road, Leamington Spa, CV31 3PP.
Tel: *01926-426559.* **Fax:** *01926-317867.*

RUGBY

Rugby Art Gallery & Museum P
St. Matthews Street, Rugby, CV21 3BZ.
Tel: *01788-542687.*

STRATFORD-UPON-AVON

Montpellier Gallery C
8 Chapel Street, Stratford-upon-Avon, CV37 3EP.
Tel: *01789-261161.* **Fax:** *01789-261161.*

WARWICK

Church Street Gallery
5 Church Street, Warwick, CV34 4AB.

Mason Watts Fine Art
60 Smith Street, Warwick, CV34 4HU.

Warwick Gallery C
14 Smith Street, Warwick, CV34 4HH.
Tel: *01926-495880.*

Wolverhampton

WOLVERHAMPTON

Bilston Art Gallery and Museum PS
Mount Pleasant, Bilston, Wolverhampton WV14 7LU.
Tel: *01902-552507.* **Fax:** *01902-552504.*

Wolverhampton Art Gallery *PS*
Lichfield Street, Wolverhampton WV1 1DU.
Tel: *01902-552055.*
Fax: *01902-552053.*
Email *info.wag@dial.pipex.com*
Ws *http://www.artgall.scit.wlv.ac.uk*
Opening times: *Mon-Sat 10-5. Free entry.*
Nearest Station: *Wolverhampton.*
Personnel: *Head of Arts & Museums:* Nicholas Dodd BA AMA.
Marketing Officer: Helen Large.

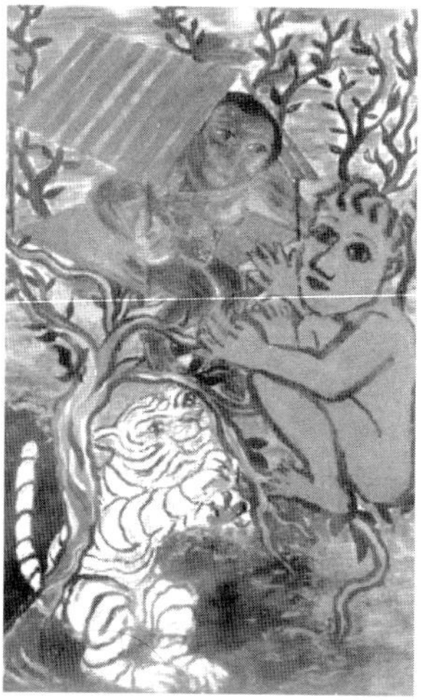

Wolverhampton has the largest collection of Contemporary Art in the region. Beautiful Victorian galleries show 18th and 19th Century paintings. We also have one of the best public collections of Pop Art in the country. An exciting programme of exhibitions, from international to local, is planned for 1999/2000, and will be accompanied by a range of workshops and activities. We are pleased to have been voted 1998 Best Museum of Fine Art. Our new "Ways of Seeing" room offers hands-on ways of looking at art for children and adults alike. Don't miss our tempting Tearoom and excellent Gallery Shop.
Services and Facilities:
Café. Commissioning Service. Craftshop. Disabled Access. Friends/Society. Lectures. Museum Shop. Shop.
Work Stocked and Sold:
Cer. Cra. Jew.
Price range: £10 - £100.

North West

Bolton

BOLTON

Bolton Museum, Art Gallery & Aquarium *P*
Le Mans Crescent, Bolton BL1 1SE.
Tel: *01204-522311 ext 2191.*
Fax: *01204-391352.*

Bury

BURY

Bury Art Gallery and Museum *PS*
Moss Street, Bury BL9 0DR.
Tel: *0161-253 5878.* **Fax:** *0161-253 5915.*
Email *artgallery@bury.gov.uk*
Opening times: *Tue-Sat 10-5.*
Nearest Station: *Bury (Metrolink - Tram).*
Personnel: *Curator:* Richard Burns.

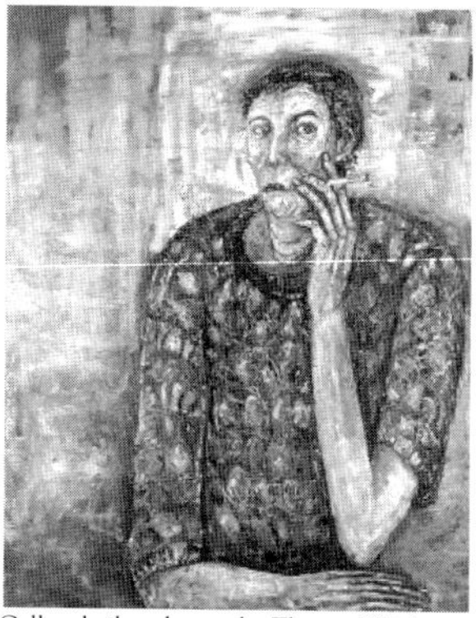

Gallery built to house the Thomas Wrigley collection of Victorian paintings and ceramics, given to Bury in 1897. Work by Turner, Constable, Landseer and Cox is still on permanent view. Burra, Pasmore, Lowry are among the artists in the 20th century collection, and works by contemporary artists are regularly added. Varied programme of contemporary art exhibitions included Ulrich Rückriem, Chris Foster, Craig Cooper and John Baldwin. Manchester Academy of Fine Arts (MAFA) Annual Open Exhibition is currently held in Bury. Decorative art collection highlights are Wedgwood and local Royal Lancastrian studio pottery. Stained glass mosaics decorate the Gallery.
Services and Facilities:
Disabled Access. Guided Tours. Lectures. Shop.

Cheshire

NORTHWICH

Weaver Gallery
45 Castle Street, Northwich, CW8 1EY.
Tel: *01606-871191.*

PRESTBURY

Artizana *C*
The Village, Prestbury, SK10 4DG.
Tel: *01625-827582.* **Fax:** *01625-827582.*

SANDBACH

dukes oak contemporary art gallery *C*
Dukes Oak, Brereton, Sandbach, CW11 1SD.
Tel: *01477-532337.*

WARRINGTON

Castle Park Arts Centre
Off Fountain Lane, Frodsham, Warrington, WA6 6SE.
Tel: *01928-35832.*

Warrington Museum & Art Gallery *P*
Bold Street, Warrington, WA1 1JG.
Tel: *01925-630550/444400.*

WINSFORD

Cheshire Visual Arts
Woodford Lodge, Woodford Lane, Winsford, CW7 4EH.
Tel: *01606-557328.*

Woodford Visual Art Centre
Woodford Lane West, Winsford, CW7 4EH.
Tel: *01606-557328.* **Fax:** *01606-862113.*

Lancashire

ACCRINGTON

Haworth Art Gallery *P*
Haworth Park, Manchester Road, Accrington, BB5 2JS.
Tel: *01254-233782.* **Fax:** *01254-301954.*

BLACKBURN

Blackburn Museum and Art Gallery *P*
Museum Street, Blackburn, BB1 7AJ.
Tel: *01254-667130.* **Fax:** *01254-680870.*

Lewis Textile Museum *P*
Exchange Street, Blackburn, BB1 7JN.
Tel: *01254-667130.*

The Street
Blackburn Central Library, Town Hall Street, Blackburn, BB2 1AH.
Tel: *01254-661221.*
Fax: *01254-690539.*

Witton Country Park Visitor Centre
Preston Old Road, Blackburn, BB2 2TP.
Tel: *01254-55423.*

BLACKPOOL

Grundy Art Gallery *P*
Queen Street, Blackpool, FY1 1PX.
Tel: *01253-751701.*
Fax: *01253-26370.*

BURNLEY

Towneley Hall Art Gallery & Museums *P*
Burnley, BB11 3RQ.
Tel: *01282-424213.*
Fax: *01282-424213.*

Wheatley Lane Library
Wheatley Lane, Burnley, BB12 9QH.
Tel: *01282-693160.*

Ab Artists' Books **App** Applied Art **Cer** Ceramics **Cra** Crafts **Dec** Decorative **Dr** Drawing **Fur** Furniture

CHORLEY

Astley Hall Museum and Art Gallery *P*
Astley Park, Chorley, PR7 1NP.
Tel: *01257-515555.* **Fax:** *01257-515556.*

LANCASTER

City Museum *P*
Market Square, Lancaster, LA1 1HT.
Tel: *01524-64637.* **Fax:** *01524-841692.*

Peter Scott Gallery *PS*
University of Lancaster, Lancaster, LA1 4YW.
Tel: *01524-593057.* **Fax:** *01524-592603.*
Email *m.p.gavagan@lancaster.ac.uk*
Ws *http://www.lancs.ac.uk/users/PETERSCOTT/Scott.htm*
Opening times: *Mon-Fri 11-4; late Thurs 6-8.30pm.*
Nearest Station: *Lancaster.*
Personnel: *Director:* Mary Gavagan.

PETER SCOTT GALLERY

University gallery open to the public, admission free, disabled access. The gallery has three display areas. On two levels, the main gallery presents a varied programme of temporary exhibitions. The Irene Manton Room houses and shows changing displays from the University Art Collection. The John Chambers Ceramics Room permanently shows the Royal Lancastrian Pottery collection and exhibitions of contemporary ceramics. Sculpture trail around university grounds. Exhibitions for hire.
Services and Facilities:
Bar. Disabled Access. Guided Tours. Parking. Restaurant. Shop.
Work Stocked and Sold:
Cer. Dr. Pa. Pr. Sc.

PRESTON

County & Regimental Museum *P*
Stanley Street, Preston, PR1 4YP.
Tel: *01772-264075.*

Harris Museum & Art Gallery *PS*
Market Square, Preston, PR1 2PP.
Tel: *01772-258248.* **Fax:** *01772-886764.*
Email *harris@pbch.demon.co.uk*
Opening times: *Mon-Sat 10-5. Closed on public holidays.*
Nearest Station: *Preston.*
Personnel: *Museum & Art Officer:* Alexandra Walker.
Fine Art collections mainly British 18th-20th century paintings, drawings and prints. Includes works by the Devis family, Newsham bequest of 19th century paintings and sculpture. A collection of British ceramics, glass and costume includes Cedric Houghton bequest of ceramics. A lively and varied programme of temporary exhibitions. Limited orange badge parking only. Lift. Chairlifts to Mezzanine Galleries. Wheelchair Ramp.

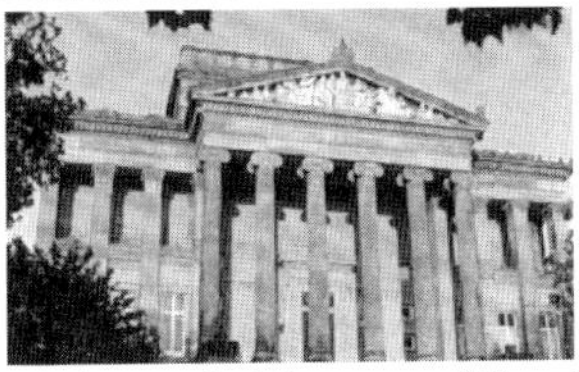

Refreshments. Guided tours are available and an education service to complement the permanent collection and exhibitions.
Services and Facilities:
Café. Disabled Access. Framing. Friends/Society. Guided Tours. Museum Shop. Shop.

Samlesbury Hall
Preston New Road, Samlesbury, Preston, PR5 OUP.
Tel: *01254-812010.*

Liverpool

LIVERPOOL

Acorn Gallery
16-18 Newington, Liverpool, L1 4ED
Tel: *0151-709 5423.* **Fax:** *0151-709 0759.*

Artreach Ltd
Unit B61, Brunswick Enterprise, Liverpool, L3 4BD.
Tel: *0151-708 7620.*

Bluecoat Display Centre *C*
Bluecoat Chambers, School Lane, Liverpool, L1 3BX.
Tel: *0151-709 4014.* **Fax:** *0151-707 0048.*

Liverpool Museum *P*
William Brown Street, Liverpool, L3 8EN.
Tel: *0151-478 4399.* **Fax:** *0151-478 4390.*

Liverpool University Exhibition
Abercromby Square, P.O. Box.147, Liverpool, L69 3BX.
Tel: *0151-794 2000.*

Open Eye Gallery *P*
28-32 Wood Street, Liverpool, L1 4AQ.
Tel: *0151-709 9460.* **Fax:** *0151-709 3059.*
Email *info@openeye.u-net.com*
Opening times: *Tues-Fri 10.30-5.30, Sat 10.30-5.*
Nearest Station: *Liverpool Central.*
Personnel: *Director:* Paul Mellor. *Gallery Manager:* Dave Williams. *Education Officer:* Helen James.
Open Eye is an organisation which develops, promotes, enables, celebrates, challenges and contextualises contemporary and historical art practices which uses or acknowledges a photographic language or technology for Merseyside and the greater North West region. The aims of the organisation are to:- Develop: new artists, existing artists, informal educational programmes, formal educational programmes, training opportunities, bridges to new and existing audiences, curatorial skills and awareness, collaboration; Create: opportunities for new work, exhibitions (external, internal and virtual), technical support services, pathways to facilities; Disseminate: touring exhibitions,

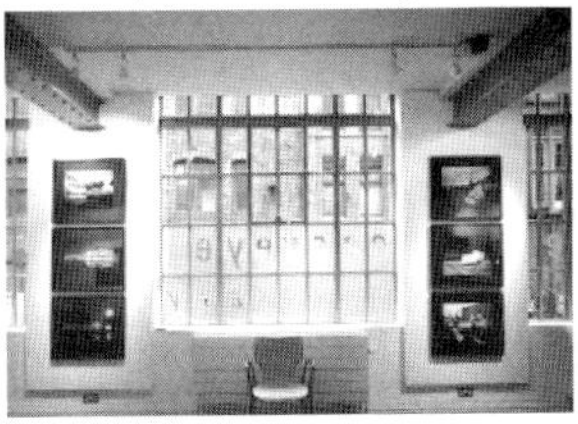

publications (both image and text), archived resources, the mission.
Services and Facilities:
Commissioning Service. Disabled Access. Gallery space for hire.

Sudley House *P*
Mossley Hill Road, Aigburth, Liverpool, L18 8BX.
Tel: *0151-724 3245.* **Fax:** *0151-478 4190.*
Ws *http://www.nmgm.org.uk*
Opening times: *Mon-Sat 10-5, Sun 12-5.*
Nearest Station: *Aigburth.*
Personnel: *Keeper of Art Galleries:* Julian Treuherz.
Sudley is undoubtedly one of Merseyside's gems. Situated in the leafy suburb of Mossley Hill, it was the home of George Holt (1825-1896) a founder of Lamport and Holt Shipping line. On display is a fine collection of late 18th and 19th century British paintings including two of Turner's most ambitious and dazzling works. There are superb paintings by Gainsborough, Bonnington and the Pre-Raphaelites and a group of 19th century sculptures ranging from Neo-classical marbles to decorative bronzes.
Services and Facilities:
Café. Disabled Access. Friends/Society. Lectures. Parking.

Tate Gallery Liverpool
Albert Dock, Liverpool, L3 4BB.
Tel: *0151-709 3223.* **Fax:** *0151-709 3122.*
Email *liverpoolinfo@tate.org.uk*
Ws *http://www.tate.org.uk*
Opening times: *Tues-Sun 10-6, closed Mon, except Bank Holidays. Also closed 24-26 Dec, 1 Jan.*
Personnel: *Director:* Lewis Biggs.
Opened in May 1988, Tate Gallery Liverpool is housed in a Victorian warehouse converted by the distinguished architect James Stirling. Attracting more than half a million visitors a year, the gallery offers a unique opportunity to see the best of the national collection of 20th c. art through a changing programme of displays, as well as special loan exhibitions. Audience development is central to the gallery's aim, and the education programme, comprising workshops, talks, study days and outreach projects, is recognised as among the most innovative in the country. A £6.96 million development scheme, completed in 1998, has transformed previously undeveloped spaces of the Grade I listed building into new galleries on the top floor

which will allow more of the national collection of modern art to be shown in Liverpool. An auditorium, seminar room, education suite, and information areas are now provided with disabled access substantially improved. The ground floor development includes the re-design of the entrance as well as a new dockside shop and cafe-bar with views across the Albert Dock. Group Talks.

Services and Facilities:
Bar. Bookshop. Café. Disabled Access. Friends/Society. Guided Tours. Lectures. Shop. Workshop Facilities.

University of Liverpool Art Gallery *PS*
3 Abercromby Square, Liverpool L69 3BX.
Tel: *0151-794 2348.*
Fax: *0151-794 2343.*
Email *acompton@liv.ac.uk*
Opening times: *Mon, Tues, Thurs 12-2, Wed, Fri 12-4. Closed: Weekends, Bank Holidays and August. Admission free.*
Nearest Station: *Lime Street.*
Personnel: *Curator:* Ann Compton. *Assistant Curator:* Matthew H. Clough.
The art gallery displays a selection of the finest works of art belonging to the University of Liverpool. Among the highlights are a representative group of English watercolours, paintings by Joseph Wright of Derby and J.M.W. Turner, rare oil paintings by the wild-life artist J.J. Audubon, a fine selection of early English porcelain, stained glass cartoons by Edward Burne-Jones, portraits by August John, sculpture by John Foley and Lord Leighton and important works by leading twentieth century artists, including Sir Jacob Epstein, Lucian Freud and Dame Elizabeth Frink. The collection has grown up over the last hundred years through the generosity of local benefactors, supplemented more recently by purchases. These gifts and acquisitions of paintings, watercolours, sculpture, medals, silver, ceramics, furniture and textiles are both a fine collection of British art and an integral part of the University's history since its foundation in 1881. The presentation of the Art Gallery complements the elegant Georgian terrace house in Abercromby Square it occupies. A fine selection of clocks, furniture, carpets and tapestries lends a domestic atmosphere to this charming gallery. Only a small part of the University's substantial collection is on display in the Art Gallery; a tour of art around the Precinct is available from the Curator. Postcards and publications are on sale at the entrance to the Art Gallery. Coffee and light refreshments are available in Staff House next door to the Art Gallery at 4-5 Abercromby Square. Free lunchtime gallery talks are organised in term time, please telephone for details. No prior booking necessary.
Services and Facilities:
Café. Gallery space for hire. Lectures. Museum Shop.

Walker Art Gallery *P*
William Brown Street, Liverpool, L3 8EL.
Tel: *0151-207 0001/0151-478 4199.*
Fax: *0151-478 4190.*
Ws *http://www.nmgm.org.uk*
Opening times: *Mon-Sat 10-5, Sun 12-5.*
Nearest Station: *Lime Street.*
Personnel: *Director:* Mr R Foster. *Keeper:* Mr J B Treuherz.
Founded in 1877, the gallery exhibits an internationally important collection of art from the 14th to the 20th century. It is especially rich in European Old Masters, Victorian and Pre-Raphaelite pictures and modern British works. Includes the award-winning Sculpture Gallery, Medieval and Renaissance, eighteenth century and High Victorian galleries. There is an exciting exhibitions programme, including Britain's premier painting biennial, the John Moores Liverpool Exhibition. The John Moores is the only national, open submission exhibition of British painting besides the Royal Academy and the first prize-winning painting becomes part of the Walker's outstanding collection of contemporary art.
Services and Facilities:
Café. Disabled Access. Friends/Society. Lectures. Parking. Shop.

Manchester

MANCHESTER

Beech Road Gallery
70 Beech Road, Chorlton, Manchester M21.
Tel: *0161-881 4912.*

Castlefield Gallery
5 Campfield Avenue Arcade, Manchester.
Tel: *0161-832 8034.*

Colin Jellicoe Gallery *C*
82 Portland Street, Manchester M1 4QX.
Tel: *0161-236 2716.*
Opening times: *Tue-Fri 11-5, Sats 1-5.*
Nearest Station: *Piccadilly or Oxford Road.*
Personnel: *Directors:* Colin Jellicoe, Alan Behar.

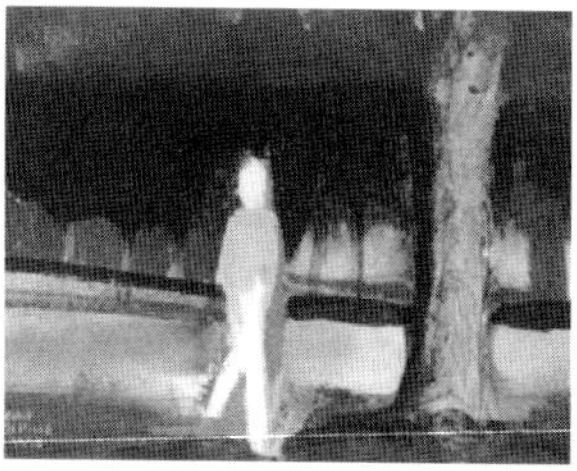

Sixty gallery artists including Colin Jellicoe (pictured) exhibiting drawings, paintings and graphics in 35th Winter Ex to April 3, 36th Summer Ex to Oct 30, 36th Winter Ex to April 2000. Group show at Mariners Gallery St. Ives, Cornwall July 31 - August 13 1999. Most works priced £50-£450. Founded 1963.
Services and Facilities:
Framing. Gallery space for hire.
Work Stocked and Sold:
Dr. Pa. Pr.
Price range: £50 - £450.
For artists see *Commercial Gallery Artists.*

Cornerhouse *PS*
70 Oxford Street, Manchester M1 5NH.
Tel: *0161-228 7621.*
Fax: *0161-236 7323.*

The Gallery, Manchester's Art House *C*
131 Portland Street, Manchester M1 4PY.
Tel: *0161-237 3551.*
Fax: *0161-228 3621.*

Manchester Central Library
St. Peter's Square, Manchester M2 5PD.
Tel: *0161-234 1900.*

Manchester City Art Gallery *PS*
Mosley Street/Princess Street, Manchester M2 3JL.
Tel: *0161-236 5244.*
Fax: *0161-236 7369.*

Manchester Craft Centre
17 Oak Street, Smithfield, Manchester M4 5JD.
Tel: *0161-832 4274.*
Fax: *0161-832 3416.*

Manchester Metropolitan University (Holden Gallery) *P*
Grosvenor Building, Manchester Metropolitan University, Cavendish, All Saints, Manchester M15 6BR.
Tel: *0161-247 1708, 0161-247 2000.*
Fax: *0161-236 0820, 0161-247 6393.*

The Museum of Science & Industry in Manchester *P*
Liverpool Road, Castlefield, Manchester M3 4FP.
Tel: *0161-832 2244.* **Fax:** *0161-833 2184.*

Philips Contemporary Art *C*
37, Ducie Street Piccadilly, Manchester
Tel: *0161-236 2707.*

Rainmaker Gallery Of Contemporary Native American Indian Art *C*
41 Lapwing Lane, West Didbury, Manchester M20 2NT.
Tel: *0161-4480 1495.*
Fax: *0161-4480 1495.*

Tib Lane Gallery *C*
14a Tib Lane (off Cross Street), Manchester M2 4JA.
Tel: *0161-834 6928.*
Opening times: *Open during exhibitions 11-2, 3-5, Sat 11-1; closed Sun.*
Personnel: *Director:* J.M. Green.
Founded in 1959, Tib Lane Gallery continues to exhibit British, mainly figurative 20th Century paintings, watercolours, drawings etc. and some sculpture, particularly bronzes by Adrian Sorrell. Solo and mixed exhibitions between September and the end of June each year show the work of well-established artists (Frink, Herman, Sutherland, Valette, Vaughan etc.) as well as that by many artists whose work, though distinguished, is less widely known. Conservation and Framing.

Ab Artists' Books **App** Applied Art **Cer** Ceramics **Cra** Crafts **Dec** Decorative **Dr** Drawing **Fur** Furniture

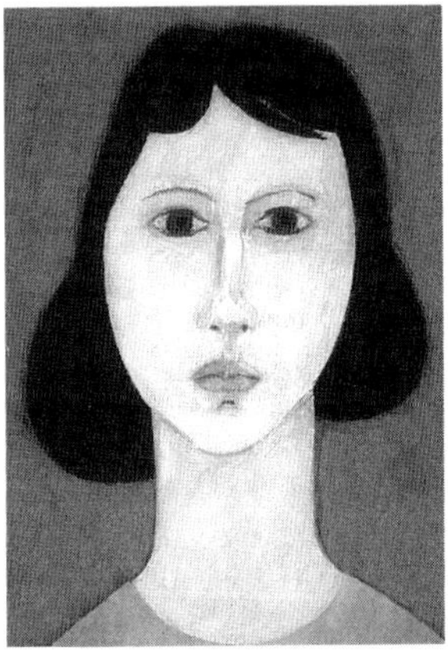

Services and Facilities:
Art Consultancy. Art for Offices. Commissioning Service. Framing. Restoration. Valuation.
Work Stocked and Sold:
Dr. Pa. Sc.
Price range: From £100.
For artists see *Commercial Gallery Artists.*

Via Communications
9 Market Buildings, Thomas Street, Northern Quarter, Manchester M4 1EU.

The Whitworth Art Gallery
University of Manchester, Oxford Road, Manchester M15 6ER.
Tel: *0161-275 7450.*
Fax: *0161-275 7451.*
Opening times: *Mon-Sat 10-5, Sun 2-5. Free admission.*
Personnel: *Director:* Alistair Smith. *Marketing Officer:* Emma Marshall.
Founded in 1889, the Whitworth is famous for its collections of British watercolours, prints, drawings, modern art, sculpture and the largest textile and wallpaper holdings outside London. A lively programme of temporary exhibitions and changing displays from the gallery's collections runs throughout the year. Works not currently on show can be seen by appointment in the Study Rooms.
Gallery Bistro.
Services and Facilities:
Bookshop. Disabled Access. Friends/Society. Guided Tours. Lectures. Parking. Restaurant. Shop.

Oldham

OLDHAM

Oldham Art Gallery P
Union Street, Oldham OL1 1DN.
Tel: *0161-911 4653 / 4650.*
Fax: *0161-627 1025.*

Saddleworth Museum & Art Gallery P
High Street, Uppermill, Oldham OL3 6HS.
Tel: *01457-874093/870336.*

Rochdale

ROCHDALE

Rochdale Art Gallery P
Esplanade Arts & Heritage Centre, Esplanade, Rochdale OL16 1AQ.
Tel: *01706-342154.*
Fax: *01706-342154.*

Salford

SALFORD

Chapman Gallery
University of Salford, The Crescent, Salford M5 4WT.
Tel: *0161-745 5000 ext 3219.*

Salford Museum & Art Gallery PS
Peel Park, The Crescent, Salford M5 4WU.
Tel: *0161-736 2649.*
Fax: *0161-745 9490.*
Opening times: *Mon-Fri 10-4.45, Sat & Sun 1-5. Admission Free.*
Nearest Station: *Salford Crescent.*

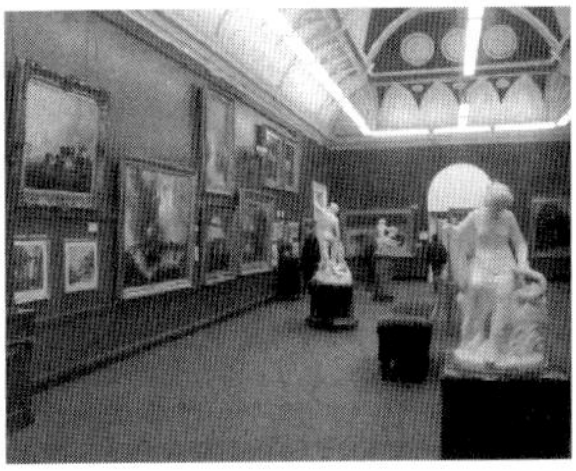

L S Lowry Gallery displaying over 100 of the best paintings and drawings from the City's vast collection of work by the artist. In addition, there is a gallery of fine Victorian paintings and decorative arts and temporary exhibitions of contemporary art, craft, social history and photography. Also a reconstruction of a cobbled Victorian Street complete with carriages and authentic sounds.
Services and Facilities:
Café. Disabled Access. Friends/Society. Gallery space for hire. Museum Shop. Parking.
For artists see *Commercial Gallery Artists.*

Viewpoint Photography Gallery
Fire Station Square, The Crescent, Salford M5 4NZ.
Tel: *0161-737 1040, 0161-736 9448.*
Fax: *0161-737 1091.*

Sefton

SOUTHPORT

Atkinson Art Gallery
Lord Street, Southport, PR8 1DH.
Tel: *01704-533133 Ext. 2111.*
Fax: *0151-934 2107.*

St. Helens

ST. HELENS

St. Helens Museum & Art Gallery P
College Street, St. Helens, WA10 1TW.
Tel: *01744-616614, 24061 ext 2961.*

Stockport

STOCKPORT

Stockport Art Gallery C
Wellington Road South, Stockport SK3 8AB.
Tel: *0161-474 4453.* **Fax:** *0161-480 4960.*

Tameside

STALYBRIDGE

Astley Cheetham Art Gallery PS
Trinity Street, Stalybridge, SK15 2BN.
Tel: *0161-338 2708.*

Wigan

LEIGH

Turnpike Gallery PS
Civic Square, Leigh WN7 1EB.
Tel: *01942-404469.* **Fax:** *01942-404447.*
Email *trngal@globalnet.co.uk*
Opening times: *Mon,Thur,Fri 9.30-5.30, Tues 10-5.30, Wed 9.30-5, Sat 10-3.*
Nearest Station: *Atherton.*
Personnel: *Gallery Officer:* Andrea Hawkins.
The Turnpike Gallery is a modern purpose built gallery 3200 sq. feet in size situated on the first floor of the Turnpike Centre. The temporary exhibitions programme reflects a variety of visual arts practices, and promotes contemporary art by regional, national and international artists. There is an Arts Education service for schools and exciting Outreach activities for the public organised throughout the year. Small changing display of prints from the permanent collection include work by Patrick Caulfield and Andy Warhol. "1999 artist in residence Astrid Greenbury". Free admission, large print guides and toilets.
Services and Facilities:
Disabled Access. Guided Tours. Lectures. Parking. Workshop Facilities.

Wirral

BEBINGTON

Lady Lever Art Gallery P
Port Sunlight, Bebington, L62 5EQ.
Tel: *0151-478 4136.* **Fax:** *0151-478 4140.*

Ws *http://www.nmgm.org.uk*
Opening times: *Mon-Sat 10-5, Sun 12-5.*
Nearest Station: *Bebington.*
Personnel: *Curator:* Julian Treuherz.
Opened in 1922. The gallery was founded and built by Philanthropist and soap manufacturer William Hesketh Lever, later the first Viscount Leverhulme, and houses his personal collection of works of art. These include Pre-Raphaelites, 18th and 19th century paintings, 18th century furniture, Chinese ceramics, Wedgwood, sculpture, embroideries and tapestries. The Lady Lever Art Gallery is named in memory of Lever's wife and forms the centre piece of the garden village Lever built for his workforce. Of special note is a series of superb carved or inlaid cabinets, some by Chippendale and paintings by Reynolds, Wilson, Sargent, Burne-Jones and Leighton.
Services and Facilities:
Café. Disabled Access. Friends/Society. Parking. Shop.

BIRKENHEAD

Blackthorn Galleries C
2a Price Street, Hamilton Quarter, Birkenhead, CH41 6JN.
Tel: *0151-649 0099.*
Fax: *0151-649 0088.*
Email *ogilvie@galleries.u-net.com*
Ws *http://www.galleries.u-net.com*
Opening times: *Mon-Fri 9.30-5.30. Sat 10-5.*
Nearest Station: *Hamilton Square (Mersey Rail).*
Personnel: *Director (M.D.):* Iain Ogilvie. *Arts Director:* Chris Wells.
The Blackthorn galleries exists to promote the work of its stable of artists/designers in the UK and further afield, to raise the awareness of fine art and contemporary design in its locale and to provide a platform for artists and designers to show their work in a professional and creative environment. We have a world-wide vision and plans are progressing to open 4 "twin" galleries in Europe, 1 in Georgia USA and another in Romania.
We exhibit and sell an exciting combination of work; fine art paintings, sculpture, photography, ceramics, glass and contemporary jewellery. See Internet - http://www.galleries.u-net.com for more details.
Services and Facilities:
Art for Offices. Craftshop. Gallery space for hire. Shop. Workshop Facilities.
Work Stocked and Sold:
Cer. Gla. Jew. Pa. Ph. Pr. Sc.
Price range: £15 - £2,500.
For artists see *Commercial Gallery Artists.*

Williamson Art Gallery and Museum P
Slatey Road, Birkenhead, L43 4UE.
Tel: *0151-652 4177.*
Fax: *0151-670 0253.*

HESWALL

Dee Fine Arts
182 Telegraph Road, Heswall, L60 OAJ.
Tel: *0151-342 6657.*

Yorkshire & Humberside

Bradford

BRADFORD

Bradford Art Galleries and Museums P
Headquarters, Cartwright Hall, Lister Park, Bradford BD9 4NS.
Tel: *01274-493313.*
Fax: *01274-481045.*

Cartwright Hall Art Gallery PS
(Bradford Metropolitan Council), Lister Park, Bradford BD9 4NS.
Tel: *01274-493313.*
Fax: *01274-481045.*

The Colour Museum PS
Perkin House, PO Box 244, 1 Providence Street, Bradford BD1 2PW.
Tel: *01274-390955.*
Fax: *01274-392888.*

National Museum of Photography, Film and Television P
Temporary Address: The Art Mill, Upper Parkgate, Little Germany, Bradford BD1 5BJ.
Tel: *01274-72748.*
Fax: *01274-394540.*

South Square Gallery C
Thornton Road, Bradford BD13 3LD.
Tel: *01274-834747.*

University of Bradford
Gallery II, University of Bradford, Chesham Building, (off Great Horton Road), Bradford BD7 1DP.
Tel: *01274-383365.* **Fax:** *01274-305340.*

KEIGHLEY

Bronte Parsonage Museum P
Haworth, Keighley, BD22 8DR.
Tel: *01535-642323.*
Fax: *01535-647131.*

Cliffe Castle Art Gallery
Spring Gardens Lane, Keighley, BD20 6LH.
Tel: *01535-606593.*

Calderdale

HALIFAX

Piece Hall Art Gallery P
The Piece Hall, Halifax, HX1 1RE.
Tel: *01422-358087.*
Fax: *01422-349310.*

TODMORDEN

Todmorden Fine Art
27 Water Street, Todmorden, OL14 5AB.
Tel: *01706-814723.*

Doncaster

DONCASTER

Doncaster Museum and Art Gallery P
Chequer Road, Doncaster DN1 2AE.
Tel: *01302-734222 / 734293.*
Fax: *01302-735409.*

Hull

HULL

University of Hull Art Collection PS
University of Hull, Cottingham Road, Hull HU6 7RX.
Tel: *01482-465192 / 465035.*
Fax: *01482-465192.*
Email *j.g.bernasconi@hist.hull.ac.uk*
Ws *http://www.hull.ac.uk*
Opening times: *Mon-Fri 2-4, Wed 12.30-4 (except Public Hols.).*
Personnel: *Director:* John G. Bernasconi.
The Hull University Art Collection specialises in paintings, sculpture, drawings and prints produced in Britain 1890-1940. It includes works by Beardsley, Sickert, Steer, Lucien Pissarro, Augustus John, Stanley Spencer, Wyndham Lewis and Ben Nicholson, as well as sculpture by Epstein, Gill, Gaudier-Brzeska and Henry Moore. The Camden Town Group and Bloomsbury artists are particularly well represented. Also on display are the Thompson Collections of Chinese ceramics on long-term loan. Regular loan exhibitions are shown.
Services and Facilities:
Disabled Access. Friends/Society. Lectures.

Humberside

KINGSTON UPON HULL

Ferens Art Gallery
Queen Victoria Square, Kingston Upon Hull, HU1 3RA.

Kirklees

BATLEY

Bagshaw Museum P
Wilton Park, Batley, WF17 OAS.
Tel: *01924-326156.*

Batley Art Gallery
Market Place, Batley, WF17 5DA.
Tel: *01924-326090.* **Fax:** *01924-326308.*

DEWSBURY

Dewsbury Exhibition Gallery
Wellington Road, Dewsbury, WF13.
Tel: *0113-233 6107.*

HUDDERSFIELD

The Ark C
113 North Road, Kirkburton, Huddersfield, HD8 0RL.
Tel: *01484-605055.*

MIRFIELD

Eastthorpe Gallery
Huddersfield Road, Mirfield, WF14 8AT.
Tel: *01924-497646.*

Leeds

LEEDS

Abbey House Museum P
Kirkstall Road, Leeds LS5 3EH.
Tel: *01532-755821.*

Art.Co, Contemporary Fine Art
No. 1 Meanwood Close, Leeds LS7 2JF.
Tel: *0113-262 0056.*
Fax: *0113-262 8388.*

Bruton Gallery C
Trafalgar House, 29 Park Place, Leeds LS1 2SP.
Tel: *0113-242 2323.*
Fax: *0113-242 1447.*
Email *Helen@BrutonGallery.co.uk*
Ws *http://www.BrutonGallery.co.uk*
Opening times: *Weekdays and by arrangement.*
Nearest Station: *Leeds.*
Personnel: *Director:* Helen Robinson. *Personal Assistant:* Sonia Harman.

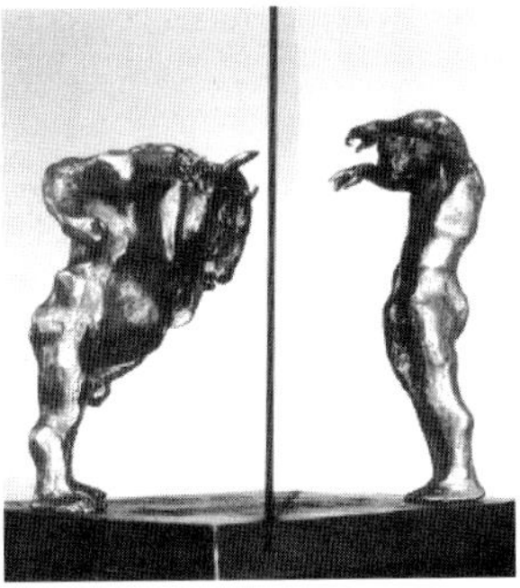

A new city centre commercial Gallery for Leeds, this beautiful, calm space is a treasure to be discovered in the Leeds art map. Previously located in Somerset and Bath, Bruton Gallery has an established reputation for selling high quality figurative sculpture by turn of the century European Masters.
We offer our clients comprehensive Fine Art Services at Museum standards. Art consultancy available for home and office, from single visual statements to a whole collection or suite refurbishment. Gallery space available for venue hire. Alongside this, Bruton showcase the work of contemporary painters and sculptors. A diverse exhibition programme features four main exhibitions a year.
Services and Facilities:
Art Consultancy. Art for Offices. Commissioning Service. Gallery space for hire. Parking. Valuation.
Work Stocked and Sold:
Dr. Pa. Pr. Sc.
Price range: £200 - £200,000.
For artists see *Commercial Gallery Artists.*

City Art Gallery
The Headrow, Leeds LS1 3AA.
Tel: *0113-2478248.*
Fax: *0113-2449689.*

The Craft Centre and Design Gallery C
City Art Gallery, The Headrow, Leeds LS1 3AB.
Tel: *0113-247 8241.*
Opening times: *Tues-Fri 10-5, Sat 10-4.*
Nearest Station: *Leeds.*
Personnel: *Director:* Hayley Walker.

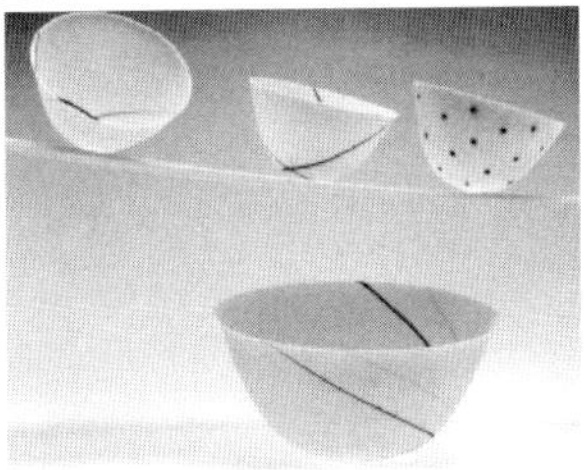

The Craft Centre and Design Gallery aims to provide 'Art for Everyone' by showing contemporary fine craft from established and new designers. A lively exhibition programme features two main exhibitions a year, jewellery and ceramics showcases, limited edition print exhibitions and a new works section. In addition displays of contemporary jewellery, studio ceramics and domesticware, textiles, limited edition prints and applied arts provide a permanent feature. All year round approximately two hundred designers show their work, making it an excellent venue to browse, to learn or to buy.
Services and Facilities:
Commissioning Service. Craftshop. Disabled Access.
Work Stocked and Sold:
App. Cer. Cra. Gla. Jew. Pr. Tx. Wd.
Price range: £10 - £3,000.
For artists see *Commercial Gallery Artists.*

The Henry Moore Institute
74 The Headrow, Leeds LS1 3AA.
Tel: *0113-234 3158 (Information line).*
Fax: *0113-246 1481.*
Email *HMST@henry-moore.ac.uk*
Opening times: *Open daily 10-5.30, Weds 10-9pm.*
Nearest Station: *Leeds City.*
Personnel: Helen Pearson.
The Henry Moore Institute, formerly a neglected group of early victorian merchants offices, has been transformed into a unique building devoted to the exhibition, study and promotion of sculpture. Situated in the heart of Leeds, the Institute houses four sculpture galleries for temporary exhibitions, also a sculpture reference library, archive and slide library. The Institute organises talks, seminars and lectures. Please call our information line for further details: 0113-234 3158.
Admission free.

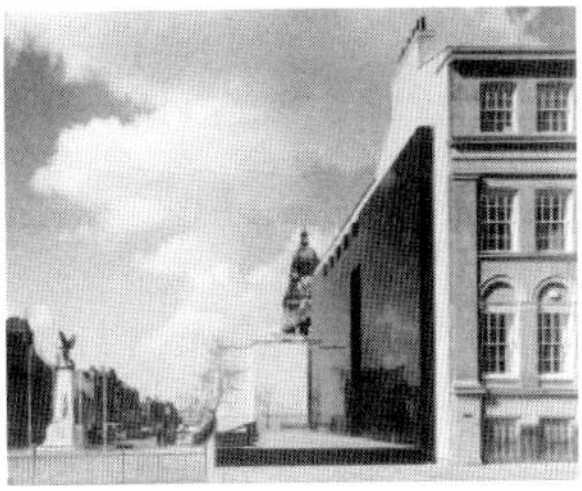

Services and Facilities:
Disabled Access. Guided Tours. Lectures. Shop.

Leeds Metropolitan University Gallery PS
Woodhouse Lane, Leeds LS1 3HE.
Tel: *0113-283 3130.* **Fax:** *0113-283 5999*
Email *c.slattery@lmu.ac.uk and m.innes@lmu.ac.uk*
Ws *http://www.lmu.ac.uk/arts*
Opening times: *Mon-Sat 11-5, Wed 11-7.*
Personnel: *Gallery Development Officers:* Claire Slattery, Moira Innes.

LEEDS METROPOLITAN UNIVERSITY
GALLERY

Leeds Metropolitan University Gallery is one of the major contemporary arts venues in the city of Leeds. It is a public gallery specialising in commissioning contemporary art exhibitions and hosting touring exhibitions by artists of national and international significance. The main programme is interjected with seasonal shows by staff and students of the University. All exhibitions are temporary - there is no permanent collection. Our exhibitions policy covers the visual arts in its widest sense.
Services and Facilities:
Bar. Disabled Access. Lectures. Workshop Facilities.

The Pavillion Photography Centre
235 Woodhouse Lane, Leeds LS2 3AP.
Tel: *0113-275 1347.*

Terrace Gallery PS
Harewood House Trust, Moor House, Harewood, Leeds LS17 9LQ.
Tel: *0113-288 6331.* **Fax:** *0113-288 6467.*
Email *business@harewood.org*
Ws *http://www.harewood.org*
Opening times: *Open daily, 9 March-31 October, 11-4.30. (Last admission 4pm).*
Nearest Station: *Leeds, Harrogate.*
Personnel: *Visual Arts Co-ordinator:* Philippa Brough.
Contemporary Art Gallery in a Country House; one of the few galleries of its kind in the UK, providing a continuum to the arts patronage which has been in existence at

Harewood for over 200 years. Exhibition programme for 1999: St. Ives Artists and their Friends in the North, 9 March - 18 July. Examination of the connection between the St. Ives based abstract painters, including Sir Terry Frost, Trevor Bell, Alan Davie, and Leeds' cultural life through the University of Leeds Gregory Fellowships in the 1950's. The Flower Show - 24 July - 31 October. A celebration and exploration of the meaning of flowers in art in the 20th century. To include work by Robert Mapplethorpe, Andy Warhol, Gillian Ayres, and David Hockney.

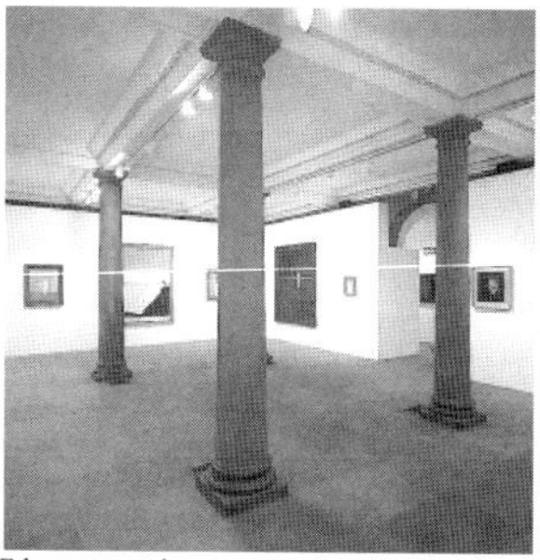

Education and interpretative events as well as programmes of free talks accompany each exhibition.
Services and Facilities:
Bookshop. Café. Disabled Access. Guided Tours. Lectures. Parking. Shop.

University Gallery Leeds *PS*
Parkinson Building, Woodhouse Lane, Leeds LS2 9JT.
Tel: *0113-233 2777.*
Email *H.M.Diaper@leeds.ac.uk*
Ws
http://www.leeds.ac.uk/library/gall/exhibs.html
Opening times: *Exhibitions Mon-Fri 10-5, Thurs 10-7.*
Nearest Station: *Leeds City.*
Personnel: *Keeper:* Dr Hilary Diaper.
Changing programme of exhibitions during each academic year, covering a wide range of historic and contemporary works in a variety of media. Wheelchair Access at north end of Parkinson Building.
Services and Facilities:
Disabled Access. Friends/Society.

WETHERBY

Green Frog Gallery *C*
2 Church Street, Wetherby, LS22 6LP.
Tel: *01937-586411.*
Fax: *01937-586411.*

Rotherham

ROTHERHAM

Art Gallery *P*
Rotherham Arts Centre, Walker Place, Rotherham S65 1JH.
Tel: *01709-382121 ext 3624.*
Fax: *01709-823650.*

Sheffield

SHEFFIELD

City Museum and Mappin Art Gallery *P*
Weston Park, Western Bank, Sheffield S10 2TP.
Tel: *0114-2768588.*
Fax: *0114-2750957.*
Opening times: *Wed-Sat 10-5, Sun 11-5, closed Mon & Tues. Opening Tuesdays 10-5 from Summer 1999.*
Personnel: *Curator of Contemporary Art:* Julie Milne.
Situated in Weston Park near the University of Sheffield, the City Museum and Mappin Art Gallery house and display the city's collections of fine and applied art, archaeology and ethnography and natural history. There is a continuous changing programme of temporary exhibitions, largely reflecting the strengths of the 19th and 20th c., visual arts collections, but with a commitment to contemporary work. Educational activities include a full schools programme plus workshops and art classes organised by the Mappin Art Workshops. Gallery and museum shop and Mappin café.
Services and Facilities:
Café. Disabled Access. Friends/Society. Museum Shop. Shop. Workshop Facilities.

Crafty People *C*
67 Barber Road, Sheffield S10 1EB.
Tel: *0114-263 1799.* **Fax:** *0114-263 1799.*
Opening times: *Mon 10-3, 4-6, Art Class 6-8, Tue & Wed closed, Thur-Sat 10-5, Sun 11-2, 2-4 Artists Group.*
Nearest Station: *Sheffield City Centre.*
Personnel: *Proprietor:* Chantal A. Pitts.
The ethos of the Crafty People gallery is to display/sell original works of art and crafts, created/designed primarily by the local community of Sheffield including items such as cards, jewellery, glass, decorative items, mobiles, paintings, fine art works, sculpture, photographic imagery, textiles, furniture, pelief and so on. Classes in a wide variety of materials are held on the premises for beginners or for artists wishing to try/explore new and varied mediums. Crafty People also provides the perfect venue for all kinds of creative people to interact with each other in a friendly, informal environment.
Commissions undertaken (numerous materials considered).
Services and Facilities:
Commissioning Service. Craftshop. Framing. Gallery space for hire. Shop.
Work Stocked and Sold:
App. Cer. Cra. Dec. Dr. Fur. Gla. Jew. Pa. Ph. Pr. Sc. Tx. Wd.
Price range: £5 - £500.
For artists see *Commercial Gallery Artists.*

Cupola Gallery *C*
178a Middlewood Road, Sheffield S61 TD.
Tel: *0114-285 2665.* **Fax:** *0114-285 2665.*
Email *cupola@globalnet.co.uk*
Opening times: *Mon-Sat 10-6.30, Sun by appointment. Please ring for details of late night opening.*
Nearest Station: *Sheffield. Tram direct from station to gallery.*
Personnel: *Manager:* Lesley Smailes. *Managing Director:* Karen Sherwood.

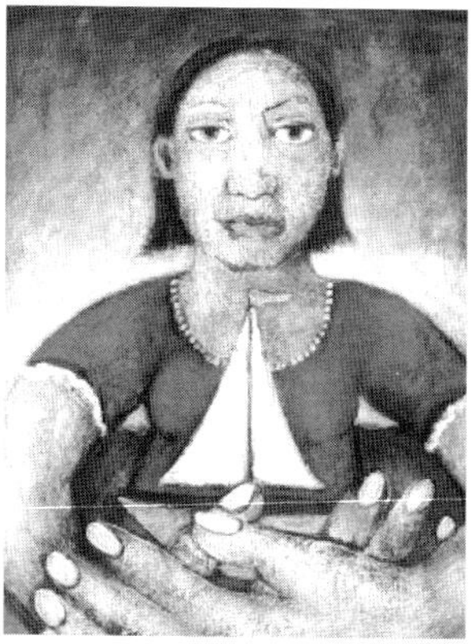

Established in 1991 Cupola is very lively and friendly, with a reputation for quality exhibitions and innovation. The gallery shows a collection of constantly evolving quality contemporary work and plays host to a breathless turnover of gallery exhibitions. New artists and makers feature extensively in Cupola, together with the more established. We operate the Artloan interest free credit system and offer free chocolate cake on Saturdays. We also offer a quality bespoke framing service where friendly and helpful staff are happy to offer advice when required. Limited Disabled Access.
Services and Facilities:
Art Consultancy. Art for Offices. Café. Commissioning Service. Craftshop. Framing. Parking. Restoration. Shop. Valuation.
Work Stocked and Sold:
Cer. Cra. Fur. Gla. Jew. Pa. Ph. Pr. Sc. Tx. Wd.
Price range: £30 - £2,000.
For artists see *Commercial Gallery Artists.*

Graves Art Gallery *P*
Surrey Street, Sheffield S1 1XZ.
Tel: *0114-273 5158.* **Fax:** *0114-273 4705.*
Opening times: *Tues-Sat 10-5. Closed Sundays. Opening Monday 10-5 from Summer 1999.*
Nearest Station: *Sheffield. Midland.*
Personnel: *Curator of Visual Art:* Anne Goodchild.
Founded 1934. The Gallery has on display paintings by famous 20th century British artists. Also on display is the stunning collection of Chinese Ivories given to the gallery by J.G. Greaves. Temporary exhibitions throughout the year include works by internationally renowned artists.
Services and Facilities:
Café. Friends/Society. Lectures. Museum Shop. Shop.

Ruskin Gallery *P*
101 Norfolk Street, Sheffield S1 2JE.
Tel: *0114-203 9416.*
Fax: *0114-203 9417.*

Opening times: *Tues-Sat 10-5, closed Sun. Opening Mondays 10-5 from Summer 1999.*
Personnel: *Principal Keeper:* Camilla Hampshire.
The Ruskin Gallery was founded by John Ruskin (1819-1900) in Sheffield in 1875. It houses the collection of the Guild of St. George which comprises paintings, water-colours, prints, photographers, minerals, plaster casts, mediaeval illuminated manuscripts and a library. This extensive collection is presented in a series of temporary exhibitions. Ruskin Craft Gallery has exhibitions of contemporary crafts.
Services and Facilities:
Friends/Society. Gallery space for hire. Museum Shop. Shop.

Untitled Photographic Gallery & Workshop
1 Brown Street, Sheffield S1 2BS.
Tel: *01742-725947.*

Wakefield

WAKEFIELD

Wakefield Art Galleries and Museums P
2nd Floor, Chantry House, 123 Kirkgate, Wakefield WF1 1ZS.
Tel: *01924-305796, Minicom 01924- 305769.*
Fax: *01924-305770.*

York

YORK

Castle Howard
York YO6 7DA.
Tel: *01653-648333.*

Kentmere House Gallery C
53 Scarcroft Hill, York YO2 1DF.
Tel: *01904-656507.* **Fax:** *01904-433949.*

Pyramid Gallery C
43 Stonegate, York YO1 2AW.
Tel: *01904-641187.*

Robert Feather Jewellery Gallery C
10 Gillygate, York YO3 7EQ.
Tel: *01904-632025.*

York City Art Gallery PS
Exhibition Square, York YO1 2EW.
Tel: *01904-551861.* **Fax:** *01904-551866.*
Opening times: *Open to the public: Mon-Sat 10-5, Sun 2.30-5, last admission each day 4.30. The Gallery is closed on 1 January, Good Friday and 25 & 26 December.*
Nearest Station: *York.*
Personnel: *Curator:* Richard Green.
Six hundred years of painting, from early Italian gold-ground panels to the art of the 20th century. Exceptional in its range and interest, the collection includes pictures by Parmigianino and Bellotto, Lely and Reynolds, Frith and Boudin, Lowry and Nash, and nudes by York-born Etty. Outstanding collection of studio pottery. Varied and exciting programme of temporary exhibitions and events. Gallery Shop. Admission free.
Services and Facilities:
Bookshop. Disabled Access. Friends/Society. Guided Tours. Lectures. Shop.

East Riding of Yorkshire

BEVERLEY

Beverley Art Gallery & Museum P
Champney Road, Beverley, HU17 9BQ.
Tel: *01482-883903 / 884956.*

BRIDLINGTON

Sewerby Hall Art Gallery and Museum (Museum of East Yorkshire) P
Sewerby Hall, Bridlington, YO15 1EA.
Tel: *01262-677874.* **Fax:** *01262-674265.*

GOOLE

Goole Museum & Art Gallery P
Carlisle Street, Goole, DN14 5AA.
Tel: *01405-768329 / 765141.*
Fax: *01405-768329.*

North Yorkshire

HARROGATE

Anstey Galleries C
33 Swan Road, Harrogate, HG1 2SA.
Tel: *01423-500102.*
Fax: *01423-500102.*

Chantry House Gallery C
Ripley, Harrogate, HG3 3AY.
Tel: *01423-771011.*
Opening times: *Apr-Sept Tues-Sat 10-5, Sun 12-5. Oct-Mar Wed-Sat 10-4, Sun 12-4.*
Personnel: *Directors:* Terry Logan, Georgina Logan.

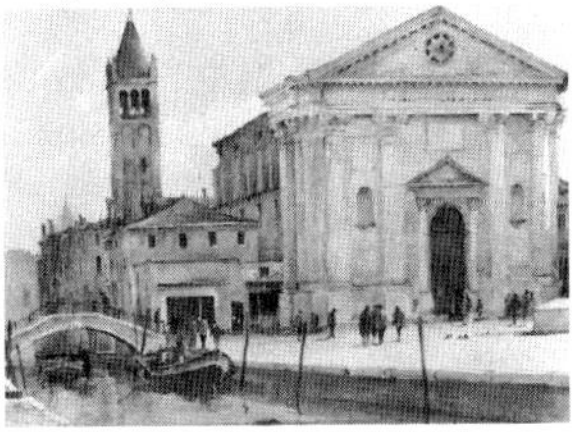

The Chantry House Gallery is situated in the beautiful and historic village of Ripley Castle, 3 miles north of Harrogate. Established in 1980, the gallery provides a show space for established artists working in a variety of media. Several exhibitions are arranged but the gallery maintains a mixed show of work by gallery artists which is ever-changing throughout the year. The Chantry House Gallery strives to provide high quality work whilst catering for a wide variety of tastes and interests.
Services and Facilities:
Art Consultancy. Art for Offices. Commissioning Service. Disabled Access. Framing.
Work Stocked and Sold:
Dr. Pa. Pr.
Price range: £10 - £1,000.
For artists see *Commercial Gallery Artists.*

Harrogate Museums and Arts P
Royal Pump Room Museum, Crown Place, Harrogate, HG1 2RY.
Tel: *01423-503340.* **Fax:** *01423-840026.*

Mercer Art Gallery
Swan Road, Harrogate, HG1 2SA.
Tel: *01423-503340.* **Fax:** *01423-840026.*

Ripley Castle P
Ripley, Harrogate, HG3 3AY.
Tel: *01423-770152.* **Fax:** *01423-771745.*

Studio Gallery
23 Cold Bath Road, Harrogate, HG2 0NL.
Tel: *01423-523284.* **Fax:** *01423-523284.*

HELMSLEY

Look Gallery C
20 Castlegate, Helmsley, YO62 5AB.
Tel: *01439-770545.*
Opening times: *Mon-Sat 10.30-5, Sun 2-5.*
Personnel: *Director:* Nicholas Coombes.
Contemporary painting, sculpture, ceramics and glass. The gallery shows a wide variety of contemporary work from living British artists. The policy of the gallery is to maintain throughout the year a mixed show of work by gallery artists. Artists represented include: Caroline Bailey, Edna Bizon, David Greenwood, Janet Skea, Robert Tilling and Simon Turvey.
Work Stocked and Sold:
Cer. Gla. Pa. Sc.
Price range: £100 - £1,000.
For artists see *Commercial Gallery Artists.*

KNARESBOROUGH

Gordon Reece Gallery
Finkle Street, Knaresborough, HG5 8AA.
Tel: *01423-866219.* **Fax:** *01423-868165.*

Old Courthouse Museum P
Castle Grounds, Knaresborough,
Tel: *01423-503340.* **Fax:** *01423-840026.*

RICHMOND

Richmondshire Museum P
Ryder's Wynd, Richmond, DL10 4JA.
Tel: *01748-825611.*

SCARBOROUGH

Crescent Arts Workshop P
The Crescent, Scarborough, YO11 2PW.
Tel: *01723-351461.*

Scarborough Art Gallery
The Crescent, Scarborough, YO11 2PW.
Tel: *01723-374553.* **Fax:** *01723-376941.*

SETTLE

Linton Court Gallery *C*
Duke Street, Settle, BD24 9DW.
Tel: *01729-822695.*
Opening times: *Please phone for information about exhibitions and opening times.*
Nearest Station: *Settle.*
Personnel: *Director:* Ann Carr.
The Gallery started in 1980 and is in a 200 year old converted hay loft. During the year there are a wide variety of exhibitions showing work of young as well as nationally known contemporary artists. Ceramics and original prints are always available.
Work Stocked and Sold:
Cer. Pa. Pr.
Price range: £100 - £3,000.
For artists see *Commercial Gallery Artists.*

THIRSK

Sion Hill Hall Museum *P*
Kirby Wiske, Thirsk, YO7 4EU.
Tel: *01845-587206.*

Zillah Bell Contemporary Art
15 Kirkgate, Thirsk, YO7 1PQ.

WHITBY

Sutcliffe Gallery
1 Flowergate, Whitby, YO21 3BA.
Tel: *01947-602239.*

West Yorkshire

HALIFAX

The Dean Clough Galleries *PS*
Halifax, HX3 5AX.
Tel: *01422-250250.*
Fax: *01422-341148.*
Email *linda@design-dimension.co.uk*
Ws *http://www.DeanClough.com*
Opening times: *Every day 10-5.*
Nearest Station: *Halifax.*
Personnel: *Director:* Roger Standen. *Arts Co-ordinator:* Chris Taylor. *Galleries Curator:* Doug Binder.
The Dean Clough Galleries are housed within a thriving industrial complex where the arts, design, business and education work together. Our aim is to create a forum for debate, celebration, learning and enjoyment and to make accessible to a wide audience a broad range of artists, designers and manufacturers. Although privately funded, the galleries profile is that of a public space and community resource.
The Dean Clough Galleries are fully sponsored by Dean Clough Industrial Park Ltd. and directed and managed on their behalf by The Design Dimension Educational Trust. For further information contact Chris Taylor, Arts Coordinator.
Services and Facilities:
Art Consultancy. Art for Offices. Bar. Bookshop. Café. Craftshop. Disabled Access. Framing. Friends/Society. Gallery space for hire. Guided Tours. Lectures. Museum Shop. Parking. Restaurant. Shop. Workshop Facilities.
Work Stocked and Sold:
Ab. App. Cer. Cra. Dec. Dr. Fur. Gla. Jew. Pa. Ph. Pr. Sc. Tx. Wd.
Price range: £30 - £3,000.
For artists see *Commercial Gallery Artists.*

HUDDERSFIELD

Lupton Square Gallery *C*
1 & 2 Lupton Square (off Westgate), Honley, Huddersfield, HD7 2AA.
Tel: *01484-666144.*
Fax: *01484-661221.*
Email *geoff@luptonsquaregallery.co.uk*
Ws *http://www.luptonsquaregallery.co.uk*
Opening times: *Fri, Sat Sun and Bank Holidays 10-5, or by appointment.*
Nearest Station: *Huddersfield.*
Personnel: Geoffrey S. Harrop.
Housed in an 18th century cottage, grade II listed building, the gallery has 3 floors of exhibition space. A wide selection of contemporary art works including metal sculpture and ceramics on show. Paintings are mainly of artists working in and around Yorkshire. A good selection of prints are available including some interesting ones from the 50's & 70's. Exhibitions are mounted periodically, please contact the gallery for details.
Services and Facilities:
Art for Offices. Commissioning Service. Framing. Parking. Shop.
Work Stocked and Sold:
Cer. Pa. Pr. Sc.
Price range: £15 - £2,000.
For artists see *Commercial Gallery Artists.*

ILKLEY

Gallery Nineteen *C*
Station Plaza, Ilkley, LS29 8HS.
Tel: *01943-602121.*
Opening times: *Wed, Thurs, Fri 10-5, Sat & Sun 10-4.*
Nearest Station: *Ilkley.*
Fine paintings and contemporary art.
Work Stocked and Sold:
Cer. Jew. Pa. Sc.
Price range: £75 - £2,000.
For artists see *Commercial Gallery Artists.*

Northern

Cumbria

ALSTON

Gossipgate Gallery *C*
The Butts, Alston, CA9 3JU.
Tel: *01434-381806.*

AMBLESIDE

Dexterity *C*
Kelsick Road, Ambleside, LA22 OBZ.
Tel: *015394-34045.*

CARLISLE

Tullie House, City Museum & Art Gallery *PS*
Castle Street, Carlisle, CA3 8TP.
Tel: *01228-534781.* **Fax:** *01228-5810249.*

COCKERMOUTH

Castlegate House
Cockermouth, CA13 9HA.
Tel: *01900-822149.*

CONISTON

Brantwood *P*
Brantwood, Coniston, LA21 8AD.
Tel: *015394-41396.* **Fax:** *015394-41263.*

EGREMONT

Lowes Court Gallery
12 Main Street, Egremont, CA22 2DW.
Tel: *01946-820693.*

KENDAL

Abbot Hall Art Gallery *PS*
Kendal, LA9 5AL.
Tel: *01539-722464.* **Fax:** *01539-722494.*
Opening times: *Open 7 days a weeks 12 February 98 - 24 December 1999, 10.30-5 (reduced hours in winter). Admission: Adult £2.80 (concessions available).*
Personnel: *Director:* Mr Edward King.

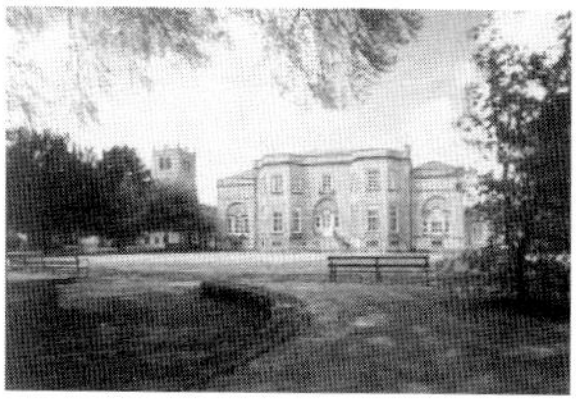

This elegant Georgian building provides a superb setting for its collection of fine art. Paintings by George Romney fill the walls of rooms furnished by Gillows of Lancaster. Touring exhibitions complement the permanent collection of 18th, 19th and 20th century British art. 1999 Temporary Exhibition Programme: Tony Bevan 12 February - 11 April, Portrait of the Artist (in prints) 12 February - 11 April, Maria Chevska 20 April - 6 June, Queen Victoria's Travels and Family 15 June - 19 September, Callum Innes 28 September - 24 December, Ruskin Pottery 6 November - 24 December. Coffee shop, Gift Shop, Free Parking, Picnic Area by river.
Services and Facilities:
Bookshop. Café. Commissioning Service. Disabled Access. Friends/Society. Guided Tours. Lectures. Museum Shop. Parking.

Brewery Arts Centre
Warehouse Gallery, 122a Highgate, Kendal, LA9 4HE.
Tel: *01539-725133.* **Fax:** *01539-730257.*

Oddfellows Gallery
Highgate, Kendal,
Tel: *01539-734669.*

Ab Artists' Books **App** Applied Art **Cer** Ceramics **Cra** Crafts **Dec** Decorative **Dr** Drawing **Fur** Furniture

KESWICK

Keswick Museum & Art Gallery *P*
Fitz Park, Station Road, Keswick, CA12 4NF.
Tel: *017687-73263.*

Thornthwaite Gallery
Thornthwaite, Keswick, CA12.
Tel: *017687-78248.*

PENRITH

Beck Stone Art Gallery
Graystoke Gill, Penrith, CA11 0UQ.
Tel: *017684-83601.*

Laburnum Ceramics
Yanwath, Penrith, CA10 2LF.
Tel: *01768-864842.*
Fax: *01768-863518.*

Penrith Museum *P*
Robinson's School, Middlegate, Penrith, CA11 7PT.
Tel: *01768-64671.*

WHITEHAVEN

The Harbour Gallery
The Beacon, Whitehaven,
Tel: *01946-592302.*

Whitehaven Museum & Art Gallery *P*
Civic Hall, Lowther Street, Whitehaven,
Tel: *01946-3111307.* **Fax:** *01946-693373.*

WORKINGTON

Carnegie Arts Centre
Finkle Street, Workington, CA14 2B.
Tel: *01900-602122.* **Fax:** *01900-604351.*

Greenhouse
Curwen Park, Workington, CA14 3YJ.
Tel: *01900-602986.*

Durham

BARNARD CASTLE

The Bowes Museum *P*
Barnard Castle, DL12 8NP.
Tel: *0183-369 0606.*
Fax: *0183-637 163.*

Castle Gallery
Witham Hall, Horsemarket, Barnard Castle, DL12.

CASTLE EDEN

Castle Eden Gallery
Castle Eden, TS27 4SD.

DARLINGTON

Bernhardt Gallery
60 Coniscliffe Road, Darlington, DL3 7RN.
Tel: *01325-356633.*

Darlington Art Gallery *P*
Crown Street, Darlington, DL1 1ND.
Tel: *01325-462034 / 469858.*
Fax: *013225-381556.*

DURHAM

Durham Art Gallery *P*
Aykley Heads, Durham, DH1 5TU.
Tel: *0191-384 2214.*
Fax: *0191-386 1770.*
Email *durham.gallery@durham.gov.uk*
Ws *http://www.durham.gov.uk*
Opening times: *Tues-Sat 10-5, Sun 2-5. Closed Mondays.*
Nearest Station: *Durham (5 mins walk).*
Personnel: *Arts Development Manager:* Zoe Channing. *Art Gallery Assistant:* Dennis Hardingham.
Situated in parkland on the northern edge of the city, the Art Gallery features a changing programme of temporary exhibitions related to all aspects of the visual arts, plus illustrated talks, films, workshops, demonstrations, lunchtime concerts and other events aimed at a wide range of visitors and special interest groups. The gallery provides a secure venue for high quality displays, including national touring exhibitions, and the 1999 programme includes 3D embroideries and contemporary textiles, Andy Capp cartoons, wildlife and landscape photography, contemporary glass and glass engraving, pop-up books, puppets and children's book illustrations.
Services and Facilities:
Café. Disabled Access. Framing. Friends/Society. Museum Shop. Parking.

Durham University Oriental Museum *PS*
Elvet Hill, Durham, DH1 3TH.
Tel: *0191-374 7911.* **Fax:** *0191-374 7911.*
Email *oriental.museum@durham.ac.uk*
Ws *http://www.dur.ac.uk/~dcm0www/omuseum.htm*
Opening times: *Weekdays 9.30-5. Weekends 2-5.*
Personnel: *Curator:* Lindy Brewster.
The Oriental Museum is a major resource for anyone in the North East who is interested in the visual arts. Its collections range from ancient Egypt to modern Japan and the major cultures of the Orient are well represented. The Museum runs a programme of lectures, day-schools and other events. Details from the Oriental Museum.
Services and Facilities:
Bookshop. Friends/Society. Lectures. Museum Shop. Parking. Shop.

Hartlepool

HARTLEPOOL

Gray Art Gallery and Museum *P*
Clarence Road, Hartlepool TS24 8BT.
Tel: *01429-266522.*

Hartlepool Art Gallery *P*
Church Square, Hartlepool TS24 8EQ.
Tel: *01429-869706.*
Fax: *01429-523408.*

Middlesbrough

MIDDLESBROUGH

Cleveland County Museums Service *P*
County Leisure Services, PO Box 41, Middlesbrough TS3 0YZ.
Tel: *01642-248155.*

Cleveland Craft Centre *C*
57 Gilkes Street, Middlesbrough TS1 5EL.
Tel: *01642-262376 / 226351.*
Fax: *01642-226351.*

Cleveland Gallery *P*
Victoria Road, Middlesbrough TS1 3QS.
Tel: *01692-262375.* **Fax:** *01692-253661.*

Dorman Museum *P*
Linthorpe Road, Middlesbrough TS5 6LA.
Tel: *01642-813781.* **Fax:** *01642-813781.*

Middlesbrough Art Gallery *P*
320 Linthorpe Road, Middlesbrough TS1 4AW.
Tel: *01642-247445.* **Fax:** *01642-813781.*

Newcastle-upon-Tyne

GATESHEAD

Baltic Flour Mills *P*
Gateshead. (Open 2000).

Design Works
William Street, Gateshead, NE10 OPJ.
Tel: *0191-495 0066.*

The Gallery, Gateshead Central Library
Prince Consort Road, Gateshead, NE8 4LN.
Tel: *0191-477 3478.* **Fax:** *0191-477 7454.*

Portcullis Craft Gallery
7 The Arcade, Metro Centre, Gateshead, NE11 9YL.
Tel: *0191-460 6345.* **Fax:** *0191-460 4285.*

Shipley Art Gallery
Prince Consort Road, Gateshead, NE8 4JB.
Tel: *0191-477 1495.* **Fax:** *0191-477 1495.*

NEWCASTLE-UPON-TYNE

Browns
First Floor, 15 Acorn Road, Jesmond, Newcastle-upon-Tyne NE2 2DJ.
Tel: *0191-281 1315.*

Chameleon Gallery
Milburn House, Dean Street, Newcastle-upon-Tyne NE1 1PQ. **Tel:** *0191-232 2819.*

Corrymella Scott Gallery *C*
5 Tankerville Terrace, Jesmond, Newcastle-upon-Tyne NE2 3AH.
Tel: *0191-281 8284, 0191-401 7513.*
Fax: *0191-281 5434.*

Gulbenkian Gallery
c/o 72 Moor Road North, Newcastle-upon-Tyne NE3 1AB.

Hatton Gallery *PS*
Newcastle University, Newcastle-upon-Tyne NE1 7RU.
Tel: *0191-222 6057.* **Fax:** *0191-222 6057.*

Laing Art Gallery
Higham Place, Newcastle-upon-Tyne.
Tel: *0191-232 7734.*

Newcastle Arts Centre
67-69 Westgate Road, Newcastle-upon-Tyne NE1 1SG. **Tel:** *0191-261 5618.*

Side Gallery
5/9 Side, Newcastle-upon-Tyne NE1 3JE.
Tel: *0191-232 2000.*

Squires Gallery
Squires Building, University of Northumbria at Newcastle, Sandyford Road, Newcastle-upon-Tyne NE1 8ST.

The University Gallery *PS*
University of Northumbria, Sandyford Road, Newcastle-upon-Tyne NE1 8ST.
Tel: *0191-227 4424.* **Fax:** *0191-227 4718.*
Email *mara-helen.wood@unn.ac.uk*
Opening times: *Mon-Thu 10-5, Fri-Sat 10-4. Closed Sundays and Bank Holidays throughout the year.*
Personnel: *Director:* Mara-Helen Wood.

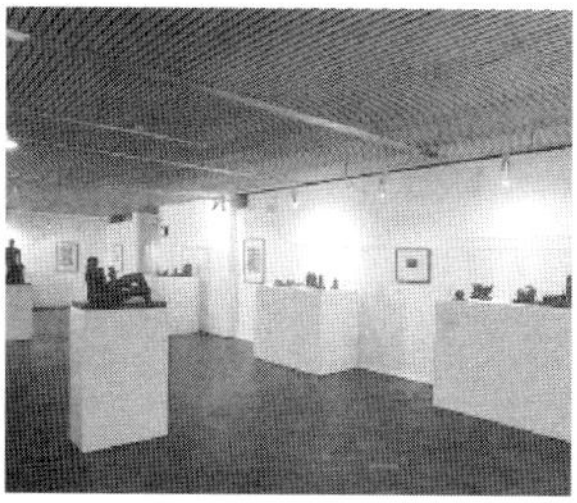

The University Gallery is recognised as a public gallery with an annual average attendance of 80,000 visitors. It presents a programme of temporary exhibitions by artists of national and international reputation, as well as exhibitions by lesser known, promising artists. Since its inception in 1977, the gallery has presented over 600 exhibitions which have ranged in character from group shows to one-man shows; thematic exhibitions of historical or topical interest; major touring exhibitions for museums and schools and an extensive programme of lectures, seminars, literary events and art classes for adults and children. The gallery is responsible for the Permanent Collection comprising over 200 paintings, drawings and prints by leading contemporary British artists including, for example, Norman Adams, Peter Greenham, Sean Scully, Albert Irvin and Victor Pasmore.
Services and Facilities:
Bookshop. Lectures.
Work Stocked and Sold:
Dr. Pa.
Price range: £50 - £5,000.
For artists see *Commercial Gallery Artists.*

North Tyneside

WALLSEND

Buddle Arts Centre *PS*
258b Station Road, Wallsend, NE28 8RH.
Tel: *0191-200 7132.*
Fax: *0191-200 7142.*
Email *buddle@ntynearts.demon.co.uk*
Opening times: *Tues-Thurs 1-5, Fri 10-5, Sat 2-5.*
Nearest Station: *BR: Newcastle, Metro: Wallsend.*
Personnel: *Principal Arts Officer:* Mike Campbell.
Mixed use arts centre including gallery space (46.5m linear hanging space) showing a range of exhibitions in various media. Main emphasis on professional artists; other shows by schools, community groups and amateur art clubs. Also occasional temporary installations and commissioned work. Outlet for new prints supplied by Northern Print Studio. The Buddle Arts Centre is managed by North Tyneside Arts.
Services and Facilities:
Bar. Commissioning Service. Disabled Access. Gallery space for hire. Parking. Workshop Facilities.
Work Stocked and Sold:
Pr.
Price range: £50 - £500.

Northumberland

ALNWICK

Bondgate Gallery *P*
22 Narrowgate, Alnwick, NE66 3JG.
Tel: *01665-576450.*

The Chatton Gallery *C*
Church House, New Road, Chatton, Alnwick, NE66 5PU.
Tel: *01668-215494.*

BELFORD

Norselands Gallery *C*
The Old School, Warenford, Belford, NE70 7HY.
Tel: *01668-213465.*

BERWICK UPON TWEED

Berwick Upon Tweed Borough Museum and Art Gallery *P*
The Clock Block, Berwick Barracks, Ravensdowne, Berwick Upon Tweed, TD15 1DQ.
Tel: *01289-330933 (Curator), 01289-330044 (Council).*
Fax: *01289-330540 (Council).*

Sallyport Gallery
48 Bridge Street, Berwick Upon Tweed, TD15 1AQ.

Three Feathers Gallery
83c Mary Gate, Berwick Upon Tweed, TD15 1BA.
Tel: *01289-307642.*

CRAMLINGTON

Cramlington Library
Forum Way, Civic Precinct, Cramlington, NE23 6QE.
Tel: *01670-714371.*

Forum Gallery
Cramlington Library, Forum Way, Civic Precinct, Cramlington,
Tel: *0167-071 4371.*

HEXHAM

Moot Hall
Market Place, Hexham,

Queens Hall Art Centre
Beaumont Street, Hexham, NE46 3LS.
Tel: *01434-606787/8.* **Fax:** *01434-606043.*

ROTHBURY

Coquet Dale Arts Centre
Front Street, Rothbury, NE65 7TZ.
Tel: *01669-621557.*

Rothbury Library and Art Gallery
Front Street, Rothbury,
Tel: *01669-620428.*

Smith & Watson Stained Glass
The Rothbury Gallery, Townfoot, Rothbury, NE65 7SL.
Tel: *01669-621156.*

STAMFORDHAM

Stamfordham Gallery
23 North Side, Stamfordham,

WARKWORTH

Dial Gallery *C*
5 Dial Place, Warkworth, NE65 0UR.
Tel: *01665-710822.*

Redcar and Cleveland

GUISBOROUGH

Art Screen Prints
7a Chaloner Street, Guisborough, TS14 6QD.
Tel: *01287-637527.*

Walton Galleries
Walton Terrace, Guisborough, TS14 6QG.
Tel: *01287-638639.*

REDCAR

Kirkleatham Old Hall Museum *P*
Kirkleatham Village, Redcar, TS10 5NW.
Tel: *01642-479500.*

SALTBURN BY THE SEA

Saltburn Gallery
21 Milton Street, Saltburn By The Sea, TS12 1DJ.
Tel: *01287-622245.*

Stockton on Tees

BILLINGHAM

Billingham Art Gallery *P*
Queensway, Billingham, TS23 2LN.
Tel: *01642-397590.* **Fax:** *01642-397590.*

STOCKTON ON TEES

Dovecot Arts Centre
Dovecot Street, Stockton on Tees TS18 1LL.
Tel: *01642-611625.*

Preston Hall Museum *P*
Yarm Road, Stockton on Tees TS18 3RH.
Tel: *01642-791424.*

Sunderland

SUNDERLAND

Northern Gallery for Contemporary Art *PS*
City Library and Arts Centre, Fawcett Street, Sunderland SR1 1RE.
Tel: *0191-514 1235.* **Fax:** *0191-514 8444.*
Opening times: *Mon/Wed 9.30-7.30, Tues/Thurs/Fri 9.30-5, Sat 9.30-4. Closed Sundays/Bank Holidays.*
Nearest Station: *Sunderland*
Personnel: *Principal Curator:* Louise Wirz. *Exhibitions Officer:* Ele Carpenter.
Located in the heart of the city, this exciting, new gallery complex has been established as a leading centre for the very best international contemporary visual art. Year-round programme of events, education and outreach. Telephone above number for current information about exhibitions and events. WC.
Services and Facilities:
Craftshop. Disabled Access. Friends/Society. Guided Tours. Lectures.
Work Stocked and Sold:
Cer. Cra. Dec. Gla. Jew. Pr. Sc. Tx. Wd.
Price range: £5 - £500.

Sunderland Museum & Art Gallery *P*
Fine and Applied Arts, Borough Road, Sunderland SR1 1PP.
Tel: *0191-565 0723.*
Fax: *0191-510 0675.*

WASHINGTON

Arts Centre *PS*
Biddick Lane, Fatfield, District 7, Washington, NE38 8AB.
Tel: *0191-219 3455.*
Fax: *0191-219 3466.*

Sun Arts
Biddick Farm, Fat Field, Washington, NE38 8AB.

North Tyneside

NORTH SHIELDS

Globe Gallery
97 Howard Street, North Shields, NE30 1NA.
Tel: *0191-259 2614.*

South Tyneside

JARROW

Bede Gallery
Springwell Park, Butchersbridge Road, Jarrow, NE32 5QA.
Tel: *0191-489 1807/420 0585.*
Fax: *0191-420 0585.*

SOUTH SHIELDS

South Shields Museum & Art Gallery *P*
Ocean Road, South Shields, NE33 2AU.
Tel: *0191-456 8740.*

SCOTTISH GALLERIES

Town/County index. Main listings.

Where this information has been provided, galleries are designated 'C' for commercial, 'P' for public gallery or museum or 'PS' for a public gallery or museum holding selling shows.

TOWN COUNTY INDEX

A/B/C

D/E/F

G/H/I

J/K/L

M/P

S/T/V/W

Aberdeen

ABERDEEN

Aberdeen Art Gallery and Museum P
Schoolhill, Aberdeen AB9 1FQ.
Tel: *01224-646333.* **Fax:** *01224-632133.*

Aberdeen Arts Centre P
33 King Street, Aberdeen AB2 3AA.
Tel: *01224-635208.*

Gallery Heinzel C
21 Spa Street, Aberdeen AB1 1PU.
Tel: *01224-625629.* **Fax:** *01224-625629.*

Grays School of Art P
Faculty of Design, The Robert Gordon University, Garthdee Road, Aberdeen AB9 2QD. **Tel:** *01224-263506 / 01224-263600.*

Hoddo Arts Trust
The Hale, Hoddo Estate, Tarves, Aberdeen AB41 0ER.
Tel: *01651-851770.*

The Lemon Tree C
5 West North Street, Aberdeen AB2 3AT.
Tel: *01224-642230.*

Peacock Printmakers Gallery C
21 Castle Street, Aberdeen AB1 1AJ.
Tel: *01224-627094 / 639539.*

The Rendezvous Gallery C
100 Forest Avenue, Aberdeen AB15 6TL.
Tel: *01224-323247.*

Vital Spark Gallery C
45 Rosemount Viaduct, Aberdeen, AB25 1NQ.
Tel: *01224-658584.* **Fax:** *01224-658583.*

Aberdeenshire

ALFORD

Syllavethy Gallery C
Montgarrie, Alford, AB33 8AQ.
Tel: *019755-62273.* **Fax:** *019755-63173.*

BALLATER

McEwan Gallery
Glengarden, Ballater, AB35 5UB.
Tel: *013397-55429.* **Fax:** *013397-55995.*
Email *rhodmcewan@easynet.co.uk*

BANFF

Warehouse Gallery
7 Quayside, Banff Harbour, Banff, AB45 1HQ.
Tel: *01261-818048.*

CULLEN

Baranoff Studio & Gallery C
6 Seafield Street, Cullen, AB56 4SH.
Tel: *01542-841410.*

ELLON

Tolquhon Gallery C
Tolquhon, Tarves, Ellon AB41 0LP.
Tel: *01651-842343.*

MACDUFF

Macduff Arts Centre
c/o Aberdeenshire Council, 1 Church Street, Macduff, AB44 1UR.
Tel: *01261-813384.*

STONEHAVEN

Riverside Gallery
30a David Street, Stonehaven, AB3 2AL.
Tel: *01569-63931.*

STRATHDON

The Lost Gallery C
Strathdon, AB36 8UJ.
Tel: *019756-51287.*
Fax: *019756-51287.*

Angus

FORFAR

Forfar Museum and Art Gallery P
Meffan Institute, 20 West High Street, Forfar, DD8 1BB.
Tel: *01307-464123.*

The Meffan Institute
20 West High Street, Forfar, DD8 1DD.
Tel: *01307-464123.*

Argyll & Bute

HELENSBURGH

The Hill House *P*
Upper Colquhoun Street, Helensburgh, G84 9AJ.
Tel: *01436-673900.* **Fax:** *01436-674685.*

South Ayrshire

AYR

Maclaurin Art Gallery *C*
Rozelle Park, Monument Road, Ayr, KA7 4NQ.
Tel: *01292-443708 / 445447.*

Rozelle House Gallery *C*
Rozelle Park, Monument Road, Ayr, KA7 4NQ.
Tel: *01292-445447.*

Scottish Borders

JEDBURGH

Mainhill Gallery *C*
Ancrum, Jedburgh, TD8 6XA.
Tel: *01835-830518.*

PEEBLES

Picture Gallery/Tweeddale Museum *P*
High Street, Peebles, EH45 8AP.
Tel: *01721-723123.*

Tweeddale Museum & Art Gallery *P*
Chambers Institute, High Street, Peebles, EH45 8AP.
Tel: *01721-720123.*

SELKIRK

Peebles Picture Gallery
c/o Municipal Buildings, High Street, Selkirk, TD7 4JX.
Tel: *01750-20096.*

Robson Gallery *P*
c/o Municipal Buildings, High Street, Selkirk, TD7 4JX.
Tel: *01750-20096.*

The Scott Gallery
Municipal Buildings, High Street, Selkirk, TD7 4JX.
Tel: *01750-20096.*

Clackmannanshire

ALLOA

Aberdona Gallery *P*
Aberdona Mains, Alloa, FK10 3QP.
Tel: *01259-752721.* **Fax:** *01259-750276.*

Alloa Museum and Gallery *P*
Speirs Centre, 29 Primrose Street, Alloa, FK10 1JJ.
Tel: *01259-213131.* **Fax:** *01259-721313.*

Dumfries & Galloway

DUMFRIES

Gracefield Arts Centre
28 Edinburgh Road, Dumfries, DG1 1JQ.
Tel: *01387-262084.* **Fax:** *01387-60453.*

Ottersburn Gallery *C*
2A Nith Avenue, Dumfries, DG1 1EF.
Tel: *01387-254860.*

Robert Burns Centre *P*
c/o Dumfries Museum, The Observatory, Dumfries, DG2 7SW.
Tel: *01387-253374.*

KIRKCUDBRIGHT

Castle Douglas Art Gallery
Council Offices, Kirkcudbright, DG6 4JG.
Tel: *01557-331643.*

Tolbooth Art Centre
c/o Council Offices, Kirkcudbright, DG6 4JG.
Tel: *01557-331643.*

STRANRAER

Stranraer Museum *P*
55 George Street, Stranraer, DG9 7JP.
Tel: *01776-705088.*

Dundee

DUNDEE

Bonar Hall *P*
The University of Dundee, Park Place, Dundee DD1 4HN.
Tel: *01382-345466.*

Duncan of Jordanstone College of Art and Design *PS*
A Faculty of the University of Dundee, Perth Road, Dundee DD1 4HT.
Tel: *01382-345330.* **Fax:** *01382-345192.*
Email *djcexhib@dundee.ac.uk*
Ws *http://www.dundee.ac.uk/*
Opening times: *Mon-Fri 9.30-8.30, Sat 9.30-4.30. Closed Sun.*
Nearest Station: *Dundee.*
Personnel: *Curator of Exhibitions:* Deirdre MacKenna.
Continually changing programme in seven exhibition spaces; five in Duncan of Jordanstone College of Art and Design, and two in the University of Dundee. The programme ranges from student and graduate work, to national and international exhibitions in Fine Art, Design, Television and Imaging, Performance, Time Based Art and Architecture. In addition University of Dundee has expanded its Visual Research Programme and facilities. Based in Dundee Contemporary Art the V.R.C. includes Centrespace, a unique project space where the public can view exciting contemporary visual art projects through development to completion. Traditional and contemporary lectures and seminars. All exhibitions and events are free and open to the public.
Services and Facilities:
Disabled Access. Guided Tours. Lectures. Parking. Restaurant.

Dundee Art Galleries and Museums *P*
Albert Square, Dundee.
Tel: *01382-223141.*

McManus Galleries *P*
Dundee Art Galleries & Museums, Albert Square, Dundee DD1 1DA.
Tel: *01382-432020 / 01382 432028.*

Seagate Gallery
36-40 Seagate, Dundee DD1 2EJ.
Tel: *01382-226331.*

Fife

ANSTRUTHER

Kellie Castle *P*
by Pittenweem, Anstruther, KY10 2RF.
Tel: *01333-720271.*
Fax: *01333-720326.*

CARDENDEN

Arts in Fife
Fife Council, Tower Block, ASDARC, Woodend Road, Cardenden, KY5 0NE.
Tel: *01592-414714 / 414727.*

CRAIL

The Courtyard Gallery *C*
42 Marketgate South, Crail, KY10 3TL.
Tel: *01333-450797.*

DUNFERMLINE

Dunfermline Museum *P*
The Small Gallery, Viewfield Terrace, Dunfermline, KY12 7HY.
Tel: *01383-721814.*

GLENROTHES

Corridor Gallery
Fife Institute, Viewfield Road, Glenrothes, KY6 2RB.
Tel: *01592-415700.*

KIRKCALDY

Kirkcaldy Museum & Art Gallery *P*
War Memorial Gardens, Kirkcaldy, KY1 1YG.
Tel: *01592-412860.*
Fax: *01592-412870.*

LEVEN

Loomshop Gallery
126 Main Street, Lower Largo, Leven, KY8 6BP.
Tel: *01333-320330.*

ST. ANDREWS

Crawford Arts Centre *PS*
93 North Street, St. Andrews, KY16 9AL.
Tel: *01334-474610.* **Fax:** *01334-479880.*

GLASGOW & EDINBURGH

East Ayrshire

CUMNOCK

Baird Institute *P*
East Ayrshire Council, 3 Lugar Street, Cumnock, KA18 1AD.
Tel: *01290-421701.*

KILMARNOCK

Dean Castle
c/o Kilmarnock & Londoun District Museums, Dick Institute, Kilmarnock, KA1 3BU.
Tel: *01563-26401.*

Dick Institute *PS*
Elmbank Avenue, Kilmarnock KA1 3BU.
Tel: *01563-526401.* **Fax:** *01563-529661.*

North Ayrshire

IRVINE

The Vennel Gallery *PS*
10 Glasgow Vennel, Irvine, KA12 0BD.
Tel: *01294-275059.* **Fax:** *01294-275059.*
Email *vennel@globalnet.co.uk*
Opening times: *October-May: Tue, Thur, Fri & Sat: 10-1 & 2-5. June-September: Mon-Sat: 10-1 & 2-5. (Closed Wednesdays).*
Nearest Station: *Irvine.*
Personnel: *Museums Curator:* Martin Bellamy. *Senior Museum Assistant:* John Gray.

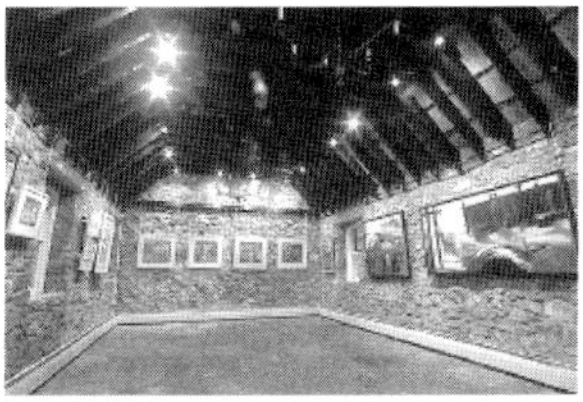

The gallery has a varied programme of exhibitions. Exhibitions tend to concentrate on contemporary Scottish fine and applied art but also include some historical shows and artists from outside Scotland. Exhibitions for 1999 include contemporary textiles, Kätue Kollwitz, video art, and the Royal Photographic Society. The gallery is situated in a restored 18th century street, and includes the Heckling Shop where Robert Burns worked.
Services and Facilities:
Craftshop. Disabled Access. Museum Shop. Workshop Facilities.

East Dunbartonshire

KIRKINTILLOCH

Auld Kirk Museum *P*
c/o East Dumbartonshire Museum, Auld Kirk Museum, The Cross, Kirkintilloch, G66 1AB.
Tel: *0141-775 1185.*

West Dunbartonshire

DUMBARTON

Dumbarton Public Library
Strathleven Place, Dumbarton, G82 1BD.
Tel: *01389-763129.*

Edinburgh

EDINBURGH

369 Gallery
233 Cowgate, Edinburgh EH1 1NQ.
Tel: *0131-225 3013.*

Bellevue Gallery *C*
4 Bellevue Crescent, Edinburgh EH3 6ND.
Tel: *0131-557 1663.* **Fax:** *0131-557 1663.*

Bourne Fine Art *C*
4 Dundas Street, Edinburgh EH3 6HZ.
Tel: *0131-557 4050.* **Fax:** *0131-557 8382.*

Calton Gallery *C*
10 Royal Terrace, Edinburgh EH7 5AB.
Tel: *0131-556 1010.* **Fax:** *0131-558 1150.*

Cameo Cinema
38 Home Street, Tolcross, Edinburgh EH3 9LZ.
Tel: *0131-228 4141.*

Carlyle's Gallery *C*
North Bridge, Edinburgh EH1 1SO.
Tel: *0131-557 5068.*

Chessel Gallery *C*
Moray House College, Holyrood Campus, Edinburgh EH8 8AQ.
Tel: *0131-556 8455.*

City Art Centre *P*
2 Market Street, Edinburgh EH1 1DE.
Tel: *0131-529 3993.* **Fax:** *0131-529 3977.*

Collective Gallery
22-28 Cockburn Street, Edinburgh EH1 1NY.
Tel: *0131-220 1260.*

Contact Gallery *C*
Grindlay Court Centre, Crindlay Street Court, Edinburgh EH3 9AR.
Tel: *0131-229 7941.*

Danish Cultural Institute
3 Doune Terrace Edinburgh EH3 6DY.
Tel: *0131-225 7189.* **Fax:** *0131-220 6162.*
Email *dci.dancult@dancult.demon.co.uk*
Opening times: *Mon-Fri 10-5.*
Personnel: *Director:* Mette Bligaard.
Exhibitions of Danish paintings, prints, photography and craft.

Dean Gallery
Belford Road, Edinburgh EH4.
Tel: *0131-624 6200.* **Fax:** *0131-343 3250.*
Opening times: *Mon-Sat 10 5, Sun 12-5*
Nearest Station: *Haymarket.*
Personnel: *Keeper:* Richard Calvocoressi. *Director of National Galleries of Scotland:* Timothy Clifford.
Opening on 27th March 1999, the new Dean Gallery provides a home for temporary exhibitions of modern and contemporary art, a major library and archive centre, along with the Sir Eduardo Paolozzi gift of sculpture and graphic art. The Dada and Surrealist collection is unrivalled in the UK. Spectacular city views, parkland and sculpture garden. Department of Administration of National Galleries of Scotland also located here.

The Dundas Street Gallery *C*
6a Dundas Street, Edinburgh EH3 6HZ.
Tel: *0131-557 4050.* **Fax:** *0131-557 8382.*

Eastern General Hospital (East and Midlothian Unit Art Fund)
Seafield Street, Edinburgh EH6 7LN.
Tel: *0131-536 7000.*

Edinburgh College of Art
Lauriston Place, Edinburgh EH3 9DF.
Tel: *0131-221 6032.* **Fax:** *0131-221 6089.*
Email *d.henderson@eca.ac.uk*
Ws *http://www.eca.ac.uk*
Opening times: *Mon-Sat 10-5.*
Personnel: *Exhibition Officer:* Diane Henderson.

Edinburgh COLLEGE *of* ART
HERIOT-WATT UNIVERSITY

Edinburgh College of Art offers an exciting programme of exhibitions, visiting lectures, conferences and concerts. Most exhibitions take place in the magnificent Neo-classical Sculpture Court which forms the heart of the college's main building. All exhibitions are open to the public and feature the work of students and staff as well as touring and specially curated exhibitions of Scottish, UK or International origin. The college also hosts major exhibitions and events as part of the Edinburgh International Festival Fringe. The

Annual Degree Show in June offers an ideal opportunity to experience the range and variety of subjects available at Edinburgh College of Art.
Services and Facilities:
Disabled Access. Gallery space for hire. Lectures.

Edinburgh Gallery
18a Dundas Street, Edinburgh EH3 6HZ.
Tel: *0131-557 5227.*

Edinburgh Printmakers C
23 Union Street, Edinburgh EH1 3LR.
Tel: *0131-557 2479.* **Fax:** *0131-558 8418.*

Edinburgh Sculpture Workshop C
25 Hawthornvale, Newhaven, Edinburgh EH6 4JT.
Tel: *0131-551 4490.* **Fax:** *0131-551 4491.*

ESU Gallery
23 Atholl Crescent, Edinburgh EH3 8HQ.
Tel: *0131-229 1528.*

Firth Gallery C
35 William Street, Edinburgh EH3 7LW.
Tel: *0131-225 2196.* **Fax:** *0131-225 2196.*

French Institute
13 Randolph Crescent, Edinburgh EH3 7TT.
Tel: *0131-225 5366.*

Fruitmarket Gallery P
45 Market Street, Edinburgh EH1 1DF.
Tel: *0131-225 2383.* **Fax:** *0131-220 3130.*

Hanover Fine Arts C
22A Dundas Street, Edinburgh EH3 6JN.
Tel: *0131-556 2181.* **Fax:** *0131-556 2181.*
Opening times: *Tue-Fri 10.30-6; Sat 10-4, Jan-Dec.*
Nearest Station: *Waverley.*
Personnel: *Proprietor:* Richard Ireland.

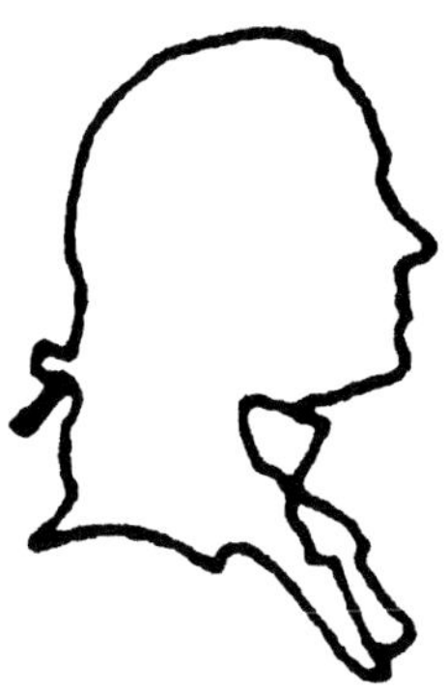

Independent owner-run commercial gallery situated in Dundas Street, right at the heart of the New Town galleries. The present policy of exhibitions (11 per year) features some established Scottish contemporary artists along with lesser-known ones, but concentrating on good quality accessible work at affordable prices. The majority of artists live or work in Scotland, but a number come from abroad, inc. Belgium, Brazil, China, Germany, India, Romania, Russia, Ukraine and the USA. Works exhibited include: oils, watercolours, original prints, ceramics, wood and stone sculpture, jewellery, wooden boxes, tiles, textiles and original/printed cards.
Services and Facilities:
Framing.
Work Stocked and Sold:
Cer. Cra. Dr. Gla. Jew. Pa. Pr. Sc. Tx. Wd.
Price range: £7 - £1,800.
For artists see *Commercial Gallery Artists.*

Ingleby Gallery C
6 Carlton Terrace, Edinburgh EH7 5DD.
Tel: *0131-556 4441.* **Fax:** *0131-556 4441.*
Email *inglebygallery@dial.pipex.com*
Opening times: *Wed-Sat 10-6 and by appointment at all other times.*
Nearest Station: *10 minutes from Waverley Station.*

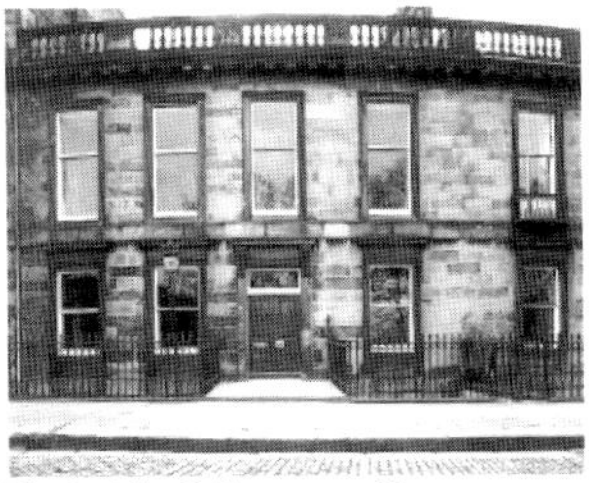

The Ingleby Gallery opened last year on the ground floor of a Georgian house overlooking the Palace of Holyrood and the site of the new Scottish Parliament. We specialise in 20th century British art and particularly in living painters, sculptors and photographers. Our first year's programme included exhibitions by Howard Hodgkin and Andy Goldsworthy; forthcoming exhibitions will include work by William Scott, Patrick Heron and Lucian Freud. We are also the major distributor of printed work by Ian Hamilton Finlay. Please contact the gallery for further details.
Work Stocked and Sold:
Cer. Pa. Ph. Pr. Sc.
Price range: £50 - £50,000.
For artists see *Commercial Gallery Artists.*

Instituto Italiano di Cultura
82 Nicholson Street, Edinburgh EH8 9EW.
Tel: *0131-668 2232.*

John Stephens Fine Art C
2A St Vincent Street, Edinburgh
Tel: *0131-557 6474.*

Kingfisher Gallery C
5 Northumberland Street, North West Lane, Edinburgh EH3 6JL.
Tel: *0131-557 5454.*
Fax: *0131-557 5454.*
Opening times: *Tue-Sat 11-4.30 or by appointment.*
Personnel: *Director:* Lena McGregor. *Director:* Ronnie McGregor. *Manager:* Loura Brooks.

Established in 1987, the Kingfisher's main focus is on presenting the very best in contemporary Scottish art to public, private and corporate clients. Over the past ten years we have introduced many artists to the Edinburgh art scene, and will continue to present a blend of both established and new talent. Our Gallery is on two levels, both benefiting from natural light. We are able to present a variety of works: paintings, sculpture, ceramics, tapestry and jewellery. There is disabled access to the ground floor only, however, provision can be made to allow as many as possible to view works here. We are easily reached from the city centre, at the heart of the New Town Gallery district.

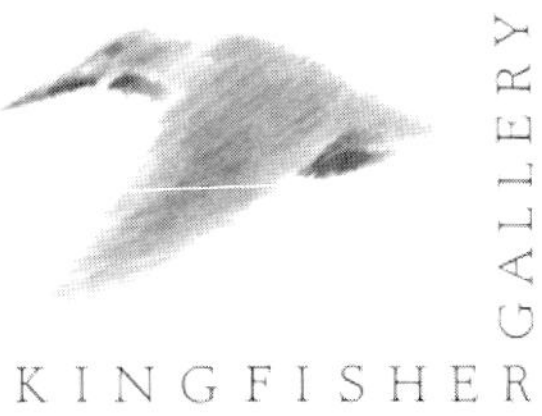

Services and Facilities:
Art Consultancy. Art for Offices. Disabled Access.
Work Stocked and Sold:
Cer. Cra. Gla. Jew. Pa. Pr. Sc.
Price range: £150 - £10,000.
For artists see *Commercial Gallery Artists.*

The Leith Gallery
93 Giles Street, Edinburgh EH6 6BZ.
Tel: *0131-553 5255.* **Fax:** *0131-553 5655.*

Lothian Fine Art
155 Dalry Road, Edinburgh EH11 2EA.
Tel: *0131-337 2055.*

Malcolm Innes Gallery C
4 Dundas Street, Edinburgh EH3 6HZ.
Tel: *0131-558 9544/5.* **Fax:** *0131-558 9525.*

National Gallery of Scotland
The Mound, Edinburgh EH2 2EL.
Tel: *0131-624 6200.* **Fax:** *0131-220 0917.*
Opening times: *Mon-Sat 10-5, Sun 2-5.*
Nearest Station: *Waverley.*
Personnel: *Director of National Galleries of Scotland:* Timothy Clifford. *Keeper, National Gallery:* Michael Clarke.
An outstanding collection of paintings, drawings and prints by the greatest artists from the Renaissance to Post-Impressionism, including Velázquez, El Greco, Rembrandt, Vermeer, Turner, Monet, Constable and Van Gogh; shown alongside the National Collection of Scottish Art - Ramsay, Raeburn, Wilkie and McTaggart. Department of Prints & Drawings is open by arrangement at Gallery front desk, Mon-Fri 10am-12.30pm and 2-4.30pm.
Services and Facilities:
Bookshop. Disabled Access. Gallery space for hire. Museum Shop. Shop.

National Library of Scotland P
George IV Bridge, Edinburgh EH1 1EW.
Tel: *0131-226 4531.*

Netherbrow Art Centre
43-45 High Street, Edinburgh EH1 1SR.
Tel: *0131-556 9579.*

Open Eye Gallery *C*
75/79 Cumberland Street, Edinburgh EH3 6RD.
Tel: *0131-557 1020.*
Fax: *0131-557 1020.*
Opening times: *Mon-Fri 10-6, Sat 10-4.*

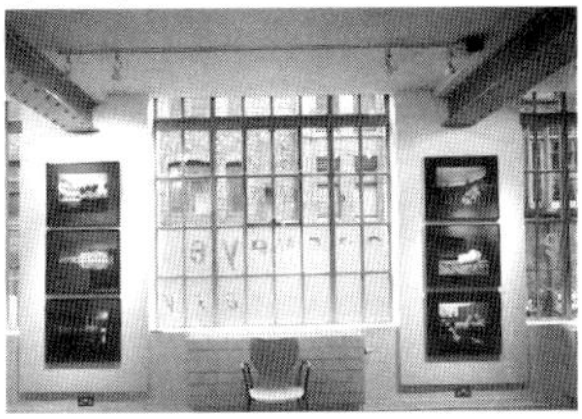

The Open Eye Gallery situated in the heart of Edinburgh's Historic Georgian New Town, equidistant between the Gallery of Modern Art and The National Gallery of Scotland. An ambitious programme of 15 exhibitions per year is organised, covering both contemporary and fine art, ranging from the work of the young contemporary to that of the established school. In addition to paintings the gallery specialises in early 20th c. prints, sculpture and contemporary crafts covering ceramics, glass, wood and jewellery.
Services and Facilities:
Art Consultancy. Art for Offices. Commissioning Service. Disabled Access. Framing. Restoration. Valuation.
Work Stocked and Sold:
Cer. Cra. Dr. Gla. Jew. Pa. Pr. Sc. Wd.
Price range: £100 - £10,000.
For artists see *Commercial Gallery Artists.*

Portfolio Gallery *P*
43 Candlemaker Row,
Edinburgh EH1 2QB.
Tel: *0131-220 1911.*
Fax: *0131-226 4287.*
Email *portfolio@ednet.co.uk*
Ws *http://www.ednet.co.uk/-portfolio*
Opening times: *Tue-Sat 12-5.30.*
Personnel: *Director:* Gloria Chalmers.
Portfolio Gallery was established in 1988 since which time it has become one of the UK's leading galleries which exhibits and promotes contemporary photographic art. The gallery is an intimate space, with an occasional programme of exhibitions from leading British, European and American photographic artists.
Portfolio Gallery also regularly commissions work by British photographers and publishes the bi-annual PORTFOLIO - The Catalogue of Contemporary Photography in Britain - which features new work by both established photographic artists and young emerging talent.
Services and Facilities:
Commissioning Service. Gallery space for hire. Lectures.

Queen's Hall
Clerk Street, Edinburgh EH8 9JG.
Tel: *0131-668 3456.*

Royal Incorporation of Architects in Scotland Gallery
15 Rutland Square, Edinburgh EH1 2BE.
Tel: *0131-229 7545.*

Royal Museum of Scotland *P*
Chambers Street, Edinburgh EH1 1JF.
Tel: *0131-225 7534.*
Fax: *0131-220 4819.*

Landings Gallery, Royal Over-Seas League *C*
Over-Seas House, 100 Princes Street, Edinburgh EH2 3AB.
Tel: *0131-225 1501.*
Fax: *0131-225 3936 / 226 3936.*
Opening times: *Open daily 10-6.*
Personnel: *Contact:* Dominic Gregory.
Situated in the heart of Edinburgh, the Landings Gallery provides a unique opportunity for young artists up to the age of 35 from the UK and Commonwealth to display their work in Scotland. All artists have been chosen through the ROSL Annual Open Exhibition, an established showcase now in its 16th year which tours to the Edinburgh College of Art each autumn after its London opening. Bi-monthly exhibitions compliment similar solo shows held at Over-Seas, London. Number of Fringe events.
Services and Facilities:
Bar. Café. Restaurant.
Work Stocked and Sold:
Dr. Pa.
Price range: £100 - £5,000.

Royal Scottish Academy *PS*
The Mound, Edinburgh EH2 2EL.
Tel: *0131-225 6671.*
Fax: *0131-225 2349.*
Opening times: *During exhibitions: Mon-Sat 10-5, Sun 2-5.*
Nearest Station: *Waverley.*
Personnel: *Administrative Secretary:* Bruce Laidlaw. *Asst. Admin. Sec.:* Margaret Wilson.

The Royal Scottish Academy

Founded in 1826. The Royal Scottish Academy is widely acknowledged as one of the foremost promoters of contemporary art in Scotland. Covering the disciplines of painting, sculpture, architecture and printmaking. The Annual Exhibition (24th April-11th July) is a key event in the Scottish Arts calendar. In addition, the RSA plays an important educational role with its unique Students' Exhibition (6th March - 17th March) together with awards and travelling scholarships.
Services and Facilities:
Art for Offices. Disabled Access. Friends/Society. Shop.

Scottish Gallery (Aitken Dott Ltd) *C*
16 Dundas Street, Edinburgh EH3 6HZ.
Tel: *0131-558 1200.* **Fax:** *0131-558 3900.*
Email *mail@scottish-gallery.co.uk*
Ws *http://www.scottish-gallery.co.uk*
Opening times: *Mon-Fri 10-6, Sat 10-4.*
Personnel: *Director:* Iain Barnet.

The Scottish Gallery, founded in 1842, specialises in 20th c. and contemporary Scottish art. The gallery has had close relationships with all the major Scottish painters of this century - The Scottish Colourists, 'The Edinburgh School' - Gillies, Redpath, MacTaggart, etc and others such as Joan Eardley. Recently we have held major shows by Blackadder, Houston, McLaren, Morrocco, Philipson, Redpath, Rae, Morrison, Michie, McClure.
An exciting and varied monthly exhibition programme is supplemented by extensive stocks of paintings. In addition we have the most prestigious selection of British Crafts in Scotland.
Services and Facilities:
Art Consultancy. Commissioning Service. Craftshop. Valuation.
Work Stocked and Sold:
App. Cer. Cra. Dr. Gla. Jew. Pa. Pr. Sc. Tx. Wd.
Price range: £20 - £20,000.
For artists see *Commercial Gallery Artists.*

Scottish National Gallery of Modern Art *P*
Belford Road, Edinburgh EH4 3DR.
Tel: *0131-624 6200.* **Fax:** *0131-343 3250.*
Opening times: *Mon-Sat 10-5, Sun 2-5.*
Nearest Station: *Haymarket.*
Personnel: *Keeper:* Richard Calvocoressi. *Director of National Galleries of Scotland:* Timothy Clifford.
Scotland's finest collection of 20th century painting, sculpture and graphic art. Includes work by Bacon, Hockney, Miro, Matisse, Moore, Paolozzi, Peploe and Picasso. Prints and drawings study room open by prior appointment, Mon-Fri 10am-12 noon, 2-4.30pm.
Services and Facilities:
Bookshop. Café. Disabled Access. Gallery space for hire. Museum Shop. Parking. Shop.

Scottish National Portrait Gallery *P*
1 Queen Street, Edinburgh EH2 1JD.
Tel: *0131-624 6200.* **Fax:** *0131-558 3691.*
Opening times: *Mon-Sat 10-5, Sun 2-5.*
Nearest Station: *Waverley.*
Personnel: *Keeper:* James Holloway. *Director of National Galleries of Scotland:* Timothy Clifford.

Portraits in all media of people who have played a significant role in Scottish history from the 16th century to the present. Also houses the National Photography Collection with regular photography exhibitions. The Print Room and Reference Archive are open by arrangement at the Gallery front desk, Mon-Fri 10am-12.00pm and 2-4.30pm.
Services and Facilities:
Bookshop. Café. Disabled Access. Gallery space for hire. Museum Shop. Shop.

Stills Gallery
23 Cockburn Street, Edinburgh EH1 1BP.
Tel: *0131-225 9876.*

Talbot Rice Gallery C
University of Edinburgh,
Old College, South Bridge, Edinburgh EH8 9YL.
Tel: *0131-650 2210-2085.*
Fax: *0131-650 2213.*
Email *val.fiddes@ed.ac.uk*
Opening times: *Tues-Sat 10-5.*
Personnel: Valerie Fiddes.
A university gallery which houses a permanent collection of old master paintings and bronzes, as well as operating a busy temporary exhibition programme. Founded in the 1970's, the gallery's commitment to the visual arts in Scotland is to provide a platform for more mature (mainly Scottish) artists to mount major solo exhibitions. Exhibitions of work from Europe and elsewhere are also shown. Education programme. Limited Disabled Access.
Services and Facilities:
Disabled Access. Friends/Society. Lectures.
Work Stocked and Sold:
Pa.

Theatre Workshop
34 Hamilton Place, Edinburgh EH3 5AX.
Tel: *0131-225 7942.*

Torrance Gallery C
29b Dundas Street, Edinburgh EH3 6QQ.
Tel: *0131-556 6366.*

Vincent Kosman Fine Art C
8 Burgess Terrace, Newington, Edinburgh EH9 2BD.
Tel: *0131-662 9990.*
Fax: *0131-662 9990.*
Opening times: *By appointment.*
Nearest Station: *Central Edinburgh.*
Personnel: Louise Kosman.
Vincent Kosman Fine Art is a small family company of art dealers and consultants established thirty years ago. We offer modern British pictures, painted 1900 to contemporary. Our stock is constantly changing, and on request we will send photographs. Viewing of our stock is by appointment only, but we are available most of the time. We also provide advice on restoration, framing, and the art market. Our prices are very competitive.
Services and Facilities:
Art Consultancy. Commissioning Service. Valuation.
Work Stocked and Sold:
Dr. Pa. Sc.
Price range: £500 - £50,000.
For artists see *Commercial Gallery Artists.*

Falkirk

FALKIRK

Callender House P
Callender Park, Falkirk.
Tel: *01324-503770.*

Glasgow

GLASGOW

90s Gallery
12 Otago Street, Kelvinbridge, Glasgow G12 8HJ.
Tel: *041-339 3158.*

Art Exposure Gallery C
19 Parnie Street, Glasgow G1 5RJ.
Tel: *0141-552 7779.*

Artbank
24 Cleveden Road, Glasgow G12 0PX.
Tel: *0141-334 6180.*

Barclay Lennie Fine Art C
203 Bath Street, Glasgow G2 4HZ.
Tel: *0141-226 5413.*

The Burrell Collection P
2060 Pollokshaws Road, Pollock Country Park, Glasgow G43 1AT.
Tel: *0141-649 7151.* **Fax:** *0141-636 0086.*

Collins Gallery PS
University of Strathclyde, 22 Richmond Street, Glasgow G1 1XQ.
Tel: *0141-553 4145.*
Fax: *0141-552 4053.*
Opening times: *Mon-Fri 10-5, Sat 12-4. Cl. public holidays and during exhibitions changeovers.*
Nearest Station: *Queen Street.*
Personnel: *Curator:* Laura Hamilton. *Exhibitions Organiser:* Morag Davidson.

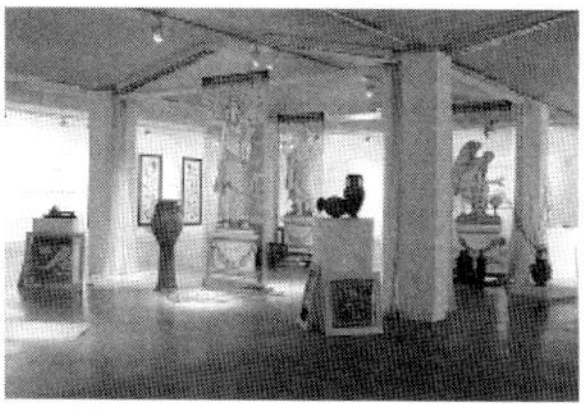

Monthly programme of temporary exhibitions ranging from contemporary Fine and Applied Art, Photography and Design, and multi-media installations to social history. Most exhibition are complemented by educational workshops, videos, performances or lectures. Plus activities for special need's groups. Permanent collection: Historic and contemporary Fine Art and Scientific Instruments.
Services and Facilities:
Café. Disabled Access. Friends/Society. Gallery space for hire. Lectures. Parking. Shop. Workshop Facilities.

Compass Gallery
178 West Regent Street, Glasgow G2 4RL.
Tel: *0141-221 6370.* **Fax:** *0141-248 1322.*
Opening times: *Mon-Sat: 10-5.30.*
Personnel: Cyril Gerber.
Glasgow's oldest established contemporary gallery with emphasis on young and mid-career artists. Changing monthly exhibitions of paintings, drawings, prints and ceramics by Scottish and international artists.
Also each July and August, "New Generation Artists", selected new graduates from Glasgow, Edinburgh, Dundee and Aberdeen Art Colleges.

Cyril Gerber Fine Art C
148 West Regent Street, Glasgow G2 2RQ.
Tel: *0141-221 3095.* **Fax:** *0141-248 1322.*
Opening times: *Mon-Sat 9.30-5.30.*
Personnel: Cyril Gerber. Jill Gerber. Stephanie Hand.
Regularly in stock: D Y Cameron, Cowie, Gaudier-Brzeska, Cadell, Eardley, Fergusson, Gillies, Peploe, Hunter, Herman, Hilton, Kay, Lanyon, Redpath, Sehilsky, McCanee, Vaughn, Gill, "Glasgow Boys" - Paterson, Wingate, Melville, Lavery, McGregor.
Contemporary: Knox, Morrocco, Shanks, Banks, Herman, Bellany, Howson. Plus several catalogued shows per year.
For artists see *Commercial Gallery Artists.*

Duncan R. Miller Fine Arts
144 West Regent Steet, Glasgow G2 2RQ.
Tel: *0141-204 0708.*

Eastwood House P
Eastwood Park, Giffnock, Glasgow G46 6UG.
Tel: *0141-638 1101.*

Ewan Mundy Fine Art
211 West George Street, Glasgow G2 2LW.
Tel: *0141-248 9755.* **Fax:** *0141-248 9744.*

Fossil Grove P
Victoria Park, Glasgow G14 1BN.
Tel: *0141-950 1448 / 287 2000.*

Gallery of Modern Art P
Queen Street, Glasgow G1 3AZ.
Tel: *0141-229 1996.* **Fax:** *0141-204 5316.*

Gatehouse Gallery C
Rouken Glen Road, Giffnock, Glasgow G46 7UG.
Tel: *0141-620 0235.*

Glasgow Print Studio Gallery C
22 King Street, Glasgow G1 5QP.
Tel: *0141-552 0704 / 1394.*
Fax: *0141-552 2919.*
Email *gallery@gpsart.co.uk*
Ws *http://www.gpsart.co.uk*
Opening times: *Tues-Sat 10-5.30.*
Personnel: Linda Meilson. John Mackechnie. Jenny Connelly. Leona Stewart.
Non-profit gallery of charitable status. Highly acclaimed for its beautiful exhibition space, the gallery hosts monthly
exhibitions of original prints, paintings and sculpture by local, national and international artists.
The gallery also organises exhibitions of original

prints by Glasgow Print Studio artists in Britain and abroad, including New York, Berlin, Munich, Moscow and Los Angeles and Iceland.
Services and Facilities:
Art Consultancy. Art for Offices. Bookshop. Disabled Access. Framing. Shop. Workshop Facilities.
Work Stocked and Sold:
Ab. App. Cer. Jew. Pr.
Price range: £25 - £2,000.
For artists see *Commercial Gallery Artists.*

Glasgow School of Art P
167 Renfrew Street, Glasgow G3 6RQ.
Tel: *0141-353 4500.* **Fax:** *0141-353 4746.*

Glasgow Tourist Board
39 St Vincent Place, Glasgow G1 2ER.
Tel: *0141-204 4480.*

Hunterian Art Gallery P
University of Glasgow, 82 Hillhead Street, Glasgow G12 8QQ.
Tel: *0141-330 5431.*
Fax: *0141-330 3618.*
Email *J.E.Barrie@museum.gla.ac.uk*
Ws *http://www.gla.ac.uk/Museum/*
Opening times: *Mon-Sat 9.30-5, (Mackintosh House closed 12.30-1.30).*
Nearest Station: *Partick (rail), Hillhead (underground).*
Personnel: *Administrator:* June Barrie.
This award-winning gallery houses the University of Glasgow's outstanding art collections. In the Main Gallery there are paintings by Rembrandt, Stubbs and Chardin, 18th century British portraits, some fine Scottish 19th and 20th century paintings, and the Estate of the American painter, J.M. Whistler, making this the largest display of his works anywhere. The Mackintosh House comprises the principal rooms from the Glasgow home of the architect Charles Rennie Mackintosh, with changing displays of his work in the Gallery above the House. Contemporary sculpture is displayed in The Sculpture Courtyard and there are temporary exhibitions from the print collection.
Services and Facilities:
Bookshop. Disabled Access. Gallery space for hire.
Work Stocked and Sold:
Pr.

John Green Fine Art C
203 Bath Street, Glasgow G2 4HJ.
Tel: *0141-221 6025.*

The Kelly Gallery
118 Douglas Street, Glasgow G2 4ET.
Tel: *0141-248 6386.*

Kelvingrove Art Gallery and Museum P
Kelvingrove, Glasgow G3 8AG.
Tel: *0141-221 9600 / 287 2000.*
Fax: *0141-305 2690 / 287 2690.*

Lillie Art Gallery
Station Road, Milngavie, Glasgow G62 8BZ.
Tel: *0141-943 3247.*
Fax: *0141-943 3246.*

Lloyd Jerome Gallery C
At The Dental Practice, 200 Bath Street, Glasgow G2 4HG.
Tel: *0141-331 0722.* **Fax:** *0131-331 0733.*

McLellan Galleries P
270 Sauchiehall Street, Glasgow G2 3EH.
Tel: *0141-331 1854.* **Fax:** *0141-332 9957.*

Michael Main Gallery
34 Gibson St, Kelvinbridge, Glasgow G12 8NX.
Tel: *0141-334 8858.*

Mitchell Library P
North Street, Glasgow G3 7DN.
Tel: *0141-305 2803.*

Museum of Transport P
1 Bunhouse Road, Kelvinhall, Glasgow G3 8DP.
Tel: *0141-287 2000 / 287 2698.* **Fax:** *0141-287 2692.*

The N S Gallery
53 Cresswell Street, Glasgow G12 9AE.
Tel: *0141-334 4240.*

Pearce Institute P
840 Govan Road, Glasgow G51 3UT.
Tel: *0141-445 1941.*

People's Palace P
Glasgow Green, Glasgow G40 1AT.
Tel: *0141-554 0223.* **Fax:** *0141-550 0892.*

Pollok House P
2060 Pollokshaws Road, Pollok Country Park, Glasgow G43 1AT.
Tel: *0141-632 0274.* **Fax:** *0141-649 0823.*

Provand's Lordship P
3 Castle Street, Glasgow G4 0RB.
Tel: *0141-552 8819.*

Roger Billcliffe Fine Art C
134 Blythswood Street, Glasgow G2 4EL.
Tel: *0141-332 4027.* **Fax:** *0141-332 6573.*

Rowan Gallery C
36 Main Street, Drymen, Glasgow G63 0BG.
Tel: *01360-660996.*

Royal Glasgow Institute of the Fine Arts
5 Oswald Street, Glasgow G1 4QR.
Tel: *0141-248 7411.* **Fax:** *0141-221 0417.*

Rutherglen Museum P
King Street, Rutherglen, Glasgow G73 1DQ.
Tel: *0141-647 0837.*

Scotland Street School, Museum of Education P
(Opposite Shields Road Underground Station), 225 Scotland Street, Glasgow G5 8QB.
Tel: *0141-429 1202.*

Springburn Museum P
Atlas Square, Ayr Street, Glasgow G21 4BW.
Tel: *0141-557 1405.*

St. Mungo Museum of Religious Life and Art P
2 Castle Street, Glasgow G4 0RH.
Tel: *0141-553 2557.* **Fax:** *0141-552 4744.*

Strathclyde Arts Centre
12 Washington Street, Glasgow G12 8PD.
Tel: *0141-221 4526.*

Street Level Photography Gallery and Workshop C
26 King Street, Glasgow G1 5QP.
Tel: *0141-552 2151.* **Fax:** *0141-552 2323.*

t. Garner Gallery
4 Parnie Street, Glasgow G1 5LR.
Tel: *0141-552 4585.*

T & R Annan & Sons Ltd
The Annan Gallery, 164 Woodlands Road, Glasgow G3 6LL.
Tel: *0141-332 0028.*

Tramway
25 Albert Drive, Glasgow G41 2PE.
Tel: *0141-422 2023.*

Transmission Gallery C
28 King Street, Tramgate, Glasgow G1 5QP.
Tel: *0141-552 4813.*

Inverclyde

GREENOCK

McLean Museum and Art Gallery P
15 Kelly Street, Greenock, PA16 8JX.
Tel: *01475-723741.*

East Lothian

GULLANE

Norrie Toch Studios
St Peters, Main Street, Gullane, EH31 2AA.
Tel: *01620-842039.*

HADDINGTON

Peter Potter Gallery C
10 The Sands, Haddington, EH41 3EY.
Tel: *01620-822080.*

West Lothian

LIVINGSTON

Balbardie Gallery P
West Lothian Council, Almondbank Campus, The Mall, Craigshill, Livingston, EH54 5BJ.
Tel: *01506-442765.*

Midlothian

LOANHEAD

Dalkeith Arts Centre P
Midlothian Council, Library HQ, 2 Clerk Street, Loanhead, EH20 9DR.
Tel: *0131-440 2210 / 0131-663 6986.*

Renfrewshire

PAISLEY

Paisley Arts Centre
New Street, Paisley, PA1 1EZ.
Tel: *0141-887 1010.*

Paisley Museum, Art Galleries and Coats Observatory *PS*
High Street, Paisley, PA1 2BA.
Tel: *0141-889 3151.*
Fax: *0141-889 9240.*

Highland

CAITHNESS

Lyth Arts Centre
by Wick, Caithness, KW1 4UD.
Tel: *01955-641270.*

CULLODEN

Culloden Library Mini Gallery
Culloden Library, Kappoch Road, Culloden, IV1 2LL.
Tel: *01463-792531.*

INVERNESS

Highland Arts
Inverness Museum & Art Gallery, Castle Wynd, Inverness, IV2 3ED.
Tel: *01463-237114.*
Fax: *01463-225293.*

Inverness Museum & Art Gallery *P*
Castle Wynd, Inverness, IV2 3ED.
Tel: *01463-237114.*

Iona Gallery
c/o Inverness Museum and Art Gallery, Castle Wynd, Inverness, IV2 3EB.
Tel: *01463-237114.*

Rhue Studio *C*
Rhue, Ullapool, IV26 2TJ.
Tel: *01854-612460.*
Fax: *01854-612460.*

Scottish Fine Arts Group
57 Church Street, Inverness, IV1 1DR.
Tel: *01463-243575 (Antique paintings) or 01808-521268 (Contemporary Art).*

Isle of Skye

DUNVEGAN

Orbost Gallery *C*
Dunvegan, IV55 8ZB.
Tel: *01470-521207.*
Opening times: *10-6 April-October, by appointment outside these months.*

Services and Facilities:
Disabled Access. Framing. Parking. Restoration.
Work Stocked and Sold:
App. Pa. Pr.
Price range: £30 - £950.
For artists see *Commercial Gallery Artists.*

PORTREE

An Tuireann Arts Centre
Struan Road, Portree, IV15 9ES.
Tel: *01478-613306.*

WATERNISH

Artizania
Captains House, Stein, Waternish, IV55 8GA.
Tel: *01470-592361.*

North Lanarkshire

BROUGHTON

Broughton Gallery *C*
Broughton Place, Nr Biggar, Broughton, ML12 6HJ.
Tel: *01899-830234.*

COATBRIDGE

Ironworks Gallery
Summerlee Heritage Trust, West Canal Street, Coatbridge, ML5 1QD.
Tel: *01236-431261.*
Fax: *01236-440429.*

South Lanarkshire

CLELAND

Cleland Arts Schoolhouse
24 Main Street, Cleland, ML1 5QN.
Tel: *01698-861740.*

Moray

ELGIN

Elgin Museum *P*
1 High Street, Elgin, IV30 1EQ.
Tel: *01343-543675.*

FORRES

Logie Steading Art Gallery *C*
Logie, Forres, IV36 0QN.
Tel: *01309-611378/278.* **Fax:** *01309-611300.*
Email *Panny@logie.co.uk*
Opening times: *Tues-Fri 11-5, Sat & Sun 12-5, April-Nov.*
Personnel: Mrs A. Laing.
The Art Gallery is in the Logie Steading which is converted farm buildings. Throughout the season there is an ever changing exhibition of individual work by predominantly Scottish artists: oils, water-colours, textiles, ceramics, sculpture, wood, cards etc. Also in the complex is an engraver, silversmith potter and tea-room. Gardens are open and plants are for sale.
Services and Facilities:
Café. Craftshop. Disabled Access. Gallery space for hire. Parking. Restaurant. Shop. Workshop Facilities.
Work Stocked and Sold:
App. Cer. Cra. Dec. Dr. Fur. Gla. Jew. Pa. Pr. Sc. Tx. Wd.
Price range: £5 - £1,500.
For artists see *Commercial Gallery Artists.*

Orkney Islands

KIRKWALL

Taukerness House Museum *P*
Broad Street, Kirkwall, KW15 1DH.
Tel: *01865-3191.*

STROMNESS

Pier Arts Centre *P*
Victoria Street, Stromness, KW16 3AA.
Tel: *01856-850209.*

Perth and Kinross

CRIEFF

Strathearn Gallery and Pottery *C*
32 West High Street, Crieff, PH7 4DL.
Tel: *01764-656100.*
Email *info@strathearn-gallery.com*
Ws *http://www.strathearn-gallery.com*
Opening times: *Mon-Sat 10-5, Sun 1-5.*
Nearest Station: *Perth.*
Personnel: *Directors:* Edith Maguire, Owen Maguire. *Contact:* Fiona Maguire.
Opened in March 1994, one of 5 Scottish galleries selected for quality by the Craft Council. We exhibit work by artists and craftspeople based in Scotland. Our annual graduates show is selected from Glasgow, Edinburgh, Dundee and Aberdeen Colleges of Art to encourage and promote new emerging talent. The Strathearn Pottery which is located in the basement of the gallery, opened in December 1995, and is run by John Maguire. You can be assured of a warm welcome in the bright and friendly atmosphere of our family run gallery.
Services and Facilities:
Commissioning Service. Disabled Access.

Work Stocked and Sold:
App. Cer. Cra. Dr. Fur. Gla. Jew. Pa. Ph. Pr. Sc. Wd.
Price range: £15 - £1,000.
For artists see *Commercial Gallery Artists.*

DUNKELD

Atholl Gallery C
6 Atholl Street, Dunkeld, PH8 0AR.
Tel: *01350-728855.* **Fax:** *01577-840636.*

PERTH

Cross Keys Art Gallery & Coffee House C
Commercial Street, Perth, PH2 7DS.
Tel: *01738-628622.* **Fax:** *01738-447976.*

The Fergusson Gallery P
Marshall Place, Perth, PH2 8NU,
Tel: *01738 -441944.*
Fax: *01738-443505.*
Opening times: *Mon-Sat 10-5. Closed Christmas/New Year.*
Nearest Station: *Perth Bus & Rail stations - Leonard St (5 mins walk from Gallery).*
Personnel: *Fine & Applied Art Officer:* Kirsten Simister.
Opened in 1992. Dedicated gallery to the life and work of the Scottish Colourist John Duncan Fergusson (1874-1961), housing the largest collection of his work in existence. Temporary exhibition programme. Archive available for consultation by appointment. MGC registered. Disabled Access (Ground Floor)/WC.
Services and Facilities:
Disabled Access. Parking. Shop.

Frames Contemporary Gallery C
10 Victoria Street, Perth, PH2 8LW.
Tel: *01738-631085.* **Fax:** *01738-631085.*
Email *hugh.goring@btinternet.com*
Ws *http://www.framesgallery.co.uk*
Opening times: *Mon-Fri 9-5.30, Sat 9-5.*
Nearest Station: *Perth.*
Personnel: *Proprietor:* Hugh Goring. *Gallery Manager:* Wanda Band.

FRAMES
CONTEMPORARY GALLERY

The Gallery specialises in contemporary Scottish Art. We hold four large mixed shows in Spring, Summer, Autumn and Winter. Each show has between 12-20 artists featuring painting, drawing, print-making, sculpture and ceramics. We have a clear policy of showing work by artists who are not only well established, but also encouraging younger, less well known artists. Particularly those who have not long left Art College.
Services and Facilities:
Art Consultancy. Art for Offices. Framing.
Work Stocked and Sold:
Cer. Dr. Pa. Sc.
Price range: £100 - £8,000.
For artists see *Commercial Gallery Artists.*

Perth Museum and Art Gallery PS
George Street, Perth, PH1 5LB.
Tel: *01738-632488.* **Fax:** *01738-443505.*
Opening times: *Mon-Sat 10-5. Closed Christmas/New Year.*
Nearest Station: *Perth (Rail & Bus).*
Personnel: *Head of Arts & Heritage:* Michael A. Taylor.
Collections of Scottish and local paintings, prints and drawings, 17th to 20th century. Temporary exhibitions programme. Catalogue paintings and drawings (1981).
Appointments necessary to view material not on display. MGC registered. Galleries opened 1935.
Services and Facilities:
Disabled Access. Lectures. Museum Shop. Parking. Workshop Facilities.

Perth Theatre Gallery
Perth Theatre, 185 High Street, Perth, PH1 5UW
Tel: *01738-638123.*

Shetland Islands

WEISDALE

Bonhoga Gallery C
Weisdale Mill, Weisdale, ZE2 9LW.
Tel: *01595-830400.*

Stirling

STIRLING

MacRobert Arts Centre Gallery P
University of Stirling, Stirling FK9 4LA.
Tel: *01786-467159.*

Smith Art Gallery & Museum P
Dumbarton Road, Stirling FK8 2RQ.
Tel: *01786-471917.* **Fax:** *01786-449523.*

VIEWFORTH

Cowane Gallery
c/o Stirling District Council, Community Services, Room 634, Ground Floor West, Viewforth,
Tel: *01786-443128.*

Western Isles

STORNOWAY

An Lanntair PS
Town Hall, South Beach, Stornoway, HS1 2BX.
Tel: *01851-703307.* **Fax:** *01851-703307.*

NOTES

WELSH GALLERIES

Town/County index. Main listings.
Where this information has been provided, galleries are designated 'C' for commercial, 'P' for public gallery or museum or 'PS' for a public gallery or museum holding selling shows.

The Gallery

Ruthin Craft Centre

A Craft Council Selected Gallery housed within a purpose built Craft Centre in the picturesque Vale of Clwyd. The Gallery shows the best of fine crafts by contemporary designer-makers form all over the British Isles. We run an exciting programme of regularly changing exhibitions which aim through a stimulating and diverse view of contemporary work, to show the breadth of excellence in the field of the applied arts.

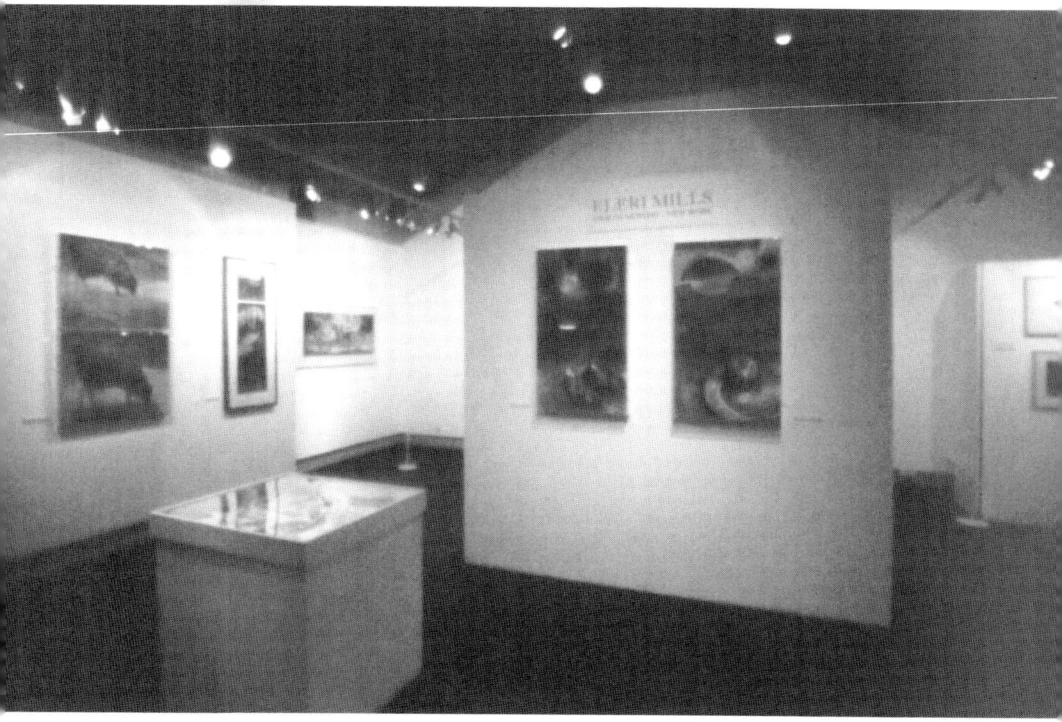

OPENING TIMES

Summer: 10.00–5.30 daily

Winter: Monday–Saturday 10.00–5.00, Sunday: 12.00–5.00.

Free admission

FACILITIES

10 Independent Craft Studios • Restaurant

Car Park • Level access and disabled toilet facilities.

Ruthin Craft Centre, Park Road, Ruthin, Denbighshire LL15 1BB Tel: 01824 704774

Ruthin Craft Centre is part of the Directorate of Planning and Economic Development of Denbighshire County Council. The Gallery Exhibition Programme is supported by the Arts Council of Wales.

Sir Ddinbych Denbighshire

TOWN COUNTY INDEX

A/B/C

Aberaeron *(Ceredigion)*
Aberdare *(Rhondda Cynon Taf)*
Aberdovey *(Gwynedd)*
Abergavenny *(Monmouthshire)*
Aberystwyth *(Ceredigion)*
Ammanford *(Carmarthenshire)*
Anglesey *(Anglesey)*
Bangor *(Gwynedd)*
Betws-y-Coed *(Gwynedd)*
Blackwood *(Caerphilly)*
Brecon *(Powys)*
Bridgend *(Bridgend)*
Caernarfon *(Gwynedd)*
Cardiff *(Cardiff)*
Cardigan *(Ceredigion)*
Carmarthen *(Carmarthenshire)*
Chepstow *(Monmouthshire)*
Criccieth *(Gwynedd)*

D/F/H

Denbigh *(Denbighshire)*
Dolgellau *(Gwynedd)*
Fishguard *(Pembrokeshire)*
Harlech *(Gwynedd)*
Haverfordwest *(Pembrokeshire)*
Hawarden *(Flintshire)*
Hay-on-Wye *(Powys)*

L/M/N

Lampeter *(Ceredigion)*
Laugharne *(Carmarthenshire)*
Llandeilo *(Carmarthenshire)*
Llandrindod Wells *(Powys)*
Llandudno *(Conwy)*
Llanelli *(Carmarthenshire)*
Llangollen *(Denbighshire)*
Machynlleth *(Powys)*
Merthyr Tydfil *(Merthyr Tydfil)*
Milford Haven *(Pembrokeshire)*
Mold *(Flintshire)*
Monmouth *(Monmouthshire)*
Montgomery *(Powys)*
Narberth *(Pembrokeshire)*
Newport *(Newport)*
Newtown *(Powys)*

P/R/S

Pembroke *(Pembrokeshire)*
Penarth *(Vale of Glamorgan)*
Pontypridd *(Rhondda Cynon Taf)*
Presteigne *(Powys)*
Pwllheli *(Gwynedd)*
Raglan *(Monmouthshire)*
Ruthin *(Denbighshire)*
St. David's *(Pembrokeshire)*
Swansea *(Swansea)*

T/U/W

Talgarth *(Powys)*
Tenby *(Pembrokeshire)*
Undy *(Monmouthshire)*
Upper Solva *(Pembrokeshire)*
Usk *(Monmouthshire)*
Welshpool *(Powys)*
Whitland *(Carmarthenshire)*
Wrexham *(Wrexham)*

Anglesey

ANGLESEY

Central Gallery
Field Street, Llangefni,
Anglesey LL77 7UR.
Tel: *01248-723527.*

Michael Webb Fine Art C
Llangristiolus, Bodorgan, Anglesey LL62 5DN.
Tel: *01407-840336.*
Opening times: *Available 7 days a week - by appointment.*
Nearest Station: *Bangor, Gwynedd.*
Personnel: *Proprietor:* Michael Webb.

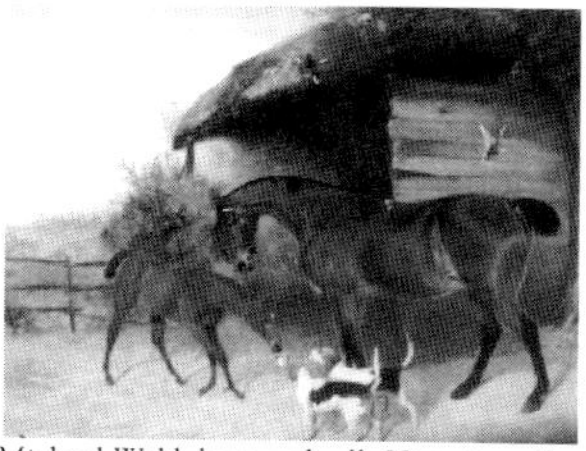

Michael Webb buys and sells Victorian oil paintings, water-colours and etchings. The list of artists given are artists I have handled in recent months; I cannot guarantee to have any particular one in stock at any one time because we do have a continuous turnover of pictures. However, we are always pleased to help you find a particular artist. We also have a collection of water-colours by the living wild life artist Owen Williams.
Services and Facilities:
Art Consultancy. Framing. Restoration. Valuation.
Work Stocked and Sold:
Dr. Pa. Pr.
Price range: £100 - £25,000.
For artists see *Commercial Gallery Artists.*

Oriel Fach
46a Castle Street, Beaumaris,
Anglesey LL58 8BB.
Tel: *01248-810445.*

Oriel Ynys Mon
Rhosmeirch, Llangefni,
Anglesey LL77 7TQ.
Tel: *01248-724444.*
Fax: *01248-750282.*

Bridgend

BRIDGEND

Nolton Gallery
66 Nolton Street, Bridgend CF31 3BP.
Tel: *01656-663278.*

Peter Wills Ceramics
Pottery and Gallery,
44 Newcastle Hill,
Bridgend CF31 4EY.
Tel: *01656-662902.*

Caerphilly

BLACKWOOD

The Gallery
Blackwood Miners' Institute, High Street,
Blackwood, NP2 1BB.
Tel: *01495-224425.* **Fax:** *01495-226457.*

Cardiff

CARDIFF

Albany Gallery C
74B Albany Road, Cardiff CF2 3RS.
Tel: *01222-487158.* **Fax:** *01222-489158.*

Cardiff Bay Arts Trust *PS*
123 Bute Street, Cardiff CF1 6AE.
Tel: *01222-488772.* **Fax:** *01222-472439.*
Email *Arts.Trust@ENABLIS.co.uk*
Opening times: *Daily office hours.*
Personnel: *Director:* Carole-Anne Davies.

Cardiff Bay Arts Trust

CBAT is a busy Public Art Consultancy which has achieved over 60 projects within its award winning public art schemes, as part of the urban regeneration strategy in Cardiff Bay. Projects undertaken include temporary and permanent works, integral and stand alone pieces in the public realm, environmental improvements, educational workshops and a changing exhibition programme. CBAT works in collaboration with residents, public authorities, the private sector, architects, artists, and craft workers in the initiation and implementation of commissions. Following the success of its work in Cardiff, CBAT is now active in other areas across the UK. Services: Consultancy and management of public art projects both urban and rural, Art for Offices, Commissioning Service.
Services and Facilities:
Art Consultancy. Art for Offices. Commissioning Service. Gallery space for hire. Guided Tours. Lectures.

Cardiff Central Library
St David's Link, Frederick Street, Cardiff CF1 4DT.
Tel: *01222-382116.*

Chapter Gallery
Market Road, Canton, Cardiff CF5 1QE.
Tel: *01222-396061.*

The Collectors Gallery
1st Floor, Cardiff Antiques Market, Morgan Arcade, Cardiff.
Tel: *01446-773324.*

Howard Gardens Gallery *PS*
University of Wales Institute Cardiff, Howard Gardens, Cardiff CF2 1SP.
Tel: *01222-506678.*
Fax: *01222-506678.*
Email *wwarrilow@uwic.ac.uk*
Opening times: *Mon-Thur 9-8pm, Fri 9-5, Sat 9-12.30.*
Nearest Station: *Cardiff Central.*
Personnel: *Director:* Walt Warrilow.

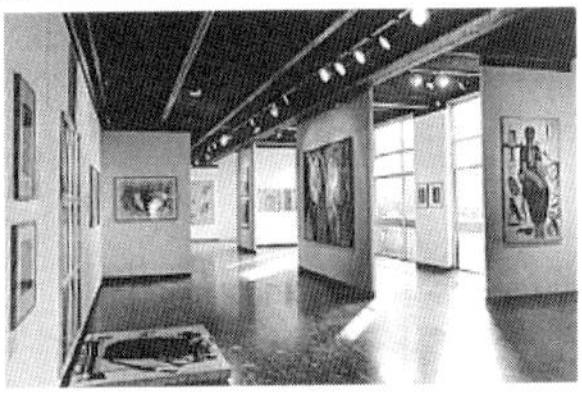

Purpose-built gallery of 264 sqm within the Faculty of Art, Design & Engineering. It has a continuous programme throughout the year which spans not only the visual and applied arts, but also other related disciplines including architecture, design, historical and cultural studies. There are complementary events, lectures, workshops etc. The gallery hosts the Faculty's final BA and MA Degree exhibitions.
Services and Facilities:
Disabled Access. Lectures. Parking. Workshop Facilities.

Manor House Fine Arts *C*
73 Pontcanna Street, Pontcanna, Cardiff CF1 9HS.
Tel: *01222-227787.*

Martin Tinney Gallery *C*
6 Windsor Place, Cardiff CF1 3BX.
Tel: *01222-641411.*
Fax: *01222-641422.*
Email *mtg@artwales.com*
Ws
http://www.ARTWALES.DIRCON.CO.UK
Opening times: *Mon-Fri 10-6, Sat 10-5.*
Personnel: Martin Tinney.
20th century and contemporary art with a strong emphasis on Welsh artists and artists who have worked in Wales. Monthly exhibitions and large stock of work by both established and emerging artists including: Leonard Beard, Neil Canning, Roger Cecil, George Chapman, Evan Charlton, Michael Crowther, Ivor Davies, John Elwyn, Merlyn Evans, Mary Griffiths, Josef Herman, Harry Holland, J.D. Innes, Augustus John, Gwen John, David Jones, Edward Morland Lewis, Mary Lloyd Jones, John Macfarlane, Sally Moore, John Piper, Edward Povey, Peter Prendergast, Gwilym Prichard, Shani Rhys James, Ceri Richards, Mark Samuel, Kevin Sinnott, Graham Sutherland, Claudia Williams, Emrys Williams, Kyffin Williams and Ernest Zobole.
Services and Facilities:
Art Consultancy. Art for Offices. Commissioning Service.
Work Stocked and Sold:
Dr. Pa. Pr. Sc.
Price range: £75 - £10,000.
For artists see *Commercial Gallery Artists.*

National Museums & Galleries of Wales *P*
National Museum & Gallery Cathays Park, Cardiff CF1 3NP.
Tel: *01222-397951.* **Fax:** *01222-373219.*
Email *Post@nmgw.ac.uk*
Ws *http://www.nmgw.ac/index.html*
Opening times: *Tue-Sun 10-5; open Bank Holiday Mondays.*
Nearest Station: *Cardiff Queen Street.*
Personnel: *Director:* Anna Southall. *Keeper of Art:* Oliver Fairclough. *Exhibitions Co-ordinator:* Deborah Spillards.
One of eight sites under the umbrella of the National Museums & Galleries of Wales, the National Museum & Gallery Cardiff is home to one of the finest collections of art treasures in Europe. The Davies collection includes works by Monet, Manet, Renoir, Van Gogh and Sisley, also bronzes by Degas and Rodin, including Rodin's Kiss. A fine collection of 18th and 19th century landscapes and important works by Welsh artists Augustus & Gwen John are displayed and there is a regular programme of changing exhibitions. Works from the museum's collection are also displayed at Turner House Gallery, Penarth, in addition to exhibitions by local art societies.
Services and Facilities:
Bookshop. Café. Disabled Access. Friends/Society. Museum Shop. Parking. Restaurant.

St. David's Hall *PS*
The Hayes, Cardiff CF1 2SH.
Tel: *01222-878500.* **Fax:** *01222-878599.*
Opening times: *Mon-Sat 10-4. Also open to concert-goers.*

St David's Hall
Neuadd Dewi Sant

St. David's Hall, the National Concert Hall of Wales, is situated in the city centre. The two main galleries currently show around 25 exhibitions each year. Exhibitions include both group and single artist shows covering a wide range of work. There is also additional space for regular photography and craft exhibitions. St. David's Hall's broad spectrum of concert hall events brings the visual arts to the attention of more than 10,000 people a week who pass through the foyers. WC.
Services and Facilities:
Bar. Café. Craftshop. Disabled Access. Friends/Society. Gallery space for hire. Restaurant. Shop.
For artists see *Commercial Gallery Artists.*

Carmarthenshire

AMMANFORD

The Gallery
38 Quay Street, Ammanford, SA18 2EN.
Tel: *01269-594959.*

CARMARTHEN

Carmarthen Museum *P*
Abergwili, Carmarthen, SA31 2JG.
Tel: *01267-231691.*

Henry Thomas Gallery
Carmarthenshire College of Technology and Art, Job's Well Road, Carmarthen, SA31 3HY.
Tel: *01554-759165 ext 4403 (Art).*
Fax: *01267-221515.*

Oriel Myrddin *C*
Church Lane, Carmarthen, SA31 1LH.
Tel: *01267-222775.*

LAUGHARNE

The Powerhouse Gallery
Behind the Clock, Laugharne, SA33 4SB.
Tel: *01994-427580.*

LLANDEILO

Fountain Fine Art
Rhosmaen Street, Llandeilo, SA19 6EN.
Tel: *01558-823328.*

The Trapp Art and Craft Centre
Llwyndewi, Trapp, Llandeilo, SA19 6TT.
Tel: *01269-850362.*

LLANELLI

Nevill Gallery
Llanelli Library, Vaughan Street, Llanelli, SA15 3AF.
Tel: *01554-773538.*

Parc Howard Mansion *P*
Felinfoel Road, Llanelli, SA15 3AS.
Tel: *01554-772029, Hire details 01554-741100..*

WHITLAND

Studio Gallery *C*
Penclippen Farm, Blaenwaun, Whitland, SA34 0JB.
Tel: *01994-448601.* **Fax:** *01994-448601.*

Ceredigion

ABERAERON

Gordon Miles Gallery
Merrihill Press, Unit 4, Clos Pengarreg Courtyard, Panteg Road, Aberaeron, SA46 0EN.
Tel: *01545-571661.*

ABERYSTWYTH

Aberystwyth Arts Centre C
Penglais, Aberystwyth, SY23 3DE.
Tel: *01970-623232 / 622895.*
Fax: *01970-622883.*

The Ceramics Gallery
Aberystwyth Arts Centre, The University of Wales, Penglais, Aberystwyth, SY23 3DE.
Tel: *01970-622460.* **Fax:** *01970-622461.*

The National Library of Wales P
Aberystwyth, SY23 3BU.
Tel: *01970-632800.* **Fax:** *01970-615709.*

Oriel Coliseum Gallery
Ceredigion Museum, Terrace Road, Aberystwyth, SY23 2AQ.
Tel: *01970-633086.* **Fax:** *01970-633084.*
Opening times:
Mon-Sun, School Holidays 10-5.
Personnel: Gwenllian Ashley.

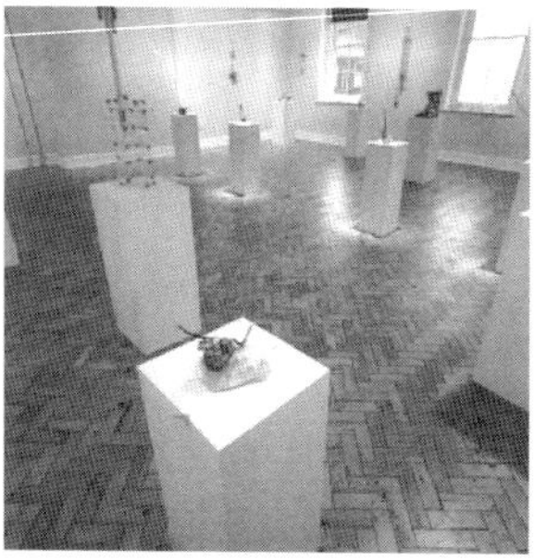

The newly refurbished gallery exhibits the best in Welsh art be it contemporary, abstract paintings or 19th Century primitive quilts. It has an exciting programme of temporary exhibitions and is attached to the Ceredigion Museum which also holds temporary exhibitions in its auditorium area. The Museum, which is housed in in an Edwardian music hall, has a fascinating permanent display of the history of life in Cardiganshire and has been described as having possibly the most beautiful museum interior in Britain.
Services and Facilities:
Gallery space for hire. Museum Shop. Shop.

School of Art Gallery & Museum PS
University of Wales, Buarth Mawr, Aberystwyth, SY23 1NE.
Tel: *01970-622460.*
Fax: *01970-622461.*
Email *nhh@aber.ac.uk*
Ws *http://www.aber.ac.uk*
Opening times: *Mon-Fri 10-5.30.*
Nearest Station: *Aberystwyth.*
Personnel: *Keeper of Art:* Robert Mayrick. *Assistant Curator:* Neil Holland.
Extensive teaching and research collection of fine and decorative art; European prints from 15th century to present, drawings, watercolours and photographs. George Powell of Nanteos collection of pictures, bronzes and objet d'art (including works on paper by Turner, Burne-Jones, Rossetti, Poynter, Rebecca and Simeon Solomon). 5,000 wood engravings for periodicals of the 1860's and a fine collection of prints representing the Etching Revival since Whistler, particularly etchings of the inter-war years. Art in Wales since 1945 and contemporary printmaking. Contemporary Welsh photography and an outstanding collection of post-war Italian photographs. Changing exhibitions from the collection,

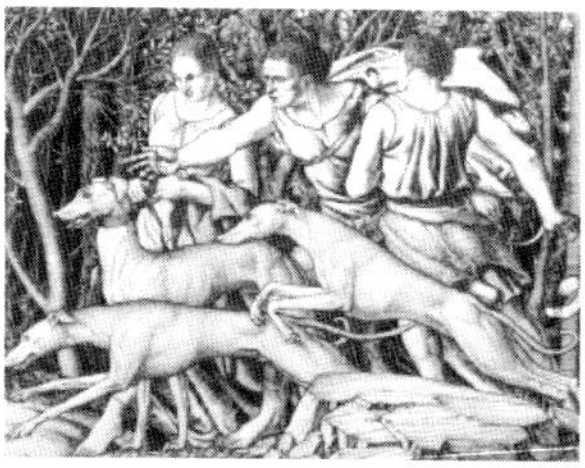

touring shows and exhibitions by staff, students and invited artists. Graphic art study collection by appointment. The School of Art Press publishes books, catalogues and research papers, and new Museum and Gallery Studies courses with the art collections at their core. Also responsible for the Ceramics Gallery at Aberystwyth Arts Centre with its important collection of early 20th century British pioneer studio pottery, contemporary British, European, American, and Japanese studio pottery, 18th & 19th century Welsh and English slip ware, Swansea and Nantgarw porcelain, Art Pottery and Oriental ceramics.
Services and Facilities:
Guided Tours. Lectures. Parking.
Work Stocked and Sold:
Ab. Dr. Pa. Ph. Pr.
Price range: £25 - £1,500.
For artists see *Commercial Gallery Artists.*

CARDIGAN

Frame by Frame
11 Black Lion Mews, Cardigan, SQ43 1HJ.
Tel: *01239-615398.*

The Studio C
3 Cambrian Quay, Cardigan, SA43 1EZ.
Tel: *01239-613711.*
Opening times: *Open all year 11-5: Easter and July-September every day; October-June closed Thursday and Sunday.*
Nearest Station: *Carmarthen.*
Personnel: David Wilson.

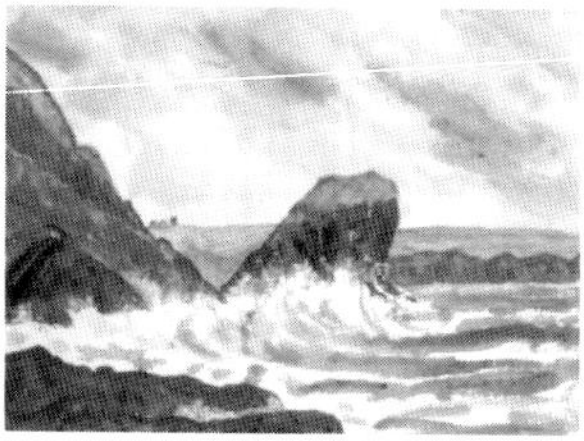

This artist-run gallery overlooking the river Teifi near the bridge is also David Wilson's studio. His paintings and prints draw their inspiration from many sources, but especially from the varied landscape and coast of West Wales. Examples of fine furniture designed by Guy Wilson are also on display.
Services and Facilities:
Art for Offices. Commissioning Service. Parking. Shop.
Work Stocked and Sold:
Dr. Fur. Pa. Pr.
Price range: £10 - £3,000.
For artists see *Commercial Gallery Artists.*

LAMPETER

St. David's University College
College Street, Lampeter, SA48 7ED.
Tel: *01570-422351.*

Y Galeri
2 Bridge Street, Lampeter, SA48 7HG.
Tel: *01570-423317.*

Conwy

LLANDUDNO

Llandudno Museum and Art Gallery P
Chardon House, 17-19 Gloddaeth Street, Llandudno, LL30 2DD. **Tel:** *01492-879130.*

Oriel Mostyn PS
12 Vaughan Street, Llandudno, LL30 1AB.
Tel: *01492-879201/870875.*
Fax: *01492-878869.*

Denbighshire

DENBIGH

Denbigh Library, Museum and Gallery P
Hall Square, Denbigh, LL16 3AU.
Tel: *01745-816313.*

LLANGOLLEN

ECTARC
The European Centre for Traditional and Regional Cultures, Parade Street, Llangollen, LL20 8RB.
Tel: *01978-861514.* **Fax:** *01978-861804.*

Royal International Pavilion
Abbey Road, Llangollen, LL20 8SW.
Tel: *01978-860111.* **Fax:** *01978-860046.*

RUTHIN

The Gallery, Ruthin Craft Centre PS
Park Road, Ruthin, LL15 1BB.
Tel: *01824-704774.* **Fax:** *01824-702060.*
Opening times: *Summer: 10-5.30 daily, Winter: Mon-Sat 10-5, Sun 12-5.*
Nearest Station: *Chester, Rhyl.*
Personnel: *Director:* Philip Hughes. Jane Gerrard.
A Craft Council Selected Gallery housed within a purpose built Craft Centre in the

picturesque Vale of Clwyd. The Gallery shows the best of fine crafts by contemporary designer-makers form all over the British Isles. We run an exciting programme of regularly changing exhibitions which aim through a stimulating and diverse view of contemporary work, to show the breadth of excellence in the field of the applied arts. We receive financial support from the Arts Council of Wales.

Services and Facilities:
Craftshop. Disabled Access. Parking. Restaurant. Shop.
Work Stocked and Sold:
App. Cer. Cra. Gla. Jew. Tx. Wd.
Price range: £5 - £5,000.

Flintshire

HAWARDEN

The Black Sheep Gallery C
The Old Stable Yard, Hawarden Castle, Hawarden, CH5 3NY.
Tel: *01244-535505.*

MOLD

Oriel Gallery *PS*
Clwyd Theatr Cymru, Mold, CH7 1YA.
Tel: *01352-756331.* **Fax:** *01352-758323.*
Email *drama@celtic.co.uk*
Opening times: *Mon-Sat 10-10.*
Nearest Station: *Chester.*
Personnel: *Curator:* J. Le Vay.

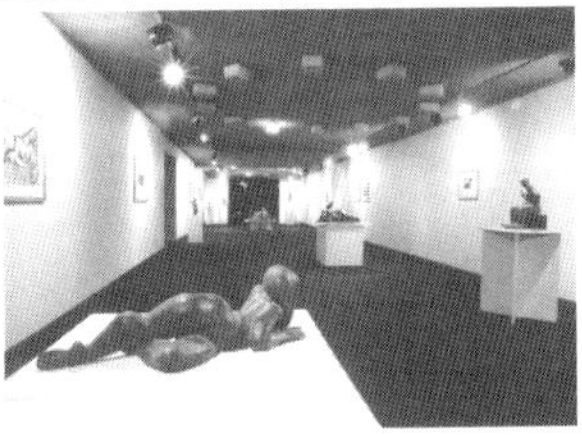

Two galleries with 110 lin. m. hanging space; emphasis on exhibiting the work of new artists in solo or group exhibitions, but work by established artists also shown. The galleries are part of a major regional multi-media Arts Centre, with annual visitor turn-over of 350,000.
Services and Facilities:
Art Consultancy. Bar. Bookshop. Café. Craftshop. Disabled Access. Gallery space for hire. Parking. Restaurant.

Vale of Glamorgan

PENARTH

Turner House
Plymouth Road, Penarth, CF64 3DM.
Tel: *01222-708870.*

The Washington Gallery
1-3 Stanwell Road, Penarth, CF64 2AB.
Tel: *01222-708047.* **Fax:** *01222-700310.*

Gwynedd

ABERDOVEY

The Gallery
11 New Street, Aberdovey, LL35 0EH.
Tel: *01654-767319, eves. 01654-710523.*

BANGOR

Bangor Museum & Art Gallery P
Ffordd Gwynedd, Bangor, LL57 1DT.
Tel: *01248-353368.*

David Windsor Gallery
201 High Street, Bangor, LL57 1NU.
Tel: *01248-364639.*

BETWS-Y-COED

The Gallery
Holyhead Road, Betws-y-Coed, LL24 0BW.
Tel: *01690-710432.*

CAERNARFON

Arfon Gallery
Palace Street, Caernarfon, LL55 1RR.
Tel: *01286-672602.* **Fax:** *01286-76728.*

Caernarfon Library
Pavilion Road, Caernarfon, LL55 1AS.
Tel: *01286-675944.*

CRICCIETH

The Chapel of Art / Capel Celfyddyd C
8 Marine Crescent, Criccieth, LL52 0EA.
Tel: *01766-523570.*
Opening times: *Open Tue-Sun 10-6, summer. Winter hours check. Closed Christmas day and Mons, except Bank holidays.*
Nearest Station: *Criccieth.*
Personnel: *Artistic Director:* Janet Kaiser.
A true centre of excellence housed in a beautifully restored Victorian chapel, in the shadow of Criccieth Castle. This intimate gallery exhibits selected contemporary fine and applied art by professional artists and makers.
Home of The International Potters' Path, we specialise in ceramics and pottery by British and European makers.
Exhibitions change every 6 to 8 weeks. Also a lively program of concerts, classes, lectures etc. all year, plus Criccieth Festival events each June. "Collectorplan" interest-free accounts for purchasing contemporary art available(an Arts Council of Wales service at selected galleries). All major credit cards accepted.
Services and Facilities:
Art Consultancy. Art for Offices. Commissioning Service. Craftshop. Disabled Access. Friends/Society. Lectures. Parking.

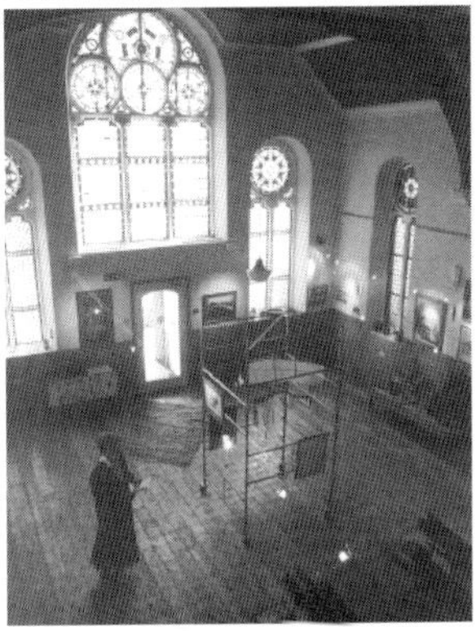

Work Stocked and Sold:
App. Cer. Cra. Dec. Dr. Fur. Gla. Pa. Ph. Sc. Tx. Wd.
Price range: £9 - £999.
For artists see *Commercial Gallery Artists.*

DOLGELLAU

The Library Gallery
Borthwog Hall, Bontddu, Dolgellau, LL40 2TT.
Tel: *01341-430271.* **Fax:** *01341-430682.*

HARLECH

The White Room Gallery at Harlech Pottery
Pentre Fail, Harlech, LL46 2YG.
Tel: *01766-247397 (after 6pm in summer)..*

PWLLHELI

Llanbedrog Pottery and Prints
The Pottery, Llanbedrog, Pwllheli, LL53 7UA.
Tel: *01758-740296.*

Oriel Plas Glyn-y-Weddw C
Llanbedrog, Pwllheli, LL53 7TT.
Tel: *01758-740763.*
Fax: *01758-740232.*
Email *oriel.glynyweddw@virgin.net*
Opening times: *Winter 11-4 except Tuesdays. Summer 11-5 except Tuesdays.*
Nearest Station: *Pwllheli (Cambrian Railway) or Bangor (Main Line).*
Personnel: *Director:* David Jeffreys.
Plas Glyn y Weddw Art Gallery, under new management, is one of the oldest public art galleries in Wales. Pictures, arts and crafts, are housed in a superb listed Victorian Gothic mansion, with fine views from the Llyn Peninsula over Cardigan Bay. There are gardens, woodland and beach walks, and a tea room in the Gallery's conservatory. Contemporary Welsh paintings form the core of the Gallery's collection, as well as changing exhibitions and a distinguished collection of porcelain.

Services and Facilities:
Café. Craftshop. Disabled Access. Friends/Society. Gallery space for hire. Lectures. Parking. Workshop Facilities.
Work Stocked and Sold:
Ab. Cer. Cra. Dr. Jew. Pa. Ph. Pr. Sc. Tx. Wd.
Price range: £30 - £6,000.
For artists see *Commercial Gallery Artists.*

Merthyr Tydfil

MERTHYR TYDFIL

Cyfarthfa Castle Museum *P*
Brecon Road, Merthyr Tydfil, CF47 8RE.
Tel: *01685-723112.*
Fax: *01685-722146.*

Monmouthshire

ABERGAVENNY

Hill Court Gallery
Hill Court, Pen Y Pound, Abergavenny, NP7 7RW.
Tel: *01873-854180.*

CHEPSTOW

The Workshop Gallery
13 Lower Church Street, Chepstow, NPH 5HJ.
Tel: *01291-624836.*

MONMOUTH

The Art Centre
Monk Street, Monmouth, NP5 3NZ.
Tel: *01600-713905.*

Beaver Art and Framing Centre
Monk Street, Monmouth, NP5 3NZ.
Tel: *01600-713905.*

Monmouth Museum *P*
Priory Street, Monmouth, NP5 3XA.
Tel: *01600-713519.*

RAGLAN

The Old Vicarage *C*
Penrhos, Raglan, NP5 2LE.
Tel: *01600-780239.*

UNDY

Art Approach
The Bon Bon, Vinegar Hill, Undy,
Tel: *01633-881999.*

USK

The Arthouse
Pen Y Parc, Llangibby, Usk, NP5 1NY.
Tel: *01633-450320.*
Fax: *01633-450552.*

Newport

NEWPORT

Newport Museum & Art Gallery *PS*
John Frost Square, Newport NP9 1PA.
Tel: *01633-840064.* **Fax:** *01633-222615.*
Opening times: *Mon-Thu 9.30-5, Fri 9.30-4.30, Sat 9.30-4.*
Personnel: *Keeper of Art:* Roger Cucksey. *Exhibitions Officer:* Sandra Jackaman.
Founded 1888. Collection of early English watercolours, oil paintings, mainly British

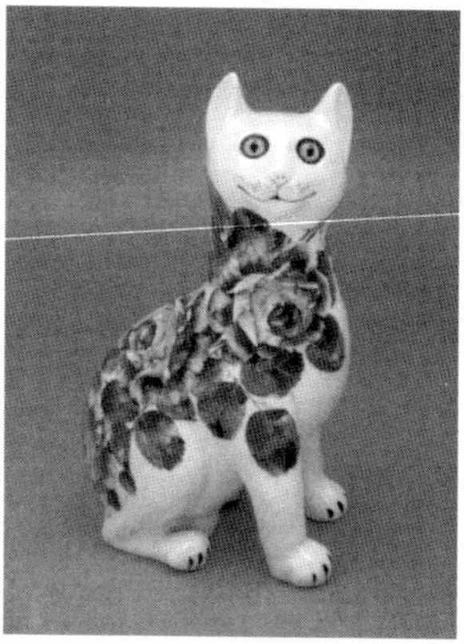

20th century with emphasis on Welsh artists. Extensive changing exhibition programme with related events and activities. The John Wait Teapot collection 1780-1980. WC.
Services and Facilities:
Café. Craftshop. Disabled Access. Lectures. Museum Shop. Shop. Valuation.
Work Stocked and Sold:
App. Cer. Cra. Dec. Dr. Fur. Gla. Jew. Pa. Ph. Pr. Sc. Tx. Wd.
Price range: Up to £1,000.

Tower Gallery
Caldicot Castle Museum, Caldicot, Newport NP6 4HU.
Tel: *01291-420241.*

Pembrokeshire

FISHGUARD

Gallery One
West Street, Fishguard, SA65 9AE.
Tel: *01348-872707.*

Oriel/Dragon Gallery
The Old Post Office, 9 West Street, Fishguard, SA65 9AE.
Tel: *01348-875175.*

West Wales Arts Centre, *C*
Castle Hill, 16 West Street, Fishguard, SA65 9AE.
Tel: *01348-873867.* **Fax:** *01348-873867.*

Workshop Wales Gallery
Lower Town, Fishguard, SA65 9LY.
Tel: *01348-872261.*

HAVERFORDWEST

The Artists Studio *C*
"Red Rails" Marloes, Haverfordwest, SA62 3BB.
Tel: *01646-636380.*

The Gallery
Haroldston House, Clay Lanes, Haverfordwest, SA61 1UH.
Tel: *01437-762611.*

Gillian Richardson
Fine Art Photography, The Gallery, Fair Winds, Spittal, Haverfordwest, SA62 5QT.
Tel: *01437-87311.*

Hamilton House Gallery
Caerfarchell, Solva, Haverfordwest, SA62 6XG.
Tel: *01437-721264.*

The Pink House
Contemporary Arts, Nine Wells, Solva, Haverfordwest, SA62 6UH.
Tel: *01437-721543.*

Trevigan Gallery
Croesgoch, Haverfordwest, SA62 5JP.
Tel: *01348-831374.*

MILFORD HAVEN

Torch Theatre
St Peters Road, Milford Haven, SA73 2BU.
Tel: *01646-694192.*

NARBERTH

The Gallery at Colby
Colby Woodland Gardens (National Trust Property), Stepaside, Narberth, SA67 8PP.
Tel: *01834-814164.*

The Golden Sheaf Gallery *C*
High Street, Narberth, SA67 7AR.
Tel: *01834-860407.* **Fax:** *01834-860407.*

NEWPORT

Carningli Centre *C*
East Street, Newport, SA42 OSY.
Tel: *01239-820724.*
Personnel: Mr C. J. Field. Mrs A. Gent.
Services and Facilities:
Commissioning Service.
Work Stocked and Sold:
Dr. Pa. Ph. Pr.
Price range: £15 - £500.
For artists see *Commercial Gallery Artists.*

Fine Arts Gallery
Carningli Centre, East Street, Newport, SA42 0SY.
Tel: *01239-820724.*

Pauline Harries Gallery
Ty Clyd, Long Street, Newport, SA42 0TL.
Tel: *01239-820404.*

The Sessions House
East Street, Newport, SA42 0SY.
Tel: *01239-820853.*

Ab Artists' Books **App** Applied Art **Cer** Ceramics **Cra** Crafts **Dec** Decorative **Dr** Drawing **Fur** Furniture

PEMBROKE

The Golden Plover Studio Gallery C
Warren, Pembroke, SA17 5HR.
Tel: *01646-661201.*
Opening times: *Telephone for details. Normally 10-6.*
Nearest Station: *Pembroke.*
Personnel: Arthur Giardelli. Bim Giardelli.
Paintings and watercolours of Pembrokeshire and other places by Bim and Arthur Giardelli - France, Italy and Far East. Fabric pictures and relief sculptures exhibited in Wales, London and abroad, including the National Museum of Wales and the Tate Gallery.
Services and Facilities:
Commissioning Service. Parking.
Work Stocked and Sold:
Dr. Pa. Sc.
Price range: £100 - £4,000.
For artists see *Commercial Gallery Artists.*

ST. DAVID'S

Albion Gallery
41 Nun Street, St. David's, SA62 6NU.
Tel: *01437-720120.*

The Gallery
Peters Lane, St. David's, SQ62 6NT.
Tel: *01437-720570.*

John Roberts Gallery
Ti Meini 16 Cross Street, St. David's, SA62 6SE.
Tel: *01437-720220.*

Saint Davids Studio Gallery C
28A High Street, St. David's, SA62 6SD.
Tel: *01437-720648, 721920.*
Opening times: *Mid Feb to early Jan 11-5 every day or by appointment.*
Nearest Station: *Haverfordwest or Fishguard.*
Personnel: *Joint Managers:* Nicola Iles, Sarah Young.

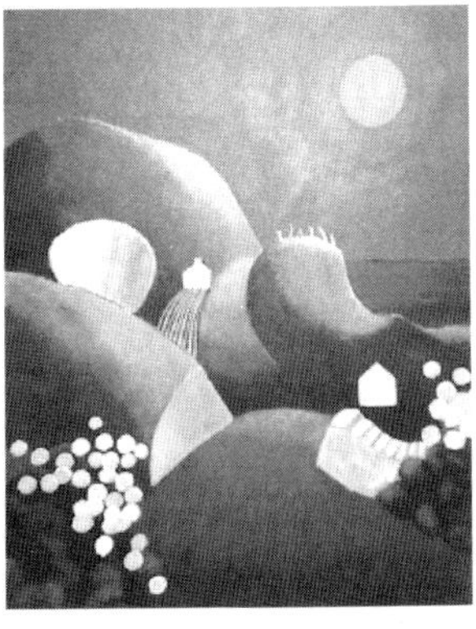

The gallery houses permanent exhibitions of original paintings by Stan Rosenthal, Nicola Iles, Sarah Young and Judith Rosenthal. It also shows the complete range of Stan Rosenthal's limited editions. Other artists' work is shown from time to time when space is available.
Services and Facilities:
Craftshop. Gallery space for hire.
Work Stocked and Sold:
Cer. Cra. Dr. Fur. Pa. Pr. Sc.
Price range: £50 - £2,500.
For artists see *Commercial Gallery Artists.*

TENBY

The Harbour Gallery and Etching Studio
1 St Julian Street, Tenby, SA70 7AY.
Tel: *01834-842370.*

Tenby Museum & Art Gallery
Castle Hill, Tenby, SA70 7BP.
Tel: *01834-842809.*
Fax: *01834-842809.*
Email *tenbymuseum@hotmail.com*
Ws *http://www.atlas-links.com*
Opening times: *Easter-end October, daily 10-5. Nov-Easter Mon-Fri 10-5.*
Nearest Station: *Tenby.*
Personnel: *Honorary Curator.* Jon Beynon.
An independent, community museum since 1878, it is situated within the castle walls in a magnificent setting, overlooking Carmarthen Bay. The art gallery houses a permanent collection of works by local artists, Augustus John, Gwen John and Nina Hamnett, and paintings of the Tenby area by leading artists since the 18th century. The recently opened New Art Gallery will display a variety of temporary exhibitions. The Local History Gallery is currently exhibiting a history of Photography in the area of South Pembrokeshire. The museum has an outstanding display of geology, archaeology, natural history and maritime history of Pembrokeshire.
Services and Facilities:
Friends/Society. Museum Shop.

UPPER SOLVA

Stan Rosenthal
Woodlands, 10 Chapel Lane, Upper Solva, SA62 6TH.
Tel: *01437-721920 or c/o 01437-720648.*
Email *stan@stanrosenthal.com*
Ws *http://www.stanrosenthal.com*
Opening times: *By appointment only.*
Nearest Station: *Haverfordwest or Fishguard.*
Personnel: *Artist:* Stan Rosenthal.
Stan Rosenthal no longer paints at the Saint Davids Studio Gallery full-time, but a full selection of his limited editions and some of his originals are still shown there. The artist now works at various sites around Wales as occasion demands, developing new images. Some of these are commissioned for posters etc., and others for production as limited editions as well as for sale as originals. He now undertakes some commission work for private collectors and corporate clients. A catalogue is available free of charge (limited editions only).
Services and Facilities:
Art Consultancy. Art for Offices. Friends/Society. Lectures.
Work Stocked and Sold: Pa. Pr.
Price range: £50 - £3,500.
For artists see *Commercial Gallery Artists.*

Powys

BRECON

The Beacons Pottery and Gallery
The Old School House, Defynnog, Brecon, LD3 8SU.
Tel: *01874-638919, Home 015504619.*

Sable and Hogg Galleries C
15 Lion Street, Brecon, LD3 7HY.
Tel: *01874-625901.*
Opening times: *Mon-Sat 10-5. Closed Wed.*
Nearest Station: *Abergavenny (20 mins away).*
Personnel: Michael Egbers.
Sales of original paintings, limited edition prints, etchings, photographs, cards. Bespoke picture framing, restoration, cleaning. Photographic work, events - social - industrial - commercial. Computer reconstruction of old photographs, copy work. Disabled access ground floor only.
Services and Facilities:
Craftshop. Framing. Gallery space for hire. Restoration. Shop. Valuation.
Work Stocked and Sold:
Cra. Pa. Ph. Pr. Wd.
Price range: £20 - £5,000.
For artists see *Commercial Gallery Artists.*

Watton Studio
37 The Watton, Brecon, LD3 7EG.
Tel: *01874-611232.*

HAY-ON-WYE

Hay Prints
9 High Town, Hay-on-Wye, HR3 5AE.
Tel: *01497-820172.*

Kilvert Gallery C
Ashbrook House, Clyro, Hay-on-Wye, HR3 5RZ.
Tel: *01497-820831.* **Fax:** *01497-820831.*

LLANDRINDOD WELLS

Porticus C
1 Middleton Street, Llandrindod Wells, LD1 5ET.
Tel: *01597-823989.*

MACHYNLLETH

The Museum Of Modern Art, Wales PS
Heol Penrallt, Machynlleth, SY20 8AJ.
Tel: *01654-703355.* **Fax:** *01654-702160.*

Opening times: *Mon Sat- 10-4. Admission free.*
Nearest Station: *Machynlleth.*
Personnel: *Chairman:* Ruth Lambert .
The Museum Of Modern Art, Wales, forms part of a cultural centre which has grown around a former chapel, The Tabernacle, in the mid-Wales market town of Machynlleth. It has a permanent collection of 20th century British Art including works by Augustus John, Peter Prendergast

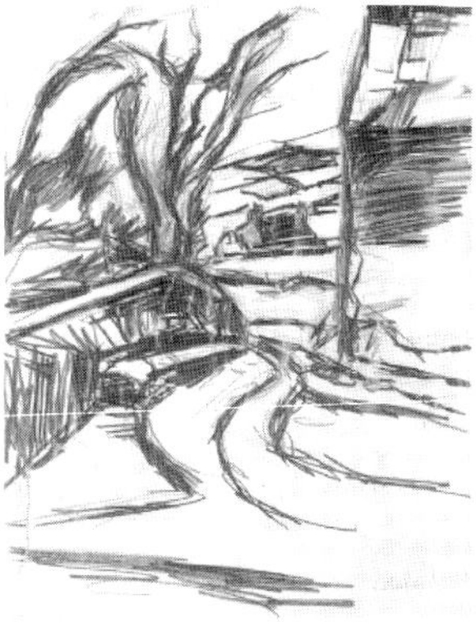

and Shani Rhys James. A special room is devoted to The Brotherhood of Ruralists. Showcase Wales is a semi-permanent exhibition featuring Wales' top artists. MOMA, Wales is particularly vibrant in August when the Tabernacle Art Competition is held in conjunction with The Machynlleth Festival. Admission Free.
Services and Facilities:
Bar. Disabled Access. Friends/Society. Gallery space for hire. Parking.
Work Stocked and Sold:
Dr. Pa. Ph. Pr. Sc.
Price range: £100 - £15,000.
For artists see *Commercial Gallery Artists.*

MONTGOMERY

Country Works Gallery *C*
Broad Street,
Montgomery, SY15 6PH.
Tel: *01686-668866.*

NEWTOWN

Oriel 31, Davies Memorial Gallery *P*
The Park, Newtown, SY16 2NZ.
Tel: *01686-625041.*
Fax: *01686-623633.*

PRESTEIGNE

The Eagle Gallery
Broad Street, New Radnor,
Presteigne, LD8 2SN.
Tel: *01544-260402.*

TALGARTH

Talgarth Library
New Street, Talgarth, LD3 0BP.
Tel: *01874-711665.*

WELSHPOOL

Welshpool Library
Brook Street, Welshpool, SY21 7PH.
Tel: *01938-553001.*

Rhondda Cynon Taf

ABERDARE

Dare Valley Country Park *PS*
Visitor Centre, Aberdare, CF44 7RG.
Tel: *01685-874672.* **Fax:** *01685-882919.*

PONTYPRIDD

Oriel y Bont
University of Glamorgan, Pontypridd, CF37 1DL.
Tel: *01443-480480 ext 2568.*
Email *asalisbu@glam.ac.uk*
Opening times: *Term time only Mon-Fri 9-5.*
Nearest Station: *Treforest.*
Personnel: *Exhibition Organiser:* Alan Salisbury (School of Humanities & Social Science).
Gallery in foyer of large building at front of the university campus. Space is roughly octagonal in shape with hanging surfaces 28' in length and 8' in height. Walls provide additional space of approx 20' x 8' also display cases. Sales not a priority. Intention is to provide arena for contemporary visual arts that will inform and extend students' visual and cultural awareness, acting as 'shop window' for institution establishing links with local community. Exhibitors usually give lectures/run workshops relating to exhibition.
Services and Facilities:
Lectures.
Work Stocked and Sold:
Cer. Dr. Pa. Ph. Pr.
Price range: £250 - £5,000.

Swansea

SWANSEA

Attic Gallery *C*
14 Cambrian Place Swansea SA1 1PQ.
Tel: *01792-653387.*
Email *roe@atticgallery.co.uk*
Ws *http://www.atticgallery.co.uk*
Opening times: *Tues-Fri 9.30-5.30, Sat 10-4.30.*
Personnel: *Directors:* Alexandra Roe, David Roe.
The gallery was established in 1962 to provide a much needed venue for contemporary artists to exhibit their work in Wales. The gallery currently shows the work of over 50 artists including a number of talented printmakers. There is an active and continuing programme of single/two artist and group exhibitions. In 1998 the gallery moved to the city's old maritime quarter and is located near the Dylan Thomas Centre. Public car park directly opposite gallery.
Services and Facilities:
Art Consultancy. Framing.
Work Stocked and Sold:
Cra. Pa. Pr. Sc.
Price range: £50 - £3,000.

Oriel Ceri Richards Gallery *PS*
Taliesin Arts Centre, University of Wales Swansea, Singleton Park, Swansea SA2 8PZ.
Tel: *01792-295526.* **Fax:** *01792-295899.*
Email *taliesin@swan.ac.uk*
Ws *http://www.whatsonwales.com*
Opening times: *Mon 11-5, Tue 11-6, Sat 12-6.*
Personnel: *Marketing Officer:* Evaline Heinzl.

Taliesin

Oriel Ceri Richards Gallery hosts approximately 10 exhibitions each year. Of these, there are three mixed shows, exhibiting a range of work from local artists and crafts people. In addition to the mixed shows, the gallery stocks an excellent range of artists and designer cards, as well as jewellery, prints, drawings, paintings, ceramics and other craft items.
Services and Facilities:
Art Consultancy. Bar. Bookshop. Café. Disabled Access. Framing. Friends/Society. Museum Shop. Parking. Shop.
Work Stocked and Sold:
Cer. Cra. Dr. Jew. Pa. Pr.

Wrexham

WREXHAM

Wrexham Arts Centre *PS*
Rhosddu Road, Wrexham LL1 1AU.
Tel: *01978-292093.*
Fax: *01978-292611.*
Email *gallery@wrexhamlib.u-net.com*
Opening times: *Mon-Fri 9.30-6.45, Sat 9.30-5, Sun closed.*
Nearest Station: *Wrexham.*
Personnel: *Visual Arts Officer:* Stephen West. *Cultural & Heritage Officer:* Hazel Hawarden. *Education Officer:* Dawn Parry. *Gallery Assistant:* Donn Critchley. *Exhibitions Assistant:* Sharon Reed.
Gallery opened 1973 to show contemporary art from Wales, Britain and International. 109 sq. metre main gallery. Foyer craft cases showing contemporary crafts for sale. Gallery 2 shows mainly local artists and groups. Exhibitions for 99/2000 include The Wales Biennale and a new installation by North Wales artist Tim Pugh entitled 'Coal'.
Services and Facilities:
Café. Craftshop. Disabled Access. Lectures. Parking. Workshop Facilities.
Work Stocked and Sold:
Ph.

IRISH GALLERIES

Town/County index. Main listings.

Where this information has been provided, galleries are designated 'C' for commercial, 'P' for public gallery or museum or 'PS' for a public gallery or museum holding selling shows.

TOWN COUNTY INDEX

A/B

C/D

E/F/G

H/I/J

K/L/M

N/O/P

Q/R/S

T/U/V/W

Antrim

BELFAST

The Bell Gallery
13 Adelaide Park, Malone Road, Belfast, BT9 6FX.
Tel: *01232-662998.* **Fax:** *01232-381524.*

Catalyst Arts
5 Exchange Place, Belfast, BT1 2NA.
Tel: *01232-313303.*

Cavehill Gallery
18 Old Cavehill Road, Belfast, BT15 5GT.
Tel: *01232-776784.*

Cresent Arts Centre
2-4 University Road, Belfast, BT7 1NT.
Tel: *01232-242338.*

The Fenderesky Gallery at Queen's
5-6 Upper Crescent, Belfast, BT7 1NT.
Tel: *01232-235245.*

The Gallery
56-60 Dublin Road, Belfast, BT2 7HP.
Tel: *01232-321402.*

John Magee Ltd
455-457 Ormeau Road, Belfast, BT7 3GQ.
Tel: *01232-693830.* **Fax:** *01232-491009.*

Old Museum arts centre *PS*
7 College Square North, Belfast, BT1 6AR.
Tel: *01232-235053.*
Fax: *01232-322912.*
Opening times: *Mon-Sat 10-6 during exhibitions.*
Personnel: *Director:* Anne McReynolds.
Services and Facilities:
Café. Workshop Facilities.
Work Stocked and Sold:
Ph. Pr.

One Oxford Street
1 Oxford Street, Belfast, BT1 3LA.
Tel: *01232-310400.* **Fax:** *01232-310444.*

Ormeau Baths Gallery
18 A Ormeau Avenue, Belfast, BT2 8HS.
Tel: *01232-321402.* **Fax:** *01232-312232.*

Ulster Museum *PS*
Botanic Gardens, Belfast, BT9 5AB.
Tel: *01232-381251 / 383000.* **Fax:** *01232-665510 / 383003 / 383103.*
Opening times: *Mon-Fri 10-5, Sat 1-5, Sun 2-5.*
Nearest Station: *Botanic.*
Personnel: *Head of Fine and Applied Art:* S.B. Kennedy. *Exhibition Organiser:* Anne Stewart.
The Ulster Museum, an interdisciplinary institution whose origins go back to the Belfast Natural History Society Museum of 1831, contains a wide variety of fine and applied art of various periods and schools. Included in the fine art holdings are works by Thomas Gainsborough, Sir Joshua Reynolds and J.M.W. Turner and by modern masters such as Francis Bacon, Henry Moore and Stanley Spencer. Irish art from the seventeenth century to the present day is also well represented, as is modern European and American painting and sculpture. Highlights of the applied art collection include The Kildare Silver-Gilt Toilet Set and the Bute Glass Bowl and Stand, both highly important eighteenth century Irish pieces and a pair of rare Matisse wall hangings, produced in 1947.
Services and Facilities:
Bookshop. Café. Disabled Access. Friends/Society. Guided Tours. Lectures. Museum Shop. Restaurant.

LISBURN

Harmony Hills Arts Centre
Clonmore House, 54 Harmony Hill, Lisburn, BT27 4ES.
Tel: *01232-678219.*

Seymour Galleries
20 Seymour Street, Lisburn,
Tel: *01232-662685.* **Fax:** *01232-662685.*

PORTRUSH

Portrush Gallery
93-95 Main Street, Portrush, BT56 8DA.
Tel: *01265-823739.*

RANDALSTOWN

Clotworthy Arts Centre
Antrim Castle Gardens, Randalstown, BT41 4LH.
Tel: *01849-428000.* **Fax:** *01849-460360.*

Armagh

ARMAGH

Adam Gallery
28 Linenhall Street, Armagh,
Tel: *01861-526908/523654.*

Armagh County Museum *P*
The Mall East, Armagh, BT61 9BE.
Tel: *01861-523070.* **Fax:** *01861-522361.*

Hayloft Gallery *P*
Palace Stables Heritage Centre, The Palace Demesne, Armagh, BT60 4EL.
Tel: *01861-529629.* **Fax:** *01861-529630.*

CRAIGAVON

The Peacock Gallery
Pinebank House Arts Centre, Tullygally Road, Craigavon, BT65 5BY.
Tel: *01762-341618.* **Fax:** *01762-342402.*

PORTADOWN

Roy Edwards Fine Arts Ltd`
Mahon Road, Portadown, BT62 3EH.
Tel: *01762-339116.*
Fax: *01762-350179.*

Carlow

CARLOW

Pembroke Studio Gallery
1 Pembroke, Carlow,
Tel: *00353-1-503 41562.*
Fax: *00353-1-503 41562.*

Cavan

CAVAN

Cavan County Arts Service
Cavan County Library, 17 Farnham Street, Cavan,
Tel: *00353-1-493 1799.*
Fax: *00353-1-496 1565/31384.*

Clare

BALLYVAUGHAN

Dallán Gallery
Ballyvaughan,
Tel: *00353-1-657 7156.*

ENNIS

De Valera Library
Harmony Row, Ennis,
Tel: *00353-1-652 1616.*
Fax: *00353-1-652 8233.*

ENNISTYMON

Ennistymon Branch Library
The Square, Ennistymon,
Tel: *00353-1-657 1245.*

KILSHANNY

The Atlantis Gallery
Caherkinalla, Kilshanny,
Tel: *00353-1-657 4270.*

SHANNON

Seán Lemass Library
Town Centre, Shannon,
Tel: *00353-1-613 64266.*

Cork

CORK

Blackcombe Art Gallery
44a MacCurtain Street, Cork,
Tel: *00353-1-215 00040.*
Fax: *00353-1-215 00040*

Cork Arts Society Lavitt's Gallery
16 Lavitt's Quay, Cork,
Tel: *00353-1-212 77749.*
Fax: *00353-1-212 77749.*

Cork Public Museum *P*
Fitzgerald Park, Mardyke, Cork,
Tel: *00353-21 270679.*
Fax: *00353-21 270931.*

Crawford Municipal Art Gallery *P*
Emmet Place, Cork,
Tel: *00353-21-273 377.*
Fax: *00353-21-275 680.*
Email *crawford@eirenet.net*
Ws *http://www.synergy.ie/crawford*
Opening times: *Mon-Fri 10-5, Sat 10-4.30.*
Personnel: *Curator:* Peter Murray. *Exhibitions Officer:* Nuala Fenton.
Located in the heart of the city, the Crawford Municipal Art Gallery is one of Cork's most important public buildings. Amongst the important Irish artists in the collection are James Barry, Nathaniel Grogan, Walter Osborne, Paul Henry, Jack B. Yeats, Harry Clarke and Sean Keating. The collection includes a considerable number of works by contemporary Irish artists, such as Tony O'Malley, Louis le Brocquy, Barrie Cooke and Robert Ballagh. Many of the contemporary artists working in Cork are also represented, including Vivienne Roche, Maud Cotter and James Scanlon. The Crawford Gallery runs a continuing programme of temporary exhibitions, both of Irish and international art.
Services and Facilities:
Bookshop. Café. Disabled Access. Friends/Society. Guided Tours. Restaurant.

Triskel Arts Centre
Tobin Street, off South Main Street, Cork,
Tel: *00353-1-212 72022/272023.*
Fax: *00353-1-212 75945.*

MACROOM

Vangard Gallery
New Street, Macroom,
Tel: *00353-1-264 1198.*

WEST CORK

O'Kane's Green Gallery
Glengarriff Road, Bantry, West Cork,
Tel: *00353-1-275 0003.*

West Cork Arts Centre
Skibbereen, West Cork,
Tel: *00353-1-282 2090.*

Derry

COLERAINE

Riverside Gallery
Riverside Theatre, Coleraine, BT52 1SA.
Tel: *01265-324449.* **Fax:** *01265-324924.*

Town House Gallery
45 Milburn Road, Coleraine, BT52 1QT.
Tel: *01265-44869.*

DERRY

Context Gallery
The Playhouse, 5-7 Artillery Street, Derry,
Tel: *01504-264481.* **Fax:** *01504-261884.*

Gordon Galleries
7 London Street, Derry, BT48 6RQ.
Tel: *01504-374044.* **Fax:** *01504-374044.*

Orchard Gallery
Orchard Street, Derry, BT48 6EG.
Tel: *01504-269675.* **Fax:** *01504-267273.*

PORTSTEWART

Flowerfield Arts Centre
185 Coleraine Road, Portstewart, BT55 7HV.
Tel: *01265-833959.*

Donegal

GLEANN CHOLM CILLE

Foras Cultúir Uladh - Ulster Cultural Institute
Gleann Cholm Cille,
Tel: *00353-1-733 0248 (Apr-Sept).*

LETTERKENNY

Donegal County Museum *P*
High Road, Letterkenny,
Tel: *00353-1-742 4613.*

Glebe House and Gallery
Church Hill, Letterkenny,
Tel: *00353-1-743 7071.*
Fax: *00353-1-743 7072.*

Port Gallery
86a Upper Main Street, Letterkenny,
Tel: *00353-1-742 5073.*

Down

BANGOR

North Down Visitors and Heritage Centre *PS*
Town Hall, Castle Park Ave,Bangor, BT20 4BT.
Tel: *01247-270371 ext 275.* **Fax:** *01247-271370.*

COMBER

Castle Espie Gallery
78 Ballydrain Road, Comber,
Tel: *01247-872517.*

Salem Gallery
29 Mill Street, Comber,
Tel: *01247-874455.*

DONAGHADEE

The Cleft Art Gallery
3 Market House, New Street, Donaghadee,
Tel: *01247-888502.*

DOWNPATRICK

Down Arts Centre
2-6 Irish Street, Downpatrick, BT30 6BN.
Tel: *01396-615283.* **Fax:** *01369-616621.*

HILLSBOROUGH

Shambles Art Gallery
Dromore Road/Park Lane, Hillsborough,
Tel: *01232-667528.*
Fax: *01232-681469.*

HOLYWOOD

Priory Art Gallery
10 Shore Road, Holywood, BT18 9HX.
Tel: *01232-428173/424570.*

NEWCASTLE

Grant Fine Art C
87c Bryansford Road, Newcastle,
Tel: *013967-22349.*
Fax: *013967-22349.*

Newcastle Art Gallery
18-22 Main Street, Newcastle,
Tel: *013967-23555.*

NEWTOWNARDS

Ards Arts Centre
Townhall, Conway Square, Newtownards, BT23 4DD.
Tel: *01247-810803.* **Fax:** *01247-823131.*

Dublin

DALKEY

The James Gallery
7 Railway Road, Dalkey,
Tel: *00353-1-285 8703.*

DUBLIN

The Architecture Centre
The Royal Institute of the Architects of Ireland, 8 Merrion Square, Dublin 2,
Tel: *00353-1-676 1703.*
Fax: *00353-1-661 0948.*

Cambridge Fine Arts Ltd
Gainboro House, 24 Suffolk Street, Dublin 2,
Tel: *00353-1-677 4652.*

Crafts Council Gallery
Powerscourt Town House, South William Street, Dublin 2,
Tel: *00353-1-679 7368.*
Fax: *00353-1-679 9197.*

Davis Gallery C
11 Capel Street, Dublin 1,
Tel: *00353-1-872 6969.*
Fax: *00353-1-872 5580.*
Opening times: *Mon-Fri 10-5, Sat 11-5.*
Personnel: *Owner:* Gerald Davis.

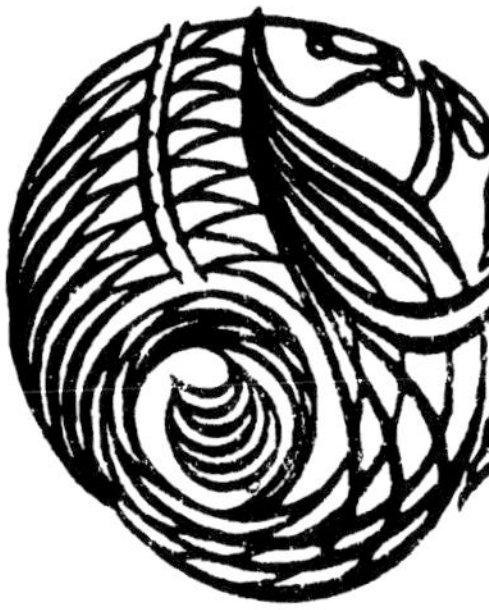

Dublin's longest running commercial gallery of Modern Art. Specialising in original works in all media by artists living in Ireland. Gallery also available for rent.
Services and Facilities:
Art Consultancy. Art for Offices. Gallery space for hire.
Work Stocked and Sold:
Cra. Pa. Sc.
Price range: £50 - £3,000.
For artists see *Commercial Gallery Artists.*

Designyard
12 East Essex Street, Dublin 2,
Tel: *00353-1-677 8453/677 8467.*
Fax: *00353-1-677 8482.*

Douglas Hyde Gallery
Trinity College, Nassau Street, Dublin 2.
Tel: *00353-1-702 1116.*
Fax: *00353-1-677 2694 (attn: DHG).*

The Gallery of Photography
Meeting House Square, Temple Bar, Dublin 2,
Tel: *00353-1-671 4654.*
Fax: *00353-1-671 4654.*

Gorry Gallery
20 Molesworth Street, Dublin 2,
Tel: *00353-1-679 5319.*
Fax: *00353-1-679 5319.*

Graphic Studio Dublin Gallery C
Through the Arch, Off Cope Street, Temple Bar, Dublin 2,
Tel: *00353-1-679 8021.*
Fax: *00353-1-679 4575.*
Opening times: *Mon-Fri 10.30-6, Sat 11-5.*
Personnel: *Administrator:* Karen O'Connor.
Graphic Studio Gallery is the oldest gallery in Dublin dealing exclusively in contemporary original prints: etchings, lithographs, monoprints, screen, relief and carborundum prints by prominent and emerging Irish artists. The gallery is part of Graphic Studio Dublin Workshop, a print studio established in 1962, to provide printmaking facilities for artists. A wide choice of work is available ranging from the work of well known artists to that of recent college graduates, representing work by over one hundred Irish artists. All prints are handmade in limited editions and are numbered and signed by the artist.
Services and Facilities:
Framing. Gallery space for hire.
Work Stocked and Sold:
Pr.
Price range: £40 - £1,500.
For artists see *Commercial Gallery Artists.*

Green on Red Gallery
26-28 Lombard Street East, Dublin 2,
Tel: *00353-1-661 3881.*
Fax: *00353-1-661 3881.*
Opening times: *Mon-Fri 11-6, Sat 11-3.*
Personnel: *Director:* Jerome O Drisceoil. *Administrator:* Alison Scott.
Services and Facilities:
Gallery space for hire.
Work Stocked and Sold:
Pa. Ph. Pr. Sc.

Guinness Gallery
Foxrock Village, Dublin 18,
Tel: *00353-1-289 7955.*

Guinness Hop Store
Crane Street, (off Thomas Street), Dublin 8,
Tel: *00353-1-453 6700.*
Fax: *00353-1-453 3631.*

Hallward Gallery
64 Merrion Square, Dublin 2,
Tel: *00353-1-662 1482.*

Hugh Lane Municipal Gallery of Modern Art
Charlemont House, Parnell Square North, Dublin 1.
Tel: *00353-1-874 1903.*
Fax: *00353-1-872 2182.*
Email *hughlane@iol.ie*
Opening times: *Tues-Thurs 9.30-6, Fri-Sat 9.30-5, Sun 11-5.*
Nearest Station: *Connolly.*
Personnel: *Director:* Barbara Dawson.
The gallery contains the second largest collection of fine art in Ireland, concentrating primarily from the mid 19th century to contemporary art practice. The nucleus of the collection was assembled by the late Sir Hugh Lane whose reputation as a dealer and collector in these islands was legendary. It was he who bought the now famous Renoir's Les Parapluies and Manet's Concert aux Tuileries for a Gallery of Modern Art in Dublin. Also included in the collection are works by Whistler, Sargent, Augustus John, Fantin-Latour, Monet, Degas, Bonnard and Vlaminck. The Gallery devotes a considerable amount of its purchasing fund to the acquisition of contemporary Irish art, as well as international art. Recent acquisitions include Sean Scully, Agnes Martin, Nikki de St. Phalle and the young Scottish landscape artist, Barbara Rae.
Services and Facilities:
Bookshop. Disabled Access. Friends/Society. Guided Tours. Lectures. Restaurant.

Irish Museum Of Modern Art
Royal Hospital, Military Road, Kilmainham, Dublin 8.
Tel: *00353-1-612 9900.*
Fax: *00353-1-612 9999.*
Email *info@modernart.ie*
Opening times: *Tue-Sat 10-5.30, Sun and bank hols 12-5.30.*
Personnel: *Director:* Declan McGonagle. *Senior Curator: Exhibitions:* Brenda McParland. *Senior Curator: Collection :* Catherine Marshall. *Senior Curator: Education & Community:* Helen O'Donoghue.
The Museum presents a wide cross-section of Irish and international art of the 20th century, from its own collection and through temporary exhibitions. There is also a busy Community and Education Programme and an Artists Work Programme, based in the studio and workshop blocks at the Museum. Talks, seminars, music and other events also form part of the Museum's work. The Museum is housed in the Royal Hospital Kilmainham, a large elegant 17th century building said to be the finest of its period in Ireland. Gardens/Grounds. Heritage Video.
Services and Facilities:
Bookshop. Café. Disabled Access. Friends/Society. Guided Tours. Lectures. Parking. Workshop Facilities.

Kerlin Gallery C
Anne's Lane, South Anne Street, Dublin 2,
Tel: *00353-1-670 9093.*
Fax: *00353-1-670 9096.*
Email *gallery@kerlin.ie*
Ws *www.kerlin.ie*
Opening times: *Mon-Fri 10-5.45, Sat 11-4.30.*
Personnel: *Directors:* John Kennedy, David Fitzgerald.
Work Stocked and Sold:
Pa. Ph. Pr. Sc.
For artists see *Commercial Gallery Artists.*

Milmo-Penny Fine Art Ltd C
55 Ailesbury Road, Ballsbridge, Dublin 4,
Tel: *00353-1-269 3486.*
Fax: *00353-1-283 0414.*

National Gallery of Ireland P
Merrion Square West, Dublin 2.
Tel: *00353-1-661 5133.*
Fax: *00353-1-661 5372.*

New Apollo Gallery C
18 Duke Street, Dublin 2,
Tel: *00353-1-671 2609.*
Fax: *00353-1-679 7558.*

Oisín Art Gallery
10 Marino Mart, Fairview, Dublin 3,
Tel: *00353-1-833 3456.*
Fax: *00353-1-833 5197.*

Oisín Art Gallery
44 Westland Row, Dublin 2,
Tel: *00353-1-661 1315.*
Fax: *00353-1-661 0464.*

Oriel Gallery
17 Clare Street, Dublin 2,
Tel: *00353-1-676 3410.*

RHA Gallagher Gallery
15 Ely Place, Dublin 2,
Tel: *00353-1-661 2558.*
Fax: *00353-1-661 0762.*

Rubicon Gallery C
1st Floor, 10 St. Stephens Green, Dublin 2,
Tel: *00353-1-670 8055.*
Fax: *00353-1-670 8057.*
Email *rubi@iol.ie*
Opening times: *Mon-Sat 11-5.30.*
Nearest Station: *Grafton St.*
Personnel: *Director:* Josephine Kelliher.

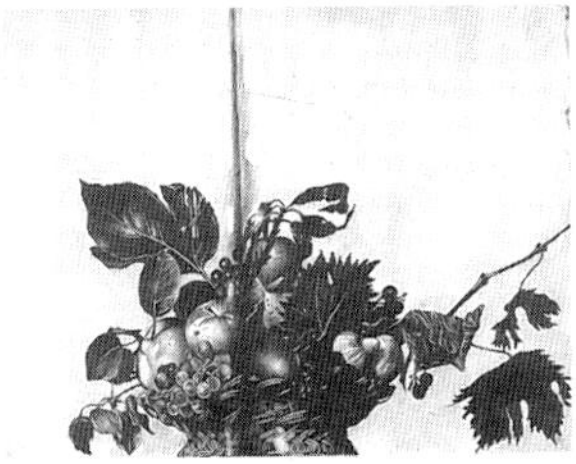

The Rubicon Gallery shows contemporary painting, drawing and sculpture by Irish and International artists and holds work by several International contemporary printmakers. It is a beautifully lit, well proportioned space overlooking St. Stephens Green. It was established in 1990, and schedules 12/14 exhibitions showing the work of a single artist, and also programmes approximately two themed groups shows or curated exhibitions every year. The gallery works closely with the other important Dublin Galleries to promote contemporary Irish Art and also works with Galleries in U.K. & U.S.A. in exchange exhibitions and joint projects.
Services and Facilities:
Art Consultancy. Art for Offices. Commissioning Service. Framing. Gallery space for hire. Valuation.
Work Stocked and Sold:
Dr. Pa. Pr. Sc.
Price range: £400 - £20,000.
For artists see *Commercial Gallery Artists.*

The Solomon Gallery C
Powerscourt Town House, South William Street, Dublin 2.
Tel: *00353-1-679 4237.*
Fax: *00353-1-671 5262.*
Email *solomon@indigo.ie*
Ws *http://indigo.ie/~solomon*
Opening times: *Mon-Sat 10-5.30.*
Personnel: *Owner:* Suzanne MacDougald. *Director:* Tara Murphy.
The Solomon Gallery was established in 1980 and is situated in the original drawing-room of an 18th Century Georgian townhouse formerly owned by Lord Powerscourt. Now considered one of Ireland's leading contemporary art galleries, the Solomon has built its reputation on representing Irish and international painters and sculptors working primarily in a figurative style. The Solomon Gallery also deals in fine Irish period paintings and sculpture. Exhibitions are mounted every three to four weeks. Artists include: Martin Mooney, Rowan Gillespie, Brian Ballard, Hector McDonnell, John Lessore, Sarah Spackman, Elizabeth Cope, Francis Tansey, Peter Collis RHA and Patrick O'Reilly. Export facilities available.
Services and Facilities:
Art Consultancy. Art for Offices. Commissioning Service. Valuation.
Work Stocked and Sold:
Dr. Gla. Pa. Sc.
Price range: £40 - £10,000.
For artists see *Commercial Gallery Artists.*

Taylor Galleries
34 Kildare Street, Dublin 2,
Tel: *00353-1-676 6055.*
Fax: *00353-1-676 8305.*

Temple Bar Gallery & Studios PS
5-9 Temple Bar, Dublin 2,
Tel: *00353-1-671 0073.*
Fax: *00353-1-677 7527.*
Email *tbgs@indigo.ie*
Ws *http://www.paddynet.ie/tbgs*
Opening times: *Sat 11-6, Sun 2-6.*
Personnel: *Director:* Norah Norton. *Administrator:* Vaari Claffey.
Temple Bar Gallery and Studios is located in the centre of Dublin's cultural quarter. The building contains a gallery, an atrium exhibition space on three floors and 30 artists studios. The work selected and exhibited is by emerging and established contemporary artists. Artists curated shows are regularly facilitated. Ancillary programming supports artist led initiatives inside and outside the TBGS&S space and provides a forum for artists and curators through debates and discussions on contemporary arts issues. Three studios are reserved for artists working on specific short-term projects and International residencies. Studio members are open to International studio exchanges.
Services and Facilities:
Art Consultancy. Art for Offices. Commissioning Service. Disabled Access. Friends/Society. Guided Tours. Lectures.
Work Stocked and Sold:
Dr. Pa. Ph. Sc.
Price range: £10 - £10,000.

Wyvern Gallery
2 Temple Lane, Temple Bar, Dublin 2,
Tel: *00353-1-679 9589.*

HOWTH

Howth Harbour Gallery
6 Abbey Street, Howth,
Tel: *00353-1-839 3366.*

SKERRIES

Village Art Gallery
Thomas Hand Street, Skerries,
Tel: *00353-1-849 2236.*

Galway

CONNEMARA

An Dánlann
Casla, Connemara,
Tel: *00353-1-917 2141.*

GALWAY

Galway Arts Centre
47 Dominick Street, (also 23 Nun's Island, Galway), Galway,
Tel: *00353-1-916 5888.*
Fax: *00353-1-916 8642.*

The Grainstore Gallery
Lower Abbeygate Street, Galway,
Tel: *00353-1-916 6620.*

The Kenny Gallery
High Street, Galway,
Tel: *00353-1-916 1014/61021.*
Fax: *00353-1-916 8544.*

OUGHTERARD

West Shore Gallery
Camp Street, Oughterard,
Tel: *00353-1-918 2562.*

Kerry

KILLARNEY

The Frank Lewis Gallery
6 Bridewell Lane, Killarney,
Tel: *00353-1-643 1108/34843 - after hours 00353-1-643 1734.*
Fax: *00353-1-643 1570.*

The Killarney Art Gallery
52 High Street, Killarney,
Tel: *00353-1-643 4628.*

LISTOWEL

St. John's Art & Heritage Centre *PS*
The Square, Listowel,
Tel: *00353-1-682 2566.*
Fax: *00353-1-682 3485.*
Ws *http://www.iol.ie/kerry-insight/stjohns.html*
Opening times: *Open all year. 9.30-6, 7-11pm (show nights.)*
Nearest Station: *Tralee.*
Personnel: *Manager:* Joe Murphy.
A weekly programme of theatre, music, dance, exhibitions, featuring the best of local, national and international artists. Group rates negotiable. Also Youth Arts Programme.
Services and Facilities:
Café. Disabled Access. Gallery space for hire. Parking. Shop. Workshop Facilities.

TRALEE

Bín Bán Gallery
124 Lower Rock Street, Tralee,
Tel: *00353-1-662 2520.*

Siamsa Tíre Theatre/Arts Centre
Tralee,
Tel: *00353-1-662 3055.*
Fax: *00353-1-662 7276.*

The Wellspring Gallery
16 Denny Street, Tralee,
Tel: *00353-1-662 1218.*
Fax: *00353-1-662 3870.*

Kildare

KILCOCK

Kilcock Art Gallery
School Street, Kilcock,
Tel: *00353-1-628 7619/628 8586/00353-1-885 78283.*

Kilkenny

KILKENNY

Butler Gallery *PS*
The Castle, Kilkenny,
Tel: *00353-1-566 1106.*
Fax: *00353-1-567 0031.*
Email *butlergal@indigo.ie*
Ws *http://www.Butlergallery.com*
Opening times: *Open 10-7 mid-March-Nov; 10-5 Sep-Nov; 10-12.45, 2-5 Nov-mid-March; closed Monday.*
Nearest Station: *Kilkenny.*
Personnel: *Administrator:* Nathalie Weadick.
The Butler Gallery is a non-commercial non-profit making gallery, whose purpose is to promote the arts on a national, international and regional basis. Specifically we aim to show art of the highest possible standard, covering all mediums, with a successful mix of internationally renowned, established and emerging artists. Previous shows include Sol le Witt, Richard Long, Sean Scully and James Turrell. The Butler Gallery also has a impressive collection of art including names such as Leech, Yeats, Lavery, Jellet, Turrell and Cooke.
Services and Facilities:
Bookshop. Café. Friends/Society. Guided Tours. Lectures.

Leitrim

CARRICK-ON-SHANNON

Old Barrel Store Arts Centre
The Quays, Carrick-on-Shannon,
Tel: *00353-1-782 0911 /after hours 00353-1-784 2093.*

Limerick

LIMERICK

Chris Doswell's Gallery
The Basement, 28 Mallow Street, Limerick,
Tel: *00353-1-613 18292.*

Dolmen Gallery
Honan's Quay, Limerick,
Tel: *00353-1-614 17929.*

Limerick City Gallery of Art
Pery Square, Limerick,
Tel: *00353-1-613 10633.*
Fax: *00353-1-614 15266.*

Muse Gallery
75 O'Connell Street, Limerick,
Tel: *00353-1-613 14699.*

University of Limerick - AV Gallery *P*
University of Limerick, Limerick,
Tel: *00353-1-61 202040.*
Fax: *00353-1-61 202938.*

Longford

LONFORD

Carroll Gallery
6 Keon's Terrace, Lonford,
Tel: *00353-1-434 1148.*

Louth

CARLINGFORD

Artistic License
The Old Coach House, Dundalk Street, Carlingford,
Tel: *00353-1-417 3745.*
Fax: *00353-1-427 3745.*

DUNDALK

The Basement Gallery
The Town Hall, Dundalk,
Tel: *00353-1-423 2276.*
Fax: *00353-1-423 6171.*

Mayo

ACHILL ISLAND

Western Light Art Gallery
The Sandybanks, Keel, Achill Island,
Tel: *00353-1-984 3325.* **Fax:** *00353-1-984 3325.*

CLAREMORRIS

Claremorris Gallery
James Street, Claremorris, **Tel:** *00353-1-947 1348.*

Monaghan

MONAGHAN

Market House Gallery
Tourist Office, Market House, Monaghan,
Tel: *00353-1-478 1122.*

Sligo

RIVERSTOWN

Taylor's Art Gallery
Taunagh, Riverstown,
Tel: *00353-1-716 5138.*
Fax: *00353-1-716 5138.*

SLIGO

Sligo Art Gallery
Yeats Memorial Building, Hyde Bridge, Sligo,
Tel: *00353-1-714 5847.*
Fax: *00353-1-716 2301.*

Tipperary

BIRDHILL

The Lucy Erridge Gallery
Birdhill,
Tel: *00353-1-613 79366.*
Fax: *00353-1-613 02459.*

Westmeath

ATHLONE

Dolan Moore Gallery
33 Church Street, Athlone,
Tel: *00353-1-902 78507.*

Wexford

BUNCLODY

The Chantry Gallery
Bunclody,
Tel: *00353-1-547 7482.*

GOREY

Woodland Arts & Crafts Gallery
Tinnock, Gorey,
Tel: *00353-1-402 37474.*

Wicklow

BRAY

Craft Art Gallery
74 Main Street, Bray,
Tel: *00353-1-286 6728.*

The Hangman Gallery
2 Westbourne Terrace, Quinnsborough Road, Bray,
Tel: *00353-1-286 6208.*
Fax: *00353-1-286 6207.*

WICKLOW

Renaissance III Gallery
County Buildings, Wicklow,
Tel: *00353-1-404 67324.*
Fax: *00353-1-404 67792.*

NOTES

PRINTS AND PRINTMAKING

Fine press printers/publishers.
Print publishers/dealers/galleries.
Print workshops.

Fine Press Printers/Publishers

Basement Press
Basement Flat, 29 Burrell Road, Ipswich, IP2 8AH.
Tel: *01473-601596.*

Circle Press C
26 St. Luke's Mews, London W11 1DF.
Tel: *0171-792 9298.*

Delos Press
11 School Road, Moseley, Birmingham B13 9ET.
Tel: *0121-449 1406.*

First Folio Cards
Hollow Cottage, Charingworth, Chipping Campden, GL55 6NY.
Tel: *01386-593477.*

Golden Apple Press
Pebble Court Cottage, Swinbrook, Burford, OX18 4DY.
Tel: *01993-824097.*

Hayloft Press
99 Oakfield Road, Birmingham B29 7HW.
Tel: *0121-472 1768.*

Incline Press
11A Printer Street, Oldham OL1 1PN.
Tel: *0161-627 1966.*

Jones and Palmer Ltd.
95 Carver Street, Birmingham B1 3AR.
Tel: *0121-236 9007; isdn: 0121-200 8380.*
Fax: *0121-236 5513.*
Email *info@jonesandpalmer.co.uk*
Personnel: *Sales:* David Binch.
Printer of post cards, preview cards, exhibition catalogues. Comprehensive size range and unique colour proof service. Mail order. Price list and information pack on request.
Jones and Palmer Ltd. also produce high quality colour print for all the requirements of the art and commercial worlds.

Ken Ferguson
20 Lanercost Park, Cramlington, NE23 6RU.
Tel: *01670-733927.*

Nine Elms Press
21 Gwendolen Avenue, London SW15 6ET.
Tel: *0181-788 4029.*

Old School Press
The Old School, The Green, Hinton Charterhouse, Bath, BA3 6BJ.

Oleander Press
17 Stansgate Avenue, Cambridge, CB2 2QZ.
Tel: *01223-244688.*

Prospect Hill Press
35 Bank Street, Herne Bay, CT6 5AW.

Redlake Press
Brook House, Clun, SY7 8LY.
Tel: *01588-640524.*

Ruth Bader Gilbert
8 Portland Road, Oxford, OX2 7EY.
Tel: *01865-559176.*

Tern Press
Saint Mary's Cottage, Great Hales Street, Market Drayton, TF9 1JN.
Tel: *01630-652153.*

Woodcraft Press
152 Hadlow Road, Tonbridge, TN9 1PB.
Tel: *01732-359206.*

The Yew Tree Press
Park Place, Aldsworth, Cheltenham, GL54 3QZ.
Tel: *01451-844487.*

Publishers/ Dealers/Galleries

Advanced Graphics London C
C103 and B206 Faircharm, 8-12 Creekside, London SE8 3DX.
Tel: *0181-691 1330.* **Fax:** *0181-694 9930.*
Opening times: *Mon-Fri 9.30-6, evenings & weekends by appointment.*
Nearest Underground: *BR: Deptford.*
Personnel: Robert Saich. Louise Peck. Julie Barnetson.

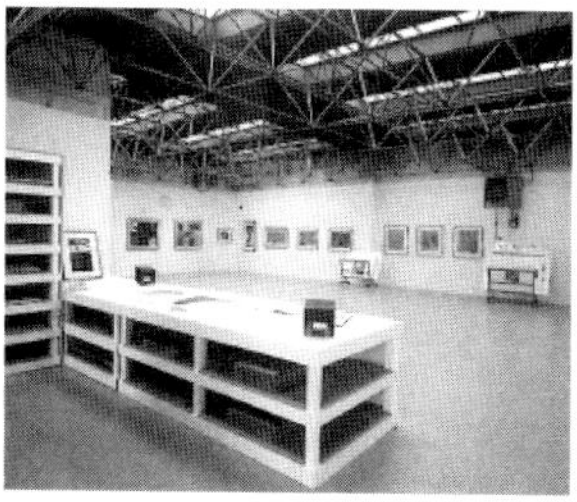

Printers and publishers of limited edition original prints, specialising in silkscreen and woodblock. Own publications include prints made directly with the following artists: Craigie Aitchison, Stephen Bartlett, Basil Beattie, Paul Benjamins, Neil Canning, Anthony Frost, Donald Hamilton Fraser, Tom Hammick, John Hoyland, James Hugonin, Albert Irvin, Trevor Jones, Anita Klein, John McLean, Matthew Radford, Ray Richardson and Kate Whiteford. Printing clients include Alan Cristea Gallery; CCA Galleries; Flowers Graphics and The Obsession of Dance Company.
Services and Facilities:
Art for Offices. Disabled Access. Parking.
Work Stocked and Sold:
Ab. Pr.
Price range: £180 - £1,000.
For artists see *Commercial Gallery Artists.*

Anderson O'Day Graphics C
5 St. Quintin Avenue, London W10 6NX.
Tel: *0181-969 8085.* **Fax:** *0181-960 3641.*
Opening times: *Mon-Fri 9.30-6 by appointment.*
Nearest Underground: *Ladbroke Grove.*
Personnel: Don Anderson.
Major publishers of contemporary limited edition prints since 1971, we produce over 50 new editions each year. We are also dealers and distributors of a wide range of contemporary artists in media including etching, screen-printing, lithography, woodcut etc. Artists include Ackroyd, Daniels, Davey Winter, Delderfield, Irvin, I. Jones, McLean, Neiland, Neville, O'Neill, Rowe, Shave and Wilkinson. Trade catalogue on request.**Pr.**
Price range: £75 - £1,500.
For artists see *Commercial Gallery Artists.*

Art from Scotland C
65 The Shore, Port of Leigh, Edinburgh EH6 6RA.
Tel: *0131-555 5580.* **Fax:** *0131-553 5655.*

The Art Group Ltd C
146 Royal College Street, London NW1 0TA.
Tel: *0171-482 3206.* **Fax:** *0171-284 0435.*

Brandler Galleries C
1 Coptfold Road, Brentwood, CM14 4BM.
Tel: *01277-222269.* **Fax:** *01277-222786.*
Email *art.british@dial.pipex.com*
Ws *http://www.brandler-galleries.com and www.thesaurus.co.uk/brandler*
Opening times: *Tues-Sat 10-5.30.*
Nearest Station: *Brentwood 400 yds, Shenfield 1 mile.*
Personnel: *Director:* John Brandler. Linda Rodrigues.

Brandler Galleries

A friendly gallery just 2 miles from exit 28 on the M25 with free parking. A wide selection of prints and paintings by British old and modern masters. As we purchase virtually all our stock we have to choose the best examples. Without the London overheads our clients know they get a much better deal on the same artists, without having to fight to get into London with all its problems. We are happy to send photographs or E-Mail images before your trip. Clients include banks, insurance companies and collectors all wanting the best art at realistic prices.
Services and Facilities:
Art Consultancy. Art for Offices. Commissioning Service. Framing. Parking. Restoration. Valuation.
Work Stocked and Sold:
Cer. Dr. Pa. Pr. Sc.
Price range: £50 - £65,000.

Cambridge Contemporary Art C
6 Trinity Street, Cambridge, CB2 1SU.
Tel: *01223-324222.* **Fax:** *01223-315606.*
Email *cam.cont.art@dial.pipex.com*
Ws *http://www.artcambridge.co.uk*
Opening times: *Mon-Sat 9-5.30.*
Nearest Station: *Cambridge.*
Personnel: *Director:* Denise Collins. *Gallery Manager:* Rosy Gounaris.
Cambridge Contemporary Art is the largest commercial art gallery in Cambridge with the best selection of hand made limited edition modern and contemporary prints by acknowledged masters, established artists and young talent. The work is highlighted through constantly changing displays and a varied

exhibition programme. Our private and corporate customers benefit from a wide range of services making the gallery the first port of call for any art enquiry.
Artists include: Karolina Larusdottir, Charlotte Cornish, Anita Klein, Donald Hamilton Fraser, Dorothy Stirling, Elisabeth Frink, Ray Richardson, Craigie Aitchison, Henri Matisse, Marc Chagall, Bert Irvin and John Piper.

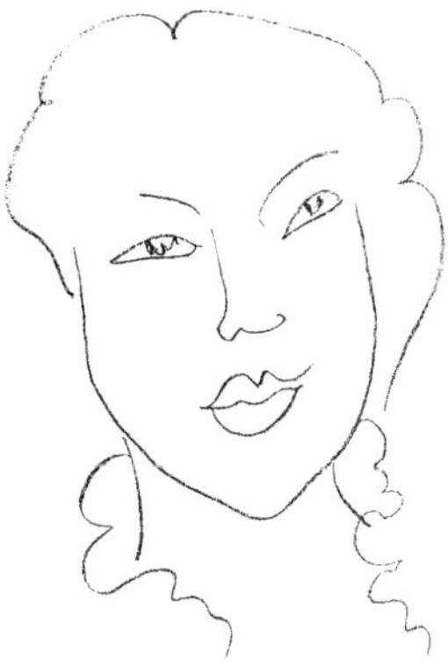

Services and Facilities:
Art Consultancy. Art for Offices. Commissioning Service. Craftshop. Disabled Access. Framing. Friends/Society. Restoration. Shop.
Work Stocked and Sold:
Ab. App. Cer. Cra. Dec. Fur. Gla. Pa. Pr. Sc. Tx. Wd.
Price range: £50 - £5,000.

Connaught Galleries
44 Connaught Street, London W2.
Tel: *0171-723 1660.* **Fax:** *0171-723 1660.*
Opening times: *Mon-Fri 10-6.30, Sat 10-1.*
Nearest Underground: *Paddington, Lancaster Gate, Marble Arch.*
Personnel: *Partner:* Michael Hollamby.
Wood and aluminium framing. Mirrors to order, or from stock. Dry-mounting. Mount cutting. Shrinkwrapping. Easels and artist supplies. Glass supplied or cut. Frame repairs. Picture restoration. A wide range of prints and posters in stock or to order from extensive catalogues. Limited edition fine art prints. Limited edition fine art figurines. Glass and perspex display cases and display domes and bases.
Services and Facilities:
Art for Offices. Framing. Gallery space for hire. Parking. Restoration. Shop. Workshop Facilities.

Curwen Gallery
4 Windmill Street, (off Charlotte Street), London W1P 1HF.
Tel: *0171-636 1459.* **Fax:** *0171-436 3059.*

Editions Alecto C
Head Office: The Court House, Lower Woodford, Salisbury, SP4 6NQ.
Tel: *01722-782544.* **Fax:** *01722-782669.*
Email *Alectouk@aol.com*
Opening times: *By appointment.*
Nearest Station: *Salisbury.*
Personnel: *Director:* Joe Studholme.
London Office: 121/123 Rotherhithe Street, London SE16 4NF. Tel: 0171-237 7117, Fax: 0171-237 1163, Email: Alectouk@aol.com.
Publishing house established 1962 now specialising in historical editions, hand printed and hand coloured, from plates and blocks and in facsimile. New and current publications include: Mark Catesby's "Natural History of Carolina, Florida and the Bahama Islands", in association with the Royal Library, Windsor; Ferdinand Bauer's watercolours of the zoological specimens collected on the first circumnavigation of Australia by Commander Matthew Flinders in HMS Investigator 1801-1803, in association with the British Museum (Natural History); and the Millennium Edition of William the Conqueror's "Domesday Book", in association with the Public Record Office. Stock of contemporary prints include David Hockney, Allen Jones, Tom Phillips, Patrick Procktor, George Segal and Eduardo Paolozzi. New projects usually four per annum, please enquire.
Services and Facilities:
Art Consultancy. Art for Offices. Commissioning Service.
Work Stocked and Sold:
Ab. Pr.
Price range: £50 - £100,000.

Elizabeth Harvey-Lee - Original Prints c.1490 - c.1940. C
1 West Cottages, Middle Aston Road, North Aston, Oxford, OX6 3QB.
Tel: *01869-347164.* **Fax:** *01869-347956.*
Opening times: *By appointment.*
Nearest Station: *Bicester North, Banbury or Oxford (equidistant).*
Personnel: *Proprietor:* Elizabeth Harvey-Lee.

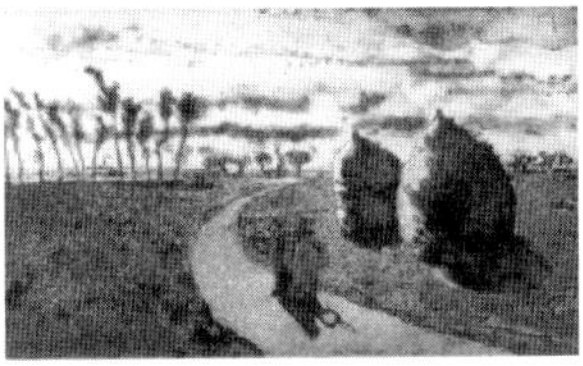

Private printdealer, offering a large range of fine etchings and engravings. Interesting and unusual old masters and 19th & 20th century British & European artists; both major and minor masters of printmaking from five centuries. Two fully illustrated new stock catalogues each year (annual subscription £12 or U.S.$25). Previous reference catalogues still available:- LASTING IMPRESSIONS - A Survey of the Techniques & History of Printmaking c.1490-c.1940, (£15 + pp). MISTRESSES OF THE GRAPHIC ARTS - Famous & Forgotten Women Printmakers c.1550-c.1950, (£13.50 + pp). Regular exhibitor at the London Original Print Fair at the Royal Academy and at the June and November Olympia Fine Art & Antiques Fairs.
Services and Facilities:
Lectures.
Work Stocked and Sold:
Pr.
Price range: £100 - £6,000.
For artists see *Commercial Gallery Artists.*

Graham Clarke C
White Cottage, Green Lane, Boughton Monchelsea, Maidstone, ME17 4LF.
Tel: *01622-743938.* **Fax:** *01622-747229.*
Opening times: *Open by appointment.*
Personnel: Dawn Masters.
Publisher and sole international distributor for Graham Clarke the artist, writer and humorist. His original etchings are produced entirely by hand using traditional processes in strictly limited editions; no photomechanical methods are used in their production. Watercolours, books, greetings cards and hand cut arch-topped mounts for the etchings are also available. Price lists and illustrations of recent images will be sent on request. Studio open by appointment.
Work Stocked and Sold:
Ab. Dr. Pa. Pr.
Price range: £50 - £2,000.

Greenwich Printmakers Association C
1a Greenwich Market, London SE10 9HZ.
Tel: *0181-858 1569.*
Email *longitude0.co.uk/printmakers/*
Ws *http://www.longitude0.co.uk/printmakers/*
Opening times: *Tues-Sun 10.30-5.30.*
Nearest Underground: *Greenwich (British Rail), Island Gardens (Docklands).*
Personnel: *Manager:* John Hurley.

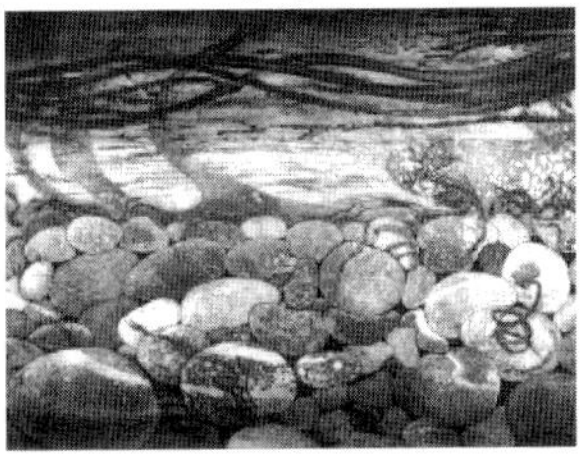

Founded 1979. The Greenwich Printmakers is a co-operative of 45 artists including some of the country's leading printmakers as well as recent graduates. Mixed exhibitions of etchings, lithographs, silk screen, relief prints, watercolours and drawings. Price range £25-£500. Each fortnight one artists work is specially featured in a mini-exhibition. Work not on display is in plan chests for browsing.
Services and Facilities:
Art for Offices. Commissioning Service.
Work Stocked and Sold:
Dr. Pr.
Price range: £30 - £400.
For artists see *Commercial Gallery Artists.*

Gresham Studio
4 Chapel Street, Duxford, CB2 4RY
Tel: *01223-576558.* **Fax:** *01223-576559.*

Hanga Ten C
Hurlingham Studios, Ranelagh Gardens, London SW6 3PA
Tel: *0171-371 9677, Mobile: 0780-115 1981.*
Fax: *0171-371 9677.*

Email *japanart@hangaten.demon.co.uk*
Opening times: *By appointment.*
Nearest Underground: *Putney Bridge.*
Personnel: Hely Norton.

版画店 *Hanga Ten*

Contemporary Japanese Prints

Hanga Ten is a new gallery specialising in modern and contemporary Japanese prints, hand-picked in Japan. Artists represented include many internationally known printmakers such as SHINODA Toko, ENDO Susumu and TAKAHASHI Rikio, but also those at the beginning of their careers. Techniques cover all printing methods: woodblock, silkscreen, lithograph, intaglio and combination processes. Artistic expression is also diverse, ranging from minimalist and abstract compositions to traditional Japanese themes. All the artists have one thing in common: their immense creative talent and the quality of their work, a reflection of their technical excellence and the genius of Japan's papermakers.
Work Stocked and Sold:
Pr.
Price range: £35 - £3,000.

Kensington Church Street Antique Centre C
58-60 Kensington Church Street
London W8 4DB
Tel: *0171-937 0425.* **Fax:** *0181-686 5610.*

Marlborough Graphics C
6 Albemarle Street, London W1X 4BY.
Tel: *0171-629 5161.* **Fax:** *0171-495 0641.*
Ws *http://www.icollector.com*
Opening times: *Mon-Fri 10-5.30, Sat 10-12.30.*
Nearest Underground: *Green Park.*
Personnel: *Director:* David Case. *Assistants:* Nicola Togneri, A. Bankes.

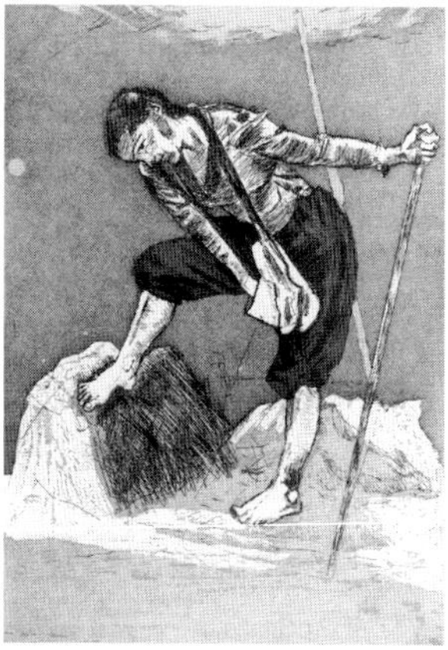

The leading dealers in Freud etchings. Contemporary publications and prints available by the following gallery artists: Arikha, Auerbach, Conroy, Davies, Hambling, Jacklin, Kliff, Kitaj, Le Brun, Oulton, Pasmore, Paul, Piper and Rego. Modern Master prints available by: Bacon, Hepworth, Kokoschka, Matisse, Miro, Moore, Nicholson, Picasso and Sutherland. A portfolio of coloured etchings by Paula Rego will be published in 1999 and we have recent publications by Ken Kiff, Christopher Le Brun and Celia Paul. You will find us at ART99, The Original Print Fair at the R.A. and the Glasgow Art Fair this year.
Services and Facilities:
Art Consultancy. Art for Offices. Framing. Valuation.
Work Stocked and Sold:
Ab. Dr. Ph. Pr.
Price range: £300 - £60,000.

The Medici Society Ltd
7 Grafton Street, London W1X 3LA.
Tel: *0171-629 5675.* **Fax:** *0171-495 2997.*
Opening times: *9-5.*
Nearest Underground: *Green Park.*

THE MEDICI SOCIETY LIMITED · MAGNVS LAVRENT IVS MEDICES

Established in 1908, The Medici Society was founded to publish fine art prints at reasonable prices, a tradition upheld today using the latest methods of production. In addition to work from most periods of Art History, Medici are now publishing contemporary prints from currently exhibiting artists. There is also a large range of Children's prints. A print catalogue and price list are available on request, as are details of other Medici publications. These include: Fine Art greeting cards, stationery, postcards and art and children's books.
Services and Facilities:
Framing. Shop.
Work Stocked and Sold:
Pr.
For artists see *Commercial Gallery Artists.*

Pratt Contemporary Art/Pratt Editions C
The Gallery, Ightham, Sevenoaks, TN15 9HH.
Tel: *01732-882326/884417.*
Fax: *01732-885502.*
Opening times: *Open seven days a week by appointment.*
Nearest Station: *Charing Cross to Sevenoaks or Victoria to Borough Green.*
Personnel: *Directors:* Bernard Pratt, Susan Pratt.
Established in 1976. Printers and publishers of original limited edition prints working directly with artists: screenprints, etchings, drypoints, woodcuts, monotypes, artists' books. Proofing and editioning service. Artists include: Ana Maria Pacheco, Seyed Edalatpour, Julian Grater, Akram Rahmanzadeh, Kristian Krokfors, Mick Rooney RA, Michael Kenny RA, Marcus Rees Roberts, Denise Walker, Leonam Nogueira Fleury, Richard Davies. Also handles and exhibits sculpture, paintings and drawings by artists represented (see Regional Galleries).

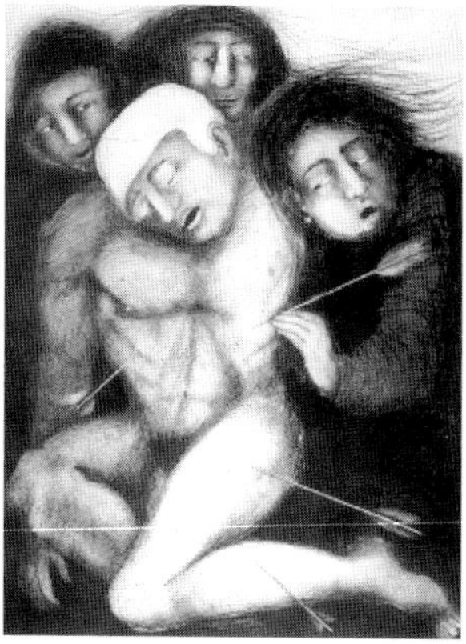

Services and Facilities:
Art Consultancy. Commissioning Service. Framing.
Work Stocked and Sold:
Ab. Dr. Pa. Pr. Sc.
Price range: £50 - £150,000.

St. Barnabas Press
10b Saint Barnabas Road, Cambridge, CB1 2BY.
Tel: *01223-576221.*
Fax: *01223-576204.*

Tina Holley
Cae Dasydd, Llanfrothen, LL48 6SN.
Tel: *01766-890474.*

The Wild Hawthorn Press
Saint Paulinus, Brough Park, Richmond, DL10 7PJ.
Tel: *01748-812127.* **Fax:** *01748-812127.*

Print Workshops

Abacus (Colour Printers) Ltd C
Lowick Green, Lowick, Ulverston, LA12 8DX.
Tel: *01229-885361.* **Fax:** *01229 -885348.*
Opening times: *Mon-Sat 9-5.*
Personnel: *Directors:* John Sutcliffe, Vicki Sutcliffe.
Specialist printers to the art world - nationwide! Mail order postcards, greetings cards, posters, catalogues from your own art work. All work is in house to ensure maximum print quality and accuracy of colour to the original art work. Print members of the Fine Art Trade Guild for 10 years.
Services and Facilities:
Parking.

Active Graphics
Unit 12, Eastmead Trading Estate, Lavant, Chichester, PO18 0DB.
Tel: *01243-787230.* **Fax:** *01243-787258.*

Art House Editions C
25 Bruton Street, London W1X 7AB.
Tel: *0171-491 3337.*

Artichoke Print Workshop C
Unit 51, Shakespeare Business Centre, 245 Coldharbour Lane, London SW9 8RR.
Tel: *0171-924 0600.*

Artizan Editions
Unit 6, Hove Business Centre, Font Hill Road, Hove, BN3 6HA.
Tel: *01273-773959.*

Bath Artist Printmakers C
7 Lower Borough Walls, Bath, BA1 1QS
Tel: *01225-446136.*

Belfast Print Workshop C
185 Stranmillis Road, Belfast, BT9 5EE.
Tel: *01232-687223.* **Fax:** *01232-687223.*
Opening times: *Mon, Wed, Fri 10-5, Tues & Thurs 10-9.*
Personnel: *Manager:* James Allen.
Open access workshop for artists/printmakers offering facilities for etching, screenprinting, stone lithography and relief printing. A darkroom is also available with black-and-white enlarger and process camera.

Bond Art C
P.O. Box 647, London E3 5UB.
Tel: *01225-892009.*

Bookworks C
19 Holywell Row, London EC2A 4JB.
Tel: *0171-247 2536.*

Bristol Printmaker's Workshop C
MacArthur Building, Cross Ferry Road, Bristol BS1.
Tel: *0117-924 9167.*

Coriander C
56 Kings Bridge Crescent, Southall, UB1 2DL.
Tel: *0181-893 6888.*

Curwen Chilford Prints C
Chilford Hall, Linton, Cambridge, CB1 6LE.
Tel: *01223-893544.* **Fax:** *01223-893544.*
Opening times: *Mon-Fri 9-5.30.*
Nearest Station: *Cambridge.*
Personnel: *Directors:* Stanley Jones, Sam Alper, Simon Alper.
Fine art printing studio established in 1958 by the Curwen Press for the production of limited edition artists' prints. Specialists in continuous tone lithography with facilities for direct and offset printing from stone and plate. Silkscreen printer for hand drawn and photographic process work. Technical expertise offered to painters and sculptors in all forms of experimental printmaking. Publishers of limited edition prints. Recent artists who have worked at the studio include: Gillian Ayres, Prunella Clough, Bernard Dunstan, Kitaj, Eduardo Paolozzi, Ken Kiff, Paul Hogarth, Chloe Cheese, John Hoyland, Albert Irvin, Ana Maria Pacheco, Josef Herman, Patrick Heron, Richard Deacon and Jane Corsellis.
Services and Facilities:
Art for Offices. Café. Commissioning Service. Disabled Access. Parking. **Pr. Sc.**
Price range: £65 - £2,000.

Edinburgh Printmakers C
23 Union Street, Edinburgh EH1 3LR.
Tel: *0131-557 2479.* **Fax:** *0131-558 8418.*

Enitharmon Press C
38 St. George Avenue, London N7 0HD.
Tel: *0171-607 7144.*

Four Impressions C
Cherry Tree Cottage, 12 Bassetsbury Lane, High Wycombe, HP11 1QU.
Tel: *01494-443607.*

Glasgow Print Studio Workshop C
22 King Street, Glasgow G1 5QP.
Tel: *0141-552 0704.* **Fax:** *0141-552 2919.*

Half Moon Printmakers C
10 Beckwith Road, London SE24 9LG.
Tel: *0171-733 9166.*

Harwood King Fine Art C
Euro Business Park, New Road, Newhaven, BN9.
Tel: *01273-512554.*

Milton Keynes Printmakers C
South Pavilion, Courtyard Arts Centre, Parklands, Great Linford, MK14 5DZ.
Tel: *01908-583845.*

Northern Print Studios C
42-47 Fish Quay, North Shields, NE30 1JA.
Tel: *0191-259 1996.* **Fax:** *0191-259 1699.*

Oxford Guild of Printmakers C
The Stoke House, Shipton Oliffe, GL54 4JF.
Tel: *01242-820073.*

Oxford Printmakers' Coop C
Christadelphian Hall, Tyndale Road, Oxford, OX4 1JL
Tel: *01865-726472.*

Poole Printmakers C
5 Bowling Green Alley, Poole BH15 1AG.
Tel: *01202-393776.*

Porthmeor Printmakers Workshop
Penwith Galleries, Back Road West, St. Ives, TR18 5BL.
Tel: *01736-61125.*

Sarah James Printmaking C
32 Staple Gardens, Winchester, SO23 8SR.
Tel: *01962-877860.*

The Sheffield Print Workshop C
Heeley Bank Centre, Heeley Bank Road, Sheffield S2 3GL.
Tel: *0114-250 8449.*

St. Barnabas Press
10b Saint Barnabas Road, Cambridge, CB1 2BY.
Tel: *01223-576221.* **Fax:** *01223-576204.*
Opening times: *Mon-Sat 10-10, additional hours for members.*
Nearest Station: *Cambridge.*
Personnel: James Hill.
Editioning and proofing by contract or co-publication, with Open Access facilities and Studio space, founded by James Hill in 1993. One aim of the Press is to give experienced printmakers access to fully equipped areas of Etching, Screenprinting, Relief Printing, Stone-Lithograph and allied photo-reprographic facilities. Also available to those with little or no experience are evening classes, short courses & individual supervised sessions. The Press works with Artists taking an experimental approach to printmaking, mixing the process using Jame's 11 years experience of collaborating in producing High Quality, Original Prints.
Services and Facilities:
Commissioning Service. Framing. Lectures. Parking. Restoration. Shop. Workshop Facilities.

Studio Prints
159 Queen's Crescent, London, NW5 4EA.
Tel: *0171-485 4527.* **Fax:** *0171-485 4527.*
Opening times: *Telephone for appointment.*
Nearest Underground: *Chalk Farm, Kentish Town.*
Personnel: *Partners:* Dorothea Wight, M. Balakjian.
Editioning workshop for intaglio and mezzotint. Technical expertise available on an hourly or daily basis. Artists who have worked at the studio recently include: Frank Auerbach, Stephen Conray, Lucien Freud, Ken Kiff, Celia Paul and Glen Suho.

Zink Editions C
33 Charlotte Road, London EC2A 3PB.
Tel: *0171-739 7207.*

Printmaking Other

The Printmakers Council
Clerkenwell Workshop, 31, Clerkenwell Close, London EC1R 0AT.
Tel: *0171-250 1927.*
Ws
http://www.printmaker.co.uk/pmc/index.html
Opening times: *Wed & Thurs 2-6.*
Nearest Underground: *Farringdon.*
Personnel: *President:* Mr Stanley Jones. *Administrator:* Helen Ward.
The Printmakers Council is a non-profitmaking artist-run group. Their objectives are to promote the use of both traditional and innovative printmaking techniques by:- holding exhibitions of prints, providing information on prints and printmaking to both its membership and the public, encouraging co-operation and exchanges between members, other associations and interested individuals. Exhibitions in major London venues and throughout the UK. Exchange shows recently in Paris, Landau Germany and Fremantle Australia. A slide index of members work is held in the London office for consultation. Membership is open to all printmakers.

THE INTERNET

'Virtual' galleries (work may be viewed on the internet).
Internet Design companies.
Listing of all establishments in this Directory with internet addresses.

Internet Galleries

Art Arena Gallery C

16 Crane Furlong, Highworth, SN6 7JX
Tel: *01793-766818.* **Fax:** *01793-766818.*
Email *katy@artarena.force9.co.uk*
Ws *http://www.artarena.force9.co.uk*
Opening times: *24 hours a day, as it is on the internet.*
Personnel: *Artist & Owner:* Katy Kianush-Wallace.

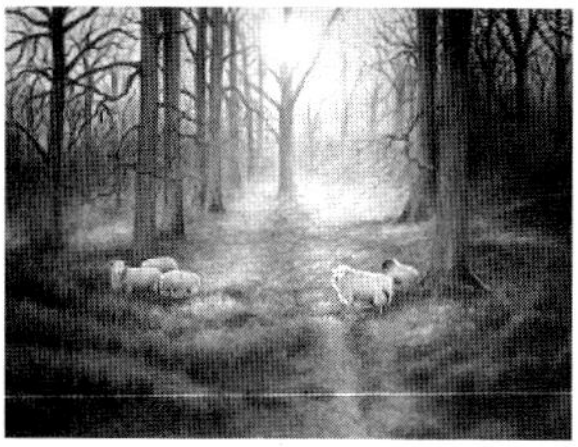

Art Arena is a Virtual Gallery providing a comprehensive and varied collection of original Landscapes, Portraits, Miniatures, and Greeting Card designs by an award winning artist. The artist's varied use of media and painting techniques, and the multiplicity of subjects treated encourage appreciation of of her art on many levels.
Art Arena brings together two of Iran's well known and established literary figures, to give an insight into modern Persian poetry and prose.
In addition to this, it opens a window onto Persian history, art, and culture.
Art Arena is host to the National Acrylic Painters' Association Web Site.
Services and Facilities:
Bookshop. Friends/Society.
Work Stocked and Sold:
Dr. Pa.
Price range: £200 - £3,500.
For artists see *Commercial Gallery Artists.*

Axis

Leeds Metropolitan University, Calverley Street, Leeds LS1 3HE.
Tel: *0113-245 7946.* **Fax:** *0113-245 7950.*
Email *axis@gn.apc.org*
Ws *http://www.lmu.ac.uk/ces/axis*
Opening times: *Mon-Fri 9-5.*
Personnel: *Principal Information Officer:* Cath Bentley.

AXIS
For Information on Visual Artists

Axis is a visual arts service providing information about contemporary artists and craftspeople living/working in Britain. The information is displayed on a computer database, the Axis database. The Axis database contains each artist's CV and up to nine images of their work. Nearly 2,500 are registered. The Axis database is available at Axispoints around the UK. Alternatively, information can be provided over the phone and by post. Printouts of CVs and artwork images are available at nominal cost. Axis is mainly funded by the Arts Councils of England, Scotland and Wales.

Jonathan Poole C

Compton Cassey Gallery, Nr. Withington, Cheltenham, GL54 4DE.
Tel: *01242-890224.* **Fax:** *01242-890479.*
Email *jonathanpoole@comptoncassey.demon.co.uk*
Ws *http://www.jonathanpoole.co.uk*
Personnel: Jonathan Poole. Maggie Mallen.
European representatives for John Lennon and Miles Davis Estates. Exhibition organisers with venues in Europe and the Middle East. Contemporary Sculpture, Paintings and Sculpture by Jonathan Poole and Bobby Plisnier.
Services and Facilities:
Art Consultancy. Art for Offices. Gallery space for hire. Valuation.
Work Stocked and Sold:
Dr. Pa. Pr. Sc.
Price range: £50 - £15,000.

London Art

Tel: *0171-404 5520.*
Ws *http://www.londonart.co.uk*

The New Masters Ltd. C

Tel: *0171-409 3456.*
Fax: *0171-491 3950.*
Email *BalfourH@aol.com.uk*
Ws *www.newmasters.co.uk*
Nearest Underground: *Victoria*
Personnel: *Director:* Peter Davis. *P.A:* Lisa Constanti.
The New Masters is a virtual art gallery featuring the selected works of art teachers and their most gifted students. This presents a unique opportunity to secure original works carried out in the top European art nurseries that we believe could be the masterpieces of the future, whilst creating a unique focus for the home or office.
Works may be purchased either by credit card or cheque and are returnable within 14 days if unsuitable.
Art colleges are invited to submit works they consider would be appropriate by visiting the Web Site or by telephoning or faxing our numbers. If the studio is in the London area, we will even send a photographer.

No.1 Gallery C

138 Weyhill Road, Andover, SP10 3BG.
Tel: *01264-358851.*
Fax: *01264-358821.*
Email *info@no1artgallery.com*
Ws *www.no1artgallery.com*
Opening times: *24 hours a day on the Internet.*
Personnel: *Directors:* Cliff Leach, Gillian Leach. *General Manager:* Carolyne Burbridge.
No.1 Gallery is one of the fastest growing Internet art galleries in the UK, offering original works of art by new and established artists for exhibition and sale.
The gallery halls exhibit an extensive range of paintings, drawings, textiles, ceramics, sculpture and alternatives by talented artists plus news and events.
Unique to No.1 Gallery is the unrivalled service offered to buyers and artists worldwide. After browsing the site, select a piece of art, purchase on-line and have the art work delivered to your door.
Providing a comprehensive, holistic service to private and corporate buyers, investors and interior designers worldwide. No.1 Gallery's driving force is to bring art to the people, breaking down the intimidating barriers of the art establishment.
Services and Facilities:
Art for Offices. Commissioning Service.
Work Stocked and Sold:
Cer. Dr. Pa. Sc. Tx.

Panvertu Galleries C

8 Prince Consort, Chislehurst, BR7 5SB.
Tel: *0181-467 1694.*
Fax: *0181-295 0378.*
Email *info@panvertu.com*
Ws *www.panvertu.com*
Opening times: *24 hours, 365 days.*
Personnel: *Sales Director:* David Wiseman. *Managing Director:* Roger Lawson.
The world's finest art for sale on the Internet. Specialising in original works of art and offering a single source to locate works by a specific artist or genre of paintings at prices from £300-£100,000.
Galleries around the globe contribute their finest paintings for sale. The widest possible selection to find a single work or to fill an office or location.
Simple selection by price, age, artist. Auction section to bid for specific works and a 'picture of the week' feature. Come and browse or contact us if you want to display works from your gallery.
Services and Facilities:
Gallery space for hire.
Work Stocked and Sold:
Pa.
Price range: £300 - £100,000.
For artists see *Commercial Gallery Artists.*

Wondermall

14 Devonshire Square, London EC2M 4YT.
Tel: *0171-247 6347.*
Fax: *0171-247 6609.*
Email *gallery@wondermall.co.uk*
Ws *http://www.wondermall.co.uk*
Opening times: *24 Hours a day.*
Nearest Underground: *Liverpool Street.*
Personnel: *Sales & Marketing Manager:* Kevin Dukes.
Wondermall Gallery.
Wondermall is a virtual shopping mall, which aims to sell British and European goods to the Japanese consumer in Japanese, it is the first e-commerce site to do this.
As part of this heavily promoted bilingual site there is a gallery showing the work of British and European fine and applied artists. Artists, agents or galleries may submit examples of their work in any format with a brief description and biography. Work will be shown in themed exhibitions free of charge, commission only being charged on works sold or commissions taken at a modest rate.
Services and Facilities:
Art for Offices. Commissioning Service. Craftshop. Gallery space for hire. Shop.

www.aarti.co.uk C
'Bygones', The Street, Rickinghall, Diss, IP22 1EG.
Tel: *01379-898966, 01379-890608.*
Fax: *0870-055 7896.*
Email *margaret@aarti.demon.co.uk*
Ws *http://www.aarti.co.uk*
Opening times: *24 Hours a day 7 days a week.*
Personnel: *Director:* Margaret Horrocks.

AARTI

AARTI provides an affordable opportunity for artists and craftspersons to present their own exhibitions on the Internet. This is a new website at the time of printing. Only £7.50 for 10 works for one year. For more information call 01379-890608, e-mail: margaret@aarti.demon.co.uk, web site: www.aarti.co.uk. Artists choose what to exhibit including details about themselves and forthcoming events
Services and Facilities:
Commissioning Service. Craftshop. Gallery space for hire.
Work Stocked and Sold:
Cra. Dec. Dr. Pa. Sc.
Price range: £90 - £2,000.
For artists see *Commercial Gallery Artists.*

Internet Design

Art On The Web
9 Rosslyn Mansions, 21 Goldhurst Terrace, London NW6 3HD.
Tel: *0171-624 5266.* **Fax:** *0171-681 4775.*
Email *gizbor@globalnet.co.uk*
Ws *http://www.lenkoran.co.uk*
Opening times: *By appointment.*
Nearest Underground: *Finchley Road.*
Personnel: *Managing Director:* Gary A. Bortz.

Art on the Web specialises in web site design and promotion for fine art and antique dealers.
The world wide web provides a vast marketplace for dealers to advertise, interact with and sell goods to new clients. Our unique combination of a broad-based knowledge of art and antiques, understanding of the tools of graphic and web site design, and familiarity with the ins and out of on-line promotion enable us to offer a superior package of services to the fine arts and antiques trade. We are prepared to undertake projects ranging from basic to complex database-driven interactive sites.
Services and Facilities:
Art Consultancy.

Other Internet Sites

Listed below are other internet sites by establishment type.

Art Book Publishers

Ashgate Publishing/Scolar Press
http://www.ashgate.com
Macmillan Publishers Ltd. The Dictionary of Art
http://www.groveartmusic.com
Oxford University Press
http://www.oup.co.uk
Thames & Hudson
thttp://www.hameshudson.co.uk

Art Bookshops

Arts Bibliographic
http://www.artsbib.com

Art Consultants

Alexandra Wettstein
http://graffiti.virgin.net/alexandra.wettstein/
Art Contact Ltd
http://www.artcontact.co.uk
The Art Loss Register
http://www.artloss.com
Brandler Galleries
http://www.brandler-galleries.com and www.thesaurus.co.uk/brandler
Business Art Galleries
http://www.curwen.demon.co.uk
Egee Art Consultancy
http://www.egeeart.com
Fine Art Commissions Ltd.
http://www.facl.com

Art Education

The Arts Institute at Bournemouth
http://www.arts-inst-bournemouth.ac.uk
Barnfield College
http://www.barnfield.ac.uk
Bath Spa University College
http://www.bathspa.ac.uk
Birkbeck College
URLhttp://www.bbk.ac.uk/
Byam Shaw School of Art
http://www.byam-shaw.ac.uk
Carmarthenshire College
http://www.ccta.ac.uk
Cavendish College
http://www.cavendish.ac.uk
Chelsea College of Art and Design (London Institute)
http://www.linst.ac.uk
The Cheshire School of Art & Design, Mid-Cheshire College
http://www.midchesh.u-net.com
Christie's Education
http://www.christies.com
Cumbria College of Art and Design
http://www.cumbriacollart.ac.uk
Dartington College of Arts
http://www.dartington.ac.uk
Edinburgh College of Art
http://www.eca.ac.uk
Glasgow University
http://www.arts.gla.ac.uk/ArtHist/decarts.htm
Goldsmiths College
http://www.gold.ac.uk/
The Institute
http://www.hgsi.ac.uk
Lancaster University, School of Creative Arts, The Art Department
http://www.lancs.ac.uk/users/art/
Nottingham Trent University
http://www.ntu.ac.uk/vpa
Oxford Brookes University
http://www.brookes.ac.uk/schools/apm/fineart
Plymouth College of Art and Design
http://www.pcad.plym.ac.uk
Ruskin School of Drawing and Fine Art
http://www.ruskin-sch.ox.ac.uk/
The Slade School of Fine Art
http://www.ucl.ac.uk/slade/
Swindon College
http://www.swindon-college.ac.uk/
University of Central England in Birmingham
http://www.uce.ac.uk/
University of Plymouth
http://www.fae.plym.ac.uk/
Westminster College
www.westminster-cfe.ac.uk

Art in Country Houses

Harewood House Trust
http://www.harewood.org

Art Societies

Association of Art Historians
http://www.gold.ac.uk/aah
The British Society of Master Glass Painters
http://www.proteusweb.com/bsmgp
Contemporary Art Society
http://www.contempart.org.uk
The Design and Artists Copyright Society Ltd
http://www.dacs.co.uk
National Acrylic Painters' Association
http://www.artarena.force9.co.uk/napa; America http://www.watercolor-online.com/NAPA/

National Association of Memorial Masons
http://www.namm.org.uk
Public Monuments and Sculpture Association
http://www.unn.ac.uk/~hcv3
Royal Academy of Arts
http://www.RoyalAcademy.org.uk
The Royal Photographic Society
http://www.rps.org
Scottish Sculpture Trust
http://www.sstq.demon.co.uk
Society of Women Artists
http://www.mcis.net.uk/swa

Artists Materials

Alec Tiranti Ltd.
thttp://www.tiranti.co.uk
Daler-Rowney
http://www.daler-rowney.com

Arts Councils

Arts Council of England
http://www.artscouncil.org.uk
Arts Council of Wales
http://www.ccc-acw.org.uk
An Chomhairle Ealaíon
http://www.artscouncil.ie

Auction Houses

Panvertu Galleries
www.panvertu.com
Phillips Fine Art Auctioneers and Valuers
http://www.phillips-auctions.com
Woolley & Wallis
http://www.auctions-on-line.com/woolleywallis

Conservators & Restorers

Abbott & Holder
http://www.artefact.co.uk/AaH.html
Fine Art Commissions Ltd.
http://www.facl.com
Simon R. Gillespie
http://www.art-connection.com

Electronic Services

Thesaurus Group Ltd
thesaurus.co.uk/

Fairs & Festivals

The Contemporary Print Show & The Contemporary Print Fair
http://www.artnet.co.uk
Penman Art Fairs
http://www.penmanfairs.demon.co.uk

Fine Art Founders

Bronze Age Sculpture Foundry
http://www.netcomuk.co.uk/-duncanh
Burleighfield Arts Limited
http://www.polestarltd/sculpture/
Leander Architectural
http://www.leanderarch.demon.co.uk

Fine Art Magazines

Art Review
http://www.art-review.co.uk
Crafts Magazine
http://www.craftscouncil.org.uk

Fine Art Printers

The Postcard Company
http://www.thepostcardcompany.com

Fine Art Printers - Art Cards

Thought Factory
http://www.kpegroup@aol.com

Fine Press Printers/Publishers

Old School Press
http://www.praxis.co.uk/ppuk/osp.htm

Framing Supplies

Peak Rock
http://peakrock.com

Gallery Hanging Supplies

Peak Rock
http://peakrock.com

Gallery Space for Hire

Abbott & Holder
http://www.artefact.co.uk/AaH.html
The Air Gallery
http://www.airgallery.co.uk
The Barber Institute of Fine Arts
http://www.barber.org.uk
modern gallery
http://www.artnet.co.uk
Westminster Gallery
http://www.wch.co.uk

Information Services

The Art Loss Register
http://www.artloss.com
Axis
http://www.lmu.ac.uk/ces/axis
National Irish Visual Arts Library
http://www.ncad.ie

Insurance Companies

Hiscox plc.
http://www.hiscox.co.uk

Irish Galleries

Butler Gallery
http://www.Butlergallery.com
Crawford Municipal Art Gallery
http://www.synergy.ie/crawford
Kerlin Gallery
www.kerlin.ie
The Solomon Gallery
http://indigo.ie/~solomon
St. John's Art & Heritage Centre
http://www.iol.ie/kerry-insight/stjohns.html
Temple Bar Gallery & Studios
http://www.paddynet.ie/tbgs

London Commercial Galleries

Abbott & Holder
http://www.artefact.co.uk/AaH.html
Adrian Sassoon
http://www.adriansassoon.com
The Air Gallery
http://www.airgallery.co.uk
Albemarle Gallery
http://www.i-i.net/albemarlegallery
Alex Wengraf
http://www.wengraf.com
Alexandra Gallery
http://www.alexandragallery.demon.co.uk
Artlondon
http://www.artlondon.com
The Association Gallery
http://www.aophoto.co.uk
Barry Davies Oriental Art
http://www.antiques-on-line.com/barrydavies
BCA Boukamel Contemporary Art
http://www.bca-gallery.com
Beldam Gallery
http://www.brunel.ac.uk./depts/arts
Bengstrom
http://www.bengstromart.co.uk
BritArt.com
http://www.britart.com
The Bruton Street Gallery
http://www.artnet.com/bruton.html
Cadogan Contemporary Art
http://www.artcad.co.uk
Catto Gallery
http://www.catto.co.uk
Colville Place Gallery
http://www.romanesque.co.uk/gallery.html
Curwen Gallery
http://www.curwen.demon.co.uk
Daniel Katz Ltd
http://www.katz.co.uk
Davies & Tooth
http://www.art-net.co.uk/banca/too-dav
Fleur de Lys Gallery
http://www.fleur-de-lys.com
Galleria Enterprise
http://www.galleria-art.co.uk

Hanging Space
Skypages
Houldsworth Fine Art
http://www.art-connection.com
IAP Fine Art
http://www.BritArt.com
Julian Hartnoll
http://www.art-on-line.com\hartnoll
Lamont Gallery
http://www.lamontart.com
Linda Blackstone Gallery
http://www.blackstoneart.com
Lisson Gallery
http://www.lisson.co.uk
London Print Studio
http://www.200.co.uk/~z8000007
Marlborough Graphics
http://www.icollector.com
Matthiesen Fine Art Limited
http://www.Europeanpaintings.com
The McHardy Sculpture Company
http://www.mchardy-sculpture.com
Mercury Gallery
http://www.mercury-gallery.co.uk
New Academy Gallery and Business Art Galleries
http://www.curwcn.dcmon.co.uk
The October Gallery
http://www.ecotechnics.edu/index-og.html
Piccadilly Gallery Ltd.
http://www.piccadillygall.demon.co.uk
Plazzotta Ltd
http://www.plazzotta.co.uk
Portal Gallery
http://www.portal-gallery.com
The Special Photographer's Company
http://www.specialphoto.co.uk
Spink-Leger
http://www.spinkandson.co.uk
Stern Art Dealers
http://www.stern-art.com
Whitford Fine Art
http://www.artnet.com/whitford.html
William Thuillier
http://www.thuillart.com
Wiseman Originals
http://www.wisemanoriginals.com

London Public Galleries

198 Gallery
http://www.globalnet.co.uk/~198glry
Bank of England Museum
http://www.bankofengland.co.uk
Barbican Art Gallery
http://www.uk-calling.co.uk
Ben Uri Art Society
http://www.ort.org/benuri/
Bethnal Green Museum of Childhood
http://www.vam.ac.uk/bgm/welcome.html
Bhownagree and Today Galleries
http://www.commonwealth.org.uk
Chalk Farm Gallery
http://www.chalk-farm-gallery.co.uk
Estorick Collection of Modern Italian Art
http://www.estorickcollection.com
Geffrye Museum
http://www.lattimore.co.uk/geffrye
Goethe-Institut London
http://www.goethe.de/gr/lon/enindex.htm
Hayward Gallery
http://www.hayward-gallery.org.uk
The Horniman Museum and Gardens
http://www.horniman.demon.co.uk
Imperial War Museum
http://www.iwm.org.uk
Institute of Contemporary Arts
http://www.illumin.co.uk/ica/
Museum of Installation
http://www.moi.dircon.co.uk
The Museum of London
http://www.museumoflondon.org.uk
Museum of the Moving Image
http://www.bfi.org.uk/museum
National Army Museum
http://www.failte.com/nam/
National Gallery
http://www.nationalgallery.org.uk
National Portrait Gallery
http://www.npg.org.uk
Orleans House Gallery
http://www.guidetorichmond.co.uk/orleans.html
Royal Academy of Arts
http://www.RoyalAcademy.org.uk
South London Gallery
http://www.southlondonart.co.uk
Studio Glass Gallery
http://www.studioglass.co.uk
TWO10 Gallery
http://www.wellcome.ac.uk
Victoria and Albert Museum The National Museum of Art and Design
http://www.vam.ac.uk
Wallace Collection
http://www.demon.co.uk/heritage/wallace
William Morris Gallery and Brangwyn Gift
http://www.lbwf.gov.uk

Packers & Shippers

Art Services
http://www.artservices@ukbusiness.com.
Oxford Exhibition Services
www.oxex.demon.co.uk

Photographers

The Photography of Art
www.books.mcmail.com/photo.htm

Print Publishers/Dealers/Galleries

Brandler Galleries
http://www.brandler-galleries.com and www.thesaurus.co.uk/brandler
Cambridge Contemporary Art
http://www.artcambridge.co.uk
Curwen Gallery
http://www.curwen.demon.co.uk
Greenwich Printmakers Association
http://www.longitude0.co.uk/printmakers/
Marlborough Graphics
http://www.icollector.com

Print Workshops

Glasgow Print Studio Workshop
http://www.gpsart.co.uk

Regional Art Boards

South West Arts
http://www.swa.co.uk
West Midlands Arts
http://www.arts.org.uk/
Yorkshire & Humberside Arts
http://www.arts.org.uk

Regional Galleries

Arnolfini Gallery
http://www.channel.org.uk/arnolfini
Ashmolean Museum of Art and Archaeology
http://www.ashmol.ox.ac.uk/
The Barber Institute of Fine Arts
http://www.barber.org.uk
Blackthorn Galleries
http://www.galleries.u-net.com
The Bonington Gallery
http://www.ntu.ac.uk/gallery/
Bourne Gallery
http://www.bournegallery.com
Brancaster Staithe and Burnham Deepdale/Micromouse Limited
http://www.users.zetnet.co.uk/deepdale
Brandler Galleries
http://www.brandler-galleries.com and www.thesaurus.co.uk/brandler
Broughton House Gallery
http://www.broughtonhouse gallery.uksw.com
Bruton Gallery
http://www.BrutonGallery.co.uk
Cambridge Contemporary Art
http://www.artcambridge.co.uk
Christ Church Picture Gallery
http://www.chch.ox.ac.uk
Contemporary Fine Art Gallery & Sculpture Park
http://www.CFAG.co.UK
Corrymella Scott Gallery
http://www.corymella.co.uk
Dansel Gallery
http://www.wdi.co.uk/dansel
The Dean Clough Galleries
http://www.DeanClough.com
Devon Guild of Craftsmen
http:/www.crafts.org.uk
Djanogly Art Gallery
http://www.nottingham.ac.uk/artscentre/
Durham Art Gallery
http://www.durham.gov.uk
Durham University Oriental Museum
http://www.dur.ac.uk/~dcm0www/omuseum.htm

Fox Talbot Museum of Photography
http://www.Fox-Talbot.org.uk/Fox-Talbot
The Gallery, Gateshead Central Library
http://www.wamses.unn.ac.uk
The Gallery
http://www1.btwebworld.com/carpathian/
The Heffer Gallery
http://www.heffers.co.uk
The Henry Moore Foundation
http://www.henry-moore-fdn.co.uk/hnt
Herbert Art Gallery and Museum
http://www.coventry.org/coventry-museums
The Hunt Gallery
http://www.thehuntgallery.com
Ikon Gallery
http://www.dialspace.dial.pipex.com/ikon/
Foyer Gallery
http://www.surrart.ac.uk
Jonathan Poole
http://www.jonathanpoole.co.uk
Lady Lever Art Gallery
http://www.nmgm.org.uk
Leeds Metropolitan University Gallery
http://www.lmu.ac.uk/arts
Lion Gallery
http://www.cogent-comms.co.uk/lion.htm
Lupton Square Gallery
http://www.luptonsquaregallery.co.uk
Manchester City Art Gallery
http://www.u-net.com/set/mcag/cag.html
Margaret Harvey Gallery and University Gallery
http://www.herts.ac.uk/artdes/
The Museum of Science & Industry in Manchester
http://www.edes.co.uk/mussci
Nevill Gallery
http://www.nevillgallery.com
Norwich Castle Museum
http://www.norfolk.gov.uk/tourism/museums/museums/htm
Parkview Fine Paintings
//ourworld.compuserve.com/homepages/parkviewpaintings
Peter Scott Gallery
http://www.lancs.ac.uk/users/PETERSCOTT/Scott.htm
Portsmouth City Museum and Records Office
http://www.xpcclsde@hants.gov.uk
Royal Albert Memorial Museum & Art Gallery
http://www.exeter.gov.uk
The Royal Photographic Society
http://www.rps.org
Russell-Cotes Art Gallery and Museum
To be announced soon.
The Stanley Picker Gallery for the Arts
http://www.JPEGDESIGN.CO.UK
Sudley House
http://www.nmgm.org.uk
Tate Gallery Liverpool
http://www.tate.org.uk
Tate Gallery St. Ives
http://www.tate.org.uk
Terrace Gallery
http://www.harewood.org
University Gallery Leeds
http://www.leeds.ac.uk/library/gall/exhibs.html
University of Essex Gallery
http://www.essex.ac.uk
University of Hull Art Collection
http://www.hull.ac.uk
Walker Art Gallery
http://www.nmgm.org.uk
Warwick Gallery
http://members.aol.com/ukgallery
Watershed Exhibitions
http://www.watershed.co.uk
Wolverhampton Art Gallery
http://www.artgall.scit.w/v.ac.uk
Wysing Arts
http://www.wysing.demon.co.uk

Scottish Galleries

An Lanntair
http://www.lanntair.com
Duncan of Jordanstone College of Art and Design
http://www.dundee.ac.uk/
Edinburgh College of Art
http://www.eca.ac.uk
Frames Contemporary Gallery
http://www.framesgallery.co.uk
Glasgow Print Studio Gallery
http://www.gpsart.co.uk
Hunterian Art Gallery
http://www.gla.ac.uk/Museum/
Paisley Museum, Art Galleries and Coats Observatory
http://www.cqm.co.uk/www/sdc/leisurestart.html
Portfolio Gallery
http://www.ednet.co.uk/-portfolio
Scottish Gallery (Aitken Dott Ltd)
http://www.scottish-gallery.co.uk
Strathearn Gallery and Pottery
http://www.strathearn-gallery.com

Sculpture Parks

The Henry Moore Foundation
http://www.henry-moore-fdn.co.uk/hmf
Scottish Sculpture Workshop
http://www.ssw.org.uk
Sculpture at Goodwood
http://www.sculpture.org.uk

Studio Space for Hire

S.P.A.C.E. Studios
http://www.ecna.org

Welsh Galleries

Attic Gallery
http://www.atticgallery.co.uk
The Ceramics Gallery
http://www.aber.ac.uk
Martin Tinney Gallery
http://www.ARTWALES.DIRCON.CO.UK
The National Library of Wales
http://www.llgc.org.uk
National Museums & Galleries of Wales
http://www.nmgw.ac/index.html
Oriel Ceri Richards Gallery
http://www.whatsonwales.com
School of Art Gallery & Museum
http://www.aber.ac.uk
Stan Rosenthal
http://www.stanrosenthal.com
Tenby Museum & Art Gallery
http://www.atlas-links.com

AUCTION HOUSES

THE ART WORLD
DIRECTORY

Bonham's
Montpelier Street, Knightsbridge, London SW7 1HH.
Tel: *0171-584 9161, 0171-393 3962/3900.*
Fax: *0171-589 4072, 0171-393 3905.*

Cheffins Grain & Comins C
2 Clifton Road, Cambridge, CB1 4BW.
Tel: *01223-213343.*
Fax: *01223-413396.*

Christie's
8 King Street, St James's, London SW1Y 6QT.
Tel: *0171-839 9060.*

Christie's
85 Old Brompton Road, London SW7 3LD.
Tel: *0171-321 3120, 0171-581 7611.*
Fax: *0171-581 3679.*

Christie's Scotland
164-166 Bath Street, Glasgow G2 4TB.

Grays Auction Rooms C
5-7 Buck Street, London NW1.
Tel: *0171-284 2026.*

Harman Healy
340 Grays Inn Road, London WC1X.
Tel: *0171-833 5885.*

Henry Spencer & Son
20 The Square, Retford, DN22 6BX.

Lloyds International Auction Galleries
118 Putney Road, London SW15 2NQ.
Tel: *0181-788 7777.*

Mallams
St. Michael's Street, Oxford, OX1 2EB.

Outhwaite & Litherland
Kingsway Galleries, Fontenoy Street, Liverpool, L3 2BE.

Panvertu Galleries
8 Prince Consort, Chislehurst, BR7 5SB.
Tel: *0181-467 1694.*
Fax: *0181-295 0378.*
Email *info@panvertu.com*
Ws *www.panvertu.com*
Opening times: *24 hours, 365 days.*
Personnel: *Sales Director:* David Wiseman. *Managing Director:* Roger Lawson.
The world's finest art for sale on the Internet. Specialising in original works of art and offering a single source to locate works by a specific artist or genre of paintings at prices from £300-£100,000.
Galleries around the globe contribute their finest paintings for sale. The widest possible selection to find a single work or to fill an office or location.
Simple selection by price, age, artist. Auction section to bid for specific works and a 'picture of the week' feature. Come and browse or contact us if you want to display works from your gallery.
Services and Facilities:
Gallery space for hire.
Work Stocked and Sold:
Pa.
Price range: £300 - £100,000.

Phillips Fine Art Auctioneers & Valuers
101 New Bond Street, London W1Y 0AS.
Tel: *0171-629 6602.*
Fax: *0171-629 8876.*
Ws *http://www.phillips-auctions.com*
Opening times: *Mon-Fri 8.30-5 & most Sundays for viewing 2-5.*
Nearest Underground: *Bond Street.*
Personnel: *Chairman:* Christopher Weston. *Managing Director:* Roger Hollest.
Phillips hold Fine Art auctions at their Bond Street premises throughout the year.
Established in 1796, they have 23 salesrooms in Britain, all staffed by experienced specialists and valuers, who are happy to advise on all aspects of buying and selling at auction.
The Bond Street salesroom specialises in Fine Furniture, Paintings, Ceramics, Jewellery, Silver, Clocks, Watches, Oriental Works of Art, Textiles, Books, Musical Instruments, Works of Art, Stamps, Medals and Decorative Arts.
The salesrooms are normally open for viewing 2 to 3 days before an auction, and visitors are always welcome.
Services and Facilities:
Art for Offices. Valuation.
Work Stocked and Sold:
Dr. Pa. Sc.

Phillips West
2 Salem Road, London W2.
Tel: *0171-221 5303.*

Russel Balwin & Bright
Rylelands Road, Leominster, HR6 8NZ.

Sotheby's
34-35 New Bond Street, London W1A 2AA.
Tel: *0171-493 8080, Telex 24454.*
Fax: *0171-408 5989.*

Sotheby's
Summers Place, Billingshurst, RH14 9AD.
Tel: *01403-783933.*
Fax: *01403-785153.*

Southgate Auction Rooms
55 High Street, Southgate, London N14 6LD.
Tel: *0181-886 7888.*
Fax: *0181-982 5065.*

Stanley Gibbons
399 Strand, London WC2R OLX.
Tel: *0171-836 8444.*

Thompson Anthony
7 Kensington Park Gardens, London W11.
Tel: *0171-221 5072.*

TWK
8 Seymour Place, London W1H.
Tel: *0171-724 7144.*

Woolley & Wallis
Salisbury Salerooms, 51-61 Castle Street, Salisbury, SP1 3SU.
Tel: *01722-424500.*
Fax: *01722-424508.*

ART IN COUNTRY HOUSES

THE ART WORLD
DIRECTORY

Ascott House
Ascott Estate Office Wing, Leighton Buzzard, LU7 0PS.
Tel: *01296-688242.* **Fax:** *01296-681904.*

Blenheim Palace *P*
Woodstock, OX20 1PX.
Tel: *01993-811091.* **Fax:** *01993-813527.*

Blickling Hall
Blickling, Aylsham, NR11 6NF.
Tel: *01263-733471.* **Fax:** *01263-734924.*

Bodelwyddan Castle
Bodelwyddan, Rhyl, LL18 5YA.
Tel: *01745-583539 / 584060.*
Fax: *01745-584563.*

Bowhill
Selkirk,
Tel: *01750-22204.* **Fax:** *01750-22204.*
Opening times: *House: public opening in July. Country Park: May-Aug. Times and dates vary annually. Educational parties by appointment throughout the year.*
Nearest Station: *Edinburgh Waverly 40m, Berwick 40m.*
Personnel: The Duke of Buccleuch.

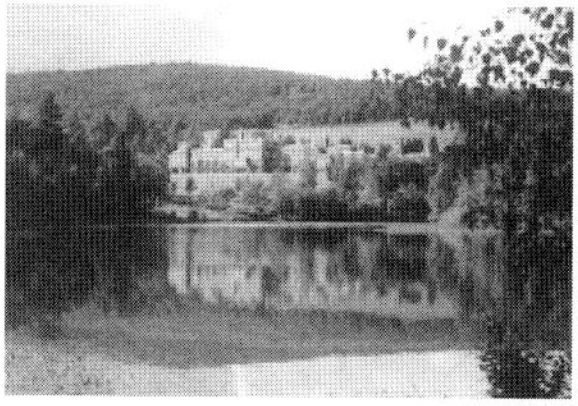

This part of the renowned Buccleuch Collection includes Canaletto's Whitehall, a key Ruiysdael, and several Guardis, works by Gainsborough, Reynolds, Claude, Vernet, Raeburn and Wilkie. French furniture 1680-1780. Porcelain includes a Sèvres set made for Madame du Barry. Lecture theatre, arts courses, visitor centre, conference centre, audio visual. Bowhill Little Theatre (drama, music, dance). Gardens/Grounds. Adventure Playground. Education Service.
Services and Facilities:
Café. Disabled Access. Gallery space for hire. Guided Tours. Lectures. Parking. Restaurant. Shop.

Brodie Castle
Brodie, Forres, IV36 0TE.
Tel: *01309-641371.* **Fax:** *01309-641600.*

Bryn Bras Castle
Llanrug, Nr Llanberis, Caernarfon, LL55 4RE.
Tel: *01286-870210.*

Chirk Castle
Chirk Wrexham, LL14 5AF.
Tel: *01691-777701.* **Fax:** *01691-774706.*

Dalmeny House
South Queensferry, EH30 9TQ.
Tel: *0131-331 1888.* **Fax:** *0131-331 1788.*
Opening times: *July & August: Mon-Tue 12-5.30, Sun 1-5.30 (last admission 4.45). Closed other days except by appointment.*
Nearest Station: *Dalmeny.*
Personnel: *Administrator:* Mrs Linda Edgar.
Family home of the Earl and Countess of Rosebery in spectacular situation on the shores of the Firth of Forth, yet only 7 miles west of Edinburgh. Built in 1817 by William Wilkins. Contains superb collections of works of art, Rothschild French furniture, tapestries and porcelain. Rosebery collection of Napoleonic memorabilia and paintings. Early Scottish furniture and books. Fine British portraits. Gardens/Grounds. Teashop.
Services and Facilities:
Café. Disabled Access. Guided Tours. Parking.

Drumlanrig Castle
Thornhill, DG3 4AQ.
Tel: *01848-330248.* **Fax:** *01848-600244.*
Email *bre@drumlanrigcastle.org.uk*
Opening times: *Please phone for details of opening times.*
Personnel: *Administrator/Archivist:* Mr Andrew Fisher.
Renowned Buccleuch collection includes Rembrandt's Old Woman Reading, Holbein's Sir Nicholas Carew, Leonardo da Vinci's Madonna with the Yarnwinder, Merton's Countess of Dalkeith. Cabinets made for Versailles, much French and English furniture 1680-1750 and 1670 silver chandelier. Gardens/Grounds.
Services and Facilities:
Craftshop. Disabled Access. Guided Tours. Lectures. Parking. Restaurant. Shop.

Dunrobin Castle and Museum
Dunrobin Castle, Golspie, KW10 6RR.
Tel: *01408-633177.* **Fax:** *01408-633800.*

Eastnor Castle
Portcullis Office, Eastnor, Ledbury, HR8 1RN.
Tel: *01531 633160.* **Fax:** *01531 631776.*

Euston Hall
Estate Office, Euston, Thetford, IP24 2QP.
Tel: *01842-766366.*

Floors Castle
Roxburghe Estates Office, Kelso, TD5 7SF.
Tel: *01573-223333.* **Fax:** *01573-226056.*

Glamis Castle
Glamis, DD8 1RL.
Tel: *01307-840202.* **Fax:** *01307-840257.*

Harewood House Trust
Moor House, Harewood, Leeds LS17 9LQ.
Tel: *0113-288 6331.* **Fax:** *0113-288 6467.*
Email *business@harewood.org*
Ws *http://www.harewood.org*
Opening times: *Open daily: 9 March - 31 October. (Last admission 4pm).*
Nearest Station: *Leeds & Harrogate.*
Personnel: *Visual Arts Administrator:* Philippa Brough.
Home of the Earl and Countess of Harewood, now a Designated Museum run by the Harewood House Trust. Important English and Italian collection of paintings as well as fine Chippendale furniture and Sèvres porcelain. The strong exhibition programme includes in the Watercolour Rooms, "Girtin in the North", 9 March - 13 June, a choice selection of Girtin's northern landscapes, followed by "Harewood Masterpieces", 19 March - 31 October, Harewood's own Turners, not seen since Spring 1997.

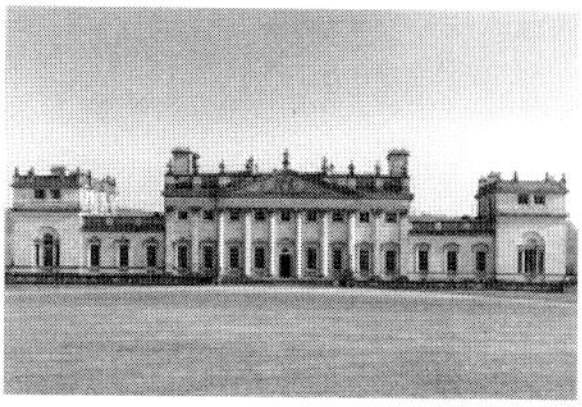

Throughout the House, The China Room: new display of the Harewood Sèvres porcelain, The Ante Room: "The Yorkshire Princess" and Harewood's Royal connections, a new display, The Library and The Spanish Library: "Off the Shelf", more revelations of rare and beautiful books drawn from Harewood's extensive libraries. For information about the contemporary gallery, The Terrace Gallery, please see separate entry.
Services and Facilities:
Bookshop. Café. Craftshop. Disabled Access. Friends/Society. Guided Tours. Lectures. Museum Shop. Parking. Shop.

Hatfield House
Hatfield, AL9 5NQ.
Tel: *01707-262823.* **Fax:** *01707-275719.*
Opening times: *25 Mar-26 Sept, daily, except Mon (but open Bank Hols) and Fri weekdays, 12-4 (guided tours), weekends 1-4.30.*
Nearest Station: *Hatfield (opposite main gates).*
Personnel: The Marquess of Salisbury.

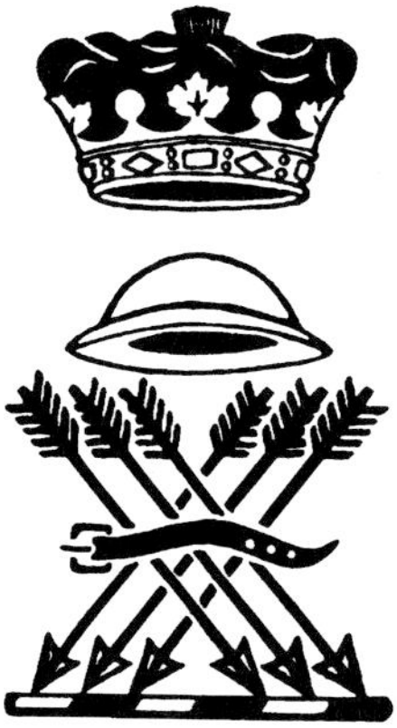

Portraits of each generation of Cecil family since Wm. Cecil, Lord Burghley. Artists include Reynolds, Lawrence, Romney and Richmond. Rainbow and Ermine portraits of Queen Elizabeth I and A Fête at Bermondsey, c. 1570, by Joris Hoefnagel. Catalogue of paintings (by Erna Auerbach) available (458 entries). WC, Gardens/Grounds.
Services and Facilities:
Café. Disabled Access. Guided Tours. Parking. Restaurant. Shop.

Hopetoun House
South Queensferry, EH30 9SL.
Tel: *0131-331 2451.*

House of the Binns
Linlithgow, EH49 7NA.
Tel: *0150683-4255.*

Knebworth House
Knebworth, SG3 6PY.
Tel: *01438-813303 / 812661.*
Fax: *01438-811908.*

Leeds Castle
Maidstone, ME17 1PL.
Tel: *01622-765400.* **Fax:** *01622-735616.*
Opening times: *Open All Year. Mar-Oct 10-5*. Castle 11-5.30*. Nov-Feb 10-3*. Castle 10.15-3.30*. (*Last admission).*
Nearest Station: *Bearsted.*
Personnel: *Curator:* Andrew Wells.

A fine collection of early English Furniture, English and Continental tapestries and pictures. Leeds Castle a Royal Palace for over three centuries has been called the 'loveliest castle in the world'. Within 500 acres of parkland other attractions include a unique Dog Collar Museum, a duckery, an aviary, maze and grotto, greenhouses and a vineyard.
Services and Facilities:
Bar. Café. Disabled Access. Guided Tours. Museum Shop. Parking. Restaurant. Shop.

Losely House
Guildford, GU3 1HS.
Tel: *01483-304440.* **Fax:** *01483-302036.*

Lotherton Hall
(Leeds City Art Galleries), Aberford, LS25 3EB.
Tel: *0113-281 3259.*

Manderston
Duns, TD11 3PP.
Tel: *01361-883450.* **Fax:** *01361-882010.*

Melbourne Hall P
Melbourne, DE73 1EN.
Tel: *01332-862502.* **Fax:** *01332-862263.*

Penshurst Place and Gardens
Penhurst, Tonbridge, TN11 8DG.
Tel: *01892-870307.*
Fax: *01892-810866.*

Ragley Hall
Alcester, B49 5NJ.
Tel: *01789-762090.* **Fax:** *01789-764791.*

Sudeley Castle
Winchcombe,
Tel: *01242-602308.* **Fax:** *01242-602959.*

Tatton Park
Knutsford, WA16 6QN.
Tel: *01565-654822.* **Fax:** *01565-650179.*

Temple Newsam House
Leeds City Council, Leeds LS15 0AE.
Tel: *01532-647321 or 0113-264 7321/264 1358.* **Fax:** *01532-602285 or 0113-260 2285.*

Towneley Hall
Burnley, BB11 3RQ.
Tel: *01282-424213.*
Fax: *01282-361138.*

Traquair House
Innerleithen, EH44 6PW.
Tel: *01896-830323.*
Fax: *01896-830639.*

Tredegar House and Park P
Coedkernew, Newport NP1 9YW.
Tel: *01633-815880.* **Fax:** *01633-815895.*

Turton Tower P
Chapeltown Road, Turton BL7 0HG.
Tel: *01204-852203.*
Fax: *01204-853759.*

Wilton House
Wilton, Salisbury, SP2 0BJ.
Tel: *01722-746720.*
Fax: *01722-744447.*
Opening times: *27 Mar-31 Oct 1999, Daily: 10.30-5.30 (last admission 4.30). House only closed 21-23 May 1999.*
Nearest Station: *Salisbury.*
Personnel: *Tourism Assistant:* Sally Watkins.

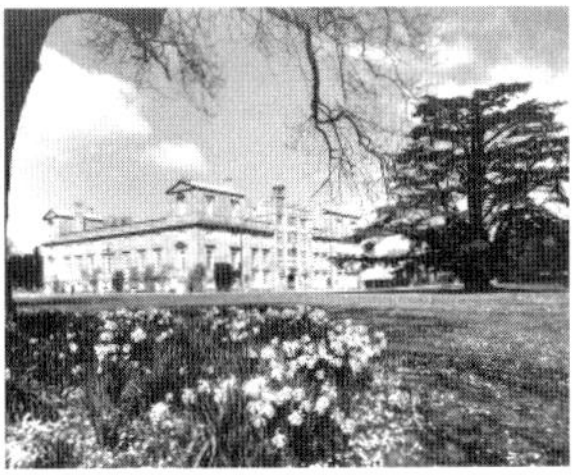

Wilton House has a superb private art collection, with over 200 paintings on show to the public. These include: winter landscapes by Pieter Brueghel the Younger and Jan Brueghel, Democritus by Ribera, The Card Players by Lucas van Leyden and works by Rubens, David Teniers, Lorenzo Lotto, Andrea del Sarto, Hugo van der Goes and Gerard Ter Borch. Portrait artists featured include Mytens, Sir Peter Lely, Sir Joshua Reynolds, Sir William Beechey, Gerrit van Honthorst, Pompeo Batoni and the nine Van Dyck's in the Double Cube Room. There are landscapes by Samuel Scott, George Lambert and Richard Wilson and a unique set of 55 paintings in gouache of the haute école riding school by the Baron d'Eisenberg. Featured exhibition for 1999 - Sir Anthony Van Dyck (400th anniversary of his birth). Gardens/ Grounds.
Services and Facilities:
Bar. Bookshop. Café. Disabled Access. Gallery space for hire. Parking. Restaurant. Shop.

Woburn Abbey
Woburn, MK43 0TP.
Tel: *01525-290666.* **Fax:** *01525-290271.*
Opening times: *11-4 (5 Sundays & Bank Holidays).*
Nearest Station: *Flitwick or Milton Keynes.*
Personnel: *Controller:* Mr W. Lash.
Woburn Abbey is the home of the Marquess and Marchioness of Tavistock and their family. One of the most important private art collections in the world can be seen here, including paintings by Van Dyck, Gainsborough, Reynolds, Velazquez and Canaletto. The collection also includes French and English 18th century furniture, silver and gold. The tour of the Abbey covers three floors, including the vaults, filled with exquisite French, Japanese, German and English porcelain. There is an Antiques Centre, coffee shop and gift shops. Open daily from March 21st to September 26th, and weekends only from 2nd October - 31st October.
Services and Facilities:
Café. Guided Tours. Museum Shop. Parking.

SCULPTURE PARKS

Barbara Hepworth Museum and Sculpture Park
Barnoon Hill, St. Ives,
Tel: *01736-792226.*

The Chilford Hall Sculpture Centre *C*
Linton,
Tel: *01223-892641.* **Fax:** *01223-894056.*

Chiltern Sculpture Trail
25A Cave Street, (Site location Cowlease Wood, between Stokenchurch and Watlington, Oxon), Oxford, OX4 1BA.
Tel: *01865-723684.*

Edinburgh Sculpture
25 Hawthornvale, Edinburgh EH6 4JT.
Tel: *0131-551 4490.* **Fax:** *0131-551 4490.*

The Garden Gallery *C*
Rookery Lane, Broughton, Stockbridge, SO20 8AZ.
Tel: *01794-301144.* **Fax:** *01794-301761.*
Email *gardgall@aol.com*
Opening times: *Early May-end July, Tues/Thurs/Sat 10-5. Other days and months by arrangement. Please ring.*
Nearest Station: *Grateley, Nr. Andover*
Personnel: *Director & Proprietor:* Rachel Bebb.

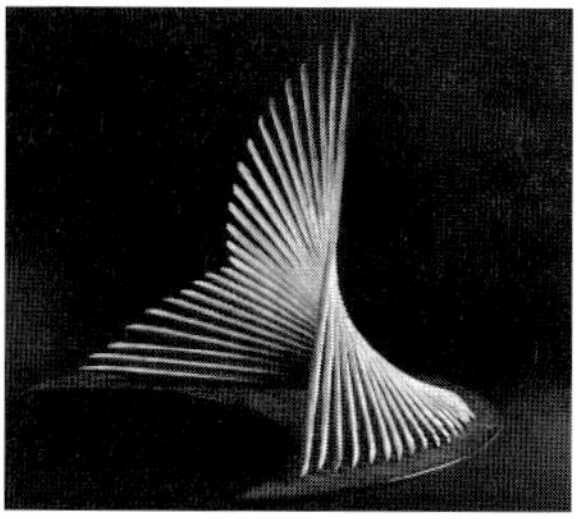

The Garden Gallery exhibits a wide range of innovative work by artists creating exciting, individual sculpture, pots and furniture for gardens. The elemental nature of stone, clay, bronze and wood establishes an empathy with plants, trees, landscape, water and light. Sculpture, a fine pot, or imaginatively-designed seat enhance a garden or landscape. Please enquire about exhibitions. Visits by arrangement are welcome. A portfolio of photographs of artists' work can be viewed. Commissions can be arranged. A garden design service is available.
Services and Facilities:
Art Consultancy. Art for Offices. Commissioning Service. Disabled Access. Lectures. Parking.
Work Stocked and Sold:
Cer. Fur. Sc.
Price range: £20 - £40,000.
For artists see *Commercial Gallery Artists.*

The Grizedale Society *PS*
Grizedale, Hawkshead, Ambleside, LA22 0QJ.
Tel: *01229-860291.* **Fax:** *01229-860050.*

Hannah Peschar Gallery *C*
Black and White Cottage, Standon Lane, Ockley, Dorking, RH5 5QR.
Tel: *01306-627269.* **Fax:** *01306-627662.*

The Henry Moore Foundation
Dane Tree House, Perry Green, Much Hadham, SG10 6EE.
Tel: *01279-843333.* **Fax:** *01279-843647.*

New Art Centre Sculpture Park and Gallery *C*
Roche Court, East Winterslow, Salisbury, SP5 1BG.
Tel: *01980-862244.* **Fax:** *01980-862447.*
Email *Nac@globalnet.co.uk*
Opening times: *Open every day all year round, 11-4.*
Personnel: *Gallery Manager:* Helen Simpson.
20th Century sculpture from Europe and the USA. Works from the Estate of Barbara Hepworth, Nevelson, Gormley, Armitage, Butler, King, Kenny, Frink and others. All works for sale. Lettering exhibition in the Walled Garden including works by Devereux and Peever and others. New gallery designed by award winning architects Munkenbeck + Marshall opening autumn 1998 as a space to show ceramics and paintings in addition to sculpture.
Services and Facilities:
Art Consultancy. Art for Offices. Commissioning Service. Guided Tours.
Work Stocked and Sold:
Cer. Fur. Pa. Sc. Wd.
For artists see *Commercial Gallery Artists.*

Scottish Sculpture Workshop
1 Main Street, Lumsden, Huntly, AB54 4JN.
Tel: *01464-861372.* **Fax:** *01464-861550.*

Sculpture at Goodwood *PS*
Hat Hill Copse, Goodwood, Chichester, PO18 0QP.
Tel: *01243-538449.* **Fax:** *01243-531853.*
Email *w@sculpture.org.uk*
Ws *http://www.sculpture.org.uk*
Opening times: *Thu/Fri/Sat 10.30-4.30 March to November. Directions: 01243-771114.*
Nearest Station: *Barnham.*
Personnel: *Founder:* Wilfred Cass.
Sculpture at Goodwood is a changing collection of contemporary British sculpture set in the beautiful grounds of Hat Hill Copse, 20 acres of woodland walks, informal gardens and rides on the southern slopes of the South Downs overlooking Chichester and the Channel coast. Artists whose work can be seen at Hat Hill include: Allen Jones, Allington, Ben-David, Caro, Chadwick, Cox, Cragg, Davies, De Monchaux, Furlong, Goldsworthy, Gregory, Hall, Hamilton-Finlay, Hicks, Isherwood, Kneale, Mach, Mistry, Nash, O'Connell, Pye, Tucker, Woodrow and many more. Compact disc imaging systems located in the information centre show retrospective surveys of the work of artists represented in the displays. Sculpture and discs are available for sale. A book on sculpture at Goodwood is published annually.
Services and Facilities:
Art Consultancy. Bookshop. Commissioning Service. Disabled Access. Parking.
Work Stocked and Sold:
Sc.
Price range: £6,000 - £660,000.
For artists see *Commercial Gallery Artists.*

Sculpture Park
Queen Mary's College, Cliddesden Road, Basingstoke, RG1 3HF.
Tel: *01256-479221.*

Yorkshire Sculpture Park *PS*
Bretton Hall, West Bretton, Wakefield WF4 4LG.
Tel: *01924-830302.* **Fax:** *01924-830044.*
Email *ysp@globalnet.co.net*
Opening times: *Summer: Grounds 10-6 daily, Galleries/Café 11-5 daily. Winter: Grounds 10-4 daily, Galleries/Café 11-4 daily.*
Nearest Station: *Wakefield Westgate.*
Personnel: *Director:* Peter Murray.
Yorkshire Sculpture Park, one of Europe's leading open-air art galleries, is set within 100 acres of beautiful 18th c. landscape, attracting over 200,000 visitors annually. It presents a programme of international open-air exhibitions alongside smaller projects, providing opportunities for the practice, understanding and enjoyment of sculpture for everyone. Two galleries and the Camellia House provide indoor space. Monumental sculptures by Henry Moore in the adjacent 96-acre Bretton Country Park is a significant collection of the artist's work. Changing displays from the collection include sculpture by Hepworth, Frink, Bourdelle, Nash, LeWitt and Paladino. A sensory trail has been developed for people with disabilities: audio guides and electric scooters available.
Services and Facilities:
Bookshop. Café. Craftshop. Disabled Access. Friends/Society. Lectures. Parking. Shop.

ART SOCIETIES & ORGANISATIONS

THE ART WORLD
DIRECTORY

56 Group Wales
18 Tydfil Place, Roath Park, Cardiff CF2 5HP.
Tel: *01222-487369.*

57 Art Group
9 Clwyd Avenue, Prestatyn, LL19 9NG.
Tel: *01745 856565.*

Aberdeen Artists Society
57 Stanley Street, Aberdeen
Tel: *01224-322691.*

An Taisce - The National Trust for Ireland
The Tailor's Hall, Back Lane, Dublin 8.
Tel: *00353-1-454 1786.* **Fax:** *00353-1-453 3255.*

The Antiquities Dealers Association (ADA)
c/o Faustus Ancient Art and Jewellry, 41 Dover Street, London W1X 3RB.
Tel: *0171-930 1864.* **Fax:** *0171-495 2882.*

Art Workers Guild
6 Queen Square, Bloomsbury, London WC1N 3AR.
Tel: *0171-837 3474.*

The Artangel Trust (Artangel)
36 St John's Lane, London EC1M 4BJ.
Tel: *0171-336 6801.* **Fax:** *0171-336 6802.*

Artists Association of Ireland (AAI)
Arthouse, Curved Street, Temple Bar, Dublin 2,
Tel: *00353-1-874 0529.* **Fax:** *00353-1-677 1585.*

Artists' General Benevolent Institution
Burlington House, Piccadilly, London W1V 0DJ.
Tel: *0171-734 1193.* **Fax:** *0171 734 1193.*
Personnel: *Secretary:* Miss April Connett-Dance.
A charity managed by artists to provide financial assistance for members of the profession who are in need, as result of illness, accident or old age. Widows of artists are also eligible to apply. The AGBI depends on voluntary contributions to carry out this work. There is also an Artists' Orphan Fund.

Artists Orphan Fund
Burlington House, Piccaddilly, London W1V 0DJ.
Tel: *0171 734 1193.*
Fax: *0171 734 1193.*

Arts World Wide (AWW)
309a Aberdeen House, 22 Highbury Grove, London N5 2DQ.
Tel: *0171-354 3030.*

Aspex Visual Arts Trust
27 Brougham Road, Southsea, Portsmouth, PO5 4PA.
Tel: *01705-812121.*

Association for Advancement Through Visual Art (ACAVA)
23-29 Faroe Road, London W14 0EL.
Tel: *0171-603 3039.*
Fax: *0171-603 3278.*

Association for Applied Arts (AAA)
6 Darnaway Street, Edinburgh EH3 6BG.
Tel: *0131-220 5070.* **Fax:** *0131-225 5079.*

Association for Business Sponsorship of the Arts (ABSA)
60 Gainsford Street, London SE1 2NY.
Tel: *0171-378 8143.* **Fax:** *0171-407 7527.*

Association of Art Galleries in Wales
Ffotogallery Wales, 31 Charles Street, Cardiff CF1 4EA.
Tel: *01222-341667.* **Fax:** *01222 341672.*

Association of Art Historians
70 Cowcross Street, London EC1M 6EJ.
Tel: *0171-490 3211.* **Fax:** *0171-490 3277.*
Email *admin.aah@btinternet.com*
Ws *http://www.gold.ac.uk/aah*
Personnel: *Administrator:* Andrew Falconer.

Registered Charity No 282579

The Association of Art Historians represents the interests of art and design historians in all aspects of the discipline including art, design, architecture, film, media and photography, cultural studies and conservation.
Members are active in museums and galleries, publishing, teaching, research and environmental work. Among the benefits offered to members are an annual conference, a quarterly journal Art History, a quarterly magazine, The Art Book, a newsletter three times a year called, Bulletin, symposia on a great variety of subjects and periods; professional interest groups with their own programme of activities - universities and colleges, art galleries and museums, freelance, schools and students. Membership is open to art and design historians and to those interested in the advancement of the study of history of art. Special subscription rates to students and the unwaged.

The Association of British Picture Restorers (ABPR)
Station Avenue, Kew, TW9 3QA.
Tel: *0181-948 5644.*
Fax: *0181-948 5644.*

Association of Illustrators (AOI)
1st Floor, 32-38 Saffron Hill, London EC1N 8FH.
Tel: *0171-831 7377.*
Fax: *0171 831 6277.*

Beca Group (BECA)
99 Windsor Road, Penarth, CF6 41JF.
Tel: *01222-703492.*

The Blake Trust
43 Gordon Square, London WC1H 0PD.
Tel: *0171-388 0708.* **Fax:** *0171 388 0854.*

British American Arts Association (BAAA)
116-118 Commercial Street, London E1 6NF.
Tel: *0171-247 5385.* **Fax:** *0171-247 5256.*

British Artists in Glass
The Glass Gallery, St. Erth, Hayle, TR27 6HT.
Tel: *01736 756577.*

British Association of Art Therapists (BAAT)
11a Richmond Road, Brighton, BN2 3RL.
Tel: *0118-926 5407.* **Fax:** *01273-685852.*

British Computer Arts Association
College Manor, Farquhar Road, London SE19 1SS.
Tel: *0181-761 9807.*

British Institute of Professional Photography (BIPP)
Fox Talbot House, Amwell End, Ware, SG12 9HN.
Tel: *01920-464011.* **Fax:** *01920-487056.*

The British Society of Master Glass Painters (BSMGP)
6 Queen Square, London WC1.
Tel: *01943-602521.* **Fax:** *01943-602521.*

The British Sporting Art Trust (BSAT)
BSAT Gallery, 99 High Street, Newmarket, CB8 8JL.
Tel: *01264-710344.* **Fax:** *01264-710114.*
Email *barnart@compuserve.com*
Personnel: *Organising Secretary:* Mrs M. Lawton.
The Trust's objectives are the formation and display of a representative collection of British sporting art, at the Trust's Vestey Galleries of Sporting Art at the National Horseracing Museum, Newmarket, and other galleries and houses open to the public. Also to support and publish research on the subject of sporting art.

CADW: Welsh Historic Monuments
Crown Building, Cathays Park, Cardiff CF1 3NQ.
Tel: *01222-500200.* **Fax:** *01222-826375.*

Charles Rennie Mackintosh Society (CRM Society)
Queen's Cross, 870 Garscube Road, Glasgow G20 7EL.
Tel: *0141-946 6600.* **Fax:** *0141-945 2321.*

The Charleston Trust
Charleston Framhouse, Nr Firle, Lewes, BN8 6LL.
Tel: *01323-811626.* **Fax:** *01323-811628.*

Contemporary Art Society (CAS)
17 Bloomsbury Square, London, WC1A 2LP.
Tel: *0171-831 7311.* **Fax:** *0171-831 7345.*
Email *cas@contempart.org.uk*
Ws *http://www.contempart.org.uk*

Opening times: *By appointment only.*
Nearest Underground: *Holborn.*
Personnel: *Director:* Gill Hedley. *Projects Director:* Cat Newton-Groves. *Collections Curator:* Mary Doyle. *Events/Membership Manager:* Kate Steel. *Registrar:* Brenda Caylor.

Contemporary Art Society

The Contemporary Art Society is a charity. We acquire paintings, sculpture, photographs, video, installation work and applied art and crafts by contemporary artist to give to member museums. We have given over 4,500 works since 1910. Date Established: 1910. Number of full members: 1,400. Membership options: Individual, joint, student, institutional and corporate. Membership fees (In same order): £30.00, £35.00, £22.50, £75.00 and £500. Membership benefits: Trips to art fairs, private views, artist studios and private collections, lectures by leading contemporary artists and critics. Discounts on major events throughout each year. Publications: Contemporary Art Society Newsletter, Quarterly. Other information: For more information on our Corporate Advisory service contact: Cat Newton-Groves.
Services and Facilities:
Art Consultancy. Art for Offices. Commissioning Service. Friends/Society. Guided Tours. Lectures.

The Contemporary Art Society for Wales (CASW)
1 Court Cottages, Michaelston Road, St. Fagans, Cardiff CF5 6EN.
Tel: *01222-595206.*

Council of Museums in Wales (CMW)
The Courtyard, Letty Street, Cathays, Cardiff CF2 4EL.
Tel: *01222-225432.* **Fax:** *01222-668516.*

Council of Regional Arts Associations
Litton Lodge, 13a Clifton Road, Winchester, SO22 5BP.
Tel: *01962-51063.*

Craft Potters Association (CPA) (CPA)
21, Carnaby Street, London W1V 1PH.
Tel: *0171-439 3377.* **Fax:** *0171-287 9954.*
Personnel: *Chairman:* Jack Doherty. *Administrator:* Tony Ainsworth.
The CPA is the only national organization representing potters. It was established in 1958 to promote and sell the work of its members and to create interest in and to educate the public in the craft. The Association owns Contemporary Ceramics a gallery for displaying potters works. Qualification for membership: Fellows and Professional members by selection: Associate membership open to everyone interested in studio ceramics. Number of full members: 150 Fellows, 150 Professional members, 500 Associate members. Membership fees: Fellow £101, Professional member £64.75, Associate £20.75. Membership benefits: Fellow; full exhibiting rights and entry in 'Potters'. Professional member; limited exhibition rights and entry in 'Potters'. Associate member: CPA News, discounts at Contemporary Ceramics and invitations to lectures and events. Members show dates: Bi-monthly exhibitions in Contemporary Ceramics, 7 Marshall Street, London. Open shows: 'Earth and Fire' Rufford, Ollerton, Notts. - Late June each year. Publications: Ceramic Review (bimonthly), CPA News (bimonthly) Potters (biannually) and technical books e.g. Clays and Glazes. We welcome applications from potters, teachers, students and ceramics enthusiasts from all parts of the UK.
Services and Facilities:
Bookshop. Craftshop. Lectures.

Crafts Council of Ireland
Powerscourt Townhouse Centre, South William Street, Dublin 2.
Tel: *00353-1-679 7368.* **Fax:** *00353-1-679 9197.*

The Crafts Council
44a, Pentonville Road, Islington, London N1 9BY.
Tel: *0171-278 7700.* **Fax:** *0171-837 6891.*

The Decorative Arts Society (DAS)
47 Combe Crescent, Bury, Pulborough, RH20 1PE.
Tel: *01798-831734.*

The Design and Artists Copyright Society Ltd
Parchment House, 13 Northburgh Street, London EC1V 0JP.
Tel: *0171-336 8811.* **Fax:** *0171-336 8822.*
Email *info@dacs.co.uk*
Ws *http://www.dacs.co.uk*
Opening times: *Office hours 10-6.*
Nearest Underground: *Barbican.*
Personnel: *Chief Executive:* Rachel Duffield.

DACS is the copyright and collecting society for the visual arts in the UK. A non-profit organisation formed by artists for artists in 1983 to administer and protect the rights of all visual creators, the Society represents over 40,000 artists of all disciplines from all over the world in matters of copyright in the UK. The Society also actively pursues infringement of members' work on their behalf.

The Design Council
Haymarket House, 1, Oxendon Street, London SW1Y 4EE.
Tel: *0171-208 2121.* **Fax:** *0171 839 6033.*

English Heritage
429 Oxford Street London W1R 2HD.

Fine Art Trade Guild
16-18 Empress Place, London SW6 1TT.
Tel: *0171-381 6616.* **Fax:** *0171-381 2596.*

The Georgian Group
6 Fitzroy Square, London W1P 6DX.
Tel: *0171-387 1720.* **Fax:** *0171-387 1721.*

Government Art Collection
c/o Dept for Culture, Media and Sport, 2-4 Cockspur Street, London SW1Y 5DH.
Tel: *0171-211 6200.*

Guild of Aviation Artists (GAvA)
DFC, Bondway Business Centre, 71 Bondway, Vauxhall Cross, London SW8 1SQ.
Tel: *0171-735 0634.* **Fax:** *0171-735 0634.*

The Guild of Glass Engravers
19, Wildwood Road, London NW11 6UL.
Tel: *0181-731 9352.*

The Guild of Railway Artists (GRA)
45 Dickins Road, Warwick, CV34 5NS.
Tel: *01926-499246.*

GWELED
Pen Roc, Rhodfa'r Môr, Aberystwyth, SY23 3DE.
Tel: *01970-623690.* **Fax:** *01970-612245.*

The Henry Moore Foundation
Dane Tree House, Perry Green, Much Hadham, SG10 6EE.
Tel: *01279-843333.* **Fax:** *01279-843647.*

Hesketh Hubbard Art Society
Mall Galleries, 17 Carlton House Terrace, London SW1Y 5BD.
Tel: *0171-930 6844.* **Fax:** *0171-839 7830.*
Personnel: *President:* Simon Whittle.
The HH is a flourishing drawing society founded in 1930 by the RBA. The society meets weekly throughout the year to draw from life models. Members include professional and amateur artists. Although not tutored, participants learn from the company of fellow artists.
Services and Facilities:
Art Consultancy. Commissioning Service. Friends/Society. Gallery space for hire. Workshop Facilities.

The Hilliard Society of Miniature Artists
15 Union Street, Wells, BA5 2PU.
Tel: *01749-674472.*
Fax: *01749 672918.*

The Institute of International Visual Arts (in IVA)
Kirkham House, 12/14 Whitfield Street, London W1P 5RD.
Tel: *0171-636 1930.*
Fax: *0171-636 1931.*

The International Association of Art, British National Committee (IAANBC)
49 Stainton Road, Sheffield S11 7AX.
Tel: *0114-266 9889.* **Fax:** *0114-266 9298.*

International Association of Art Critics
91 Eton Hall, Eton College Road, London NW3 2DH.

Irish Association of Art Historians (IAAH)
c/o National Gallery of Ireland, Merrion Square, Dublin 2,
Tel: *00353-1-661 5133.* **Fax:** *00353-1-661 5372.*

Irish Georgian Society
74 Merrion Square, Dublin 2,
Tel: *00353-1-676 7053.* **Fax:** *00353-1-662 0290.*

Irish Museums Association (IMA)
c/o 59 Lambard Street West, Dublin 8.
Tel: *00353-1-454 1947.*

Irish Watercolour Society (IWCS)
68 Crannagh Road, Rathfarnham, Dublin 14.
Tel: *00353-1-490 4248.*

Live Art Press (LAP)
49 Stainton Road, Sheffield S11 7AX.
Tel: *0114-266 9889.* **Fax:** *0114-266 9298.*

The London Group
PO Box 447, London SE22 9LL.

Manchester Academy of Fine Arts (MAFA)
4 Delph Greaves, Delph, Oldham OL3 5TY.
Tel: *01457-875718.*
Fax: *01422-370256.*
Personnel: *President:* Ian Thompson NDD DA ATC ARBS FRSA. *Vice President:* Glenys Latham Dip AD CIE. *Hon. Secretary:* Cliff Moorhouse TD. *Hon. Treasurer:* Philip Livesey FCA.
The Academy is a society of artists which seeks to promote the Fine Arts in general and the work of its members in particular; initiating exhibition and commission opportunities whilst maintaining its long historical association with the City Art Gallery. It actively encourages membership applications from committed artists, especially from the North West and aims to attract work of the highest quality from non-members into its Annual Open Exhibition.
Services and Facilities:
Friends/Society. Guided Tours. Lectures.

The Masters Photographers Association (MPA)
Hallmark House, 2 Beaumont Street, Darlington, DL1 5SZ.
Tel: *01325-356555.*
Fax: *01325-357813.*

The Museums and Galleries Commission (MGC)
16 Queen Anne's Gate, London SW1H 9AA.
Tel: *0171-233 4200.*
Fax: *0171-233 3686.*

Museums Association
42 Clerkenwell Close, London EC1R 0PA.
Tel: *0171-250 1834.* **Fax:** *0171-250 1929.*

National Acrylic Painters' Association
134 Rake Lane, Wallasey, L45 1JW.
Tel: *0151-639 2980.* **Fax:** *0151-639 2980.*
Email *katy@artarena.force9.co.uk*
Ws *http://www.artarena.force9.co.uk/napa; America http://www.watercolor-online.com/NAPA/*
Opening times: *24 hours a day, as it is on the internet.*
Personnel: *President of Association:* Alwyn Crawshaw. *Vice-President of Association:* Professor Arthur Hughes. *Director General and Founder of Association:* Kenneth J. Hodgson.
The National Acrylic Painters' Association (NAPA), founded in 1985, was evolved from the concept that acrylic paint is still largely unrecognised. The association intends to be a vehicle for collective exhibitions, which aim to promote the excellence and innovation of the medium. Since its inaugural exhibition in December 1985, there have been fourteen shows, and since 1997 the annual exhibition has been open to non-members.
Membership consists of two categories, Full and Associate, and includes not only British members, but also members from America (with its own Division), Brazil, Canada, France, Malta, Portugal, and Spain.
The Associations Patrons: The Master of the Fine Arts Trade Guild, Adrian Henri, Professor Brendan Neiland R.A., Dr. Sally A. Bulgin, Kay Greenwood-Casey.
Services and Facilities:
Bookshop. Friends/Society.
Work Stocked and Sold:
Dr. Pa.
Price range: £200 - £3,500.

National Art Collections Fund (NACF)
Millais House, 7 Cromwell Place, London SW7 2JN.
Tel: *0171-225 4800.* **Fax:** *0171-225 4848.*

National Artists Association (NAA)
Spitalfields, 21 Steward Street, London E1 6AJ.
Tel: *0171-426 0911.* **Fax:** *0171-426 0282.*

National Association for Fine Art Education
University of the West of England, Faculty of Art, Media and Design, Clanage Road, Bower Ashton, Bristol BS3 2JU.
Tel: *01179-660222.* **Fax:** *01179-763946.*

The National Association of Decorative and Fine Arts Societies (NADFAS)
All enquiries to the Administrator, NADFAS, 8 Guilford Street, London WC1N 1DT.
Tel: *0171-430 0730.* **Fax:** *0171-242 0686.*
Email *admin@nadfas.org.uk*
Personnel: *Patron:* HRH The Duchess of Gloucester, GCVO. *President:* Mr Timothy Clifford. *Administrator:* Lindley Maitland.
NADFAS is an organisation of 308 societies dedicated to the enjoyment and care of the visual arts. It arose to satisfy a need to increase the awareness of the history of art and the enjoyment which this provides. It gives active help with the problems facing museums, country houses and historic churches. Many members are trained to do straightforward tasks, such as cleaning old books, mending fabrics, cataloguing and learning to guide. Instruction is provided by museum experts and help is given by the staff of the Victoria & Albert Museum and other museums throughout the country. Young NADFAS exists to encourage those aged between 8 & 18.

National Association of Memorial Masons (NAMM)
27a Albert Street, Rugby, CV21 2SG.
Tel: *01788-542264.* **Fax:** *01788-542276.*

National Campaign for the Arts (NCA)
Francis House, Francis Street, London SW1P 1DE. **Tel:** *0171-828 4448.*

National Portraiture Association
59/60 Fitzjames Avenue, London W14 0RR.
Tel: *0171-602 0892.* **Fax:** *0171 602 0892.*

The National Society for Education in Art and Design (NSEAD)
The Gatehouse, Corsham Court, Corsham, SN13 0BZ.
Tel: *01249-714825.* **Fax:** *01249-716138.*

National Society of Painters, Sculptors and Printmakers (National Society)
122 Copse Hill, Wimbledon, London SW20 0NL. **Tel:** *0181-946 7878.*

The National Trust for Places of Historic Interest or Natural Beauty (National Trust)
36 Queen Anne's Gate, London SW1H 9AS.
Tel: *0171-222 9251.* **Fax:** *0171-222 5097.*

National Trust for Scotland (NTS)
5 Charlotte Square, Edinburgh EH2 4DU.
Tel: *0131-226 5922.* **Fax:** *0131-243 9501.*

New English Art Club
F. B. A., Mall Galleries, 17 Carlton House Terrace, London SW1Y 5BD.
Tel: *0171-930 6844.* **Fax:** *0171-839 7830.*
Personnel: *Hon. Secretary:* William Bowyer RA, RP, NEAC. *Keeper:* Charlotte Halliday NEAC.
The NEAC was formed in 1886. Its members then and now have been concerned with the fresh handling of paint and the direct observation of nature. The NEAC holds exhibitions at various galleries throughout the year, but their major annual open exhibition is at the Mall Galleries in November.
Services and Facilities:
Art Consultancy. Commissioning Service. Friends/Society. Gallery space for hire. Guided Tours. Lectures. Workshop Facilities.

Northern Ireland Museums Council (NIMC)
185 Stranmillis Road, Belfast, BT9 5DU.
Tel: *01232-661023.* **Fax:** *01232-683513.*

Oriental Ceramic Society (OCS)
30b Torrington Square, London WC1E 7JL.
Tel: *0171-636 7985.* **Fax:** *0171-580 6749.*

The Outsider Gallery
213 South Lambeth Road, London SW8 1XR.
Tel: *0171-735 2192.* **Fax:** *0171-820 9313.*

Paintings in Hospitals Sheridan Russell Gallery
16 Crawford Street, London W1H 1PF.
Tel: *0171-935 0250.* **Fax:** *0171-935 1701.*

Paisley Museum & Art Gallery (PAI)
High Street, Paisley PA1 2BA.
Tel: *0141-889 3151.* **Fax:** *0141-889 9240.*
Email *RKelsey@compuserve.com*
Opening times: *Tues-Sat 10-5.*
Nearest Station: *Paisley Gilmour St (Rail).*
Personnel: *President:* Joe Hargan PAI. *Vice President:* Dr. George Addis. *Secretary & Honorary Treasurer:* Margaret Duff. *Honorary Collector:* Ruth Donald.

To promote the best in Scottish painting, drawing and sculpture. The PAI also promotes an enjoyment of the arts in general through visits to private collections of paintings, and by holding musical recitals in their galleries. Date Established: 1876. Number of full members: 170. Other members: 150 Lay members. Qualifications for membership: Artist members are elected by a committee of management. Lay membership is open. Membership fees: £12 per year.
Membership benefits: Access to the annual exhibition, lectures, visits, musical evenings etc. Members' show dates 1999: 7th May to 5th June. Open show dates: PAI Scottish Drawing Competition Spring 2,000.
Publications: PAI Newsletter (Quarterly).
Other information: We have established the PAI Scottish Open Drawing Competition with major prizes. Distinguished member artists include Mary Armour RSA, RSW, RGI, PAI, LLD; W. M. Birnie RSW, PAI; Robert Kelsey DA, PAI, John Kingsley.
Services and Facilities:
Lectures. Museum Shop. Parking. Workshop Facilities.

Pastel Society (PS)
Mall Galleries, 17 Carlton House Terrace, London SW1Y 5BD.
Tel: *0171-930 6844.* **Fax:** *0171-839 7830.*
Personnel: *President:* Tom Coates PPRBA RP RWS NEAC. *Vice President:* Moira Huntly RI RWA RSMA.
To promote the versatility and vibrancy of the pastel medium by exhibiting the best contemporary work, both conventional and adventurous, thereby continuing the outlook of the Society's original exhibitions, such as Degas, Rodin, Sickert and Whistler. Annual exhibition in Spring. Many prizes are on offer for submitting artists.
Services and Facilities:
Art Consultancy. Commissioning Service. Friends/Society. Gallery space for hire. Guided Tours. Lectures. Workshop Facilities.

Patrons of British Art
Development Office, Tate Gallery, Millbank, London SW1P 4RG.
Tel: *0171-887 8743.* **Fax:** *0171 887 8755.*

Patrons of New Art
Development Office, Tate Gallery, Millbank, London SW1P 4RG.
Tel: *0171-887 8743.* **Fax:** *0171 887 8755.*

The Printmakers Council
Clerkenwell Workshop, 31, Clerkenwell Close, London EC1R 0AT.
Tel: *0171-250 1927.*

Public Art Forum (PAF)
Halfpenny Wharf, Torrington Street, East-the-Water, Bideford, EX39 4DP.
Tel: *01237-470440.* **Fax:** *01237-470440.*

Public Monuments and Sculpture Association (PMSA)
c/o Conway Library, Courtauld Institute, Somerset House, Strand, London WC2R 0RN.
Tel: *0171-485 0566 or 0171-873 2614/2406.*
Fax: *0171-267 1742 or 0171-873 2406.*

Royal Academy of Arts (RA)
Burlington House, Piccadilly, London W1V 0DS.
Tel: *0171-300 8000.* **Fax:** *0171-300 8001.*
Ws *http://www.RoyalAcademy.org.uk*
Opening times: *Mon-Sun 10-6.*
Nearest Underground: *Green Park & Piccadilly.*
Personnel: *Press & Promotions Officer:* Katharine Jones.
Founded in 1768, The Royal Academy is the oldest arts institution in the UK, governed by its artist members.
Its exhibition programme includes the annual Summer Exhibition of work by living artists and internationally acclaimed travelling exhibitions.
Services and Facilities:
Bookshop. Café. Disabled Access. Framing. Friends/Society. Guided Tours. Lectures. Museum Shop. Restaurant. Shop.

Royal Birmingham Society of Artists
69a New Street, Birmingham B2 4DU.
Tel: *0121-643 3768.* **Fax:** *0121-644 5298.*

Royal Cambrian Academy of Art (RCA)
Crown Lane, Conwy, LL32 8BH.
Tel: *01492-593413.*

Royal Commission on the Ancient and Historical Monuments of Wales (RCAHMW)
Crown Building, Plas Crug, Aberystwyth, SY23 1NJ.
Tel: *01970-621227.*
Fax: *01970-627701.*

Royal Commission on the Ancient and Historical Monuments of Scotland (RCAHMS)
John Sinclair House, 16 Bernard Terrace, Edinburgh EH8 9NX.
Tel: *0131-662 1456.* **Fax:** *0131-662 1477.*

Royal Commission on the Historical Monuments of England/National Monuments Record (RCHME/NMRC)
Kemble Drive, Swindon SN2 2GZ.
Tel: *01793-414600.* **Fax:** *01793-414606.*

Royal Dublin Society
Ballsbridge, Dublin 4,
Tel: *00353-1-668 0866.* **Fax:** *00353-1-660 4014.*

Royal Fine Art Commission (RFAC)
7 St James' Square, London SW1Y 4JU.
Tel: *0171-839 6537.* **Fax:** *0171-839 8475.*

The Royal Fine Art Commission for Scotland
9 Atholl Crescent, Edinburgh EH3 8HA.
Tel: *0131-229 1109.* **Fax:** *0131-229 6031.*

Royal Glasgow Institute of the Fine Arts (RGI)
5 Oswald Street, Glasgow G1 4QR.
Tel: *0141-248 7411.* **Fax:** *0141-221 0417.*

Royal Hibernian Academy R.H.A.
15 Ely Place, Dublin 2,
Tel: *00353-1-676 6212.* **Fax:** *00353-1-676 6212.*

Royal Institute of British Architects (RIBA)
66 Portland Place, London W1N 4AD.
Tel: *0171-636 4389.* **Fax:** *0171-637 5775.*

Royal Institute of Oil Painters
Mall Galleries, 17 Carlton House Terrace, London SW1Y 5BD.
Tel: *0171-930 6844.* **Fax:** *0171-839 7830.*
Personnel: *President:* Dr Richard Baines.
Founded in 1882 the ROI is the only National Art Society devoted exclusively to oil painting. Its annual exhibitions aim to show a cross section of the highest standard of work in that medium currently being produced. The annual open exhibition is held at the Mall Galleries in December.
Services and Facilities:
Art Consultancy. Commissioning Service. Friends/Society. Gallery space for hire. Guided Tours. Lectures. Workshop Facilities.

Royal Institute of Painters in Water Colours
Mall Galleries, 17 Carlton House Terrace, London SW1Y 5BD.
Tel: *0171-930 6844.* **Fax:** *0171-839 7830.*
Personnel: *President:* Ronald Maddox PRI Hon. RWS.
Founded in 1831, the RI is a major society representing British watercolour painting, holding an annual exhibition of work by members and non-members. Its aims are to promote the best in modern and traditional

uses of the medium. The annual open exhibition is held at the Mall Galleries in March/April and includes over 500 works. Many artists' awards are on offer, including the Winsor and Newton Awards for Young Artists.
Services and Facilities:
Art Consultancy. Commissioning Service. Friends/Society. Gallery space for hire. Guided Tours. Lectures. Workshop Facilities.

The Royal Photographic Society (RPS)
Octagon Galleries, Milsom Street, Bath, BA1 1DN.
Tel: *01225-462841.* **Fax:** *01225-448688.*
Email *info@rps.org*
Ws *http://www.rps.org*
Opening times: *Daily 9.30-5.30. Admission: Adults £2.50, Concessions £1.75*
Nearest Station: *Bath.*
Personnel: *Secretary General:* Barry Lane. *Curator:* Pam Roberts. *Exhibitions Officer:* Carole Sartain. *Membership Officer:* Sara Beaugeard.
Four constantly changing photographic exhibitions, holography display and museum of photography. Membership and photography workshops and lectures.
We welcome everyone with a real interest in photography - and that includes newcomers to photography, teachers, historians and scientists as well as dedicated amateurs and full time professionals. Date Established: 1853. Number of full members: 10,000. Qualifications for membership: None. Membership options: Student, overseas, family, disabled. Membership fees: Ordinary UK £77 pa, Student £28. Membership benefits: Internationally recognised Distinctions - Fellowship, Associateship and Licentiateship. Private views, free access to Octagon Galleries, darkroom for hire. Special discounts. Members' shows: See programme. Open show dates: See current Octagon Galleries Programme. Publications: The Photographic Journal - 10/12, The Imaging Science Journal - 6/12.
Services and Facilities:
Bookshop. Disabled Access. Friends/Society. Gallery space for hire. Lectures. Museum Shop. Restaurant. Shop. Workshop Facilities.

The Royal Scottish Academy (RSA)
The Mound, Edinburgh EH2 2EL.
Tel: *0131-225 6671.* **Fax:** *0131-225 2349.*
Opening times: *During exhibitions 10-5, Sun 2-5, Office 9-4.30.*
Nearest Station: *Waverley.*
Personnel: *President:* Dr Ian McKenzie-Smith RSA. *Secretary:* William Scott RSA. *Admin. Secretary:* Bruce Laidlaw. *Treasurer:* Izi Metzstein.

The Royal Scottish Academy

For the past 172 years, Scotland's foremost body of artists, The Royal Scottish Academy, has promoted the work of Scotland's leading contemporary painters, sculptors, printmakers and architects. It also gives practical and financial assistance to the young talent emerging in these disciplines from Scotland's Colleges of Art and Schools of Architecture through its unique Students' Exhibition held annually in March.

Royal Scottish Society of Painters in Water Colours (RSW)
29 Waterloo Street, Glasgow G2 6BZ.
Tel: *0141-226 3838.* **Fax:** *0141-221 1397.*

Royal Society of British Artists
Mall Galleries, 17 Carlton House Terrace, London SW1Y 5BD.
Tel: *0171-930 6844.* **Fax:** *0171-839 7830.*
Founded in 1823 the society boasts many celebrated past members including Whistler, Brangwyn and Sickert. The annual open exhibition at the Mall Galleries in September includes a diverse selection of painting and sculpture. Many prizes are awarded through the exhibition, including the De Laszlo medal.
Services and Facilities:
Art Consultancy. Commissioning Service. Friends/Society. Gallery space for hire. Guided Tours. Lectures. Workshop Facilities.

The Royal Society of British Sculptors
108 Old Brompton Road, South Kensington, London SW7 3RA.
Tel: *0171-373 5554.* **Fax:** *0171-373 9202.*

Royal Society of Marine Artists
Mall Galleries, 17 Carlton House Terrace, London SW1Y 5BD.
Tel: *0171-930 6844.* **Fax:** *0171-839 7830.*
Personnel: *President:* Bert Wright.
The RSMA was formed in 1939. The subject matter is broadly marine in character. Membership is in two categories: artist members and lay members who support the society through their appreciation. The society's Fine Diploma collection is housed in the Ferens Gallery in Hull. The annual open exhibition is held at the Mall Galleries in October.
Services and Facilities:
Art Consultancy. Commissioning Service. Friends/Society. Gallery space for hire. Guided Tours. Lectures. Workshop Facilities.

Royal Society of Miniature Painters, Sculptors and Engravers (RMS)
1 Knapp Cottages, Wyke, Gillingham, SP8 4NQ.
Tel: *01747-825718.* **Fax:** *01747-825718.*

Royal Society of Painter-Printmakers
Bankside Gallery, 48 Hopton Street, London SE1 9JH.
Tel: *0171-928 7521.* **Fax:** *0171 928 2820.*
Email *RE&RWS@bankside-gallery.demon.co.uk*
Opening times: *Tues 10-8, Wed-Fri 10-5, Sat & Sun 1-5. Closed Monday.*
Nearest Underground: *Blackfriars, Southwark is scheduled to open May 1999.*
Personnel: *Director:* Judy Dixey.
The Royal Society of Painter-Printmakers (RE) was founded in 1880 to seek recognition that an artist's prints are original artworks. Now numbering 150 Members, the RE aims to be international both in membership and scope. To this end the RE acknowledges advances in technology which open new opportunities for printmaking, and organises exchange exhibitions with outstanding printmakers world-wide. The RE has one annual exhibition of Members work in its home at Bankside Gallery, London, and shows regularly in the UK and abroad. 1999 sees a retrospective of the Society in the form of a showing of its Diploma Collection at the Ashmolean, Oxford.
Services and Facilities:
Art for Offices. Commissioning Service. Friends/Society. Lectures.

Royal Society of Portrait Painters
Mall Galleries, 17 Carlton House Terrace, London SW1Y 5BD.
Tel: *0171-930 6844.* **Fax:** *0171-839 7830.*
Personnel: *President:* Daphne Todd. *Commissions Consultant:* Katy Letman.
Formed in April 1891 and achieving the Royal Patronage in 1911 the RP aims to ensure the continuance of portraiture in this country. Distinguished artists from abroad have traditionally joined the best of British artists at the Society's annual exhibition at the Mall Galleries in May, awards include the £5,000 Ondaatje prize and RP gold medal, The Carroll Foundation Award for Young Portrait Painters and The Philip Solomon Award for Portrait Drawing.
Services and Facilities:
Art Consultancy. Commissioning Service. Friends/Society. Gallery space for hire. Guided Tours. Lectures.

Royal Watercolour Society
Bankside Gallery, 48 Hopton Street, London SE1 9JH.
Tel: *0171-928 7521.* **Fax:** *0171 928 2820.*
Email *RE&RWS@bankside-gallery.demon.co.uk*
Opening times: *Tues 10-8, Wed-Fri 10-5, Sat & Sun 1-5. Closed Monday.*
Nearest Underground: *Blackfriars, Southwark which is scheduled to open May 1999.*
Personnel: *Director:* Judy Dixey.
The Royal Watercolour Society was founded in 1804 to act as an advocate for watercolour artists and for the practice of watercolour itself. With a current Membership of eighty artists, the RWS elects new members annually and organises two major shows and one Open painting competition a year in its home at Bankside Gallery, London. The RWS welcomes both traditional and experimental approaches to the use of water-based paint on paper.
Services and Facilities:
Art for Offices. Commissioning Service. Friends/Society. Lectures.

Royal West of England Academy
Queen's Road, Clifton, Bristol BS8 1PX.
Tel: *0117-973 5129.* **Fax:** *0117-923 7874.*

RSA
The Royal Society for the Encouragement of Arts, Manufactures and Commerce, 8 John Adam Street, London WC2N 6EZ.
Tel: *0171-930 5115.* **Fax:** *0171-839 5805.*

Ruskin Society of London
351 Woodstock Road, Oxford, OX2 7NX.
Tel: *01865 310987 / 515962.*

S.A.A.C.
169/6 Great Junction Street, Edinburgh EH6 5LG
Tel: *0131-554 3365.*

Scottish Artists' Benevolent Association (SABA)
Second Floor, 5 Oswald Street, Glasgow G1 4QR.
Tel: *0141-248 7411.* **Fax:** *0141-221 0417.*

Scottish Glass Society (SGS)
32 Farington Street, Dundee DD2 1PF.
Tel: *01382-669864.*

Scottish Museums Council (SMC)
County House, 20-22 Torphichen Street, Edinburgh EH3 8JB.
Tel: *0131-229 7465.* **Fax:** *0131-229 2728.*

Scottish Potters Association (SPA)
77 Spottiswood Gardens, St. Andrews, KY16 8SB.
Tel: *01334-472303.* **Fax:** *01334-472303.*

Scottish Sculpture Trust (SST)
6 Darnaway Street, Edinburgh EH3 6BG.
Tel: *0131-220 4788.* **Fax:** *0131-220 4787.*
Email *trust@sstq.demon.co.uk*
Ws *http://www.sstq.demon.co.uk*
Personnel: *Director:* Andrew Guest.

A charitable body committed to the promotion of contemporary sculpture in Scotland, founded in 1978.
The Trust's aims are to make new opportunities for the creation and appreciation of contemporary sculpture (of the broadest definition) in Scotland. It campaigns for new space for sculpture by facilitating closer relationships between sculptors and those who make, maintain, fund and use public places. It runs a sculpture database covering both individuals and organisations in Scotland and Britain, practitioners and patrons. It stimulates communication about sculpture through publications, meetings and debates, and advises architects and artists on sculpture projects and commissions.
Services and Facilities:
Art Consultancy. Commissioning Service. Lectures.

Scottish Society for Art History
Talbot Rice Gallery, University of Edinburgh, Old College, South Bridge, Edinburgh EH8 9YL.
Tel: *0131-650 2211.*
Fax: *0131 650 2213.*

The Sculptors' Society of Ireland
119 Capel Street, Dublin 2,
Tel: *00353-1-872 2296/2364.* **Fax:** *00353-1-872 2364.*

The Sculpture Company
108 Old Brompton Road, South Kensington, London SW7 3RA.
Tel: *0171-373 8615/244 8431.* **Fax:** *0171-370 3721.*

Society of Botanical Artists (SBA)
1 Knapp Cottages, Wyke, Gillingham, SP8 4NQ.
Tel: *01747-825718.* **Fax:** *01747-825718.*

Society of Catholic Artists (SCA)
c/o 19 Cranford Close, West Wimbledon, London SW20 0DP.
Tel: *0181-947 6476.*

Society of Equestrian Artists (SEA)
63 Gordon Close, Knowle Green, Staines, TW18 1AP
Tel: *01784-889669*
Personnel: *Secretary:* John Collins. *Chairman:* Philip Gibson OBE.
To encourage the study of equine art and by mutual assistance between members promote excellence in its practice.
Services and Facilities:
Friends/Society. Workshop Facilities.

Society of Graphic Fine Art
15 Willow Way, Hatfield, AL10 9QD.
Tel: *01707-880615.*
Personnel: *President:* Jean Canter. *Vice President:* Michael Taylor. *Vice President/Publicity:* Geraldine Jones. *Hon. Treasurer:* David Brooke. *Secretary:* Mrs Sharon Curtis.
The Society of Graphic Fine Art, founded in 1919, is a professional society that exists to promote good drawing skills. Members are selected solely on their quality of work, and membership is open to any artist working in any drawing medium or any form of original printmaking. Oil painting or 'pure' watercolours are inadmissible. The society holds an annual open exhibition in central London and has been increasing its out-of-town exhibitions. Members receive a newsletter and occasional visits and painting weekends are arranged.

The Society of London Art Dealers (SLAD)
91 Jermyn Street, London SW1Y 6JB.
Tel: *0171-930 6137.* **Fax:** *0171-321 0685.*

Society of Scottish Artists (SSA)
11a, Leslie Place, Edinburgh EH4 1NF.
Tel: *0131-332 2041.*

Society of Scottish Artists and Artists Craftsmen (SAAC)
10 Wellington Street, Edinburgh EH7 5ED.
Tel: *0131-556 0244.* **Fax:** *0131-556 0244.*

Society of Wildlife Artists
Mall Galleries, 17 Carlton House Terrace, London SW1Y 5BD.
Tel: *0171-930 6844.* **Fax:** *0171-839 7830.*
Personnel: *President:* Mr Bruce Pearson.
The SWLA was formed in 1964 to foster all forms of visual art based on or representing the world's wildlife. Through art the society actively seeks to advance the interest, education, and concerns of the public in the conservation of wildlife. The annual open exhibition is held at the Mall Galleries in July. Many artists awards are on offer.
Services and Facilities:
Art Consultancy. Commissioning Service. Friends/Society. Gallery space for hire. Guided Tours. Lectures. Workshop Facilities.

Society of Women Artists (SWA)
1 Knapp Cottages, Wyke, Gillingham, SP8 4NQ.
Tel: *01747-825718.* **Fax:** *01747-826835.*
Ws *http://www.mcis.net.uk/swa*
Opening times: *10-7 excluding Sundays.*
Nearest Station: *St. James Park or Victoria.*
Personnel: *President:* Barbara Tate. *Vice Presidents:* Joyce Wyatt, Muriel Owen, Susan Millis, Joyce Rogerson. *Admin, Sec:* Pamela Henderson.

Founded in the mid-nineteenth century, the SWA Annual Open Exhibition is held in March each year at the Westminster Central Hall, Storey's Gate, London SW1, (admission free). Aim is to exhibit the best of women artists work and features approximately 700 new works by many leading artists in a range of media, including oils, pastels, etchings, miniatures, sculptures and showcase pieces. Membership is by election only but non-members may enter work. To apply for submission forms write to above address. Archives are held by V&A Museum's Archive of Art and Design, Blythe House, 23 Blythe Road, London W14 0QF. Web address: http://www.nal.vam..ac.uk/.
Services and Facilities:
Café. Commissioning Service. Disabled Access. Friends/Society. Guided Tours. Lectures. Restaurant. Workshop Facilities.
Work Stocked and Sold:
Pa. Sc.

Society of Wood Engravers (SWE)
North Lodge, Hamstead Marshall, Newbury, RG20 0JD.
Tel: *01635-524255.* **Fax:** *01635-524255.*

The Textile Society
Macclesfield Museum, Roe Street, Macclesfield, SK11 6UT.
Tel: *01625-613210.* **Fax:** *01625-617880.*

The Turner Society
BCM Box Turner, London WC1N 3XX.

United Society of Artists (UA)
207 Sunny Bank Road, Potters Bar, EN6 2NJ.
Tel: *01707-851439.* **Fax:** *01707-646613.*

Visiting Arts
11 Portland Place, London W1N 4EJ.
Tel: *0171-389 3019.* **Fax:** *0171-389 3016.*

Visual Arts and Galleries Association (VAGA)
The Old Village School, The High Street, Witcham, Ely, CB6 2LQ.
Tel: *01353-776356.* **Fax:** *01353-776356.*
Email *106341.327@compuserve.com*
Personnel: *Director:* Hilary Gresty. *Chair:* Stephen Foster.
The national association working for the public exhibition, presentation and development of the visual arts.
The Association (membership 350 organisations and individuals) works primarily as an advocacy body on behalf of museums and galleries throughout the UK. Activities include regular briefings (eg free entry to museums and galleries; lobbying MPs etc), seminars (eg contemporary collecting policy; NESTA etc). Bi-monthly newsletter.
Services and Facilities:
Art Consultancy.

Voluntary Arts Network
P.O. Box 200, Cardiff CF5 1YH.
Tel: *01222-395395.* **Fax:** *01222-397397.*

Water Colour Society of Wales (Cymdeithas Dyfrlliw Cymru)
4 Castle Road, Raglan, NP5 2JZ.
Tel: *01291-690260.*
Personnel: *Secretary:* Margaret Butler.
The Watercolour Society of Wales was established in 1959.
Contemporary developments in art and in paint technology have extended interpretation of the medium to include a wider range of essentially water-based media and techniques.
Recent exhibitions have clearly expressed this affinity with the contemporary scene, through an increasing diversity in scale and character of the works on show.
The Society exhibits in prestigious galleries throughout the year. The 1999 programme is March-April, Conway (Royal Cambrian); July-August, Penarth (Turner House); December-January 2000, Newport Museum and Gallery.

The Welsh Group
28 Rowan Way, Lisvane, Cardiff CF4 5TB.
Tel: *01222-756653.*
Fax: *01222 756653.*

NOTES

ARTS BOARDS

Arts boards.
Arts councils.

THE ART WORLD
DIRECTORY

Arts Councils

Arts Council of England
14 Great Peter Street, London SW1P 3NQ.
Tel: *0171-333 0100.* **Fax:** *0171-973 6590.*
Email *enquiries@artscouncil.org.uk*
Ws *http://www.artscouncil.org.uk*
Nearest Underground: *St. James' Park, Westminster.*
The Arts Council of England is the national funding body for the arts in England. It is responsible for developing, sustaining and promoting the arts through the distribution of public money from central government and revenue generated by the National Lottery. The Arts Council exists to help people enjoy the arts by supporting drama, music, dance and touring companies, contemporary art galleries and exhibitions, film and literature projects. National galleries and museums are directly funded by the Government. The Arts Council is fully independent, non-political body operating at arm's length from Government. Originally founded in 1946 as the Arts Council of Great Britain, autonomous arts councils for England, Scotland and Wales were set up in 1994.

Arts Council of Northern Ireland
MacNeice House, 77 Malone Road, Belfast, BT9 6AQ.
Tel: *01232-385200.* **Fax:** *01232 -661715.*
Opening times: *Mon-Thurs 9-5.30, Fri 9-5.*
Personnel: *Director of Creative Arts:* Noirin McKinney. *Public Affairs:* Damian Smyth.

ARTS COUNCIL of Northern Ireland

'The Mission of the Arts Council of Northern Ireland is to develop the arts in Northern Ireland so that as many people as possible can enjoy as many forms of art as possible to as high a standard as possible.'
The Arts Council of Northern Ireland is the prime distributor of public support for the arts. It was established in 1962 as a successor to the Committee for the Encouragement of Music and the Arts (CEMA) which had operated since 1942. The Arts Council (Northern Ireland) Order 1995 set up the Arts Council as a statutory body. In addition to providing funding for the arts, its principal functions are:- to develop and improve the knowledge, appreciation and practice of the arts; to increase public access to and participation in the arts; to advise the Department of Education and other government departments, district councils and other bodies, on matter relating to the arts; to develop and improve the knowledge, appreciation and practice of the arts; to increase the Department of Education and other government departments, district councils and other bodies, on matters relating to the arts.
Key Publication: To The Millennium: A Strategy for the Arts in Northern Ireland (1995).

Arts Council of Wales
Museum Place, Cardiff CF1 3NX.
Tel: *01222-376500.* **Fax:** *01222-221447.*
Email *information@ccc-acw.org.uk*
Ws *http://www.ccc-acw.org.uk*
Opening times: *Mon-Fri 9-5.15*
Nearest Station: *Cardiff Central.*
Personnel: *Senior Visual Arts & Craft Officer, Artform Development Division:* Peter Davies.
The Arts Council of Wales (ACW) is the national organisation with specific responsibility for the funding and development of the arts in Wales, including the visual arts and the crafts. It receives grants from central and local government of which the largest is from the Welsh Office. It is also the distributor of funds for the arts in Wales generated by the National Lottery. From these resources, ACW makes grants to support art activities and facilities. Some of this funding is allocated in the form of annual revenue grants to full-time arts organisations. ACW also operates schemes which provide financial and other forms of support for individual activities and projects. ACW is a Registered Charity and is set up by Royal Charter. ACW works through the medium of both the Welsh and English languages.

The Arts Council/An Chomhairle Ealaíon
70 Merrion Square, Dublin 2,
Tel: *00353-1-618 0200.*
Fax: *00353-1-676 1302.*
Email *info@artscouncil.ie*
Ws *http://www.artscouncil.ie*
Opening times: *9.15-5.30.*
Personnel: *Visual Arts Officer:* Oliver Dowling. *Exhibition Organiser:* Helena Gorey.

The British Council
Visual Arts, 11 Portland Place, London W1N 4EN.
Tel: *0171-389 3009.* **Fax:** *0171-389 3101.*
Email *Hymie.Dunn@britcoun.org*
Personnel: *Director:* Andrea Rose. *Grants Officer:* Katie Boot.
Grants Officer: Katie Boot, Tel: 0171-389 3045, Fax: 0171-389 3101, E-mail: Katie.Boot@britcoun.org.
Working with museums and galleries abroad as well as colleagues in British Council offices around the world, the department organises major exhibitions of British art for overseas audiences involving loans from national, regional and private collections as well as mounting touring exhibitions, drawn from its collection of over 7000 works by British artists. The Grants to Artists scheme, to recommence in April 1999, offers assistance to artists who have been invited to exhibit abroad and to overseas galleries wishing to exhibit the work of UK artists. Programmes and study tours are organised by invitation for curators from abroad wishing to update their knowledge of British art.

Scottish Arts Council
12, Manor Place, Edinburgh EH3 7DD.
Tel: *0131-226 6051.* **Fax:** *0131-225 9833.*

Regional Arts Boards

East Midlands Arts Board
Mountfields House, Epinal Way, Loughborough, LE11 0QE.
Tel: *01509-218292.* **Fax:** *01509-262214.*

Eastern Arts Board
Cherry Hinton Hall, Chery Hinton Road, Cambridge, CB1 8DW.
Tel: *01223 -215355.* **Fax:** *01223-248075.*
Email *info@eastern-arts.co.uk*
Opening times: *Mon-Fri 9-5.30.*
Nearest Station: *Cambridge.*
Personnel: *Visual Arts Officer:* Niki Braithwaite.
Eastern Arts Board is the regional funding and development agency for the east of England. It is one of ten Regional Arts Boards and covers the counties of Bedfordshire, Cambridgeshire, Essex, Hertfordshire, Lincolnshire, Norfolk and Suffolk. It receives funding from the Arts Council of England, the British Film Institute, the Crafts Council and the regions Local Authorities. The Visual and Media Arts Department supports artistic activity across contemporary visual arts, crafts, photography, multimedia, live art, cinema, television and radio.

London Arts Board
Elme House, 133 Long Acre, London WC2E 9AF.
Tel: *0171-240 1313.*

North West Arts Board
Manchester House, 22 Bridge Street, Manchester M3 3AB.
Tel: *0161-834 6644.* **Fax:** *0161-834 6969.*

Northern Arts Board
9-10 Osborne Street, Newcastle-upon-Tyne NE2 1NZ
Tel: *0191-281 6334.* **Fax:** *0191 281 3276.*

South East Arts Board
10 Mount Ephraim, Tunbridge Wells, TN4 8AS
Tel: *01892-515210 ext 213.*
Fax: *01892-549383.*

South West Arts
Bradninch Place, Gandy Street, Exeter, EX4 3LS.
Tel: *01392-218188.* **Fax:** *01392-413554.*
Email *info@swa.co.uk*
Ws *http://www.swa.co.uk*
Personnel: *Chairman:* John Prescott Thomas. *Acting Chief Executive:* Nick Capaldi.
South West Arts is the official public body for

the arts in the South West. We cover Bristol, Bath and North East Somerset, South Gloucestershire and North Somerset, Cornwall, Devon, Dorset, Gloucestershire and Somerset. We are a registered charity. Our mission is "To raise the quality of the arts in the region and make them available to the widest possible audience". We achieve our mission through information, advice, advocacy, raising funds for the arts and funding. South West Arts is the official adviser to the Arts Council of England on all Lottery applications from the region.

Southern Arts Board
13 St. Clement Street, Winchester, SO23 9DQ.
Tel: *01962-855099.* **Fax:** *01962-861186.*

West Midlands Arts
82 Granville Street, Birmingham B1 2LH.
Tel: *0121-631 3121, Lottery Line, 0121-693 6878.* **Fax:** *0121-643 7239.*

Yorkshire & Humberside Arts
21 Bond Street, Dewsbury, WF13 1AX.
Tel: *01924-455555.* **Fax:** *01924-466522.*
Email *yharts-info@geo2.poptel.org.uk*
Ws *http://www.arts.org.uk*
Opening times: *Mon-Thurs 9-5.30, Fri 9-5.*
Personnel: *Chief Executive:* Roger Lancaster.
Yorkshire and Humberside Arts serves the administrative area covered by the counties of West, South and North Yorkshire and the former county of Humberside, providing financial support for the arts in the region and developing public appreciation of the arts by improving access to, and the quality of, artistic activity.
Services and Facilities:
Art Consultancy. Disabled Access.

NOTES

EDUCATION

Institutions by course.
Awards/qualifications.
Main address listings.

THE ART WORLD
DIRECTORY

FINE ART

American Intercontinental University
Core Subjects:
Art History. Drawing. Photography.

The Arts Institute at Bournemouth
Core Subjects:
Art History. Drawing. Photography. Printmaking.

Bath Spa University College (Formerly Bath College of HE)
Core Subjects:
Sculpture.

Bretton Hall
Core Subjects:
Ceramics. Sculpture.

Byam Shaw School of Art
Core Subjects:
Drawing. Photography. Printmaking. Sculpture.

Canterbury Christ Church College

Carmarthenshire College
Core Subjects:
Art History. Drawing. Printmaking. Sculpture.

Cavendish College
Core Subjects:
Drawing. Photography. Printmaking.

Chelsea College of Art and Design (London Institute)
Core Subjects:
Media. Painting. Sculpture.

The Cheshire School of Art & Design, Mid-Cheshire College

Christie's Education
Art History.

The City Literary Institute for Adult Studies, Department of Visual Arts
Core Subjects:
Photography. Printmaking. Sculpture.

College of North East London
Core Subjects:
Drawing. Media. Photography.

Cumbria College of Art and Design
Core Subjects:
Photography. Printmaking. Sculpture.

Dartington College of Arts
Core Subjects:
Media.

Edinburgh College of Art
Core Subjects:
Ceramics. Drawing. Media. Photography. Printmaking. Sculpture. Textiles.

Goldsmiths College
Core Subjects:
Drawing. Media. Photography. Printmaking. Sculpture. Textiles.

Heatherley School of Fine Art
Core Subjects:
Art History. Drawing. Printmaking. Sculpture.

The Institute
Core Subjects:
Art History. Ceramics. Drawing. Photography. Sculpture.

Kingston University, Faculty of Design
Core Subjects:
Photography. Printmaking. Sculpture.

Lancaster University, School of Creative Arts, The Art Dept.
Core Subjects:
Art History. Drawing. Painting. Printmaking. Sculpture.

Nottingham Trent University
Core Subjects:
Drawing. Media. Photography. Printmaking. Sculpture.

Oxford Brookes University
Core Subjects:
Artist's Books. Art Theory. Drawing. Installation. Media. Painting. Photography. Printmaking. Video.

Plymouth College of Art and Design
Core Subjects:
Ceramics. Media. Photography.

Reigate School of Art and Design

Ruskin School of Drawing and Fine Art
Core Subjects:
Art History. Printmaking. Sculpture.

The Slade School of Fine Art
Core Subjects:
Media. Photography. Printmaking. Sculpture.

Swansea Institute of Higher Education
Core Subjects:
Art History. Ceramics. Drawing. Media. Photography. Printmaking.

Swindon College
Core Subjects:
Drawing.

Tameside College
Core Subjects:
Drawing. Media. Photography. Printmaking. Textiles.

University of Central England in Birmingham
Core Subjects:
Art History. Ceramics. Drawing. Media. Photography. Printmaking. Sculpture. Textiles.

University of Lincolnshire & Humberside, The Hull School of Art & Design
Core Subjects:
Art Theory. Painting. Phonic Arts. Photography. Printmaking. Sculpture. Time-based Media.

University of Plymouth
Core Subjects:
Art History. Media. Photography. Printmaking. Sculpture. Textiles. Time-based Media.

Westminster College
Core Subjects:
Media. Photography. Textiles.

York College of Further and Higher Education
Core Subjects:
Art History. Ceramics. Drawing. Media. Photography. Printmaking. Sculpture. Textiles.

INDIVIDUAL COURSES

ANIMATION

American Intercontinental University
The Arts Institute at Bournemouth
Cavendish College
The City Literary Institute for Adult Studies, Department of Visual Arts
College of North East London
Cumbria College of Art and Design
Edinburgh College of Art
Nottingham Trent University
Swansea Institute of Higher Education
University of Central England in Birmingham
University of Lincolnshire & Humberside, The Hull School of Art & Design
York College of Further and Higher Education

ARCHITECTURE

Birkbeck College
Cavendish College

Edinburgh College of Art
Nottingham Trent University
University of Lincolnshire & Humberside,
The Hull School of Art & Design

ARCHEOLOGICAL ILLUSTRATION

Swindon College

ART HISTORY

American Intercontinental University
The Arts Institute at Bournemouth
Bath Spa University College (Formerly Bath College of HE)
Birkbeck College
Chelsea College of Art and Design (London Institute)
Christie's Education
Christie's Modern Art Studies
The City Literary Institute for Adult Studies, Department of Visual Arts
Cumbria College of Art and Design
Glasgow University
The Institute
Lancaster University, School of Creative Arts, The Art Department
The New Study Centre
The Slade School of Fine Art
Swansea Institute of Higher Education
University of Central England in Birmingham
University of Plymouth
York College of Further and Higher Education

CERAMICS

The Arts Institute at Bournemouth
Barnfield College
Bath Spa University College (Formerly Bath College of HE)
Canterbury Christ Church College
Carmarthenshire College
The Cheshire School of Art & Design, Mid-Cheshire College
The City Literary Institute for Adult Studies, Department of Visual Arts
Cumbria College of Art and Design
Edinburgh College of Art
The Institute
Kingston University, Faculty of Design
Nottingham Trent University
Plymouth College of Art and Design
Swansea Institute of Higher Education
Tameside College
University of Central England in Birmingham
University of Plymouth
York College of Further and Higher Education

CONTEMPORARY ARTS

Nottingham Trent University

DECORATIVE ART

Christie's Education
Nottingham Trent University
Swansea Institute of Higher Education

FURNITURE

The Arts Institute at Bournemouth
College of North East London
Edinburgh College of Art
The Institute
Kingston University, Faculty of Design
Nottingham Trent University
University of Central England in Birmingham
University of Plymouth
York College of Further and Higher Education

ILLUSTRATION

American Intercontinental University
The Arts Institute at Bournemouth
Carmarthenshire College
The Cheshire School of Art & Design, Mid-Cheshire College
The City Literary Institute for Adult Studies, Department of Visual Arts
Edinburgh College of Art
Nottingham Trent University
Swansea Institute of Higher Education
University of Central England in Birmingham
University of Lincolnshire & Humberside,
The Hull School of Art & Design
University of Plymouth
Westminster College
York College of Further and Higher Education

JEWELLERY/SILVER

The Arts Institute at Bournemouth
The Cheshire School of Art & Design, Mid-Cheshire College
The City Literary Institute for Adult Studies, Department of Visual Arts
Cumbria College of Art and Design
Edinburgh College of Art
The Institute
Plymouth College of Art and Design
University of Central England in Birmingham
York College of Further and Higher Education

MEDIA

American Intercontinental University
Barnfield College
Carmarthenshire College
The Cheshire School of Art & Design, Mid-Cheshire College
Cumbria College of Art and Design
Dartington College of Arts
Edinburgh College of Art
Nottingham Trent University
Plymouth College of Art and Design
Swansea Institute of Higher Education
University of Central England in Birmingham
University of Lincolnshire & Humberside,
The Hull School of Art & Design
University of Plymouth
Westminster College
York College of Further and Higher Education

MULTIMEDIA

American Intercontinental University
The Arts Institute at Bournemouth
Bath Spa University College (Formerly Bath College of HE)
Carmarthenshire College
Cavendish College
The Cheshire School of Art & Design, Mid-Cheshire College
College of North East London
Cumbria College of Art and Design
Dartington College of Arts
Edinburgh College of Art
Nottingham Trent University
Plymouth College of Art and Design
Swansea Institute of Higher

Education
Tameside College
University of Central England in Birmingham
University of Plymouth
Westminster College
York College of Further and Higher Education

PAINTING

The Arts Institute at Bournemouth
Bath Spa University College (Formerly Bath College of HE)
Bretton Hall
Byam Shaw School of Art
Carmarthenshire College
Cavendish College
Chelsea College of Art and Design (London Institute)
The Cheshire School of Art & Design, Mid-Cheshire College
The City Literary Institute for Adult Studies, Department of Visual Arts
College of North East London
Cumbria College of Art and Design
Edinburgh College of Art
Heatherley School of Fine Art
The Institute
Kingston University, Faculty of Design
Lancaster University, School of Creative Arts, The Art Department
Nottingham Trent University
Ruskin School of Drawing and Fine Art
The Slade School of Fine Art
Swansea Institute of Higher Education
Tameside College
University of Plymouth
York College of Further and Higher Education

PHOTOGRAPHY

American Intercontinental University
The Arts Institute at Bournemouth
Barnfield College
Carmarthenshire College
Cavendish College
The Cheshire School of Art & Design, Mid-Cheshire College
The City Literary Institute for Adult Studies, Department of Visual Arts
College of North East London
Edinburgh College of Art
The Institute
Nottingham Trent University
Plymouth College of Art and Design
Swansea Institute of Higher Education
Tameside College
University of Central England in Birmingham
York College of Further and Higher Education

STAINED GLASS

Edinburgh College of Art
The Institute
Swansea Institute of Higher Education
York College of Further and Higher Education

TEXTILES

The Arts Institute at Bournemouth
Bath Spa University College (Formerly Bath College of HE)
Carmarthenshire College
Chelsea College of Art and Design (London Institute)
The Cheshire School of Art & Design, Mid-Cheshire College
The City Literary Institute for Adult Studies, Department of Visual Arts
College of North East London
Cumbria College of Art and Design
Edinburgh College of Art
Goldsmiths College
Nottingham Trent University
University of Central England in Birmingham
Westminster College
York College of Further and Higher Education

DESIGN COURSES

CRAFT

Swindon College

3D

The Arts Institute at Bournemouth
Bath Spa University College (Formerly Bath College of HE)
Carmarthenshire College
Cavendish College
The Cheshire School of Art & Design, Mid-Cheshire College
Edinburgh College of Art
Nottingham Trent University
Plymouth College of Art and Design
Swindon College
Tameside College
University of Central England in Birmingham
University of Plymouth
York College of Further and Higher Education

DISPLAY

The Cheshire School of Art & Design, Mid-Cheshire College
Swansea Institute of Higher Education

FASHION

Barnfield College
Carmarthenshire College
Nottingham Trent University

FURNITURE

Nottingham Trent University

GRAPHIC

American Intercontinental University
The Arts Institute at Bournemouth
Barnfield College
Bath Spa University College (Formerly Bath College of HE)
Carmarthenshire College
Cavendish College
The Cheshire School of Art & Design, Mid-Cheshire College
The City Literary Institute for Adult Studies, Department of Visual Arts
College of North East London
Cumbria College of Art and Design
Edinburgh College of Art
Nottingham Trent University
Plymouth College of Art and Design
Swansea Institute of Higher Education
Swindon College
Tameside College
University of Central England in Birmingham
University of Lincolnshire & Humberside,
The Hull School of Art & Design
University of Plymouth
Westminster College
York College of Further and Higher Education

INTERACTIVE

University of Lincolnshire & Humberside, The Hull School of Art & Design

INTERIOR

The Arts Institute at Bournemouth
Cavendish College
Chelsea College of Art and Design (London Institute)
The Cheshire School of Art & Design, Mid-Cheshire College
Edinburgh College of Art
Nottingham Trent University
Plymouth College of Art and Design
University of Central England in Birmingham
University of Lincolnshire & Humberside, The Hull School of Art & Design
Westminster College
York College of Further and Higher Education

MUSEUM & EXHIBITION

University of Lincolnshire & Humberside, The Hull School of Art & Design

PHOTOGRAPHY

The Arts Institute at Bournemouth
Carmarthenshire College
Cavendish College
The Cheshire School of Art & Design, Mid-Cheshire College
The City Literary Institute for Adult Studies, Department of Visual Arts
College of North East London
Swansea Institute of Higher Education
Tameside College
University of Plymouth
York College of Further and Higher Education

PRODUCT

Nottingham Trent University

PUBLIC ART

Chelsea College of Art and Design (London Institute)

SURFACE

Carmarthenshire College

TEXTILE

Barnfield College
Chelsea College of Art and Design (London Institute)
Nottingham Trent University

TV AND FILM

Nottingham Trent University
University of Lincolnshire & Humberside, The Hull School of Art & Design

THEATRE

Nottingham Trent University

THEORY

Swindon College

TYPOGRAPHIC

The Cheshire School of Art & Design, Mid-Cheshire College
The City Literary Institute for Adult Studies, Department of Visual Arts
College of North East London
Edinburgh College of Art
Plymouth College of Art and Design
Swansea Institute of Higher Education
Swindon College
University of Plymouth
York College of Further and Higher Education

AWARDS AND COURSE TYPES

ADULT EDUCATION

The Arts Institute at Bournemouth
Birkbeck College
Carmarthenshire College
Cavendish College
Chelsea College of Art and Design (London Institute)
The Cheshire School of Art & Design, Mid-Cheshire College
Christie's Education
The City Literary Institute for Adult Studies, Department of Visual Arts
Cumbria College of Art and Design
Edinburgh College of Art
Heatherley School of Fine Art
The Institute
The New Study Centre
Plymouth College of Art and Design
Tameside College
University of Central England in Birmingham
Westminster College
York College of Further and Higher Education

CERT. IN PORTRAITURE

Heatherley School of Fine Art

CERAMICS - DIPLOMA

The City Literary Institute for Adult Studies, Department of Visual Arts

DEGREE

American Intercontinental University
The Arts Institute at Bournemouth
Bath Spa University College (Formerly Bath College of HE)
Bretton Hall
Byam Shaw School of Art
Carmarthenshire College
Chelsea College of Art and Design (London Institute)
The Cheshire School of Art & Design, Mid-Cheshire College
Christie's Education
Cumbria College of Art and Design
Dartington College of Arts
Edinburgh College of Art
Goldsmiths College
Kingston University, Faculty of Design
Lancaster University, School of Creative Arts, The Art Department
Nottingham Trent University
Oxford Brookes University
Plymouth College of Art and Design
Ruskin School of Drawing and Fine Art
The Slade School of Fine Art
Swansea Institute of Higher Education

Swindon College
University of Central England in Birmingham
University of Lincolnshire & Humberside,
The Hull School of Art & Design
University of Plymouth

FOUNDATION

The Arts Institute at Bournemouth
Barnfield College
Byam Shaw School of Art
Carmarthenshire College
Cavendish College
Chelsea College of Art and Design (London Institute)
The Cheshire School of Art & Design, Mid-Cheshire College
The City Literary Institute for Adult Studies, Department of Visual Arts
College of North East London
Cumbria College of Art and Design
Heatherley School of Fine Art
Oxford Brookes University
Plymouth College of Art and Design
Swansea Institute of Higher Education
Tameside College
University of Central England in Birmingham
Westminster College
York College of Further and Higher Education

HNC

Barnfield College

HND

The Arts Institute at Bournemouth
Carmarthenshire College
The Cheshire School of Art & Design, Mid-Cheshire College
College of North East London
Cumbria College of Art and Design
Nottingham Trent University
Plymouth College of Art and Design
Swansea Institute of Higher Education
Swindon College
Tameside College
University of Central England in Birmingham
Westminster College
York College of Further and Higher Education

PREFOUNDATION

Carmarthenshire College
The Cheshire School of Art & Design, Mid-Cheshire College
The City Literary Institute for Adult Studies, Department of Visual Arts
College of North East London
Heatherley School of Fine Art
The Institute
Tameside College
University of Central England in Birmingham
York College of Further and Higher Education

POST GRADUATE

The Arts Institute at Bournemouth
Bath Spa University College (Formerly Bath College of HE)
Bretton Hall
Byam Shaw School of Art
Chelsea College of Art and Design (London Institute)
Christie's Education
Cumbria College of Art and Design
Dartington College of Arts
Edinburgh College of Art
Glasgow University
Goldsmiths College
Lancaster University, School of Creative Arts, The Art Department
Nottingham Trent University
Oxford Brookes University
Plymouth College of Art and Design
The Slade School of Fine Art
Swansea Institute of Higher Education
Swindon College
University of Central England in Birmingham
University of Lincolnshire & Humberside,
The Hull School of Art & Design
University of Plymouth

PRACTICAL

Byam Shaw School of Art
Heatherley School of Fine Art

TEACHER TRAINING

Bath Spa University College (Formerly Bath College of HE)
Bretton Hall
University of Central England in Birmingham
University of Plymouth

MAIN ADDRESS LISTINGS

American Intercontinental University
110 Marylebone High Street, London W1M 3DB.
Tel: *0171-467 5600.* **Fax:** *0171-935 8144.*
Email *admissions@acl.edu*
Nearest Underground: *Baker Street/Bond Street*
Personnel: *Director of Admissions:* Miss Karen Haygreen. *Program Chair, Visual Communication:* Mr Steve Jeppesen.
The Visual Communication Program at ACL provides outstanding educational quality in the fields of graphic design, illustration, photography and computer/multi-media design. The teaching program is well supported by an impressive range of industry standard equipment and facilities including three dedicated design studios, an Apple PowerMac computer design lab, a Multi-Media computer lab, a full-colour and black and white photographic darkroom, a photo studio and an animation suite as well as an extensive library with Internet research resource facilities.
We have an impressive tradition of success with graduates now working across the globe in the fields of advertising, publications, graphics and multi-media design. In fact, there is a good chance you will already have seen the work of our alumni in magazines, on billboards or on television. In 1997, a recent graduate won 5 of the British Advertising Awards including the Campaign Gold Award for Best Individual Poster; three of our students were awarded honours for their outstanding and original design work in the Royal Society for the Arts Student Design Awards and four of our graduating students were accepted on an M.A. course at one of the most selective institutions in the United Kingdom.
We believe that we can offer you a great chance to become part of this tradition of success and help you to develop the knowledge and skills needed for an exciting and fulfilling professional career.
Courses:
Animation. Art History. Design (Graphic). Fine Art. Illustration. Media. Multi-Media. Photography.
Qualifications:
Degree.

The Arts Institute at Bournemouth
Wallisdown, Poole BH12 5HH.
Tel: *01202-533011.* **Fax:** *01202-537729.*
Email *general@arts-inst-bournemouth.ac.uk*
Ws *http://www.arts-inst-bournemouth.ac.uk*
Nearest Station: *Bournemouth.*
Personnel: *Marketing Manager:* Ms Laura Stuart. *Admissions Administrator:* Mrs Annette Jones.

The Arts Institute at Bournemouth is one of the largest institutions in the UK specialising in art, design and media. The AIB has achieved an enviable reputation for the innovation and quality of its courses and in November 1998 was awarded the prestigious Queen's Anniversary Prize for excellence in education for the film industry.

the
arts institute
at bournemouth

The AIB offers a range of further education, higher education and postgraduate courses. It is the home of the Bournemouth Film School which has won international acclaim for its award-winning courses in film and animation. Please contact us for details of courses or Open Days.

Courses:
Animation. Art History. Ceramics. Design (3-D). Design (Graphic). Design (Interior). Design (Photography). Fine Art. Furniture. Illustration. Jewellery/Silversmithing. Multi-Media. Painting. Photography. Textiles.
Qualifications:
Adult Education. Degree. Foundation. HND. Post Graduate.

Barnfield College

New Bedford Road, Luton, LU2 7BF.
Tel: *01582-569631.* **Fax:** *01582-572264.*
Email *courses@barnfield.ac.uk*
Ws *http://www.barnfield.ac.uk*
Nearest Station: *Luton.*
Personnel: *Head of Art:* Mr Peter Jenner .
Barnfield College is two miles north of Luton with good rail and bus links. The department of art and design has extensive resources for the delivery of a wide range of subjects. The majority of our students progress to degree level.
Courses:
Ceramics. Design (Fashion). Design (Graphic). Design (Textile). Media. Photography.
Qualifications:
Foundation.

Bath Spa University College (Formerly Bath College of HE)

Faculty of Art and Music, Sion Hill Place, Lansdown, Bath, BA1 5SF.
Tel: *01225-875875.* **Fax:** *01225-875666.*
Email *staffinitial.surname@bathspa.ac.uk*
Ws *http://www.bathspa.ac.uk*
Nearest Station: *Bath Spa.*
Personnel: *Dean of Faculty of Art & Music:* Mr Alan Carter .
The Faculty of Art and Music, which offers undergraduate and postgraduate courses, utilises both University College campuses and is characterised by its wide use of practising artists, designers and musicians as part-time and associate lecturers. This policy ensures that students are in regular tutorial contact with staff who actively engage in research. Many of our staff operate internationally, resulting in a highly creative and professional environment at Bath Spa University College. Faculty courses have an excellent reputation for the quality of educational experience available to students. Work takes place in either refurbished or purpose-built specialist accommodation. The cities of Bath and Bristol, as well as ease of access to London, ensure excellent resources for creative study.
Courses:
Art History. Ceramics. Design (3-D). Design (Graphic). Fine Art. Multi-Media. Painting. Textiles.
Qualifications:
Degree. Post Graduate. Teacher Training.

Birkbeck College

Faculty of Continuing Education, 26 Russell Square, London WC1B 5DQ.
Tel: *0171-631 6660.* **Fax:** *0171-631 6686.*
Email *m.pickford@cems.bbk.ac.uk*
Ws *URLhttp://www.bbk.ac.uk/*
Nearest Underground: *Russell Square.*
Personnel: *Executive Officer, Art History:* Michelle Pickford.
The Faculty offers about ninety part-time day/evening courses on the history of art and architecture in various centres in the Greater London area. The courses are for adults, and all except a post-Diploma course are open to anyone, without prior qualification. The programme covers a Certificate/Diploma (equivalent to the first year of a BA); assessed courses of one or two terms; non-assessed courses; weekend study days; and a residential summer school. Classroom meetings are supplemented by gallery visits. Emphasis is on developing ways of seeing art, thinking about it and understanding critical approaches to it.
Courses:
Architecture. Art History.
Qualifications:
Adult Education.

Bretton Hall

West Bretton, Wakefield WF4 4LG.
Tel: *01924-832017.*
Fax: *01924-832016.*
Email *registry@bretton.ac.uk*
Nearest Station: *Wakefield.*
Personnel: *Head of Fine Art:* Richard Bell.
The Fine Art Degree Programme recruits to three discrete routes, each based within a subject discipline - ceramics - painting - sculpture, offering an intensive experience in developing understanding through informed studio practice.
The diversity and range of possibilities within contemporary Fine Art practice is encouraged and nurtured by a varied range of teaching strategies. This is underpinned by a clear sense of historical and contemporary social and critical issues. Studio accommodation is extensive and provides excellent provision across the area. The unique and highly stimulating environment of Bretton Hall and its surroundings, including the Yorkshire Sculpture Park, enhances this well established programme.
Courses:
Fine Art. Painting.
Qualifications:
Degree. Post Graduate. Teacher Training.

The British Sporting Art Trust

BSAT Gallery, 99 High Street, Newmarket, CB8 8JL.
Tel: *01264-710344.* **Fax:** *01264-710114.*
Email *barnart@compuserve.com*
Personnel: *Organising Secretary:* Mrs M. Lawton.
The Trust's objectives are the formation and display of a representative collection of British sporting art, at the Trust's Vestey Galleries of Sporting Art at the National Horseracing Museum, Newmarket, and other galleries and houses open to the public. Also to support and publish research on the subject of sporting art.

Byam Shaw School of Art

2 Elthorne Road, Archway, London N19 4AG.
Tel: *0171-281 4111.* **Fax:** *0171-281 1632.*
Email *info@byam-shaw.ac.uk*
Ws *http://www.byam-shaw.ac.uk*
Nearest Underground: *Archway.*
Personnel: *Director:* Alister Warman.

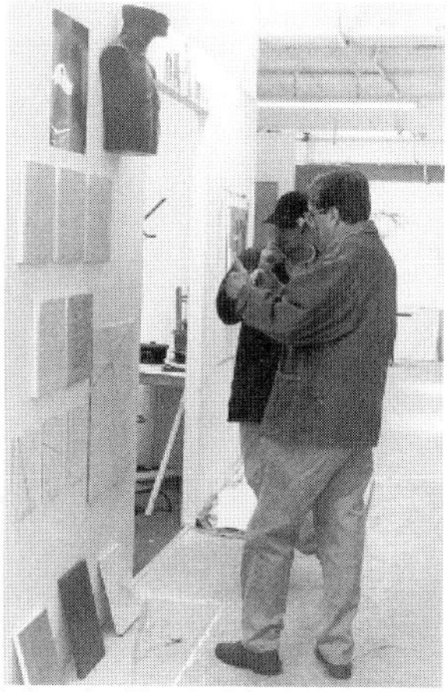

Independent Fine Art School committed to the education of intending artists. Three-year BA (Hons) in Fine Art. Foundation and Diploma Studies. Post-graduate and Short-term studies.
Courses:
Fine Art. Painting.
Qualifications:
Degree. Foundation. Post Graduate. Practical.

Canterbury Christ Church College

Department of Art and Design, North Holmes Road, Canterbury, CT1 1QU.
Tel: *01227-767700.* **Fax:** *01227-470442.*
Personnel: *Head of Department:* Mr David Shutt .
Courses:
Ceramics. Fine Art.

Carmarthenshire College

Faculty of Creative and Performing Arts, Jobswell Road, Campus, Carmarthen, SA31 3HY.
Tel: *01554-748204.* **Fax:** *01554-221515.*
Email *gailminihane@ccta.ac.uk*
Ws *http://www.ccta.ac.uk*

Opening times: *9-5, 9-4.30 Friday.*
Nearest Station: *Carmarthen.*
Personnel: *Head of Faculty:* Ms Gail Minihane . *Assistant Head of Faculty:* Mr Paul Evans.
The Faculty of Creative and Performing Arts is a large and successful one with a long established history of high quality Art and Design courses. Its broad range of courses in Art, Design and Performing Arts allow students of every level to gain qualifications relevant to their intended careers or to education at a higher level.
The Faculty is also able to offer its students a unique range of facilities from work in traditional areas of art such as Painting, Printmaking and Sculpture including Metal Casting through to a wide range of Higher Education courses which employ state of the art Digital Technology such as in Photography, Media, Textiles, Fashion and Graphics.
Courses:
Ceramics. Design (3-D). Design (Fashion). Design (Graphic). Design (Photography). Design (Surface Decoration). Fine Art. Illustration. Media. Multi-Media. Painting. Photography. Textiles.
Qualifications:
Adult Education. Degree. Foundation. Pre-foundation. HND.

Cavendish College
35-37 Alfred Place, London WC1E 7DP.
Tel: *0171-580 6043.* **Fax:** *0171-255 1591.*
Email *learn@cavendish.ac.uk OR cavendish@gpo.sonnet.co.uk*
Ws *http://www.cavendish.ac.uk*
Opening times: *Mon-Fri 9am-8pm, Sat 9-5.*
Nearest Underground: *Goodge Street.*
Personnel: *Principal:* Dr John Sanders . *Course Director:* Mr Nick Devison.
A Cavendish Diploma course provides each student with a solid foundation from which to enter their chosen field in art and design together with sound progression opportunities into higher education. All courses provide an intensive and diagnostic arena of study, enabling the student to identify and maximise their creative potential across a range of inter-related disciplines. Lectures by a large number of practising professional's give the student a clearer understanding of their chosen area of study and an insight into the routes by which they may progress towards their chosen careers. Please contact the college for further enrolment details.
Courses:
Animation. Architecture. Design (3-D). Design (Graphic). Design (Interior). Design (Photography). Fine Art. Multi-Media. Painting. Photography.
Qualifications:
Adult Education. Foundation.

Chelsea College of Art and Design (London Institute)
Manresa Road, London SW3 6LS.
Tel: *0171-514 7751.* **Fax:** *0171-514 7777.*
Ws *http://www.linst.ac.uk*
Nearest Underground: *South Kensington.*
Personnel: *Dean of Art:* Mr Andy Yates . *Dean of Design:* Mr Cliff Nicholls. *School Administrator, Art:* Mr Steve Farrow. *School Administrator, Design:* Ms Jane Edwards.
Chelsea College of Art & Design is a constituent college of the London Institute, the largest Art & Design education institute in Europe. The College offers a range of pace-setting courses for UK and overseas students, from Foundation through to MA and research degrees. The College is located in central London, the centre for most art and design activity in the United Kingdom - contemporary art galleries, design practices, trade fairs, fashion houses, as well as museums, libraries and archives.
The School of Art has two sites: Manresa Road and Bagley's Lane (SW6). The School of Design has two sites: Lime Grove (W12) and Hugon Road (SW6).
Courses:
Art History. Design (Interior). Design (Public Art). Design (Textile). Fine Art. Painting. Textiles.
Qualifications:
Adult Education. Degree. Foundation. Post Graduate.

The Cheshire School of Art & Design, Mid-Cheshire College
Hartford Campus, Hartford, Northwich, CW8 1LJ.
Tel: *01606-74444.* **Fax:** *01606-75101.*
Email *admin@midchesh.u-net.com*
Ws *http://www.midchesh.u-net.com*
Nearest Station: *BR Greenbank & Hartford.*
Personnel: *Head of Faculty:* Ms Susan Ainsworth . *Programme Leader H.E. Art & Design:* Mr Ales Ellis. *Administrator H.E. Art & Design:* Ms Debbie Cooke. *Faculty Secretary:* Ms Michelle Holt.
The Cheshire School of Art is conveniently situated close to the rural Cheshire town of Northwich. Excellent access is available to the cultural centres of Liverpool, Chester and Manchester. We offer a comprehensive range of Art and Design courses from post-school to Degree level and part-time courses for adults. Studios are well equipped and offer a level of technology comparable with that found in industry. Our government funded regional centre for design skills training for industry will be open from Easter 1999 offering courses in leading-edge design technologies.
Courses:
Ceramics. Design (3-D). Design (Display). Design (Graphic). Design (Interior). Design (Photography). Design (Typographic). Fine Art. Illustration. Jewellery/Silversmithing. Media. Multi-Media. Painting. Photography. Textiles.
Qualifications:
Adult Education. Degree. Foundation. Pre-foundation. HND.

Christie's Education
63 Old Brompton Road, London SW7 3JS.
Tel: *0171-581 3933.* **Fax:** *0171-589 0383.*
Ws *http://www.christies.com*
Opening times: *Mon-Fri 9-5.*
Nearest Underground: *South Kensington.*
Personnel: *Chairman:* Robert Cumming. *General Manager:* Caroline de Lane Lea.
Christie's Education runs a wide variety of challenging, specialist and general interest courses in the Fine and Decorative Arts. They cover all periods from classical antiquity to contemporary art, and range from fully validated diploma and university courses to short courses and evening classes. Courses are run in London, Scotland, Paris, New York and Australia. All of them place great importance on training the eye and the first hand examination of works of art, with vocational as well as academic instruction. Students are of all ages, nationalities and backgrounds, and post-graduate and mature students are well catered for.
Courses:
Art History. Decorative Art. Fine Art.
Qualifications:
Adult Education. Degree. Post Graduate.

Christie's Modern Art Studies
5 Bloomsbury Place, London WC1A 2QA.
Tel: *0171-436 3630.* **Fax:** *0171-436 3631.*
Email *courses@modernartstudies.demon.co.uk*
Personnel: *Principal:* Diana Weir. *Course Director:* Jean Hodgins.

MODERN ART STUDIES

Christies Modern Art Studies offers full and part time courses surveying key ideas and developments from Impressionism to the present day. The course includes slide lectures and gallery visits by distinguished art historians, critics and writers and also comprises visits to museums, galleries, auctions houses and study visits abroad.
Courses:
Art History.

The City Literary Institute for Adult Studies, Department of Visual Arts
Keeley House, Keeley Street, London WC2B 4BA.
Tel: *0171-430 0547.* **Fax:** *0171-583 7500.*
Email *visualarts@citylit.ac.uk*
Opening times: *10-9 teaching, 10-6 office.*
Nearest Underground: *Holborn, Covent Garden.*
Personnel: *Head of Visual Arts:* To be appointed. *Administrator:* Sarah Jones.

the City lit

The Department of Visual Arts offers a wide range of part-time courses for adults throughout the whole year. Subject areas include: Art history, basketry, bookbinding, ceramics, conservation of books, documents and ceramics, design, drawing, gilding, graphic design, jewellery, life drawing, painting, picture framing, portfolio preparation, pottery, printmaking, sculpture, stained glass and textiles. The programme provides opportunities to study weekdays, in the evening and on Saturdays. Courses vary from one day schools to year long courses.

Courses:
Animation. Art History. Ceramics. Design (Graphic). Design (Photography). Design (Typographic). Fine Art. Illustration. Jewellery/Silversmithing. Painting. Photography. Textiles.
Qualifications:
Adult Education. Diploma in Ceramics. Foundation. Pre-foundation.

College of North East London

Muswell Hill Centre, Rhodes Avenue, London N22 4UT.
Tel: *0181-802 3111.*
Fax: *0181-442 3150.*
Opening times: *9-5.*
Nearest Underground: *Bounds Green.*
Personnel: *Head of School Creative Studies:* Laura Gander Howe.

THE college OF NORTH EAST LONDON

The College of North East London has provided Further Education for over 100 years, offering a wide range of exciting full time, part time and evening courses.
The College caters for over 11000 students attracting both school leavers and mature students from London and the Home Counties.
The College offers a number of creative subjects that have attracted growing interest over the years. Amongst those offered are courses in Art & Design, Photography, Graphic Design and Multimedia. These subjects are offered at all levels, from GCSE and A Level to BTEC Foundation and Higher National Certificate (HNC).

Courses:
Animation. Design (Graphic). Design (Photography). Design (Typographic). Fine Art. Furniture. Multi-Media. Painting. Photography. Textiles.
Qualifications:
Foundation. Pre-foundation. HND.

Cumbria College of Art and Design

Brampton Road, Carlisle, CA3 9AY.
Tel: *01228-400300.*
Fax: *01228-514491.*
Email *q@cumbriacad.ac.uk*
Ws *http://www.cumbriacollart.ac.uk*
Nearest Station: *Carlisle - 1.5 miles.*
Personnel: *Marketing:* Allison J. Roberts.
Cumbria College of Art and Design - a college in the university sector - offer a wide range of courses in the study, practice, criticism and promotion of visual, performing and media arts, crafts and design, and in heritage management. These lead to the award of BA Honours degrees and Higher National Diplomas as well as a range of BTEC National Diplomas.
With the opportunity of further part time post graduate study in contemporary arts practice, cultural and heritage management, media and local history.

Courses:
Animation. Art History. Ceramics. Design (Graphic). Fine Art. Jewellery/Silversmithing. Media. Multi-Media. Painting. Textiles.
Qualifications:
Adult Education. Degree. Foundation. HND. Post Graduate.

Dartington College of Arts

Totnes, TO9 6EJ.
Tel: *01803-862224.*
Fax: *01803-863569.*
Email *registry@dartington.ac.uk*
Ws *http://www.dartington.ac.uk*
Nearest Station: *Totnes.*
Personnel: *Administrator : Registry:* Margaret Eggleton.
Established in 1961 on the beautiful Dartington Hall Estate, Dartington College of Arts is well-known as a centre for innovation in the performance arts. A recent Higher Education Funding Council assessment report commented on our "charismatic" and "innovative" teaching methods. We scored 23 out of a potential 24 points.

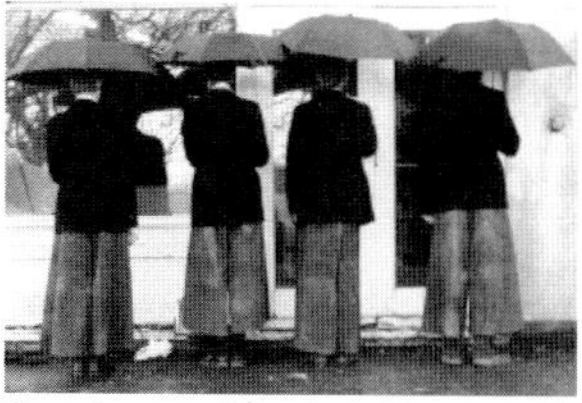

Through partnership with the University of Plymouth, undergraduate and post-graduate awards are offered in Visual Performance (visual arts and performance), Music, Theatre, Performance Writing and Arts Management. Students studying for BA (Hons) in any of these specialisms are encouraged to collaborate between disciplines and to experiment in emerging hybrid and multi-media art forms.

Courses:
Fine Art. Media. Multi-Media.
Qualifications:
Degree. Post Graduate.

Edinburgh College of Art

Lauriston Place, Edinburgh EH3 9DF.
Tel: *0131-221 6000/221 6030.*
Fax: *0131-221 6089.*
Email *registration@eca.ac.uk*
Ws *http://www.eca.ac.uk*
Personnel: *Registrar:* Marian Hall.

Edinburgh COLLEGE of ART
HERIOT-WATT UNIVERSITY

Edinburgh College of Art offers a wide range of degree courses in the fields of Art & Design and Environmental Studies.
With a student population of approximately 1700 and a reputation as a centre of excellence, the College has a lively, creative and intimate atmosphere.
Throughout the year, the College also runs a varied exhibitions programme, featuring not only work from students and staff but touring or specially curated exhibitions of local, UK or international origin.

Courses:
Animation. Architecture. Ceramics. Design (3-D). Design (Graphic). Design (Interior). Design (Typographic). Fine Art. Furniture. Illustration. Jewellery/Silversmithing. Media. Multi-Media. Painting. Photography. Architectural Stained Glass. Textiles.
Qualifications:
Adult Education. Degree. Post Graduate.

Glasgow University

History of Art Department, 7 University Gardens, Glasgow G12 8QQ.
Tel: *0141-330 4097.* **Fax:** *0141-330 3513.*
Email *J.Nicholson@arthist.arts.gla.ac.uk*
Ws *http://www.arts.gla.ac.uk/ArtHist/decarts.htm*
Personnel: Gordon McFarlan.

CHRISTIE'S SCOTLAND

UNIVERSITY of GLASGOW

This is a one year programme run in association with Christie's Scotland combining practical and academic approaches to the study of the decorative arts. Both Diploma and Master of Philosophy are offered and the emphasis of the course is on 18th, 19th, and early 20th century decorative arts seen in British, European and Far Eastern contexts. Students are provided with a sound background in the history of furniture, interiors and in various media studies such as ceramics, metalwork, glass and textiles, they are also introduced to the workings of an auction house and the art market at Christie's Glasgow.

Courses:
Art History.
Qualifications:
Post Graduate.

Goldsmiths College

Lewisham Way, New Cross, London SE14 6NW.
Tel: *0171-919 7671 Visual Arts office.*
Fax: *0171-919 7673.*
Email *visualarts@gold.ac.uk*
Ws *http://www.gold.ac.uk/*
Opening times: *Mon-Fri 9-12.00, 2-5.*
Nearest Underground: *New Cross, New Cross Gate.*
The Department of Visual Arts at Goldsmiths College is one of international distinction. In addition to teaching programmes at both undergraduate and postgraduate level, it is concerned with promoting the understanding of contemporary art through the personal endeavours of individual members of staff and through departmental initiatives. The department is divided into two study areas - Fine Art and Textiles. The department received a 5* rating (Centre of International Excellence) in the 1996 Research Assessment Exercise, one of only two University departments to be awarded such a rating for Fine Art.

Courses:
Fine Art. Textiles.
Qualifications:
Degree. Post Graduate.

Heatherley School of Fine Art

80 Upcerne Road, Chelsea, London SW10 0SH.
Tel: *0171-351 4190.* **Fax:** *0171-361 6945.*
Email *heatherleys@hotmail.com*
Opening times: *9.30-5.*
Nearest Underground: *Fulham Broadway/Sloane Square. BR: Victoria*
Personnel: *Director of Studies:* Mr Tony Mott .

HEATHERLEY'S
Chelsea - Est. 1845

Heatherleys is a small independent Art school based in Chelsea. It offers a wide range of full time and part time Fine Art courses for both beginners and experienced artists.
Professional artists specialised in their academic field tutor the courses. Heatherleys runs a highly successful foundation/portfolio course. This is for those who are looking to go on to a degree but need a structured year to prepare their portfolio. It has small classes and a high tutor to student ratio. Other courses include painting, drawing, life drawing, portraiture, sculpture, watercolour/pastel, Printmaking, the Heatherley Diploma in Portraiture, and Continuing Studies.
Courses:
Fine Art. Painting.
Qualifications:
Adult Education. Certificate in Portraiture. Foundation. Pre-foundation. Practical.

The Institute

Hampstead Garden Suburb, Central Square, London NW11 7BN.
Tel: *0181-455 9951.* **Fax:** *0181-201 8063.*
Email *office@hgsi.ac.uk*
Ws *http://www.hgsi.ac.uk*
Nearest Underground: *Golders Green.*
Personnel: *Head of Art & Creative Studies:* Bob Rothero. *Course Director:* Barbara Jackson.

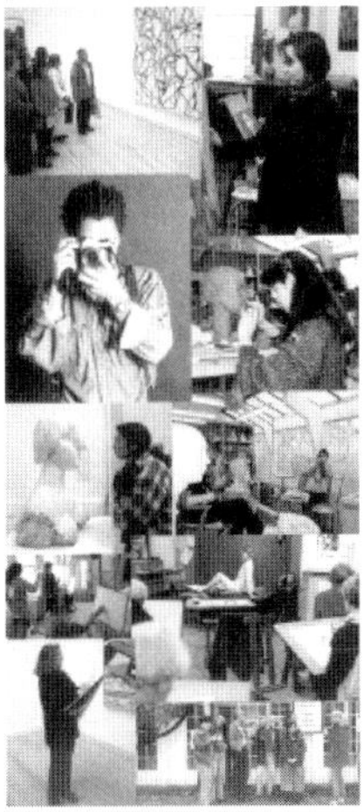

Prefoundation and Portfolio - September to March. This course in the visual arts consists of two structured terms, 27 hours per week, designed to prepare students for an art foundation course or an art degree at university. The course is suitable either for school leavers or for those mature students who wish to experience the total commitment of a full-time course in art and creative studies. Regular tutorials will be given to students as well as practical guidance and career advice. Some basic materials will be made available by the Institute but students should provide a portfolio and basic drawing equipment. A list of materials and equipment needed will be sent to successful students on acceptance to the course. Access to Art - April to June. This one term course is aimed at students interested in pursuing art to a higher level with the possibility of progressing onto the Prefoundation Course.
Courses:
Art History. Ceramics. Fine Art. Furniture. Jewellery/Silversmithing. Painting. Photography. Architectural Stained Glass.
Qualifications:
Adult Education. Pre-foundation.

Kingston University, Faculty of Design

Knights Park, Kingston upon Thames, KT1 2QJ.
Tel: *0181-547 2000.* **Fax:** *0181-547 7011.*
Email *P.Amendt@kingston.ac.uk*
Nearest Station: *Kingston-Upon-Thames.*
Personnel: *Head of School:* Prof. Bruce Russell.
Three areas: painting, sculpture, intermedia. Emphasis on student self-management and professional practice. Printmaking, photography and computer assisted imaging inductions first year. First year structured, project led, second and third years personal research. Second year transatlantic and European exchange programme. All student contribute to public art/town and gown programme and art loan scheme. 'Aftercare' graduate students network. Inhouse gallery showing staff and student self-curated shows and Stanley Picker Gallery. All courses now modular.
Courses:
Ceramics. Fine Art. Furniture. Painting.
Qualifications:
Degree.

Lancaster University, School of Creative Arts, The Art Department

Lonsdale Hall, Bailrigg, Lancaster, LA1 4YW.
Tel: *01524-593056.* **Fax:** *01524-593056.*
Email *artists@lancaster.ac.uk*
Ws *http://www.lancs.ac.uk/users/art/*
Nearest Station: *Lancaster*
Personnel: *Head of Department:* Professor Nigel Whiteley. *Admissions Tutor:* Tony Heward.
We offer two degree schemes: Art: Practice and Theory. A fine art-based degree which integrates courses in painting, drawing, sculpture and printmaking with 20th century art history. Art: History and Culture. An art-history-based degree which focuses on the 20th century and allows you to take a limited amount of practical work. M.A. in Art Practice is also available as well as Post-graduate research degrees (M.Phil and Ph.D). Lancaster is one of the leading universities in the country for the quality of teaching, research and facilities.
Courses:
Art History. Fine Art. Painting.
Qualifications:
Degree. Post Graduate.

The New Study Centre

21 Palace Gardens Terrace, London W8 4SA.
Tel: *0171-229 3393.* **Fax:** *0171-229 4220.*
Personnel: *Administrator:* Mrs J. FitzGerald.
The New Study Centre, formerly known as The Study Centre for the History of the Fine and Decorative Arts continues a tradition of more than 30 years providing opportunities for the study of art history. The New Study Centre offers a variety of courses and lectures which cover all levels of interest and experience. Courses for 1999 include The Decorative Arts Course which covers the history of European furniture (mainly English and French), pottery, porcelain, silver, glass and textiles from the sixteenth century to the present day. Lectures take place on Tuesday and Wednesday mornings. This eighteen-week course is divided into four self-contained parts. Each part may be taken separately.
For details of courses, lectures and private visits to selected country houses please contact The New Study Centre office.
Courses:
Art History.
Qualifications:
Adult Education.

Nottingham Trent University

Faculty of Art and Design, Dryden Street, Nottingham, NG1 4FZ.
Tel: *0115-848 2485.*
Fax: *0115-948 6403.*
Email *lisa.howes@ntu.ac.uk*
Ws *http://www.ntu.ac.uk/vpa*
Opening times: *Faculty fortnight. Please contact for details.*
Nearest Station: *Nottingham.*
Personnel: *Dean:* Prof. Simon Lewis .
The Faculty of Art and Design is one of the largest and foremost in Europe, offering a wide range of courses at undergraduate and postgraduate levels.
The Faculty comprises three departments: Design, Fashion and Textiles and Visual and Performing Arts. Each department provides a related portfolio of courses offering a broad spectrum of disciplines.
All facilities are of a very high standard and most are in purpose-built accommodation.
All courses involve input from distinguished professionals, specialists and consultants who visit the Faculty on a regular basis and enhance still further the academic programmes delivered by accomplished and dedicated staff teams.
Courses:
Animation. Architecture. Ceramics. Contemporary Art. Decorative Art. Design (3-D). Design (Fashion). Design (Furniture). Design (Graphic). Design (Interior). Design (Product). Design (TV & Film). Design (Textile). Design (Theatre). Fine Art. Furniture. Illustration. Media. Multi-Media. Painting. Photography. Textiles.
Qualifications:
Degree. HND. Post Graduate.

Oxford Brookes University
School of Art, Publishing & Music, Richard Hamilton Building, Headington Hill Campus, Oxford OX3 0BP.
Tel: *01865-484951.* **Fax:** *01865-484952.*
Email *apm@brookes.ac.uk*
Ws *http://www.brookes.ac.uk/schools/apm/fineart*
Opening times: *24 Hours studio access, Office and enquiries 9.30-4.30.*
Nearest Station: *Oxford.*
Personnel: *Head of School:* Mr Paul Richardson . *Principal Lecturer Fine Art:* Ms Shelly Sacks.
Single and Combines Honour Degree. The Fine Art course provides students with opportunities to develop as individual practitioners, working in a wide range of new and traditional technologies.
It interrogates art and culture through a range of theoretical and conceptual frameworks. Its interdisciplinary character assists students to link traditional skills and approaches (such as drawing, casting, painting, bookworks and printmaking) with new media for the production and manipulation of images. Creative processes from a breadth of disciplines are claimed and redeployed to contribute to new approaches to working with materials, photography, time-based media and electronic imaging.
MA/PgDip in Contemporary Arts and Music. A unique postgraduate course starting in October 1999* which offers a range of alternatives for postgraduate work in contemporary arts and new music within an interdisciplinary framework. Artists or composers may specialise in their chosen medium, collaborate with others and explore a number of interdisciplinary routes across art forms.
The course also focuses on the relation between art and/or musical composition in their social context. It aims to provide students with creative strategies for generating music, art work and interdisciplinary projects and offers direct experience of working in dialogue with the city, and the world around them.
Students will be encouraged to conceive of their work in terms of context- and site-specificity so that social location, audience relation, and performance context will become a key concern. Academic staff will help students to foster a range of appropriate links with local bodies.
* Subject to validation.
Courses:
Fine Art.
Qualifications:
Degree. Foundation. Post Graduate.

Plymouth College of Art and Design
Tavistock Place, Plymouth, PL4 8AT.
Tel: *01752-203434.* **Fax:** *01752-203444.*
Email *enquiries@pcad.plym.ac.uk*
Ws *http://www.pcad.plym.ac.uk*
Opening times: *Term time:- Mon-Thur 8am-8.30pm, Fri 8-4.30.*
Nearest Station: *Plymouth.*
Personnel: *Director of Curriculum:* Mr Adrian Ballasat. *Director of Marketing:* Ms Fay Jeffrey . *Head of School, Decorative & Fine Art:* Mr Alan Lemin. *Admissions Officer:* Mrs Jean Edmonds.
Plymouth College of Art and Design is a specialist provider of Art and Design education, and offers a wide range of full and part time programmes at further and higher education level.

The college is composed of five subject focussed schools, graphic communication, media and photography, decorative and fine arts, industrial arts and applied arts. Links with the community and local industry are encouraged to ensure that students are kept abreast of recent developments. The college also has a gallery at its main site, where former and current students as well as local artists can exhibit their work.
Courses:
Ceramics. Design (3-D). Design (Graphic). Design (Interior). Design (Typographic). Fine Art. Jewellery/Silversmithing. Media. Multi-Media. Photography.
Qualifications:
Adult Education. Degree. Foundation. HND. Post Graduate.

Reigate School of Art and Design
127 Blackborough Road, Reigate, RH2 7DE.
Tel: *01737-766137.* **Fax:** *01737-76843.*
Personnel: *Manager of Art School:* Ms Barbara Bell .
Courses:
Fine Art.

Ruskin School of Drawing and Fine Art
74 High Street, Oxford, OX1 4BG.
Tel: *01865-276940.* **Fax:** *01865-276949.*
Email *stephen.farthing@ruskin-school.ox.ac.uk*
Ws *http://www.ruskin-sch.ox.ac.uk/*
Personnel: *Ruskin Master of Drawing/Head of Department:* Mr Stephen Farthing .

The Ruskin School is the Fine Art Department at Oxford University. It benefits from a strong academic foundation, with a particular emphasis on prominent visiting lecturers, and treats the boundaries between media as permeable. Of particular note is The Laboratory, the School's research wing, which supports the production of new work deriving from collaborations between artists and experts from the worlds of science, technology and the Humanities. The Laboratory is administered by Paul Bonaventura and Antonia Payne and organises The Joseph Beuys Lectures and the Arts Council of England Helen Chadwick Fellowship on an annual basis.
Fine Art. Painting.
Qualifications:
Degree.

The Slade School of Fine Art
University College London Gower Street, London WC1E 6BT.
Tel: *0171-504 2313.* **Fax:** *0171-380 7801.*
Email *slade.enquiries@ucl.ac.uk*
Ws *http://www.ucl.ac.uk/slade/*
Nearest Underground: *Euston, Euston Square, Warren Street.*
Personnel: *Co-ordinator of Academic Affairs:* Ms Caroline Nicholas .

The Slade School of Fine Art, founded in 1871, is a department of University College London. The Slade offers the BA in Fine Art (four years, full time) and, at graduate level, the MA and MFA (two years full time), the Graduate Diploma (one year, full time) and MPhil and PhD degrees.
Students are taught by professional artists of distinction and distinguished staff teaching art history and theoretical studies. At Undergraduate level students may specialise either in Painting, Sculpture or Fine Art Media (including film, video, printmaking, photography and electronic media). Graduate students may also specialise in Theatre Design.
Courses:
Art History. Fine Art. Painting.
Qualifications:
Degree. Post Graduate.

Swansea Institute of Higher Education
Faculty of Art and Design, Townhill Road, Swansea SA2 0UT.
Tel: *01792-481285.* **Fax:** *01792-205305.*
Personnel: Dr. Bill Gaskins.
As a major centre of excellence for art & design higher education in Wales, the Faculty provides opportunities for students to study a wide variety of vocational and professional subjects or to undertake more academically oriented studies by choosing alternative theoretical and historical subjects. There is also an Art and Design Foundation programme for students preparing for higher education entry, as well as future possibilities to study for a taught postgraduate degree leading to MA or

the Research degrees of MPhil and PhD. Undergraduate awards include the BA (Hons) and HND and these are available on both a full-time and part-time basis.
Courses:
Animation. Art History. Ceramics. Decorative Art. Design (Display). Design (Graphic). Design (Photography). Design (Typographic). Fine Art. Illustration. Media. Multi-Media. Painting. Photography. Architectural Stained Glass.
Qualifications:
Degree. Foundation. HND. Post Graduate.

Swindon College
School of Art and Design, Euclid Street, Swindon SN1 2JQ.
Tel: *01793-498490.* **Fax:** *01793-422102.*
Email *chrismaule@msxchg.swindoncollege.ac.uk*
Ws *http://www.swindon-college.ac.uk/*
Nearest Station: *Swindon.*
Personnel: *Head of School of Art & Design:* Chris Maule.
Swindon College (in Association with Oxford Brookes University).
MA Process and Context of Design.
Approximate number of places: 12.
Length of course: 1 year FT, 2 years PT.
This theory and practice led course examines research methodology in relation to design practice; design in social/cultural contexts; human, industrial and consumer applications; developments in creative technology, visual methodology; new materials, ethical design, design issues and the mind.
Courses:
Archeological Illustration. Design (Craft). Design (3-D). Design (Graphic). Design (Theory). Design (Typographic). Fine Art.
Qualifications:
Degree. HND. Post Graduate.

Tameside College
Beaufort Road, Ashton-under-Lyne, Tameside OL6 6NX.
Tel: *0161-908 6760.* **Fax:** *0161-908 6611.*
Email *info@tamesidecollege.ac.uk*
Personnel: *Head of School:* Mr Steve Warton .

The School of Art and Design Media offers HNDs in Graphics, Photography, Fine Art, Fashion and Design Crafts. In addition there are GNVQs in Art and Design and in Media. There is also an Art Foundation course and a wide range of part-time classes.
The school is affiliated to the University of Salford as well as having progression links with Manchester Metropolitan and Huddersfield Universities.
Courses:
Ceramics. Design (3-D). Design (Graphic). Design (Photography). Fine Art. Multi-Media. Painting. Photography.
Qualifications:
Adult Education. Foundation. Pre-foundation. HND.

University of Central England in Birmingham
Birmingham Institute of Art & Design, Corporation Street, Costa Green, Birmingham B4 7DX.
Tel: *0121-331 5878.* **Fax:** *0121-359 0423.*
Email *John.Salmon@uce.ac.uk*
Ws *http://www.uce.ac.uk/*
Opening times: *Tuesdays during term-time. Must book in advance.*
Nearest Station: *New Street.*
Personnel: *Publicity Officer:* Ms Helen Annette .

Birmingham Institute of Art & Design is one of the largest centres for art, design and media education in the UK. Nearly four thousand full-time and part-time students presently study on five recently renovated and refurbished sites. BIAD offers a comprehensive choice of pregraduate, undergraduate and postgraduate courses and a well established higher research degrees programme.
Courses:
Animation. Art History. Ceramics. Design (3-D). Design (Graphic). Design (Interior). Fine Art. Furniture. Illustration. Jewellery/Silversmithing. Media. Multi-Media. Photography. Textiles.
Qualifications:
Adult Education. Degree. Foundation. Pre-foundation. HND. Post Graduate. Teacher Training.

University of Lincolnshire & Humberside, The Hull School of Art & Design
Queens Gardens, Hull HU1 3DQ.
Tel: *01482-440550.* **Fax:** *01482-462101.*
Email *lclark@humber.ac.uk*
Nearest Station: *Hull.*
Personnel: *Head of Art:* Mr Rob Gawthrop .
Course Descriptions: BA (Hons) Fine Art - This course is concerned with contemporary art practice and provides the facilities and academic support necessary for the student engaged in the making of art in the current climate and the ever changing world. BA (Hons) Phonic Art - This innovative course is concerned with the making of work that is derived from or is manifested through sound. This encompasses both specific and converging areas of art and music. Where music includes the creative construction, manipulation and combination of audible and inaudible material.
Entry Requirements:- Normally applicants are currently undertaking, or have successfully completed an appropriate pre-degree course or equivalent professional experience. Subject to available places all suitably qualified applicants are interviewed. Commitment and capability evidenced through interview is considered of great importance.
Rob Gawthrop (Head of Art): +44 (0) 1482 462123, rgawthrop@staff.humber.ac.uk; Course Secretary: +44 (0) 1482 462166, lclark@humber.ac.uk
Courses:
Animation. Architecture. Design (Graphic). Design (Interactive). Design (Interior). Design (Museums & Exhibitions). Design (TV & Film). Fine Art. Illustration. Media.
Qualifications:
Degree. Post Graduate.

University of Plymouth
Faculty of Arts and Education, Earl Richards Road North, Exeter, EX2 6AS.
Tel: *01392-475022.*
Fax: *01392-475012.*
Email *fae-admissions@plymouth.ac.uk*
Ws *http://www.fae.plym.ac.uk/*
Nearest Station: *Exeter St. Davids, Exeter Central.*
Personnel: *Publicity:* Ms Sue Try .

Based in Exeter and Exmouth, the Faculty of Arts & Education offers a wide range of programmes in Arts & Design disciplines at undergraduate, postgraduate and research level.
The Art & Design programme includes: Fine Art; Fine Art Contextual Practice; Design & Italian; Illustration; Photography; Typography and 3D Design. The Combined Arts programme includes: Art History; Cultural Practice; Media Arts; Visual Arts, all of which can be studied as single honours, majors or options with another subject. Art and Design is also a subject specialism in the Teacher Education programmes at upper and lower primary and secondary level.
Courses:
Art History. Ceramics. Design (3-D). Design (Graphic). Design (Photography). Design (Typographic). Fine Art. Furniture. Illustration. Media. Multi-Media. Painting.
Qualifications:
Degree. Post Graduate. Teacher Training.

Westminster College

Battersea Park Road, London SW11 4JR.
Tel: *0171-556 8000.* **Fax:** *0171-556 8082.*
Email *admissions@westminster-cfe.ac.uk*
Ws *www.westminster-cfe.ac.uk*
Opening times: *Admissions Unit, Mon-Thurs 10.30-4.30, Fri 10.30-4.00. Also Tuesdays 5-6.45 during term time.*
Nearest Underground: *Battersea Park.*
Personnel: *Head of School:* Ms Deborah See. *Head of Art & Fashion:* To be announced.

WESTMINSTER COLLEGE

At the centre of London Westminster College aims to provide quality education and training and to serve key employment sectors by providing a flexible response to the learning needs of our clients, based on our tradition and international reputation as a college of excellence.
The dynamic and expanding creative programme area, covering art and design, fashion, textiles, interior design, photography, media and multimedia and performing arts, has benefited from considerable recent investment in facilities and equipment. We cater for for students of all ages with an exciting range of full and part-time creative courses, from GCSE and A-level to Higher National Diploma.

Courses:
Design (Graphic). Design (Interior). Fine Art. Illustration. Media. Multi-Media. Textiles.
Qualifications:
Adult Education. Foundation. HND.

York College of Further and Higher Education

Tadcaster Road, Dringhouses, York YO2 1UA.
Tel: *01904-770293.* **Fax:** *01904-770499.*
Opening times: *Mon-Thur 9-8.45pm, Fri 9-6.*
Nearest Station: *York.*
Personnel: *Curriculum Manager Art, Design & Crafts:* Mr Chris Brace . *Curriculum Manager Graphics, Media & Performing Arts:* Mrs Jenny Frayna. *Hairdressing, Beauty & Fashion:* Mrs Clare Wareing.
Full time art and design courses available from York College include:- (All courses are EDEXCEL BTEC).
GNVQ Foundation in Art and Design
GNVQ Intermediate in Art and Design
GNVQ Advanced in Art and Design
Diploma in Foundation Studies
National Diploma in Sculpture for Gardens and Landscapes
National Diploma in Design Crafts
Higher National Diploma in Design Crafts
National Diploma in 3D Design: Furniture, Product and Interior
National Diploma in Graphic Design
Higher National Diploma in Graphic Design
National Diploma in Fashion Design
Higher National Diploma in Fashion Design
National Diploma in Media Studies
National Diploma in Performing Arts
National Certificate in Art and Design

Courses:
Animation. Art History. Ceramics. Design (3-D). Design (Graphic). Design (Interior). Design (Photography). Design (Typographic). Fine Art. Furniture. Illustration. Jewellery/Silversmithing. Media. Multi-Media. Painting. Photography. Architectural Stained Glass. Textiles.
Qualifications:
Adult Education. Foundation. Pre-foundation. HND.

ART MANAGEMENT & PROMOTION

Advertising Services.
Art Consultants.
Art Management.
Electronic Services.
Information Services.
Marketing Services & PR.
Public Art Agencies.

Art Consultants

Aesthetic Environment Consultancy C
79 De Freville Avenue, Cambridge, CB4 1HP.
Tel: *01223-462712.*
Email *LOIST@COMPUSERVE.COM*
Opening times: *By appointment.*
Nearest Station: *Cambridge.*
Personnel: Dr Lois Tilbrook. Simone Tilbrook.

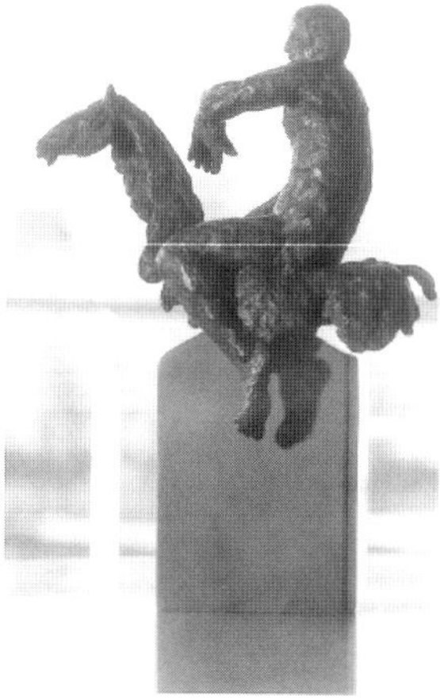

We are a professional art consultancy representing a wide base of contemporary artists in the following media: painting, sculpture, printmaking, wall hangings, glass, ceramics & photography. We offer sales, commissioning services, advice on selection and placement of works, and general aesthetic consultation. Located in the UK leading high-tech region of Cambridge, our direct involvement in the artistic community provides us with a wide base of talent and resources. Flexible rental scheme. Art for offices, the corporate sector, architects & designers, and private enquiries welcome. Initial consultation free.
Services and Facilities:
Art Consultancy. Art for Offices. Commissioning Service. Lectures.
Work Stocked and Sold:
Cer. Cra. Dr. Gla. Pa. Ph. Pr. Sc. Tx.
Price range: £200 - £20,000.

Alexandra Wettstein C
138 Ladywell Road, London SE13 7NS.
Tel: *0181-690 9556, Mobile 0411-700021.*
Fax: *0181-690 7959.*
Email *alexandra.wettstein@virgin.net*
Ws *http://graffiti.virgin.net/alexandra.wettstein/*
Opening times: *9-6 and By appointment.*
Nearest Underground: *Ladywell BR, Brockley.*
Personnel: *Proprietor:* Alexandra Wettstein.
Alexandra Wettstein deal primarily in the sale of recognised modern and contemporary art created from c.1880 to the present day. The business also deals in up and coming, but as yet less well known contemporary artists. Alexandra Wettstein has available unique works and limited edition works on paper as well as sculpture and ceramics. The company will locate specific works not in stock and provides framing, restoration and valuation services irrespective of whether or not the work was originally purchased from Alexandra Wettstein Fine Art.
Services and Facilities:
Art Consultancy. Art for Offices. Commissioning Service. Parking. Valuation.
Work Stocked and Sold:
Cer. Dr. Pa. Pr. Sc.
Price range: £50 - £150,000.
For artists see *Commercial Gallery Artists.*

Anne Berthoud
Flat 4, 1 Stanley Gardens, London W11 2ND.
Tel: *0171-229 8400.* **Fax:** *0171-221 8185.*
Opening times: *By appt.*
Nearest Underground: *Notting Hill Gate.*
Personnel: *Director:* Anne Berthoud.
Contemporary British and international paintings, drawings, prints, sculpture, ceramics and photographs. Agency and organisation of exhibitions. Anne Berthoud is also personally available for consultancy services.
Services and Facilities:
Art Consultancy. Commissioning Service. Valuation.
Work Stocked and Sold:
Cer. Dr. Pa. Ph. Pr. Sc.

Art Contact Ltd
2 Rickett Street, London SW6 1RU.
Tel: *0171-381 8655.* **Fax:** *0171-386 9015.*
Email *jt@artcontact.co.uk*
Ws *http://www.artcontact.co.uk*
Opening times: *Office hours, by appointment.*
Personnel: *Director:* Julian Thomas.
Art Consultants for office interiors and private clients. Rent or buy: Original works - Commissions - Prints - Sculpture - Limited Editions. Framing and Installation.
Services and Facilities:
Art Consultancy. Art for Offices. Commissioning Service. Framing. Restoration.
Work Stocked and Sold:
Dec. Dr. Pa. Ph. Pr. Sc. Tx.
Price range: £10 - £100,000.

Art For Offices C
International Art Consultants, The Galleries, 15 Dock Street, London E1 8JL.
Tel: *0171-481 1337.* **Fax:** *0171-481 3425.*
Email *art@artservs.demon.co.uk*
Opening times: *Open Mon-Fri 9.30-6.*
Nearest Underground: *Tower Hill, Aldgate, Aldgate East.*
Personnel: *Directors:* Andrew Hutchinson, Peter Harris. Amanda Basker.
We have 20 years experience advising architects, designers and corporate clients on the planning and implementation of art programmes. Our 10,000 square foot galleries provide a central source of art, enabling clients and specifiers to view a comprehensive range of art on a single visit to one location. We deal directly with over 800 artists and have a large visual reference library covering art in all media which is cross referenced by style and price. This makes it possible to research works of art, or artists for commission quickly and effectively. Art can be purchased, commissioned or acquired on a flexible rental basis.
Services and Facilities:
Art Consultancy. Art for Offices. Commissioning Service. Framing. Parking.
Work Stocked and Sold:
Cer. Cra. Dr. Gla. Pa. Ph. Pr. Sc. Tx. Wd.
Price range: £100 - £50,000.
For artists see *Commercial Gallery Artists.*

Art Link London
85 Mildmay Road, London N1 4PU.
Tel: *0171-249 3453.*

The Art Loss Register
12 Grosvenor Place, London SW1X 7HH.
Tel: *0171-235 3393.* **Fax:** *0171-235 1652.*
Email *artloss@artloss.com*
Ws *http://www.artloss.com*
Opening times: *8.30-6.30 (N.Y. 2-10pm).*
Nearest Underground: *Hyde Park Corner, Victoria.*
Personnel: *Managing Director:* James Emson.
The Art Loss Register is a database of stolen art with the aim of deterring art theft and reducing trade in stolen art, antiques and collectibles. Anyone who has suffered a theft can register details with the ALR. The database of 100,000+ items is constantly screened against forthcoming auction sales worldwide and against searches from law enforcement agencies, museums, galleries and any other prospective purchaser. The largest international independent database of stolen art in the world, the ALR has assisted in over £40m of recoveries. Offices in London, New York, Dusseldorf.
Services and Facilities:
Art Consultancy.

The Art Movement
120 Beaufort Mansions, Beaufort Street, London SW3 5AE.
Tel: *0171-351 0510, Mobile 0973-692494.*
Fax: *0171-351 0510.*

Axla Art Consultants C
121 Ledbury Road, London W11.
Tel: *0171-727 9724, 0171-229 7267.*

Belinda Canosa
38 St. Marys Grove, London W4 3LN.
Tel: *0181-747 0436.* **Fax:** *0181-995 1099.*

Brandler Galleries C
1 Coptfold Road, Brentwood, CM14 4BM.
Tel: *01277-222269.* **Fax:** *01277-222786.*
Email *art.british@dial.pipex.com*
Ws *http://www.brandler-galleries.com*
Opening times: *Tues-Sat 10-5.30.*
Nearest Station: *Brentwood 400 yds, Shenfield 1 mile.*
Personnel: *Director:* John Brandler. Linda Rodrigues.

Brandler Galleries

A friendly gallery just 2 miles from exit 28 on the M25 with free parking. A wide selection

of prints and paintings by British old and modern masters. As we purchase virtually all our stock we have to choose the best examples. Without the London overheads our clients know they get a much better deal on the same artists, without having to fight to get into London with all its problems. We are happy to send photographs or E-Mail images before your trip. Clients include banks, insurance companies and collectors all wanting the best art at realistic prices.
Services and Facilities:
Art Consultancy. Art for Offices. Commissioning Service. Framing. Parking. Restoration. Valuation.
Work Stocked and Sold:
Cer. Dr. Pa. Pr. Sc.
Price range: £50 - £65,000.

Business Art Galleries C
New Academy Gallery, 34 Windmill Street, Fitzrovia, London W1P 1HH.
Tel: *0171-323 4700* . **Fax:** *0171-436 3059.*
Email *business@curwen.demon.co.uk*
Ws *http://www.curwen.demon.co.uk*
Opening times: *Mon-Fri 10-6 (Thurs 10-8), Sat 11-5 (closed Bank Holiday Weekends).*
Nearest Underground: *Goodge Street, Tottenham Court Road.*
Personnel: *Directors:* John Hutchings, Jill Hutchings. *Contact:* Caroline Brown.

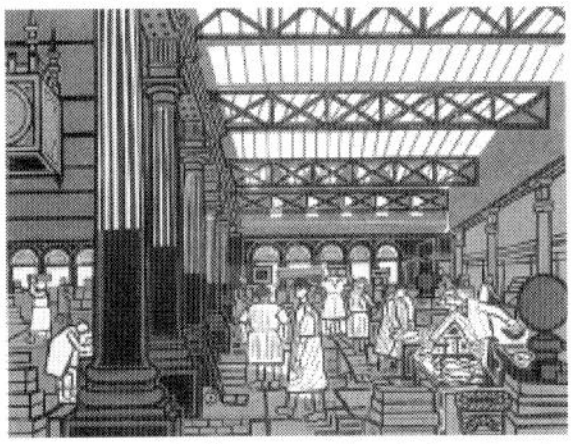

Business Art Galleries was founded within the Royal Academy of Art in 1978 and is Britain's longest established art consultants. Now an independent company, we offer a comprehensive corporate art service including: free consultations and on-site presentation, a flexible hire scheme and special commissions. Our two sister galleries, The New Academy Gallery and Curwen Gallery, provide us with an extensive permanent stock of work as well as a changing monthly programme of exhibitions (including our highly esteemed Northern Graduates show in August). This includes painting, limited edition prints and sculpture from both leading and up-and-coming contemporary British artists.
Services and Facilities:
Art Consultancy. Art for Offices. Commissioning Service.
Work Stocked and Sold:
Dr. Pa. Pr. Sc.
Price range: £50 - £20,000.
For artists see *Commercial Gallery Artists.*

CCA Galleries Corporate Art C
517-523 Fulham Road, London SW6 1HD.
Tel: *0171-386 4906.* **Fax:** *0171-386 4919.*
Opening times: *Mon-Fri 9.30-5.30.*
Nearest Underground: *Fulham Broadway.*
Personnel: *Director:* Stella Benakis.
CCA Galleries Corporate Department provides a comprehensive art service for architects, designers, specifiers and facility managers. Forming part of CCA Galleries, Europe's leading publisher of limited edition prints, our extensive range of artwork enables us to meet all creative requirements and budgets. In addition to our own publications, we source and commission works in all media. An excellent bespoke framing service is also available.
Services and Facilities:
Art Consultancy. Art for Offices. Commissioning Service. Framing.
Work Stocked and Sold:
Dr. Pa. Pr. Sc.

Conservation Management Ltd
10 Wilton Street, London SW1X 7AF.
Tel: *0171-823 2331.* **Fax:** *0171-823 2285.*
Opening times: *By appointment.*
Nearest Underground: *Victoria/Hyde Park Corner.*
Personnel: *Director:* Sally Lescher, MA (Courtauld).

CONSERVATION MANAGEMENT

Sally Lescher and associates assist private and corporate clients in putting together interesting collections of works of art. Expertise ranges from Old Master Paintings to 20th century British and contemporary art. They also provide specialist cataloguing, restoration and conservation services to museums and collectors.
Services and Facilities:
Art Consultancy. Art for Offices. Commissioning Service. Framing. Lectures. Restoration.

Coode-Adams Martin Associates
Inworth Hall, Inworth, Colchester, CO5 9SN.
Tel: *01376-561946.* **Fax:** *01376-570318.*

Davies & Tooth
5 Northfields Prospect, Putney Bridge Road, London SW18 1PE.
Tel: *0181-875 0820.* **Fax:** *0181-877 1741.*

de Putron Art Consultants Ltd.
27 Pattison Road, London NW2 2HL.
Tel: *0171-431 1125.* **Fax:** *0171-431 1125.*
Email *Lauradpac@asl.co.uk*
Opening times: *By appointment only.*
Nearest Underground: *Hampstead/Golders Green.*
Personnel: *Director:* Laura de Putron.

dp de Putron
art consultants

An art consultancy that provides a professional and comprehensive service to clients in the corporate and private sectors. It represents artists who specialise in painting, portraiture, sculpture, murals and the applied arts. These artists represent the very highest standards and are individually selected by the consultancy. They range from well-established names to the 'rising stars' who have just entered the market place. The consultancy works directly with corporate and private clients, architects and interior designers, and offers total flexibility of service irrespective of job size and complexity. Artwork can be purchased, rented or commissioned. Free consultation offered to all enquirers.
Services and Facilities:
Art Consultancy. Art for Offices. Commissioning Service.
Work Stocked and Sold:
App. Cer. Dr. Gla. Pa. Pr. Sc. Tx. Wd.
Price range: £100 - £50,000.
For artists see *Commercial Gallery Artists.*

Dickson Russell Art Management
7 Queen Anne's Gardens, Bedford Park, London, W4 1TU.
Tel: *0181-747 3066 & 0171-733 7137.*
Fax: *0181-742 7831.*
Opening times: *By appointment.*
Nearest Underground: *Turnham Green.*
Personnel: *Directors:* Rachel Dickson, Emma Russell.
Dickson Russell provides a complete range of art management services for both corporate and private clients, to include art acquisition, exhibition curation, project management for commissioned works, and maintenance of existing collections. Art of all media and from across all periods can be sourced to suit the client's business, profile and location. Additional services can include professional packing, shipping, restoration, framing, installation and photographing of artwork; catalogue literature, insurance updates and valuations are also undertaken. A professional fee is charged; no commission is taken on purchased artworks.
Services and Facilities:
Art Consultancy. Art for Offices. Commissioning Service. Framing. Restoration. Valuation.

Egee Art Consultancy C
9 Chelsea Manor Studios, Flood Street, London SW3 5SR.
Tel: *0171-351 6818.* **Fax:** *0171-376 3510.*
Email *egee.art@btinternet.com*
Ws *http://www.egeeart.com*
Opening times: *Mon-Fri 8.30-5.30, Sat by arrangement. By appointment.*
Nearest Underground: *Sloane Square or South Kensington.*
Personnel: *Director:* Dale Egee. *Sales:* Yvonne Eklund. *Art Consultant:* Kate Brown. *Administrator:* Barbara Allen.

EGEE ART CONSULTANCY

Specialists in art for the Middle East for twenty years. We have a wide range of antique and contemporary Arab and Orientalist art at our Gallery in London, our own range of editioned prints suitable for hotels and corporate interiors, and exclusive Alhambra plaques in painted resin and sterling silver. We find art that is appropriate for the Middle East, from reproductions to fine paintings and unique commissioned works. Our clients range from private collectors to governments and corporations, and we will be pleased to discuss your

artwork requirements. Please contact us for an appointment, or to request our brochures.
Services and Facilities:
Art Consultancy. Art for Offices. Commissioning Service. Framing. Restoration. Valuation.
Work Stocked and Sold:
Cra. Dr. Pa. Ph. Pr. Sc. Tx.
Price range: £50 - £35,000.
For artists see *Commercial Gallery Artists.*

Federation of British Artists
Mall Galleries, 17 Carlton House Terrace, London, SW1Y 5BD.
Tel: *0171-930 6844.*
Fax: *0171-839 7830.*

Fine Art Commissions Ltd. C
107 Walton Street, Knightsbridge, London SW3 2HT.
Tel: *0171-589 4111.*
Fax: *0171-589 3888.*
Email *facl@btinternet.com*
Ws *http://www.facl.com*
Opening times: *By appointment 10-6.*
Nearest Underground: *South Kensington or Knightsbridge.*
Personnel: *Director:* Sara Stewart.

Fine Art Commissions Ltd.

Specialists in Commissioned Art including Portraiture, Landscapes, Houses, Sculpture, Equestrian, Murals. Free advice starting with the choice of artist through to the end of the commission.
We are not governed by Members of a Society and so have a broad range of artists including established names and many talented newcomers. With an office conveniently situated in Knightsbridge we also advise on Restoration, Framing and Auction Consultancy.
Services and Facilities:
Art Consultancy. Commissioning Service. Framing. Restoration.
Work Stocked and Sold:
Dec. Pa. Sc.
Price range: £300 - £70,000.
For artists see *Commercial Gallery Artists.*

Howick Contemporary Art Ltd. (Contemporary Art Consultants)
The Side House, 18 Parkhill Road, London NW3 2YN.
Tel: *0171-284 2614.*
Fax: *0171-267 7861.*
Opening times: *Opening: normal office hours and visits by appointment only.*
Nearest Underground: *Belsize Park.*
Personnel: *Directors:* Louisa Howick, Alistair Howick.
A professional art consultancy providing a comprehensive and personal service to architects, interior designers and corporate clients on a wide range of art works. Imaginative well-researched solutions, including commissions, purchasing, and rentals within set budgets.
Clients include: BAA plc, Cable & Wireless plc, River & Rowing Museum, Henley-on-Thames, Marks & Spencer plc, Studio Downie, David Chipperfield Architects.
Services and Facilities:
Art Consultancy. Art for Offices. Commissioning Service. Framing. Parking.

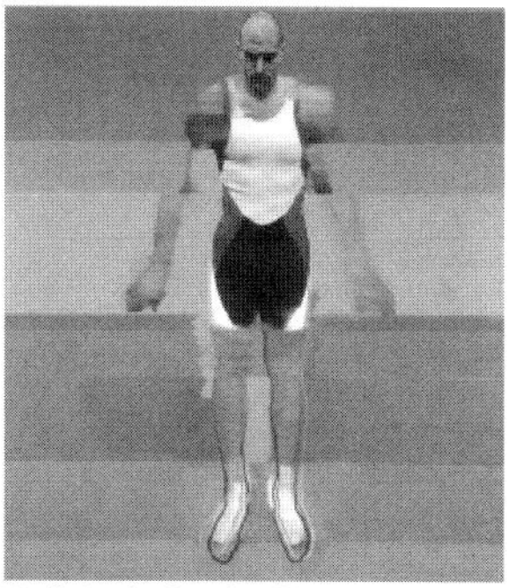

Work Stocked and Sold:
Cer. Cra. Dec. Dr. Fur. Gla. Pa. Ph. Pr. Sc. Tx. Wd.

Images, Corporate Art Consultants
19 Helenslea Avenue, Golders Green, London, NW11 8NE. **Tel:** *0181-455 3160.*

James Cox Consultancy
Lynton House, 48 Lynton Road, Rayners Lane, Harrow, HA2 9NN

Kathryn Bell/Fine Art Consultancy
Studio 123D, Canalot Production Studios, 222 Kensal Road, London W10 5BN.
Tel: *0181-960 0070.* **Fax:** *0181-960 0209.*

London Art Consultancy C
29 Hollywood Road, London, SW10.
Tel: *0171-351 7711.*

London Artforms C
Low Ground Floor, 7-15 Rosebery Avenue, London, EC1. **Tel:** *0171-837 1900.*

Louise Pickering Fine Art
79 Elms Road, London SW4 9EP.
Tel: *0171-720 4168.* **Fax:** *0171-720 9292.*
Email *lpfa@globalnet.uk*
Opening times: *By appt.*
Nearest Underground: *Clapham Common.*
Personnel: Louise Pickering.
Services and Facilities:
Art Consultancy. Art for Offices. Commissioning Service. Framing. Restoration. Valuation.
Work Stocked and Sold:
Dr. Pa. Ph. Pr. Sc.
Price range: £200 - £50,000+.
For artists see *Commercial Gallery Artists.*

Lynne Stern & Linnet Feilding
Art Consultancy & Management, 46 Bedford Row, London WC1R 4LR.
Tel: *0171-491 8905.* **Fax:** *0171-624 7072.*
A professional team with wide, independent art experience and particular expertise in working with corporate clients, architects and designers and in managing all aspects of large and small art projects, to schedule and to budget. For each client, works are selected from in-depth knowledge of established and emerging and younger generation artists, for purchase or for commissioning.

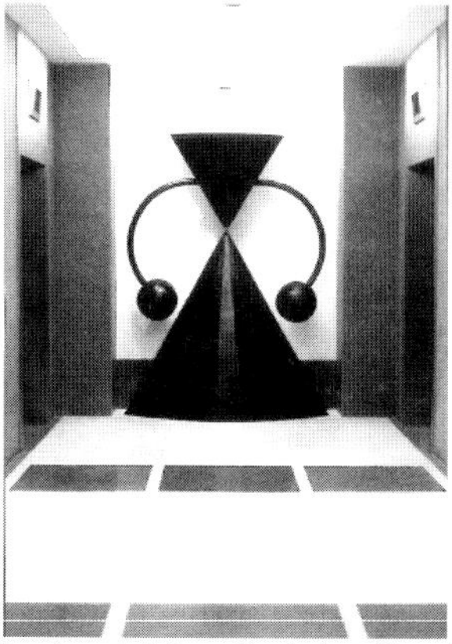

Experience includes working in the public and private art sectors, including several years in the business art section of the Royal Academy of Arts. Art management and inventory systems and maintenance including framing and hanging for existing works of art are some of the range of back-up services provided.
Client projects were awarded the Art and Work Award in 1996 and Commendation in 1998.
Services and Facilities:
Art Consultancy. Art for Offices. Commissioning Service. Lectures.

Sarah Myerscough Associates C
40 South Molton Street, London W1Y 1HB.
Tel: *0171-495 0069.* **Fax:** *0171-493 2354.*

Tanja Gertik Fine Art Consultant
First Floor, 42 Welbeck Street, London W1M 7HF. **Tel:** *0171-483 4526.*

Thomas Corman Arts
24 Daleham Gardens, London NW3 5DA.
Tel: *0171-433 1339.* **Fax:** *0171-433 1339.*
Email *tca@btinternet.com*
Opening times: *Anytime by appointment.*
Nearest Underground: *Swiss Cottage, Finchley Road, Belsize Park.*
Personnel: *Partners:* Ruth Corman, Christopher Thomas.
Thomas Corman Arts provides a professional service, working with corporate clients, architects, designers as well as private collectors. Dealing directly with over 400 young and established artists and makers from the UK and overseas, TCA has gained a reputation for working effectively with clients from the initial free consultation to the installation of artworks. Our role is to make your acquisition of art easy. TCA will source art to suit your budget, your location and your image.
Services and Facilities:
Art Consultancy. Commissioning Service. Framing.
Work Stocked and Sold:
Cer. Cra. Dec. Gla. Pa. Ph. Pr. Sc. Tx. Wd.
Price range: £100 - £50,000.

Unicorn Pictures Ltd. C
"Space 8" Hollywood Road, London SW10 9HY
Tel: *0171-376 3195.* **Fax:** *0171-351 5100.*
Opening times: *Tue-Sat 11-8, Sun 12-5.*
Nearest Underground: *Fulham Broadway, South Kensington.*
Personnel: *Director:* John Simmons FRSA. *Consultants:* Maurizio Castronovo, Michelle Dennison.

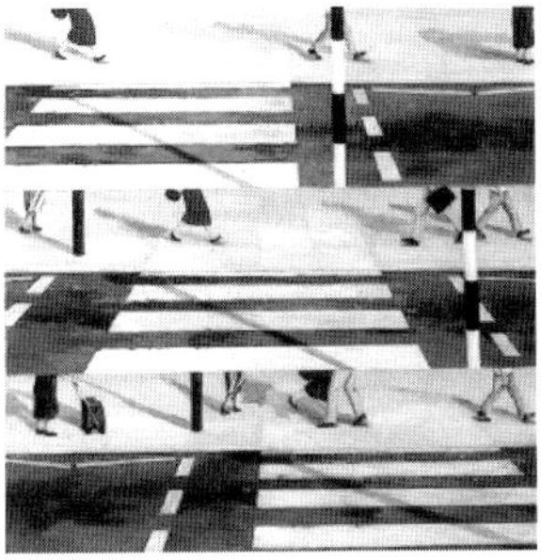

Unicorn Pictures (Established 1961) provides new and adventurous paintings and sculpture by award-winning British artists with rising reputations, to Parliamentary, corporate and private collections from their recently opened gallery in Chelsea. Creates in-house exhibitions in corporate premises, promotional events, and provides a renowned artist-in-residence scheme.
Services and Facilities:
Art Consultancy. Art for Offices. Commissioning Service.
Work Stocked and Sold:
Cer. Gla. Pa. Pr. Sc. Tx.
Price range: £300 - £8,000.

William Hardie Ltd
Fine Art Consultants and Valuers, 15a Blythswood Square, Glasgow G2 4BG.
Tel: *0141-221 6780.*
Fax: *0141-248 6237.*

Work Place Art Consultants C
Globe Studio, 62 Southwark Bridge, London SE1.
Tel: *0171-401 9494.*

Art Management

Art For Offices C
International Art Consultants, The Galleries, 15 Dock Street, London E1 8JL.
Tel: *0171-481 1337.*
Fax: *0171-481 3425.*
Email *art@artservs.demon.co.uk*
Opening times: *Open Mon-Fri 9.30-6.*
Nearest Underground: *Tower Hill, Aldgate, Aldgate East.*
Personnel: *Directors:* Andrew Hutchinson, Peter Harris. Amanda Basker.
We have 20 years experience advising architects, designers and corporate clients on the planning and implementation of art programmes.
Our 10,000 square foot galleries provide a central source of art, enabling clients and specifiers to view a comprehensive range of art on a single visit to one location. We deal directly with over 800 artists and have a large visual reference library covering art in all media which is cross referenced by style and price. This makes it possible to research works of art, or artists for commission quickly and effectively. Art can be purchased, commissioned or acquired on a flexible rental basis.
Services and Facilities:
Art Consultancy. Art for Offices. Commissioning Service. Framing. Parking.
Work Stocked and Sold:
Cer. Cra. Dr. Gla. Pa. Ph. Pr. Sc. Tx. Wd.
Price range: £100 - £50,000.

Conservation Management Ltd
10 Wilton Street, London SW1X 7AF.
Tel: *0171-823 2331.*
Fax: *0171-823 2285.*
Opening times: *By appointment.*
Nearest Underground: *Victoria/Hyde Park Corner.*
Personnel: *Director:* Sally Lescher, MA (Courtauld).
Sally Lescher and associates assist private and corporate clients in putting together interesting collections of works of art. Expertise ranges from Old Master Paintings to 20th century British and contemporary art. They also provide specialist cataloguing, restoration and conservation services to museums and collectors.
Services and Facilities:
Art Consultancy. Art for Offices. Commissioning Service. Framing. Lectures. Restoration.

Heritage Lottery Fund and the National Heritage Memorial Fund
7 Holbein Place, London SW1W 8NR.
Tel: *0171-591 6000.*
Fax: *0171-591 6001.*

Independent Public Arts C
17 Bernard Street, Leith, Edinburgh EH6 6PW.
Tel: *0131-555 0045.*
Fax: *0131-554 1850.*

Electronic Services

The LMR Computer Consultancy
19 South Walk, Wickham, BR4 9JA.
Tel: *0181-462 7740.*
Fax: *0181-462 7739.*

Thesaurus Group Ltd
Mill Court, Furlongs, Newport, PO30 2AA.
Tel: *01983-826000.*
Fax: *01983-826201.*
Ws *thesaurus.co.uk/*
Personnel: *Managing Director:* John Woracker.
Comprehensive pre-sale information products based on auction data from around the world giving the user access to in excess of 7,000 sales and 4 million objects each year from over 600 auction houses in the UK and North America.
Services and Facilities:
Bookshop. Valuation.

Information Services

The Art Loss Register
12 Grosvenor Place, London SW1X 7HH.
Tel: *0171-235 3393.*
Fax: *0171-235 1652.*
Email *artloss@artloss.com*
Ws *http://www.artloss.com*
Opening times: *8.30-6.30 (N.Y. 2-10pm).*
Nearest Underground: *Hyde Park Corner, Victoria.*
Personnel: *Managing Director:* James Emson.
The Art Loss Register is a database of stolen art with the aim of deterring art theft and reducing trade in stolen art, antiques and collectibles. Anyone who has suffered a theft can register details with the ALR.
The database of 100,000+ items is constantly screened against forthcoming auction sales worldwide and against searches from law enforcement agencies, museums, galleries and any other prospective purchaser. The largest international independent database of stolen art in the world, the ALR has assisted in over £40m of recoveries. Offices in London, New York, Dusseldorf.
Services and Facilities:
Art Consultancy.

Art Sales Index Ltd
1 Thames Street, Weybridge, KT13 8JG.
Tel: *01932-856426.*
Fax: *01932-842482.*

Artists' General Benevolent Institution
Burlington House, Piccadilly, London W1V 0DJ.
Tel: *0171-734 1193.*
Fax: *0171 734 1193.*

Artsinform
Cooper House, 2 Michael Road, London SW6 2AD.
Tel: *0171-610 9991.*
Fax: *0171-610 9992.*

Axis
Leeds Metropolitan University, Calverley Street, Leeds LS1 3HE.
Tel: *0113-245 7946.*
Fax: *0113-245 7950.*
Email *axis@gn.apc.org*
Ws *http://www.lmu.ac.uk/ces/axis*
Opening times: *Mon-Fri 9-5.*
Personnel: *Principal Information Officer:* Cath Bentley.

AXIS
For Information on Visual Artists

Axis is a visual arts service providing information about contemporary artists and craftspeople living/working in Britain. The information is displayed on a computer database, the Axis database. The Axis database contains each artist's CV and up to nine images of their work. Nearly 2,500 are registered. The Axis database is available at Axispoints around the UK. Alternatively, information can be provided over the phone and by post. Printouts of CVs and artwork images are available at nominal cost. Axis is mainly funded by the Arts Councils of England, Scotland and Wales.

International Arts Bureau

4 Baden Place, Crosby Row, London SE1 1YW.
Tel: *0171-403 6454 (Admin).*
Fax: *0171-403 2009.*
Email *iab@mcmail.com (general)*
Opening times: *9.30-5.30.*
Nearest Underground: *London Bridge.*
Personnel: *Director:* Rod Fisher. *Manager:* Valerie Synmoie.

International Arts Bureau

The International Arts Bureau is an independent agency providing information, advice, research, publications, training and consultancy on international arts issues. The Bureau offers:- a free enquiry service open five day a week (between 10-1pm and 2-5pm) - contact can be made by telephone (0171-403 7001) or by letter, email (enquiry.iab@mcmail.com) or fax; free monthly one-to-one funding advice surgeries; a bi-monthly journal, the International Arts Navigator outlining key European Union policy developments, prospective legislation, international funding programmes and case studies (available on subscription) tailored training courses and information seminars on a range of international arts issues.
Services and Facilities:
Art Consultancy.

National Irish Visual Arts Library

100 Thomas Street, Dublin 8,
Tel: *00353-1-6364200.*
Fax: *00353-1-6364207.*
Email *annehodge@ncad.ie*
Ws *http://www.ncad.ie*
Opening times: *Mon 10-1, Tue & Wed 10-1, 2-5, Thur 2-8, Fri 10-1, 2-8.*
Personnel: *Administrator:* Anne Hodge. *Librarian:* Edward Murphy.
Based in the National College of Art and Design, the Library is a unique research facility which holds information on Irish art and design.
The core collection (amassed over the last 20 years) comprises files on individual artists (2000) and galleries (200). A wide variety of ephemera make up each file: exhibition catalogues, invitation cards, pricelists, press releases, press cuttings and correspondence.
Other areas covered include: design, craft, art collections, societies, public art, Irish art abroad and special exhibitions. Monographs, artists' books, slides and videos also form part of the collections. Donations of relevant material are always welcome.
Services and Facilities:
Disabled Access.

Marketing Services and PR

Alan Sykes Promotions

Talkin Head Farm, Brampton, CA8 1LT.
Tel: *016977-2228.* **Fax:** *016977-2228.*

Art Market Research

85 Stoke Newington Church, London N16.
Tel: *0171-249 8071.*

Brian Potter and Associates

12 Ryeworth Road, Charlton Kings, Cheltenham, GL52 6LH.
Tel: *01242-529121.* **Fax:** *01242-513495.*

James Kessell Design Consultants

Meadows Edge, Gibraltar, Aylesbury, HP17 8TY.
Tel: *01296-747446.*
Fax: *01844-292150.*

John Haywood Press and Public Relations C

67 Gordon House, Glamis Road, London E1 9ED.
Tel: *0171-481 3073.*

Layzell Public Relations for the Arts

98 Castle Street, Woodbridge, IP12 1HL.
Tel: *01394-386139.*
Fax: *01394-385149.*
Email *layzellpr@compuserve.com*
Personnel: *Director:* Alistair Layzell.
Layzell Public Relations for the Arts specialise in publicity for art exhibitions and events, artists and books on the arts. Marketing Services.

Parker Harris Partnership

15 Church Street, Esher, KT10 8YZ.
Tel: *01372-462190.*
Fax: *01372-460032.*
Email *info@parkerharris.co.uk*
Opening times: *Open daily 9-5.*
Personnel: *Partners:* Penny Harris, Emma Parker.

PARKER HARRIS

Parker Harris and Company specialise in all aspects of arts administration, exhibition organising, press and public relations. As well as organising national touring events such as the Jerwood Painting Prize, The Hunting Art Prizes and the Singer Friedlander/Sunday Times Watercolour Competition, they also arrange one man shows throughout the UK and Europe, liaising between artist, gallery, buyer and press.

Sue Bond Public Relations C

Boxted Hall, Boxted, Bury St. Edmunds, IP29 4JT.
Tel: *01787-282288.* **Fax:** *01787-282119.*

Yvonne Courtney PR

5a Bramber Road, London W1A 9PA.
Tel: *0171-795 6001.*

Public Art Agencies

Cardiff Bay Arts Trust

123 Bute Street, Cardiff CF1 6AE.
Tel: *01222-488772.* **Fax:** *01222-472439.*
Email *Arts.Trust@ENABLIS.co.uk*
Opening times: *Daily office hours.*
Personnel: *Director:* Carole-Anne Davies.

Cardiff Bay Arts Trust

CBAT is a busy Public Art Consultancy which has achieved over 60 projects within its award winning public art schemes, as part of the urban regeneration strategy in Cardiff Bay. Projects undertaken include temporary and permanent works, integral and stand alone pieces in the public realm, environmental improvements, educational workshops and a changing exhibition programme. CBAT works in collaboration with residents, public authorities, the private sector, architects, artists, and craft workers in the initiation and implementation of commissions. Following the success of its work in Cardiff, CBAT is now active in other areas across the UK. Services: Consultancy and management of public art projects both urban and rural, Art for Offices, Commissioning Service.
Services and Facilities:
Art Consultancy. Art for Offices. Commissioning Service. Gallery space for hire. Guided Tours. Lectures.

Cywaith Cymru - Artworks Wales

2 John Street, Cardiff CF1 5AE.
Tel: *01222-489543.* **Fax:** *01222-465458.*
Personnel: *Director:* Tamara Krikorian.

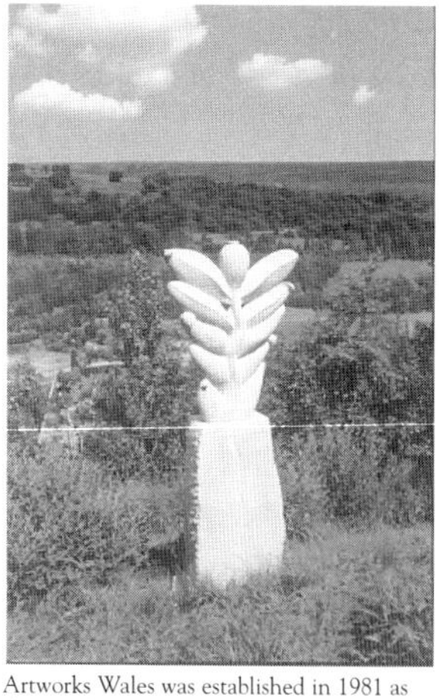

Artworks Wales was established in 1981 as the Welsh Sculpture Trust to encourage the placing of art in the environment through commissions, exhibitions and residencies.

The wide range of work covered by the organisation is supported by a strong commitment to the cultural life of Wales, seeking to bring about new work which is particular to its environment and of which reflects the culture from which it comes. Cywaith Cymru works closely with local authorities, industry, environmental groups and arts organisations. It encourages creative collaboration between artists, architects, landscape architects and developers.
Registered charity No. 512006.
Services and Facilities:
Art Consultancy. Commissioning Service.

Free Form Arts Trust
38 Dalston Lane, London E8 3AZ.
Tel: *0171-249 3394.* **Fax:** *0171-249 8499.*

Public Art Commissions Agency
Studio 6, Victoria Works, Vittoria Street, Jewellery Quarter, Birmingham B1 3PE.
Tel: *0121-212 4454.* **Fax:** *0121-212 4426.*
Personnel: *Director:* Vivien Lovell.
London office:- c/o 116 Commercial Street, London E1 6NF. The Public Art Commissions Agency is constituted as a company limited by guarantee, registered as an educational charity, and governed by a Council of Trustees. The Agency works nationally with a wide range of public and private sector clients. Organisation objectives: the Agency's aim is to develop and carry out a programme of visual arts commissions and residencies by professional artists and craftspeople. It ensures that work of the highest quality is produced in a context of appropriate consultation with the community for which it is intended; advocates, through collaboration with the appropriate professional and statutory bodies, that the visual arts are fully integrated into projects of architectural or environmental design. Presentations, seminars, workshops organised.
Services and Facilities:
Art Consultancy. Commissioning Service. Lectures. Workshop Facilities.

Public Art Development Trust
3rd Floor, Kirkham House, 12-14 Whitfield Street, London W1P 5RD.
Tel: *0171-580 9977.* **Fax:** *0171-580 8540.*

ART SERVICES

ART INSURANCE

Brokers.
Companies.
Loss adjusters.

Insurance Brokers

Aon UK
Briar Cliff House, Kings Head, Farnborough, GU4 7TE.
Tel: *01252-807321.* **Fax:** *01252-807330.*

Blackwall Green (Jewellery and Fine Art)
Lambert Fenchurch House, Friary Court, Crutched Friars, London EC3N 2NP.
Tel: *0171-560 3000, Telex 8814631.*
Fax: *0171-560 3649.*

Byas Mosley & Co. Ltd.
International Fine Art Division, William Byas House, 14-18 St. Clare Street, London WC3N 1JX.
Tel: *0171-481 0101.* **Fax:** *0171-480 5303.*

Crowley Colosso
Friary Court, Crutched Friars, London EC3N 2NP.
Tel: *0171-560 3000.* **Fax:** *0171-560 3655.*

HSBC Gibbs (HCA) Ltd.
Bishops Court, 27/33 Artillery Lane, London E1 7LP.
Tel: *0171-661 2360.* **Fax:** *0171-377 2175.*
Opening times: *9.30-5.30 Mon-Fri.*
Nearest Underground: *Liverpool Street.*
Personnel: Bob Diggory. Tony Barratt.
Specialist insurance brokers for Art Dealers; Antique Dealers; Auction Houses; Shippers and Packers; Art Galleries and Museums; Historic Houses; Private Collections; Corporate Collections; Exhibitions; Transits; Art Trade Fairs and Jewellery. Official insurance brokers for "Art 97". A member of the HSBC Group.

Jardine Insurance Brokers Int. Ltd.
Jardine House, 6 Crutched Friars, London EC3N 2HT.
Tel: *0171-528 4100, 0171-528 4444.*

Needham Jobson & Co. C
Byron House, 102 Wimbledon Hill Road, London SW19 7PB.
Tel: *0181-944 8870.* **Fax:** *0181-944 8816.*

SBJ Speciality Limited
One Hundred Whitechapel, London E1 1JG.
Tel: *0171-816 2000.* **Fax:** *0171-816 2121.*

Personnel: *Directors:* Christopher Bailey-West, David Lock.
Dedicated specialist in the insurance of Fine Arts & Collectables for Private Collectors, Galleries, Museums and others connected to the art world. For further information contact Christopher Bailey-West or David Lock.

Sedgwick Fine Art
Sedgwick House, The Sedgwick Centre, London E1 8DX.
Tel: *0171-377 3456.* **Fax:** *0171-377 3199.*

Sneath, Kent & Stuart Ltd.
Stuart House, 53/55 Scrutton Street, London EC2A 4QQ.
Tel: *0171-739 5646.* **Fax:** *0171-739 6467.*

Willis Corroon Fine Art
Ten Trinity Square, London EC3P 3AX.
Tel: *0171-975 2173.* **Fax:** *0171-975 2447.*

Windsor Insurance Brokers Ltd., Fine Art and Antiques Division
Lyon House, 160-166 Borough High Street, London SE1 1JR.
Tel: *0171-407 7144.* **Fax:** *0171-378 6676.*
Email *paul.tasker@windsor.co.uk*
Opening times: 8-6.
Nearest Underground: *London Bridge.*
Personnel: *Account Executives:* David Beck, Peter Clifford.

Brokers to: LAPADA; The Fine Art Trade Guild, IDDA and BAFRA. Instant Premium Indications. Specialist Brokers to Contemporary Art Dealers, Private Collections, Antique and Fine Art Dealers, Interior Decorators. Fairs - Brokers to: World of Drawings and Watercolours, 20th Century Art Fair, Fine Art and Antiques Fair, Olympia, Chelsea Antiques Fair to name a few.

Insurance Chartered Loss Adjusters

Cunningham Ellis & Buckle Fine Arts
Suite 772 Lloyds, One Lime Street, London EC3M 7DQ
Tel: *0171-283 0529.* **Fax:** *0171-283 0528.*
Email *hodgsonp@ellisandbuckle.co.uk*
Opening times: *8am-8pm.*
Nearest Underground: *Bank.*
Personnel: *Lloyds Director:* Paul Hodgson.
In October 1998, Ellis & Buckle and Cunningham UK merged to become Cunningham Ellis & Buckle. Operationally, the new business is based on the structure of Ellis & Buckle, which was originally formed in 1914 to provide loss adjusting services. The merger has expanded the company's national and international representation and, currently, it is the largest Claims and Incident Management organisation in the UK. Cunningham Ellis & Buckle is part of the Lindsey Morden Group who have 400 offices in 40 countries providing Claims and Risk Management services worldwide.
Services and Facilities:
Art Consultancy. Lectures. Valuation.

Insurance Companies

Hiscox plc.
1 Great St. Helen's, London EC3A 6HX.
Tel: *0171-448 6000.* **Fax:** *0171-448 6797.*
Email *enquiry@hiscox.co.uk*
Ws *http://www.hiscox.co.uk*
Personnel: Robert Read. Annabel Fell-Clark. Emma O'Neill.

Hiscox plc is one of the leading specialist insurers in the UK, representing 30 years' experience and knowledge of providing individually tailored insurance. By combining efficiency of service, speed and fairness of claims payment, Hiscox offers an unparalleled ranged of products to the discerning individual.
Services and Facilities:
Café.

Nordstern Art Insurance Ltd.
78 Leadenhall Street, London EC3A 3DH.
Tel: *0171-626 5001.* **Fax:** *0171-626 4606.*

Insurance Other

Society of Amateur Artists
PO Box 50, Newark, NG23 5GY.
Tel: *01949-844050.* **Fax:** *01949-844051.*

CONSERVATION & RESTORATION

THE ART WORLD
DIRECTORY

Abbott & Holder C
30 Museum Street, London WC1A 1LH.
Tel: *0171-637 3981.* **Fax:** *0171-631 0575.*
Email *abbott.holder@virgin.net*
Ws *http://www.artefact.co.uk/AaH.html*
Opening times: *Mon-Sat 9.30-6, Thurs 9.30-7.*
Nearest Underground: *Tottenham Court Road.*
Personnel: *Partners:* Phillip Athill, John Abbott.
Over 1000 English watercolours,, drawings and prints (with some oils) 1780-1990 displayed on three gallery floors. Founded in 1936 our policy has always been to sell pictures that can be bought from income and our price range is from £50-£5,000. We have an in-house conservator and are happy to give free advice of cleaning, restoring and framing. Every seven weeks we issue a LIST introducing 300 works to stock and announcing any particular exhibition we are featuring. Our LISTS are free and will be sent in application.
Services and Facilities:
Art Consultancy. Framing. Gallery space for hire. Restoration. Valuation.
Work Stocked and Sold:
Pr.
Price range: £50 - £5,000.

Clare Finn & Co.
38 Cornwall Gardens, London SW7 4AA.
Tel: *0171-937 1895.*
Fax: *0171-937 4198.*

Connaught Galleries
44 Connaught Street, London W2.
Tel: *0171-723 1660.* **Fax:** *0171-723 1660.*
Opening times: *Mon-Fri 10-6.30, Sat 10-1.*
Nearest Underground: *Paddington, Lancaster Gate, Marble Arch.*
Personnel: *Partner:* Michael Hollamby.
Wood and aluminium framing. Mirrors to order, or from stock. Dry-mounting. Mount cutting. Shrinkwrapping. Easels and artist supplies. Glass supplied or cut. Frame repairs. Picture restoration. A wide range of prints and posters in stock or to order from extensive catalogues. Limited edition fine art prints. Limited edition fine art figurines. Glass and perspex display cases and display domes and bases.
Services and Facilities:
Art for Offices. Framing. Gallery space for hire. Parking. Restoration. Shop. Workshop Facilities.

Conservation Management Ltd
10 Wilton Street, London SW1X 7AF.
Tel: *0171-823 2331.* **Fax:** *0171-823 2285.*
Opening times: *By appointment.*
Nearest Underground: *Victoria/Hyde Park Corner.*
Personnel: *Director:* Sally Lescher, MA (Courtauld).
Sally Lescher and associates assist private and corporate clients in putting together interesting collections of works of art.
Expertise ranges from Old Master Paintings to 20th century British and contemporary art. They also
provide specialist cataloguing, restoration and conservation services to museums and collectors.
Services and Facilities:
Art Consultancy. Art for Offices. Commissioning Service. Framing. Lectures. Restoration.

The Conservation Studio
Sparsholt, Winchester, SO21 SQH.
Tel: *01962-776495.* **Fax:** *01962-776495.*
Email *WinStudio@aol.com*
Opening times: *By appointment only.*
Personnel: Paul Congdon-Clelford.
Member of IPC; FATG; ABPR; GADR. The Conservation Studio specialises in the restoration and conservation of oil paintings on canvas and panel; water colours and other works of art on paper. The Studio are conservators to Museums, Galleries and Institutions including private collections. Services: Home consultations, collection and delivery throughout most of Britain.
Services and Facilities:
Art Consultancy. Parking. Restoration.

De Beer Studios
9 Old Bond Street, London W1X.
Tel: *0171-629 1470.*

Deborah Bates Paper Conservation & Gallery
191 St. John's Hill, Battersea, London SW11 1TH.
Tel: *0171-223 1629.* **Fax:** *0171-207 1330.*
Opening times: *Studio: Mon-Fri 10-6. Gallery: Mon-Sat 10-4.*
Nearest Underground: *Clapham Junction.*
Personnel: *Proprietor:* Deborah Bates.
Established in 1980 the conservation practice offers studio and on site conservation and restoration of works of art on paper: watercolours, prints, drawings and pastels for private collectors, galleries and institutions. All staff fully qualified. Large, well equipped studio. Insurance work undertaken (flood and fire damage). Appraisal and estimates are given free. Condition and treatment reports. Framing service and advice on storage and display for preventative conservation. Delivery and collection can be arranged. Member of the Institute of Paper Conservation and listed on the register maintained by the Museum & Galleries Commission. Gallery specialising in contemporary art.
Services and Facilities:
Restoration.

Fine Art Commissions Ltd.
107 Walton Street, Knightsbridge, London SW3 2HT.
Tel: *0171-589 4111.* **Fax:** *0171-589 3888.*
Email *facl@btinternet.com*
Ws *http://www.facl.com*
Opening times: *By appointment 10-6.*
Nearest Underground: *South Kensington or Knightsbridge.*
Personnel: *Director:* Sara Stewart.

Fine Art Commissions Ltd.

Specialists in Commissioned Art including Portraiture, Landscapes, Houses, Sculpture, Equestrian, Murals. Free advice starting with the choice of artist through to the end of the commission. We are not governed by Members of a Society and so have a broad range of artists including established names and many talented new-comers. With an office conveniently situated in Knightsbridge we also advise on Restoration, Framing and Auction Consultancy.
Services and Facilities:
Art Consultancy. Commissioning Service. Framing. Restoration.
Work Stocked and Sold:
Dec. Pa. Sc.
Price range: £300 - £70,000.

G. Bignell Paper Conservation
45 Coronet Street, London N1.
Tel: *0171-729 3161.*

Graeme Storey
The Grange, Maesbrook, Oswestry, SY10 8QP.
Tel: *0169-185260.*

Hahn & Son C
47 Albemarle Street, London, W1X 8FE.
Tel: *0171-493 1630, 0171-493 9196.*

James Wray Picture Conservation
Wood Farm, Ipswich Road, Otley Ipswich,
Tel: *01473-890286.*

Lees Fine Art Restorers
Unit 11, Wellington Close, Ledbury Road, London W11.
Tel: *0171-229 3521.*

Lowe & Butcher
Neckinger Mills, 162-164 Abbey Street, London SE1.
Tel: *0171-237 1113.*

Patricia Garner
Arragon Conservation Studio, 55 Arragon Road, Twickenham, TW1 3NG.
Tel: *0181-892 1819, 0181-286 6153.*
Fax: *0181-891 0115.*

Paul Mitchell Ltd
99 New Bond Street, London W1Y 9LF.
Tel: *0171-493 8732 / 0860.*
Fax: *0171-409 7136.*

Plowden and Smith C
190 St. Ann's Hill, Wandsworth, London SW18 2RT.
Tel: *0181-874 4005.* **Fax:** *0181-874 7248.*

Preservations Solutions
60 Queens Gardens, London W2.
Tel: *0171-724 4744.*

Rankins (Glass) Company Ltd.
The London Glass Centre, 24-34 Pearson Street, London E2 8JD.
Tel: *0171-729 4200.*
Fax: *0171-729 7135/9197.*
Personnel: Stephanie Graham.
Holders of the Royal Warrant for supplying low-reflective glass, Rankins are independent glass processors and glaziers situated in the east end of London. We specialise in fire-resistant, conservation and low-reflective glass and carry substantial stocks of these and all standard float glass products. With our vast range of equipment we can offer all the different forms of glass processing required by the end user as well as design advice when required. For further information please call the Rankin Sales Office.

S. Firnberg Paper Conservation
Home Farm, Salters Lane, Ludgershall,
Nr. Aylesbury, HP18 9NY.

Simon R. Gillespie
16 Albemarle Street, London W1X.
Tel: *0171-493 0988.*
Fax: *0171-493 0955.*
Email *Simon.R.Gillespie@btinternet.com*
Ws *http://www.art-connection.com*
Opening times: *Mon-Fri 9-6.*
Nearest Underground: *Green Park.*
Personnel: *Partner:* Simon Gillespie.

Undertaking the restoration of oil paintings on panel or canvas, early English pictures, old masters and portraits.
Our West End studio has been specialising in Conservation and Restoration for the past twenty years. We work with small collections and individuals as well as large Institutions, Clubs and Galleries. We offer advice on all aspects of paintings - including lighting, framing, hanging and humidity control. In addition, we are pleased to give assistance with the acquisition or disposal of paintings.
Member UKIC - IIC - included in the register maintained by Museums and Galleries Commission.
Services and Facilities:
Art Consultancy. Art for Offices. Framing. Restoration. Valuation.

Sophia Fairclough
Studio 5, Whitehouse Mews, 37-39 Westminster Bridge Road, London SE1 7QD.
Tel: *0171-261 0735.*
Fax: *0171-261 0735.*

The Studio
55 Arragon Road, Twickenham, TW1 3NG.
Tel: *0181-892 1819.*

Trade Picture Services
Neckinger Mills, Abbey Street, London SE1.
Tel: *0171-237 4388.*

UCL Painting Analysis
43 Gordon Square, London WC1H.
Tel: *0171-383 2090.*

Witney Restorations Ltd.
Unit 17, Hanborough Business Park, Main Road, Long Hanborough, OX7 2LH.
Tel: *01993-883336.*
Fax: *01993-779852.*

NOTES

NOTES

FINE ART PRINTERS

Fine Art Printers.
Art cards.

Fine Art Printers

Abacus (Colour Printers) Ltd
Lowick Green, Lowick, Ulverston, LA12 8DX.
Tel: *01229-885361.* **Fax:** *01229 -885348.*
Opening times: *Mon-Sat 9-5.*
Personnel: *Directors:* John Sutcliffe, Vicki Sutcliffe.
Specialist printers to the art world - nationwide! Mail order postcards, greetings cards, posters, catalogues from your own art work. All work is in house to ensure maximum print quality and accuracy of colour to the original art work. Print members of the Fine Art Trade Guild for 10 years.
Services and Facilities:
Parking.

Amica Fine Art Printing Ltd.
F1 Park Hall, 40 Martell Road, London SE21 8EN.
Tel: *0181-670 6060.* **Fax:** *0181-670 0060.*

BAS Printers Ltd.
Over Wallop, Stockbridge, SO20 8JD.
Tel: *01264-781711.* **Fax:** *01264-781116.*

Broad Oak Colour
Units A & B, 254 Broad Oak Road, Canterbury, CT2 7QH.
Tel: *01227-767856.* **Fax:** *01227-762599.*

Dayfold Fine Art Printers C
Dayfold House, Black Moor Road, Verwood, BH31 6BE.
Tel: *01202-827141.* **Fax:** *01202-825841.*

Fidelity Colour Fine Art Prints
8-10-12 Hornsby Square, Southfields, Lamdon, SS15 6SD.
Tel: *01268-544066.* **Fax:** *01268-418977.*

J.A. Repro
Unit 2, Stephens Industrial Estate, 635 Warwick Road, Tyseley, Birmingham B11 2EZ.
Tel: *0973-232834.*

J.Thomson Colour Printers
14 Carnoustie Place, Glasgow G5 8PB.
Tel: *0141-429 1094.* **Fax:** *0141-429 5638.*

Napier Jones
187 Gordon Road, London SE15 3RT.
Tel: *0171-277 8677.*
Fax: *0171-639 3320.*
Email *print@napierjones.ltd.uk*
Opening times: *7-6.*
Nearest Underground: *Peckham.*
Personnel: *Managing Director:* Jennifer Jones. *Director:* Peter Clements.

NAPIER·JONES
PRINTERS

Napier Jones has an established reputation for quality care in preparation, proofing and printing. We work with designers or directly with galleries or artists to design if needed or produce catalogues, cards or other literature for which we win awards. Limited edition or open prints up to 28 x 40 inches (720 x 1020 mm). Call us for more information.

Newcastle Fine Art Printers
9A Marquis Court, Low Prudhoe,
Tel: *01661-831086.*

Northumberland Fine Art Printers
West Farm, Kenton Bar, Ponteland Road, Newcastle-upon-Tyne NE3 3EJ.
Tel: *0191-286 2596.*

The Pale Green Press
Unit 30, Cranwell Close, Violet Road, London E3 3QY.
Tel: *0171-538 0330.*
Fax: *0171-538 3691.*

The Postcard Company
Graham & Sons (Printers) Ltd., 51 Gortin Road, Omagh, BT79 7HZ.
Tel: *01662-249222.*
Fax: *01662-249886.*
Email *sales@thepostcardcompany.com*
Ws *http://www.thepostcardcompany.com*
Opening times: *Mon-Thur 8.30-5.15, Fri 8.30-1.15.*
Personnel: *Marketing Executive:* Wendy Braden.

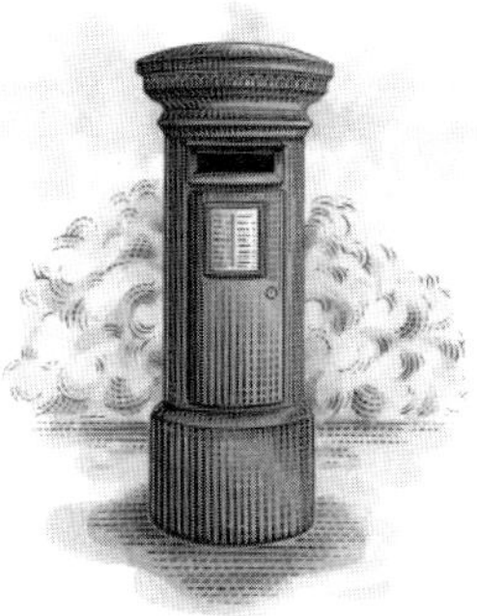

THE
POSTCARD
COMPANY

Manufacturers of high quality full-colour and black and white postcards, product cards, greetings cards, business cards and promotional material to artists, craftspeople, photographers and graphic designers in UK, Ireland and Europe. Offering an unrivalled service with a quick order turnaround of 10 working days and the Lowest Prices in UK and Ireland. For example, 500 postcards for £62 + VAT. PHONE NOW FOR OUR FREE SAMPLE PACK!!

Ranelagh Colour Printers
Park End, South Hill Park, London NW3 2SG.
Tel: *0171-435 4400.* **Fax:** *0171-435 5635.*

Severnside Printers Ltd.
Upton-upon-Severn, WR8 0HG.
Tel: *01684-594521.* **Fax:** *01684-594344.*

St. Ives Printing & Publishing Company C
High Street, St. Ives, TR26 1RS.
Tel: *01736-798951.* **Fax:** *01736-795020.*
Opening times: *Mon-Fri 9-5.*
Personnel: *Director:* Toni Carver.
Contact: Andrew Richards.
The St. Ives Printing & Publishing Company, situated as we are, amongst the 'Art Colony' of St. Ives, our printing craftsmen are fully aware of the needs of individual painters, photographers and galleries to have their work reproduced to the highest standard. It is in meeting these high expectations that St. Ives Printing & Publishing Company has gained a national reputation for its quality of fine art reproduction, while at the same time, keeping its prices competitive.
Phone now for our free sample pack and price list - Tel: 01736-798951.

Walker Print Ltd.
Dept. AR Classic House, 4th Floor, 174 Old Street, London EC1V 9BP.
Tel: *0171-253 1200.* **Fax:** *0171-253 0890.*

Fine Art Printers Art Cards

Loudmouth Postcards
The Workstation, 15 Paternoster Row, Sheffield S1 2BX.
Tel: *0114-275 3175.* **Fax:** *0114-249 4028.*

Thought Factory
Group House, 40 Waterside Road, Hamilton Industrial Park, Leicester LE5 1TL.
Tel: *0116-276 5302.* **Fax:** *0116-246 0506.*

West One Postcards
32 Great Pulteney Street, London W1R 3DE.
Tel: *0171-734 1588.* **Fax:** *0171-434 2061.*
Personnel: Ian Brewster.
Private view and production postcards - from £125 for 1,000 full colour cards including black text on the reverse. We also supply presentation folders, envelopes, invoice pads, stationary, posters, catalogues. Design, artwork and finishing services available.

FOUNDERS

THE ART WORLD
DIRECTORY

Morris Singer Ltd
Highfield Industrial Estate, Church Lane, Lasham,
Hampshire GU34 5SQ
Tel: 01256 381033 Fax: 01256 381565
Contact: David J Vallance

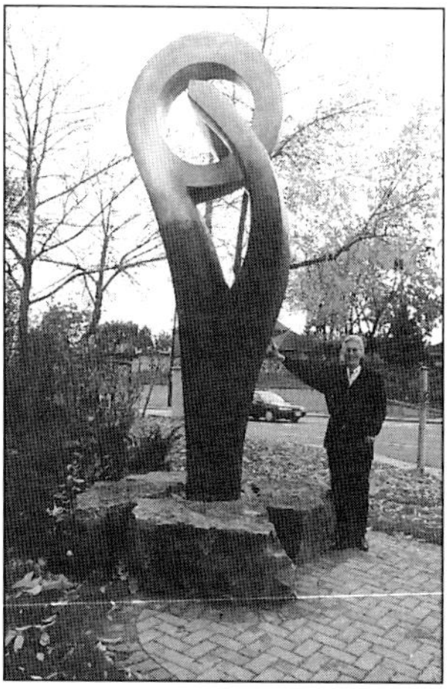

Annie Harris, 'Circle of Life', 14' high, Sunny Brook Hospital, Toronto, Canada

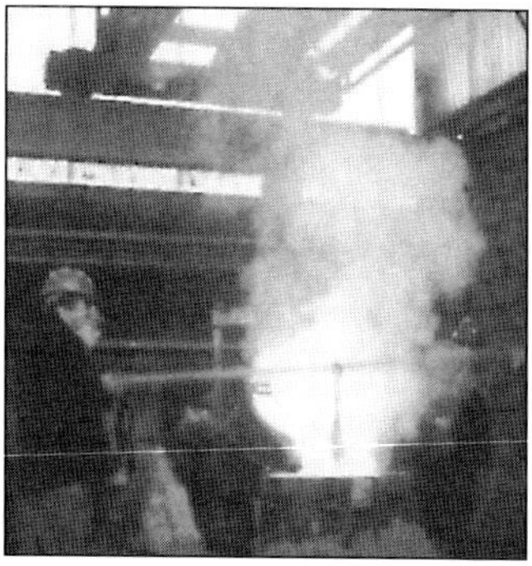

Casting in process at Morris Singer

Whenever you place a commission with Morris Singer Ltd., you have the confidence of knowing that it has the backing of almost 150 years of experience and many of the great artists within that time have commissioned the services of Morris Singer. Whether you work is large or small, anywhere in the world, then we will be happy to enlarge, cast, erect on site and provide all of the comprehensive services you would expect from the foremost company. We are south of exit 5 or 6 on the M3. Please phone for a map.

LOST WAX & SAND CAST BRONZE

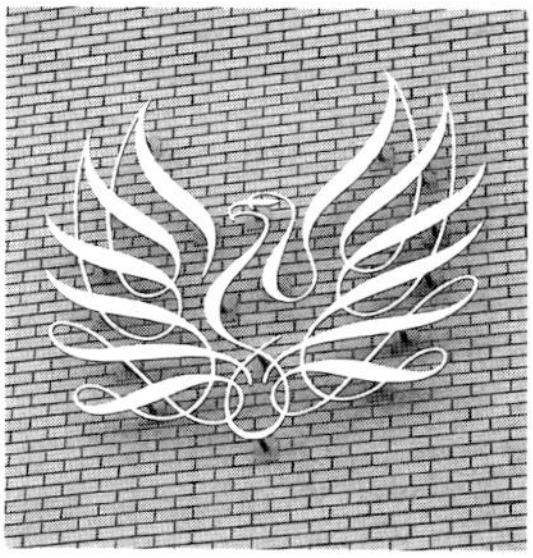

This cast bronze phoenix measures 2400mm square and is typical of Leander's ability to produce fine one-off castings to budget and deadline.

The company also produces sculptural castings, signs, plaques and memorials in a range of metals.

Leander Architectural

(Sand castings)
Fletcher Foundry, Hallstead Close,
Dove Holes, Buxton, SK17 8BP
tel 01298-814941 fax 01298-814970
email ted@leanderarch.demon.co.uk

(Lost wax castings)
Tanat Art Foundry
Llanrhaeadr-ym-Mochnant, Powys
tel 01691-780078
fax 01691-780563

AB Fine Art Foundry
1 Fawe Street, London E14 6PD.
Tel: *0171-515 8052.*
Fax: *0171-987 7339.*
Personnel: Henry Abercrombie.
Jerry Hughes.
A B Fine Art Foundry Ltd employs only craftspeople with a fine art background, ensuring an empathy with individual sculptors and their work.
The foundry offers a complete range of services: scaling up - armature building - mould making - lost wax and sand casting - patination - repair and restoration etc.
We have a record of reliability in meeting deadlines and maintaining high quality and good value for money.
1,700 sq ft. studio available for individual projects. If casting your work into bronze interests you and you would like to visit the workshops or discuss any projects, please phone and we will be happy to help and advise.

Alden Arts
8 Reynolds Place, Crawley,
Tel: *01293-535411.*

Art Bronze Foundry (London) Ltd
1 Michael Road, London SW6.
Tel: *0171-736 7292.*

Art Cast
36 Southwell Road, London SE5.
Tel: *0171-733 8424.*

Beltane Studios Ltd
2 Soonhope Farm Holdings,
Peebles, EH45 8BH.
Tel: *01721-724888.*

Bronze Age Sculpture Foundry
272 Island Row, Limehouse, Docklands,
London E14 7HY.
Tel: *0171-538 1388.* **Fax:** *0171-538 9723.*
Email *duncanh@netcomuk.co.uk*
Ws *http://www.netcomuk.co.uk/-duncanh*
Opening times: 9-6.
Nearest Underground: *Limehouse (Docklands Light Rail).*

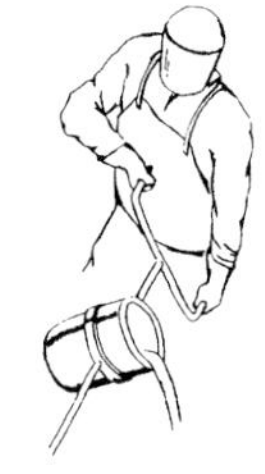

Bronze Age

Personnel: *Proprietor:* Mark Kennedy.
Situated in London's Docklands within ten minutes of Tower Bridge, Bronze Age offers a unique personalised service to artists, using the lost wax casting technique.
Services and Facilities:
Parking.

The Bronze Works
Yaff, 111 Matilda Street, Sheffield S14 QF.
Tel: *0114-2726452.* **Fax:** *0114-2761769.*

Burleighfield Arts Limited
Sculpture Casting Studio, Loudwater,
High Wycombe, HP10 9RF.
Tel: *01494-521341.* **Fax:** *01494-461953.*

Casteck Ltd.
Unity Works, 42 Victoria Street, Hockley,
Birmingham B1 3OE.
Tel: *0121-233 1334.* **Fax:** *0121-523 7469.*

Castle Fine Arts Foundry
Hillview, Sandford, Oswestry, SY11 4GX.
Tel: *01691-610780/610672/610269.*

Century Bronze
9 Camton Street, Birmingham BAT 6AR.
Tel: *0121-212 0840.*

Colin Reid Glass
New Mills, Stod Road, Stroud, GL3 1RN.
Tel: *01453-751421.*

East Coast Casting Ltd
Old Iron Foundry, Norwich Road,
Carbrooke, Watton,
Tel: *01953-881741.*

Euro Cast
Michael House, 48 Carver Street,
Birmingham B1 3AS.
Tel: *0121-233 2266.* **Fax:** *0121-233 9731.*

Firth Rixon
PO Box 6, Heath Road, Darleston, Wednesbury,
Tel: *0121-568 6222.*

Harrison Castings Ltd
Gough Road, Leicester.
Tel: *01533-769351.*

John Longbottom (Ironfounders)
Broomhill Road, Bonnybridge, FK4 2AN.
Tel: *01324-812860.*

Leander Architectural
Fletcher Foundry, Hallsteads Close,
Doves Holes, Buxton,
Tel: *01298-814941.* **Fax:** *01298-814970.*
Email *ted@leanderarch.demon.co.uk*
Ws *http://www.leanderarch.demon.co.uk*
Opening times: *8-5.30.*
Nearest Station: *Dove Holes.*
Personnel: *Partner:* Ted McAvoy.
Leander operate a sand cast bronze and aluminium foundry specialising in plaques and bas-reliefs.
The company has in-house pattern and modelling facilities and a wide range of graphic production techniques. Leander has acquired a deserved reputation for undertaking complex and graphically precise castings in any quantity and to tight schedules. Clients include sculptors, community arts groups, English Heritage, CADW and many local authorities. Many plaques and signs are cast for export because of the foundry's experience in working with different languages and script forms.
Services and Facilities:
Disabled Access. Parking. Workshop Facilities.

Livingstone Art Founders
Maidstone Road, Matfield,
Tonbridge, TN12 7LQ.
Tel: *01892-722474.* **Fax:** *01892-722474.*

LS Sculpture Casting
Southfield Farm, North Lane,
Weston-on-the-Green, Bicester, OX6 6RG.
Tel: *01869-350904.* **Fax:** *01869-350904.*

Lunts Castings Ltd
Middlemore Road, Birmingham B21 0BJ.
Tel: *0121-551 4301.* **Fax:** *0121-523 7954.*
Opening times: *7.30-5.*
Nearest Station: *Birmingham New Street.*
Personnel: *Managing Director:* A.J. Limb.
Lunts Castings Ltd. have built on an enviable reputation for quality and service at very competitive prices, enabling the sculptor to price to sell. We offer a collection/delivery service of both waxes and bronze. Casting is carried out for most non-ferrous and precious metals, i.e. bronze, brass, silver and gold. Many well-known sculptors are moving to the Lunts complete casting service, so put us to the test.

Mike Davis Foundry
St. James Street, New Bradwell, Milton Keynes,
MK13 0BW
Tel: *01908-315841.* **Fax:** *01908-511363.*

Morris Singer Ltd
Bond Close, Kingsland, Basingstoke, RG24 0PT.
Tel: *01256-24033.*
Fax: *01256-844565.*
Personnel: *Contact:* David J. Vallance.
Whenever you place a commission with Morris Singer Ltd., you have the confidence of knowing that it has the backing of almost 150 years of experience and many of the great artists within that time have commissioned the services of Morris Singer.
Whether your work is large or small, anywhere in the world, then we will be happy to enlarge, cast, erect on site and provide all the comprehensive services you would expect from the foremost company.
We are very close to exit 6 on the M3.

Nautilus Fine Art Foundry
Head Office and Works,
11 Swinborne Drive, Springwood Industrial Estate, Braintree, CM7 2YP.
Tel: *01376-343222 or 0181-692 1309.*
Fax: *01376-343480.*
Opening times: *7.30am-5.30pm.*
Nearest Station: *Braintree.*
Personnel: *Manager:* Paul Joyce.
Nautilus is now recognised as a leader in the art casting profession. By employing only those considered to be the best in their respective disciplines, we achieve a quality second-to-none.
The facilities we can offer and the range of materials, processes and patinations available, together with our studio facilities in both Braintree and London, has resulted in us becoming one of the most comprehensive of any art foundry. To fully appreciate all that Nautilus can offer, with an opportunity to discuss your requirements with our production team, please contact Paul Joyce to arrange a visit.

FRAMERS

Framers.
Frames for hire.
Period frames.
Dry Mounters.

THE ART WORLD DIRECTORY

Framers

Academy Arts Centre
Winton Road, Petersfield, GU32 3HA.
Tel: *01730-261624.* **Fax:** *01730-231499.*
Email *NIXY@COMPUSERVE.COM*
Opening times: *Mon-Sat 9-5.30.*
Nearest Station: *Petersfield.*
Personnel: *Gallery Director:* Nick Yellop. *Art Centre Manager:* Geoff Harris. *Exhibition Administrator:* Wendy Drake.
A recently expanded centre for the arts close to Petersfield town centre. Academy Art Centre comprises one of the largest artists materials suppliers in the south of England. Services include a bespoke picture framing department where decades of experience come together with extensive ranges of mouldings and mounts. Our Contemporary Art Gallery specialises in original works of art, and provides Art Consultancy to Commerce and Industry for selection of suitable works of art for offices and reception areas. Further expansion of the Academy Art Centre in 1999 will herald an inspiring start to the millennium for the artists in Hampshire, Surrey and West Sussex.
Services and Facilities:
Art for Offices. Commissioning Service. Framing. Gallery space for hire. Parking. Shop.

Academy Framing Royal Academy of Arts
Burlington House, Piccadilly, London W1V 0DS.
Tel: *0171-300 5646 & 5647.*
Fax: *0171-300 8001.*

Alec Drew Picture Frames Ltd
5/7 Cale Street, Chelsea Green, London SW3 3QT.
Tel: *0171-352 8716.* **Fax:** *0171-352 8716.*
Opening times: *Mon-Fri 9-5, Wed 9-6, Sat 9.30-1.*
Nearest Underground: *Sloane Square/South Kensington.*
We are well situated bespoke framers, working to a conservation standard offering a wide range of traditional and modern Factory Mouldings and Hand-Made Frames. We can also put you in touch with restorers, picture hangers, or other specialists.
Services and Facilities:
Framing. Restoration.

Arnold Wiggins & Sons Ltd
4 Bury Street, London SW1.
Tel: *0171-925 0195.*

Art For Offices
International Art Consultants, The Galleries, 15 Dock Street, London E1 8JL.
Tel: *0171-481 1337.* **Fax:** *0171-481 3425.*

Art & Soul
G14 Belgravia Workshops, 157-163 Marlborough Road, London N19 4NF.
Tel: *0171-263 0421.* **Fax:** *0171-263 0421.*
Opening times: *Tues-Fri 9-5. Closed 1-2. Sat : am. (Phone to check time/holidays).*
Nearest Underground: *Archway, Finsbury Park.*
Personnel: *Owner:* Rebecca Bramwell.
Art & Soul offer a quality framing service to the creative market. In stock are an excellent range of simple and stylish mouldings for every taste and budget. Being based in the

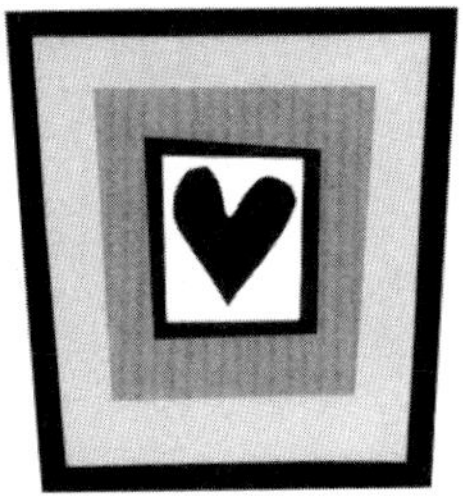

art & soul.

workshop allows a friendly flexible approach with fair prices for quality work. Please phone for details and a booklet.
Services and Facilities:
Framing. Parking.

Art & Wood Supplies
220 North End Road, London W14.
Tel: *0171-385 4683.*

Art Works
50 High Street, Walton-on-Thames, KT12 1BY.
Tel: *0800-834409.*

Artbeat
703 Fulham Road, London SW6.
Tel: *0171-736 0337.*

Artbook London
The Chambers, Chelsea Harbour, London SW10 0XF.
Tel: *0171-349 0666.* **Fax:** *0171-349 0202.*

Artefact Picture Framers
36 Windmill Street, London W1P 1HF.
Tel: *0171-580 4878, Freephone 0500-850085.*

Articles
460 Fulham Road, London SW6.
Tel: *0171-381 3204.*

Artistic Impressions
62a Queens Road, London SE15.
Tel: *0171-580 4878.*

Ashworth & Thompson
12 Baron Street, London N1.
Tel: *0171-837 6836.*

Belgravia Frameworks
9 Kinnerton Street, Belgravia, London SW1X 8EA.
Tel: *0171-245 1112.* **Fax:** *0171-245 1156.*

Bishopsgate Framing Gallery
228 Bishopsgate, London EC2M 4QD
Tel: *0171-247 2320.* **Fax:** *0171-247 2320.*

Bloomsbury Framing Co.
42 Theobalds Road, London WC1.
Tel: *0171-404 8140.*

Blue Jay Frames
Possingworth Craft Workshops, Blackboys East, Heathfield, TN22 5HE.
Tel: *01435-866258.* **Fax:** *01435-868473.*

C.C. Galleries
420 Roman Road, London E3.
Tel: *0171-980 2888.*

Chelsea Frame Works
106 Finborough Road, London SW10.
Tel: *0171-373 0180.*

Circa 48
17b Brecknock Road, London, N7.
Tel: *0171-485 9249.*

Connaught Galleries
44 Connaught Street, London W2.
Tel: *0171-723 1660.* **Fax:** *0171-723 1660.*
Opening times: *Mon-Fri 10-6.30, Sat 10-1.*
Nearest Underground: *Paddington, Lancaster Gate, Marble Arch.*
Personnel: *Partner:* Michael Hollamby.
Wood and aluminium framing. Mirrors to order, or from stock. Dry-mounting. Mount cutting. Shrinkwrapping. Easels and artist supplies. Glass supplied or cut. Frame repairs. Picture restoration. A wide range of prints and posters in stock or to order from extensive catalogues. Limited edition fine art prints. Limited edition fine art figurines. Glass and perspex display cases and display domes and bases.
Services and Facilities:
Art for Offices. Framing. Gallery space for hire. Parking. Restoration. Shop. Workshop Facilities.

Cork Street Framing
8 Bramber Street, London W14.
Tel: *0171-381 9211.*

The Cottage Gallery
11/12 High Street, Huntingdon, PF18 6TE.
Tel: *01480-411521.* **Fax:** *01480-386521.*
Opening times: *Mon-Sat 9-5.30, Sun 10-4.*
Nearest Station: *Huntingdon.*
Personnel: *Proprietor:* John Nind. *Manageress:* Amanda Burrell.

The Cottage GALLERY framing service

We offer a complete picture framing service. Sticheries and tapestries stretched mounted and framed. Ready made and clip frames at competitive prices. We offer a picture cleaning and professional restoration service. We have over 3,000 sq. ft. of framing workshops therefore we can stock a range of over 300 different picture frame mouldings, we can supply 123 colours of mount board from stock. Natural wood can be stained to specified colours to match a colour scheme. Emergency same day panic service. Free delivery and collection within 20 mile radius. We have a constantly updated selection of original work,

limited edition prints, woodcuts and print catalogues and 'old' photographs. Our team of staff are always available to help and advise.
Services and Facilities:
Commissioning Service. Framing. Restoration. Shop. Valuation. Workshop Facilities.

Court Frames Mayfair
8 Bourdon Street or 5-7 Sedley Place, (off Berkeley Square), London W1X 9HX.
Tel: *0171-493 3265.* **Fax:** *0171-493 8369.*

Coutts Framing
75 Blythe Road, Hammersmith, London W14.
Tel: *0171-603 7475.*

Dixon Bate Framing
94-98 Fairfield Street, Manchester M1 2WR.
Tel: *0161-273 6974.*
Fax: *0161-274 4865.*
Opening times: *Mon-Fri 8.30-5.30, Sat 9-1.*
Personnel: *Managing Director:* Jon Davies.

DIXON
BATE
FRAMING

One of the finest contemporary framers in the country. Bespoke hand-finished frames for the fine art market. Specialists in natural hardwoods and softwoods, stained/coloured/gilded/finished to your requirements. The largest selection of fames available in the North West, all produced with individual attention. Full conservation framing service to the highest possible standards. Servicing artists, dealers, galleries, private & public collections nationwide. Outstanding and beautiful framing at a sensible price.
Services and Facilities:
Framing. Parking.

Drury Lane Gallery
Unit 4, 30-35 Drury Lane, London WC2B 5RH.
Tel: *0171-379 7161.* **Fax:** *0171-379 7161.*

Falconer Trade Framing
17 Ferdinand Street, Chalk Farm, London, NW1.
Tel: *0171-267 7777.*

Fletcher Gallery Services
12 Kinghorn Street, London EC1A 7HT.
Tel: *0171-726 4811.* **Fax:** *0171-606 1826.*

Flying Fox Framing
54 Penton Street, London, N1 9QA.
Tel: *0171-833 3569.*

Frame Designs
57 Ebury Street, London SW1.
Tel: *0171-730 0533 / 0171-823 6521.*

Frame Emporium
589-591 Holloway Road, London, N19 4DJ.
Tel: *0171-263 8973.* **Fax:** *0171-281 1766.*

Frame Factory
1E Gleneagle Road, London SW16.
Tel: *0181-677 1882.*

Framery
3 Academy Buildings, Fanshaw Street, London N1.
Tel: *0171-729 7677.*

Frameworks
9 Kinnerton Street, London SW1..
Tel: *0171-245 1112.*

Framing Matters
301 King Street, Hammersmith, London W6 9NH.
Tel: *0171-748 6631.*

Frasco International
40 Moreton Street, London SW1V.
Tel: *0171-834 7773 / 7834.*

Gallery 181 Framing and Just Mirrors
141 Greyhound Road, London W6 8NJ.
Tel: *0171-385 9613.*

Glaze & Frame
408 Harrow Road, London W9 2HU.
Tel: *0171-266 5379.*

Hadleigh Frames
11 Benwell Road, London N7.
Tel: *0171-700 1192.*

Harvard Enterprises
36-40 York Way, London N1.
Tel: *0171-278 7138.*

Holborn Galleries
70 Chancery Lane, London WC2A.
Tel: *0171-404 0678.*

International Art Supplies
CP House, Otterspool Way, Watford, WD2 8HG.
Tel: *01923-210042.* **Fax:** *01923-240899.*

Islington Frames
8 Essex Road, London N1.
Tel: *0171-359 8031.*

John Campbell, Picture Framers
164 Walton Street, Kensington, London, SW3 2JL.
Tel: *0171-581 1775, 0171-584 9268.*
Fax: *0171-581 3499.*

John Gilbert
30-34 Woodfield Place, London W9.
Tel: *0171-289 3198.*

John Jones Art Centre Ltd.
Stroud Green Road, Finsbury Park, London N4 3JG.
Tel: *0171-281 5439.* **Fax:** *0171-281 5956.*

Kevin D'arts
Unit 6, Southern Row, London W10.
Tel: *0181-964 0238.*

Kingsbridge Arts
141 Dawes Road, London SW6.
Tel: *0171-381 1133.*

Lenny Villa
386a York Way, London N7 9LW.
Tel: *0171-700 5010.*

Little Venice Frames
12 Clifton Road, London W9.
Tel: *0171-286 6500.*

Mainline Mouldings
Unit 3 Hollygate Lane Industrial Park, Cotgrave, Nottingham, NG12 3JW.
Tel: *0115-989 0076.* **Fax:** *0115-989 9488.*

Mosta Posta
86 Southwark Street, London SE1.
Tel: *0171-620 4070.*

New Frames
37 Beak Street, London W1.
Tel: *0171-437 8881.*

Old Church Galleries
320 Kings Road, London, SW3 5UH.
Tel: *0171-351 4649.* **Fax:** *0171-351 4449.*

Oxford Exhibition Services
Station Road, Uffington, SN7 7QD.
Tel: *01367-820713.* **Fax:** *01367-820504.*

A comprehensive framing service for Museums and Galleries.
And at Unit G6,Tavern Quay, Rope Street, Rotherhithe, London SE16 1TD.
Tel: 0171-237 5646, fax: 0171-232 2254.

Services and Facilities: *Framing.*

Paul Mitchell Ltd
99 New Bond Street, London W1Y 9LF.
Tel: *0171-493 8732 / 0860.*
Fax: *0171-409 7136.*

Peter Allen
27 Union Street, London SE1.
Tel: *0171-357 8002.*

Picturesque
16 St Marys Street, Chepstow, NP6 5EW.
Tel: *01291-623000.*

Popner Picture Framing
352 Old York Road, (Formerly York Road), Wandsworth, London SW18 1SS.
Tel: *0181-871 4808.*

Portobello Framers
316 Portabello Road, London W10 5RU.

Richard Tindall
151 Tower Bridge Road, London SE1.
Tel: *0171-403 0500.*

Simon Beaugie Picture Framers
Manor Farm Workshops, Kingsnorth, Ashford, TN26 1NL.
Tel: *01233-733353, Mobile 0973-232947.*
Fax: *01233-733353.*

Steve Maddox Specialist Picture Framers
Hardy House, 62 Trafalgar Road, Moseley, Birmingham B13 8BU.
Tel: *0121-449 3868.*

Timothy Newbery
39 Warple Way, London W3 0RX.
Tel: *0181-749 7002.*

Wessex Wood Mouldings
Beeston Road, Mileham,
Tel: *01328-700200, 01794-519500.*
Fax: *02438-700777, 01794-519505.*

Zella Gallery
2 Park Walk, Fulham Road, London SW10 0AD.
Tel: *0171-351 0588.* **Fax:** *0171-352 4752.*

Frames for Hire

b2 Exhibitions
5 Peary Place, Bethnal Green, London E2 0QW.
Tel: *0181-983 1109.*

James Cox
Lynton House, 48 Lynton Road; Rayners Lane, Harrow, HA2 9NN

Period Frames/ Restoration

Bourlet Fine Art Frames
32 Connaugh Street, London W2.
Tel: *0171-724 4837.*

Brian Nicholson
Unit 1/2, St Mary's Workshop, Henderson Street, Leith,
Tel: *0131-553 6811.*

Colin Lacey Gallery
38 Ledbury Road, London W11.
Tel: *0171-229 9105.*

Connaught Galleries
44 Connaught Street, London W2.
Tel: *0171-723 1660.* **Fax:** *0171-723 1660.*
Opening times: *Mon-Fri 10-6.30, Sat 10-1.*
Nearest Underground: *Paddington, Lancaster Gate, Marble Arch.*
Personnel: *Partner:* Michael Hollamby.
Wood and aluminium framing. Mirrors to order, or from stock. Dry-mounting. Mount cutting. Shrinkwrapping. Easels and artist supplies. Glass supplied or cut. Frame repairs. Picture restoration. A wide range of prints and posters in stock or to order from extensive catalogues. Limited edition fine art prints. Limited edition fine art figurines. Glass and perspex display cases and display domes and bases.
Services and Facilities:
Art for Offices. Framing. Gallery space for hire. Parking. Restoration. Shop. Workshop Facilities.

Daggett
153 Portobello Road, London, W11 2DV.
Tel: *0171-229 2248.*

The Greenwich Gallery
9 Nevada Street, Greenwich, London, SE10 9JL.
Tel: *0181-305 1666.*
Fax: *0181-305 1666.*

Howard & Stone Conservators
Unit 27 Penny Bank Chambers, 33-35 St. Johns Square, London, EC1.
Tel: *0171-490 0813.*

Jack Hopson Conservation
Holes Lane, Olney, MK46 4BX.
Tel: *01234-712306.*

John Tannous
115 Harwood Road, London, SW6.
Tel: *0171-736 7999.* **Fax:** *0171-371 5237.*

Keith Elliot, Bespoke Framer
The Old Meeting Hall, Maltby Lane, Barton-Upon-Humber, DN18 5PY.
Tel: *01652-660380.*

Marguerite Marr
403 Elm Tree Court, Elm Tree Road, London, NW8.
Tel: *0171-289 0877.*

Patricia Garner
Arragon Conservation Studio, 55 Arragon Road, Twickenham, TW1 3NG.
Tel: *0181-892 1819, 0181-286 6153.*
Fax: *0181-891 0115.*

Sebastian D'Orsai
8 Kensington Mall, London, W8.
Tel: *0171-229 3888.*

Dry Mounters

A. Bliss
5 Bakers Row, London EC1R 3HF.
Tel: *0171-837 4959.*
Fax: *0171-837 8244.*
Email *Edward.Bliss@btinternet.com*
Opening times: *Mon-Fri 9-6.*
Nearest Underground: *Farringdon.*
Personnel: *Partner:* Edward Mawby.
A. BLISS are dry mounting specialists with over 40 years experience. Our workshops in Clerkenwell (with off-street parking) are equipped with the largest and most up to date machinery whilst retaining a traditional hot mounting facility, indispensable for many types of work. We are aware of conservation issues and can advise on the most appropriate methods of mounting most types of media on to a wide variety of materials including aluminium and cloth.
Services and Facilities:
Framing.

NOTES

MATERIALS & EQUIPMENT

Framing supplies.
Artists' materials.
Gallery hanging supplies.
Sculpture Services.

THE ART WORLD
DIRECTORY

Framing Supplies

Arqadia
2 Wolseley Road, Kempston Bedford, MK42 7AD.
Tel: *01234-857488, Sales Order: 01234-852777.* **Fax:** *01234-840190, Sales Order: 840735, Accounts: 852984, Export Sales: 854897.*
Email *sales@arqadia.co.uk*
Ws *http://www.arqadia.co.uk*
Arqadia is the UK's award-winning supplier of mouldings, mountboard, ready-made frames and equipment. In business for almost 25 years, it supplies an extensive range of well over 3000 mouldings - from decorative to plain, from washed to veneered. The Arqadia Mountboard range is divided into three - Standard boards for everyday framing, Inspirations for creativity, and the Muses Collection, for the protection of art. Arqadia's ready-mades collection offers everything from swept and decorative to plain and wood. The Company is a member of the Fine Art Trade Guild and is the Guild's 1997 and 1998 Exemplar Company of the Year.

Connaught Galleries
44 Connaught Street, London W2.
Tel: *0171-723 1660.* **Fax:** *0171-723 1660.*
Opening times: *Mon-Fri 10-6.30, Sat 10-1.*
Nearest Underground: *Paddington, Lancaster Gate, Marble Arch.*
Personnel: *Partner:* Michael Hollamby.
Wood and aluminium framing. Mirrors to order, or from stock. Dry-mounting. Mount cutting. Shrinkwrapping. Easels and artist supplies. Glass supplied or cut. Frame repairs. Picture restoration. A wide range of prints and posters in stock or to order from extensive catalogues. Limited edition fine art prints. Limited edition fine art figurines. Glass and perspex display cases and display domes and bases.
Services and Facilities:
Art for Offices. Framing. Gallery space for hire. Parking. Restoration. Shop. Workshop Facilities.

Frank B. Scragg & Co
68 Vittoria Street, Birmingham B1 3PB.
Tel: *0121-236 7219.* **Fax:** *0121-236 3633.*
Personnel: Mr J. B. Lewis.
Frank B. Scragg & Company are a long established company dealing in a wide range of supplies for framing and hanging pictures. For galleries, there is brass rail with hooks and chain, together with a system of sliding rods and adjustable hooks, available in various finishes. Scragg's also supply all manner of framing accessories including wire, cord, hooks and rings. A free illustrated catalogue and price list is available on request.

Nielsen UK
Unit 7, Frogmore Estate, Acton, London, NW10 7NQ.
Tel: *0181-961 0010.*
Fax: *0181-961 6368.*
Personnel: *Sales Manager:* Stuart Northage.
Manufacturer and supplier of large range of aluminium and wood picture frame mouldings and mountboard.

nielsen®

Manufacturer of alphamat artcare archival boards utilising microchamber technology to protect framed art from many acid gases which cause artwork to deteriorate.

Peak Rock
Unit 30, DRCA Business Centre, Charlotte Despard Avenue, London SW11 5HD.
Tel: *0171-498 8444, Mobile 07050-108555.*
Fax: *0171-498 8333.*

Artists Materials

Academy Arts Centre C
Winton Road, Petersfield, GU32 3HA.
Tel: *01730-261624.* **Fax:** *01730-231499.*
Email *NIXY@COMPUSERVE.COM*
Opening times: *Mon-Sat 9-5.30.*
Nearest Station: *Petersfield.*
Personnel: *Gallery Director:* Nick Yellop. *Art Centre Manager:* Geoff Harris. *Exhibition Administrator:* Wendy Drake.
A recently expanded centre for the arts close to Petersfield town centre. Academy Art Centre comprises one of the largest artists materials suppliers in the south of England. Services include a bespoke picture framing department where decades of experience come together with extensive ranges of mouldings and mounts.
Our Contemporary Art Gallery specialises in original works of art, and provides Art Consultancy to Commerce and Industry for selection of suitable works of art for offices and reception areas. Further expansion of the Academy Art Centre in 1999 will herald an inspiring start to the millennium for the artists in Hampshire, Surrey and West Sussex.
Services and Facilities:
Art for Offices. Commissioning Service. Framing. Gallery space for hire. Parking. Shop.

Alec Tiranti Ltd. C
27 Warren Street, London W1.
Tel: *0171-636 8565.* **Fax:** *0171-636 8565.*
Email *sales@tiranti.co.uk*
Ws *thttp://www.tiranti.co.uk*
Opening times: *Mon-Fri 9-5.30, Sat 9.30-1.*
Personnel: *Managing Director:* Susan Tiranti Lyons, ACIS. *Director:* Jonathan Lyons.

Established 1895 & still a family business. Shop & Administration: 70 High Street, Theale, Reading, Berks., RG7 5AR. Open : Mon-Fri 8.30-5pm, Sat 9.30-1pm. Tel: 0118-930 2775; Fax: 0118-932 3487; Web Site: www.tiranti.co.uk; E-mail: enquiries@tiranti.co.uk. Manufacturers and suppliers of a complete range of sculptors' tools, materials and studio equipment. Publish an extensive catalogue covering tools for stonecarving, woodcarving and modelling. Materials for making flexible rubber moulds, special plasters, clays, waxes, Chavant non-drying clays, polyester resins and cold cast resin metals, white metals and pewter, gilding supplies, modelling and carving stands.
Services and Facilities:
Shop.

Connaught Galleries
44 Connaught Street, London W2.
Tel: *0171-723 1660.*
Fax: *0171-723 1660.*
Opening times: *Mon-Fri 10-6.30, Sat 10-1.*
Nearest Underground: *Paddington, Lancaster Gate, Marble Arch.*
Personnel: *Partner:* Michael Hollamby.
Wood and aluminium framing. Mirrors to order, or from stock. Dry-mounting. Mount cutting. Shrinkwrapping. Easels and artist supplies. Glass supplied or cut. Frame repairs. Picture restoration. A wide range of prints and posters in stock or to order from extensive catalogues. Limited edition fine art prints. Limited edition fine art figurines. Glass and perspex display cases and display domes and bases.
Services and Facilities:
Art for Offices. Framing. Gallery space for hire. Parking. Restoration. Shop. Workshop Facilities.

Cowling & Wilcox Ltd.
26-28 Broadwick Street, London W1V 1FG.
Tel: *0171-734 9557.* **Fax:** *0171-434 4513.*
Opening times: *Mon-Fri 9-6, Sat 10-5.*
Nearest Underground: *Oxford Circus, Piccadilly Circus.*
Personnel: *Sales:* Jane Goodwin.

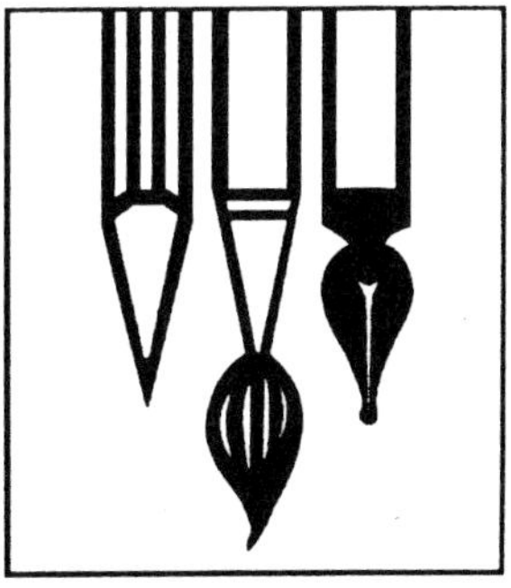

Widest selection of portfolios, carrying cases and presentation books in Central London. Photographic display and Agency books are also available. We stock a full range of Fine Art, Craft and Graphic materials catering for all ages and levels. Our shop is conveniently located in Central London where we have

knowledgeable staff to help and advise you. We offer student discount and a worldwide mail order service. Please contact us for a free stock list.
Services and Facilities:
Shop.

L. Cornelissen & Son
105 Great Russell Street, London WC1B 3RY.
Tel: *0171-636 1045.*

Lamley Art Supplies
5 Exhibition Road, London SW7 2HE.
Tel: *0171-589 1276.*

Langford & Hill
4th Floor, Hardy House, 16-18 Beak Street, Regent Street, London W1R.
Tel: *0171-439 0181.*

Liquitex Uk
Ampthill Road, Bedford, MK42 9RS.

London Graphic Centre
254 Upper Richmond Road, London SW15 6TQ.
Tel: *0171-785 9797.*

Product Caran D'ache/Jakar International Ltd
Hillside House, 2-6 Friern Park, London N12 9BX.
Tel: *0181-445 6376.* **Fax:** *0181-445 2714.*
Personnel: *General Manager:* D.W. Finney.
Exclusive distributors in the UK and Ireland of Caran D'ache (Switzerland) Artists' Materials in addition to many Art Products in the Jakar catalogue.

Russell & Chapple Ltd., 'The Artists Canvas Company'
23 Monmouth Street, Shaftsbury Avenue, London WC2H 9DE.
Tel: *0171-836 7521.* **Fax:** *0171-497 0554.*
Opening times: *Mon-Fri 8.30-5. Sat 10-5.*

RUSSELL & CHAPPLE LTD
EST. 1770

Our specialist ground floor canvas shop offers an unrivalled choice of Artists Canvases, from 8oz to 16oz per square yard, and from 36" to 162" width. While our first floor fine art shop has a cornucopia of artists' materials, including: Artists Paper, Boards, Easels, Paints, Pastels, Brushes, Pencils and General Artists Paraphernalia, in qualities aimed at professional artists, art students and serious amateur painters. We welcome mail order customers as well as personal shoppers.
Services and Facilities:
Shop.

Staedtler (UK) Ltd
Pontyclun, CF72 8YJ.
Tel: *01443-237421.* **Fax:** *01443-237440.*
Staedtler (UK) Limited is one of the leading manufacturers of drawing and writing equipment. A comprehensive range of art and craft products are available, suitable for all needs, ranging from the amateur to the professional artist or crafter.

STAEDTLER

1999 sees the introduction of FIMO into Staedtler's creative range, this will run alongside established product's such as Easy Metal, a stunning range of leaf metal finishes, Idea & Colour, a collection of stimulating paint techniques, an extensive collection of stylish Moulds and airdrying modelling products. The creative range also includes Mars Lumograph sketching pencils, pigment Liners, and Calligraphy Pens, along with Karat Aquarell Water-soluble Pencils and Crayons.

Gallery Hanging Supplies

Absolute
The Old School House, 66 Leonard Street, London EC2A 4LW.

Connaught Galleries
44 Connaught Street, London W2.
Tel: *0171-723 1660.* **Fax:** *0171-723 1660.*
Opening times: *Mon-Fri 10-6.30, Sat 10-1.*
Nearest Underground: *Paddington, Lancaster Gate, Marble Arch.*
Personnel: *Partner:* Michael Hollamby.
Wood and aluminium framing. Mirrors to order, or from stock. Dry-mounting. Mount cutting. Shrinkwrapping. Easels and artist supplies. Glass supplied or cut. Frame repairs. Picture restoration. A wide range of prints and posters in stock or to order from extensive catalogues. Limited edition fine art prints. Limited edition fine art figurines. Glass and perspex display cases and display domes and bases.
Services and Facilities:
Art for Offices. Framing. Gallery space for hire. Parking. Restoration. Shop. Workshop Facilities.

Frank B. Scragg & Co
68 Vittoria Street, Birmingham B1 3PB.
Tel: *0121-236 7219.*
Fax: *0121-236 3633.*
Personnel: Mr J. B. Lewis.
Frank B. Scragg & Company are a long established company dealing in a wide range of supplies for framing and hanging pictures. For galleries, there is brass rail with hooks and chain, together with a system of sliding rods and adjustable hooks, available in various finishes. Scragg's also supply all manner of framing accessories including wire, cord, hooks and rings. A free illustrated catalogue and price list is available on request.

Nielsen UK
Unit 7, Frogmore Estate, Acton, London, NW10 7NQ.
Tel: *0181-961 0010.*
Fax: *0181-961 6368.*
Personnel: *Sales Manager:* Stuart Northage.
Manufacturer and supplier of large range of aluminium and wood picture frame mouldings and mountboard.

nielsen®

Manufacturer of alphamat artcare archival boards utilising microchamber technology to protect framed art from many acid gases which cause artwork to deteriorate.

Oxford Exhibition Services
Station Road, Uffington, SN7 7QD.
Tel: *01367-820713.* **Fax:** *01367-820504.*
Email *enquiries@oxex.demon.co.uk*
Ws *www.oxex.demon.co.uk*

And at Unit G6,Tavern Quay, Rope Street, Rotherhithe, London SE16 1TD. Tel: 0171-237 5646, fax: 0171-232 2254.
Services and Facilities: Design and construction of exhibition furniture for hire or purchase; display cases, plinths, display screens, lighting, installations, packing crates, storage. See also: Packers and Shippers and Framers.
Services and Facilities:
Framing.

Peak Rock
Unit 30, DRCA Business Centre, Charlotte Despard Avenue, London SW11 5HD.
Tel: *0171-498 8444, Mobile 07050-108555.*
Fax: *0171-498 8333.*

Materials General

Conservation By Design
Timecare Works, 60 Park Road West, Bedford, MK41 7SL.
Tel: *01234-217258.*
Fax: *01234-328164.*
Email *info@conservation-by-design.co.uk*
Ws *http://www.conservation-by-design.co.uk*
Personnel: Stuart Welch. Philip Chamock. Rachel Bridger.
Conservation By Design is a company dedicated to the design and supply of high quality conservation, storage and display products including acid free boxes, safe transparent polyester album pages, acid free papers and mounting board and a wide range of furniture including plan chests, picture racking, mobile shelving and museum standard glass showcases.

Sculpture Services

Benson-Sedgewick Engineering Ltd.
Dagenham, RM8 1QE.
Tel: *0181-593 0212.* **Fax:** *0181-592 8240.*
Personnel: A. Benson.

PACKERS & SHIPPERS

THE ART WORLD
DIRECTORY

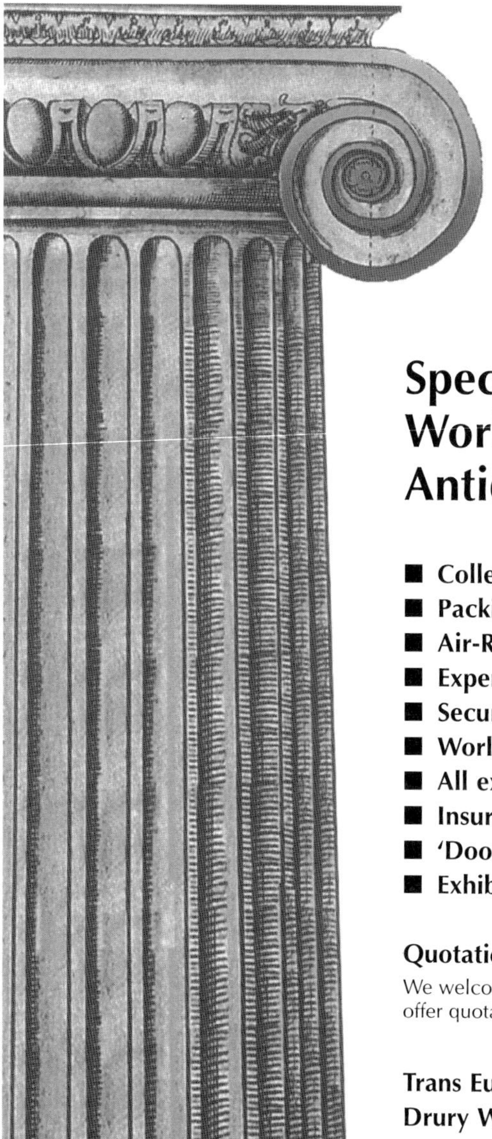

Packers & Shippers

01 Art Services
282 Richmond Road, London E8 3QS.
Tel: *0181-533 6124.* **Fax:** *0181-533 2718.*
Opening times: *Mon-Fri 9-6.*
Personnel: Elizabeth Cooper.
01 Art Services Ltd is a reputable company specialising in fine art transportation and installation in London and the UK. Handling and installation of single works and exhibitions. Storage space available.

All Wheel Drive
4 Clevedale, Downend, Bristol B216 2SQ.
Tel: *0117-9836 627520/01836-627520 /01272-570158.* **Fax:** *01272-820505.*

Anglo Pacific International Plc
Unit 1, Bush Industrial Estate, Standard Road, N. Acton, London NW10 6DF.
Tel: *0181-838 8008.* **Fax:** *0181-453 0225.*
Email *gerryward@anglopacific.co.uk*
Opening times: *8-6.*
Nearest Underground: *North Acton.*
Personnel: Gerry Ward.
Specialist Packers and Shippers serving the whole world from a London head office. Offering a full range of services to meet the needs of Artists, Dealers, Collectors, Exhibitions organisers etc. Contact Gerry, Mary or Malcolm for a free estimate or just friendly advice.

Art Handle
9 Sophia's Walk, Cathedral Road, Cardiff CF1 9LL.
Tel: *01222-233390, Mobile 0850-681004.*
Fax: *01222-233390.*

Art Move Ltd
Unit 3, Grant Road, London SW11 2NU.
Tel: *07000 ART MOVE .*
Fax: *0171-223 0241.*
Email *artmove@dircon.co.uk*
Opening times: *Mon-Fri 9-5.30 and by appointment.*
Nearest Underground: *Clapham Junction.*
Local, national and international transport. Climate-controlled Secure Storage approved by Museum and Galleries Commission. Worldwide Shipping. Picture Hanging and Sculpture Installation for trade, corporate and private clients. Packing and case making. Photography. Gilding and Conservation.
Services and Facilities:
Framing. Restoration.

Art Services
134 Queens Road, London SE15 2HR.
Tel: *0171-635 7555.* **Fax:** *0171-737 2631.*
Email *ReesM@ArtServices.co.uk*
Ws *http://www.artservices@ukbusiness.com.*
Opening times: *Open 8.30-5.30.*
Personnel: *Manager:* Rees Martin. *National Transport (0171-635 2130):* Steve Glynn. *International Transport (0171-635 2137):* Jo Pearson. *Storage & Installation:* Patrick Onione.
Specialists in all aspects of Fine Art Handling. Experts in packing, case making, import and export services, exhibition and sculpture installation, national and international transport (specialist air ride, climate control vehicles). High security and climate controlled storage facilities at our 4 acre site.

Artlink Transport
102 Main Street, Milngavie, Glasgow.
Tel: *0141-956 5320.*

C'ART
Unit 7, Brunel Court, Enterprise Drive, Off Station Road, Four Ashes, Wolverhampton WV10 7DF.
Tel: *01902-791797.*
Fax: *01902-790687.*
Personnel: Angus Macdonald.
Ideally placed on the M6/M5 axis for competitive art and craft transport throughout Britain in custom built vehicles; onward transport to Europe. Shipping and airfreight arranged worldwide. Packing and casemaking available. Hanging of single works or exhibitions; public art installation.

Cadogan Tate Fine Art Removals Ltd.
Cadogan House, Huthe Road, North Kensington, London NW10 6RS.
Tel: *0181-969 6969.* **Fax:** *0181-960 4567.*

David Williams Specialised Transport
20 Lammas Road, Watton At Stone, SG14 3RH.
Tel: *01920-830031.*
Fax: *01920-830576.*
Opening times: *Mon-Fri 8-8.*
Specialising in all aspects of the transportation and installation of sculpture, for private and public exhibitions. Case packing, shipping, storage, national and international transport.

Davies Turner Worldwide Movers Ltd.
Overseas House, Stewarts Road, London SW8 4UG.
Tel: *0171-622 4393.*
Fax: *0171-720 3897.*

Hedley's Humpers Ltd. C
Units 2, 3 & 4, 97 Victoria Road, London NW10 6ND.
Tel: *0181-965 8733.*
Fax: *0181-965 0249.*

Lockson International Shippers, Packers & Removals of Fine Arts & Antiques
29 Broomfield Street, London EC14 6BX.
Tel: *0171-515 8600.*
Fax: *0171-515 4043.*

Momart Limited (a wholly owned subsidiary of Momart International Plc)
199-205 Richmond Road, London E8 3NJ.
Tel: *0181-986 3624.* **Fax:** *0181-533 0122.*
Personnel: *Managing Director:* Scot Blyth.
Specialists in all aspects of Fine Art handling; experts in packing, case making, import and export services, private and exhibition installation, national and international transport (using air ride, climate control, fine art vehicles), high security storage.

Oxford Exhibition Services
Unit 7, Tavern Quay, Rope Street, London SE16 1TD.
Tel: *0171-237 5646.*
Fax: *0171-232 2254.*
Email *enquiries@oxex.demon.co.uk*
Ws *www.oxex.demon.co.uk*

Also at Station Road, Uffington, Oxon SN7 7QD. Tel: 01367-820713, fax: 01367-820504. Oxford Exhibition Services offer a wide range of specialist fine art handling services to museums and galleries in the UK and abroad. Established in 1986 its London and Oxfordshire based staff are committed to maintaining high standards in the packing, domestic and international transport, display and storage of art works and other unique objects.

Pitt & Scott Ltd.
Eden Grove, London N7.
Tel: *0171-607 7321/0171-607 0566.*

Robinson & Foster Ltd
75/81 Burnaby Street, London SW10 0NS.
Tel: *0171-393 3993.*
Fax: *0171-393 3906.*

Shuttle Services
Unit 4 Level 1, 36 Lime Street, Newcastle-upon-Tyne NE1 2PQ.
Tel: *0191-230 0505 / 0191-281 1397, Mobile 0831-854518.*
Fax: *0191-230 1515.*
Email *Shuttle-Service@onyxnet.co.uk*
Personnel: *Director:* Ron Eadon.

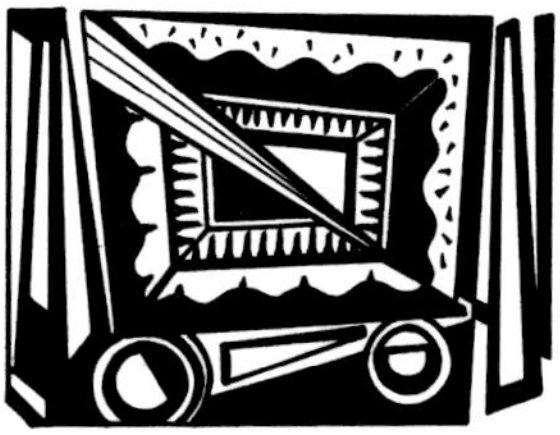

Specialise in the transportation and packing of artworks, exhibitions and antiques, with weekly runs to London, the Midlands and Scotland in air-ride vehicles. The company has experience of delivering and collecting works throughout Europe and Scandinavian countries, and can fulfil the conditions for the transport of items to be covered by the Government Indemnity Scheme.

T. Rogers & Co. Ltd. C
P.O. Box 8, 1a Broughton Street, London SW8 3QL.
Tel: *0171-622 9151.*
Fax: *0171-627 3318.*
Storage, packing, removal, shipping and forwarding of all works of art. Customs bonded warehousing.

Trans Euro Fine Art Division C
Trans Euro Worldwide Movers, Drury Way, Brent Park, London NW10 0JN.
Tel: *0181-784 0100.*
Fax: *0181-459 3376.*
Email *richarde@transeuro.com*
Opening times: *Mon-Fri 8-6.*
Personnel: *General Manager:* Roy Pateman. Richard Edwards. Richard Bullivant.

Providing specialist packing and worldwide transportation services for the safe movement of works of art of all kinds. Secure environment controlled storage available for short and long terms. 'Climate Controlled' UK and European transport on 'Air Ride' vehicles. International exhibition transport and handling.

Transnic Ltd.
Arch 434, Gordon Grove, London SE5 9DW.
Tel: *0171-738 7555.*

Transportomatic Ltd.
Ladford Covert, Ladforfields Business Park, Seighford, Stafford, ST18 9QL.
Tel: *01785-282892.* **Fax:** *01785-282802.*

Vulcan International C
Unit 13/14, Ascot Road, Clockhouse Lane, Feltham, TW14 8QF.
Tel: *01784-244152.* **Fax:** *01784-248183.*

Wingate & Johnston Ltd. C
134 Queens Road, London, SE15 2HR.
Tel: *0171-732 8123.* **Fax:** *0171-732 2631.*
Personnel: *Manager:* Michel Letendrie.

NOTES

NOTES

PHOTOGRAPHY

A. C. Cooper
10 Pollen Street, London W1R 9PH.
Tel: *0171-629 7585.*

Alan Crumlish
11 Kirklee Terrace Lane, Glasgow G12 0TL.
Tel: *0141-339 5790.*

Anthony Marshall
2 Riverside Cottages, New Lumford, Bakewell, DE45 1GH.
Tel: *01629-814787.*

Antonia Reeve
11 Grosvenor Crescent, Edinburgh EH12 5EL.
Tel: *0131-337 4640.*

ASP Photography
281 Sydenham Road, London SE26 5EN.
Tel: *0181-676 0836; Mobile 0956-897302.*

b2 Photographic
5 Peary Place (off Roman Road), Bethnal Green, London E2 0QW.
Tel: *0181-983 1109.*

Chris Boyle
272 Newchurch Road, Rawtenstall, BB4 7SN.
Tel: *01706-215958/0161-832 2244 ext 245; Mobile 0802-680601.*

Coopers of Regent Street
207 Regent Street, London W1R 7DD.
Tel: *0171-629 6745.* **Fax:** *0171-493 4488.*

Davies Colour Ltd
168 Sloper Road, Cardiff CF1 8AA.
Tel: *01222-230565.*

Dawes & Billings Photographic
42 Goldstone Road, Hove, BN3 3RH.
Tel: *01273-722971.* **Fax:** *01273-722971.*

Dennis Gilbert
11/15 Furmage Street, London SW18 4DF.
Tel: *0181-870 9051.*

Frank Thurston Photography
c/o Royal College of Art, Kensington Gore, London SW7.
Tel: *0171-584 5020 x286. 0171-584 7881.*

Gabriel Weissman Applied & Fine Art
21 Cable Street Studios, 566 Cable Street, London E1 9HB.
Tel: *0171-780 9096.*

Graham P. Matthews
Delfyd Farm, Llangennith, SA3 1JL.
Tel: *01792-386217.* **Fax:** *01792-386295.*

Hayward Associates C
Unit 1, Shelley Farm, Ower, Romsey, SO51 6AS. **Tel:** *07000-442992.*

Ian Jackson Photography
Oakgate, Southampton Road, Cadnam, SO4 2NA.
Tel: *01703-814010.* **Fax:** *01703-814002.*

Imagetrend
12 Chesterford Gardens, London NW3 7DE.
Tel: *0171-435 7383.*

Incorporated Photographer
14 East Rise, Llanisben, Cardiff CP4 5RJ.
Tel: *01222-751368.*

J.R. Photography
15 Westward Close, Uttoxeter, ST14 7BJ.
Tel: *01889-565061; Mobile 0836-717783.* **Fax:** *01889-567039.*

James Austin Fine Art Photography
Wysing Arts, Fox Road, Bourne, Cambridge, CB3 7TX.
Tel: *01954-718871.* **Fax:** *01954-718500.*
Opening times: 9-6.
Nearest Station: *Cambridge/Royston.*
Personnel: James Austin.
Extensive experience of fine art photography. Clients include National Trust, English Heritage, Crafts Council, Christie's, Kettle's Yard, Cambridge Colleges, Private Collections, Artists, Craftsmen and Architects. Subjects covered include architecture, paintings, sculpture, ceramics, glass, textiles and jewellery. Catalogue photography for Waddington Galleries, Tate Gallery, London and Liverpool, Henry Moore Foundation, Van Gogh Museum, Sainsbury Centre for Visual Arts (including catalogue of Robert and Lisa Sainsbury collection). Commissioned work for many books on architecture, arts and crafts. Photographic library extensively used by History of Art departments of universities throughout the world, and by numerous publications on history of art and architecture.
Services and Facilities:
Disabled Access. Parking.

John Carmichael
2 Scotts Avenue, Bromley, BR2 0LQ.
Tel: *0181-464 5869.*

John Hoodless
36 Seymour Avenue, Morden, SM4 4RD.
Tel: *0181-330 3234/01323-762547; Mobile 0378-385732.*

John Penna
2 Hylands Road, Epson, KT18 7ED.
Tel: *01372-721678.*

John R. Simmons
21 Park Mansions, Prince of Wales Drive, London SW11.
Tel: *0171-622 0448.*

Keith Meadley Photography
2 Sadberge Court, Osbaldswick, York YO1 3DR. **Tel:** *01904-611109.*

Kenneth Smith
6 Lussielaw Road, Edinburgh EH9 3BX.
Tel: *0131-667 6159.*

Leith Photography
447 Edgeware Road, London W2.
Tel: *0171-723 5551.*

Michael Hoppen Photography
Alexandra Studios, 3 Jubilee Place, London SW3 3TD.
Tel: *0171-352 3649.* **Fax:** *0171-352 3669.*

Mike Smith
Durham University Oriental Museum, Elvet Hill, Durham, DH1 3TH.
Tel: *0191-374 7911.*

Norman R. Kent
Unit 5, 14 Castelnau, Barnes, London SW13 9RU.
Tel: *0181-741 9133.*

Paul Medley
Oxford,
Tel: *01865-72316.*

Peter Waltham
Lincolnshire Archives, St. Rumbolds Street, Lincoln, LN2 5AB.
Tel: *01522-526204.*

The Photography of Art
159 Kennington Lane, London SE11 4EZ.
Tel: *0171-735 2432/0705/007 0216.*
Fax: *0171-735 2627.*

Prudence Cuming Associates
28-29 Dover Street, London W1X 3PA.
Tel: *0171-629 6430.*

Raymond Fifield
12 Lutton Bank, Lutton, Spalding, PE12 9LJ.
Tel: *01406-363951.*

Rodney Todd-White & Son
3 Clifford Street, London W1X 1RA.
Tel: *0171-734 9070.* **Fax:** *0171-287 9727.*
Opening times: 9-6.
Personnel: Michael Todd-White.

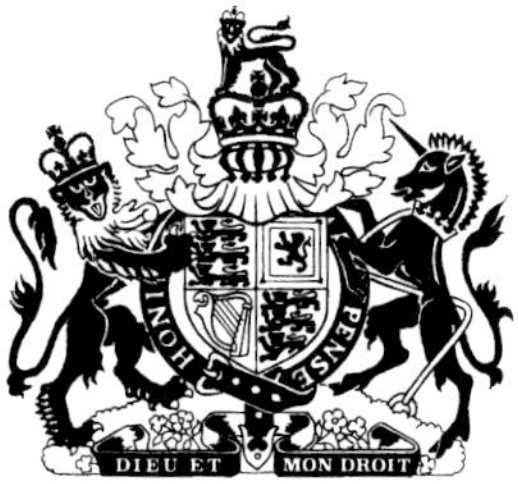

RODNEY TODD-WHITE & SON. A partnership established in 1962 between Rodney Todd-White and Michael Todd-White. All negatives held since then. Location and studio photography undertaken for galleries, artists, insurers and private collectors. Specialists in supplying 5x4 and 10x8 transparencies, hand colour prints and black and white hand prints.

SPACE FOR HIRE

Gallery hire.
Studio hire.

THE ART WORLD DIRECTORY

Gallery Space for Hire

Abbott & Holder C
30 Museum Street, London WC1A 1LH.
Tel: *0171-637 3981.* **Fax:** *0171-631 0575.*

The Air Gallery C
32 Dover Street, London W1X 3RA.
Tel: *0171-409 1255.* **Fax:** *0171-409 1856.*
Email *admin@airgallery.co.uk*
Ws *http://www.airgallery.co.uk*
Opening times: *10-6.*
Nearest Underground: *Green Park.*

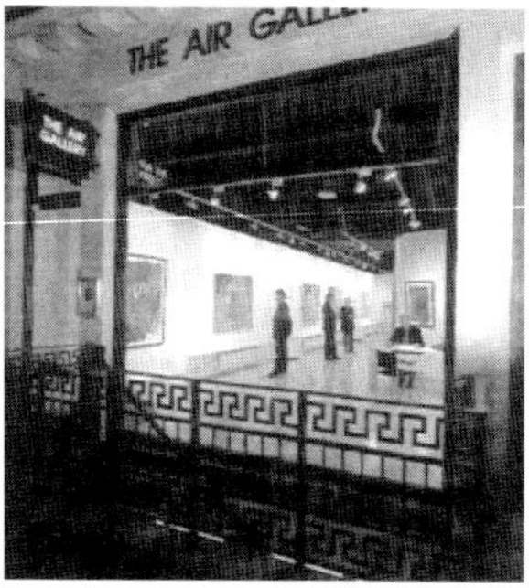

The Air Gallery offers 2 superbly equipped galleries (120m2 and 70m2) at the heart of Londons' exclusive gallery district. The galleries can either be hired separately or together for large exhibitions. A mailing list is available to all hirers, and in-house PR and exhibition organising services are available on request. Please call us and ask to see our illustrated brochure.
Services and Facilities:
Art Consultancy. Art for Offices. Commissioning Service. Gallery space for hire.

Alchemy Gallery C
157 Farringdon Road, London EC1R 3AD.
Tel: *0171-278 5666.* **Fax:** *0171-278 9666.*

Art Connoisseur Gallery C
95-97 Crawford Street, London W1H 1AN.
Tel: *0171-258 3835.* **Fax:** *0171-258 3532.*

Atrium Gallery, Whiteleys
Whiteleys, Queensway, London W2 4YN.
Tel: *0171-229 8844.* **Fax:** *0171-792 8921.*

The Barber Institute of Fine Arts
The University of Birmingham, Edgbaston, Birmingham B15 2TS.
Tel: *0121-414 7333.* **Fax:** *0121-414 3370.*
Email *info@barber.org.uk*
Ws *http://www.barber.org.uk*
Opening times: *Mon-Sat 10-5, Sun 2-5.*
Nearest Station: *New Street (Main line), University (Cross City Line).*
Personnel: *Director:* Professor Richard Verdi. *Senior Curator:* Paul Spencer-Longhurst. *Administrator:* Sophie Wilson.
One of the finest small picture galleries in the world housing an outstanding collection of old masters and modern paintings including masterpieces by Bellini, Rubens, Poussin, Murillo, Gainsborough, Rossetti, Whistler and Magritte. Among the Impressionist pictures are major works by Manet, Monet, Renoir,

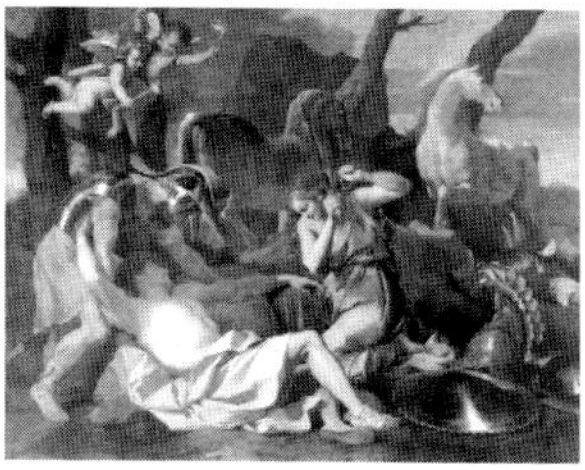

Degas, Gauguin and Van Gogh. The Institute regularly holds concerts, lectures and recitals - all of which are open to the public. It is also available for hire for seminars, receptions, concerts and private views.
Services and Facilities:
Disabled Access. Friends/Society. Gallery space for hire. Guided Tours. Lectures. Museum Shop. Parking.
Work Stocked and Sold:
Pa.

Bird & Davis Ltd
45 Holmes Road, Kentish Town, London NW5 3AN.
Tel: *0171-485 3797.* **Fax:** *0171-284 0509.*

The Coningsby Gallery C
30 Tottenham Street, London W1 9PN.
Tel: *0171-636 7478.* **Fax:** *0171-580 7017.*
Opening times: *Mon-Fri 11-6.*
Nearest Underground: *Goodge Street*
Personnel: Andrew Coningsby.

the coningsby gallery

Specialists in the exhibition and marketing of contemporary art photographers, illustrators and fine artists who work, or are interested in working, in the applied arts markets of advertising, design and publishing. Wide variety of hire and promotional options.
Services and Facilities:
Art Consultancy. Art for Offices. Commissioning Service. Gallery space for hire.
Work Stocked and Sold:
App. Cra. Dr. Pa. Ph. Pr. Sc.
Price range: £200 - £8,000.

Connaught Galleries
44 Connaught Street, London W2.
Tel: *0171-723 1660.* **Fax:** *0171-723 1660.*
Opening times: *Mon-Fri 10-6.30, Sat 10-1.*
Nearest Underground: *Paddington, Lancaster Gate, Marble Arch.*
Personnel: *Partner:* Michael Hollamby.
Wood and aluminium framing. Mirrors to order, or from stock. Dry-mounting. Mount cutting. Shrinkwrapping. Easels and artist supplies. Glass supplied or cut. Frame repairs. Picture restoration. A wide range of prints and posters in stock or to order from extensive catalogues. Limited edition fine art prints. Limited edition fine art figurines. Glass and perspex display cases and display domes and bases.
Services and Facilities:
Art for Offices. Framing. Gallery space for hire. Parking. Restoration. Shop. Workshop Facilities.

Ebury Galleries
200 Ebury Street, London, SW1.
Tel: *0171-730 8999.*

Gallery 47 C
47 Great Russell Street, Bloomsbury, London WC1B 3PA.
Tel: *0171-637 4577, 0181-663 6746.*

The Gallery in Cork Street and Gallery 27 C
28 Cork Street, London W1X 1HB.
Tel: *0171-287 8408.*
Fax: *0171-287 2018.*
Opening times: *Mon-Fri 10-6, Sat 11-4.*
Nearest Underground:
Green Park/Piccadilly.
Personnel: *Manager:* Caroline Edwards.

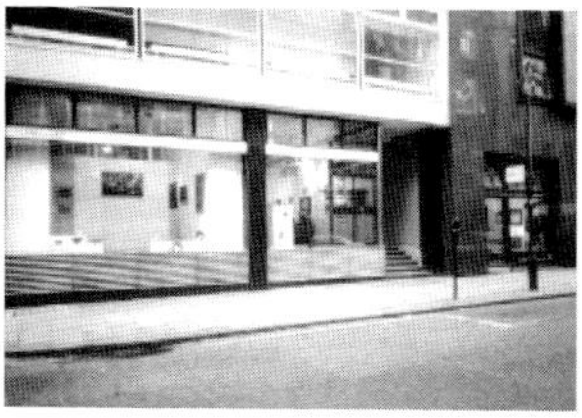

The Gallery in Cork Street and Gallery 27 are two stunning galleries of international reputation in "Europe's Leading Art Street". The Gallery in Cork Street Ltd. offers our clients a unique opportunity to hold exhibitions entirely under their control in Cork Street. The Gallery in Cork Street: 125m2 of versatile prime display area, 60 linear m of wall space, full height double window frontage. Gallery 27: 100m2 of versatile prime display area, 50 linear m of wall space, large window frontage. Excellent Presentation. Full Management and Facility support. Exclusive mailing list. Organisation services available by arrangement.
Services and Facilities:
Gallery space for hire.

Hanover Galleries C
11-13 Hanover Street, Liverpool, L1 3DN.
Tel: *0151-709 3073.*
Opening times: *Tues-Sat 10.30-5.*
Personnel: *Director:* E.P. Austin.
Two spacious and prestigious galleries of exceptional standard, on ground and first floors, inter-connected by a spiral staircase, wall run 85ft and 81ft respectively. Both have good natural light and 30 fully adjustable track spots per gallery. Available for rent. Details on request.
Services and Facilities:
Gallery space for hire.

Highgate Gallery
11 South Grove, Highgate, London N6 6BS.
Tel: *0181-340 3343.* **Fax:** *0181-340 5632.*
Email *admin@hlsi.demon.co.uk*
Opening times: *Wed-Fri 1-5, Sat 11-4, Sun 11-5.*
Nearest Underground: *Archway.*
Personnel: *Administrator:* Linden Nicoll. Hazel Solomon.

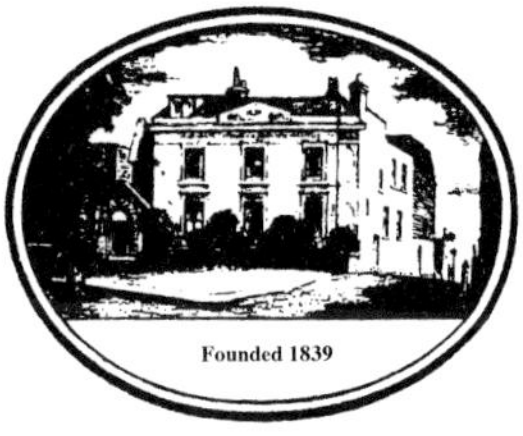

This unique C19 gallery is housed in the Highgate Literary and Scientific Institution, a busy social and cultural centre in Highgate Village. The gallery is top-lit and spacious with 75' x 6' clear hanging space and excellent exhibition lighting. Rates are reasonable. There are nine exhibitions a year, usually of two weeks each. Slides and/or photos should be sent to the Exhibition Committee plus a CV. Ring the Administrator on 0181-340 3343 for further details.
Services and Facilities:
Disabled Access. Gallery space for hire.

Lauderdale House Community Arts Centre *PS*
Waterlow Park, Highgate Hill, London N6 5HG.
Tel: *0181-348 8716/341 2032.*
Fax: *0181-341 4892.*
Opening times: *Tues-Fri 11-4, Sun 12-5. (check events). Sats (dependent on private bookings).*
Nearest Underground: *Archway (Northern Line).*
Personnel: *Director:* Carolyn Naish. *General Manager:* Katherine Ives. *Arts Education Assistant:* Lucy Ribeiro.

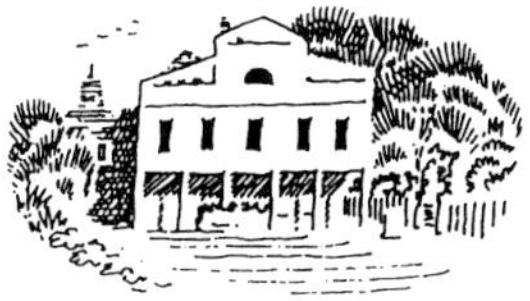

Old Tudor building from 1580, set in Waterlow Park. Reopened in 1978 by Lauderdale House Society Charity. Community Arts and Education Centre. Approx. 38 exhibitions a year, admission free, varying from fine art, photography, local history, to special exhibitions by local groups, societies and schools. Four gallery spaces for hire as follows - Lower Gallery £300, Upper Gallery £170, Entrance Hall £110, and Long Gallery £300. These prices are for a fortnight (Mon to Mon) and include a Private View evening. Space can be shared among artists, no commission on sales and no selection, but artists must manage show professionally. Limited Disabled Access.
Services and Facilities:
Friends/Society. Gallery space for hire. Restaurant. Workshop Facilities.

Mall Galleries
17 Carlton House Terrace, London SW1Y 5BD.
Tel: *0171-930 6844.* **Fax:** *0171-839 7830.*

modern gallery
6a Goodge Place, London W1P 1FL.
Tel: *0171-436 4007.* **Fax:** *0171-436 2755.*
Email *clivej@artnet.co.uk*
Ws *http://www.artnet.co.uk*
Opening times: *10-6.*
Nearest Underground: *Goodge Street, Tottenham Court Road.*
Personnel: *Director:* Clive Jennings.

m o d e r n
g a l l e r y

modern gallery is a new space owned and managed by the organisers of The Contemporary Print Show. In addition its own exhibition programme, the gallery is also available for hire. Located in Fitzrovia, an area well known for its galleries, modern gallery is a beautiful light ground floor space facing on to Goodge Street. Modestly sized at 200 sq ft, it is particularly suitable for smaller pieces, artists' prints, works on paper and photographs. Hire charges are reasonable with no commission; additional services (PR mailing list, listings, internet page, gallery staff etc.) are available if required.
Services and Facilities:
Art Consultancy. Art for Offices. Commissioning Service. Gallery space for hire.
Work Stocked and Sold:
Dr. Pa. Ph. Pr.
Price range: £50 - £5,000.
For artists see *Commercial Gallery Artists.*

Open Space Gallery
131 Lower Marsh, London SE1 7AE.
Tel: *0171-261 1353.*

Sackville Gallery *C*
26 Sackville Street, London W1X 1DA.
Tel: *0171-734 8104.* **Fax:** *0171-734 8104.*

Soar Gallery *C*
4 Launceston Place, London W8 5RL.

Westminster Gallery *P*
Central Hall, Storey's Gate, London SW1 9NH.
Tel: *0171-222 8010.* **Fax:** *0171-222 6883.*
Email *events@wch.co.uk*
Ws *http://www.wch.co.uk*
Opening times: *Various.*
Nearest Underground: *Within walking distance of Victoria, Charing Cross & Waterloo main line stations. U/ground: Westminster & St. James's Park.*
Personnel: *Senior Events Officer:* Ms Cathy Williamson.
The Westminster Gallery offers an elegant, spacious and versatile exhibition area. The three rooms the gallery occupies can be hired individually or as a whole and are available throughout the year. Lighting, hanging and display facilities are easily managed. The adjacent café is open daily and is very happy to assist with refreshments for your private viewings.
Services and Facilities:
Café. Disabled Access. Gallery space for hire. Guided Tours.

Yarrow Gallery
Art Department, Oundle School, Glapthorn Road, Oundle, Peterborough, PE8 4EN.
Tel: *01832-274034.* **Fax:** *01832-274034.*
Opening times: *Mon-Fri 10.30-1 & 2.30-5, Sun 2.30-5.*
Nearest Station: *Peterborough.*
Personnel: *Director:* Roger Page.
School-sponsored exhibitions and available for hire.
Services and Facilities:
Gallery space for hire.

Studio Space for Hire

ACME
44 Copperfield Road, London E3 4RR.
Tel: *0181-981 6811.* **Fax:** *0181-983 0567.*

The Cable Street Studios
Thames House, 566 Cable Street, Limehouse, London E1 9HB.
Tel: *0171-790 1309.* **Fax:** *0171-790 1309.*

Florence Trust Studios *C*
St. Saviour's, Aberdeen Park, Highbury, London N5 2AR.
Tel: *0171-354 4771.* **Fax:** *0171-354 4771.*
Nearest Underground:
Highbury & Islington.
Personnel: *Director:* Rod McIntosh.

Great Western Studios *C*
Westbourne Park, London W2.
Tel: *0171-221 0100.*

Hertford Road Studios
12-14 Hertford Road, London N1.
Tel: *0171-241 0651.*

Roseangle Gallery
17 Roseangle, Dundee.
Tel: *0138-322429.*

S.P.A.C.E. Studios
8 Hoxton Street, London N1 6NG.
Tel: *0171-613 1925.* **Fax:** *0171-613 1996.*
Email *spacestudios@easynet.co.uk*
Ws *http://www.ecna.org*
Personnel: *Director:* Charlotte Robinson. *Studios Manager:* Fiona Furness.
A registered non-profit making charity established by artists in 1968. S.P.A.C.E. Studios aims to provide secure well-managed studios for visual artists. Studio buildings are situated in East and South East London.

Prices per sq. ft. include rates, buildings insurance, maintenance and administration. Vacant studios can be let short term or long term. Sub-lets and shares are also available. Some sites are subject to waiting list. Phone for application and registration pack. Funded by the London Arts Board.

Sculpture House
54-56 Mill Place, Kingston upon Thames, KT1 2LR.

South and North Arts
133 Rye Lane, Peckham, London SE15 4ST.
Tel: *0171-635 8742.*

Wimbledon Art Studios
Holman & Williams House, Riverside Road, London SW17 0BA.
Tel: *0181-879 1100.* **Fax:** *0181-944 5162.*
Opening times: *24 hours/day, 7 days/week.*
Nearest Underground: *Earlsfield & Tooting Broadway.*
Personnel: *Director:* Nigel Holman.

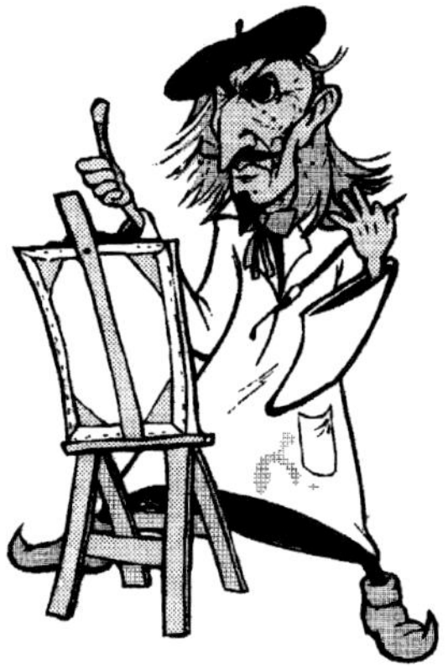

South London's largest art studios complex, offering a wide range of spaces, starting at £19/week shared and £27/week individual, on monthly terms. Currently studios are available, due to a major building programme in the last few months. Excellent natural light, 24 hours access, high ceilings, dry & secure. Very successful twice yearly exhibitions, shared models, good local public transport & parking. This friendly positive environment for creative people, has been developed with the aid of commercial sponsorship. Currently there are over 100 artists undertaking painting, sculpture, ceramics, drawing, mixed media and print making. Other disciplines are also welcome.
Services and Facilities:
Art for Offices. Parking. Workshop Facilities.

NOTES

PUBLISHING

Bookshops.
Book Publishers.
Magazines.

THE ART WORLD
DIRECTORY

Art Book Publishers

Academy Group Ltd
Academy Editions, 42 Leinster Gardens, London W2 3AN.
Tel: *0171-402 2141.*

AN Publications
PO Box 23, Sunderland SR4 6DG.
Tel: *0191-514 3600.*
Fax: *0191-564 1600.*

The Apple Press
6 Blundell Street, London N7 9BH.
Tel: *0171-700 8521.*

Art Sales Index Ltd
1 Thames Street, Weybridge, KT13 3JG.
Tel: *01932-856426.*

Ashgate Publishing/Scolar Press
Gower House, Croft Road, Aldershot, GU11 3HR.
Tel: *01252-331551.* **Fax:** *01252-344405.*
Email *info@ashgatepub.demon.co.uk*
Ws *http://www.ashgate.com*
Personnel: Helen Kennedy.
Editorial: 11 Mecklenburgh Square, London, WC1N 2AD; Tel: 0171-837 6300; Fax: 0171-837 6322; Email: ashgate@mecklenburgh.demon.co.uk;
Contact: Pamela Edwardes.
In 1998 we will publish a new, expanded and updated edition of the classic Handbook of Modern British Painting and Printmaking 1900-1990, plus new works on Glyn Philpot, Forrest Reid, C.W. Nevinson, Mary Potter, amongst others. As part of our expanding programme of Ashgate Art History titles we will continue to publish recent research, monographs or collected essays dealing with all aspects of art and architectural history. Please visit our website to find out about new titles and/or telephone to request a copy of our current art books catalogue.

Aurum Press Ltd
25 Bedford Avenue, London WC1B 3AT.
Tel: *0171-637 3225.*

British Museum Press
46 Bloomsbury Street, London WC1B 3QQ.
Tel: *0171-323 1234.*

BT Batsford
583 Fulham Road, London SW6 5BY.
Tel: *0171-486 8484.*

Cambridge University Press
The Edinburgh Building, Shaftesbury Road, Cambridge, CB2 2RU.
Tel: *01223-312393.*

Caroline Mornement Craft Galleries
Burton Cottage Farm, East Coker, Yeovil, BA22 9LS.
Tel: *01935-862731.*

Cassell Plc
Wellington House, 125 Strand, London WC2R 0BB.
Tel: *0171-420 5582.*

Collins & Brown Publishers
London House, Parkgate Road, London SW11 4NQ.
Tel: *0171-924 2575.*

Constable and Company
3 The Lanchesters, 162 Fulham Palace Road, London W6 9ER.
Tel: *0181-741 3663.*

David & Charles
Brunel House, Forde Road, Newton Abbott, TQ1Z 4PN.
Tel: *01626-61121.*

Dorling Kindersley
9 Henrietta Street, London WC2E 8PS.
Tel: *0171-836 5411.*

Faber & Faber
3 Queen Square, London WC1N 3AU.
Tel: *0171-465 0045.*

Garnet Publishing
8 Southern Court, South Street, Reading, RG1 4QF.
Tel: *01189-597847.*

Gerald Duckworth & Co Ltd
48 Hoxton Square, London N1 6PB.
Tel: *0171-729 5986.*

Hamilyn Octupus
Michelin House, 81 Fulham Road, London SW3 6RB. **Tel:** *0171-581 9393.*

Harry N.Abrams Inc
Lynton House, 7-12 Tavistock Square, London WC1H 9LB.
Tel: *0171-391 65643.*

Hodder & Stoughton
Hodder Headline Book Publishing Ltd 338 Euston Road, London NW1.
Tel: *0171-873 6000.*

J.A.B. Publishing
Suite 2, Arran Place, Valnord Road, St. Peter Port, Gu1 1TL
Tel: *01481-722460.*

Little, Brown & Company
Brettenham House, Lancaster Place, London WC2E 7EN.
Tel: *0171-911 8000.*

Macmillan Publishers Ltd. The Dictionary of Art
25 Eccleston Place, London SW1W 9NF.
Tel: *0171-881 8356.* **Fax:** *0171-881 8357.*

Manchester University Press
Oxford Road, Manchester M13 9NR.
Tel: *0161-273 5539.* **Fax:** *0161-274 3346.*

Methuen London Ltd
Michelin House, 81 Fulham Road, London SW3 5DT.
Tel: *0171-581 9393.*

The MIT Press Ltd
Fitzroy House, 11 Chenies Street, London WC1E 7ET.
Tel: *0171-306 0603.*

Octupus Books Ltd
Michelin House, 81 Fulham Road, London SW3 6RB.
Tel: *0171-581 9393.*

Orion Publishing
Orion House, 5 Upper St Martins Lane, London WC2H 9EA.
Tel: *0171-240 3444.*

Oxford University Press
Great Clarendon Street, Oxford, OX2 6DP.
Tel: *01865-556767.* **Fax:** *01865-556646.*
Ws *http://www.oup.co.uk*

OXFORD
UNIVERSITY PRESS

Oxford University Press is an international publishing house which publishes books across almost every academic subject and has become known for the highest standards of academic excellence and quality of production. It publishes a wide range of art books including the new OXFORD HISTORY OF ART series, a major collection of ground-breaking, authoritative, and beautifully illustrated paperbacks by art historians at the forefront of new thinking.

Paragon Press C
92 Horwood Road, London SW6 4QH.
Tel: *0171-736 4024.*

Pavilion
26 Upper Ground, London SE1 9DP.
Tel: *0171-620 1666.*

Phaidon Press
Regents Wharf, All Saints Street, London N1 9PA.
Tel: *0171-843 1000.*

Random House Publishing
20 Vauxhall Bridge Road, London SW1V 2SA.
Tel: *0171-973 9670.*

Reaktion Books
11 Rathbone Place, London W1P 1DE.
Tel: *0171-580 9928.*

Routledge
11 New Fetter Lane, London EC4P 4EE.
Tel: *0171-583 9855.*

Sansom & Company / Art Dictionaries Ltd.
81g Pembroke Road Clifton Bristol BS8 3EA
Tel: *0117-973 7207.* **Fax:** *0117-973 8991.*
Personnel: *Publishing Director:* John Sansom.
Specialise in artist biographies 1880-2000. Recent titles include Lamorna Birch, Gaudier-Brzeska, Walter Langley, Bernard Leach, Brian Pearce, Claude Rogers, George Sweet, Alfred Wallis. Welcome proposals from art historians and writers.

Through Art Dictionaries Ltd., publish David Buckman's THE DICTIONARY OF ARTISTS IN BRITAIN SINCE 1945, with over 10,000 profiles of painters, printmakers,

Art
DICTIONARIES

sculptors and video and installation artists. Running to c. 1.5 million words, this is the most comprehensive reference for collectors, art historians, curators and dealers researching artists active from mid-end decades of the twentieth century.

Scolar Publishing
Croft Road, Aldershot, GU12 4DY.
Tel: *01252-331551.*

Thames & Hudson
181A High Holborn, London WC1V 7QX.
Tel: *0171-845 5000.*
Email *sales@thbooks.demon.co.uk*
Ws *thttp://www.hameshudson.co.uk*

Thames and Hudson

V&A Publications
160 Brompton Road, London SW3 1HW.
Tel: *0171-938 9663.*

White Cockade
71 Lonsdale Road, Oxford, OX2 7ES.
Tel: *01865-510411.* **Fax:** *01865-514034.*
Email *pk@whitecockade.demon.co.uk*
Personnel: *Director:* Perilla Kinchin.

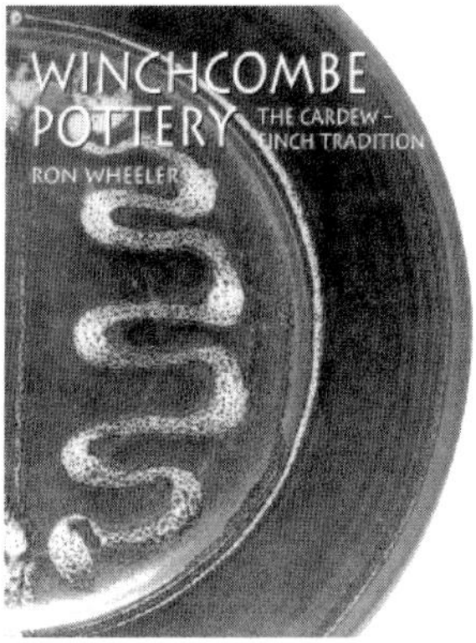

White Cockade publishes a small list of well-reviewed illustrated books in the field of the decorative arts, architectural and design history and social history, often in collaboration with museums. The most recent title is Winchcombe Pottery: The Cardew-Finch Tradition, the first book on Britain's longest surviving studio pottery. Other subjects include Charles Rennie Mackintosh's architectural writings; the Glasgow tea rooms; Glasgow's Great Exhibitions; George Walton, pioneer of the Glasgow Style; and the furniture designer-maker Edward Barnsley, who kept alive the ideals of the Arts and Crafts movement late into the twentieth century.

Yale University Press
23 Pond Street, London NW3 2PN.
Tel: *0171-431 4422.*

Art Bookshops

Arts Bibliographic
37 Cumberland Business Park,
Cumberland Avenue, London, NW10 7SL.
Tel: *0181-961 4277.*
Fax: *0181-961 8246.*
Email *sales@artsbib.com*
Ws *http://www.artsbib.com*
Arts Bibliographic is not a bookshop as such, it is a firm of library suppliers specialising in books and catalogues on art and design. Their expert services are now available to the general public as well via a website providing mail-order facilities and information on the latest publications: www.artsbib.com.

Atrium Bookshop
5 Cork Street, London W1.
Tel: *0171-495 0073.*

Beyond Words
42-44 Cockburn Street, Edinburgh EH1 1PB.
Tel: *0131-226 6636.*
Fax: *0131-226 6676.*

Blackwell's Art & Poster Shop
27 Broad Street, Oxford, OX1 2AS.
Tel: *01865-792792.*
Fax: *01865-794143.*

Dillons Arts Bookshop
8 Long Acre, London WC2.
Tel: *0171-836 1359.*

Foyles Bookshop
Charing Cross Road,
London, WC2H 0EB.
Tel: *0171-437 5660.*

Hayward Gallery Bookshop
Hayward Gallery, South Bank,
London SE1.
Tel: *0171-928 3144.*

ICA Bookshop
Institute of Contemporary Arts,
The Mall, London SW1.
Tel: *0171-930 0493.*

Paisley Fine Books
17 Corsebar Crescent, Paisley, PA2 9QA.
Tel: *0141-884 2661.*

Waterstone's Bookshop
193 Kensington High Street, London, W8.
Tel: *0171-937 8432.*

Zwemmers
24 Litchfield Street, London WC2M 9NJ.
Tel: *0171-379 7886/0171-240 699 /0171-240 4158.*
Fax: *0171-836 7049.*

Fine Art Magazines

Antiques Bulletin
2 Hampton Court Road, Harborn,
Birmingham B17 9AE.

Antiques Trade Gazette
17 Whitcomb Street, London, WC2H 7PL.
Tel: *0171-930 7192.*

Apollo
1 Castle Lane London SW1E 6DR.
Tel: *0171-233 8906.* **Fax:** *0171-233 7159.*

Art Monthly
Suite 17, 126 Charing Cross Road,
London WC2H 0DG.
Tel: *0171-497 0726.* **Fax:** *0171-497 0726.*

The Art Newspaper
27-29 Vauxhall Grove, London SW8 1SY.
Tel: *0171-735 3332.* **Fax:** *0171-735 3332.*

Art Review
Hereford House, 23-24 Smithfield Street,
London EC1A 9LF.
Tel: *0171-236 4880.*
Fax: *0171-236 4881.*
Email *info@art-review.co.uk*
Ws *http://www.art-review.co.uk*
Opening times: *We never close.*
Personnel: *Editor:* David Lee.
Advertisement Manager: Louisa Utting.

art REVIEW

Britain's leading monthly art magazine. Annual UK subscription £38; USA $79; Europe £48; Rest of World £48. Also publishers of the Art Review Art World Directory.

Artists & Illustrators
The Fitzpatrick Building, 188-194 York Way,
London N7 9QR.
Tel: *0171-700 8500.* **Fax:** *0171-700 4985.*
Personnel: *Publisher:* Zarina Hawkins.
Editor: Laura Gasgoigne.
Manager: Paul Harris.

Artists & Illustrators

The UK's best selling practical art magazine, available the first Monday of each month. Amateur and professional artists and illustrators will find inspiration and advice on a wide range of materials and techniques. Step by Step Demonstrations and Interviews provide an insight into working methods, Business File covers aspects of a career in art plus the latest news on exhibitions, books, courses, competitions and opportunities. Cover price £2.40; one year subscription £23.10 (saving £5.70) - call 01858-435307 for further details. Organisers of the annual Artists & Illustrators Exhibition - call 0171-700 8504 for further information.

Artists Newsletter
PO Box 23, Sunderland SR4 6DG.
Tel: *0191-567 3589.* **Fax:** *0191-564 1600.*

The Artists' Publishing Company
Caxton House, 63-65 High Street, Tenterden, TN30 6BD.
Tel: *01580-763315/3673.* **Fax:** *01580 765411.*
Personnel: *Managing Director:* Dr Sally Bulgin.
Publisher of two, monthly instructional fine art magazines offering professional painting instruction in all media: Leisure Painter, for the amateur and student. Editor: Irene A. Briers. The Artist, for the serious amateur and semi-professional. Editor: Dr Sally Bulgin. Both magazines give up-to-date information on books, videos and art products; tuition and exhibition listings, painting courses and holidays. An invaluable marketplace for all forms of art tuition and fine arts services. Both magazines cost £2.10 per issue; subscription: £23.00.

Contemporary Visual Arts
Suite K101, Tower Bridge Business Complex, Clements Road, London SE16 4DG.
Tel: *0171-823 8373.* **Fax:** *0171-823 7969.*

Crafts Magazine
Crafts Council, 44a Pentonville Road, Islington, London N1 9BY.
Tel: *0171-278 7700.* **Fax:** *0171-837 0858.*
Email *crafts@craftscouncil.org.uk*
Ws *http://www.craftscouncil.org.uk*
Nearest Underground: *Angel.*
Personnel: *Editor:* Geraldine Rudge.
Sales & Marketing Manager: Nichola Bath.

CRAFTS

From the avant-garde to classic collectors pieces, from domestic pottery to public art commissions on the grand scale, Crafts is the only British magazine to highlight and explore the very best of the decorative and applied arts. Disciplines covered include textiles, jewellery, wood, ceramics, metalwork, furniture, fashion accessories, calligraphy, glass, and automata. Published bi-monthly by the Crafts Council Crafts, is the essential reference for both specialists and those with a general interest in visual culture.
Services and Facilities:
Commissioning Service.

Frieze
21 Denmark Street, London WC2H 8NE.
Tel: *0171-379 1533.* **Fax:** *0171-379 1521.*

Modern Painters
Universal House, 251 Tottenham Court Road, London W1P 9AD.
Tel: *0171-636 6058.* **Fax:** *0171-580 5615.*

Print Quarterly Publications
80 Carlton Hill, London NW8 0ER.

RA Magazine
Royal Academy of Arts, Piccadilly, London W1.
Tel: *0171-439 7438.* **Fax:** *0171-287 9023.*

Tate Magazine
Blueprint Media Ltd., Christ Church, Cosway Street, London NW1 5NJ. **Tel:** *0171-706 4596.*

NOTES

COMMERCIAL GALLERIES BY MEDIA

This section lists establishments by media speciality. Use this section to find the gallery stocking the media you require.

THE ART WORLD
DIRECTORY

Artists' Books

Applied Art

Ceramics

Crafts

Decorative Art

Drawing

Furniture

Glass

Jewellery

Painting

Photography

Prints

Sculpture

Textiles

Wood

NOTES

ART UNDER £1,000

Galleries selling work priced under £1,000.

COMMERCIAL GALLERY ARTISTS

This section lists, by gallery, a sample of the artists the gallery represents, stocks or sells.

198 GALLERY
(Page 74)
Aliyu, Hassan
Cooper, Clement
Donkor, Godfried
Ettienne, Glen
Imani, Pablo
Jones, Sheila
Kelly, George
Manning, Jenni
Watson, Raymond

ABBOTSBURY STUDIOS
(Page 93)
Skinner, John

ABBOTT & HOLDER
(Page 53)
Absolon, John
Adam, Robert
Ardizzone, Edward
Austin, Samuel
Barrett, George
Becker, Harry
Bourne, James
Brangwyn, Frank
Callow, William
Carmichael, John W.
Carrington, Dora
Clausen, George
Collins, Cecil
Cox, David
Davis, Anthony
De Wint, Peter
Diboin, Thomas
Dulac, Edmund
Emett, Rowland
Farington, Joseph
Faulkner, John
Fielding, A.V. Copley
Fraser, (Family)
Fripp, George
Frost, George
Glover, John
Goodall, Edward A.
Hills, Robert
Holland, James
La Cave, Peter
Lear, Edward
Lessore, Thérèse
Minro, Dr. Thomas
Minton, John
Morley, Harry
Pitchforth, Vivian
Pont, Graham Laidlaw
Reynolds, Alan
Rowbotham, Thomas L.
Rowlandson, Thomas
Sandby, Paul
Searle, Ronald
Sickert, Walter
Strang, William
Sunderland, Thomas
Topolski, Feliks
Varley, John
Vaughan, Keith
Welch, Denton
Wood, Christopher

ADAM GALLERY
(Page 89)
Bond, Marj
Cartwright, Richard
Davie, Alan
Denaro, Melita
Foord, Susan
Frost, Sir Terry
Graham, Brian
Harvey, Gail
Heron, Patrick
Hilton, Roger
Hitchens, Ivon
Hockney, David
Hoyland, John
Kent, Colin
Lanyon, Peter
Lin, Hsiao Mei
Macmiadhachain, Padraig
McDowell, Leo
Moore, Henry
Newton, Algernon
Nicholson, Ben
Philipson, Robin
Piper, John
Piper, John
Roberts, William
Robertson, James
Scott, William
Selby, William
Suddaby, Rowland
Wood, Christopher

ADVANCED GRAPHICS LONDON
(Page 160)
Aitchison, Craigie
Bartlett, Stephen
Beattie, Basil
Bellany, John
Benjamins, Paul
Bennett, Mick
Canning, Neil
Caulfield, Patrick
Fraser, Donald Hamilton
Frost, Anthony
Halter, Ardyn
Hammick, Tom
Hoyland, John
Hugonin, James
Irvin, Bert
Jones, Trevor
Keane, John
Klein, Anita
McLean, John
Moon, Mick
Radford, Matthew
Richardson, Ray
Setch, Terry
Walker, John
Whiteford, Kate
Wragg, Gary

ALAN CRISTEA GALLERY
(Page 53)
Avery, Milton
Ayres, Gillian
Baselitz, Georg
Blake, Peter
Braque, Georges
Caulfield, Patrick
Chillida, Eduardo
Craig-Martin, Michael
Davey, Grenville
Dibbets, Jan
Dine, Jim
Dubuffet, Jean
Flanagan, Barry
Fulton, Hamish
Gabo, Naum
Hamilton, Richard
Hodgkin, Howard
Hoyland, John
Inshaw, David
Johns, Jasper
Jones, Allen
Judd, Donald
Langlands and Bell
Léger, Fernand
Lichtenstein, Roy
Mansen, Matthias
Manser, Antje
Matisse, Henri
McKeever, Ian
Milroy, Lisa
Miró, Joan
Moon, Mick
Motherwell, Robert
Nicholson, Ben
Opie, Julian
Paladino, Mimmo
Penck, A.R.
Picasso, Pablo
Rauschenberg, Robert
Rosenquist, James
Salle, David
Scully, Sean
Self, Colin
Stella, Frank
Sultan, Donald
Tapiès, Antoni
Tilson, Joe
Walker, John
Warhol, Andy
Winner, Gerd

ALBEMARLE GALLERY
(Page 53)
Al-Atar, Suad
Alarcon, Aracely
Alderliesten, Kees
Barlow, Jeremy
Berber, Mersad
Dominguez, Goyo
Escofet, Miriam
Faulkner, Iain
Formin, Igor
Gallarda, Michael
Gatherer, Stuart Luke
Gosling, Annabel
Gran, Elena & Michel
Hurtado, Fabio
King, Alan
Krasnovsky, Alexy
Landa, Julien
Liepke, Malcolm
Liu, Jincheng
Markus, Csaba
McAllister, Ian
McDowell, Leo
McKean, Graham
Narkevich, Elena
Raissis, Aris
Roberts, Steven
Roldan, Alfredo
Saunders, Robert
Schwartz, Daniel
Smuling, Inrid
Van Hoylandt, Werner
Williams, Antony

ALEXANDRA WETTSTEIN
(Page 208)
Bailey, Belinda
Barker, Dale Devereux
Caulfield, Patrick
Chadwick, Lynn
Cooper, Eileen
Frost, Sir Terry
Garfield, Rachel
Jones, Allen
Keiller, Anna
Kitaj, R.B.
Kowalsky, Elaine
Matisse, Henri
McKellar, Robert
Miró, Joan
Moore, Henry
Newington, Charles
Paolozzi, Eduardo
Pasmore, Victor
Picasso, Pablo
Piper, Edward
Piper, John
Sutherland, Graham
Sykes, Sandy
Tilson, Joe
Wakita, Aijiro

ALTERNATIVE ART MARKET
(Page 53)
Aitchison, Bob
Anderson, Jim
Bingham, Dolures
Cabey, Josef
Carrett, James
Chesterman, Martin
Conquy, Walter
Cuttle, Sue
Davis, Steve
Deeson, Tobi
Delimabritto, Tania
Drew Edwards, Lucille
Edgar, Carol
Francis, Sarah
Gacillanes, Enrique
Gillilan, Helen
Gretton, Keith
Grice, Justine
Harris, Sarah
Hickman, Gill
Hodgen, Joanne
Howorth, James
Joseph, Ian
Knott, Lin
Lewis, Sanchia
Marshall, Stuart
Nazim, Nazim
Pengilly, Caria
Reyes, Arturo
Rose, Jenny
Runache, Jenny
Staniforth, Catherine
Till, Tobias
Tisdall, Sarah

ANDERSON GALLERY
(Page 114)
Bowen, Clive
Bowman, Sarah
Campbell, James
Cardew, Ara
Cardew, Seth
Cookson, Delan
Doherty, Jack
Dunbar, Emma
Fieler, Helen
Goldsmith, Robert

Hilton, Roger
Hitchens, Ivon
Hodge, Anthony
Holland, Michael
Howard, Ashley
Jeffrey, Jill
Lambert, Nigel
Millais, Fiona
Morrell Barnett, Christine
Moy, Judith
Nicholson, Ben
Nicholson, Winifred
Piper, John
Prosser, Debbie
Purser, Keith
Rowe, Judith
Sickert, Walter
Stephens, Jenny
Stevenson, Paul
Vaughan, Keith
Wells, John

Anderson O'Day Graphics
(Page 160)
Ackroyd, Norman
Cole, Yvonne
Crossley, Anthony
Daniels, Harvey
Davey Winter, Jean
Delderfield, Delia
Farrow, Carol
Frost, Sir Terry
Irvin, Bert
Jones, Ian
McLean, Bruce
Neiland, Brendan
Neville, Alison
O'Neill, Mary Rose
Piper, John
Rowe, Carl
Shave, Terry
Virgils, Katherine
Wilkinson, Donald

Anne Faggionato
(Page 54)
Bacon, Francis
Balthus
Baselitz, Georg
Bonnard, Pierre
Degas, Edgar
Gauguin, Paul
Giacometti, Alberto
Hepworth, Barbara
Hirst
Lichtenstein, Roy
Matisse, Henri
Miró, Joan
Monet, Claude
Moore, Henry
Picasso, Pablo
Quinn
Rodin
Warhol, Andy
Whiteread, Rachel

Annely Juda Fine Art
(Page 54)
Ackling, Roger
Caro, Anthony
Chillida, Eduardo
Christo
Clough, Prunella
Fulton, Hamish
Funakoshi, Katsura
Gabo, Naum
Green, Alan
Hall, Nigel
Hockney, David
Kawamata, Tadashi
Leapman, Edwina
Malevich, Kasimir
Moholy-Nagy, Laszlo
Nash, David
Popova, Liubov
Reynolds, Alan
Rodchenko, Alexander
Vordemberge-Gildewart, Friedrich

The Antique & Book Collector
(Page 99)
Belleroche, Albert
Copley, John
Drury, Paul
Fishwick, Clifford
Fraser, Eric
Gaudier-Brzeska, Henri
Gill, Eric
Grant, Duncan
Hermes, Gertrude
Hilton, Roger
Jones, Barbara
Jones, David
Knight, Laura
Lord, Elyse
Nash, John
Paolozzi, Eduardo
Pissarro, Orovida
Spencer, Stanley
Tanner, Robin
Tindle, David
Vaughan, Keith

Art Arena Gallery
(Page 168)
Kianush, Katy

Art For Offices
(Page 208)
Benbow, Zoe
Blik, Maurice
Booth, Martin
Brown, John
Canning, Neil
Carter, Lara
Cinalli, Ricardo
Duffy, Terry
Ford, Anita
Freshwater, Sally
Godwin, Mark
Hayes, Peter
Hewitson, Eric
Hewitt, Annabel
Homma, Kaori
Humphreys, Ian
Jacobson, David
Jennings, Helyne
Jones, Graham
Krikhaar, Anthony
Lichterman, Heidi
Lucien, Simon
Marriot, Neale
Olins, Rob
Palin, Les
Plummer, Brian
Ribbons, Ian
Seligman, Lincoln
Simpson, Chris
Stok, William
Virgils, Katherine
Whadcock, Richard

The Art Supermarket
(Page 54)
Atkins, David
Avsec, Naomi
Bauman, Lydia
Boyne, David
Braga, Celio
Casano, Rosana
Chapman, Kevin
Codina, Joseph
Colombo, Cecile
Cooper, Lucian
de Val, Manuel
Duffin, John
Eustace, David
Halsey, Mark
Knubley, Alex
Mayes, Emerson
McGregor, Mhairi
Milne, Christine
Notman, Marion
Prat, Jordi
Read, James
Sabala
Thompson, Ian
Waring, Janet
West, Sarah

Artworks Gallery
(Page 94)
Bates, Merete
Greenup, John
Hughes, Susan
Launder, June
McKee, Samantha
Mowlam, Geoff
Sealy, Gina

Avalon Art
(Page 91)
Beer, David
Bray, Barrie
Bray, Heather
Dalgarno, Barbara
Dayton, John
Dunstan, Sarah
Evans, Bernard
Fisher, Tom
Frost, Luke
Gore & Flumeri
Hawkes, Gabrielle
Hiddleston, Stephen
Hoskin, Amanda
Hoskin, Catherine
Laurie, Ian
Lodey, Richard
McClary, Louise
Pilcher, Esther
Scott, Carol
Sherlock, Darrel
Smith, Jason
Smith, Nicole
Styles, Linda
Styles & Ward
Talbot, Sarah
West, Oliver
Wilson, Ges
Winterton, Claire

BCA Boukamel Cont. Art
(Page 55)
Bach, Elvira
Braham, Philip
Castelli, Luciano
Chia, Sandro
Clemente, Francesco
Currie, Ken
Delebecque, François
Delprat, Hélène
Fetting, Rainer
Garouste, Gérard
Hödicke, K.H.
Lüpertz, Markus
Mcintyre, Keith
Mourad, Joumana
Nele, E.R.
Penck, A.R.
Spoerri, Daniel
Tatafiore, Ernesto
Traquandi, Gérard
Wiszniewski, Adrian

Beaux Arts
(Page 89)
Adams, Norman
Ayrton, Michael
Barker, Patrick
Barns-Graham, Wilhelmina
Bealing, Nicola
Bellany, John
Blackadder, Elizabeth
Boydell, Lucy
Chadwick, Lynn
Cinalli, Ricardo
Entwisle, Mark
Fedden, Mary
Feiler, Paul
Fraser, Donald Hamilton
Frink, Elisabeth
Frost, Sir Terry
Gatfield, Rupert
Glendinning, Lucy
Hanscomb, Brian
Hartley, Ben
Henry, Sean
Herman, Josef
Holland, Harry
Holzhandler, Dora
Jammet, Lin
Kane, Martin
Klein, Anita
Knox, Jack
Lanyon, Andrew
Mackenzie, Alexander
MacPherson, Neil
McDonald, James
McLean, Donna
McRae, Jennifer
Mount, Paul
Musgrave, Olivia
Nolan, Sir Sydney
Organ, Robert
Paltenghi, Julian
Pearce, Bryan
Penny, Giles
Philipson, Sir Robin
Piper, Edward
Piper, John
Ray, Roy
Richardson, Ray
Turpin, Louis
Ustinov, Igor
Volk, Patricia

Bowyer, William
Bratby, John
Brown, Ralph
Camp, Jeffrey
Casson, Sir Hugh
Cockrill, Maurice
Constable, John
Cox, Paul
Cuming, Fred
Dring, William
Dunlop, Ronald O.
Dunstan, Bernard
Eurich, Richard
Fedden, Mary
Frink, Elisabeth
Gainsborough, Thomas
Gore, Frederick
Gosse, Sylvia
Green, Anthony
Hartill, Brenda
Hayes, Colin
Hepple, Norman
Hitchens, Ivon
Hockney, David
Howard, Ken
Jacklin, Bill
John, Augustus
Kenny, Michael
Larusdottir, Karolina
Lawrence, John Frederick
Lowry, L.S.
Millar, John
Moore, Henry
Phillips, Tom
Piper, John
Potter, Beatrix
Rooney, Mick
Russell, Calvin
Shepard, E. H.
Shepherd, David
Smith, Stan
Stage, Ruth
Sutherland, Emma
Sutton, Linda
Sutton, Philip
Tindle, David
Turner, J.M.W.
Weight, Carel

Brian Sinfield Gallery
(Page 98)
Armfield, Diana
Arnup, Sally
Cordery, Don
Crook, P.J.
Cuming, Fred
Hemingway, Andrew
Herman, Josef
Ryder, Sue
Smith, Richard
Tabner, Len
Ward, John
Williams, Jacqueline
Wootton, Olive

Broughton House Gallery
(Page 105)
Aked, G. D.
Balzola, Asun
Borlase, Deirdre
Cornford, Christopher
Cunliffe, Christopher
English, Andy
Hartley, Marie
Hazelwood, David
Hellewell, Jack
Hemming, Caroline
January, Libby
Jesson, Robin
Kennedy, Richard
Kraczyna, Swietlan
Lawrence, John
Lewis, Ffiona
Lickfold, Gail
Lister, Raymond
Lodge, Jean
Mattioli, Carlo
McGuinness, Tom
Mommens, Norman
Morsman, Phil
Muñoz, Rie
Newbolt, Clare
Newbolt, Thomas
Piper, John
Raverat, Gwen
Richards, Ceri
Schloss, Edith
Shreve, Peter
Vannithone, Soun

Bruton Gallery
(Page 121)
Ayrton, Michael
Bourdelle, Emile-Antoine
Brown, Ralph
Claudel, Camille
Cornet
Crowe, Victoria
Dalcu, Jules-Aimé
Eurich, Richard
Foster, Tony
Howie, James
Maillol, Aristide
Moore, Henry
O'Reilly, Joseph
Philipson, Sir Robin
Pilkington, Cathie
Rodin, Auguste
Sacksick, Gilles
Smith, Ken
Tarr, Deborah
Wiérick, Robert

The Bruton Street Gallery
(Page 56)
Backhouse, David
Boncompain
Boydell, Lucy
Broadbent, Stephen
Bueno, Pinedo
Cameron, Ronald
Carrick, Ian
Crozier, William
De Bruyne, Anne
Eck, Francis
Foreman, William
Gales, Simon
Gibbs, Leonie
Graham, David
Llacer, Teresa
Macdonald, Alan
Mendjisky, Serge
Nadal, Carlos
Quanne, Michael
Royo
Thursby, Peter
Tweed, Jill
Vayreda, C.

Business Art Galleries
(Page 209)
Atherton, Barry
Barry, Jo
Bawden, Edward
Bigger, Clare
Blackburn, Kenneth
Blackmore, Clive
Blake, Naomi
Boyd Harte, Glynn
Brokenshire, John
Cecil, Roger
Corsellis, Jane
Creswell, Alexander
Dingwall, Phoebe
Dover, Peter
Dunstan, Bernard
Fraser, Donald Hamilton
Frink, Elisabeth
Gibbs, Jonathan
Gore, Frederick
Hartill, Brenda
Hepworth, Barbara
Herman, Josef
Hocking, Susan-Jayne
Holliday, Sarah
Hoyland, John
Jawahirilal, Lallitha
Jones, Stanley
Kotzen, Thirza
Macara, Andrew
Macmiadhachain, Padraig
Mandl, Anita
Martin, Ruth
Mierins, Laimonis
Moore, Henry
Noach, Michèle
Norris, Linda
Oki, Yuji
Piper, John
Richards, Ceri
Richmond, Robin
Rizvi, Jacqueline
Roberts, Keith
Ryan, Paul
Schwarz, Hans
von Stumm, Johannes
Walker, Richard
Williams, Jago Max
Wouda, Marjan
Wray, Peter

Cadogan Contemporary Art
(Page 56)
Alcock, Emma
Ballard, Brian
Bealing, Nicola
Grant, Keith
Iskhakov, Timur
Johnstone, Andrew
Le Grice, Jeremy
Leaman, Bridget
Mann, Sargy
McClure, Daphne
McClure, Emma
Mei Lin, Hsiao
Neal, Arthur
Yavorskya, Svetlana

Cambridge Contemporary Art
(Page 105)
Aitchison, Craigie
Bendall-Brunello, Tiziana
Bond, Marj
Bridge, Eoghan
Cartwright, Reg
Chagall, Marc
Clarke, Jonathan
Cornish, Charlotte
Dove, Stanley
Falcke, Emma
Foster, Barbara
Fraser, Donald Hamilton
Frink, Elisabeth
Gleeson, David
Hollidge, Jane
Hyslop, Aliisa
Irvin, Bert
Klein, Anita
Larusdottir, Karolina
Loizou, Renos
Macinnes, Jock
Maddox, Ronald
Matisse, Henri
McInnes, Sheila
McVeigh, Michael
Murfitt, Stephen
Newland, Jeremy
Newland, Jeremy
Palser, Alice
Patterson, Ann Ross
Picasso, Pablo
Piper, John
Richardson, Ray
Richarson, Ilana
Russ, Michael
Smith, Sophie
Spence, Annora
Stirling, Dorothy
Tuff, Richard
Welch, Robin

Carningli Centre
(Page 148)
Batt, Richard
Coles, Bill
Farrell, Alan
Flack, Robert
Horton, Sheila
Hughes, Robert
King, Michael
Mason, Ann
Whitaker, Rita
Williams, Paul

CCA Galleries Ltd
(Page 56)
Crew, Lee
Frost, Sir Terry
Hamilton-Fraser, Donald
König, Heidi
Millington, Terence
Piper, John
Piper, Luke
Poulton, Jane
Richardson, Ilana
Ruffhead, Andrew
Spare, Richard
Spence, Annora
Swain, Hannah
Taylor, Frank
Tuff, Richard
Vettriano, Jack

Chantry House Gallery
(Page 123)
Allen, David
Anderson, Athena

Barker, Neville
Berzins, Valteris
Braithwaite, Kevin
Crossley, Donald
Cudworth, Jack
Curgenven, Michael
Durkin, Tom
Gray, Len
Halsey, Mark
Haste, J. Barrie
Howell, David
Jones, Mike
Keeton, Richard
Lazzerini, Giuliana
Logan, Georgina
Logan, Lynda
Logan, Terry
Mayes, Emerson
Nettleship, Patrick
Parkin, John
Roxby, Brian
Rush, Maureen
Saville, Michael
Schofield, Helen
Sibson, John
Simone, Neil
Velard, Paula
Whatmore, Nel

The Chapel Gallery
(Page 93)
Atridge, Claire
Ayles, Roberta
Bannochie, Priscilla
Belsher, Holly
Benfield, John
Betowski, Noel
Bird, Buddy
Brown, Caroline
Calder, Matt
Chapple, Dan
Chivers, Bruce
Cockram, Roger
Cookson, Delan
De Choisy, Kevin
Faulkener, Felix
Godfrey, Richard
Goldberg, Nary
Hahn, Carl
Hanscomb, Brian
Harford, Chloe
Hawkins, Chris
Highet, Hilary
Howse, Karen
Hyde, Marylin
Jackson, Paul
Keeley, Laurel
King, Sarah
Leather, Peet
Marsh, Suzie
Martin, Jane
Mills, Jane
Moss, Michael
Napiorkowska, Danka
Newell, Eleanor
Polyblank, Rebecca
Polyblank, Veronica
Price, Trevor
Prinol, Chris
Raeburn, Elizabeth
Reeves, Peter
Rivans, Maria
Rudge, Dillon
Sewart, Vicky
Sollis, Rob
Stein, Gillian
Taja
Theobald, Jane
Truman, Jan
Wall, David
Williams, Heather
Zellinski, Pauline

The Chapel of Art / Capel Celfyddyd
(Page 147)
Aplin, Kay
Boenigk, Dagmar
Brown, Celia
Cheshire, Richard
Clay, Andie
Coles, Howard
Elsworth, Carole
Evans, Polly Marix
Frith, David
Gardner, Jan
Gould, Teena
Grosvenor, David
Hamer, Frank
Hamer, Janet
Ingham, Eta
John, Linda
Kay, Jay F.
King, Sue
Kojelyté, Diava
Morgan, Ann
Morris, Nancy
Napier, Jean
Piatigorsky, Max
Pritchard, David
Reading, John
Rice, Bill
Snape, Alan
Spashett, Anne
Swann, Bill
Templeman, Angharad
Templeman, Rhian
Watkins, Jim
Wilkinson, Fiona Brown
Wilkinson, Ray
Williams, Karen
Williams-Ellis, Bronwyn

Colin Jellicoe Gallery
(Page 118)
Abbott, Nolan
Avellano, Ambrose
Baumforth, David
Bell, John
Blenkinsopp, John
Bocai, Maria Daniela
Brady, Flo
Brown, Sally
Cousset, Jean-Marie
Cownie, Allan
Davey, Peter Granville
Dobson, Martin
Gardner, Reg
Gilbert, Colin
Granville
Granville, Nicholas
Harrison, Michael
Hawtin, John
Henry, Sue
Hesketh, Michael
Higginson, Cliff
Hill, Debbie
Jellicoe, Colin
Jones, Alwyn Dempster
Kelly, Francis
Key, Geoffrey
Lawley, Christine
Leach, Krys
Leigh, Teresa
Martin, Christina
Mayer, William
Mitchell, Sue
Noble, Chris
Persson, Kariona
Picking, John
Porter, Robert
Ritchie, Paul
Rothmer, Dorothy
Sanderson, Jean
Simione, Giovanni
Skovgaard, Kim
Stanley, Dave
Sykes, George
Tatham, Susan
Thornton, Barry
Whittall, Sylvia
Williams, Enid
Williams, Jackie
Williams, Peter

The Coningsby Gallery
(Page 56)
Archer/Quinnell
Bellingham, Barbara
Burston, Oliver
Crowther, Peter
Davis, Paul
Fraser, Ewan
Friedman, Jim
Gissing, Nicky
Haygarth, Stuart
Hoogslag, Nanette
Huntley/Muir
Jarzbowska, Tamsin
Kitching, Alan
Loco, Gone
Mann and Man
Marsham, Sophie
Maynard, Peter
Zap Art

The Contemporary Print Show & The Contemporary Print Fair
(Page 41)
Ayres, Gillian
Bassett, Clare
Baxter, Sandra
Blackadder, Elizabeth
Blake, Peter
Brett, Simon
Buckland-Wright, John
Byrne, John
Carpenter, Pip
Craig-Martin, Michael
Desmet, Anne
Ferguson-Lees, Dominic
Ford, Peter
Fraser, Donald Hamilton
Freud, Lucian
Frost, Sir Terry
Fulton, Hamish
Hammick, Tom
Hockney, David
Hodgkin, Howard
Houston, John
Hoyland, John
Huxley, Jonathan
Ingamells, Andrew
Inshaw, David
Irvin, Bert
Jones, Trevor
Kalinovich, Konstantin
Kiff, Ken
Klein, Anita
Koenig, Heidi
Kudryashov, Oleg
Le Brun, Christopher
Lee, Jessie
Lewandowski, Simon
McKeever, Ian
McLean, Bruce
Meyer, Klaus
Milroy, Lisa
Moxley, Susan
Oulton, Thérèse
Paladino, Mimmo
Perring, Susie
Petterson, Melvyn
Rae, Barbara
Rego, Paula
Richardson, Ray
Rollo, Sonia
Russell, Victoria
Sykes, Sandy

The Cottage Gallery
(Page 106)
Bartlett, Mikaela
Beaver, David
Berry Patterson, Penny
Cameron, Barbara
Carsberg, Natasha
Castellano-Haycock, Cinzia
Coles, Fiona
Garner, Olivia
Gosling, Oliver
Hawdon, Paul
Maberley, James
Marsters, Geoff
Morse, Colin
Murfin, Michael
Osborne, Tricia
Richardson, Phillip
Ronaldson, Bruce
Ross, Nigel
Sewell, Marc
Smith, Jane
Street, Cynthia
Tracey, Sue
Waters, Alan
White, Peter
Winbolt, Pam

The Craft Centre and Design Gallery
(Page 121)
Ackroyd, Norman
Ambery-Smith, Vicki
Barnes, Roger
Bendall-Brunello, Tiziana
Blakeney, Anthony
Bottle, Neil
Briggs, Jessica
Carnac, Helen
Coleman, John
Degen, Joel
Eden, Michael
Eden, Victoria
Finlay, Anne
Forrest, Marianne

Forrester, Trevor
Hale, Jennie
Hicks, Jeremy
Hill, Andrew
Jackson-Currie, Lorna
Keith, Sara
Kirby, Sarah
Klein, Anita
Klevan, Gail
Krinos, Daphne
Larusdottir, Karolina
Lewin, Linda
McPake, John
Mercedes-Wear, Anna
Morton, Grainne
Murphy, Kathie
Muskett and Mazzullo
Perry, Janet
Perry, Jo
Perry, Sarah
Porter, Diana
Preston, Paul
Pugh, Martyn
Richards, Victoria
Royle, Guy
Rylatt, Ian
Slattery, Nicola
Smith, Martin
Smythe, Helen
Strickland, Lesley
Theakston, Anthony
Vallis, Alan
Van Liefferinge, Katrien
White, David

Crafty People
(Page 122)
Aukland, Rick
Battell, Carol
Bradshaw, Karen
Connell, Jeff
Cookson, Paul
Driver, Nigel
Fowler, John
Frisby, Steve
Gage, Lea
Ganley, Amanda
Garnett, John
Hanaghan, Lionel
Helliwell, E. and K.
Hudson, Kay
James, David
Jones, David
Kearon, Martin
McAssey, Martin
McDermot, John
McNamara, Jim
McNamara, Sadie
Nettleship, John and Myra
Parnell, Carolyn
Pitts, Chantal
Price, Richard J.R.
Sutton, Carol
Williamson, Lynn
Young, David

Cupola Gallery
(Page 122)
Bassett, Clare
Baxter, Sandra
Bendall-Brunello, Tiziana
Briggs, Jessica
Brokenshire, John
Button, Corinna
Carson-Shaw, David
Charles, Jane
Fay, Helen
Gladden, Peter
Graham, Victor-Stuart
Grover, Emma
Hardwick, Bruce
Haxworth, Hetty
Hodnett, Lyn
Hudson, Caroline
Jackson, Brian
Langan, Jane
Langford, Martin
Lee, Jessie
McDade, Sarah
Palliser, Neil
Parrott, Helen
Ross, Vivienne
Westergaard, Hanne
Wood, Paul

Curwen Gallery
(Page 57)
Ayres, Gillian
Bawden, Gillian
Beattie, Basil
Blackburn, Kenneth
Boyd Harte, Glynn
Clough, Prunella
Dingwall, Phoebe
Farrow, Kieron
Frink, Elisabeth
Gibbs, Jonathan
Hepworth, Barbara
Herman, Josef
Holden, Don
Hoyland, John
Irvin, Bert
Jawahirilal, Lallitha
Jones, Stanley
Kotzen, Thirza
Martin, Ruth
McRae, Jennifer
Mierins, Laimonis
Moore, Henry
Oki, Yuji
Piper, John
Richards, Ceri
Richmond, Robin
Rizvi, Sophia
Ryan, Paul
Tominaga, Kenichi
von Stumm, Johannes
Wouda, Marjan

Cyril Gerber Fine Art
(Page 136)
Banks, Lesley
Bellany, John
Cadell, F.C.B
Cameron, D.Y.
Cowie, James
Eardley, Joan
Fergusson, J.D.
Gaudier-Brzeska, Henri
Gill, Eric
Gillies, William G.
Herman, Josef
Hilton, Roger
Howson, Peter
Hunter, Leslie
Kay, James
Knox, Jack
Lanyon, Peter
Lavery, John
McCance, William
Melville, Arthur
Morrocco, Alberto
Paterson, James
Peploe, S.J.
Redpath, Anne
Schilsky, Eric
Shanks, Tom
Vaughan, Keith

Daniel Katz Ltd
(Page 57)
Canova, Antonio
Clodion
Da Fiesole, Mino
Da Ravenna, Severo
Fanelli, Francesco
Foggini, G-B
Giambologna
Gibson, John
Lombardo, Tullio
Susini, Antonio
Tacca, Ferdinand
Tacca, Pictro
Thorwaldsen, Bertel
Wilton, Joseph

Danusha Fine Arts
(Page 57)
Atayan, Gayane
Holimbievska, Tetyana
Magro, Petro
Shusterman, Roman
Shyshko, Grygoriy
Tytenko, Panas
Vitkovskyi, Lev
Volobuev, Eugeniy
Yablonska, Tetyana
Yalanskyi, Andriy

Davis Gallery
(Page 154)
Cahill, Patrick
Clear, Ciaran
Crowe, Dee
Davis, Gerald
Hayes, Olivia
Kelly, Joe
Klitz, Tony
Oakley, George
Pearson, Peter
Treacy, Liam
Viale, Patrick

de Putron Art Consultants Ltd.
(Page 209)
Adams, Alastair
Amin, Sherif
Aplin, Kay
Aust, Rushton
Barratt, Sophia
Becker, Bernard
Bennett, Austin
Bisset, Anna
Black, Simon
Brason, Paul
Bryon, Beverly
Carpanini, David
Churchill, Martin
Clay, Andie
David, Michele
Davies, Ivor
Dwyer, Judy
Farquharson, Mo
Ferrey, Petrina
Fiennes, Susannah
Godlieb, Jennifer
Hamilton, Susie
Harrington, Heidi
Hawken, Anthony
Jarvis, Martin
Jones, Catrin
Killin, Mhairi
Kinley, Susan
Klapez, Ivan
Larsen, Patricia
Lord, Bernard
Lovegrove, Catherine
Maclean, Diane
Masoero, Jeanne
Maxwell, Mark
McNiven, Peter
Medway, Sarah
Morgan, Howard
Morland, Louise
Morris, Stuart
Nicholas, Peter
O'Leary, Clare
Patsalides, John
Pavlenko, Sergei
Pearse, Deborah
Piatigorsky, Max
Radford, Diane
White, Laura
Whitehead, Rhonda
Willson, Graeme

The Dean Clough Galleries
(Page 124)
Attree, Jake
Babayan, Karen
Binder, Doug
Brown, Jo
Cronshaw, Edward
Darnley, Frank
Dawson, Stuart
Gaffney, Sheila
Gorner, Jo
Gratton, Ralph
Jameson, Katherine
Judd, Ian
Lockey, Jayne
North, Suzanne
Rados, Ivan
Sacker, Chris
Sahaja
Schwab, Linda
Sykes, Barbara
Taylor, Chris
Wincer, Richard
Wood, Tom

Devon Guild of Craftsmen
(Page 92)
Anderson, Blandine
Andrews, Tim
Bowen, Clive
Bowen, Clive
Cockram, Roger
De Trey, Marianne
Edmunds, Rebecca
Highet, Hilary
Hone, Juliet
Honnor, Michael
Keeley, Laurel
Kellam, Colin

Kendall, Jessamine
Langley, Siddy
Leach, David
Leach, John
Lloyd, Andrew
Maltby, John
Mann, Tony
Martin, Malcolm
McKay, Ian
Peters, Alan
Regester, Dave
Searle, Teresa
Stoyel, Janet
Taja
Vincent, Carole

Egee Art Consultancy
(Page 209)
Al Fakhri, Patricia
Azzawi, Dia
Berchere, N.
Carter, Owen
Contreras, Don Rafael
Cooke, Jonathan
Corrodi, Hermann
Deutsch, Lugwig
Diab, Rachid
Eastham, Peter
Ermes, Ali Omar
Forray, Count Ivan
Fromentin, Eugéne
Géricault, Théodore
Harrison, Christopher
Hartman, Lesley Ann
Hugronje, Snouck
Iacovleff, Alexandre
Kebir, Abdeldrim
Koreichi, Rachid
Lamplough, A.O.
Lewis, Jane
Lubroth, Mil
Marrash, Hania
Massoudy, Hassan
McNab, Tiffany
Miller, Francis St. Clair
Murphy, James
Nasiri, Rafa
Neville, Alison
Newington, Charles
Niati, Houria
Noire, Maxim
Pascale, P.
Philippoteau, Felix
Preziosi, Amedeo
Prisse D'Avennes, A.C.T.
Racim, Mohammed
Raymonde, A.M.
Richmond, Ernest
Roberts, David
Rousseau, Henri
Shimy, Awad El
Siti, Walid Mustafa
Van Loo, Carle
Vernet, Horace
Von Mayr, Heinrich
Warren, Sarah
Wyld, William
Zenderoudi, Hussein

Elizabeth Harvey-Lee - Original Prints c.1490 - c.1940.
(Page 161)
Auerbach, Arnold
Austin, Robert
Bewick, Thomas
Blampied, Edmund
Bone, Muirhead
Brangwyn, Frank
Callot, Jacques
Cameron, David Young
Constable, John
Copley, John
Cowern, R.T.
Daumier, Honoré
Dodd, Francis
Dürer, Albrecht
Freeth, H.A.
Gabain, Ethel
Goeneutte, Norbert
Goltzius, Hendrik
Goya, Francisco
Griggs, F.L.
Haden, Francis Seymour
Kermode, William
Laboureur, Jean-Emile
Lalanne, Maximillien
Legrand, Louis
Lord, Elyse
McBey, James
Menpes, Mortimer
Nash, Paul
Nevinson, C.R.W.
Orlik, Emile
Palmer, Samuel
Pissarro, Camille
Pissarro, Orovida
Ranft, Richard
Rembrandt, Vanrijn
Roussel, Theodore
Short, Frank
Sparks, Nathaniel
Sutherland, Graham
Taylor, C.W.
Toulouse-Lautrec, Henri de
Tournour, Sister Morparet
Tunnicliffe, Charles Frederick
Unwin, Francis
Utrillo, Maurice
Valadon, Suzanne
Walcot, William
Whistler, James McNeil
Wolfsfeld, Erich

Finchley Fine Art Galleries
(Page 58)
Aston, Charles Reginold
Callow, George
Callow, John
Callow, William
Cashmore, Francis Milton
Cook, Herbert Moxom
Dominicus, Achille De
Gould, David
Greig, James
Marks, Richmond
Mearns, Fanny Lois
Muncaster, Claude
Newton, Alfred Pizzey
Rochard, Francois Theodore
Rosher, Charles
Rutt, Henry
Scarselli, A.
Scott, Henry
Simmons, Eyres
St. John, Edwin
Stewart, Lawson J.
Tuke, Henry Scott
Walenn, Gilbert
Willett, Arthur

Fine Art Commissions Ltd.
(Page 210)
Alsop, Roger
Barrow, Julian
Beckett, Robert
Bovill, Katrina
Broome, Helena
Browning, Mary
Chancellor, Zara
Churchill, Robert
Clements Wright, Naomi
Dewsbury, Gerald
Dyer, Simon
Farquharson, Mo
Foster, Richard
Gilbert, Terence
Hann, Priscilla
Heathcote, Peregrine
Heseltine, Michael
Hilleary, Alasdair
Hodge, Marcus
Hoffman, Jessica
Jacques, Timothy
James, Andrew
Laubin, Carl
Lester, Guy
Mackie, Hamish
Maley, Tom
Michael, Peter
Millner, Etienne
Money, Pandora
Morgan, Howard
Munslow, Angela
Noakes, Michael
Oakshett, Anthony
Odescalchi, Tin
Paik, Anna
Pavlenko, Sergei
Pearson Cooper, Michelle
Philipps, Clare
Philipps, Nicky
Philipps, Susie
Platt, Theo
Rampling, Madeleine
Sancha, Carlow
Scott Bolton, Tin
Stultiens, Jeff
Terry, Francis
Tkachuk, Alla
Williams-Ellis, David
Wraith, Robert
Yeo, Jonathan

Flowers East
(Page 58)
Barton, Glenys
Bellany, John
Boyd & Evans
Chambers, Stephen
Clough, Prunella
Cohen, Bernard
Cuddihy, Mikey
Daley, Anthony
Dutkiewicz, Edward
Faulkner, Amanda
Forster, Noel
Frost, Sir Terry
Gibbons, John
Gouk, Alan
Hahn, Friedemann
Hepher, David
Herman, Josef
Hicks, Nicola
Hirst, Derek
Hodgson, Carole
Howson, Peter
Hughes, Patrick
Jeffries, Neil
Jones, Lucy
Jones, Trevor
Keane, John
Kirby, John
Kondracki, Henry
Lewis, Tim
Loker, John
Mara, Tim
Neagu, Paul
Osuga, Jiro
Payne, Freya
Phillips, Tom
Rothenstein, Michael
Schierenberg, Tai-Shan
Self, Jo
Sinnott, Kevin
Smith, Jack
Smith, Richard
Stahl, Andrew
Sutton, Trevor
Tait, Renny
Wragg, Gary

Frames Contemporary Gallery
(Page 139)
Bourne, Peter
Gray, Janice
Littlejohn, William
MacQueen, Charles
Woodside, Christine

Francis Graham-Dixon Gallery
(Page 58)
Andersen, Emily
Berger, Sybille
Boepple, Willard
Carter, John
Dixon, Jane
Durrant, Jennifer
Farrer, Julia
Girling, Sheila
Hopkins, Clyde
Ingham, Bryan
James, Merlin
Kolár, Jirí
Kudryashov, Oleg
McLean, John
Morris, Mali
Roberts, Derek
Smallhorn, Sophie
Thesiger, Amanda
Verran, Virginia
Zechner, Johanes

Frederick Gallery
(Page 109)
Arnold, Christopher
Burman, John
Campbell, Andrew
Chatten, Geoffrey
Cherry, Maureen
Coulter, Michael
Durban, Ronald
Glass, Margaret
Green, Jasmine
Hann, Hannah

Hazelwood, David
King, Andrew
Laurance, Martin
Leech, Raymond
Lomax, Patricia
Loveday, Ross
Merchor, Oswaldo
Morgan, Richard
Parsons, Richard
Patchett, John
Quantrill, David
Richardson, Ann
Richardson, Louise
Riley, Sue
Smith, Madeline
Stocker, Tony
Thompson, Kevin
Woodard, Adrian

GALERIE MODERNE / LE STYLE LALIQUE
(Page 59)
Lalique, René

THE GALLERY DORCHESTER
(Page 94)
Barry, Jo
Brown, Stephen
Cadman, Michael
Clemson, Katie
Cuthbert, David
Cuthbert, Ros
Deakin, Liz
Desmet, Anne
Ellis, Edwina
Emerson, Keyna
Gradidge, Daphne
Hicklin, Jason
Hill, Dennis
Jesty, Ron
Lunn, Jean
Marshallsay, Fred
Pickering, Robin
Pikesley, Richard
Rose, Alison
Salt, Jeffy
Simpson, Alan
Toms, Peter
Uht, John

GALLERY NINETEEN
(Page 124)
Bailey, Caroline
Carter, Alan
Curgenven, Michael
Dixon, Kevin
Groves, Fred
Thorp, Selina
Ward, Eric

GALLERY OF MODERN ART
(Page 59)
Allen, St. Claire
Bauman, Lydia
Boulting, Bridget
Brogan, Honor
Bruguera, Lluis
Burke, Peter
Carswell, Robbie
Clarke, Pat
Davis, Derek
Davis, Ruth
Freeman, Barbara
Freudenthal, Peter
Gill, Bobby
Gratz, Thomas
Hamilton-Finlay, Ian
Harley Peters, Jonet
Harvey, Jake
Hirvimaki, Veiko
Hodgson, Carole
Holmsen, Brit
Holtom, Robin
Hulland, Ann
Hunt, Helen
Hunt, Kate
Jaquet, Francoise
Jones, Mary Lloyd
Katz, Tamara
McGowan, Richard
Mellon, Erik
Mulholland, Susan
O'Brien, Donagh
Parhizgar, Monir
Rogers, John Boydell
Royston, Gwen Joy
Shakspeare, William
Sivertsen, Jan
Williams, Lois
Willis, Simon
Wilson, Julia

THE GALLERY
(Page 103)
Ambrose, John
Barker, Jon
Beecroft, Yvonne
Haas, Pamela
Hudson, Sheila
Markovich, Violeta
O'Keeffe, Rory
Organ, Bryan
Osborne, James
Relph, Sue
Strang, Michael
Walton, Janice

THE GARDEN GALLERY
(Page 180)
Ackroyd, Jane
Bawden, Richard
Bent, Richard
Berlin, Greta
Brown, John
Clahane, Daniel
Clarke, Peter
Constable, Sasha
Erland, Sukey
Falcke, Emma
Ford, Susan
French, Neal
Genders, Carolyn
Goodman, Amy
Hawken, Anthony
Hessenberg, Karin
Hodgson, Carole
Hubbard, Deidre
James, Harriet
Jones, Jenifer
Konu, Michael
Leach, Ben
Lush, Emma
Maxwell, Lyn Constable
Mayer, Charlotte
McGuigan, Bernard
Milborrow, Jim
Moss, Anne-Marie
Mussi, Cleo
Peever, Alec
Penny, Giles
Plowman, Chris
Pryce, Vivien ap Rhys
Ralph, Alex
Richards, Christine-Ann
Sinclair, Helen
Skelton, Helen Mary
Vou Marx, Maggie
Woodford, Johnny
Wynne, Althea

GLASGOW PRINT STUDIO GALLERY
(Page 136)
Blackadder, Elizabeth
Byrne, John
Cook, Ashley
Currie, Ken
Duffin, Stuart
Gonzalez, Roberto
Houston, John
Howson, Peter
Lamb, Elspeth
Mach, David
Mackenzie, Tom
MacPherson, Neil
McDonald, James
McLean, Bruce
McLellan, Abigail
Rae, Barbara
Richardson, Ray
Taylor, John
Teh, Hock-Avn
Wiszniewski, Adrian

THE GOLDEN PLOVER STUDIO GALLERY
(Page 149)
Giardelli, Arthur
Giardelli, Bim

THE GOLDMARK GALLERY
(Page 113)
Ayrton, Michael
Bawden, Edward
Brangwyn, Frank
Burman, Barry
Chagall, Marc
Chapman, George
Farrington, John
Gibbings, Robert
Gill, Eric
Graham, Rigby
Gross, Anthony
Kokoschka, Oskar
Kossoff, Leon
Large, George
Miró, Joan
Moreton, Nicolas
Piper, John
Richards, Ceri
Stringer, Simon
Sutherland, Graham
Wootton, Olive

GORING MILL GALLERY
(Page 98)
Brazier, Connie
Cash, Angela
Chiles, Trish
Chilton, Linda
Clandon, Penny
Clements, Caroline
Coombs, Trevor
Couling, Paula
Dudding, Valerie
Emmerich, Anita
Farrell, David
Findlay, Kate
Firth, Jo
Foster, Stephen
Gillmore, Olwen
Hall, Mary
Hallett, Ted
Halliday, Mary
Handley, Betty
Hanson, Helen
Hulse, Caroline
Joslyn, Bob
Macaulay, Kerry
Marek, Stanley
Markin, Mavis
Millis, Susan
Monostori, Helen
Morgan, David
O'Neill, Sarah
Parkin, Jane
Pidoux, Janet
Piper, Brenda
Pitt, Gale
Rawlings, Ray
Rogerson, Joyce
Saward, Ann
Seddon, Joyce
Sim, David
Symes, Marion
Target, Connie
Ward, Derek
Welch, Rosemary
Whittle, Janet
Wyatt, Joyce
Zelin, Linda

GRAHAM CLARKE
(Page 101)
Clarke, Graham

GRAPHIC STUDIO DUBLIN GALLERY
(Page 154)
Aghajanian, Sophie
Bardon, Jean
Benson, Carmel
Bewick, Pauline
Bourke, Brian
Breakey, John
Cooney, Jackie
Cronin, John
Crozier, William
Cuffe, Grainne
Cuffe, Siobhan
Cullen, Charles
Cullen, Michael
Delargy, Diamuid
Doyle, Cliona
Duncan, Jead
Egan, Felim
Farrell, Michael
Flood, Taffina
Frew, Ivan
Gorman, Richard
Grahame, John
Hannan, Valerie
Hanratty, Alice
Hickey, Patrick
Jones, Peter
Kane, Michael
Keating, John

Lane, Jennifer
Lawlor, Stephen
Le Brocquy, Louis
Lennon, Ciaran
Madden, Anne
Maguire, Brian
Maher, Alice
McCreary, James
Monreal, Alfonso
Nolan, James O.
O'Donnell, Ruth
O'Donoghue, Tighe
O'Malley, Jane
O'Malley, Tony
O'Neill, Mary Rose
Pye, Patrick
Reilly, Marc
Sheridan, Vincent
Simonds Gooding, Maria
Staunton, Tracy
Tyrrell, Charles

Greenwich Printmakers Association
(Page 161)
Aida, Emiko
Alves, Timothy
Atkinson, Jane
Barham, Jean
Black, Maureen
Bowyer, David
Carpenter, Pip
Carreck, Libby
Coleborn, Deanne
Cossey, Mary
Croft, Diana
Crozier, Kathleen
Davies, Louise
De Monchaux, Ruth
Dell, Mickey
Gilbert, Ellen
Golding, Gillian
Gracia, Carmen
Graubart, Ellen
Hammond, Audrey
Hanson, Helen
Harris, Donald
Irvin, Joanna
Johnson, Annette
Klein, Anita
Marshall, Elaine
Morris, Elizabeth
Pateman, Theresa
Perring, Susie
Price, Trevor
Robson, Sally
Rollo, Sonia
Ronay, Jenny
Salmon, Christopher
Salter, Anthony
Sands, Susan
Scovell, Audrey
Solly, Phillip
Stone, Kirsten
Strachan, Peter
Sullock, Julie
Weaver, Felicity
Wright, Kevin
Zaleki, Barbara

Grove Contemporary Arts
(Page 115)
Ayre, Thelma
Bradbury, Robin
Dunbabin, Chris
Pulford, Charlie
Rogers, John Boydell

H. Arts
(Page 101)
Beesley, John
Hart, Tony
Leonard, Neil
Prickett, Bill
Ramsey, Paul

Hales Gallery
(Page 59)
Beddington, Sarah
Bick, Andrew
Callan, Jonathan
Carter, Claire
Dawson, Ian
De Goede, Leo
Dean, Judith
Heath, Claude
Hyde, James
Leapman, David
Lowe, Rachael
McGinn, Martin
Takahashi, Tomoko
Wilson, Keith
Woods, Richard

Hanga Ten
(Page 59)
Akiyama, Iwao
Araki, Shinko
Brayer, Sarah
Colyer, Ted
Endo, Susumu
Hagiwara, Hideo
Ihara, Kaori
Ikegami, Isao
Imamura, Yoshio
Iwami, Reika
Kaneko, Kunio
Kinoshita, Keisuke
Maki, Haku
Mori, Yoshitoshi
Nakazawa, Shin'ichi
Okamoto, Shogo
Ouchi, Makoto
Sawada, Tetsuro
Shinoda, Toko
Sugiura, Kazutoshi
Tachibana, Seiko
Takahashi, Rikio
Wako, Shuji
Yamada, Juliane
Young, Karyn

Hanging Space
(Page 60)
Asimi
Barbor, Sam
Born, Boris
Burbridge, Claire
Constant, Victoria
Fraser, Patrick
Helm, Zebedee
Hosking-Smith, Carol
McCormick, Liza
Segura, Gabriela
Smith, Kate
Walford, Juliet
Walsh, David

Hanover Fine Arts
(Page 134)
Alred, Richard
Anderson, Libby
Arnstein, Sylvia
Bathgate, John
Bochkov, Valery
Boyle, Lorna
Briggs, Maureen
Browning, Demetra
Brydon, Lindsay
Cairncross, Mike
Clark, Fay
Conboy, Kathleen
Cosman, Octavian
Couper, Carolyn
Craig, Ronald A.H.
Crawford, Anne
Fernandes, Regina
Fish, Margo E.
Hanley, Lynn
Hepworth, Susan
Jaques, Avril
Jaques, Richard
Johnstone, Ian S.
Kudriavtseva, Natasha
MacDonald, Allan
Macvicar, Marily
Magro, Petro
Mastin, Ian
McMillan, Margaret
Merrilees, Roberta
Neustein, Ella
O'Donnell, Bernie
Philip, Jackie
Phillips, Sheena
Sharp, Elizabeth
Shyshko, Grygoriy
Standen, Peter
Stevenson, Wendy
Strachan, Una
Stubbs, Rosemary
Sutherland, Alan
Theys, Freddy
Tytenko, Panas
Vitkovskyi, Lev
Volobuev, Eugeniy
Watling, John
Watts, Enid Foote
Wilkinson, Sarah
Yalanskyi, Andriy
Znoba, Valentin

Hart Gallery
(Page 60)
Baldwin, Gordon
Bevan, Jenny
Blackburn, David
Bot, G.W.
Bowen, Sian
Buthod-Garcon, Giséle
Carter, Chris
Champy, Claude
De Waal, Edmund
Devereux, Richard
Dilworth, Steve
Doig, Maxwell
Draper, Kenneth
Freeman, Barbara
Graham, Brian
Greaves, Derrick
Hartman, John
Henderson, Ewen
Koch, Gabrielle
MacAlpine, Jean
Maltby, John
Middlemiss, Jon
Owen, Elspeth
Perry, Richard
Roberts, David
Rogers, Phil
Ross, Duncan
Sheppard, Michael
Stringer, Simon
Taylor, Sutton
Virot, Camille
Walker-Barker, David
West, Jenny
West, Steve
Whittaker, Malcolm
Wood, Tom
Wright, Austin

Highgate Fine Art
(Page 60)
Adams, Norman
Andrewes, Eliza
Atkinson, Anthony
Bawden, Richard
Betowski, Noel
Blow, Sandra
Boyd, Jamie
Bratby, John
Brill, Reginald
Browne, Piers
Casson, Hugh
Cronyn, Hugh
Cuming, Fred
Cundall, Charles
Dinner, Tony
Donovan, James
Easton, Arthur
Feilden, Lucy
Flint-Shipman, Andrew
Géas, Luce
Gore, Frederick
Gowing, Lawrence
Green, Anthony
Guaitamacchi, Bruno
Harrison, Claude
Hay, Ian
Hepburn, Alan
Hobhouse, Robert
Howard, Ken
Ingamells, Andrew
Irwin, Flavia
Kenning, David
Lawton, Teresa
lowndes, Rosemary
McWhirter, Ishbel
Patterson, Doug
Pedraza, Jorge
Pettit, Roy
Pugno-Vandni, Francesca
Quirke, Michael
Richardson, Philip
Rizvi, Jacqueline
Robbins, Richard
Robinson, Paul
Roca, Francesc
Scherbakova, Tanya
Soan, Hazel
Sorel, Agathe
Whitehead, Rhonda
Wilson, Stuart
Wolfe, Edward
Wolff, Phyllis
Zeh, Ulrich

Lamb, Judi
Lebor, Brenda
Mann, Maurice
Moroney, Ken
Murray, John
Stewart, Alex
Weisbort, George
Wright, Dominic

KERLIN GALLERY
(Page 155)
Clemente, Francesco
Cooke, Barrie
Cross, Dorothy
Doherty, Willie
Egan, Felim
Eun-Mo, Chung
Francis, Mark
Godbold, David
Gorman, Richard
Hamilton, Richard
Hodgkin, Howard
Kippenberger, Martin
Magill, Elizabeth
Maguire, Brian
McKenna, Stephen
McKeown, William
Ní Chiosáin, Fionnuala
O'Dowd, Gwen
Oehien, Albert
Paladino, Mimmo
Prendergast, Kathy
Scott, William
Scully, Sean
Seawright, Paul
Shanahan, Séan
Sugimoto, Hiroshi
Taylor, Marcus
Ungers, Sibylle
Warhol, Andy

KINGFISHER GALLERY
(Page 134)
Anderson, Anne
Bailey, Christopher
Baillie, William
Ballantyne, Margaret
Balmer, Barbara
Barrie, Mardi
Birrell, George
Black, Dorothy
Boag, Francis
Bourne, Peter
Bridge, Eoghan
Conboy, Kathleen
Downham, Sara
Flynn, Theresa
Fraser, Donald Hamilton
Grossart, Gay
Harrigan, James
Jaques, Avril
Kelsey, Robert
Knox, Liz
Lassen, Jeanette
Lenaghan, Brenda
Littlejohn, William
Manby, Simon
Melrose, Janet
Miller, Moray
Paterson, Anda
Paterson, Susie
Pickard, Baajie
Pyrie, Jenny A.
Robertson, Iain
Simmers, Connie
Smith, Andrew
Spence, James
Stubbs, Rosemary
Thomson, Alastair W.
Wardman, Clare
Watt, Tom
Wegmuller, Ann

LENA BOYLE FINE ART
(Page 62)
Brown, Bonnie
Byars, Hugh
Cary, Caroline
Coghill, Sarah
Cohen, Alfred
Fedden, Mary
Frink, Elisabeth
Garwood, Jason
Gilbert, Dennis
Hall, Clifford
Hart, Simon
Herman, Josef
Howson, Peter
Hutton, Sarah
Inwood, Derek
John, Augustus
Johnstone, Gwyneth
Macmiadhachain, Padraig
McAdam Clark, Caroline
Moore, Henry
Newcomb, Mary
Newcomb, Tessa
Nice, Derek
Pasmore, Mary
Sell, Charlotte
Sutton, Philip
Trevelyan, Julian
Ward, Henry
Weight, Carel

LINDA BLACKSTONE GALLERY
(Page 62)
Batchelor, Valerie
Blockley, G. John
Bloom, Enid
Bolton, Richard
Brennand, Catherine
Brown, John
Butlin, Anne-Marie
Cullen, Patrick
Davis, Pamela
Farrell, Don
Gyles, Pauline
Harrison, Stephanie
Huntly, Moira
Kavanagh, Paul
Kennedy, Matt Barber
Kent, Colin
King, Robert
Ledger, Janet
Lidzey, John
Majzlik, Alois
Manifold, Debra
McDowell, Leo
Meacher, Neil
Mitchell, Brenda
Outram, Steven
Paine, Ken
Parsons, Arthur
Plincke, J. Richard
Read, Sue
Simmonds, Jackie
Simpson, Alan
Sutton, Charles
Sykes, David
Thompson, Andrew
Turner, Jacquie
Uht, John

LINTON COURT GALLERY
(Page 124)
Adams, Norman
Borlase, Deirdre
Butt, Anna
Cook, David
Holmes, Katharine
North, Kitty
Roberts, Tony

LISSON GALLERY
(Page 63)
Allington, Edward
Art & Language
Baldessari, John
Bismuth, Pierre
Borland, Christine
Burgin, Victor
Burton, Scott
Casebere, James
Coleman, James
Collishaw, Mat
Cragg, Tony
Deacon, Richard
Dujourie, Lili
Floyer, Ceal
Gerber, Gaylen
Gordon, Douglas
Graham, Dan
Graham, Rodney
Grenville, Davey
Hilliard, John
Hosking, Mark
Houshiary, Shirazeh
Joseph, Peter
Judd, Donald
Kapoor, Anish
Kawara, On
Latham, John
Lewitt, Sol
Linke, Simon
Mangold, Robert
Martin, Jason
McCollum, Allan
McCracken, John
Monk, Jonathan
Mossman, Anna
Muñoz, Juan
Murphy, John
Newman, Avis
Opie, Julian
Oursler, Tony
Paolini, Giulio
Patterson, Simon
Schütte, Thomas
Ufan, Lee
Vercruysse, Jan
Wentworth, Richard
West, Franz
Wilson, Jane & Louise

LOGIE STEADING ART GALLERY
(Page 138)
Awlson, Walter
Barton, Michael
Barton, Peter
Black, John
Cameron, Elizabeth
Carter, Pam
Christie, John
Hutchenson, Andrew
Munro, Arlette
Munro, Ian
Nicolson, John
Ross, Irene
Sharpe, Chris
Smith, Bill
Smith, Clare
Smith, Julian
Stowell, Judith

LOOK GALLERY
(Page 123)
Baglee, Arthur
Bailey, Caroline
Barker, Neville
Bell, Catherine
Bizon, Edna
Browne, Piers
Carruthers, Rosemary
Cheall, John
Egerton, John
Fearn, Raymond
Gillespie, Bridget
Gordon, Frank
Greenwood, David
Heath, Andrew
Henley, David
Janin, Philippe
Jones, Derek
Jones, Mike
Lazzerini, Giuliana
Luckham, Alan
Massie, Ian Scott
McCarthy, Peter
Naylor, John
Oliver, Raymond
Parker, Ian
Pierson, Rosalind
Platts, David
Ruggeri, Anne-Marie
Skea, Janet
Taunton, Adrian
Tilling, Robert
Tulloh, Phoebe
Turvey, Simon
Walton, Jackie
Westergaard, Hanne

LOUISE PICKERING FINE ART
(Page 210)
Craig-Martin, Michael
Di Stefano, Arturo
Dibbetts, Jan
Dine, Jim
Doig, Peter
Hodgkin, Howard
Hughes, Patrick
Langlands and Bell
McKeever, Ian
Tait, Renny
Thompson, Estelle

LUMLEY CAZALET
(Page 63)
Belleroche, Albert
Braque, Georges
Chagall, Marc
Frink, Elisabeth
Helleu, Paul
Hockney, David
Matisse, Henri

Miró, Joan
Picasso, Pablo
Tissot, J.J.

LUPTON SQUARE GALLERY
(Page 124)
Abrahams, Rosemary
Bowman, Malcolm
Boyson, Alan
Brown, Susan
Burgess, Jane
Collier, Maureen
Court, Stephen
Cross, Diane
Fairchild-Woodard, Roy
Greenwood, David
Hutton, Sarah
Kirkby-Geddes, Mick
Mead, Pauline
Mountain, Keith
Muchan, Paul
North, Suzanne
Palliser, Neil
Pasmore, Victor
Rados, Ivan
Spence, Annora
Thornton, Barry
Walton, Jackie

MARLBOROUGH GRAPHICS
(Page 64)
Arikha, Avigdor
Auerbach, Frank
Bacon, Francis
Davies, John
Freud, Lucian
Hambling, Maggi
Hepworth, Barbara
Jacklin, Bill
Kiff, Ken
Kitaj, R.B.
Le Brun, Christopher
Matisse, Henri
Miró, Joan
Moore, Henry
Nicholson, Ben
Oulton, Thérèse
Pasmore, Victor
Paul, Celia
Picasso, Pablo
Piper, John
Rego, Paula
Richards, Ceri
Sutherland, Graham
Tilson, Joe
Winner, Gerd
Yifei, Chen

MARLENE ELEINI
(Page 64)
Bray, Sarah
Brooks, Alan
Cretton, Tom
Frost, Sir Terry
Hubbuch, Karl
Hugonin, James
Law, Bob
Olivier, Richon
Rickett, Sophie
Rollins, Tim & KOS
Walker, John
Yehuda, Verdi

MARTIN TINNEY GALLERY
(Page 145)
Canning, Neil
Cecil, Roger
Chappell, Dick
Crowther, Michael
Davies, Ivor
Elwyn, John
Griffiths, Mary
Herman, Josef
Holland, Harry
James, Shani Rhys
John, Augustus
John, Gwen
Jones, David
Lloyd-Jones, Mary
Mabbutt, Mary
Macfarlane, John
Moore, Sally
Müller, Sigrid
Piper, John
Povey, Edward
Prendergast, Peter
Prichard, Gwilym
Richards, Ceri
Samuel, Mark
Sinnott, Kevin
Tudur, Dewi
Volk, Patricia
Williams, Claudia
Williams, Emrys
Williams, Kyffin
Williams, Vivienne
Zobole, Ernest

MATTHIESEN FINE ART LIMITED
(Page 64)
Bassano, Jacopo
Batoni, Pompeo
Bellotto, Bernardo
Botticelli, Sandro
Boucher, Francois
Canaletto, Antonio
Carracciolo, Giovanni Battista
Chardin, Jean-Baptiste-Siméon
Courbet, Gustave
Delacroix, Eugène
Di Paolo , Giovanni
Dossi, Dosso
Fragonard, Jean-Honoré
Gaddi, Agnolo
Ingres, Jean-Auguste-Dominique
Lanfranco, Giovanni
Nattier, Jean-Marc
Pater, Jean Baptiste
Romanino, Girolamo
Rosa, Salvator
Solimena, Francesco
Tiepolo, Giambattista
Vernet, Horace
Vouet, Simon

THE MCHARDY SCULPTURE COMPANY
(Page 64)
Bell, Sandra
Bennett, Holly
Berelowitz, Jill
Bermejo, Vega
Blik, Maurice
Bodie, Marc

Brook, Dorothy
Cameron, Ronald
Cohen, Agi
Cregeen, David
Daniels, Stephen
Dickens, Sophie
Freeman, Richard
Frohlich-Wiener, Irene
Gibbs, Leonie
Gioia, Angelo
Glendinning, Lucy
Godden, Nicola
Hooke, Robert
Hubbard, Deidre
Huggins, John
Konu, Michael
Lecerf, Odette
Lovell, Margaret
MacDonell, Alasdair Neil
MacDonell, Sally
Owen, Glynis
Penny, Giles
Pomeroy, Tim
Rattenbury, Jim
Robinson, Peter Lyell
Roud, Adam
Samson, Hana
Sandys, Edwina
Thursby, Peter
Volk, Patricia
Wall, Terence
Wheeler, Alexandra
White, Laura
Willis, Neil
Wozniak, Florian

MEDICI GALLERIES
(Page 64)
Casseldine, Nigel
Chandler, Colin
Crittenden, James
Deymonaz, Andre
Henshaw, Nicola
Hill, Thomas
Magill, Anne
Martin, Malcolm
Penny, Charles
Raybould, Howard
Raynes, Polly
Rich, Mary
Sanders, Jeremy
Tonks, Godfrey
Wilson, Althea

THE MEDICI SOCIETY LTD
(Page 162)
Brett, Molly
Brueghel, Pieter
Constable, John
Edwards, Carlotta
Elsley, Arthur
Holbein, Hans the Younger
Lowry, L.S.
Millais, Sir John
Raphael
Renoir, Pierre
Scott, Sir Peter
Sherwin, Frank
Strevens, John
Tarrant, Margaret
Turner, J.M.W.
Ward, Vernon

MERCURY GALLERY
(Page 64)
Abbassy, Samira
Blackadder, Elizabeth
Boulton, Janet
Callender, Robert
Gentleman, David
Hirst, Barry
Houston, John
Kenny, Michael
Laurie, Simon
Remfry, David
Rimmington, Eric
Sutherland, Carol Ann

MICHAEL WEBB FINE ART
(Page 144)
Armfield, Edward
Armfield, George
Bond, W.J.J.C.
Breakspear, John
Breanski, Alfred Jnr
Browne, E. of Coventry
Calvert, Henry
Cleminson, Robert
Cockram, George
Cox, David
Duncan, Edward
Fielding, Copley
Foster, Birket
Fox, Henry Charles
Gregory, George
Hagarty, Mary S.
Hardy, Thomas Bush
Hart, Thomas
Holland, James
Holland, John
Howard, Squire
Ireland, Thomas
Jamieson, Alex
Kelly, Talbot
King, H.J. Yeend
Knell, William Callcott
Knowles, Fred J.
Lines, Henry H.
Maiden, Joseph
Martin, E.H.
Mason, Frank H.
Nightingale, Basil
Passey, Charles
Powell, Alfred
Richardson, Charles
Rickman, Philip C.
Roe, Clarence
Roe, Colin Graeme
Rope, George Thomas
Shalders, George
Sherrin, Daniel
Simone
Spencelash, Charles
Tunnicliffe, Charles Frederick
Valter, Florence
Wainwright, T.F.
Walker, Eaton
Wane, Richard
Watson, Robert
Watson, William R.C. Jnr
Williams, Owen

MODERN GALLERY
(Page 243)
Ayres, Gillian
Bassett, Clare
Baxter, Sandra

Blackadder, Elizabeth
Blake, Peter
Brett, Simon
Buckland-Wright, John
Byrne, John
Carpenter, Pip
Craig-Martin, Michael
Desmet, Anne
Ferguson-Lees, Dominic
Ford, Peter
Fraser, Donald Hamilton
Freud, Lucian
Frost, Sir Terry
Fulton, Hamish
Hammick, Tom
Hockney, David
Hodgkin, Howard
Houston, John
Hoyland, John
Huxley, Jonathan
Ingamells, Andrew
Inshaw, David
Irvin, Bert
Jones, Trevor
Kalinovich, Konstantin
Kiff, Ken
Klein, Anita
Koenig, Heidi
Kudryashov, Oleg
Le Brun, Christopher
Lee, Jessie
Lewandowski, Simon
McKeever, Ian
McLean, Bruce
Meyer, Klaus
Milroy, Lisa
Moxley, Susan
Oulton, Thérèse
Paladino, Mimmo
Perring, Susie
Petterson, Melvyn
Rae, Barbara
Rego, Paula
Richardson, Ray
Rollo, Sonia
Russell, Victoria
Sykes, Sandy

The Museum Of Modern Art, Wales
(Page 149)
Arnold, Ann
Arnold, Graham
Bala, Iwan
Blundell, Martyn
Boydell Rogers, John
Burgess, Cefyn
Cecil, Roger
Davies, Ogwyn
Isaac, Bert
Lloyd-Jones, Mary
Oliver, Richard
Parry, Iwan Gwyn
Prichard, Gwilym
Stuart Burns, Brendan
Williams, Claudia
Yeomans, Geoff

Narwhal Inuit Art Gallery
(Page 65)
Aaluk, Paul
Aculiak, Johnny
Alikashuak, Alex
Alikaswa, Mark
Anguhadluq, Luke
Anowtalik, Luke
Arlook, George
Atchealak, Davie
Curley, Tony
Echalook, Lucassie
Emerak, Mark
Evik, Tommy
Houston, James
Ipellie, Family
Ishulutaq, Elisapee
Kalvak, Helen
Kananginak
Kenojuak, Ashevak
Kigiuna, Annie
Kolola, Akeego
Mamnguqsualuk, Victoria
Manumie, Tukiki
Mayoreak, Ashoona
Meeko, Family
Nanogak, Agnes
Napatchie, Noah
Noah, William
Ohaituk, Family
Oonark, Jessie
Papikatuk, Markoosie
Pitseolak, Ashoona
Pootoogook, Mosesee
Pootoogook, Nujalia
Pudlo, Pudlat
Qinnuayuak, Lucy
Saggiatok, Johnny
Sagouk, Towatuga
Sala, Family
Shaa, Qiatsuq
Tapanie, Tommy
Tikkivik, Etuk
Tookoome, Simon
Tutsweetok, Lucy
Uppik, Simeonie

Nevill Gallery
(Page 100)
Alexander, Matthew
Armour-Chelu, Ian
Bailey, Clifford
Bellany, John
Chaplin, Michael
Clarke, Graham
Cuming, Fred
Flyn, Diana
Greenwood, Ernest
Haskins, Joan
Hedley, Paul
Howat, Andrew
Johns, Phil
Kay, Pamela
Madgwick, Clive
Napp, David
Yardley, Bruce

New Academy Gallery and Business Art Galleries
(Page 65)
Atherton, Barry
Barry, Jo
Belsky, Franta
Bigger, Clare
Blackmore, Clive
Blake, Naomi
Brokenshire, John
Cecil, Roger
Chinnery, Clare
Corsellis, Jane
Creswell, Alexander
Dover, Peter
Dunstan, Bernard
Fraser, Donald Hamilton
Gore, Frederick
Grant, Alistair
Hartill, Brenda
Hocking, Susan-Jayne
Holliday, Sarah
Macara, Andrew
Macmiadhachain, Padraig
Mandl, Anita
Noach, Michèle
Norris, Linda
Piper, John
Rizvi, Jacqueline
Roberts, Keith
Rubens, Zoe
Schwarz, Hans
Walker, Richard
Williams, Jago Max
Wray, Peter

New Art Centre Sculpture Park and Gallery
(Page 180)
Adams, Robert
Armitage, Kenneth
Aylieff, Felicity
Barratt, Oliver
Berlin, Sven
Berman, Brenda
Booth, Chris
Breeze, Gary
Burke, Peter
Butler, Reg
Chadwick, Lynn
Colonna, Marzia
Crowther, Alison
Dalwood, Hubert
Das Gupta, John
Devereux, Richard
Devonald, Anthony
Edwards, John
Frink, Elisabeth
Gormley, Antony
Grellier, Paul
Habicher, Eduard
Harrisson, Tim
Hepworth, Barbara
Hermes, Gertrude
Hilliard, Karen
Jackson, Rachel
Jennings, Martin
Johanson, Anna
Johns, Greg
Jones, Allen
Jones, Jenifer
Kennethson, George
Kenny, Michael
King, Phillip
Kneale, Bryan
Lasdun, William
Lim, Kim
Lowe, Jean
Lyons, Michael
McCrum, Bridget
McWilliam, F.E.
Meadows, Bernard
Morris, Derek
Mount, Paul
Mowbray, Joanna
Neilson, John
Nevelson, Louise
Paolozzi, Eduardo
Peever, Alec
Peever, Fiona
Perry, Richard
Rance, Victoria
Rennertz, Karl Manfred
Renshaw, Richard
Roberts Holmes, Paul
Rosa, Alvaro de la
Sadiq
Salisbury, James
Spencer Watson, Mary
Stahler, Franz
Stirling, Annet
Thewlis, Alan
Thomas, Simon
Twyford, Kit
Viney, Tony
Watts, Meical
Wilks, Claire
Wright, Austin

New Ashgate Gallery
(Page 102)
Angus, Nancy
Belsher, Holly
Blow, Sandra
Brown, Ruta
Caines, Susan
Clapcott, Helen
Constantinides, Joanna
Dean, Graham
Draper, Kenneth
Dunbar, Emma
Eastop, Geoffrey
Fairclough, Michael
Gray, Nick
Grevatte, Jenny
Hayes, Peter
Kiely, David
Klein, Anita
Lawson, Sonia
Leach, David
Malenoir, Mary
Maltby, John
Martini, Babette
Millais, Fiona
New, Keith
Parkinson, Peter
Phipps, Howard
Robertson, Carol
Ross, Vivienne
Salmon, Chris
See-Paynton, Colin
Smith, Pippa
Spackman, Sarah
Theakston, Anthony
Vlassopoulis, Tina
Whishaw, Anthony
Zelinski, Pauline

New Grafton Gallery
(Page 65)
Adlington, Mark
Bailey, Julian
Bowey, Olwyn
Bowyer, Jason
Brooke, Peter
Campion, Oliver
Campion, Sue
Chalmers, Sarah
Coates, Tom
Craigmyl, Anthea
Cuming, Fred

Fayette, L.
Fielding, A.V.S.
Forbes, E.A.S.
Forbes, L.
Fortye, W.H.
Foster, M.B.
Fraser, R.W.
Fuller, L.J.
Garden, W.F.
Gaskin, A.J.
Gibb, H.P.
Goddard, C.
Goodall, J.S.
Goodisin, A.
Hope, L.E.R.
Laurent, J.
Leeuw, A. de
Maze, Paul
McLeod, Janette
Menpes, Mortimer
Noel, J.P.
Pyne, G.
Rosell, A.
Stannard, H.J.S.
Turner, W.
Widgery, F.J.

PENWITH GALLERIES
(Page 91)
Barns-Graham, Wilhelmina
Bedding, John
Bourne, Bob
Cardew, Ara
Cardew, Seth
Chandler, Jill
Conn, Roy
Corser, Trevor
Cross, Tom
Crossley, Bob
Culwick, Robert
Dove, Stephen
Emanuel, John
Feiler, Paul
Freeman, Ralph
Frost, Sir Terry
Hilton, Rose
Jones, Robert
Leach, Janet
Legrice, Jeremy
Maeckelberghe, Margo
Marshall, William
McClure, Daphne
McDowall, Carole
McNally, Kathy
Miles, June
Mitchell, Denis
Mount, Paul
Nicholson, Kate
O'Casey, Breon
O'Malley, Tony
Oliner, Sheila
Pearce, Bryan
Pender, Jack
Praed, Michael
Ritman, Lieke
Semmens, Jennifer
Stork, Mary
Sumray, Maurice
Symonds, Ken
Tribe, Barbara
Walker, Rod
Walker, Roy
Ward, Peter
Wells, John
Wilson, Vincent

PETERS BARN GALLERY
(Page 104)
Bailey, Walter
Bryars, Jill
Chaikin, Michael
Dupré, Marie-Frederique
Gregory, Ian
Hoskins, Steven
Jupp, Mo
Keeler, Walter
Munn, Annabel
Pearson, Colin
Schroeder, Kjersti
Scott, Sally
Sula, Artur

PICCADILLY GALLERY LTD.
(Page 66)
Berg, Adrian
Green, Anthony
Greenland, Martin
Held, Julie
Kelly, John
Morley, John
Murfin, Michael
Ovenden, Graham
Parker, Alan
Tumim, Matilda
Turnbull, Peter
Wilkins, William

PLAZZOTTA LTD
(Page 67)
Plazzotta, Enzo

PORTAL GALLERY
(Page 67)
Allin, John
Anderson, Eddie
Aris, Fred
Broomfield, Frances
Byrne, John
Carter, Bernard
Cartwright, Reg
Castle, Barry
Castle, Philip
Cheepen, David
Clark, Terry
Cook, Beryl
Copas, Ronnie
Copeland, Mark
Cornner, Haydn
Cudworth, Nick
Easby, Steve
Grainger, James
Harrison, Claude
Lawman, Peter
Le Bas, Philip
Lewis, Jane
Lloyd, James
Lyon, Charlotte
McNaught, James
Neville, Pat
Pepper, Reg
Riches, Lizzie
Rooney, Mick
Rozot, Isabelle
Taplin, Guy
Turpin, Emma
Ward, Graham
Williams, Kit

POSK GALLERY
(Page 67)
Baranowska, Janina
Borkowski, Andrzej
Dankiewicz, Krystyna
Dawidowski, Andrzej
Elaszkiewicz, Andrzej
Falkowski, Wojciech
Gierc, Danuta
Hojak-Mysko, Elzbieta
Jaczynska, Maria
Jaffe, Ilona
Lotringer, Ludwig
Lubomirski de Voux, Stefan
Lurczynski, Mieczyslaw
Nekanda-Trepko, Halina
Piesakowska, Danuta
Pytel, Zygmunt
Skolimowski, Staszka
Slaski, Peter
Smart, Alan
Werner, Aleksander
Zoltowski, Adam
Zwolinska-Brzeski, Teresa

PRATT CONTEMPORARY ART/PRATT EDITIONS
(Page 101)
Davies, Richard
Edalatpour, Seyed
Grater, Julian
Kenny, Michael
Krokfors, Kristian
Nogueira Fleury, Leonam
Pacheco, Ana Maria
Rahmanzadeh, Akram
Rees Roberts, Marcus
Rooney, Mick
Walker, Denise

PRIMAVERA
(Page 105)
Barker, Patrick
Batterham, Richard
Bauman, Lydia
Beard, Peter
Betts, Malcolm
Blanthorn, Brian
Bowen, Clive
Brennand Wood, Michael
Caines, Susan
Cartwright, Ashley
Constantinides, Joanna
Cornwell, Jeremy
Cowen, Gina
Creese, Susannah
Crouch, Andrew
De Waal, Edmund
Fanshawe Kato, Jill
Forrest, Marianne
Gilmour, Judith
Harris, Charmain
Henley, Nicola
Hough, Catherine
Hussey, Dan
Krinos, Daphne
Lambert, Anna
Layton, Peter
Leach, David
Long, Maurice
Mackmaidhachain, Padraig
Maltby, John
Mannheim, Catherine
Martin, Guy
McDowell, Leo
Meddings, Camilla
Newcomb, Tessa
Newell, Stephen
Owen, Elspeth
Pearson, Colin
Race, Robert
Ramshaw, Wendy
Ray, Jane
Scott, Mike
Spira, Rupert
Taplin, Guy
Tookey, Fleur
Watson, Janet

PRYORY ART
(Page 67)
Bennett, Hafdis
Berry, Renu
Burgess, Andres
Cardash, Alan
De Beaumorel, G.
Espeth, Katrine
Gerrard, Charlotte
Goldschuidt, Eileen
Goode, Natalie
Gori, Emanuele
Keulshiemer, Pam
Konyn, Gillian
Lass, Cindy
Lewers, Jessica
Lowe, Roz
Nastasic, Drasan
Oberheumer, Christopher
Parsons, Stella
Rockberger, Polly
Simler, Marilyn
Todd, Janet

PYMS GALLERY
(Page 68)
Clausen, George
Forbes, Stanhope
Harpignies, H.J.
Henry, Paul
Hone, Nathaniel
Jellett, Mainie
John, Augustus
Keating, Sean
La Thangue, H.H.
Lavery, John
Leech, William
McDonnell, Hector
Millet, Jean-Francois
O'Conor, Roderic
Orpen, William
Osborne, Walter
Pryde, James
Sickert, Walter
Swanzy, Mary
Yeats, Jack B.

REBECCA HOSSACK GALLERY
(Page 68)
Bauman, Lydia
Berman, Carole
Bowen, Dean
Casson, Lucy
Davie, Joseph
De Stempel, Sophie
Farrelly, Jimmy
Faucon, Bernard
Flockhart, Helen
Fransella, Graham

Fuller, Moss
Harker, Janet
Hastings, Eveline
Henderson, Sue
Houghton, Barrie
Morgan, Jane
Neusten, Barrie
Spafford, Iola
Thomas, Glynn
Tookey, John
Wade, Richard
Westwood, Neil

THE SOLOMON GALLERY
(Page 155)
Ballard, Brian
Blackshaw, Basil
Chihuly, Dale
Collis, Peter
Cope, Elizabeth
Duncan, Ana
Geoghegan, Trevor
Gillespie, Rowan
Kingston, Richard
Longueville, James
Lynn, Bob
McAllister, Therese
McDonnell, Hector
McEntagart, Brett
McWilliam, F.E.
Mooney, Martin
O'Reilly, Patrick
Poskitt, Frances
Richardson, Victor
Spackman, Sarah
Stuart, Imogen
Tansey, Francis
Warren, Michael
Wejchert, Alexandra
Yeats, Jack B.

ST. DAVID'S HALL
(Page 145)
Beard, Leonard
Chapman, June
Darlison, John
Dewsbury, Gerald
Evans, David
Giles Hobbs, Annie
Hawkins, Des
Howell, Joyce
Howells, Pat
Hughes-Williams, Sylvia
Hurn, Daphne
Hurst, Dora
Lowry, Arnold
Lush, Helen
McDonagh, Sue
Owen, Cyril
Owen, Shirley Anne
Traynor, Mary
Waugh, Trevor
Whalley, Ann
Williams, David
Woods, Anne

STAN ROSENTHAL
(Page 149)
Rosenthal, Stanley

STAR GALLERY
(Page 103)
Armitage, David
Blight, John
Cooper, Michael
Dubrey, Henrietta
Fedden, Mary
Hammick, Tom
Lloyd-Jones, Mary
Messer, Peter
Mockford, Harold
Rix, Ruth
Rooney, Mick
Traherne, Margaret
Williams, Charles

STERN ART DEALERS
(Page 69)
Armfield, Edward
Bale, Thomas Charles
Bates, David
Clark, James
Clemenson, Robert
Cousin, Charles
de Breanski, Alfred
de Breanski, Gustave
Ellis, Edwin
Epstein, Jacob
Goodall, Frederick
Haldon, Trevor
Hines, Theodor
Hollums, Frances Mabel
Horlor, Joseph
Hulk, Abraham Jnr.
Kadar, Bela
King, H.J. Yeend
Kramer, Jacob
Maze, Paul
Meadows, William
Morris, Alfred
Niemun, Edward J.
Paice, George
Parker, Henry H.
Passey, Charles
Perez, Alonzo
Pike, Sidney
Pissarro, Camille
Pissarro, Georges Manzana
Pissarro, H. Claude
Pissarro, Lelia
Pissarro, Lucien
Pissarro, Ludovic-Rodo
Pissarro, Orovida
Pissarro, Paulemile
Pollentine, Alfred
Schafer, Henri
Sherrin, Daniel
Spinks, Thomas
Steele, Edwin
Thornley, William
Vickers, A.H.
Walbourn, Ernest

STRATHEARN GALLERY AND POTTERY
(Page 138)
Awlson, Walter
Bell, John
Bourne, Peter
Bushe, Chris
Campbell, Catriona
Gray, Janice
Halstead, Rebecca
Harkess, Claire
Hollands, Emma
Maclean, Sonas
Maguire, Fiona
Maguire, John
McCarthy, Liz
McStay, Adrienne
Meikle, Annabel
Morrison, John Lowrie
Muir, Graham
Pretsell, Philomena
Robinson, Neil
Scobie, Lara

THE STUDIO
(Page 146)
Wilson, David
Wilson, Guy

TIB LANE GALLERY
(Page 118)
Baker, Barbara
Billsborough, Jim
Burton, Morag
Cebertowicz, Janina
Clayton, Peter
Connell, Joan
Davies, John
Ehrlich, Georg
Foerster, Florian
Freer, Allen
Frink, Elisabeth
Grimshaw, Trevor
Halliday, Irene
Henderson, Sue
Herman, Josef
Howard, Ghislaine
Kramer, Jacob
Lacoux, John
Lloyd, James
McIntyre, Donald
McKinlay, Don
Nash, John
Ousey, Harry
Radford, Gordon
Richardson, Bob
Rutherford, Harry
Sarkis, Vera
Selwyn, William
Shaw, David Carson
Sorrell, Adrian
Spafford, Iola
Stubbs, Rosemary
Sutherland, Joan
Thompson, Alan
Vallette, Adolphe
Vaughan, Keith
Wood, Michael
Woods, Brian

UNICORN PICTURES LTD.
(Page 70)
Ashman, Malcolm
Black, Simon
Cameron, Peter
Carr, Francis
Cordero, Philip
Creswell, Alexander
Crocker, Andrew
Day, Paul
Elliott, Richard
Gallwey, Kay
Handon, Paul
Johnson, Frank
List, Caroline
Maconochie, James
Marshall, Steven
Roberts, Trevor
Rubinstein, Gerda
Rudd, Bob
Shanahan, David
Shiels, Charlie
Stevens, Christopher
Wiskey, Joshua

UNIT 2 GALLERY
(Page 109)
Allen, Gabrielle
Aplin, Kay
Armstrong, Pat
Arnull, Nick
Barker, Jane
Barlow, Mike
Bates, Amanda
Bolt, Rachael
Bourne, Mary
Brown, Sarah
Bruce, Angela
Burnell, Jan
Clarke, Shaun
Cooke, David
Cooke, Rosemarie
Crouchman, Clare
Eeles, Tony
Foster, Sally-Ann
Galanides, Therasa
Gandy, Paul
Green, Francesca
Halligan, Janet
Harvey, Rebecca
Head, Viv
Heale, Meg
Hicks, Peter
Hoare, Wendy
Hurst, Dagmar
Illsley, Will
Kaffash, Gila
Knibs, Vic
Langworth, Stewart
Leigh, Joyce
Lockwood, Barry
Logan, Frank
Marix-Evans, Polly
McFarlane, Kathleen
Morgan, Annette
Peddie, Crofton
Plunkett, Tim
Russell, Caroline
Skeels, Rebecca
Skinner, Graham
Spencer, Lucy
Spriet, Cristal
Thompson, Fiona
Wagh, Ibrahim
Warner, Carmen
Waters, Alan
Wilson, Andrew

THE UNIVERSITY GALLERY
(Page 126)
Cornish, Norman
McGuinness, Tom

VINCENT KOSMAN FINE ART
(Page 136)
Armstrong, John
Bell, Vanessa
Bomberg, David
Brown, Hugh Boycott
Connard, Philip
Crosbie, William
Duncan, John
Dunlop, Ronald O.

Fedden, Mary
Fergusson, J.D.
Gertler, Mark
Gill, Eric
Gillies, William
Gore, Frederick
Gosse, Sylvia
Grant, Duncan
Hall, Clifford
Hamilton, Maggie
Harvey, Harold
Hayward, Arthur
Hilton, Roger
Houston, George
Kennedy, Cecil
Lee Hankey, William
Maitland, Paul
Manson, James B.
Maze, Paul
McClure, David
McIntyre, Donald
Meninsky, Bernard
Methuen, Lord
Morrocco, Alberto
Mostyn, Tom
Nicholson, William
Park, James Stuart
Park, John A.
Paterson, James
Paterson, Viola
Phillipson, Robin
Redpath, Anne
Robertson, Eric
Roussel, Theodore
Russell, Gyrth
Smith, Matthew
Trevelyan, Julian
Vaughan, Keith
Williams, Terrick
Wolfe, Edward
Wolmark, Alfred
Zinkeisen, Doris

THE WALK
(Page 70)
Banks, Nick
Bartlett, Adrian
Carr, David
Clarke, Denis
Feilden, Lucy
Milne, Vincent
Morris, Sue
Mortimer, Sophie
Sen, Neera
Snow, Peter

THE WEST END GALLERY
(Page 112)
Hacker, Sophie
Hobbs, Paul
Lamb, Jean

WHITFORD FINE ART
(Page 71)
Bendall, Mildred
Bissiere, Roger
Bogart, Bram
Boty, Pauline
Bradley, Martin
Bratby, John
Bunny, Rupert
Caulfield, Patrick
Caziel
Clarke, Geoffrey
Cockrill, Maurice
Davie, Alan
Donaldson, Antony
Francis, Mike
Frost, Sir Terry
Gear, William
Gilbert, Stephan
Heath, Adrian
Henri, Adrian
Herman, Josef
Heron, Patrick
Hilton, Roger
Hull, John
Jones, Allen
Kidner, Michael
Lacasse, Joseph
Laing, Gerald
Mack, Heinz
Mara, Pol
Martin, Henri
Maze, Paul
Melville, John
Nolan, Sir Sydney
Paolozzi, Eduardo
Penrose, Roland
Phillips, Peter
Riley, Bridget
Russell, John Peter
Sedgley, Peter
Smith, Matthew
Souverbie, Jean
Souza, Frank Newton
Survage, Leopold
Tilson, Joe
Tucker, William
Van Hoeydonck, Paul
Wall, Brian
Wilson, Frank Awray
Wolfe, Edward
Wolmark, Alfred

WISEMAN ORIGINALS
(Page 71)
Aitchison, Craigie
Braque, Georges
Chagall, Marc
Freud, Lucian
Frink, Elisabeth
Frost, Sir Terry
Giacometti, Alberto
Heron, Patrick
Hockney, David
Hodgkin, Howard
Hoyland, John
Matisse, Henri
Miró, Joan
Moore, Henry
Picasso, Pablo
Scott, William
Scully, Sean

WOLSELEY FINE ARTS
(Page 71)
Ardizzone, Edward
Bomberg, David
Bonnard, Pierre
Buckland-Wright, John
Denis, Maurice
Derain, André
Dobson, Frank
Dunoyer de Segonzac, André
Gill, Eric
Grant, Duncan
Gretta
Hagreen, Philip
Holloway, Edgar
Jones, David
Klemann, Paul
Lhote, André
Marquet, Albert
Nash, Paul
Pascin, Jules
Piper, John
Raverat, Gwen
Roussel, Ker Xavier
Spencer, Stanley
Theodosiou, Panico
Underwood, Leon
Volk, Patricia
Vuillard, Edouard
Watts, Peter
Yale, Brian

WOODBINE COTTAGE GALLERY
(Page 108)
Bailey, Katy
Beech, Juliet
Bibby, Rob
Bramble, Steven
Colquitt, Peter
Cupitt, Susan
Curgenven, Michael
English, Andy
Foster, Patience
Gregory, Mac
Hollinshead, David
Ladbrook, Christine
Lagadec, Jean
Lincoln, John
Micallef, Antony
Milliken, Rob
Moon, Liz
Moore, Sarah
Neal, Richard
Simpson, Juliet
Williams, Louise
Yorath, Liz
Yorath, Rowan

WWW.AARTI.CO.UK
(Page 168)
Addinall, Ruth
McCafferty, Liz
Middleton, Susan
Oxborrow, Edmond
Potts, Suzi

ZELLA GALLERY
(Page 71)
Arden, Kitty
Bako Bittner, Eva
Bassett, Clare
Browne, Piers
Burley, Maggie
Caymax, Katrien
Clayton, Inge
Devereux Barker, Dale
Devereux, Jenny
Epps, Melanie
Fay, Helen
Fraser, Cameron
Graver, Mark
Grigor, Rachel
Hartill, Brenda
Hunter, Michael
Katsuragi, Camille
March, Carl
McMurray, Katty
Neville, Alison
Noach, Michèle
Perring, Susie
Price, Trevor
Rollo, Sonia
Searle, Ronald
Shea, Kiva
St. Clair Miller, Frances
Theys, Freddy
Whadcock, Richard
Woods, Belinda

NOTES

ARTISTS' INDEX

This section lists by artist, the establishments where the artist's work may bought.

THE ART WORLD
DIRECTORY

A

D

E

F

G

H

I

J

N

O

P

Q

R

S

T

U

V

W

Y

Z

GALLERY SERVICES

This section lists establishments offering additional services.

THE ART WORLD
DIRECTORY

Art Consultancy

Art for Offices

Commissioning

Disabled Access

Space for Hire

Valuation

Workshop facilities

NOTES

GENERAL INDEX

Alphabetical index to all entries.

THE ART WORLD DIRECTORY

C

H

M

N

O

P

Q

R

S

GENERAL INDEX

X/Y/Z

ADVERTISER'S INDEX